On Slavery's Border

Missouri's Small-Slaveholding Households, 1815–1865

DIANE MUTTI BURKE

The University of Georgia Press

ATHENS AND LONDON

Sections of Chapters 3 and 4 reprinted from *Women in Missouri History: In Search of Power and Influence*, edited by LeeAnn Whites, Mary C. Neth, and Gary R. Kremer, by permission of the University of Missouri Press. Copyright © 2004 by the Curators of the University of Missouri. Sections of Chapter 5 reprinted from *Searching for their Places: Women in the South Across Four Centuries*, edited by Thomas H. Appleton, Jr., and Angela Boswell, by permission of the University of Missouri Press. Copyright © 2003 by the Curators of the University of Missouri.

LIBRARY OF CONGRESS CATALOGING-IN-PUBLICATION DATA

Burke, Diane Mutti.
    On slavery's border : Missouri's small-slaveholding households, 1815–1865 / Diane Mutti Burke.
        p.   cm. — (Early American places)
    Includes bibliographical references and index.
ISBN-13: 978-0-8203-3636-7 (hardcover : alk. paper)
ISBN-10: 0-8203-3636-x (hardcover : alk. paper)
ISBN-13: 978-0-8203-3683-1 (pbk. : alk. paper)
ISBN-10: 0-8203-3683-1 (pbk. : alk. paper)
    1. Slavery—Missouri—History—19th century.   2. Slaveholders—Missouri—History—19th century.   3. Households—Missouri—History—19th century.   4. Farm life—Missouri—History—19th century.   5. Slaves—Missouri—Social conditions—19th century.   6. African Americans—Missouri—Social conditions—19th century.   7. Whites—Missouri—Social conditions—19th century.   8. Missouri—Race relations—History—19th century.   9. Missouri—Social conditions—19th century.   10. Border States (U.S. Civil War)—Social conditions—Case studies.   I. Title.
E445.M67B87   2010
977.8'03—dc22
                                                                    2010026523

British Cataloging-in-Publication Data available

FRONTISPIECE: County Map of the States of Iowa and Missouri. W. H. Gamble. This 1861 map of the states of Iowa and Missouri shows the location of county lines, towns, waterways, and railroads on the eve of the Civil War. This map was created by W. H. Gamble and published by S. A. Mitchell Jr. of Philadelphia. Courtesy of the State Historical Society of Missouri.

For David, Matthew, Maggie, and Ellie

Contents

Acknowledgments

Growing up in Kansas City, I understood that Missouri was a border state during the Civil War, and I also had a vague notion that the region was not a land of large plantations; however, I was never taught the history of slavery in the state. When choosing a topic for an undergraduate honors thesis, I decided to explore the experiences of the slaves and slaveholders who lived in my natal state. Without fully understanding it at the time, I stumbled into a historiographically significant project. I have been researching and writing on this topic ever since, and along the way I have benefited from the assistance and guidance of many wonderful individuals. I hope to thank them all, but I know that with a project spanning so many years I may inadvertently omit someone who helped me.

I have profited from wonderful advice and support from a number of professors and faculty mentors at both Dartmouth College and Emory University. Jere Daniell, Michael Green, and Margaret Darrow inspired me to learn and think about eighteenth- and nineteenth-century United States and European history, and Mary Kelley and Sydney Nathans skillfully mentored me as I wrote my undergraduate thesis. At Emory University, I benefited from sitting in the classrooms of Jonathan Prude, Margot Finn, and Susan Socolow, as well as Mary Odem, who both taught me well and served as a model for balancing teaching, scholarship, and motherhood. Dan Carter was of great assistance in the initial phase of the process, and Eugene Genovese graciously stepped in when

Dr. Carter moved to another university, lending his incredible breadth of knowledge on southern slavery and society to this project. Throughout the years, James Roark has been a constant source of advice and support. He carefully read drafts of chapters and articles and has been enthusiastic about the need for a new study of Missouri slavery since we first talked of it. Finally, I am deeply grateful to Elizabeth Fox-Genovese, for her unfailing encouragement over the years. She was supportive of my decisions and she helped improve my project and encouraged me both personally and professionally in so many ways. I only wish that she could be here to witness the publication of this book.

I often learned nearly as much from my outstanding peers as I did from my professors. I benefited from lively historical debates with Dan Costello, Sarah Gardner, David Freeman, and Jeffrey Young, around both the seminar and the cafeteria table. The members of my writing group, Christine Jacobson Carter, Ellen Rafshoon, Yael Fletcher, Annette Parks, Ruth Dickens, Naomi Nelson, Stacey Horstmann Gatti, Jaclyn Stanke, and Belle Tuten, offered helpful criticisms of early drafts of chapters. Traveling with Jacki Stanke and Sarah Gardner made research road trips much more enjoyable. Steve Goodson and Ann Short Chirhart, who were further along in the process, always were sources of advice and encouragement. Good friends, Christine Carter, Ellen Rafshoon, Ruth Dickens, and Laura Crawley, shared with me the joys and frustrations of balancing graduate school and motherhood.

I deeply appreciate the History Department at the University of Missouri–Kansas City for giving me the opportunity to live and work in my hometown. My wonderful colleagues and students have made UMKC a wonderful place to teach, as well as research and write. I first must thank my department chairs Louis Potts and Gary Ebersole, who have been extremely supportive of my work over the past six years. In addition, Dean Karen Vorst granted me a leave from teaching during a crucial juncture in the revision process. Gail Green and Amy Brost provided amazing administrative support. Scott Walters patiently endured making multiple revisions to his maps, and graduate students Jennifer Farr, Clinton Lawson, and Chainy Folsom spent hours transcribing microfilm, tracking down documents and photographs, and double-checking my statistics and citations. My colleagues Pellom McDaniels, Louis Potts, and Linna Funk Place have served as excellent sounding boards for my ideas about nineteenth-century Missouri history. Lynda Payne, Miriam Forman-Brunell, Andrew Bergerson, Carla Klausner, Dennis Merrill, and Linda Mitchell have provided me with sound scholarly and professional advice, and James Falls, Mary Ann Wynkoop, Dave Freeman, Viviana Grieco, Shona Kelly Wray, and especially John Herron have made life in Cockefair Hall a lot more enjoyable.

Funding from a number of universities and foundations made the research and writing of this book possible. The McGuire Grant for African American Studies at Dartmouth College funded early research trips to Chapel Hill, North Carolina, and Columbia, Missouri. While at Emory, I received generous graduate fellowships and numerous travel grants from both the History and the Women's Studies Departments, as well as an Andrew W. Mellon Foundation Southern Studies Dissertation Fellowship which provided me with a fifth year of funding. The Beveridge Grant from the American Historical Association and the Mississippi Delta Initiative Grant from the National Park Service funded additional research trips, and a grant from the Earhart Foundation allowed me to finish the manuscript. In the course of working on book revisions I received a Faculty Research Grant from the University of Missouri–Kansas City, a Supreme Court of Missouri Historical Society Robert Eldridge Seiler Fellowship from the Missouri State Archives, and the Richard S. Brownlee Fund Grant from the State Historical Society of Missouri. I am especially grateful to the University of Missouri Research Board for funding a year-long leave from teaching that allowed me to accept a postdoctoral fellowship at the Gilder Lehrman Center for the Study of Slavery, Resistance, and Abolition at Yale University. The time spent in New Haven away from professional and personal obligations was restorative, productive, and invaluable to the writing process.

I have been fortunate to work in wonderful archives while researching this book. The staffs at the National Archives in Washington, D.C., the Missouri State Archives, and the Missouri History Museum, particularly Jeff Meyer, were extremely helpful. The interlibrary loan librarians at Emory University and the University of Missouri–Kansas City, especially David Bauer, as well as Tammy Green from the University of Missouri–Columbia, went above and beyond to assist me. I have received tremendous support and assistance from the staff at the State Historical Society of Missouri and would like to specifically thank Gary Kremer, Lynn Gentzler, Christine Montgomery, and Loucile Malone. John Rodrigue first invited me to visit the Freedmen and Southern Society Project at the University of Maryland during graduate school, and it was then that I came to understand the importance of the work done there. Leslie Rowland graciously opened up the project's well-organized photocopy archive to me and patiently assisted me in my attempts to understand the

Civil War military records related to emancipation in Missouri. I could not have written this book without the tremendous archival resources found at the Western Historical Manuscript Collection–Columbia. During the early years of working on this project, Randy Roberts, Cindy Stewart, and Diane Ayotte were an incredible source of knowledge of Missouri's archival resources, and the current archivists has been just as attentive to my research needs. I especially enjoyed the long stretches of time that I spent at the Kansas City branch of WHMC. Marilyn Burlingame, Bettie Swiontek, Jennifer Parker, and David Boutros were part of this project from the beginning, and more recently Peter Foley has helped during the final stages of manuscript preparation. They advised me, spent countless hours photocopying for me, and provided me with enjoyable breaks from reading documents.

I sincerely appreciate the remarkable generosity shown to me by family and friends while on research trips. Becky Eustance Kohn invited me to stay with her in Baltimore while working at the National Archives, and Nancy Staab hosted me in Chapel Hill, North Carolina. My brothers, Jim and John Mutti, and their college roommates, as well as my then future sister-in-law, Megan Poole Mutti, allowed me to stay with them for weeks on end while working in Columbia, Missouri. The long dinners and good conversations enjoyed with friends and family after the archives closed made the trips both personally and professionally satisfying.

My professional debts are numerous, and I only hope that I will not forget any of the many exceptional scholars who have helped me along the way. Dennis Boman graciously shared his massive and detailed database of the Abiel Leonard Papers, enabling me to quickly identify only those documents related to the Leonard family and slaves in an otherwise overwhelmingly large collection. I have benefited tremendously from the outstanding comments made about my work by panelists and audience members at numerous conferences throughout the years, including Edward Baptist, Beverly Bond, Stephanie Camp, Barbara Fields, Louis Gerteis, Michael Johnson, Wilma King, Barbara Krauthamer, Allan Kulikoff, Virginia Laas, James Oakes, Julie Saville, Kimberley Phillips, Leslie Rowland, Quintard Taylor, and Marli Weiner. The fine editing skills of LeeAnn Whites, Mary Neth, Gary Kremer, Angela Boswell, and Thomas Appleton Jr. helped shape the articles that served as the foundation for two chapters of this book. David Blight, Dana Schaffer, Tom Thurston, Melissa McGrath, Glenda Gilmore, Bonnie Martin, John Wood Sweet, and Honor Sachs welcomed me to New Haven and helped make my stay there pleasant. Jonathan Earle, Catherine Clinton, Leslie

Schwalm, Daina Ramey Berry, Theda Perdue, and Ann Short Chirhart have offered excellent scholarly and professional advice. Steve McIntyre, Kim Schreck, Traci Wilson-Kleekamp, Tom Spencer, Jeremy Neely, and Kim Warren have made working and researching in this region much more enjoyable. Years ago, LeeAnn Whites kindly introduced me to her graduate students who were working on women's history and issues of race in Missouri. I have benefited from her advice and friendship ever since. I sincerely appreciate the friends who took the time to read drafts of book chapters and offered valuable suggestions for improvement. My UMKC colleagues John Herron, Linna Funk Place, Lynda Payne, Louis Potts, Rebecca Lee, and Shona Kelly Wray all read my work. Jessica Millward generously reviewed a chapter in the midst of a major move, and long-time friend Kim Schreck took a significant amount of time away from her busy schedule to read and comment on a large portion of the book. The intelligent and insightful suggestions made by the two anonymous readers from the University of Georgia Press pushed me to expand my arguments in ways that I believe have greatly improved the book. Tim Roberts, the editor of Early American Places, guided me through the final stages of the book's production, and Teresa Jesionowski skillfully helped me improve my prose. I also am grateful to the Andrew W. Mellon Foundation for generously funding the Early American Places series, the wonderful editorial and marketing staff at the University of Georgia Press, and especially Derek Krissoff, who has patiently explained to me the mysteries of publishing and who has been a joy to work with on this project.

Last, and most important, I must acknowledge the incredible support that I have received from my friends and family. Jenny Jessee, Beca Solberg McPherson, Megan Poole Mutti, Julie Medlock, Jennifer Frost, and Laura Hammond have served as sources of encouragement and have enriched my life with their wonderful friendships. My uncle, Ed Mutti Jr., has assisted me in countless ways throughout the years. My parents, Jim and Carla Mutti, have generously supported me and have encouraged my love of history since my childhood. They generously allowed their grown daughter to stay at their Kansas City home for weeks on end while I worked at local archives. My mother deserves special recognition both for occasionally serving as my research assistant and for frequently caring for my children while I worked. I wish to thank my children, Matthew, Maggie, and Ellie, for keeping me laughing and helping me maintain a balanced perspective. They patiently tolerated the photocopied documents and chapter drafts scattered throughout the house and frequently seeing their mother with a computer in her lap, yet, they always enthusiastically supported the project—offering me research facts and words of advice along the way. I especially must thank David Burke, who has literally lived with this book as long as I have. Words cannot express how much I appreciate the selfless love and support he has given me throughout these many years.

ON SLAVERY'S BORDER

Introduction

*Slavery in western Missouri was like slavery in northern Kentucky—much
more a domestic than commercial institution. Family servants constituted
the bulk of ownership, and few white families owned more than one family
of blacks. The social habits were those of the farm and not the plantation.
The white owner, with his sons, labored in the same fields with the negro,
both old and young. The mistress guided the industries in the house in
both colors. . . . These conditions cultivated between the races strong
personal and reciprocal attachments. The negroes were members of the
family; the blights of ownership were at a minimum.*

—JOHN GIDEON HASKELL
"THE PASSING OF SLAVERY IN WESTERN MISSOURI"

Forty years after the Civil War, John G. Haskell evoked a world of slaveholding and slavery that differed significantly from the descriptions of
large cotton or rice plantations, complete with the big house and the slave
quarters, that have become the quintessential representation of the antebellum South. Haskell described slavery in Missouri as a highly personal
system of economic and social relations, much more "domestic" than
what prevailed in the plantation South.[1] This idealized portrayal provokes the question of whether the experience of slavery and slaveholding was actually different in Missouri than elsewhere. Many of Haskell's
contemporaries would have agreed with his assessment; white Missourians who remembered slavery in the state often touted the virtues of
the former institution. This argument about the benign nature of border slavery reached back to the antebellum years when Missourians had
a vested interest in promoting their image as benevolent slaveholders.
Ironically, during this same time, some slaves also imagined that conditions were better in Missouri than down river in the cotton kingdom. In
fact, Missouri and its sister border states were set apart from the larger
slaveholding states in many nineteenth-century Americans' minds, and
even fellow Southerners viewed them with suspicion. On the eve of the
Civil War, southern intellectuals and politicians openly expressed concerns that Missouri, with its marginal system of slavery, was not firmly
united in common cause with the rest of the slave South.[2]

In the decades following the war, beliefs about the mild nature of border state slavery became more firmly entrenched in people's collective consciousness. Missourians' memories of the Civil War were complicated by the vicious guerrilla violence that had plagued the region for more than a decade. Missourians of southern persuasion felt the sting of Confederate defeat deeply, but perhaps even more so in light of the often personal nature of the conflict in a state with residents with divided loyalties. Most individuals who recorded their memories of the war primarily were interested in cataloguing the atrocities of Union forces who "occupied" the Missouri countryside and "Jayhawkers"—Union troops who raided into western Missouri from Kansas—but many also made it a priority to describe the perfection of their slaveholding society before it was devastated by the war. The faithful slaves who populated the state's farms were a special focus of their descriptions of antebellum Missouri. Although there are glimpses of discontented enslaved people in reminiscences of the war, by and large white Missourians argued that their slaves suffered for nothing, were content in their enslavement, and were reluctant to leave their owners. White Southerners told similar stories, of course, as they celebrated a world that was no longer and justified both their Lost Cause and the South's emerging system of racial segregation. Missourians enhanced this well-known southern story of slavery by repeatedly emphasizing the highly familial nature of the small-scale system of slavery that once existed in the state. It was not surprising, therefore, that Haskell described Missouri slavery as domestic, because contemporary white Missourians assured him that it had been so. Divided in their loyalties during the war, as the twentieth century approached, many white Missourians began to closely align themselves with the South and Jim Crow, and their memories of border state slavery bolstered their contemporary racial system.[3]

Nineteenth-century American writers also reinforced the image of a milder border state slavery. In *Uncle Tom's Cabin,* Harriet Beecher Stowe painted a sympathetic portrait of the Shelbys of Kentucky, who did the best that they could as they worked within a flawed and immoral slavery system. Mr. Shelby consented to the sale of Eliza's young son and Uncle Tom only after his financial incompetency threatened the loss of all members of his beloved and loyal slave family. Perhaps most enduring in Americans' minds, however, are Mark Twain's Huck and Jim, who floated together down the Mississippi River in search of freedom. The unlikely friendship that was forged between the poor white boy and the runaway slave man had its roots in a border state slavery culture. In contrast to Stowe, Twain knew personally of what he wrote because he had spent his childhood in the river town of Hannibal, Missouri, in a world immersed in slavery. Samuel Clemens grew up with slaves in his parents' household. He witnessed firsthand the horrors of border state slavery: how people were brutalized and families were torn apart. Yet, he also understood how slaves and owners might learn to function together within a small-slaveholding household, and ultimately how they might recognize one another's humanity, as had Huck and Jim. Twain readily accepted, and in fact defended, slavery in his youth, but as he aged he came to understand the complexities of the institution, reaching the conclusion that it was morally wrong. He worked to square his memories of the bucolic Missouri river community, which he so eloquently described in his books, with the horrors of slavery. At some level, Twain reconciled these early experiences of growing up on slavery's border as he wrote his masterpiece, *Huckleberry Finn,* and breathed life into Jim, perhaps the most well known, albeit fictional, Missouri slave.[4]

This image of benign border slavery has persisted in spite of the more complex picture painted by the individuals who actually endured enslavement in the state. Those interviewed by the Works Progress Administration in the 1930s remembered their experiences in slavery in a myriad of ways, ranging from kind treatment at the hands of their owners to the worst forms of psychological and physical abuse. The life story of William Wells Brown, escaped Missouri slave and abolitionist lecturer and novelist, also represents the broad range of experiences faced by enslaved Missourians. Likely mindful of white Missourians' boasts that they treated their slaves more humanely than elsewhere, Brown argued that their so-called kind treatment was meaningless, because ultimately slavery "decrees that the slave shall not worship God according to the dictates of his own conscience; it denies him the word of God; it makes him a chattel, and sells him in the market to the highest bidder; it decrees that he shall not protect the wife of his bosom; it takes from him every right which God gave him. Clothing and food are nothing compared with liberty. What care I for clothing or food, while I am the slave of another?"[5]

Nineteenth-century white Americans' collective memory, in combination with cultural references, resulted in the myth of mild border slavery trumping formerly enslaved Missourians' criticisms of the system. A paucity of historical research on small slaveholdings and border state slavery has compounded this tendency. Although historians have not taken the story of benign border slavery at face value, few have explored the actual experiences of the slaves and slaveholders who lived in the border states. Scholars have devoted pages to debunking the moonlight and magnolia myth, exploring aspects of antebellum plantation life such as the treatment of slaves, material conditions, slaveholders' and slaves' family lives, differences according to age and gender, slavery in manufacturing and urban areas, and southern churches and communities. These important correctives by and large have neglected the experiences of the many black and white Southerners who lived on small-slaveholding farms in the upland or border South, however, thus allowing for the belief that slavery was easier to endure in the border states.[6]

Indeed, the history of slaves and slaveholders on large plantations tells only one aspect of the story of slavery in the American South. Far more than half of the whites who owned slaves, and almost half of slaves, lived on farms rather than plantations. The census of 1860 shows that throughout the South as a whole, 80 percent of slaveholding families owned fewer than twenty slaves—the number most often used to define a plantation; 88 percent of slaveholding families owned fewer than ten slaves and around 50 percent owned only one. In 1989, the economic historian Robert Fogel called on scholars to examine small-scale slavery; he noted that although nearly half of American slaves lived on slaveholding units of fewer than twenty slaves, most historians ignore the question of slavery on farms and concentrate their inquiries on the planters and slaves living in the plantation belt instead.[7]

Scholars have made some limited observations about small-scale slavery in their larger works on the plantation South, although there has been little focused research in this area. There are a few studies of small slaveholding at the macro level, explorations of the mind-set of upwardly mobile small slaveholders and the economy and politics of small-slaveholding regions, but with few exceptions, there has been little emphasis on small-scale slavery at the level of the household. Historians have not comprehensively explored how the everyday lives of the slaves and slaveholders who lived on the South's many small slaveholdings may have differed from those who lived on plantations. They simply have not opened the doors of small slaveholders' homes and examined the relationships and the lives of the individuals found within: how owners and slaves lived and worked with one another each day; how the circumstances of small-scale slavery affected their family lives; and how they socialized with their neighbors.[8]

This tendency to ignore the effects of slaveholding size has been accompanied by a proclivity to neglect regional differences in slavery and slaveholding. In the introduction to a 1974 collection of essays that focuses on local histories of slavery, the historians Eugene Genovese and Elinor Miller first challenged their peers to explore the potential influence of region on the experience of slavery. Although scholars have made significant strides toward rectifying this neglect through examinations of slavery in places as diverse as Texas, Maryland, Appalachia, and upcountry Virginia and North Carolina, this work is far from complete. The state of Missouri has been particularly neglected in larger studies of slavery and southern society. Missouri traditionally has been considered to be on the periphery of the slave South, and, therefore, few scholars have included it in their larger examinations of southern slavery. Yet, the state was settled overwhelmingly by Southerners and from the beginning slavery was at the base of the state's economic and social system. Even though slaves accounted for only 10 percent of Missouri's population in 1860, there were large communities of slaveholders and slaves in many of the counties bordering the Missouri and the Mississippi Rivers, where the slave population often exceeded 25 percent. In these locations, migrants from the Upper South created a slave society with small-scale slavery at its core. Despite the importance of slavery to Missouri's economy and society and the repeated involvement of the state in the ongoing sectional conflict, few scholars have concentrated on this significant slave state and little of their work has been published. There are a few focused studies of various aspects of Missouri slavery, such as the trial of an enslaved woman who murdered her master, slavery and agriculture, slave crime, and slave education, but the last general study of slavery in the state was Harrison Trexler's *Slavery in Missouri,* which was published in 1914. None of these works has comprehensively explored the everyday lives of Missouri's many small-slaveholding families and the slaves with whom they shared their lives.[9]

On Slavery's Border uses a bottom-up approach to examine how the experience of slavery and slaveholding was influenced both by the size of slaveholding and by geography. In a place such as Missouri, slavery developed into a region of small slaveholdings precisely because of its geographic location; both climate and proximity to free states discouraged the migration of planters and conversely encouraged the migration of slaveholders of lesser means. Small slaveholders were marginalized in much of the South, but in Missouri they dominated, creating a slavery culture that differed socially, politically, and economically from that of plantation regions. This book outlines the history and economics of slavery in Missouri, but the primary focus is how small-scale slavery affected the families and communities of both slaves and owners, as well as the many ways their lives intersected. The relatively small size of slaveholdings had profound implications for the lived experiences of the many Missourians involved with slavery, ultimately influencing their economic strategies, labor relations, and family and community lives. The personal and work interactions of Missouri slavery were intimate, exposing both slaves and owners to a vast array of human exchanges ranging from empathy and cooperation to hatred and brutal violence. Although white Missourians long argued that slavery was more benign in their border location, the historical evidence suggests that this was not true in most cases. Slavery differed in significant ways in Missouri, but this never translated into an overall "better" system of bondage. Missouri slavery was often just as cruel and exploitative as anywhere in the South.

While the relations between slaves and owners were at the core of their life experience, perhaps more profound was the effect of small-scale slavery on Missourians' family and community lives. Slaveholders were concerned with harnessing the economic potential of their farms in order to enhance the possibility that their children would maintain racial and class prerogatives in the future, and they structured their farming, labor management, and child-rearing decisions to ensure this outcome. At the same time that slaveholders worked to shore up slavery in a marginalized border location through the development of flexible economic strategies, such as hiring, granting slaves liberal geographic mobility in order to accommodate their fragile families and communities, and confrontations with those who dissented against slavery, black Missourians struggled—and often succeeded—to maintain family and community ties in the absence of resident nuclear families and slave-quarter communities. In the end, border slavery rapidly disintegrated in the wake of an assault on the system from forces both internal and external during the years of the Civil War.

The experiences of Paulina and Thomas Stratton, who migrated to Missouri from Virginia in 1855 with five children and eleven slaves, beautifully represent those of a typical small-slaveholding family. Paulina Stratton indicated in her diary that although her family initially struggled, the Strattons and their slaves eventually built a prosperous farming operation in Missouri. Slaveholding status afforded the Strattons social capital, allowing them to quickly integrate into the community. The Stratton slaves also met their enslaved neighbors while hired out, running errands, and attending local social gatherings. The relations between the Strattons and their slaves were influenced by the close proximity in which they lived and worked. The slaves knew their owners' weaknesses and, according to Paulina Stratton, authority over them slowly eroded throughout the years. Relations were not always strained between owners and slaves, however: there were also cases of mutual assistance and even glimpses of affection. The Strattons' slaves left during the Civil War, yet the relationship between former slaves and owners did not end with emancipation. Paulina Stratton continued to look out for the welfare of her former bondpeople even after they no longer lived with her. These relations, like those of the Strattons' small-slaveholding neighbors, were fraught with the ambiguity that accompanied the intimate interaction between slaves and slaveholders on Missouri's small holdings. As the Stratton case suggests, the study of small-scale slavery in Missouri sheds light on the lives of these historically neglected Southerners. Slaveholders' and slaves' existence on the border of slavery, both geographically and figuratively, represents the diverse experiences of slavery found within the antebellum South.[10]

* * *

On Slavery's Border is not a history of the institution of slavery in Missouri. Although legal codes and the politics of slavery provide a framework, this exploration of Missouri slavery instead focuses on the everyday lives of slaveholders and slaves. The best unit of analysis for this study is the small-slaveholding household. As defined by the historian Elizabeth Fox-Genovese, the southern household was a social and economic unit that encompassed the productive and reproductive activities of all who resided on an individual farm or plantation. She and others have argued that the male heads of southern households, regardless of slaveholding status, by law and custom were granted mastery over all their dependents, men, women, and children, slave and free, and represented their interests to those in the world outside their enclosure. Southern men spoke of these household relations in familial terms, considering those residing within their households, both white and black, as their family, and argued that they governed their dependents through a paternalistic impulse. Scholars of southern women have made particularly insightful arguments about the relations between the black and white women who lived within these households, suggesting that the master served as the pivotal figure in all human relations because only men were imbued with tangible power in southern society. The organization of southern households and the relations among those living within them set them apart from the homes of the emerging northern middle class in significant ways. The big house especially was deemed an ideologically significant site of family and domesticity, but the historian Thavolia Glymph has argued that privileging plantation homes as private domestic space misses the point that these homes were also sites of work, where labor relations were intensely contested.[11]

This definition of the household is of particular significance on small slaveholdings where black and white residents were such an integral part of one another's lives. While historically many individual studies of plantation slavery have focused on discrete members of southern households—only slaveholders, only slaves, or only women—I argue that the intimacy of small-slaveholding household relations makes it illogical to concentrate on one race or gender. Rather, the study of small slaveholdings lends itself to an exploration of the lives of all members of the household—slave and free, male and female, young and old. This book examines the varied dimensions of enslaved and slaveholding Missourians' lives, including their work relations, families, and communities. In addition, their life experiences were greatly influenced by their gender-defined work and social roles, as well as their ages.

On Slavery's Border has a loose chronological organization, beginning with the movement of upland Southerners to Missouri and ending with the destruction of slavery during the Civil War, but by and large this book is arranged topically, as I explore Missouri slaveholders' and slaves' relations of work, families, and communities. Chapters 2 through 6 revolve around important systemic and relational topics, such as the child-rearing and fiscal strategies of small slaveholders, the economics of Missouri slavery, relations between slaves and owners within small-slaveholding households, the challenges faced by enslaved families, and sociability among black and white residents of Missouri's rural neighborhoods. In all chapters except the two that focus on families, I have worked to integrate discussions of both slaves and slaveholders, believing that the nature of small-scale slavery demands an exploration of the experiences of all household members. Keeping true to these topical foci demands the separation of some material; for example, I include information about slave sales in four different chapters: the use of slave sales as a means of financing slaveholders' lifestyles in Chapter 2; the economics of slave sales in Chapter 3; the threat of sale as a factor in slaves' decisions to resist in Chapter 4; and the destruction of slave families due to sales in Chapter 5. These continued discussions across chapters may leave readers with temporarily unanswered questions, but in the end separating the threads of the argument furthers the goals of my overarching arguments about small-slaveholding households.

Chapter 1, "They came like an Avalanche," outlines the ways in which Missouri's geographic location on the South's northwestern border influenced the development of slavery. Settlers hailing from the backcountry of the Upper South flocked to the Mississippi and Missouri River valleys hoping to better their economic and social conditions. Missouri proved a haven for small slaveholders; nearly 90 percent owned ten or fewer slaves. Once in the West, both slaveholders and slaves quickly set about building farms and communities that resembled those they left behind in their eastern homes, but the thousands of westward-migrating Southerners far surpassed their original intentions of replicating an eastern small-slaveholding paradigm and instead created a distinctive slave society in which small slaveholders reigned supreme.

Chapter 2, "Households in the Middle Ground," examines the experiences of the white families who lived in the "big house." Foremost in the minds of those who risked the move westward was the potential for improving the financial and social circumstances of their families and, thus, most of the economic and child-rearing decisions made by Missouri's small slaveholders had this priority at their core. A few Missouri slaveholders acquired the trappings of planter gentility, but most had more modest aspirations. Instead, gender expectations and the work regime of the farm household defined the everyday lives of most middling and small slaveholders and influenced the relationships between husbands and wives and also parents' expectations for their children. Living on the border between the North and the South, as well as on the margins of slaveholding, the sensibilities of both the southern planter class and the northern middle class altered white Missourians' cultural expectations. Decisions about their farms—and ultimately about the lives of their slaves—were affected both by their priorities for their own children and the limitations imposed on them by small-scale slavery.

Chapter 3, "I was at home with the Negroes at work," describes the economic structure of Missouri's small-slaveholding households. Although slavery was entrenched in the state as an economic, political, and social system, the profile of most slaveholding households reflected that of the family farm rather than the plantation. The economic conditions of Missouri slavery influenced the work conditions of both slaves and owners. Missouri farmers did not require many laborers to successfully practice diversified agriculture. Overseers were rarely needed; instead, slave owners worked alongside their slaves, supervising and supplementing their labor in the homes and fields. Expansion created a persistent demand for slave labor, and slaveholders found it profitable to hire out underemployed slaves in the ubiquitous slave-hiring system. This active labor market also decreased the number of slaves sold from the state, thus increasing the possibility that bondpeople would remain near their families and friends.

Chapter 4, "May we as one family live in peace and harmony," explores how the intimacy of small-scale slavery fostered personal relationships between slaves and slaveholders. Eugene Genovese once wrote, "Cruel, unjust, exploitative, oppressive, slavery bound two people together in bitter antagonism while creating an organic relationship so complex and ambivalent that neither could express the simplest human feelings without reference to the other." In some ways these words came to pass on Missouri's small slaveholdings. Indeed, the relations of farm life allowed slaves and owners to influence one another's lives in profound ways. Slaves and slaveholders alike were bound together by common gender and work experiences, but these intimate relations were often double-edged for slaves. Daily interaction afforded slaves resistance opportunities and eroded the authority of their owners but at the same time exposed them to slavery's worst abuses. On the one hand, slaves were well placed to understand the personalities of their owners and used this knowledge to their advantage. The marginal economic conditions of small-scale slavery coupled with the tenuous nature of life on the border encouraged slave resistance and undermined the authority of owners. Some owners also felt an affinity with those with whom they lived and worked so closely, resulting in better treatment of favored slaves. On the other hand, slaves often were exposed to the worst forms of physical and psychological abuse, including sexual exploitation of slave women. In the end, the quality of these relationships often depended on owners' personalities and whims.[12]

It was difficult for small slaveholders and their slaves to extricate themselves from one another when they lived and worked so intimately, yet they created some social spaces that were segregated by race. Slaves did not have the freedom to determine their circumstances as did white Missourians. Many Missouri slaves, for example, were denied daily access to crucial support systems, such as the resident nuclear family and the slave-quarter community. Chapter 5, "Mah pappy belong to a neighbor," describes how the conditions of small-scale slavery affected enslaved families. Small slaveholdings meant that most slave marriage partners came from neighboring farms, and these "abroad" unions profoundly influenced gender dynamics, notions of authority, and the economy within slave households. It was difficult for abroad slave men to provide their wives and children with emotional and economic support when they visited only once a week. Most women cared for the daily needs of their children alone, thereby augmenting the matrifocal tendencies of slave households. Small-scale slavery left many families vulnerable to both temporary and permanent separation through hiring, migration, estate divisions, and sales. But in spite of the many challenges, Missouri slaves tenaciously created and maintained family ties that often survived for many years.

Chapter 6, "We all lived neighbors," describes how black and white Missourians created both integrated and segregated social spaces. All members of the community—slaveholders, nonslaveholders, slaves, and free blacks—interacted socially as they worked together, attended weddings and funerals, and met one another at neighborhood stores or churches. Not all community spaces were shared, however. White Missourians of all classes socialized together at schools, courthouses, militia musters, and at voluntary association meetings, and black Missourians fashioned vibrant interfarm communities, forging ties as they traveled throughout their neighborhoods while running errands for their owners, during hiring assignments, or visiting family members. Owners frequently allowed slaves to celebrate with family and friends at weddings, births, and funerals, but slaves also clandestinely attended brush arbor religious services, visited their lovers, or gambled and danced at parties in the woods. Missouri bondpeople compensated for their truncated families by forging relationships with others in the greater slave network—evidence of adaptability and agency in their lives.

Chapter 7, "The War Within," explores how the multiple tensions always latent in Missouri slavery were dramatically exposed during the years of the Civil War. In the 1840s and 1850s, Missourians increasingly developed ties to the northern marketplace, making it difficult for slaveholders to decide between their pragmatic economic interests and their historical and cultural ties to the South. Slaveholding farmers, not planters, became regional powerbrokers, significantly affecting the sociopolitical economy. Life on the margins of slavery affected the dynamics of white Missourians' families and neighborhoods, as well as influenced their economic and political decisions. Communities were ripped asunder during the war years, with neighbors literally fighting neighbors. Many of the issues of small-scale slavery were exacerbated by these unfolding events. Midway through the war slave men flocked into the ranks of the occupying federal army, and their wives and children fled to nearby military camps or the adjoining free states. Many white Missourians clung tenaciously, and often violently, to slavery even as the system began to collapse from within. Demonstrating agency yet again, Missouri slaves struck a fatal blow to slavery long before they were emancipated in January 1865.

* * *

Slavery existed throughout rural Missouri, although the emphasis of this book is on the experiences of the slaves and slaveholders living in the counties bordering the Mississippi and Missouri Rivers. It was in these areas with large populations of slaves and slaveholders that a slave society flourished. For statistical analysis, I often refer to the ten counties with the largest slave populations in 1860, but occasionally I profile five counties that I believe represent the diverse demographic and geographic makeup of Missouri's slaveholding counties. Chariton, Clay, and Cooper Counties are all located along the Missouri River in the western half of the state in the region commonly referred to as Little Dixie. By the end of the antebellum years, many of the most populous slaveholding counties were located in this Little Dixie region. In 1860, slaves constituted 27 percent of the total population of Clay County, and the slave population in both Cooper and Chariton Counties hovered at a little over 20 percent. With a few notable exceptions, Marion and Ste. Genevieve Counties are representative of the many counties located along the Mississippi River and throughout the state, with slaves constituting a less substantial percentage of their total population.[13]

This book does not address the many slaves who lived in the city of St. Louis, unless their experiences directly related to those of bondpeople living in the Missouri countryside. The city was a vibrant place where people and ideas occasionally fused but more frequently clashed—both German and Irish immigrants and residents of southern origins mingled on the streets of the city, and slave and free laborers existed side by side in the city's worksites. All of Missouri was within the economic and social orbit of St. Louis, and the city was vitally important to the political history of the state during the antebellum years. In fact, St. Louis was at the epicenter of the state's response to the Civil War. The unique experiences of urban slaves—who by and large were owned by small slaveholders as well—are outside the purview of this study, however.[14]

Neither does this book explore the lives of Missouri's free black population. Until the United States Supreme Court put the practice to an abrupt end with its 1857 ruling on the Dred Scott case, for years the Missouri Supreme Court had rather liberally interpreted the law when it came to individual slaves' challenges to their status and often had ruled that those who had lived for an extended time in free states or territories had a right to their freedom. While a sizable free black population lived in St. Louis in the last decades before the Civil War, there were never many free blacks in the Missouri countryside.[15]

This study instead concentrates on the experiences of the thousands of small slaveholders and their slaves who lived and worked throughout rural Missouri. A vast majority of these men, women, and children spent their lives on the state's farms, although some also lived in the towns that dotted the countryside. Occasionally, small planters find their way into this analysis of small slaveholders. Their stories are included in this study because in most cases these men and women began their slaveholding lives in a modest way, and even at the pinnacle of their economic power a vast majority owned fewer than fifty slaves. In addition, Missouri's small planters lived in a society dominated by small-scale slavery, and in the end, their cultural framework ultimately was similar to that of their less affluent neighbors.

Between numerous manuscript collections, government documents, newspapers, and church records, materials related to slaveholding families and white society are abundant. Researching the lives of Missouri slaves and their communities is more challenging, however. There are five valuable former-slave biographies and autobiographies from Missouri—those of William Wells Brown, Henry C. Bruce, Archer Alexander, Mattie J. Jackson, and Lucy A. Delany. In addition, there are a few more than a hundred Works Progress Administration interviews of former Missouri slaves. An equally significant and little used source for the study of slaves' families and communities are the Civil War pension claims of formerly enslaved soldiers. The claims of hundreds of Missouri soldiers, all of whom served in the 65th Regiment of the United States Colored Infantry, and their dependents provide extensive information about slaves' marriages and families, as well as exciting glimpses of extended family ties and interfarm slave neighborhoods.[16]

Many of the historical records used in this book present challenges when it comes to questions of validity. Historians and literary scholars long have recognized that fugitive slaves often had the help of abolitionist editors as they crafted their accounts to adhere to the antislavery genre. Many others have questioned the use of the Great Depression–era

Federal Writers' Project interviews, usually referred to as the WPA narratives, as a definitive source for the study of slavery. Concerns about the narratives abound: many interviewers recorded the testimony using their own interpretation of the subjects' dialect; and interviewees may have held back or altered testimony given to white interviewers, ingratiated themselves to interviewers because of a belief that government aid was forthcoming, forgotten the past due to failing memories in their old age, or may have remembered slavery favorably during times of economic hardship. Indeed, many former slaves recounted stories of favorable treatment at the hands of their owners, and the stories of former Missouri slaves were no different in this regard. At face value, these stories seem to support the myth of benign slavery, but the reality is complex. In contrast to those who recalled kind treatment, many other former Missouri slaves reported devastating physical and sexual abuse, as well as the emotional trauma of divided families due to sales. Concerns about altered testimony are not unfounded, but I strongly believe that it would be a mistake to reject these positive memories, or indeed the WPA narratives, out of hand. A variety of historical sources from Missouri support the argument that the intimacies of small slaveholdings occasionally engendered these types of relationships. In fact, the historian Stephen Crawford, in his quantitative study of the WPA slave narratives, found that one of the greatest determinants of a slave's quality of life was the size of his or her owner's holding. In the South at large, slaves who lived on farms generally fared better than those who lived on plantations, but as William Wells Brown so aptly stated, slavery was slavery no matter the circumstances.[17]

Civil War pension claims also are inherently problematic for use as historical sources because prospective pensioners often set out to game the system in order to ensure the successful receipt of a monthly pension check. Pensioners generally fit into two categories: former soldiers who could prove that they suffered from a disability linked to their military service or the widows, children, parents, and younger siblings of deceased soldiers. By the end of the century, Civil War pensions essentially had become old-age benefits for former soldiers and their widows. In this project I have used only the pensions filed by dependents because they provide more information about the family and community lives of people during slavery. Widows and orphans were asked to prove the validity of marriages and the legitimacy of paternity in the absence of legal proof of weddings and births, and parents and siblings were required to show that the deceased soldier had contributed to them financially during slavery and would have been their primary means of support in its aftermath. Potential pensioners solicited testimony from the deceased soldiers' former comrades, relatives, neighbors, ministers, doctors, and former owners in order to prove their cases. One benefit of pension testimony is that the cases used in this book were submitted in the years directly after emancipation and, therefore, do not suffer from the same issues of potentially faulty memories as the WPA interviews. In addition, those testifying were by and large reporting on their lives as adults during slavery, providing information about migration, hiring and sales, work, treatment by owners, religion, family medical history, and their own family and community histories. The pension records potentially are biased, however, by the fact that would-be pensioners frequently molded the descriptions of their relationships to meet the white middle-class gender expectations and standards of morality promoted by the federal government and occasionally solicited fraudulent testimony from friends, relatives, and local whites. Oftentimes, attorneys were heavily involved in the process, benefiting financially from claims they filed whether or not they were granted. In addition, many of the witnesses deposed were illiterate and dependent on white attorneys and agents to record their testimony. As a result, the language of the depositions often reads in the stilted tone of legal documents, although the witnesses were asked to attest to the validity of the recorded words by signing the document with either their mark or their signature.[18]

Concerns about validity are not confined to evidence left by former slaves, however. The letters and diaries written by Missouri slaveholders are also grossly biased, especially since white owners viewed their slaves through a lens of racial superiority. In addition, white Missourians were concerned with promoting the institution of slavery in the years preceding the Civil War and often wished to present testimony as to the humane nature of slavery in the state. Government records and newspapers often are no less problematic. Official records and newspaper accounts involving slaves were written by white Missourians and reflect their perspective. Even Union military officers were racially biased in their observations about Missouri slaves, although they also viewed Missouri slaveholders with suspicion even when they professed Unionist sentiments.

I have done my best to recognize problems of evidence and potential biases in the many types of sources used in this book and have worked to analyze Missouri slavery and slaveholding in this light. A case in point is the pension records. The United States Pension Bureau scrutinized the files of potential pensioners hoping to ferret out cases of fraud. While the pension officers' judgments frequently were tainted by their own class and racially bound beliefs about the proper sexual and domestic conduct of women, the disputed cases have the advantage of presenting a broad range of evidence from multiple witnesses. I was able to shift through oftentimes conflicting stories to arrive at a reasonable conclusion as to the facts of the case. In addition, I was able to juxtapose the accounts of slavery presented by the pension cases with those remembered by the WPA interviewees, as well as those of white Missourians. Careful readings and comparisons help to avoid some of the pitfalls of using pension records and slave narratives, but ultimately these historical sources are no more or less suspect than those left by white Missourians. The story of slavery in Missouri simply would be incomplete without the voices of the people who suffered under the system. Ultimately, I used the weight of corroborating evidence from a myriad of sources as I constructed my arguments. The reality is that most historical sources regarding slavery fall prey to individuals' subjective memories of an institution that is overwhelmingly burdened by America's devastating legacy of slavery and racism.

I have transcribed all of the sources verbatim, without any corrections or the addition of punctuation, and with a full understanding that many of Missouri slaves' words were filtered through the pen of a white person. Words that were underlined in the sources appear in italics. I have used the [sic] notation only in the instances when I believed the spelling mistakes could be construed as my own and brackets when I substituted a tense, added capitalization, or added a missing word to make the quotation more readable.[19]

1 / "They came like an Avalanche": The Development of a Small-Slaveholding Promised Land

During the winter of 1855, Thomas and Paulina Stratton prepared to move their children and slaves from western Virginia to their new home in central Missouri. This was the Strattons' second move in less than five years, each one undertaken with the hope of improving their circumstances. The couple lived with Thomas's widowed mother, Mary Ann Stratton, in her Roanoke County, Virginia, home after their marriage in 1842. Thomas farmed his mother's Roanoke River bottomland with the labor of a small combined slave workforce—partly owned by him and partly owned by Mary Ann. Paulina, Mary Ann, and the slave women maintained the home and barnyard and contributed to the household economy by weaving and making carpets for neighbors. The Strattons' living arrangement was fraught with conflict, however, because Mary Ann constantly challenged Paulina's attempts to exert authority over household affairs. In 1851, Thomas and Paulina purchased their own farm in northwestern Virginia in a bid to escape this stifling economic dependency but soon discovered that they could not get ahead in mountainous Kanawha County; those who came earlier, including some Stratton kin, had already claimed the most productive and mineral-rich land. As much as Paulina hoped the situation would improve, the poisoned household dynamics were altered little by the move because Mary Ann and her slaves accompanied them to their new home. Within a few short years, Thomas decided to push farther westward in search of a better chance. His aspirations were modest; he never planned to own vast tracts of land or a large number of slaves, but instead he wished to replicate his present life on more fertile, less expensive soil, hopefully bettering his family's prospects in the process.[1]

Like most southern men, Thomas Stratton made the decision to move, and his wife, children, and slaves had little choice but to follow him. Paulina mourned the thought of leaving neighbors and kin in her native Virginia and feared moving "amongst Strangers," although she was somewhat comforted by the fact that Thomas's sister and family would live nearby. The Stratton slaves also faced the move with trepidation because, unlike their owners who could maintain contact through letters, they knew their ties to abroad spouses and neighbors would be permanently severed. These fears were compounded when Mary Ann Stratton died on the eve of the move. A palpable air of uncertainty and despair hovered over the slave cabins in the days before the division of Mary Ann's estate and the moving sale. With little recognition that her slaves' concerns in many ways mirrored her own, Paulina offhandedly remarked that the bondwoman Patience was especially "uneasy about what will become of her dreads a separation from her children."[2]

In mid-March, the Strattons and their slaves hauled their belongings down the mountainside to the banks of the Kanawha River and embarked on the *Salem* for their journey westward, arriving in Boonville, Missouri, twelve days later. Despite her apprehension, Paulina found the steamboat ride pleasant because extended family members and Kanawha neighbors were also on board. The Stratton slaves likely took a different view, however. A few days into the voyage, Thomas's brother-in-law disembarked at Paducah, Kentucky, with the bondpeople that he had purchased from Mary Ann's estate, splitting Patience from her young sons and breaking apart an extended kin group. Those who remained with Thomas and Paulina almost certainly shared the emotions of their mistress when she viewed her new Missouri home and recorded in her diary, "I felt almost heartbroken. It looked so lonesome and desolate I cryed like a child for sometime."[3]

The Strattons and their slaves initially struggled to prosper in Missouri, contending with a series of natural disasters, including drought, sickness of family members and slaves, and the death of livestock. Although gaining a financial foothold was at first elusive, establishing themselves socially in the new land was not nearly as formidable a task for the Strattons and their slaves as it had been for the tens of thousands who had migrated before them. They settled on an already improved 500-acre farm in southwestern Cooper County, an area largely populated by small slaveholders, yeomen, and slaves who hailed from Kentucky and Virginia. The Strattons quickly engaged in the social life of the neighborhood, joining the Cumberland Presbyterian Church, enrolling their children in the nearby one-room schoolhouse, and making friends with their new neighbors. The Strattons' ownership of eleven slaves made them substantial slaveholders by local standards, and the social status bestowed on them as owners of human property presumably helped them forge connections with the upper echelon of society and eased their transition into their new life. In time, the Stratton slaves also adjusted to their new home, although they likely continued to yearn for family and friends left behind even as they established new relationships in Missouri.[4]

Long before the Strattons' arrival, many generations of migrating slaveholders and their slaves already had created a society in Missouri that was patterned after that found in their original homes, bringing with them cultural and economic expectations, including slavery, and transferring them to what was at the time the western edge of American settlement. Missouri's unique geography and history, and the migration patterns that resulted, lay at the heart of the distinctive slave society that emerged on the northwestern border of the slave South. French settlers first brought slaves of African descent to the region decades before the arrival of the first American settlers. After the United States acquired the territory in 1803, Missouri quickly emerged as a prime destination for small-slaveholding farmers and yeomen from the backcountry areas of the Upper South, and they flocked to the region in order to capitalize on the fertile bottomlands of two of the nation's greatest rivers. Never a destination for the South's largest planters, as late as 1860, most Missouri slaveholders owned only a few slaves. Over time, Missouri grew into a region of farmers engaged in diversified agricultural production and light industry rather than an outpost of the cotton kingdom. Although others also decided to make Missouri their home, upland Southerners were demographically prevalent and, therefore, ultimately had the greatest influence on the development of the new land. They fashioned a society that was dominated socially and economically by small slaveholders, thereby altering Missourians' experience of slavery and slaveholding.

Slavery in the Borderlands

The slave society that eventually developed in Missouri had its roots in more than a century of French and Spanish colonial settlement.

African slaves were already a significant presence in the Upper Mississippi Valley by the 1730s, farming the expansive bottomlands on the Illinois side of the Mississippi River and accompanying fur trappers and lead and salt miners west of the river into what later became known as Missouri. It was not until the middle of the eighteenth century that the French established permanent settlements on the western bank of the Mississippi River. European settlement was sparse in Missouri during the early years, although the population increased dramatically in 1763 when French *habitants* living on the Illinois bank crossed over the Mississippi to escape impending British rule after the French defeat in the French and Indian War. Soon after, the French transferred Louisiana to Spain in appreciation of its wartime assistance.[5]

The historian Stephen Aron has dubbed colonial Missouri a "confluence region," for not only do three of America's greatest rivers merge there, but during the eighteenth century this area on the imperial periphery was a meeting place of many peoples and cultures. Missouri was viewed as a place of boundless opportunities from the earliest years of European settlement. A moderate climate, with long growing seasons, mild winters, and ample rainfall, in addition to the rich alluvial soil of the bottomlands of the Missouri and Mississippi Rivers and their extensive tributary systems, supported bountiful harvests; timber was plentiful, and the forests and prairies teemed with abundant game. French families, like the Chouteaus, became wealthy through their trapping and trading connections with native peoples like the Osage, but the rivers and their connections to the Atlantic world were the greatest blessing of the location. From the start, settlers capitalized on distant markets as they shipped their crops and furs down the Missouri and Mississippi Rivers to New Orleans and the transatlantic and coastal trade. Even those who came with little could live comfortably in this "best, 'poor man's country.'"[6]

By the end of the thirty years of Spanish colonial rule, a fairly complex society had developed in Upper Louisiana with a population that had expanded from 1,000 inhabitants, mostly of French and African decent, to 3,083 by 1796. The cultural, economic, religious, and social character of the settlements retained a French character; even the architecture and physical layout of Upper Louisiana's villages had a French flavor. *Habitants* and their slaves cultivated their section of the enclosed common field on the outer edge of villages, growing corn, wheat, tobacco, hemp, and a variety of vegetables and fruits, as well as tending to fowl and free-range cattle and hogs. Farmers sent excess produce to supply Lower

Louisianans, but the fur trade remained the most important commercial venture and primary export. Men commonly left their wives and slaves in charge of their businesses and farms for months at a time while they hunted and trapped in Louisiana's interior. French settlers and slaves also worked the lead mines that were located southwest of St. Louis.[7]

Slaves were integral members of society, making up 38 percent of the population of Upper Louisiana in 1772, and were engaged in most aspects of colonial life, working in the homes, fields, mines, and businesses. These operations remained on a small scale, however, unlike in Lower Louisiana where a plantation society was simultaneously developing. The Code Noir regulated all activities and interactions of Louisiana's slaves and slaveholders during both French and Spanish rule. The law was influenced by the state-supported Catholic Church and afforded enslaved people many protections, such as adequate material conditions, restricted work hours, and limits on physical punishment. The church also encouraged baptism, instruction in the Catholic faith, Christian marriage, and banned the sexual exploitation of women and breaking up families through sale. Conversely, restrictions placed on slaves were limited; they could not carry arms, cohabitate with someone not of their race, or gain manumission without governmental authorization. But in actual practice, a protective slave code did not translate into better conditions for enslaved Louisianans. As was true in Latin America, the laws were never fully enforced, especially not those statutes favoring slaves. There as elsewhere, owners could be violent or abusive, and individuals responded to their servitude with acts of resistance and mitigated their conditions through the support of their families and fellow bondpeople. Any benefits gained from living in Upper Louisiana came not from the law, but from a milder climate and work regime than was found in the West Indies or Lower Louisiana.[8]

The Spanish, like the French before them, hoped to use Missouri as a buffer colony between their settlements in the Spanish Southwest and the British, and later the Americans, to the east, but it quickly became apparent that few French or Spanish settlers would move to Upper Louisiana. The Spanish first encouraged Native Americans, such as the Shawnee and the Delaware, to relocate west of the Mississippi, although they never came in large numbers. In 1787, in spite of their concerns about American encroachment, the Spanish opened the Mississippi River to navigation and invited Americans to move to Upper Louisiana. Enticed by offers of free land, nearly three hundred Americans, including many slaves, moved west between 1787 and 1789, but by the mid-1790s, the

Spanish government actively recruited American settlers by distributing handbills with promises of liberal land grants, an absence of taxes, and peaceful relations with local Indians. American pioneers, such as Thomas Hardeman and Daniel Boone, heeded the call and began migrating into the area after 1796, bringing their families and frequently their slaves.[9]

The first Americans who ventured westward were those already on the vanguard of American expansion. Hunters from Virginia and North Carolina first crossed into the trans-Appalachian west as early as the years following the French and Indian War in order to take advantage of the abundant wild game in Kentucky and Tennessee. It was not long before many also coveted the region's fertile soil, looking to establish permanent homes in a place with enough available land to accommodate future generations. Americans poured westward in the years following the Revolutionary War and staked claims to land in Kentucky and Tennessee through grants from colonial governors, Revolutionary War bounties, and rights of preemption for squatters who first settled and improved the land. Representative of these pioneers was Daniel Boone, who in 1769 first crossed over the Appalachians in search of promising hunting grounds but by 1775 had relocated his family to central Kentucky. Thomas Hardeman was another early pioneer who moved in the late 1770s with his family to the Watauga River Valley in what would become Tennessee, to escape tenancy in western Virginia. At the end of the Revolutionary War, Hardeman, along with many of his fellow war veterans, was lured farther westward by the prospect of inexpensive and fertile lands in the Cumberland River basin of Tennessee, but by the mid-1780s, he had moved his family yet again to near present-day Nashville, where he, his wife, their many children, and his few slaves carved a farm out of the forest.[10]

By the turn of the nineteenth century, American settlers were pushing against the outer limits of the American frontier on the border of Upper Louisiana, settling lands nearly adjacent to the Mississippi River. Many were increasingly dissatisfied with their circumstances; especially troublesome were the countless overlapping land boundary disputes that resulted from haphazard surveying, a land distribution system that favored the wealthy and well connected, and widespread speculation. On the losing end of this litigious land game were many western pioneers, like Daniel Boone, who had first settled the area. The Spanish offer of land in Upper Louisiana promised freedom from both disputed claims and the attorneys who most benefited from the resulting protracted legal battles. Many would have preferred moving to American territory rather than Spanish, but their options were limited by the 1787 exclusion of slavery from the Northwest Territory, encouraging upland Southerners, and especially slaveholders, to migrate to Upper Louisiana instead. They hoped that the climate and soil of Upper Louisiana would allow them to reestablish their modest lifestyles on the newest frontier. French *habitants* continued to dominate Upper Louisiana socially and economically, but Americans quickly outnumbered them, and by 1804, three-fifths of the nearly ten thousand nonnative residents of Missouri hailed from the United States.[11]

Despite their great success recruiting settlers, the Spanish, like the French before them, were frustrated by the high costs of administering Louisiana and leapt at the favorable terms provided by France in the 1800 Treaty of San Ildefonso to rid themselves of the expensive colony. When the reinstated French colonial power promptly closed the port of New Orleans to foreign traffic, President Thomas Jefferson sent James Monroe to join other American diplomats in France to negotiate for its purchase. Meanwhile, the French, cutting their losses in America after the protracted rebellion in St. Domingue, offered to sell all of Louisiana to the United States for $15 million. Upper Louisianans were shocked that the territory had been purchased by the United States, having just received word of the impending transfer of the colony to the French, and were especially concerned that the American government might not extend full rights of citizenship to them or recognize the massive grants of land that the departing Spanish officials had recently made to local residents, particularly the French Creole elite. They also were anxious about the status of their two thousand slaves, fearing that the Americans would outlaw slavery as they had in the Northwest Territory. Most troubling was the potential of unrest among the slave population created by rumors of impending freedom.[12]

The Americans quickly alleviated these concerns by setting up a system to review land claims and instituting a slave code that was patterned after that of Virginia and was stricter than the Code Noir. Americans poured into the territory once property rights appeared secure, and the population of Missouri doubled to around twenty thousand inhabitants by the eve of the War of 1812. The newcomers pushed into the interior, hopping over the rough terrain west of St. Louis and settling as far west as the soon-to-be fabled Boon's Lick region, which was conveniently located along the Missouri River in the central part of the present-day state. Migration temporarily slowed due to massive earthquakes that struck southeastern Missouri in December 1811, rearranging the Mississippi River and the land along its shores. Yet, despite this and fears of Indian attack during the War of 1812, Americans—overwhelmingly from the Upper South—flooded into the Missouri Territory in the years of peace and prosperity that followed the war, establishing a pattern of migration that persisted until the Civil War. John Mason Peck, an itinerant Baptist minister, observed that in the years directly following 1815: "Then the 'new-comers,' like a mountain torrent, poured into the country.... [T]hey came like an avalanche. It seemed as though Kentucky and Tennessee were breaking up and moving to the 'Far West.' Caravan after caravan passed over the prairies of Illinois, crossing the 'great river' at St. Louis, all bound to the Boone's Lick." The fertile and extensive bottomlands of the Missouri River and its tributaries and the adjacent undulating prairie lands soon became legendary. Observers such as Gottfried Duden and Timothy Flint reported the existence of primordial hardwood forests filled with oak, ash, and walnut trees, prairies covered with a variety of grasses that grew taller than the height of a grown man, and deep, rich bottom soil with so few rocks that it was easily plowed and so fertile that its nutrients would not be depleted in a lifetime.[13]

It was not long before Missouri's population grew large enough to meet the requirements for statehood and a firestorm erupted on the national political stage over the possibility of its entrance as a slave state. The controversy dismayed residents because few within Missouri questioned their legal right to the human property that they had brought with them into the territory. They deeply resented Missouri's role as a pawn in the nascent sectional struggle, believing that the state rather than the federal government had the constitutional right to determine internal affairs. Crisis at last was averted by the Missouri Compromise, and statehood was secured without restrictions on slavery. The citizens promptly elected delegates to the Constitutional Convention, which wrote a state constitution with strong protections for slavery, thus recognizing the economic, social, and political importance of the institution. Migration increased dramatically after Missouri's admission to statehood in 1821 confirmed the previously ambiguous status of slavery, and the region quickly emerged as a prime destination for those who felt constricted by lack of access to land and economic and political opportunities in the eastern states of the Upper South. Although there were occasional lulls in migration created by economic downturns and social and political uncertainty, the forty-year period from 1821 to 1860 was one of extraordinary movement of settlers from Kentucky, Tennessee, North Carolina, and Virginia to Missouri.[14]

"Virginians, Carolinians, Tennesseeans, and Kentuckians are moving in great force"

The society that emerged in Missouri was created by thousands of individual decisions to pull up roots in the East and transplant them in western soil. Missouri's geographic location continued to determine the region's demographic and historic destiny after statehood. Certain individuals were attracted to Missouri because of what the land and climate had to offer, but for every upland Southerner who determined that his or her future lay in the West there were many more who had little or no choice but to accompany their husbands, fathers, and owners westward. Over time these many newcomers influenced the society that emerged; even those who had no voice in the migration decision profoundly shaped the character of the place. In the end, the tens of thousands of new Missourians created a society and culture in Missouri that was deeply influenced by their experiences with agriculture and slavery in their original homes.

Indeed, more than a quarter of a million free people from the Upper South, many of them small slaveholders, migrated to Missouri between 1820 and 1860. Neither planters from the Upper South nor migrants of any class from the Lower South moved to Missouri in great numbers; by 1850 the states of the Lower South had supplied fewer settlers than those from the free states. "[S]carcely a Yankee has moved onto the country this year," the *Missouri Gazette* observed in 1820. "At the same time Virginians, Carolinians, Tennesseeans, and Kentuckians are moving in great force." Although after 1830 an increasing number of Northerners and German and Irish immigrants arrived, the United States Census of 1850 demonstrates, by conservative estimate, that two-thirds of the people of Missouri could still trace their origins back to the four Upper South feeder states.[15]

Residents throughout the southeastern states struggled with depleted soil and access to affordable land, and as the antebellum years progressed many became increasingly dissatisfied with their economic circumstances and reasoned that they could improve their prospects in the West. Expansion and migration were long a part of white Southerners' regional, class, and racial identities. They considered access to abundant, inexpensive, fertile land—and ample slave labor to exploit it—the keys to achieving success in the slaveholders' republic. Many southeastern slaveholders believed they could improve their economic and social circumstances on the southern frontier, where they could capitalize on international demand for agricultural products, like cotton and sugar, which grew so well in the warm southern climate. Yeomen, small slaveholders, and planters moved to all of the nation's southwestern territories and states, but the resources, cultural roots, and expectations of migrants often influenced their choice of destination. Planters from the South Carolina Low Country or the Virginia Tidewater, for example, brought their many slaves with them to the frontiers of the cotton kingdom, settling in Alabama and Mississippi, Middle Florida, Louisiana, and eventually eastern Texas in the first half of the nineteenth century. At the same time, many of the less affluent slaveholders from the Upper South chose to move in a more westward direction, first to Kentucky and Tennessee and later to Missouri and northern Arkansas, where they cultivated crops, ranging from tobacco, cotton, and hemp to wheat and corn. They hoped that they could achieve their economic, social, and political goals in the western border states, establishing lives that were similar yet improved on their present ones.[16]

Many Missouri migrants came from the backcountry areas of the Upper South and, therefore, had never personally participated in a full-scale plantation culture. In 1818, Nicholas Patterson described the first large wave of Missouri pioneers: "They, or their fathers, came from the backwoods of the Carolinas, and the less cultivated part of Kentucky and Tennessee." German and Scotch-Irish settlers originally populated the southern backcountry beginning in the eighteenth century, and although slavery was crucial to the region, a majority of the residents did not own slaves. Some upland farmers used the labor of a few slaves to produce a variety of agricultural products, such as grains, tobacco, and livestock, for both household use and sale in the commercial marketplace. Slaveholdings in these areas were by and large modest; depending on the location, between 70 and 90 percent of slaveholders owned ten or fewer slaves. Other small slaveholders and yeomen came to Missouri from areas of the Upper South, such as the Kentucky bluegrass region, that were dominated by planters, but chose to move westward in search of a place where they would not be in direct competition with the economic and political elite. In either case, migrants' choice of Missouri as their destination was directly a result of both their history and their future expectations.[17]

Many migrants brought their backcountry slavery and agricultural customs westward with them to Missouri. Following traditional patterns of migration along parallel latitudes, Upper South migrants were attracted to Missouri because of its relative proximity and similarities to their home states. They believed that they could replicate in Missouri a farming and slaveholding experience much like the one that they left in the East. The state's climate was suitable for the production of corn, wheat, tobacco, hemp, and livestock, all grown for southern and later national and international markets. First and foremost, however, these migrants were enticed westward by the promise of reasonably priced fertile land in the bottomlands of the Missouri and Mississippi Rivers and their tributaries.[18]

Most Upper South migrants believed their small-slaveholding paradigm was more easily replicated in Missouri than in the cotton belt of the southwestern frontier. By the third decade of the nineteenth century, Missouri had emerged as a magnet for southern slaveholding families of limited means. After statehood, an increasing number of slaveholders were willing to risk their valuable property on a venture to Missouri. Timothy Flint, a Presbyterian missionary, marveled at the "power and strength" of the migration of pioneers from the "western and southern states," at the number of a hundred a day, bringing "a hundred cattle, besides hogs, horses, and sheep, to each wagon; and from three or four to twenty slaves." He enjoyed the "pleasing and patriarchal scene" of the many slaves accompanying their owners westward and romantically described these captive migrants as having "delight in their countenances, for their labours are suspended and their imagination excited. . . . The slaves generally seem fond of their masters, and quite as much delighted and interested in the immigration, as the master." By 1860, slaveholders and slaves lived in every Missouri county, although a vast majority settled along or near the Missouri and Mississippi Rivers in order to capitalize on the link to commercial markets. The counties straddling the Missouri River in the western two-thirds of the state, later known as Little Dixie, ultimately held the largest concentrations of slaves. In fact, both the slave and free population in the state grew through migration and natural increase during the forty years following statehood, expanding from 10,222 enslaved people in 1820 to 114,931 in 1860, and from 56,017 free people to 1,063,489 during these same years (see table 1).[19]

Wealthy planters who owned more than fifty slaves did not migrate to the state, and even planters who owned from twenty to fifty slaves never came in great numbers. The North Carolinian Walter R. Lenoir, with his slave force of twenty-three slaves, was one of the wealthiest migrants to Missouri. The same geographic and demographic features that enticed small slaveholders to move to Missouri by and large discouraged most southern planters and even many who aspired to join their ranks. In the end, most southern men on the make were deterred by Missouri's lack of extensive cotton production. Missouri settlers initially had experimented with cotton but found it too risky to produce commercially because the region's 180-day average growing season was shorter than optimal. The little cotton grown in the state was mostly for personal and local market consumption.[20]

Planters also were concerned that slaves—often their greatest source of wealth—were less secure in the southern borderlands. Missouri was surrounded by free states or unsettled territory on three sides, and two of the nation's greatest rivers, the Mississippi and the Missouri, flow through and along the boundaries of the state. Major arteries of trade, these rivers also could carry slaves to freedom. Although there was not an epidemic of Missouri runaways, it is true that for those who did escape, the chances of success, at least compared to the Lower South, were increased by the state's geography. Some potential slaveholding migrants pointed to this threat as a reason not to come to Missouri. In 1851, the North Carolinian J. A. Reinhardt spoke with a man who had recently left Missouri for Mississippi because he lived "near the Illinois line and his negroes become two troublesome runing over to Illinois and he had trouble getting them again." And Thomas Copes of St. Charles, Missouri, chose to sell his slave in Mississippi, observing, "The sole object in disposing of him is the danger of loosing [sic] him here. We are on the edge of the state of Illinois, and they can make their escape across that state to Canada. And do do it every day." Additionally distressing was the violence that erupted on Missouri's western border during the 1850s and the opportunities that the armed conflict created for slave flight.[21]

Many potential migrants believed that Missouri's pivotal role in several of the nation's sectional controversies was indeed cause for concern. Missouri slaveholders worried that slaves were more susceptible to abolitionist interference because of the state's border location. The situation appeared especially dire in the decades preceding the Civil War, when a large number of foreign immigrants and Northerners settled in the state, and abolitionists and free-soil settlers traversed Missouri en route to new homes in Kansas Territory. Some potential migrants, and even many Missourians, believed that slavery was compromised by these developments, but in the end concerns about the newcomers were grossly exaggerated. A few new Missourians held antislavery views, but, outside of St. Louis, they could not effectively organize before the war because proslavery Missourians systematically squelched any dissenting voices. In reality, most Missourians tacitly supported slavery. By and large those who opposed slavery—for moral reasons or more likely because they believed that slavery stifled yeomen and white laborers economically— chose to migrate to free states instead. Most Missourians supported slavery as a system of labor and of social and racial control. In addition, many nonslaveholders had an important economic interest in slavery because they routinely hired the labor of other people's slaves. Some northern migrants enthusiastically embraced slavery. One noteworthy example is Abiel Leonard, who was born in Vermont, studied at Dartmouth College, and moved around 1818 to Missouri, where he married a woman from a wealthy Kentucky slaveholding family and eventually became a prominent Howard County slaveholder, farmer, attorney, and state supreme court justice.[22]

In the end, most southern families with a large number of slaves and ample access to capital believed that the southwestern frontier was a more logical place to create a successful economic future. They ceded the settlement of slavery's northwestern border to less affluent small slaveholders and yeomen from the Upper South, hundreds of thousands of whom flocked to Missouri during the first six decades of the nineteenth century.

"We are now in the midst of a moving poeple [sic]"

All southern pioneers traveled along similar routes to Missouri. In the early days of American settlement, when the lack of good roads made land travel extremely challenging, many followed the rivers to their new homes. They came on flatboats down the Tennessee, Cumberland, and Ohio River systems, until they at last met the Mississippi River, where they faced the challenge of propelling their crafts against its treacherous currents, often with the assistance of French boatmen pulling them up the shore. Despite the difficulties, this was the most practical route to Missouri in the days before steamboats or adequate roads. Sarah Barton Murphy, recently widowed, made just such a trip from Tennessee in 1802, with her children and two slaves, from her home on the Holston River. She joined her three grown sons on land in the interior west of Ste. Genevieve that her late husband, William, had claimed the year before.[23]

After the first steamboats began traversing the waters of the Upper

Mississippi and Missouri Rivers in 1817 and 1819 respectively—although regular steamboat travel was not established until later—many travelers chose this less arduous and quicker mode of transport. It was expensive to move an entire family, with baggage and slaves, by steamboat, however. Selden C. Slater calculated that it cost him $125 to move three white adults, three slave "boys," two horses, and a wagon from Virginia to St. Joseph, Missouri, in 1848. A few years later, the Strattons also journeyed by water with their four children and eleven slaves, changing boats as they traveled down the Kanawha and Ohio and up the Mississippi and Missouri. Although they sold most of their belongings before the move, they shipped some household items westward, spending approximately $200 in the process. Slater, Stratton, and others reported the expense and hassle of lodging slaves, often in jails, on the Kentucky side of the Ohio River for fear that they would flee while the boat docked in free-state towns like Cincinnati. Although the expense could be great, this mode of travel was preferable to the potential hardships of the overland route, and many migrants, such as Paulina Stratton, described the trip as a pleasant one. Even Henry Bruce, a former slave, remembered his boyhood trip from Virginia to Missouri with his master as an exciting break from his daily routine and described his first ride on a steamboat as a "most wonderful experience."[24]

Other southern migrants, especially those with fewer means, chose the less expensive overland option. There were a number of trails from the Upper South to Missouri, but many families from places such as Virginia traveled a route that took them down the Shenandoah Valley, over the Cumberland Gap, across northwestern Tennessee, central Kentucky, and portions of southern Indiana and Illinois, eventually crossing the Mississippi River at St. Louis. Sarah Evalina Lenoir and Sarah Ann Quarles Chandler traveled similar paths from North Carolina and Virginia respectively. Although both were members of prosperous slaveholding families, their wealth and status did not shield them from the hardships of the long journey. Depending on the road and weather conditions and the distance traveled, such a trip lasted from six weeks to many months. Sarah Chandler and her small children were privileged enough to travel in a carriage, but in many cases the family's belongings displaced women and children from wagons and carts. Most bondpeople made the exhausting journey by foot, although a fortunate few reported riding in wagons. At first, both free and enslaved travelers slept in tents, but in later years some found lodging in inns and private homes. It was not unusual for families to travel in the company of kin and friends or with others they met en route. Throngs of migrants clogged the roads during the antebellum years; some were destined for the twenty-fourth state while in the later decades others merely pushed through on their way farther west. As late as 1857, Martha J. Woods observed as she traversed the road to Missouri: "We are now in the midst of a moving poeple [sic] as I never saw anything like it, we are constantly meeting and passing movers."[25]

Tens of thousands left their homes in the East with hopes of creating a brighter future in the new land, but life in Missouri did not meet everyone's expectations. Although many settled permanently, others eventually moved onward in search of something better. Those who ventured to Missouri were represented by what contemporary Nicholas Patterson described as "three classes" of people: transients, who squatted on the land and moved on as settlement encroached; temporary landowners, who viewed land as a fluid commodity to be sold when better prospects beckoned them elsewhere; and established landowners, who viewed Missouri as their permanent home. All three types of settlers were found throughout Missouri during the antebellum years.[26]

The more transient settlers were usually those on the vanguard of frontier development. During the early years, they were pushed out of Kentucky and Tennessee by a lack of economic opportunity. Later, many abandoned the backcountry areas of Virginia and North Carolina for the same reason. Although they dispersed throughout Missouri during the first half of the nineteenth century, by the time of the Civil War, many had settled in the sparsely populated Ozark Mountains. Much of this transient class was made up of those who had few economic resources and no slaves. Public land auctions and the arrival of permanent settlers in the area forced many squatters off land that they could not afford to purchase. The same forces that first propelled these men and women westward caused them to sell their "improvements" to the newly arrived and take their chances elsewhere on the ever-moving frontier.[27]

Initially, the federal government owned most land in Missouri, although some tracts were privately held through earlier grants of land from the French and Spanish colonial governments, military bounties, or New Madrid earthquake claims, which were offered to replace settlers' damaged land in southeastern Missouri with unsettled—and frequently better—land in other parts of the state. The problem of confirmation of land titles plagued the United States government for decades because these early grants often were difficult to validate and frequently were purchased by speculators, but once a majority of claims were settled in an area, the balance of the land went up for sale at public auction. The minimum bid for land was $1.25 an acre, and it was sold in allotments as small as eighty acres. The value of land varied across time and from place to place, but prime land in central Missouri sold for as high as $10 to $20 an acre in the mid-1830s. The 1814 Preemption Act granted squatters the first right to purchase their land, but many were forced to sell their improvements to others because of financial constraints. J. Calvin Berry wrote from Platte County of the possibility of acquiring land from capital-poor squatters as late as 1842: "Though the land is held by premption [sic], and a family on every quarter section in the whole county, but there are a great many farmers who have not the money, and cannot get, to enter their land."[28]

The second group of settlers who came to antebellum Missouri could afford to purchase unsettled or even already improved land. These migrants were more financially secure than the first group, and some owned a few slaves. They built sturdy homes and outbuildings, cleared extensive fields, and began crop production for household use and commercial sale. These newcomers often remained in the same area for a decade or more and became integrated into their communities, but ultimately they were willing to sell their land and move if they felt constricted by their neighbors or perceived better prospects elsewhere. Many, like the Hardemans, within the course of two generations, moved from the eastern seaboard to Kentucky or Tennessee and later to Missouri, only to pick up and move again to Texas or Oregon. In 1844, Waldo P. Johnson described Missourians, many of them substantial landowners, who were caught up by "Oregon fever" and "Texas Excitement" and left for these new frontiers: "[T]here are men in this country who become dissatisfied whenever others settle within ten miles of them; they feel cramped and want more room & without thinking much about consequences, they pull up stakes, and strike for Oregon or Texas." These families often viewed Missouri as a stopping point on their way to somewhere else. As time passed, there were increasingly fewer options for slaveholders choosing to move onward. A good number of Missouri slaveholders moved to Texas with their slave property; a few, such as Judge Hays of Marshall, sold their slaves and joined the pioneers traveling the overland trails to Oregon; and thousands of men were struck by California gold fever, satisfying their wanderlust by attempting to strike it rich during a year or two stay in the West. Others shed their blood, or that of their perceived enemies, in a fruitless attempt to secure their right to carry slave property into the new Kansas Territory.[29]

The final category of migrants—often in financial circumstances not much different from those of the people who moved onward—chose to make Missouri their permanent home. They often invested their resources in enhancing the commercial agricultural potential of their farms through an improvement of their property and an augmentation of their labor force. These persistent families often became the core members of their communities, transforming the wild landscape into cultivated farmlands punctuated by thriving towns. Those who remained are the primary focus of this study, for as the institution builders, they established the churches and schools, opened businesses, built fine homes, ran for political offices, and remained to improve their position economically and socially. Many of those who persisted were slaveholders. Wealthier members of the community, they had more to risk by moving onward.[30]

It is difficult to provide an accurate timetable for the development of Missouri because various geographic areas were settled during different decades. By the late 1830s the Boon's Lick was densely populated, for example, while the Platte Purchase, along the state's northwestern border, had only recently been opened to settlement. Migrants had populated almost all of the state, with the exception of the mountainous Ozarks, by the beginning of the Civil War, however. As a recent arrival observed in 1859: "There are people moving in from all quarters. Missouri is filling up fast—land raising every day." In 1820 only 550,000 acres of public land had been sold, but by 1860 around 20,000,000 acres (nearly half the area of the state) were in private hands.[31]

Once migrants arrived in Missouri they quickly filled up the riverine lands and extended into the interior. At first they settled near the forests that lined the rivers and streams, in order to capitalize on the readily available source of wood and water and the possibility of easy transport of goods offered by the waterways. Many also mistakenly believed that the woodlands were more fertile than the prairies that covered substantial portions of the state. In the early years, some settlers held the widely shared assumption that the grasslands would not support crops because trees did not grow there, while in actuality these lands had greater organic content than the woodlands. Aside from this prejudice, most farmers could not easily break the tough tall grass prairie soil, embedded with a knotted mass of grass roots, with only a shovel or a moldboard plow. In addition, attacks from biting insects discouraged all but the most persistent settlers. It was not until the 1840s and 1850s with the advent of improved agricultural equipment and the coming of the railroads that Missouri's expansive grasslands were fully exploited. Usually the closest the initial pioneers came to settling the prairie was to live at its edge, where they took advantage of the grasses for their livestock.[32]

It was a large investment to relocate to Missouri; the expense of travel to the West and of buying land, seed, implements, and livestock, and building homes, barns, and outbuildings was substantial. Farmers without slaves often were forced to hire help in order to clear their initial acreage. R. Douglas Hurt, an agricultural historian, has estimated that, in the end, it could cost nearly $2,000 to move to and settle in Missouri, and even more if the family owned slaves. Even though travel in the winter was unpleasant, it was ideal if newcomers arrived in Missouri in time to clear the land for spring planting. Those who arrived in the late spring or early summer were forced to wait until the following year to plant a crop. Most new arrivals purchased land and set about improving it, but some could not purchase initially for lack of capital and squatted or rented until they could afford to buy. Once in the new country, most families quickly built modest cabins of horizontally stacked logs—often initially without glass windows or wooden floors—for their families and slaves and then turned their attention toward clearing fields for cultivation. Farmers, their grown sons, and slaves cut out the underbrush in the wooded areas, girdled the larger trees, intending to remove them for firewood once dead, and in the meanwhile, planted their crops among their decaying skeletons in order to make their first harvest. These years of self-sufficiency usually were limited, however, for most settlers quickly brought more acreage into cultivation and began to engage in diversified farming, growing crops such as corn, flax, and clover, as well as raising hogs, sheep, and cattle. From the beginning, Missourians took advantage of the state's fortuitous river system that provided easy access to the growing national and international markets and began to commercially raise livestock and grow cash crops such as tobacco and hemp. Settlers set about transforming land that they viewed as untamed into cultivated farmland, and over time they also fashioned a built environment to reflect their cultural preferences. Missourians believed that their manipulations of the physical environment brought order to it and considered it a moral imperative to transform the frontier into what they understood as civilization. The newcomers also set about to create a social and political order that resembled the one based on racial and class prerogatives that most had experienced in their original eastern homes. The transformation was swift, especially in the lands along the river, which were quickly claimed by upcountry slaveholding farmers. The labor of thousands of slaves of African descent dramatically increased the economic potential of the new land, and relegating bonded workers to the bottom social rung ensured the dominance of white Missourians.[33]

In the later antebellum years, some migrants were able to bypass this initial frontier stage and the labor-intensive process of building from nothing. Wealthier slaveholders, such as Walter Lenoir and Thomas Stratton, were concerned about the risks of relocating and carefully weighed their choices, often traveling to Missouri to scout out possible homes. In 1834, Walter Raleigh Lenoir sent his nephew William from North Carolina to identify a promising location where he might settle his family and twenty-three slaves the following year. Twenty years later, Thomas Stratton made scouting trips to both Texas and Missouri before purchasing in central Missouri. Each man employed a different settlement strategy once he arrived in Missouri. Walter Lenoir first rented until he could find suitable property, and meanwhile discovered that hiring out his slave men in the surrounding neighborhood was an excellent source of capital in a cash-poor land. He wrote soon after his arrival in Boone County: "In adopting this course I will have less care on my mind and can have more time to explore the country dureing [sic] the next season." Hiring out slaves provided many slaveholders with an income while they waited for their first harvest. As one Missourian explained, "[T]hose who have negroes can hire them very readily for Cash these advantages enable the Emigrant to live at little expence untill they/he can situate themselves/himself and raise grain." In contrast, Thomas Stratton purchased already improved acreage in Cooper County's New Lebanon Township before his move, and once he arrived in Missouri he quickly set about putting in crops with the assistance of his small slave force.[34]

Slaveholders who came in later years were at an advantage over those who had moved earlier. Many knew that when they arrived family and friends would greet them and help ease their transition into their new neighborhoods. Those who migrated in the years after 1830 were able to establish themselves in settled communities, which resembled those that they had left in the East. With the exception of the Platte Purchase, by the mid-1830s most locations—especially those riverine counties most attractive to slaveholding migrants—contained numerous businesses, churches, and at least one school. It was possible for those with sufficient capital, like Thomas Stratton, to purchase improved property in well-developed townships with such amenities.

Another economic strategy pursued by ambitious newcomers, especially young men, was to move to Missouri in order to establish a business or practice a profession. Lawyers, doctors, and merchants found the frontier profitable, as initially men of their professions were scarce. Early settlers commonly complained of the exorbitant fees charged by doctors or of merchants gouging them with high prices as they took advantage of sales to newcomers and in later years in outfitting pioneers traveling on their way to the far West. Although many of these professional men were able to support themselves and their families handsomely from the proceeds of their businesses or practices, they often chose to engage in farming as well. Abiel Leonard and William Napton were both attorneys and later judges who used slave labor to cultivate their farms. The attorney Waldo P. Johnson explained to his brother in Virginia why it was an imperative to purchase land: "[I]t gives a man an importance in the community that he would not otherwise have, and here as well as elsewhere, the people are disposed to encourage and patronize those who do not specially need their aid." Johnson believed that owning land would elevate his social standing and thus increase his legal clientele. He also may have been responding to the American, and particularly southern, cultural assumption that independent, and even civilized, men should be connected to the land. What remained unsaid—perhaps there was no need to say it to a Virginia man—is that the status of a southern man improved considerably through the ownership and mastery of slaves. In this sense, Missourians' priorities were no different from those of white men in any other slave state.[35]

"Come onto [this] country with out hesertating aney longer"

The decision to leave eastern homes for an uncertain future in the West was rarely an easy one to make. Potential migrants had to balance the comforts and connections of home with the possibility of a more prosperous life in the West. Most left with a heavy heart, wondering if they would ever see their family and friends again, and were comforted by the hope that they might meet again in heaven. Men often reasoned that the great sacrifice of leaving loved ones behind was worth it if they improved their economic situation in Missouri. Jesse Mellon conveyed the feelings of many when he wrote to his mother in 1839: "I am in hopes you will rejoice to here [sic] that I have bettered my self and famely so much by comeing out here I would like veary much to see you agane and I am in hopes I will tho if I should not I am in hopes to meet you where parting will be no more." Few women were consulted about the decision to migrate, and some did not share their husbands' enthusiasm for the idea. Many placed a greater premium on kinship ties and were reluctant to leave their families and friends for a westward venture. Others feared the physical hardships of the arduous journey and settlement on the frontier. In general, women were much less likely than men to believe that worldly gain was worth the pain of leaving loved ones behind. Typical was Sarah Evalina Lenoir, who soundly rejected the economic determinism of her husband, Walter Raleigh Lenoir, and others like him, reckoning that "when I think of the kind friends we have left it is most too great a sacrifice to be reconciled to for the sake of a little more of this worlds goods."[36]

Sentiments about migration were never entirely bound by gender, however. Although it is true that white men migrated westward in order to better themselves and that many of their wives and mothers regretted leaving their homes, there was a much greater range of motivations and emotions than this assessment acknowledges. Some women wished to move westward in order to escape unfavorable situations—either personal or economic. Paulina Stratton initially wished to move to Missouri to get away from her mother-in-law, for example, although she did not find relocating as appealing after Mary Ann Stratton's unexpected death. Many women were fascinated by the trip westward, recording every detail of what they saw around them, taking the hardships of the journey in stride, whereas some, like Elizabeth Ann Cooley, were conflicted: "I . . . regret leaving home . . . I fear I will never be satisfied if I am here. I remember and with great regret the good water of Carroll [North Carolina], and if there, I remember the rich productive soil of Mo. I fear my peace of mind is forever shaken." Once on the western frontier, men and women equally missed their family members and actively showed an interest in maintaining kinship ties, although men were the most likely to sing the praises of their new home in order to entice relatives to move westward. Waldo Johnson lamented to his mother in 1845: "The reflection that the Earth has performed one complete revolution since I bid, perhaps a final adieu to everything on earth, which had then, or yet has, a place near my heart, fills my mind with the deepest melancholy." But men, more often than women, reconciled this loss by what could be gained in Missouri. A. A. Edwards explained best in 1834: "This is not pleasant for me to think about, and much more unpleasant to talk about, for I have [fond] ties in Old Virginia that will be hard to sever, and *friends* although few, that I will never meet with [anyw]here. still when one's welfare and interest is at sta[ke it] is best to nerve himself up to the point and summ[on u]p resolution sufficient to leave both friends and cou[ntry]."[37]

When migrants first arrived in Missouri, many experienced pangs of loneliness, compounded by the fact that neighbors often lived miles apart during the early years of settlement. Henry Brackenridge told of a family so secluded before statehood that they did not know the name of the president of the United States. This story may be apocryphal, but it conveys the dislocation many newcomers felt from all that they had left behind in the East. Indeed, the very land seemed foreign from what they had known before. Unfamiliar flora, fauna, and even weather patterns were experienced, deciphered, and conquered; forests were felled, wetlands drained, fields groomed, houses, barns, and outbuildings constructed, and businesses, schools, and churches established. Initially, many expressed concerns about the lack of civilizing forces on the frontier. Reverend Timothy Flint claimed that a good number believed that when they crossed the Mississippi River they had traveled "beyond the Sabbath." Newcomers, particularly women, yearned for the familiar institutions that reminded them of home. Migrants regretted finding few churches, especially of their chosen denomination, yearning for a place to seek solace in an unfamiliar country. During the later antebellum years, slaveholding families generally settled in the most populous and well-developed parts of Missouri, thereby escaping such isolation, yet many, like Paulina Stratton, still felt lonely on arrival despite their presence in well-established neighborhoods. Eventually, most established new friendships, joined religious and civic organizations, and became more satisfied with their chosen homes.[38]

Slaves' feelings about migration were by and large unambiguous, however. Timothy Flint's description of slaves traveling with "delight in their countenances" rings patently false. Enslaved migrants obviously had no voice in the decision to come to Missouri, and many experienced heart-wrenching dislocation as they were forcibly marched westward. By whatever means eastern slaves arrived in Missouri—either through slaveholder migration or the domestic slave trade, the end result was typically the same: the vast majority were separated from immediate family members and extended kin and were removed from familiar places and routines.[39]

Between 1790 and 1860 more than a million American slaves were transported from the Upper South to the Lower South. The same economic forces that propelled seaboard planters westward encouraged those who remained to sell their slaves into the domestic slave trade. Exhausted soil forced a transition from the cultivation of tobacco to small grains and resulted in a declining need for labor in places such as Virginia, Maryland, and North Carolina, at the same time that a demand for labor emerged on the southwestern frontier as planters needed more and more workers to cultivate cotton. Owners in the Upper South were rich in slaves, and they converted this vast economic resource into cash as they jettisoned part of their labor force to the Deep South. Historians have estimated that in the years between 1810 and 1860 throughout the South as a whole 50 to 70 percent of enslaved migrants were forcibly transported between regions in speculators' coffles.[40]

As in the other western states, the slave population of Missouri increased dramatically during the antebellum years. The historian Michael Tadman includes Missouri in a list of net "importing" states throughout its antebellum history, calculating that in each decade after 1810 there was a net increase in the number of slaves living in Missouri that was greater than what would have come from natural reproduction. Clearly, Missourians were responding to the demand for labor by importing slaves into the state. Tadman argues that a majority of slaves brought westward from the Upper South came to Missouri with traders rather than their owners. He examined the age structure of slave populations throughout the South to determine the number of people who were transported through the domestic slave trade, reasoning that the trade resulted in populations with higher percentages of individuals of prime productive age, since planters usually migrated with slaves who spanned the age spectrum. He believes that the demographics of the Missouri slave population reflect the pattern of migration by the slave trade.[41]

Indeed, there are scattered references to slaves coming to Missouri in traders' coffles. In 1849, the *Liberty Tribune* advertised the sale of twenty-five "choice young negroes" from twelve to twenty years of age in Platte County, which had recently been opened to settlement: "from the plough boys and hemp breakers, from the nurses, house girls and seamstresses, to the cooks, washers and ironers—the above negroes have just arrived from old Virginia, under the best discipline, bought with care, sound and healthy, and titles good." A few months later the same paper reported that a Maryland trader was en route to Missouri with a "gang of nearly one hundred negroes." In the years before the war, Emma Knight's mother was sold and shipped west "from Virginia or down south some place. Dey brought her in a box car with lots of other colored people. Dere was several cars full, with men in one car, women in another, and de younger ones in another, and de babies in another with some of the women to care for dem." Although it cannot be determined whether they actually came as part of the slave trade, two other former slaves claimed that their parents were brought to Missouri when they were children without their mothers or fathers accompanying them.[42]

Some of those transported westward indeed were children; most lost all contact with family members when they were sold. Malinda Discus's mother "was separated from her parents when eleven years old and brought to Missouri from Tennessee. She never saw any of her folks again and the last words her mother said to her was: 'Daughter, if I never see you again any more on earth, come to heaven and I will see you there.'" Margaret Nickens's parents, one from Kentucky and the other from Virginia, also came West as part of the domestic slave trade. She recalled their story: "Dey never seen dere parents no more. Dey watched for a long time among de colored people and asked who dey was when dey thought some body looked like dere parents, but never could find dem. Dey was so small when dey left, dey didn't even remember dere names."[43]

The manuscript records from Missouri, including slave narratives and pension claims, strongly suggest that most slaves accompanied their owners westward rather than were brought through the interstate slave trade, however. Many former slaves, such as Sarah Graves and Martha Ann Woods, reported coming to Missouri with their owners, their mothers, and their siblings, leaving their fathers with their owners in their home states. Others were sent to Missouri from various states in the Upper South as part of an intergenerational transfer of property; often given as gifts to slaveholders' children or when estates were divided. Jeanette Leonard and Melinda Napton received slaves from their fathers' Kentucky and Tennessee estates, and William Fleetwood brought the slaves he had inherited after his father's death, a woman named Elizabeth and her four small children, back to Missouri with him from North Carolina.[44]

Other Missouri slaveholders looked to relatives and friends in their home states, which were exporting slaves in large numbers, to hand select and purchase bondpeople for them. Always wary of the inflated claims of traders, prospective buyers attempted to instill a bit more quality control into their purchases, as well as save the speculator's price markup. Thomas Houston asked his relatives in North Carolina to watch for and buy for him two "young, smart, and likely" slave boys from twelve to sixteen years old. Eventually he hoped to increase his male workforce to ten or twelve—not a modest holding by any means. When the Napton or Leonard families were in need of a slave driver or a cook, Melinda Napton and Jeanette Leonard asked their fathers to assist in locating them. Although in the end, many Missouri slaveholders preferred buying slaves in the local slave trading market to acquiring unknown slaves from afar.[45]

Whether brought to Missouri through the slave trade or by their owners, the result was often the same; enslaved people were separated from those for whom they cared. Large planters might transport complete slave quarters with them when they relocated, thereby maintaining the family and community ties of many of their bondpeople, but this was not usually the experience of those living on the multitude of smaller holdings in the Upper South. In regions dominated by small-scale slavery, kin often were scattered among many different slaveholdings both because individuals commonly formed romantic attachments and friendships with those living on neighboring farms and because family members frequently were sold or dispersed among heirs when their owners died. In areas closer to the eastern seaboard, complex relationships developed over generations between slaves living within slave quarters and on nearby farms and plantations, and individuals often maintained at least limited contact with loved ones who lived within the general neighborhood. When slaveholders migrated westward, many of these relationships were destroyed. Migration or long-distance sales were of great consequence for slaves, as it was likely that they would forever lose contact with the family and friends who remained behind. The ultimate fear of most was that their owners would sell them or move them away from loved ones. The emotional response of the Strattons' slave woman is indicative of many who faced the uncertainty of estate divisions and migration. Patience's fears were well founded, of course; she was ultimately parted from some of her children.[46]

Most slaves were separated from at least some family members when their owners migrated to Missouri. Sarah Waggoner and her mother never saw her abroad father again after her master came from Kentucky, and Nancy Jackson lost contact with her husband when her master brought her from Virginia. Harvey Lamm brought his slave Margarett and her two children to Boone County, Missouri, from Kentucky in 1850, "[s]eperating her from her husband, who belonged to W^mGrey, but who was not willing to come to Mo." Jane Washington explained how she was torn from her husband, who was owned by another slaveholder, when her master moved from Kentucky: "Marser wouldn't sell him and marser wouldn't sell me is what parted us." Washington resisted her owner's callous disregard for her personal life in one of the few ways open to her; she refused to remarry for nine years. Another slave, forced by her master to remarry, chose a man she knew to be infertile in order to thwart the designs of her owner and preserve the memory of her Virginia husband, whom she had left behind when she was forced westward. Some slaves protested their owners' attempts to remove them from loved ones by running away and thus depriving them of their property. Virginia slave William Brown was incensed by his owner's refusal of an offer to purchase him made by the owner of his wife and children on the eve of relocating to Missouri. Brown's owner would not take the $220 offered for the 60-year-old slave man, saying, "I can get that out of him in Missouri in three years." En route to Missouri by water, Brown's master housed almost all his slaves on the Kentucky side of the Ohio River when the boat docked in Cincinnati but trusted Brown to remain on board to tend to his horses. Brown seized the opportunity, walked off the boat, and made his way to freedom in Canada.[47]

Some owners empathized with the difficulty of their slaves' situation and rewarded their sacrifice. A few, such as David Thomson, agreed to sell or purchase individual bondpeople in order to keep abroad families intact. Others, such as Walter Lenoir, came westward with too many slaves to be of use on a Missouri farm but chose to hire them out rather than sell them. Lenoir considered this decision a financial sacrifice, explaining that "it would be to my advantage to sell 8 or 10 negroes at the present high prices and purchase land with the money. But they have conducted themselves well, and had left their connections under the expectation of remaining with me, therefore feel disposed to do by them as I would have them do by me if I was in their stead." Many more, such as Thomas Stratton, selectively decided which slaves to keep together when they migrated. Stratton allowed an elderly slave woman to remain in Virginia with her free black husband and sold a young slave woman, Charity, to his brother-in-law so that she might remain with kin, yet he separated Patience's two eldest sons from her. Other owners made similar decisions, bringing productive laborers and the young with them westward and leaving the elderly or sickly behind.[48]

Often knowing only one another, owners and slaves were forced into a heightened interdependency, turning inward as they labored together to establish housekeeping, prepare the land, and plant their first crops. While still living in Virginia, Paulina Stratton relentlessly complained about her slaves and their numerous acts of resistance, but during the first year in Missouri her diary was suspiciously silent on matters of slave management. The unfamiliar surroundings temporarily altered the relationship between the Strattons and their slaves while both were busy establishing the farm and acclimating themselves to the new environment.

These improved relations were often at significant psychological and emotional cost to enslaved migrants. C. P. Tate reported to his brother soon after he moved to Missouri that his slave family had grown well enough to almost do "a mans work" and that his slave Sally was behaving much better now that he had taken "full command of her." Sally may have been emotionally broken by the move westward and her forced separation from her husband because, as Tate explained, "she still has her ill nature spell but soon gets over them as she has not her husband to back her in them." The move likely placed bondpeople in less favorable conditions to resist because although many acts of resistance were solitary, they often relied on kin and neighbors to reinforce their efforts. Disconnected from their social support systems, and likely agonizing over it, many were temporarily subdued in their servitude. As with white settlers, there was a period of adjustment for the newly arrived as their bodies acclimated to the climate and diseases of the new land, and as they interjected themselves into the social life of the neighborhood and familiarized themselves with the physical spaces where local bondpeople met and mingled on their own terms. Newcomers commonly remained close to home until they made these connections and gained knowledge of their surroundings.[49]

The only link between the migrants and their loved ones in the East was an occasional letter. White migrants devotedly engaged in epistolary exchanges, often despite limited literacy; few black migrants had this luxury. In later years, when travel became easier by steamboat and rail, some more affluent white Missourians were able to visit their relatives in their former homes in the East. Most had to rely on the often untrustworthy and slow mails to bring them news of family and friends, however. Letters were such a precious commodity that when relatives and friends did not write for great lengths of time they could count on a vigorous chastisement. Death from disease was common, so letters frequently opened with the phrase, "I am . . . writ[ing] you a few lines informing you that I am still in the land of the living," but it was not uncommon to send letters reporting the deaths of loved ones or family slaves, especially the elderly and the very young. Once the general health of family members was established, writers usually informed their readers of news of neighbors, kin, and slaves, the prospects for a good crop that year, and local politics.[50]

Both men and women wrote to their kin about individual slaves and their adaptation to the circumstances of migration and especially about their sicknesses and deaths. Compassionate owners, understanding the pain caused by the separation of enslaved families, included messages in their letters from their bondpeople to their family members owned by white relatives and friends. Oftentimes the message was as simple as, "The negroes desire to be remembered to their kinfolk." Jeanette Leonard brought family slaves to Missouri from her father Benjamin Reeves's home in Kentucky, and white family members frequently relayed messages between slave relatives living in different states. On her own initiative, Octavia Blackwell Chilton sent information about those owned by her to their kin who still lived in Virginia. Owners were especially accommodating if slaves' messages portrayed their decision to migrate in a positive light, perhaps believing that a report that even enslaved migrants were pleased with the new country emphatically endorsed their decision to remove westward. Robert Brown's slave William asked him to tell "his Father & Mother that he likes the county [sic] much better now than he did at first & hopes to like first rate after a while." Brown added that William did not appreciate "the cold weather but says it's a first rate country for black folks to get plenty to eat in."[51]

Migrants hoped that their relatives and friends in the East would eventually decide to venture westward as well; bondpeople might even look forward to reunions with family if their owners' kin moved to Missouri. Aside from economic considerations, the greatest inducement for a family to leave its eastern home for Missouri was to follow kin who had already made the journey. Part of the "avalanche" of settlers from the Upper South was directly linked to the fact that family and friends followed one another westward.[52]

The development of the New Lebanon community in southwestern Cooper County, Missouri, is a prime example of the importance of chain migration to the settlement of the West. Members of the Lebanon Cumberland Presbyterian congregation, which was located in what is now Logan County, Kentucky, were among the first to settle New Lebanon. This group of early pioneers hailed from the southwestern Kentucky epicenter of Cumberland Presbyterianism, a sect that had broken away from the Presbyterian Synod because of theological differences following the Great Kentucky Revival. Although the entire congregation did not leave Kentucky, dozens of interconnected families followed one another westward over a twenty-year period. As early as 1819, Lebanon's minister, Finis Ewing, one of the original founders of the Cumberland Presbyterians, observed that nearly half of his congregation had removed westward, most bound for central Missouri, and many more families were on the verge of leaving Kentucky. In 1820, a core group of Lebanon congregants established the New Lebanon Cumberland Presbyterian Church in southwestern Cooper County. Multifaceted and intertwined strands of kinship, friendship, and Christian fellowship pulled additional migrants westward. Over time, the original Lebanon congregants had become increasingly interrelated through marriage, and it was typical for brothers and sisters to follow one another westward, as well as the siblings of their spouses, creating a chain of migrants that encompassed a large part of the original Kentucky community, including individuals outside of the original congregation, many of whom were Baptists.[53]

The adult children of John and Catherine Cordry were swept up in the movement of their Logan County neighbors to southwestern Cooper County in the first two decades after Missouri statehood. Seven out of nine of the Cordry siblings made the decision to move to Cooper County; a married sister and her family remained in Kentucky, and another married sister and her husband moved to Illinois. John Cordry was the first to move to Cooper County, bringing his wife, Martha, and young children as early as 1828. John's two brothers Charles and James followed with their wives and children in the fall of 1830 and were accompanied by their widowed mother, Catherine. It appears that their sister Elizabeth arrived in Missouri with her husband, Samuel Finley, soon after. By 1835, the youngest Cordry sibling, Elijah, had moved his family to the area, and in 1837, the year after the death of the matriarch, Catherine, Sally Cordry Mann and her husband, Andrew, and their children made the decision to join her siblings in the West. Not only did most of the Cordrys move to Missouri, but many of their in-laws did as well. A number of the siblings of Margaret Murphy Cordry, the wife of James, also moved to the New Lebanon area with their spouses and children. The Cordrys and their many connections went on to become prominent members of the community, serving as founders of the West Fork Baptist Church and School and establishing sizable farms that frequently were operated by slave labor.[54]

Most Missourians embarked on a course of selling the virtues of their new home to their family and friends who remained in the East rather than leave their decision to chance. Often these descriptions of Missouri were so glowing that they must be read with a skeptical eye. A common vein that runs through these letters was an attempt to disparage eastern homes in order to enhance the desirability of Missouri. One such account was that of Samuel Ralston who wrote to North Carolina relatives about the advantages of Missouri "over poor 'let well enough alone' North Carolina. Missouri, at this time has more inducements for emigration *than any state in the Union* and more particularly to the agricultural class." He went on to "recommend, and urge you to become a citizen of this State, and suffer me to request that you will use every exertion in your power to induce our friends in Carolina to do likewise." Others were more balanced in their approach, assessing both the positive and the negative aspects of migration to the new land. In the end, their letters usually contained many more positive descriptions than otherwise, declaring that they were very pleased with their new home. Thomas Duggins believed that his father and mother would do "much better than Virginia with the same industry and economy," but he feared that they would "undergo a great many little hardships and privations" that would be difficult to endure because of their advanced age. Often new settlers suggested to their eastern relatives to "come out . . . and judge for yourself," informing them that once in Missouri they would never wish to return to the worn-out lands of home. Ethelbert Lewis wrote in 1838, "The more I see of Mo. the better I am pleased. But I advise any of my friends who think of migrating to see for them selves."[55]

Most correspondents gave the prospect of economic betterment as the primary reason to migrate. Recent settlers, such as J. R. Bohannon, often compared the fertile land in Missouri to the spent soil of their former homes and claimed that "I am delighted with the country Old Va. can never hold me again." A. A. Edwards wrote in 1834 that he would never return to his old home because he could not imagine how he could "make a living by cultivating that poor Forrest land," especially when he compared it with "the products of this fertile country." William Powell emphatically informed his brother: " [W]e dont want the land aney richer it is richer nough." And their father professed that "it is the greatest Country for Corn Tobacco and hogs Cowes and horses that Ever was known" and that he would not give up his 240 acres of fertile Missouri land "for ten thousand acres of the best land in Caswell [North Carolina]." Martha Allen informed her aunt in 1857, "I think if you could see the hevy crops of grain you would be wiling to leave them red nobs to go where you could see good crops without so much labor." Others commented about the ability to produce more per acre in the fertile Missouri soil with less labor: "[T]hey make at least one third more here to the acre than you do with half the labor." Most assured their relatives and friends that they were doing well in their new homes. John Burch explained: "I live fully as well here as I did in Maryland, except that I have not wine every day, as I had there." He encouraged his uncle to come to Missouri and bring his daughters with him as he was "persuaded, your Girls would marry much better here, than in the old country, for you well know that a new country always for men of enterprise." Justus Post agreed, claiming that Missouri was "the best country for an industrious and enterprising man to get rich in that I ever saw."[56]

Those writing to their relatives and friends in the East knew that they wished for information in addition to the economic potential of the country. Often correspondents attempted to dispel fears about the unsettled state of society and especially about the rumored unhealthy nature of frontier Missouri. In an 1834 act of boosterism, Walter Lenoir described the citizens of Boone County, Missouri, as friendly, moral, and religious people, who mostly hailed from Kentucky and Virginia. Lenoir went on to enumerate the businesses, schools, and fine brick houses in Columbia. Clarinda Tate observed that the people of Callaway County "all appear very genteel and extremely kind," while James Robinson claimed that the residents of Washington County "dress here in an expensive and fashionable stile more so than in any part of the old states with which I am acquainted." Others, like John Slater who migrated to the Platte Purchase in 1848, cautioned relatives and friends in the East not to expect too much when they arrived, observing that there was "not that real refinement of manners nor the fashionable etiquette of which Eastern Virginia boasts so much." He expected that northwest Missouri would "advance in intelligence & refinement" in the near future since in the river counties of "Clay, Jackson, Lafayette, or Saline these advantages can be procured to a considerable extent," although he observed that migrants paid a premium for land in these more settled locations.[57]

Individuals also made migration decisions based on the reputed "health of the country," choosing to settle on land that their experience led them to believe was "salubrious." They struggled to reconcile the fact that the land in the river and creek bottoms was often most fertile but at the same time was most unhealthy, embedded with the mysterious and troublesome "miasmatic" qualities of wet lowlands. Settlers quickly learned that those individuals who lived in or near these low-lying spots were likely to wear the sallow complexion of those who suffered from the ague, or malaria as it is known today, but they had no understanding that the mosquitoes who lived in these environments were vectors of the disease rather than the water or air itself. "The best and richest land is most sickly, poor high land more healthy than low bottom land," complained a newcomer to his brother in England. Eventually settlers either built their homes on higher ground and sent their bonded laborers into the unhealthy bottoms to work the fields near the rivers and creeks or directed those same workers to drain the wetlands or cut down the strand of riverside timber and convert the area to farmland. Walter Lenoir tellingly assured his friend in North Carolina that the people of Boone County "enjoy as good health as in any part of the world" if they refrained from settling too near the river and creeks.[58]

Letter writers frequently advised potential migrants of the best places to settle—those areas with the best quality and healthiest land at the lowest prices and with the best society. They recommended the ideal time of the year in which to travel and even provided suggestions for how to successfully dispose of their property in the East. Almost all writers encouraged potential migrants to bring a substantial amount of hard money, as the currency situation in the state remained tenuous throughout the antebellum years. Some, like John Burch, even suggested what belongings to bring: "[S]ell everything except their Negroes not even making a reserve of their Beds and Bedcovers. Goods of every sort are certainly much cheaper here than I ever knew them in Maryland."[59]

Whereas some acknowledged the initial hardships of migration, most believed that the rewards were sufficient to outweigh any inconveniences. Few admitted that they had made the wrong decision in coming to Missouri, perhaps precisely because they wished to encourage the migration of family and friends. If an eastern relative received word that a relative was unhappy, Missourians usually denied the rumor. Most were unwilling to admit that Missouri had not lived up to their expectations or that they had failed financially in the new land—most likely difficult admissions to make, especially if those at home had discouraged migration. Rather than give up and return to their eastern homes, most instead urged their family and friends to "Come on to [this] Country with out hesertating aney longer."[60]

The Small Slaveholders' El Dorado

Migration to Missouri peaked in 1835, but settlers from the Upper South flocked to the state up until the eve of the Civil War; the Little Dixie counties, located along the Missouri River in the western two-thirds of the state, continued to grow throughout the antebellum years. The state's unique geography and history influenced the type of settlers who ventured to Missouri, and over time, the sheer weight of their numbers altered the course of development. Slavery was a vibrant economic and social institution in Missouri, and although some fissures began to appear after the 1840s because of the influx of Northerners and foreign immigrants and the conflict over slavery in Kansas, it remained important to the state. The society crafted by the thousands of small slaveholders and their slaves had slavery at its foundation. The institution touched most aspects of Missouri life, but the predominance of small-scale slavery resulted in a slavery and slaveholding experience that differed in significant ways from that in the East. Even though by 1860 slaves made up a little less than 10 percent of the total population of the state, slavery was central to the economy and society of antebellum Missouri nonetheless.[61]

Missouri emerged as a prime destination for small slaveholders and yeomen who hailed from the Upper South. These backcountry men and women were led westward by a dream of economic betterment for the present and future generations of their families in the small slaveholders' "el dorado." They quickly recognized the potential for success in this new land dominated by others like themselves. Missouri's climate was suitable for production of corn, wheat, tobacco, hemp, and livestock, all of which Missouri farmers raised for markets in the Lower South, where planters were too busy cultivating cotton and sugarcane to waste valuable time growing food products or producing hemp baling and bagging for their cotton. More than the climate dictated Missourians' economic decisions, however. A plantation society on a large scale never developed in Missouri. Intensive labor was required for the cultivation of Missouri's two cash crops of hemp and tobacco, but planters never migrated in the numbers necessary to make large-scale production a possibility. Those who accumulated the number of slaves required for planter classification usually amassed them over time after they arrived in Missouri. Even so, in comparison to slaveholders in the Lower South, few Missourians ever achieved planter status, and larger slaveholders, like Walter Lenoir, rarely used slaves in large-scale production of exclusively cash crops. Most Missouri owners instead pursued agricultural practices that merged diversified agriculture with the production of staples. They developed alternative economic strategies, such as the lucrative practice of hiring out excess slave laborers, to keep their workers occupied; other pursued interests in light industry.[62]

Slaveholdings by and large remained small in Missouri. The percentage of slaveholders owning ten or fewer slaves remained substantially higher in Missouri than along the eastern seaboard or in the Lower South. In 1860, at least 90 percent of slaveholders in 74 of Missouri's 113 counties owned ten or fewer slaves. By contrast, in Alabama there was

FIGURE 1. Buchanan County. Views. St. Joseph. Circa 1851. Engraving from
Herrmann J. Meyer, *United States Illustrated,* 1853. Founded less than a
decade before, St. Joseph was a thriving river community by the early 1850s.
The town's location on the banks of the Missouri River in northwestern
Missouri made it a prime launching spot for people traveling overland to the
far West. This image reflects the prosperity of the state's river towns in the
decades preceding the Civil War. Courtesy of the State Historical Society of
Missouri.

not a single county with as high a percentage of small slaveholders. In
addition, in both 1850 and 1860, 86 percent of Missouri slaves lived on
holdings of fewer than twenty slaves. In the South as a whole, only 49.4
percent of slaves in 1850 and 47.2 percent in 1860 lived on small holdings.
With the exception of Delaware, with its tiny slave population, Missouri
boasted a higher percentage of slaves living on small holdings than any
other slave state.[63]

The predominance of small-scale slavery influenced almost all aspects
of life in Missouri—even the landscape differed from plantation regions.
Most Missouri counties boasted of a few large estates that usually were
patterned after those found in Kentucky and Virginia, but more common were the thousands of modest farms that were scattered throughout the countryside. Interspersed between these households were small

hamlets and towns, at first located along the waterways and at crossroads and later along railroad lines, where white and black Missourians associated with one another and connected with the greater world. Central to the life of these communities were the local churches, schools, country stores, mills, and courthouses. Although Missourians' daily lives were spent with those living on their own farms, most were linked with neighbors through bonds of kinship, business, and friendship and could look forward to regular opportunities to interact socially with others who lived nearby.

The paucity of planters assured that small slaveholders dominated the state economically, socially, and politically; indeed at the time some argued that the state was a promised land for small slaveholders. In Missouri, unlike in the older eastern states, there was no competition from a wealthy and dominant planter elite. Small slaveholders stepped into this breech and assumed a leadership role. Not surprisingly, the Little Dixie region, with its great concentration of slaves and slaveholders, proved to be the most politically and economically important part of the state during most of the antebellum years. Enslaved Missourians helped to create this world as well. Not only were they instrumental in literally building Missouri's towns and farms, in the process adding to the wealth of their owners, but all the while they fashioned their own social networks by nurturing bonds of family and friendship and cultivating a rich religious and cultural life. These strands of love and affection connected them to others across farm boundaries and sustained a secret inner world invisible to most white Missourians. In the end, the thousands of westward migrating slaveholders far surpassed their original intentions of replicating the eastern small-slaveholding paradigm, and instead created a distinctive slave society in which small slaveholders reigned supreme.[64]

2 / Households in the Middle Ground: Small Slaveholders' Family Strategies

In the late 1850s, Martha McDonald, a Missouri school girl, meticulously copied the following words, attributed to Alexander Hamilton, into her classroom notebook, suggesting that they held deep meaning for her.

> How to Build a Happy Home
>   Six things are requisite. Integrity must be the architect, tidiness the upholster. It must be warmed by affection, lighted up with cheerfulness, and industry must be the ventilator renewing the atmosphere and bringing in fresh salubrity day by day while over all as a protecting canopy and glory nothing will suffice except the blessing of God.[1]

Middle-class Americans of the time would have appreciated the sentiments expressed in these lines as a model for the ideal home, and Martha likely recognized them as values embraced by her own family. Martha's account of her youth spent on Missouri's western border paints a portrait that rivals that of any northeastern middle-class domestic haven and suggests that her parents, Silas and Sarah McDonald, heeded Hamilton's advice and provided their children with a home befitting their status as small slaveholders and members of the merchant class. The McDonalds' values mirrored those of their small-slaveholding peers, reflecting their focus on creating a household and farming environment that would promote their goals for their families.[2]

Martha McDonald France spent her childhood in a bustling St. Joseph, Missouri, household that included her parents, seven siblings, and her paternal grandmother. She wrote of her mother preparing strawberries, ice cream, and cake to welcome her father home from a journey and of the flower-lined front walk of the McDonald home. Martha frequently chronicled the many times when the family played together; her father took the children swimming, hiking, hunting for rabbits, and on gooseberry-picking expeditions. Family members also attended church, school exhibitions, and public celebrations together. Martha recorded the fun shared by her younger siblings as they cavorted around the yard, and in the evenings, family members relaxed while Martha or her siblings played the guitar and piano, entertaining their many guests. The McDonalds frequently gathered together in the parlor or in their mother's or their grandmother's room: "[A]ll here Father, Mother, Brothers, Sisters all who hold each other dear." When the evening of camaraderie ended, Silas McDonald sang his little sons to sleep.[3]

The McDonalds also labored together on the family's farm. Silas and his son Dan hoed the garden, and the children of both sexes helped during hay harvesting time. Martha clearly loved raking hay, partly because the "new mown hay smells so sweet," but also because she saw it as a chance for the family to spend time together. She remembered one day in July 1856 when they labored with their father in the fields: "All of us helped him put up twenty hay-cocks after sun-down. . . . We are going to make some more this evening. We all worked till it blistered our hands." The McDonalds owned six slaves, a man, a woman, and four children, in 1860, yet they barely registered in Martha's description of middle-class domestic life on Missouri's western border. Slavery was central to the McDonalds' family life as was the case in other Missouri households, but more often than not slaves faded into the background in small slaveholders' accounts of their personal and family experiences.[4]

On the surface, the McDonalds' expectations and concerns for their family were similar to those of many other nineteenth-century upper- and middle-class Americans. Historians have argued that the domestic ideals that had emerged by midcentury were rooted in the ongoing transformation of the family that resulted from rapid economic and social change in the northeastern United States. In the urbanizing and industrializing North, middle-class men increasingly left their residences for work in the emerging marketplace, while women managed their homes and cared for their children. Women now produced fewer goods for household consumption and, therefore, refocused their energies on their roles as wives and mothers. These economic and social developments coincided with a new emphasis and celebration of women's "natural" maternal and moral attributes. Women were expected to be their children's first teachers, educating them to be responsible republican citizens, hard workers, and stalwart Christians. Men and women were described as living in separate spheres, with each playing important and complementary roles. Husbands and wives ideally were companions and helpmates, who worked together for the good of the entire family. Only after women attended to their domestic responsibilities were they free to expand their talents outward from their sphere in order to perfect the greater society through their involvement in maternal associations, churches, and reform movements. The ideals of separate spheres and domesticity permeated the print culture of the day and were the standards by which all others of differing regions, classes, and ethnic backgrounds were measured, whether or not the realities of their lives resembled the rhetoric. Even the McDonalds, who made their home on what was then considered the western edge of American civilization, were not immune to the power of these ideals.[5]

There is some debate, however, as to what extent southern slaveholders such as the McDonalds adopted northern middle-class notions of separate spheres and domesticity. Clearly, the economic and social dimensions of southern plantation slavery resulted in household compositions and social realities that differed from those of northern bourgeois families. Yet, throughout the antebellum period educated southern men and women often read literature produced in the North, especially periodicals and evangelical texts, which promoted ideals of domesticity. It was not until the 1830s that southern publishing houses began to produce much literature aimed at a southern audience, and even then, authors co-opted ideas about family life and gender roles promoted by northern writers and altered them to fit the parameters of southern life. They in turn used this southern version of domesticity to bolster the slavery system and tout their region's cultural superiority.[6]

Slaveholding Southerners embraced the notions of companionate marriage, women's superior morality, and child-centered households, but they altered these ideals to accommodate the realities of life in a slave society. Scholars have argued that southern men's and women's lives did not neatly fit within the parameters of the separate-spheres ideology articulated by the northern middle class. In the South, men and women, management and workers, instead lived and worked together within the confines of the household. The plantation or farm was the site of both the reproductive and productive energies of slaveholders and slaves. No matter the number of slaves owned, the definition of independent white manhood was the ownership of property and the mastery of a house-hold. White men, regardless of slaveholding status, were the head of all dependents, including wives, children, and slaves, who lived within their households and they represented their interests to the outside world. The ultimate authority that slaveholding men held over their slaves was the foundation of this power, but gender relations played a vital role as well. Southerners believed that white men's mastery was grounded in a God-given order, in which all individuals played important roles yet knew their appropriate social places.[7]

Elite Southerners agreed with many of their northern contemporaries' ideas about gender difference and its implications for family life. As in the North, the ideal southern woman was to be submissive and helpful to her husband, pious, pure, and dedicated to her children. She also was charged with creating a comfortable home for her family, one that lived up to nineteenth-century standards of domesticity. Husbands and wives should form bonds of love and affection, and mothers and fathers should play gender-specific and complementary roles in the upbringing of their children. Southerners patently rejected the northern emphasis on indi-vidualism, especially as it regarded women. In theory, women's subor-dinate position did not allow much room for independent action either within their homes or in the greater world. Slaveholding women wielded little power in society and were instead encouraged to use their influence within their own households. They rarely expanded their reforming pro-clivities past the confines of their own fences and instead focused their attention on their families and slaves. In a particularly southern version of domestic ideology, slaveholding women were expected to extend their moral authority and Christian charity not only to their husbands, chil-dren, and kin but also to their slaves. In reality, although slaveholding women lacked significant influence in public life, they exercised con-siderable power within their own households over their family's slaves, especially the women and children, often securing dominance through violence and intimidation. Many women enjoyed the authority, although truncated, granted by this definition of southern womanhood.[8]

Merchant and professional families like the McDonalds were perhaps in a better position than most Missourians to create a home life that approached the domestic ideal. The men who headed these households often traveled for their work and were exposed to cultural ideas accepted by the middle class in the eastern United States. In addition, these mid-dle-class Southerners generally were well attuned to the prescriptive lit-erature of the day, and many strove to emulate the family ideals espoused in these books and periodicals. Not only were these families aware of bourgeois domestic standards, but they were also in the position to embrace them. Professional and business families often had more disposable income and leisure time that farm families, and many also lived in town in close proximity to schools and other cultural institutions. The McDonalds lived near the growing community of St. Joseph and had the means to take advantage of the educational and social opportunities offered there.[9]

In contrast, the rhetoric of romantic love, companionate marriage, and domesticity espoused by both the northern middle class and southern planters did not always fit the reality of many Missouri small slaveholders' economic and social circumstances, and, therefore, it was difficult for them to achieve the full embodiment of these ideals. Much like many of their neighbors, the Strattons owned a small number of slaves and spent their lives on modest farms in the upper and border South. The family's migration patterns, household composition, and economic circumstances were similar to those of thousands of other small slaveholders. It is true that small slaveholders lived in the long shadow of the planter class and shared many of the same cultural values, but their lives differed from planters in significant ways. The marriages and family lives created by many small slaveholders, like the Strattons, in many ways better resembled the experiences of yeomen farmers than of planters. Whether they lived in the Low Country of South Carolina, the Nanticoke Valley of New York, or on the prairies of Sugar Creek, Illinois, antebellum farm families hoped to ensure the economic sustainability of their households before they heavily entered into the commercial marketplace. Regardless of whether or not they owned slaves, family members were important sources of labor on these farms, directly leading to decisions to produce large families. Women contributed to the household economy through domestic production of textiles, dairy, and poultry. Over time, farmers increasingly produced more for the marketplace, especially if they had access to waterways or as the railroad arrived in the hinterlands, but most continued to grow a significant portion of their crops for household consumption. The economic dynamics of rural households were similar across regions, but the historian Stephanie McCurry and others have argued that there was a particular quality to yeoman households in the South. In similar fashion to planters, southern yeomen operated as the masters of all those living within their enclosures, including their wives, children, and slaves.[10]

Missouri small slaveholders' decisions about their farms and businesses were directly influenced by their family values and strategies, and those decisions in turn were affected by the realities of life on slavery's border. Most Missouri slaveholders, both those living in town and on farms, lived modestly by the standards of the South's planter elite. Everything in Missouri was on a smaller scale—from the construction of their homes to the ways they passed wealth on to the next generation. A few attempted to emulate the lifestyles and priorities of southern planters, but most simply had neither the economic means nor the leisure time to do so. Instead, Missourians were driven by practical concerns. Rather than simply reproducing slaveholding status, they were consumed with maintaining the economic viability of their households in the present and providing their children with a good start on their futures. This was no easy feat when some Missouri slaveholding households operated on slim economic margins. Like so many other aspects of their lives, their beliefs about family life developed out of their limitations. The result was family strategies that did not simply replicate those of planters, but instead shared some commonalities with the traditional expectations of southern yeomen and northern farmers, as well as the emerging sensibilities of the northern middle class.

Small-slaveholding Missourians' lives and priorities were practical and based on the everyday realities of work, slave management, family, kin, and community. In most cases, their farms and plantations were modest in scale; not only did they have fewer acres in cultivation than most southern planters, but they also employed many fewer slaves. While many hoped to better their lives through additional purchases of land or slaves, small slaveholders' main concern was the immediate support of their families and keeping their property unencumbered by debt. Crop mixes, housing choices, and labor strategies all focused on this ultimate goal. With few exceptions, family members were expected to contribute to the economy of the household in a manner befitting their age and gender, especially because of the small number of adult slaves found on most farms. The viability of the household rather than the needs of individuals was the ultimate consideration. Only when this primary goal was met did most small slaveholders consider expenditures such as building better houses, providing an advanced education for their children, or giving adult children land or slaves. They hoped their children would replicate their class status in the next generation, but they knew that they alone could not provide them with the means to reproduce wealth. Most parents instead provided their children with the tools, but not always the actual resources, to prosper in their adulthoods. They also relied on kinship and community networks to assist in this endeavor through reciprocal labor exchanges as they collectively worked toward each family's ultimate financial goal.[11]

More than the number of slaves influenced Missourians' family strategies, however. Although initially settled by migrants from the Upper South, Missouri's border location drew people from throughout the nation and even abroad. As time progressed, rural Missourians were likely to live near neighbors with origins outside of the South. Although most who moved to Missouri supported slavery, this mixture of people and cultures resulted in a society that reflected this middle ground. From the start, Missourians were connected to the outside world through the rivers and were exposed to print culture and ideas from throughout the nation. Cultural expectations collided and were reformulated in Missouri's slaveholding regions. The result was a fusion of family values that suited the western lifestyles of Missouri's small slaveholders. They, like so many others in different times and different contexts, learned to alter the expectations they came with to fit the realities of their lives on the edge of the frontier. Although their lifestyles may not have approached those of their planter counterparts, Missouri's slaveholders were the elite of their time and place. They developed cultural values that reflected this status, while at the same time accommodating the realities of their lives as slaveholders on a smaller scale.

Missouri's small-slaveholding families lived in all types of circumstances. Most common were those, like the Strattons, Woods, or Haines, who resided on the state's many farms. Others lived in the hundreds of towns scattered throughout the state. Merchant and professional families, like the Scotts, McDonalds, and Belts, and their few slaves, often lived in the many hamlets that dotted the banks of the Missouri and Mississippi Rivers. Dr. Alfred Patton and his wife, Priscilla, and their four young children inhabited the central Missouri town of Rocheport, and John Helm moved his family to Hannibal to establish a legal practice and help develop the Hannibal–St. Joseph railroad line. Other men, such as Abiel Leonard and William Napton, left their wives and children at home on their farms while they pursued legal and political careers in the state's urban centers. The economic circumstances and career paths of Missouri slaveholders varied greatly, as did the household responsibilities of their wives. Some couples built large homes, while others lived in modest dwellings. Some managed many slaves, and others only a few. Individual families made very different decisions about the size of their families and the ways they prepared their children for adulthood. These families' stories reveal that although the life experiences and family strategies of Missouri's slaveholders differed in many ways from those of planters, they also did not follow a template specific to a small-slaveholding class for how their households and families were organized. Instead, they pursued strategies that reflected their diverse experiences and often compensated for the limitations inherent in small-scale slavery.[12]

To a certain extent, the manuscript records influence the analysis of Missouri's small-slaveholding families. The families most likely to leave extensive letters outlining their home lives and experiences were often those who were physically separated from one another. Farming families far outweighed merchant and professional families in the aggregate, but their papers are not as well represented in the archives. Men who traveled for business, such as merchants, politicians, and attorneys, were more likely to correspond with their wives and children while they were away, often for months at a time. Family members frequently exchanged letters on a weekly basis, relaying news and discussing household concerns. In addition, the wives of professional and businessmen frequently had more free time to correspond with their husbands or write in journals because their household responsibilities were far less involved than those of women who managed farm households. They often lived in town, supervised fewer slaves, and, interestingly, some also had fewer children, suggesting that professional families were beginning to limit the number of their children like their northeastern bourgeois counterparts. There was simply not a need for a large number of children to serve as workers if they did not live on a farm. Affluent children also were more likely to attend the region's colleges and academies and correspond with family members who remained at home. All of these factors increased the likelihood that they would record their families' stories.[13]

In most cases, Missouri slaveholders were silent about the enslaved people who worked, and often lived, in their homes, especially when describing their own family lives. The presence of slaves was such a regular aspect of everyday life that many owners mentioned them only at points of conflict. In the end, slaveholders focused their attention on what was best for their own families, and their slaves generally figured into the story only in as much as they furthered that principal goal. Slaves produced the crops and goods that provided slaveholding families with the means to purchase the fine furnishings that equipped their homes in the domestic standards of the day, as well as to pay tuition bills to educate their children in a manner befitting their race and class. Worse yet, the hire or sale of slave men, women, and children frequently provided the funding for these priorities. Slave women and young girls cooked the meals, cleaned the houses, and washed the clothes of white families. As standards of housewifery dramatically increased in the years preceding the war, the labor of slave women became even more crucial to slaveholders' attempts to achieve what they deemed a respectable family and home life. White Missourians considered this domestic work so important that they willingly entered the slave-sale and -hiring market to achieve what they saw as essential objectives for their families. In the end, the lifestyles of Missouri slaveholders were acquired on the backs of their slaves and at the expense of their personal lives and the integrity of their families.[14]

"Each year of *my* married life, has increased my happiness"

At the center of Missouri's small-slaveholding families was the relationship between husbands and wives. As was true of other upper- and middle-class Americans, over the course of the early nineteenth century men and women became less focused on family and community concerns as they sought marriage companions and began to search for life mates to whom they were personally attracted. The ideal marriage was one in which couples were mutually supportive and shared strong bonds of love and affection. This companionate ideal does not suggest that men and women were equitable partners in the marriage relationship, however. Law, custom, and religion anointed husbands the masters of their households, and wives were expected to submissively defer to their will. Although not social equals, wives were expected to be notable companions to their mates, creating for them homes that adhered to the demanding expectations of domesticity and representing them favorably socially.[15]

The realities of small slaveholding often undercut the ability of Missouri couples to fully enact the ideals of modern bourgeois marriage promoted in the literature read by middle-class Americans. Indeed, the descriptions of companionate marriages would not have rung true to many Missouri couples, who focused most of their attention on the everyday concerns of running a farm, managing slaves, and providing for their children. Merchant and professional couples were more likely to embody these domestic ideals because they often resided in town and ran less extensive households, but couples living in farm households were required to invest much of their time in the work of the farm. The economic limitations of small-scale slavery necessitated the labor of all members of the household, leaving less free time to create the domestic havens suggested by the rhetoric. In the end, many Missouri slaveholding couples combined the emerging family values of the middle class with more traditional ideas of household sustainability and husbands and wives as helpmates.[16]

Most young Missouri men and women of the slaveholding class expected to marry and set up households much like those of their parents, but they first needed opportunities to identify and court their potential life mates. Young people were the Missourians who were most actively engaged in the social activities of their local towns and neighborhoods. Parties and gatherings gave the young the chance to socialize with one another in group settings. These events generally were not formal, but more often reflected the fluid and casual sociability of the countryside. In Missouri, neighbors commonly associated with others within their cultural group, regardless of their slaveholding status; upcountry Southerners socialized with one another, and settlers of German descent socialized together, for example. Young men and women participated in rounds of visiting, Christmas dances, sleigh rides, and church services, as well as school exhibitions, picnics, and Fourth of July festivities. Parents usually encouraged this social interaction and recognized that it was the means by which their children could meet their future spouses. Parents generally did not choose marriage partners for their children, although they did attempt to engineer the choice by encouraging them to socialize with the "right" sorts of people, namely those who shared their cultural values and ideally class status. Paulina Stratton recorded the names and commented on the suitability as potential husbands of the many young men who visited the Stratton home in the years preceding the marriages of her daughters, Agnes and Bettie. Others, like William and Melinda Napton, promoted their sons' attendance at local dances. Some young people took matters into their own hands and created more innovative excuses for fellowship. Martha McDonald and her teenage siblings organized a social club during the winter of 1862 and dubbed it first the Rural Club and later the Rustic Club. The membership included young women and men from throughout their Buchanan County neighborhood. Girls held all the leadership positions, and the club had no other purpose but to provide a venue for socializing. In fact, Martha McDonald's future husband, Charles France, was a member of the Rustics.[17]

Young men and women of marrying age understood the importance of selecting an ideal mate and used these social opportunities to explore their options. As was true throughout the ages, the right choice of marriage partner was crucial to the future happiness of Missouri men and women. This was especially the case for women in a society where slave-holding men wielded so much power. In Missouri, as elsewhere, laws regarding conjugal relations overwhelmingly privileged men. Under the legal definition of *feme covert,* a woman's husband controlled all the family's property—even that which the wife brought into the marriage, unless her male relatives drew up a prenuptial contract. In addition, southern law and custom designated a tremendous amount of power to white men, who were considered masters of their households. Consequently, women's fathers and husbands were central forces in their lives and had tremendous power to control their destinies. Women who married intemperate, fiscally irresponsible, lazy, or abusive men could be in for a lifetime of suffering. The historian Anya Jabour argues that many young southern women sincerely believed that finding their love match was the means by which they could ensure a happy marriage, reasoning that if they selected a mate with whom they shared deep and abiding love they might be able to manipulate their husbands' affections in order to curb any inclination toward abuse. Young women often relied on men's public reputations and the council of friends and family as they made their choices. Mary Belt worried that her husband John's brother Thompson would follow her unmarried sister Ann to Texas after she moved there with her parents. She harbored grave concerns about the potential match because of Thompson's excessive drinking, but in the end, Ann heeded her sister's and brother-in-law's advice and married another suitor. Paulina Stratton discouraged her seventeen-year-old daughter, Bettie, from accepting a proposal from a young man she deemed unacceptable by arguing that she was too young to consider marriage. Bettie ultimately listened to her mother and waited a few years until she consented to marry another man. Ultimately it was incumbent on women to make the right choice. William Napton wrote to his wife, Melinda, about a legislative bill that would provide some legal protections to married women. He believed that the bill was unnecessary and instead held women responsible for their decisions: "If the ladies will take the precaution to marry honest men, they will need no protection from the law; if they marry knaves, the laws will be inefficient to protect them." Napton was clearly naive in his belief that women always were able to judge the real character of their suitors, but he was correct that the law could not protect them from bad husbands.[18]

Group courting rituals did not always allow couples to get to know one another very well, and, consequently, many men and women knew less than was ideal about one another before their wedding day. Priscilla

Patton reflected on her own marriage at the time of her daughter Annie's wedding and confessed that it took many years of marriage before she and her husband, Alfred, got to know each other and became "accustomed to his ways or he to mine." Other courting couples thwarted convention and stole away for private meetings, where they might be in a better position to deepen their intimacy. Martha McDonald and Charles France entered into a secret engagement and even contemplated elopement. There is no record of whether or not the two married without the blessing of Martha's parents, but if they did all must quickly have been forgiven because within months of the wedding her mother was writing affectionate letters to the couple in their new Colorado home.[19]

In fact, Missouri couples most often used the informal social opportunities approved by their parents to forge connections with young people of the opposite sex who lived nearby. This comfortable familiarity with their neighbors may have given them at least some sense of the character and reputation of their intendeds. An analysis of the marriages of Cooper County couples indicates that the machinations of their elders usually led to unions that they likely deemed suitable. Young people from slaveholding families most often chose spouses from within their own class or at the least from families who also hailed from the Upper South and who owned similar amounts of property. Usually the prospective spouse came from within the local social network and sometimes even within the extended kinship group; marriage between first cousins, siblings who married siblings, and marriage to the sibling of a deceased spouse were all common patterns. There were some cases of men and women who married outsiders, however. Both Abiel Leonard and William Napton were born in northern states and came to Missouri with little to offer but their superior educations and abundant talents. After establishing successful legal careers, both men won the hands of the young daughters of successful planters. Missouri women married at relatively young ages, although men traditionally waited longer to marry, as was the case in the marriages of the Leonards and the Naptons. In a sample of marriages from Cooper County in the decade before the Civil War, women typically married in their late teens or early twenties, whereas the majority of men were closer to thirty. Most small-slaveholding parents had little to offer their children when they married; therefore, young men may have waited to marry, working long enough to establish a career or acquire the resources to set up housekeeping.[20]

Weddings customarily took place soon after the couple agreed to marry. These usually modest affairs often took place in the home of the

FIGURE 2. Abiel Leonard. Abiel Leonard (1797–1863) was a Howard County slaveholder, attorney, and politician. Born in Vermont, he moved to Missouri in 1819 where he established a successful legal practice. Abiel Leonard reached prominence in Missouri political circles, eventually serving as a justice on the Missouri Supreme Court in the 1850s. He remained loyal to the Union during the Civil War. This photograph was first published in L. C. Krauthoff, "The Supreme Court of Missouri," in *The Green Bag* in April 1891. Courtesy of the State Historical Society of Missouri.

bride's parents and were officiated by the family's pastor. It was common for the couple's immediate family and a few special friends to attend the ceremony, which was usually followed by a small party, frequently with a cake. Throughout the years, Paulina Stratton noted the marriages of her three oldest children and those of their friends. She described her daughter Agnes's simple wedding to the son of a local small slaveholder in 1861: "Agnes married at 6 'clock Mr Neal married them. We had a small Party Amanda Divers and Bob Stoneman waited." The informal nature of these ceremonies is suggested by the fact that Sallie Starke's brother Bud left to attend a "Preaching" rather than stay to witness his sister exchange vows with the Stratton's son John Calvin. Paulina Stratton attended few of the neighborhood weddings herself, although her children frequently witnessed the nuptials of their friends.[21]

Once married, women's happiness was bound up with that of their

FIGURE 3. Jeanette Reeves Leonard. Jeanette Reeves Leonard (1812–1895) was the daughter of Benjamin H. Reeves, a successful Kentucky planter and politician. After her marriage to Abiel Leonard in 1830, the couple built Oakwood, where they raised their seven children. Jeanette Leonard was a capable manager of the household and farm, while her husband traveled extensively for his legal career. Courtesy of the Western Historical Manuscript Collection. Abiel Leonard (1797–1863) Papers, 1782–1910, 1932, n.d.

husbands. Whereas men often found validation in their careers and civic roles in addition to their position within their households, most women found personal satisfaction and rooted their sense of self in their roles as wives, mothers, mistresses, and daughters. These culturally ascribed gender roles, coupled with the great legal power afforded men, made it especially important for women to make wise choices of their life partners. Some men used their social and legal authority to control their wives' mobility and expenditures, and a few used this power to humiliate them through physical and emotional abuse or engagement in indiscreet extramarital affairs. There were many other couples for whom the bloom of romantic love quickly wore off and who settled into a humdrum coexistence as they worked together to manage their domestic and business affairs.[22]

A few couples dissolved their unhappy unions through a formal divorce; a step that required approval from the Missouri state legislature.

There were few legal grounds for divorce, and many of those available were applied with a double standard. Men often sought divorce because of their wives' adultery, whereas women had little recourse if their husbands engaged in similar behavior—especially if the husband's sexual partner was a slave woman. It was even difficult for women to sue for divorce on grounds of abuse, although desertion was sometimes considered favorably by the legislature, especially if the local community feared that it might be responsible for the support of an indigent woman and her children. Few Missouri couples chose to pursue divorce, both because of fears of public disapproval and because of the difficulties inherent in moving the case through the legislative process. Women also understood that a divorce would likely end in the loss of the property that they brought into the marriage—as well as that accumulated during it—and the custody of their children.[23]

In many cases, small-slaveholding women may have been in a less favorable position to control their circumstances than planter wives. A woman's connections to wealthy male relatives often determined her ability to leave an abusive or unfaithful husband. Eliza Sappington Pearson acquired an annulment of her marriage after she learned that her husband had another wife and child in Georgia because her wealthy and politically connected father, Dr. John Sappington, pushed the dissolution of the marriage through the legislature and volunteered to financially support her and her children. Eliza later married her late sisters' husband, Claiborne Fox Jackson—a politically ambitious man who first married the two younger Sappington sisters (both died soon after their weddings) and willingly married a third Sappington daughter to preserve this socially desirable and financially lucrative family connection. Less affluent or well-connected women had little option than to stay with an adulterous or cruel husband. Wealthier women also might defuse an unhappy or volatile marital situation by traveling to visit relatives or inviting them for extended stays, but small slaveholders often did not have the means to travel away from their troubles, and their modest homes did not always have the space to accommodate relatives and friends who might serve as buffers between unhappy husbands and wives. They instead had little recourse but to work and live together each day, tending to their children, slaves, and farms, and simply making the most of an unhappy situation. Justina Woods wrote her sister about the simmering hostility that existed between the small-slaveholding couple with whom she boarded: "[T]hey are some punkins, he never calls her name, no more than if there never was such a person and she never talks of him but she tell all his faults and means [*sic*] things that he has done and all such as that." Later, she observed of the Jeffries' dysfunctional marriage: "Last Sunday she asked him when he was going to Washington [Missouri], he answered her by asking her when she was going to *Hell.*"[24]

The profound unhappiness of some marriages occasionally was manifested in much more dramatic ways. The historian Adam Rothman argues that southern men and women married with an expectation of love, fidelity, and mutual support, but trouble ensued when one or the other shattered these expectations. Adultery on the part of husbands suggests male prerogatives and beliefs about the sexual availability of slave women and lower-class white women, whereas wives' infidelity might instead be a reflection on the state of the marriage. One Cooper County woman had an affair with a married neighbor named Mr. Saunders while her husband was away on a six-week-long business trip to Arkansas. The family's slave woman reportedly caught her mistress in a compromising position with Saunders, who ostensibly was helping her with chores around the house. When her husband returned, the adulterous wife informed him that while he was gone, "Saunders had been very kind to her, was her best friend, and that without him, she would have suffered," perhaps hinting to her husband that he failed to offer her the emotional support she desired.[25]

Marital harmony often was shattered when husbands' and wives' expectations for their relationship and their understanding of acceptable gender roles did not match with the behavior of one or both of the marriage partners. Spousal abuse was common throughout nineteenth-century America, but the pervasiveness of violence in a slave society made it even more likely that Southerners would turn to physical confrontations to solve their relationship problems. Occasionally disharmonious marriages ended in tragedy, as when Rebecca Hawkins, who suffered under an abusive husband, enlisted the aid of her slave man and woman in an attempted poisoning of her spouse with rats' bane. The slave woman betrayed her mistress and confessed to assisting Hawkins in the crime of "mingling poison with the food and drink of her husband." Wives were more often victims of husbands' violent rage, however, as when a drunken James Layton brutally bludgeoned his wife, Mary, to death within earshot of their young son, or when John Wise beat his wife, Christina, with a stick and then suggested that neighborhood slaves were the likely murderers.[26]

Most men and women did not make such poor matches, nor did they initiate divorce proceedings, but this does not suggest that they were part of harmonious or romantic relationships. In a letter written to her fiancé on the eve of their marriage, Paulina Donald predicted a blissful future life with Thomas Stratton in which their "days shall glide sweetly and swiftly by," but in reality their marriage never approached her romantic expectations. Rather than soul mates, Thomas and Paulina instead served as helpmates to each other, as was the case within many other rural households. Husbands and wives were expected to fulfill gendered expectations of shared responsibility for the management of the productive and reproductive functions of the household. The marriages of couples such as Paulina and Thomas Stratton revolved around the daily work of the farm and home, work that necessitated the labor of all members of the household both black and white. Paulina, with the assistance of her two eldest daughters and two female slaves, was responsible for the family's home and barnyard with child care, household management, sewing, gardening, and cows and fowl all under her purview. Thomas worked with their one slave man, Ike, their eldest son, and the younger slave boys to operate the farm. At best the Strattons appear to have co-existed with each other as they worked together for the common good.[27]

Paulina made it clear in her diary that her marriage to Thomas Stratton was never a happy one. She suggested that Thomas often sided with his mother in the rancorous relationship between the two women, and she complained that he was not as kind as he once was and that he did not respect her needs or opinions. It disturbed her that he never reported to her news of the neighborhood or consulted with her about his plans. Paulina strongly disagreed with the way that Thomas managed his slave man, Ike, but Thomas became angry when she confronted him about his misplaced trust. "It seems hard to see things doing so different from what I would like and not allowed to speak. But it is my duty to obey and I will try and do it," she lamented. She was afraid to purchase the smallest incidental item for fear of displeasing her husband. Paulina never indicated that Thomas was physically abusive, but instead suggested that he was excessively controlling. She chafed under this dependency, and always perceived Thomas as tyrannical, especially resenting his curtailment of her and the children's mobility, such as when Thomas limited Agnes's and Bettie's attendance at neighborhood social gatherings. Paulina in fact blamed Thomas for driving the girls toward early marriages. Most upsetting, he frequently kept her from attending the church services she loved. She wrote in 1862: "[Q]uite a cold day I wanted to go to Lebanon to hear Mr Godby but Mr S would not let me. I was truly hurt he cares nothing for preaching and will hardly ever let me go. If he can get his paper It is all he cares for. And he never gratifies me in any thing. But it is my dutie to Submit. . . . I chose my lot and must abide by It."[28]

Paulina worried that her marital troubles were a result of her disobedience to God, fearing that "god is Punishing me for disobeying him in not marrying one whose heart was with God." She understood that her heavenly father wished for husbands and wives to stand equally before him in faith, but instead she chose a man she knew was not redeemed. She desperately prayed for her husband's salvation, hoping not only that he would share eternity with her, but that his conversion would improve the quality of their marriage and unify them on child-rearing and slave-management issues in this life. Paulina's faith taught her that she should be submissive to her husband in all matters, despite his lack of faith. She also knew that she must not be abrasive in her attempts to convert him. Although she usually worked to bring about his salvation through example, she occasionally used more direct tactics. After her husband yelled at her for her harassing evangelizing she began to leave letters begging him to consider his eternal state. In the end, Paulina utterly failed to influence the one individual who held the greatest power to improve her lot in life; Thomas Stratton never gave in to his wife's pleas for his soul.[29]

Thomas's views of the marriage are largely unknown, outside of the actions and few words attributed to him by his wife. The story is written from Paulina's perspective, of course, so it is difficult to know the true nature of the relationships within the Stratton household. It is unclear how often Paulina actually acted on the frustrations that she vented in the pages of her journal. She described some altercations and frequently referred to losing her temper, but in the end we only know what Paulina chose to tell us. There is no record of how Thomas and Paulina interacted day to day, but the diary clearly reveals that their relationship was not close or open enough for Paulina to express her real feelings and concerns directly to her husband. In the end, she felt as if she was unable to command even those aspects of life over which southern slaveholding women maintained limited influence and authority—her slaves, her children, and her religious life. In response, she constructed a sense of herself as isolated and victimized. Thomas may have been partly correct in his retort to his wife that she "was constantly thinking about something to make [her] unhappy and made everybody else unhappy around [her]."[30]

Other marriages among slaveholders, like that between William and Melinda Napton, more fully embodied the companionate ideal. The

Naptons were married in 1838 when William was thirty years old and Melinda merely eighteen. Melinda was the daughter of Thomas Williams, a judge and member of the Knoxville, Tennessee, gentry. She met William during a long stay at the home of her sister Cynthia Smith, who was married to a wealthy Saline County, Missouri, planter. Melinda's father provided the young couple with one thousand acres of Saline County land and a few slaves upon their marriage, yet the Naptons struggled financially throughout their married life, primarily because of their extremely large family. The couple's main source of income was William's job as a Missouri State Supreme Court justice, and he spent nine months of the year away from his wife and ten children. The Naptons acquitted themselves as Missouri gentry, even though for most of their marriage they were not slaveholders on a grand scale and often complained of financial constraints. In 1850, the Naptons owned thirteen slaves, although by 1860 they commanded forty-five slaves—twenty-nine owned by them, many recently inherited from Melinda's father, and sixteen owned by an orphaned niece for whom Napton served as guardian.[31]

William and Melinda exchanged hundreds of letters over the course of their married life filled with information about their family and farm, the books they read, their friends and neighbors, William's work, and state and national politics. They looked forward to receiving the other's letters and chastised each other when they did not arrive in a timely manner. Melinda saved William's letters to read during the few quiet moments in her day after she undressed for bed and sat before the fire. She often wrote him with the paper on her lap and her foot rocking a baby in the cradle. William and Melinda playfully addressed each other by pet names such as "My Dear Old Man" and "My dearest" in these communications. The Naptons' marriage was not without stresses and occasional misunderstandings and disagreements, but by and large William and Melinda enjoyed physical intimacy and each other's companionship. William spent the long months that he was away at his work yearning for his wife. At one point early in their marriage, he complained that he was "most horribly tired of living by myself . . . in this lonely condition" and professed, "I am nearly dead to see you." Even after the birth of eight children, Melinda observed, "I'm sure, no young girl was ever more anxious to see her sweetheart, than I am to see, my dear old man." The deep and abiding love that William and Melinda shared pours forth from the pages of their letters. On the tenth anniversary of their marriage, Melinda asked William if he was happier now than he was when they were first married. She reflected, "If you are not, I know I am sorry, for each year of *my* married life, has increased my happiness. May the Almighty giver of all good, spare to me, my blessed old man, & darling children." The roles that Melinda and William played within their marriage were very conventional—he fashioned himself as her urbane and educated superior while she represented the domestic ideal, but among Missouri slaveholders, the Naptons' marriage perhaps best represents the nineteenth-century romantic ideal. William's and Melinda's elevated social position, educations, and immersion in contemporary literature and print culture likely contributed to their acceptance of ideas of marriage that were circulating in the cultural currents of the day.[32]

Dwelling Places

Missouri's small-slaveholding couples built homes for their families in a literal sense as well as a figurative one. Ultimately, the physical spaces in which white Missourians lived reflected their values and the ways in which they experienced their family lives. Affluent slaveholders erected fine brick or clapboard homes by the eve of the Civil War, but as in other aspects of their lives, their big houses were constructed on a much smaller scale than in the plantation South. Most Missourians engaged in a vernacular or folk architecture, designing homes from the memories of those they had lived in or seen in their original eastern homes rather than consulting any formal plans. They generally used the native materials available to them in the construction of these buildings, although a few wealthier Missourians imported design elements for their homes from the East or abroad. Floor plans and the size of homes changed over time and reflected both the material means of their owners and changing cultural expectations about the ideal home, but as was often the case in Missouri, there was a tension between the model and the reality. As much as Missourians tried to create a spatial distinction between public and private as was dictated by domestic ideology, the ideal could never be as well articulated in Missouri as in the North—both because of slavery and because of the predominantly rural way of life.[33]

Early settlers adapted the designs of their homes from what they knew in the East to the realities of life on the frontier. Most newcomers first built single pen houses, approximately sixteen-foot square or rectangular one-room cabins made of native logs and chinking, in order to provide a roof over the heads of their families. Some slaveholders lived in these log houses for years, although over time many renovated them to increase living space and accommodate their growing families. It was quite common for Missourians to build a second single pen cabin along side the first with a covered walkway, or dogtrot, connecting the two structures. These open areas were frequently closed in later, creating a two-room house with a central hall and a fireplace at either end. The entire family, and sometimes even their slaves, lived together in these cramped spaces. Personal and even family privacy would have been nearly impossible, and the friction of the constant interaction among household residents increased tensions or at the worst led to violent altercations. As late as the Civil War, many Missourians continued to live in these log structures. Steve Brown, a former slave, remembered his owners as living in a large log home "with a big porch," and, although he owned many slaves, Smoky Eulenberg's master lived in a large double log house "wid a open hall in between." Justina Woods described the squalid living conditions of the small-slaveholding family with whom she boarded while teaching school in southeastern Missouri, whining to her sister: "I am not in the habit of complaining about my boarding, but this place beats the bugs, every things is so nasty that I can hardly eat." Woods's aforementioned description of the Jeffries' volatile marriage suggests that more than poor housekeeping was at issue in their household. Some Missourians abandoned their original cabins to their slaves after they built finer homes, but many merely covered the log structures with clapboard siding or used the older buildings as the core of larger renovated structures.[34]

A number of more affluent Missourians ended the antebellum years living in homes patterned after the gracious structures that they remembered from Virginia or Kentucky, often naming their homes after these same places. Some of these houses were built of brick, while others were sided with whitewashed clapboard. The structures varied in size, but they often consisted of a central hall plan, with one or two rooms on either side and a second story that duplicated the first with a staircase leading up from the hall below. It was common for homeowners to add additions to their homes as their resources allowed, often in the form of a rear ell. These larger homes allowed families to differentiate space for private and public use. Often the front rooms served as parlors, with some homes boasting both a formal public receiving room and private family sitting room. Dining rooms typically were located toward the back of the house close to either an interior kitchen or a southern-style summer kitchen that was often constructed a short distance from the main house. The sleeping chambers were usually upstairs, with parents and babies slumbering in one room and older children in another. If the home was large

FIGURE 4. Oakwood. Abiel and Jeanette Leonard built their home on the outskirts of Fayette, Missouri, in Howard County, in the mid-1830s. The house is typical of the homes of affluent Missouri slaveholders. The original two-story brick house represents the central hall federal style that includes one room and a fireplace on each side of the structure. The house has a single-story rear ell that was enlarged to two stories in 1850–51. A front portico, similar to the one in this image, was added in 1856. Courtesy of the Historical American Building Survey, Library of Congress.

enough, children's sleeping quarters might be segregated by gender. The yards of rural homes were littered with numerous outbuildings, including outdoor kitchens, barns, smokehouses, slave cabins, chicken coops, privies, sheds, corn cribs, and occasionally fruit-drying or ice houses. All these outbuildings typically were located a short distance from the main house.[35]

As much as slaveholding Missourians imagined they were distinguishing space that was accessible to outsiders from that reserved for their families, the realities of slavery never allowed for their homes to be truly private spaces. Slave men, women, and children were present, often in the background, during many intimate moments of slaveholders' lives. Slaves prepared their owners' food, served at their tables, helped care for their children, slept on pallets at the foot of their beds, and assisted with nursing them during times of sickness and death. In general, as the historian Thavolia Glymph has argued, slavery also turned the private home into a place of work, where enslaved men, women, and children often contested the terms of their labor, as well as their relations with their owners. White Missourians generally chose to ignore their servants' ubiquitous presence in the shadows of their homes, refusing to recognize that all the while black Missourians were quietly accumulating information about both their owners and the white world. In the end, private moments shared between slaveholding family members might well become public knowledge within the greater neighborhood as slaves relayed what they had learned.[36]

The limitations to the articulation of proper domesticity aside, Missourians increasingly hoped to emulate the family ideals set forth in the periodicals, novels, and advice manuals of the day. Missouri slaveholding women, such as Elvira Scott, were prolific readers of *Harper's* and *Godey's Lady's Book,* as well as publications originating from southern presses. Not only did this literature suggest the proper way to order relations within households, including those between parents and children, husbands and wives, and masters and servants, but it also recommended the right way to order and equip the physical space of the home. The interior furnishings of Missouri homes depended on the financial means of the owners. Some modest homeowners possessed few furnishings, but the more affluent purchased the many consumer goods flooding American markets in the mid-nineteenth century. Riverboat transportation made it possible for Missourians to furnish their homes with commercial items comparable to middle-class homes in the East. Manufactured furniture, wallpaper, glassware, and plush fabric for draperies were bought in St. Louis shops or were ordered by local merchants from eastern suppliers. Weston resident Elizabeth Coleman justified to her parents why she had ordered fine furnishings for her parlor, including divans, a set of chairs, and a piano, by explaining: "[W]hen a person is making they have to Spend I, would rather have it that way than in blacks." Not all Missouri slaveholders lived in fine style, but some believed that it was a priority to construct and furnish homes that would rival those in the East.[37]

Decisions about the construction of new homes and the ways to furnish them varied greatly among Missouri slaveholders. Many, like the Strattons, were very conservative in their expenditures. They repaired their original house rather than build a nicer new one, and they purchased a few items to make it more comfortable. Other more affluent slaveholders placed a premium on appearances and comfort and expended a large portion of their income on their property. John Helm spared no expense as he constructed his new home in Hannibal, Missouri. He was a wealthy attorney and slaveholder who had invested heavily in the construction of the Hannibal and St. Joseph railroad line. It took months for John and Mary Helm to design their home and oversee its construction by their slave men and local tradesmen in 1852 and 1853. Once finished, the house was large enough to accommodate their five children and eleven slaves. Their daughter Lizzie described the house as including six chambers, a set of double parlors, and a dining room. The Helms chose to house both their slaves and their family inside the large town home. The basement included three rooms to accommodate their slaves and "the largest widest Hall you ever saw for the negro children and us to play in." There was some disagreement between John and Mary about the optimal size for the rooms in the house. "You know Ma is so much opposed to small rooms and papa to large ones that I thought we might have had some of both sorts, but some how or other I find where papa and Ma cannot agree Ma always has it her way—how it is I don't know but expect to learn by the time I am as old as she is," Lizzie Helm marveled to her sister. As was the case with the McDonalds, little mention was made of the enslaved inhabitants of the Helm household in the family's many letters.[38]

William Napton also made it a priority to build a fine home and develop his farm into an estate, even though he stretched his finances to complete his vision. Napton's focus on his property likely had its roots in his social insecurities as an outsider, and therefore, he wished to erect a visible symbol of his mastery and worthiness to inhabit the lofty social position to which he had risen. Throughout the years, William and Melinda corresponded about planting flowers, shrubs, and trees at Elk Hill, and in 1859 they built a two-story addition to the house that included a dining room, kitchen, and pantry downstairs, and three additional bedrooms upstairs. The expansion of the home was partly due to the large size of the Napton family, but William clearly was consumed with shaping Elk Hill into something to be admired. "[I]f we continue to live at Elk Hill, we had as well make every thing around us as comfortable & attractive as possible, even at some sacrifice. I don't want to live poor & die rich, nor do I want to leave any over our debts upon you & the children. But a thousand dollars will not break us up either way," he once observed. Although he professed to hate his separations from his family, William frequently pointed to improvements to Elk Hill as a primary reason to remain employed as a judge.[39]

Many Missouri slaveholders understood their property as a reflection of their values, as well as a symbol of their social prominence. This was likely their primary goal when they constructed "plantations" patterned after those of the Virginia and Kentucky gentry. In most cases these homes were on a smaller scale than those in the East, yet Missouri slaveholders wished to signify to white and black members of their communities that they were the social leaders in their western world. As much as they valued their property and saw it as a reflection of their worth, Missouri slaveholders invested even more energy and resources in their children.

"My heart is very much bound up in this dear baby"

Missouri slaveholding families were child centered, as was the case with other Americans of similar social standing. During the first half of the nineteenth century middle- and upper-class American parents began to focus their attention and resources on nurturing their children in order to successfully launch them into adulthood. This was especially the case in urban areas in the North where fathers increasingly worked outside of the home and the labor of children was no longer necessary. Mothers spent less time on domestic production and focused their attention on the reproductive aspects of their gender roles. They were their children's first teachers—not only instructing them in their letters and numbers but also inculcating them with the values of their class. Children spent their earliest years under their mother's nurturing care and only moved outside of the home once they were ready to attend school. Fathers took great interest in the development of their children as well, paying special attention to their education and moral progress. Parents provided their children with structure and discipline but also showered them with affection. In all, mothers' and fathers' energies and resources were focused on preparing their children for their adulthoods. Most parents did not have the financial means to set their children up for life so they instead provided them with the tools to make their own way in the world. This assistance often came in the form of an education.[40]

Southern planter families embraced many of the same ideals of family life. They too showered their children with love and affection, and they too concentrated their energies and finances on preparing their progeny for their adult lives. As in northern middle-class homes, southern mothers' primary occupation was the rearing of their children. Mothers usually nurtured and nursed their babies and spent many hours overseeing their young children's educations, even as slave nurses frequently assisted them with caring for their children's physical needs. Southern fathers also took a keen interest in the education of their children, working to prepare them for their place as members of the ruling class. Southern parents generally were more permissive than their northern counterparts, but this is not to suggest that they were any less interested in instilling the values of industry, self-control, and frugality that were so highly valued by the northern middle class.[41]

A major point of difference between northern and southern parents was the propensity of Southerners to produce large families well into the nineteenth century. The size of the American family began to gradually decline over the course of the century, and urban middle-class families, who had little need for the labor of their children and instead wished to concentrate their limited resources on fewer children, were on the vanguard of this change. Various forms of contraception made this declining birth rate possible, although few Southerners used these devices until the twentieth century. The only birth control used by most southern women was the time-honored practice of breast-feeding their children into the second year in order to delay pregnancy. Despite their large families, most planters provided their children with an education as well as a legacy; the bequest was often in the form of land for sons and slaves for daughters.[42]

Missouri slaveholders followed childbirth patterns and child-rearing practices similar to those of planters. Most mothers and fathers valued their children and made financial and career decisions based on the best interests of their families, but as was the case with many other aspects of their lives, their more limited means made it difficult for most to provide their children the same advantages afforded planters' offspring. Small-slaveholding women were much more involved in the care of their children because their smaller slave forces necessitated this labor. Educational opportunities were limited in rural Missouri and many parents were forced to take an active role in the education of their children. Not all small-slaveholding families could afford tuition at the region's academies or colleges, nor could they launch their children into their adulthoods in grand style. In fact, many of Missouri's small slaveholders made parenting decisions that in many ways resembled those of northern middle-class and farm families rather than planter families. Most Missouri slaveholding families remained large during the antebellum years, and although many fathers and mothers were concerned about the expense of caring for and educating their children, most were happy to gain extra hands to assist them on their farms. As was true in middle-class families, small-slaveholding parents focused on providing their children with the tools, rather than the actual means, to make their own way in the world.[43]

Most Missouri slaveholding parents were thrilled by the birth of a healthy baby, and there is little indication that parents held back from forming emotional attachments to their infants because of concerns that they might die prematurely in an age of high infant mortality. Both fathers and mothers wrote lovingly of their new babies and apprised relatives and friends of their growth and progress. They bragged about their children outright, observing how advanced or attractive they were. Mary Belt wrote to her mother about how delighted she and her husband were in their young son: "Georgia is growing very fast, he gets prettier and smarter. Mr Belt is as foolish about him as he ever was about sonny." A month later, Mary Belt continued to revel in Georgia's many antics, reporting to her mother that "he is commenced talking he will take a cup in his hand and wave it and holler hurrah. hurrah." Over the years, Melinda Napton gushed to her husband about her babies. She reflected about one son in 1847: "My dear delightful, sweet, beautiful Charley is the most precious thing that ever lived, and is constantly thinking his mother will eat him up." Three year later she chastised her husband for not giving their only daughter proper consideration: "You did not send Molly a kiss in your last letter. Now my good fellow—you are to pet this baby—if you never did any thing else—and to make a greater fuss with the little girl than you ever did with the boys. A father's only daughter—will be a treasure in after years." And in 1858, she worried over the health of her baby boy, Lewis: "My heart is very much bound up in this dear baby, and I felt uneasy about him. It appears to me, I never loved a child so much, but I suppose I did love all the others, just as much."[44]

Parents held their older children in similar esteem and dedicated much of their time, energy, and resources to raising them. They worried over their children's health and education, and concentrated their attention on their moral development. Plenty of time was given over to instruction and discipline; however, parents also enjoyed the company of their children as they read to or played with them. As children grew toward adulthood, parents forged enduring bonds with their offspring, especially those of the same gender. Soon after the move to Missouri, Paulina Stratton developed a fulfilling relationship with her teenage daughters, Agnes and Bettie, turning to them for emotional support and clearly enjoying their company.[45]

The family life of small slaveholders John and Mary Helm, in addition to that of the McDonalds, perhaps best reflects northern middle-class standards. Helm moved his family from Louisville, Kentucky, to Hannibal in the early 1850s when he was named director of the Hannibal and St. Joseph Railroad. He also pursued a legal career there. Letters between family members and the older Helm children, who were away at school, suggest a comfortable family life. The epistles relayed information about the construction of the family's new home and the daily activities of the younger children, who frequently played in the yard and fed the chickens. The older children bragged about their siblings' progress with school work and proclaimed that their baby sister was "the sweatest [sic] child in Hannibal or in the state of Missouri or in the United States." The girls even complained about wearing their older sister's hand-me-down frocks. The Helm children also conveyed news about one another's health and welfare and worried while they were parted. More than once they mentioned their mother's ill health and were concerned about her frequent "sick head aches." John and Mary Helm fretted about their children while they were away as well. In 1852, Lizzie Helm suggested to her sister Sallie, who was attending school in Kentucky, that she carefully guard her words when she wrote to their mother: "Sister Sallie we do all want to see you so much, but you had better mind how you write to Ma that you want to come home so bad, unless you do indeed want to come home for it makes her cry and then she says she ought not to have left you and talks of going for you. The other day when she got your letter in which you said so much about wanting to see us all so bad. Ma cried and talked of going right off for you but papa laughed her out of the notion."[46]

Not all Missouri slaveholding households were scenes of domestic bliss, however. Gus Smith, a former slave in Osage County, told a harrowing story of the violence and abuse that his neighbor Mr. Thornton perpetrated on the residents of his household. Thornton was known to be a cruel master, but his violent temper was not only directed at his slaves—he also beat his grown son to death with the handle of a cowhide whip. Thornton granted his son permission to leave on a Saturday evening to court a young woman and instructed him to return the following evening, but when the boy sauntered into his father's fields mid way through the day on Monday, he met his violent end. Ironically, Thornton treated his son much the same way he might have treated a slave man who had returned late from visiting his abroad wife. When the boy expired ten hours after the beating, and the men in the neighborhood "began to plan a lynching party," Thornton took his slaves and fled the jurisdiction, never to be heard from again.[47]

Violence was pervasive in many small-slaveholding households, although not usually as extreme as in the case of the Thorntons, and, therefore, it is not surprising that parents routinely physically disciplined their children. Paulina Stratton disliked striking her children, but reasoned to herself that resorting to violence was more a sign of her children's disobedience than her own inability to control her temper. Stratton blamed her children and slaves for her violent turns, but her diary suggests that a low level of violence continuously permeated the Stratton household. Stratton even slapped her baby daughter for the annoying, although developmentally appropriate, offense of repeatedly throwing her spoon on the floor. She, like many other Missouri parents, sincerely believed that physical punishment was a necessary step in breaking the will of a potentially wayward child. Most slaveholding parents were not excessively violent, but they also were not afraid to turn to the rod if it helped them to impress upon their children the prized values of discipline and obedience. Slaveholders were less restrained when they physically disciplined their slaves, however. Paulina Stratton, Priscilla Patton, and Elvira Scott frequently lamented that they were unable to control their tempers with their slaves, as well as their children.[48]

Missouri slaveholding parents thought that teaching discipline was necessary, but most also embraced contemporary middle-class ideals about childhood and child rearing, and believed that children should be showered with affection and given ample time to play. Children's material possessions were not great, but slaveholding children frequently played with toys, such as dolls, balls, and wagons, which often suited the purpose of preparing them for their gender roles as adults. Girls were encouraged to emulate the experiences of adult women, and, therefore, Beverly Helm was thrilled when her cousins gave her a doll bed and bedding. In contrast, boys were expected to engage in physical play that would foster independence and competition. The McDonald boys reveled in all kinds of outdoor play, including going sledding in the wintertime. Many traveling parents, like William Napton, bought their children gifts as a token of their affection. Fathers especially fielded requests from their children, but were more likely to oblige if the desired item was practical. Abiel Leonard happily acquiesced when his daughter Mary requested a knife to make her own pens like the other girls at her school. He bought knives for both Mary and her sister Martha and observed to the girls that he hoped that making their own pens would improve their penmanship. Even presents came at the cost of a life lesson.[49]

Missouri parents held their children in great esteem, but they were always cognizant of their important role in training them for their adult lives. Parents ultimately hoped that they would prepare their children to assume their proper places as male and female members of the dominant class and race. From an early age, parents believed that they should be role models for their children and sought to provide a good example of upright living, as well as teach them the values of their class. Many parents believed that a strong Christian faith would provide the best foundation for achieving this goal and were consumed with concerns about the state of their children's souls. Antebellum gender expectations charged women with a special role in bringing about their children's salvation. Mothers, such as Paulina Stratton and Priscilla Patton, took this directive to heart and often worried that they were not up to the task. Patton prayed in 1855: "I have many responsible duties. My children require great time a[nd] patience. I try to bring them up as a christian mother, but often fail in many things. Help me Heavenly Father to do aright." Stratton also recognized that she did not always live up to the dictates of her faith and constantly worried that her occasionally ungovernable temper would not set the proper example for her children. She brought her children with her to church service on Sunday mornings and provided them with religious instruction on Sunday afternoons. She was especially gratified when her older daughters, Agnes and Bettie, experienced conversion and joined the church in August 1856.[50]

Parents also modeled the values of hard work, thriftiness, and piety through example. Priscilla Patton, fearing that she might die during a grave illness, penned letters to her children that both reflected her parenting values and her expectations for their futures. She wished to provide her children with constructive criticisms and used the letters as a vehicle both to assess their personal weaknesses and provide direction for their future improvement. In the process, she revealed both her own priorities and the gender expectations of the small-slaveholding class. She encouraged her daughter Annie, 11, to be a "diligent scholar," observing that "[y]our mind is capable of acquiring knowledge and your memory is retentive, all you lack is *application*." Patton also criticized her daughter for sometimes being "jealous" and "suspicious," and advised, "You must, if you wish to be happy or a christian study to conquer that irritable complaining temper. Oh! my dear, it will be a dark cloud over your pathway of life." Annie was encouraged to "[e]ndevour to cultivate a sweet, cheerful, kind, and loving heart, then you will be happy, and beloved"—admirable attributes for girls and women of her time, class, and place. Patton advised her three sons to be obedient to their father, find "firmness of purpose," "assocociate with persons of worth, intelligence and respecability," be honest and thrifty, and to work hard and persevere. She encouraged her eldest son, Tommy, 13, to "[s]trive to be *first*. those who aim high do not fall very far below the mark" and warned him not to "float along with the drift, but make a name for goodness and greatness." Patton's letters to her children resembled those written by middle- or upper-class parents from either the North or the South. She was interested in instilling values that would serve her children well as they worked to achieve respectability in their future lives as members of the slaveholding class. That she penned these lines on the eve of the Civil War is even more poignant. Within a few short years, Alfred and Priscilla Patton, who sided with the South, found their comfortable Rocheport, Missouri, life utterly turned on end when they were forced to flee their home.[51]

Although the historical record is largely silent on the issue, slaveholding children also learned about mastery over slaves through the example of their parents. As children grew older, they were no longer encouraged to play with slave children and instead practiced their future roles as masters and mistresses. It was common for white children to begin to assert their dominance over slave children, the individuals over whom they held at least limited power. Thomas Jefferson's acute observation that slavery taught white children tyranny proved to be the case for small-slaveholding children as well. Certainly, children were likely to emulate the abuse that they saw white adults perpetrate against slaves. Slave children likely found discipline at the hands of the white children with whom they often played especially intolerable, and they sometimes resisted their playmates' attempts to discipline them. When a slaveholding child slapped Lucinda Patterson when she accidentally pulled up a garden plant instead of a weed: "I got so mad at her, I taken up a hoe and run her all the way in the big house, and of course I got whipped for that." The mistress beat Sarah Graves after her daughter unfairly accused the slave girl of kicking dirt on a white bride's dress. Graves still bore the marks of the beating in her old age. When the master also began to whip her, Graves informed him that his daughter was a "Damned lyin' devil." Interestingly, he believed her story, and the white child received the whipping instead for telling a lie. There is no way to know the motivations of the white girl, but it is likely that she accused Graves of an offense for which she was actually guilty. She calculated at a young age that white adults would likely believe her story, yet her bluff was called when Graves successfully appealed to her master.[52]

Occasionally white children's rehearsals of adult power relations turned even more violent. Justina Woods witnessed a disturbing scene when she broke up an altercation between the white and black children while her landlords, the Jeffries, were away from the farm one day. "They raised a row in the kitchen this morning, I went in and the oldest white boy (who is fifteen) had a butcher knife drawed on a little darky, I walked up to him and took it out of his hand and told him to walk in the house, he drew up his fist but never said a word," Woods reported in a letter to her sister. When she went inside the house to retrieve a carriage whip, the perpetrator ran off with his two younger brothers. Woods worried that as his teacher she would have to discipline him at a future date. Although she understood that she would have more authority within her own schoolhouse, she feared that "he will get smart there some day and then one of us will get hurt and likely both of us, because I will conquer or die in the struggle." Although there is no way to know for certain, Woods's description of the Jeffries' disorderly household suggests that the children likely imitated the behavior of their elders. Justina Woods characterized the marriage and home life of this particular small-slave-holding family as outside of the pale, but the incident with the slave child suggests that the Jeffries' home was an unpleasant and likely dangerous place for their slaves as well.[53]

Frequent references to education in letters and diaries suggest that Missouri slaveholding parents were more concerned about the formal schooling of their children, however. The quality of education provided to slaveholding children depended on both the means and the inclination of their parents. Educational opportunities were limited in antebellum Missouri; in some areas of the state schools were not available, and in most places the quality of education was poor. White children were taught in a variety of locations, including their homes, local subscription schools, and regional academies and colleges. If educated, many parents chose to teach their youngest children at home, and some mothers, like Melinda Napton and Mary Ann Kendley, often spent hours overseeing the education of their children. Napton taught her many children what she termed "the common branches" before they were sent away to school. Fathers often kept apprised of their children's educational progress, although some, like William Napton, took a more active role and introduced them to more advanced subjects such as Latin. A few wealthier parents arranged to hire tutors to privately instruct their children and occasionally those of relatives and friends. William Napton made just such an arrangement when he agreed to employ a young man to tutor his sons in exchange for board and instruction in reading the law, and Abiel Leonard employed a female tutor for a few years to instruct his children and two of his nieces.[54]

Other parents sent their children to the local one-room schoolhouses that dotted the Missouri countryside. The state legislature supported the concept of public education in theory yet never found the political will to adequately fund their mandates. Neighboring landowners often joined together to construct school buildings for the benefit of the local white children. Some schools were partly financed through the rental or sale of Section 16 of each township as stipulated by the federal Land Ordinance of 1785, the law that outlined how federal land would be surveyed and sold in future territories, but this did not cover the costs of running the schools over the long term. In most cases, a locally elected school board hired teachers who were paid through subscriptions. Parents decided the appropriate amount of schooling for each child and pledged to pay for the subscribed days whether or not their children attended. The West Fork School, located in south-central Cooper County, was one such public school. In February 1852, legal voters who resided in the district decided to build a one-room schoolhouse and elected trustees to govern the school. A tax was levied to pay for construction of the school building, and local parents paid the teacher's salary through subscription. During the 1859 school term, the rate was four cents per day per pupil. Both male and female teachers taught at the school and earned a salary of approximately $35 a month. The school term usually lasted for four to five months with both boys and girls, ranging in age from five to eighteen, attending classes in the 18-by-22-foot building. The children were taught reading, writing, arithmetic, grammar, orthography, and geography. Slaveholding and yeomen children attended the school together. In 1860, for example, only seven out of twenty families owned slaves, and both slaveholders and yeomen farmers served as trustees of the school.[55]

In many cases, slaveholding parents had received little formal education as children and, therefore, believed that an elementary education was sufficient for their own children. There is no record of Thomas and Paulina Stratton's educational background, although it is clear from their ability to communicate that both had received a respectable degree of schooling. When it came to their own children, the Strattons chose the West Fork School rather than an academy in a distant town. Paulina never revealed why she and Thomas decided on this particular educational course for their children, but a lack of resources may have been a determining factor since farming did not provide the disposable income available to professional or business men. They also may not have considered the education of their children a high priority. The Strattons appear not to have been driven by concerns about class status, and their economic strategies and decisions were usually modest in scale. Thomas Stratton was able to educate four children for seven dollars during the 1859–1860 school term, a bargain compared to the hundreds of dollars it would have cost to send the older children to an academy. Sixteen-year-old Mary Agnes and fourteen-year-old Bettie attended the school for fifty-seven and forty-seven days respectively, which was above average attendance among the students. Eleven-year-old John attended school for twenty-six days, and five-year-old Lena for only eleven days. The Strattons may have believed that the education gained at West Fork was perfectly sufficient for children who likely would spend their lives working a farm.[56]

Other slaveholding parents pursued formal education for their children at the many academies and colleges founded in the region in the years preceding the Civil War. The establishment of advanced schools in Missouri followed patterns that had emerged throughout the nation during the antebellum years. There were few local educational opportunities during the early years of statehood, and some elite Missourians sent their sons east to attend schools in states whence their parents had migrated. As the years progressed, elite Missourians sought to establish their own institutions of higher learning in response to national educational trends that resulted from concerns about regional identity, changing ideas about women's education, and denominational competition. The result was the founding of academies and colleges for both young men and women. After 1830 there was tremendous growth in the number of institutions of higher learning throughout the state. Protestant denominations established the first Missouri colleges for the purpose of educating ministers. Many of these institutions were located in central and western Missouri and were attended by the sons of the slaveholding and middle classes. They included Westminster College (first called Fulton College), founded by the Presbyterians and opened in Callaway County in 1849; William Jewell College, founded by the Baptists and opened in Clay County in 1850; and Central College, founded by the Methodists and opened in Howard County in 1857. There were also a host of private academies for young men scattered throughout the region that had no denominational affiliation, such as the Masonic College, which opened in Lexington in 1845. In 1839, the leading men of Boone County, Missouri, secured the University of Missouri, the first public university west of the Mississippi River, for their community through the promise of land and financial support, and the school opened its doors to young men in the spring of 1841.[57]

Missouri's young women were not forgotten during the educational advancements of the antebellum years. Most elite Missourians believed in the education of their daughters as well as their sons. Although some may have promoted girls' education with a mind toward improving their marriage prospects, it appears that others followed a northeastern model and educated their daughters with the expectation that they would teach before marriage. Female seminaries were founded throughout the state; they included Columbia Female Academy (later Columbia Female Baptist Academy and now Stephens College), which opened in Boone County in 1833; Clay Seminary, which opened in Clay County in 1855; and the more substantial Christian Female College (now Columbia College), which opened in Boone County in 1851.[58]

The proliferation of academies and colleges during the 1840s and 1850s suggests the importance that many Missouri parents placed on the education of their children. Parents who lived near a town that boasted of an educational institution could save the expense of boarding their child at school, but those who had to pay room and board, as well as tuition, could spend upwards of $200 a year. A young woman attending a ten-month term at the Clay Seminary in 1860 could expect to pay $150 for board, washing, and lights and $38 for the collegiate department's general education, as well as additional expenses for music lessons, ornamental and visual arts, French, German, Latin or Greek, and advanced mathematics, such as analytical geometry and calculus. Parents paid comparable amounts or more for a son's education, although perhaps this was palatable if the result was preparation for a career. The reality was that a great many Missouri parents were willing to incur the expense of sending their children away to school. While most students attended school a short distance from their homes, others, like John Helm and William Napton, sent their children to what they perceived as the best institutions in the region. One historical study of Clay Seminary found that although the majority of the students who attended the school came from surrounding counties and were the daughters of slaveholders, a number of parents of lesser means chose to send their children there as well. Many of those were members of the professional and merchant classes, who obviously valued the idea of women's education and perhaps saw it as a means of upward mobility.[59]

A driving force in William Napton's life was the pursuit of an excellent higher education for his nine sons. Had money been no object, he would have preferred to send all of his sons back East to attend one of his alma maters, Princeton or the University of Virginia, and indeed he sent some of his sons to school in the East. That said, at one point Napton showed little patience for an acquaintance who chose to send his son to a school in Kentucky, observing that the "school is not better than ours—has no reputation at all & if it had, the best policy is to educate our sons here where they expect to live." Napton was constantly making inquires into the quality of education offered at local institutions of higher learning. He reported to his wife in 1852: "I have made some enquiries about the Columbia school, but they have not proved very satisfactory. I believe from what I can learn that the Lexington school is about as good, & if so it will be greatly more convenient for us. I hardly see how we shall be able to send the boys off any where, unless some unexpected wind fall should put me in funds. Times are hard." Napton was less eager to send his only daughter away to school, fearing, as did many parents, that "these ladies boarding schools are the ruin of many a girl." He would consent only if he was assured that Molly was under the care and guidance of "some lady *known* to be of the right sort." His reluctance to provide Molly with a formal education may have signified deeper reservations about educating women. He regaled his wife with a story of a woman at his boarding house who chastised him for neglecting Molly's formal education: "Mrs Bay was abusing me very much at table yesterday for not sending Molly to school. She goes in for educating the girls—called me a heathen said she would have me mobbed." He finally relented and enrolled Molly in boarding school. As the historian Christopher Phillips has observed, the Naptons' great financial sacrifice paid off as the education of their sons launched many into successful professional careers.[60]

The Naptons' family values and expectations resembled those of the northern middle class and southern planters, even as it stretched their financial resources. William Napton never believed that his salary or the profits from his farm were enough to support his growing family in the manner that they required or deserved. He wished to send his eldest son Billy to the University of Virginia in 1857, but knew that the cost to send him would be around $500 in addition to another $500 to educate three other sons locally. On a salary of $2,500 annually this would leave only $1,500 to support the rest of his family. The birth of his eighth son prompted him to write a letter to his friend and political ally, Claiborne Fox Jackson, arguing for a raise: "Well, this boy renders an increase of salary necessary. $2500 a year is a small support for a man who has four sons who ought to be at college, & four more at home." He asked Jackson to take his case to the state legislators and ask them to better support public servants: "You know & every observant man knows, that a man who devotes nine months out the year to public employments & is absent from home all that time, is not destined to make any thing at farming or any other pursuit . . . can't believe but that a judge of our highest court is to live as he does, without books, with his children at the plough & with his wife & daughters [sic] and himself on bacon & corn." Napton, of course, owned a large farm and a number of slaves by 1857, yet the circumstances of his exceedingly large family made it difficult for him to provide for his children in the manner he hoped.[61]

Once enrolled at school, parents expected that their children of both genders would work hard and acquit themselves well. Foremost, they hoped their offspring would gain control of their personal habits, learning to be industrious in their labors and economical in their expenditures, in addition to mastering the required academic subjects. Letters between home and school reveal parents' continued role in the nurture of their children as they moved toward adulthood. Henry Coleman advised his son Weston, who attended Masonic College in Lexington, to excel at his studies. Not only was achievement at the annual examination important for self-fulfillment and to meet the expectations of his family, but it was crucial that he perform well in the eyes of the school and local community. Coleman warned his son: "As the progress in there studies of every one in the College will be carefully scrutinized when the examination some one and the public will look upon those who have made the most progress with smiles and delight while those who have made but little progress will be pitied and neglected as things unworthy of notice." Reputations were made and social connections forged even at the secondary school level, and parents wanted their children to keep this always in their minds.[62]

Many slaveholding parents looked upon education as providing their children with tools to their future success. They inherently understood that they did not command the kind of wealth that would allow them to secure their children's future through inheritance alone and instead struggled to provide their children with an education that could either establish them in a career or would place them in social circles that would promote the possibility of a successful marriage match. In this way, parents believed that they could launch their children into the slaveholding class, but most often it would take the exertions of their offspring to assure their continued place in it.

"Divided equally among my children"

Much was revealed about Missouri slaveholders' expectations and priorities at the moments of sickness and death in the family. Missouri remained an unhealthy place throughout the antebellum years; death from disease, complications during childbirth, and accidents were a common part of everyday life. Few parents could expect to raise all of their children to adulthood, and many children experienced the death of a parent before they reached their maturity. Missourians often exposed their feelings about their families in the moments in which they contemplated the death of a loved one or their own impending demise.[63]

As was true elsewhere in the nineteenth century, Missouri children were especially susceptible to sickness and death. A few parents nonchalantly described the death of their children. For example, Henry Coleman reported to his son who was away at school: "We have had the Misfortune to loose [sic] your little Sister *Emma*, who died yesterday morning at 9 Oclock. Her disease was Bronchites or billious diahriea. We buried her on the same evening at 6 ½ oclock." More often, parents wrote about the deaths of their children in heart-wrenching prose. Jonathan Haines relayed the anguishing story of the sickness of three of his children and the eventual death of his daughter Katherine. He felt complicit in his daughter's untimely death because of his choice of a new and, tragically, incompetent doctor. After he realized that the doctor was unable to save her, Haines "walked the house to and fro lamenting my sad condishion until between midnight and day." It was only after another, more capable, doctor was found that two of his children recovered, but it was too late for Katherine. He grieved the death of his "dear and loving daughter" but felt the pain more acutely because he believed that she did not "have a fair shake for her life I do not think it would have hurt me as bad but to think that she was murdered in the manner that she was is more than I can bar." Haines seemed somewhat consoled by the "wish of some of my family" to name a newborn daughter after her recently departed sister. Two years later the family lost another daughter, Charity, but Haines had learned his lesson and brought in a parade of doctors to minister to her in the month before her death. He wrote of the experience, "I am greatly discorged to think that the choise of my children is taken away from me." He described Charity's deathbed scene in great detail, explaining how she called her family to her bedside to "express the love she had for us all."[64]

The death of a parent caused the greatest disruption in the life of the family, however. When a wife and mother died, the family suffered for want of someone to manage the domestic concerns of the household, and if the children were still young, to nurture them. In 1862, William Napton was devastated when Melinda died during the birth of their eleventh child, a stillborn son. The six Napton children still living at home were left in their father's care, although he quickly enlisted his unmarried sister, Malvena, to step into the mothering role. In fact, it was quite common for widowers to ask unmarried female relatives to assist with motherless children or for the children to be sent away to a relative's home, although it often was not long before many grieving widowers took another wife.[65]

Although the death of a mother might cause untold emotional trauma, the death of the husband and father frequently resulted in the financial dislocation of the family. Paulina Stratton was shocked at Thomas's unexpected death after a brief illness in November 1863. Paulina had incessantly complained about Thomas during the last years of their marriage, but she began to glorify him soon after his death, ignoring all of the negative aspects of their marriage and dwelling only on the positive as she poured out her troubles in the pages of her diary. Thomas's death and the loss of her slaves during the war left Paulina in desperate financial circumstances, and she was forced to turn to her son-in-law for assistance. During the years ahead, she always held onto the belief that had her husband still been alive she and her youngest children would have prospered. Elizabeth Haines deeply mourned the death of her husband, Jonathan, as well. Although she also missed their four daughters who preceded him in death, she lamented to a relative: "the los of my children is n[o]thing to my companion it seams like theare is no company hear for me." Widows, like Elizabeth Haines and Paulina Stratton, were forced to quickly learn how to make their way in a world that was run by men. Small-slaveholding men typically left their estates in the hands of their wives, but most often the women looked to male relatives for assistance as they navigated the legal system and worked to provide for their children. Although some widows continued to run their homes and farms with the aid of slave labor, many widows hired out most of their bondpeople and supported their families with the proceeds.[66]

The decisions made by Missouri slaveholders in anticipation of their deaths lay bare both their family values and the economic limitations under which they operated. Unlike wealthy planters, who often distributed land and slaves to their children both during their lifetimes and after their deaths, most Missouri slaveholders had limited assets. A few were able to provide their children with small gifts of land, goods, cash, or slaves upon their marriages or as they entered their adulthoods, however. Joseph Staples indicated in his will that he had previously given each of his children a slave and stipulated that, minus his wife's portion and the value of the slaves already given, his estate should be equally divided among his children. Travese Davis asked that his wife maintain full control of his property until his two youngest sons reached majority, and then it should be divided among these three heirs. His seven older children were willed only one dollar apiece because he had already distributed to them their share of his property.[67]

Most sons and daughters were forced to wait until the death of both parents to inherit the family's wealth. Slaveholders were more interested than most Missourians in dictating how their estates would be distributed to their heirs. Of the 229 wills entered into probate in Cooper County from 1818 to 1866 at least 40 percent involved the distribution of slaves. In Cooper County, a little over 70 percent of slaveholders divided their property equally among their children. There was a slight tendency for parents to favor sons in the early years, but overall there was a strong effort to be equitable. Southern planters also dispensed with primogeniture as the nineteenth century progressed, but they demonstrated a pattern of giving land to sons and slaves to daughters. Most Missouri slaveholders could not bequeath in this manner because they did not own large tracts of land or large numbers of slaves. They instead distributed their more limited assets in ways that made sense to each individual family. Although wives were occasionally willed a dower portion or an equal share of the estate, it was quite common for slaveholding men to leave all of their property in the hands of their wives for use during their lifetimes, stipulating that the estate should be divided equally among the children upon her death. There were various schemes for distributing property—combinations of land, slaves, personal property, livestock, and cash, all dictated by the circumstances of particular slaveholding households. It was not usual for testators to designate which slave should be given to which child, for example.[68]

The most many slaveholding parents could do was to provide their children with the tools to make their own way in the world and many believed that a good education would accomplish this goal. Alfred Wilson asked that those of his children who had not yet received an education at the time of his death should be provided with an education, and Achilles Eubank stipulated that his children should be given a "common education and to be decently raised" in the case that his wife should also die. Joseph Arnold requested that his son Joseph should be enrolled in Georgetown Military Academy in Kentucky if "he proves capable and studious." In the case that he was a lackluster scholar, Joseph's father asked that he should not be "placed behind a counter where he will be too apt to become familiarized with arts of deception, with his mind intent only on frivolities, and have his intellect annihilated." It is unclear why Arnold was so contemptuous of merchants, but he may have wished that his son would pursue a future in agriculture. He also demanded that Joseph Arnold Jr.'s bequest should be diminished to one tenth if he "contracted habits of idleness and dissipation." Apparently, Joseph Arnold intended to parent even from beyond the grave.[69]

Slaveholders' dreams for their children's futures were more often than not fulfilled at the expense of their slave men, women, and children. The fact that relatively small estates were dispersed among many heirs meant that slave families were often divided upon settlement. Although a few owners stipulated that families should be kept together, in most cases the division among slaveholding family members meant the separation of slave families. The careful and equal distribution of property often resulted in mothers and their children each given to a different slaveholding heir. Although slaveholding family members lived in close proximity, many miles sometimes separated their households. Some owners actually acknowledged the link between the welfare of their children and the fate of their slaves when they specifically allowed their family slaves to be sold in order to fulfill the mandates of their will. Alfred Wilson indicated that his slaves could be sold if it was necessary to pay for the education that he wished to provide to his youngest children. Wilson appeared unconcerned that his children might reach for a bright future while another family was destroyed. Missouri slaves were already faced with many challenges as they worked to protect their families. Slaveholders' hopes for their own children proved to be yet another.[70]

3 / "I was at home with the Negroes at work": Labor within Missouri's Small-Slaveholding Households

Stephen Hempstead kept a journal of life on his farm five miles outside of the city of St. Louis from his arrival in 1811 until his death in 1831. Year in and year out Hempstead faithfully chronicled both the mundane and profound happenings in his own life and the life of his wife, Mary, as well as those of his many children, grandchildren, and few slaves. He noted births, marriages, and deaths, but he also devoted significant attention to the everyday workings of his home and farm, regularly beginning his diary entries with the words, "I was at home," and continuing with detailed descriptions of seemingly endless but necessary labor.[1]

Hempstead and his farmhands, as on most Missouri slaveholdings, worked together to maintain the agricultural operations of his farm. Two or three men—including his own slave men and hired men both slave and free—worked with him raising corn, wheat, oats, flax, various feed grasses, fruits, vegetables, and livestock. Hempstead also intermittently employed his slave men, and occasionally hired skilled laborers, on various construction projects around the farm. Household members consumed much of what they grew, but the nearby city of St. Louis provided a ready market for excess production. Hempstead often sent his slave men to the local mill and into the city with a wagonload of produce for sale. Like many Missourians, he actively used the local slave-hiring market, thereby maintaining flexibility in his labor force by hiring slaves when he needed extra help and hiring out his own slaves when work on the farm slackened. He also frequently exchanged slave laborers with his neighbors and kin in the area. Hempstead readily sold slaves whom he believed had become intractable, however, including a man who for years figured prominently in his accounting of tasks performed around the farm. Mary Hempstead engaged the labor of slave women in the completion of her endless household duties, but unlike her husband, she faced ongoing difficulties in securing steady domestic help. The Hempsteads both bought and hired a succession of slave women to assist Mary during their two decades in Missouri. It clearly was a priority for the Hempsteads, as it was for many Missourians, to employ slaves in both their home and their fields.[2]

The Hempsteads were an affluent early Missouri slaveholding family, yet the description of their St. Louis County small-slaveholding farm scarcely resembled that of southern plantations. Although slavery was firmly entrenched in the state as an economic, political, and social system, the profile of the vast majority of Missouri slaveholding households in many ways better reflected farms than plantations. Missouri was never a land of large estates where slaves devoted most of their labor to the production of cash crops, but instead was populated by farmers who produced a wide variety of crops and products for household use and market sale. Largely self-sufficient producers, Missouri farmers grew both small and large grain crops for household consumption, and they regularly dined on produce from their own vegetable gardens and orchards, as well as meat from their swine, cattle, and poultry. Yet from the beginning of American settlement, Missourians took advantage of the river system and produced and marketed sizable tobacco, hemp, corn, and wheat crops, as well as livestock specifically for the market. Commercial production granted settlers the means to achieve their financial priorities, providing them with the necessary cash and credit to improve their property, purchase more land and slaves, and provide for their families. Those producers with access to ample land and labor had the potential to thrive in Missouri. As early as 1816, J. Clemens described the promise the new land held: "In Short this Country possesses so many advantages that those who acquire lands here in time can not fail to reap a rich harvest. . . . Capitalists coming to this country who have a Sufficiency of hands to attend to the raising of wheat Tobacco or Hemp . . . the river at all Seasons afford him a quick outlet to any port he pleases."[3]

As children of the Upper South, most white Missourians considered racially based slavery to be at the foundation of the society that they helped to create on slavery's border. Relegating enslaved people of African descent to the bottom rung of the social ladder ensured the dominance of all whites regardless of their class status and allowed for the existence of a "natural" order based on race, gender, and age with white men dominating all those who lived within their households. Yet, white women and children were empowered in this society as well because they too were considered superior to the slave men, women, and children with whom they lived and worked. Whatever social benefits that slavery provided white Missourians it was foremost a system of labor, however. Slaveholders generally structured the labor regime within their households to reflect their preexisting racial and gender assumptions, as well as the realities of life on the small-slaveholding farms of the border South. Slaves were not the only people who labored in Missouri's fields, homes, mines, and businesses, but most white Missourians believed that their race made them especially well suited to the most undesirable and strenuous of tasks and that whites were preordained to supervise this labor.[4]

Slavery was central to Missouri's economy and labor system, although demographic diversity existed within the state—some geographic areas were settled more heavily by nonslaveholding and even free-state migrants and thus counted among their residents fewer slaves. There were slaves in all Missouri counties by 1850; however, the numbers varied greatly throughout the state. Howard County in Little Dixie had a population of 4,890 slaves, whereas Dodge County on the Iowa border had only two. Russel L. Gerlach, a geographer, has calculated that twenty-six Missouri counties, mostly bordering the Missouri and Mississippi Rivers, held slave populations of at least 1,000 in 1850, accounting for 77 percent of the slaves in the state. Conversely, another twenty-five counties, primarily located in northern Missouri and in the Ozark Mountains, had slave populations of less than a hundred. Not surprisingly, the support for slavery was strongest in Missouri's river counties where the largest number of slaveholders and slaves resided, but throughout the state—no matter the number of slaves in the immediate proximity—there existed a preference for slave over free labor. Slavery retained favor as both a social and a labor system in Missouri in spite of the fact that it differed in significant ways from the better-known plantation paradigm. Missourians adapted slavery to an agricultural economy that mixed cash crops with food crop production and necessitated a labor force that was flexible. Ultimately, they structured the economics of their households in ways that they believed would help them realize their financial and social goals for their families (see table 2).[5]

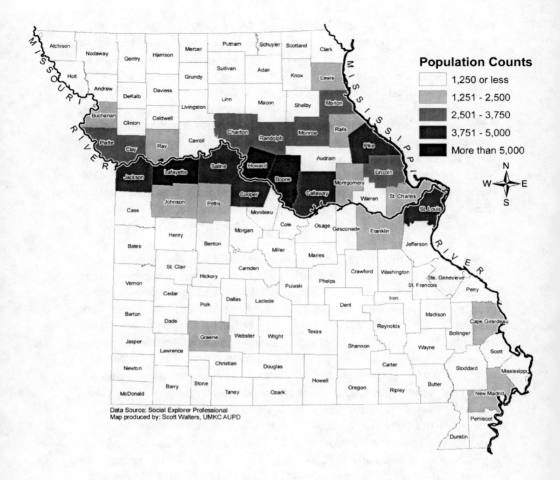

MAP 2. Slave Population of Missouri Counties, 1860. This map illustrates the distribution of the slave population in Missouri counties in 1860. While there were slaves in every Missouri county in 1860, this map clearly shows that most slaves were held in the counties straddling the Missouri and Mississippi Rivers, with the largest concentration in the central and western part of the state. Map created by Scott Walters.

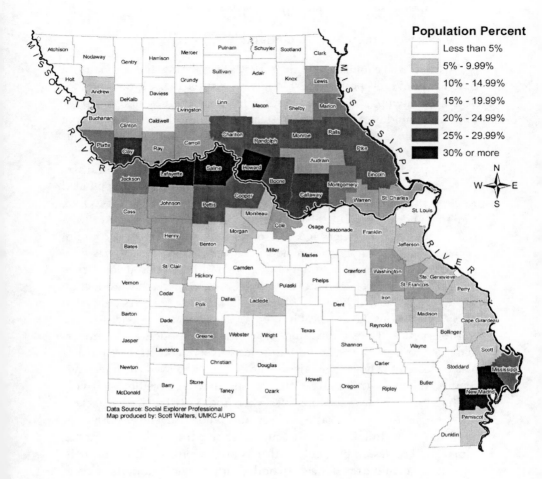

MAP 3. Slaves as a Percentage of the Total Population, Missouri Counties, 1860. This map illustrates the distribution of slaves as a percentage of the total population of Missouri counties in 1860. The map suggests that slaves accounted for a sizable percentage of the population in a vast number of Missouri counties. The counties with the largest slave populations and those with slaves as the greatest percentage of the total population do not always coincide. St. Louis County is a prime example: it had the seventh largest slave population, but slaves accounted for only 2 percent of the total population. Map created by Scott Walters.

"Negroes were, therefore, in demand"

Missouri slaveholders and their slaves, emulating the agricultural practices and crop preferences of Upper South farmers, grew corn, tobacco, and hemp, and raised hogs, cattle, horses, mules, and sheep for both household use and the marketplace. The labor demands stemming from the cultivation of these diverse agricultural products largely influenced Missouri farmers' decisions about their workforce.[6]

Corn production was at the foundation of Missouri's agricultural system, as was the case for those upland Southerners who had populated Kentucky, Tennessee, as well as the states of the Old Northwest—Ohio, Indiana, and Illinois—in the decades preceding the settlement of Missouri. Southerners by heritage, Missourians cultivated corn because of preference and utility: it was a staple of the southern diet; it was used to feed livestock; and it did not require milling. Missourians grew 17,332,524 bushels of "Indian" corn by 1840 and increased production to 72,892,157 bushels by 1860. In contrast, Missouri farmers cultivated only 4,227,586 bushels of wheat in 1860. Corn production was closely tied to the practice of raising livestock for both consumption and commercial sale. Pork was a staple of Missourians' everyday diets, and farmers also exported the hogs they raised. At first they employed the free-range method typical of the rural South, but later they used feedlots—driving the hogs to riverside processing sites where they were butchered, packed, and shipped to distant markets. They also tended sheep for both their wool and meat, and developed a flourishing breeding industry for cattle, horses, and mules. In particular, farmers bred and raised draft animals, such as mules and oxen, for sale to both southern clients and those coming through Missouri on their way to the far West. In addition, the state became a major producer of beef, as well as the eastern terminus for cattle driven out of the southwestern United States. By 1860, Missouri livestock was valued at $53,693,673, surpassing Kentucky and Tennessee as the major southern producer of swine; and the state emerged as a leading producer of horses, mules, cattle, and sheep as well.[7]

Cleared land, access to markets, and an available labor source were the keys to expansion of market crops; therefore, Missouri's slaveholders were well positioned to engage in substantial commodity production. Yet few Missouri farmers planted commercial crops on a large scale and ran their farms with gang labor like on the plantations of the South; most instead chose to cultivate cash crops on a smaller scale, planting some acres in tobacco and hemp and the rest primarily in corn and grasses.

Rather than a single cash crop, farmers practiced diversified agriculture, producing multiple crops on alternate fields. They chose a crop mix that would keep their workers busy throughout the course of the year, cultivating sustenance and feed crops during lulls in the growing and harvesting of cash crops.[8]

Many farmers in the East, whose intensive cultivation of tobacco had exhausted the soil, turned to Missouri as a promising new place for production. The state never really rivaled Kentucky's output, but as early as 1840, Missourians produced 9,057,913 pounds of tobacco, and increased that amount to 25,086,196 pounds by 1860. In the late antebellum years, Missouri tobacco was sold in New Orleans and Baltimore and supplied both American and European consumers. Migrants from the Upper South also brought hemp cultivation westward to Missouri, eventually cultivating 19,267 tons of primarily dew-rotted hemp by 1860. Hemp rose with the fortunes of cotton as it was mainly used for bagging and rope to transport southern cotton crops. A shipping and manufacturing industry emerged in St. Louis and other river towns that focused on the processing and transporting of Missouri's cash crops. Factory workers in places such as Brunswick and Arrow Rock processed tobacco purchased from local farmers into chewing tobacco and cigars. Rope and bagging manufacturers established ropewalks and factories all along the Missouri River to process hemp for products used in the southern cotton trade. These manufactured goods were shipped down river to St. Louis and then on to southern markets.[9]

The cultivation and processing of both tobacco and hemp required intensive labor throughout the year. Tobacco plants required vigilant care, demanding grueling hours of tedious toil during the growing, harvesting, and curing processes. One individual could realistically be responsible for approximately four acres of tobacco, or 4,000 pounds worth a year. Workers began with the preparation of tobacco fields in the early months of each year, followed by multiple sowings of specially prepared tobacco beds in late February or early March. A few months later, the plants were transplanted into the fields, where they required constant tending throughout the summer months. Workers "hilled" the plants to reinforce them, "primed" away the unwanted lower leaves, "topped" the terminal buds, and continually pinched hornworms and hoed cutworms away from the plants. The tobacco leaves were harvested manually in September, hung and dried in "hands" in a tobacco shed or barn (and in later years smoke-cured), and finally stripped and bound for shipping at the end of the year. Slaveholders and nonslaveholders alike cultivated tobacco, but only those with access to laborers could expand production.[10]

The harvesting of hemp was more physically demanding work than most white men willingly would engage, and, therefore, in many Missourians' minds the development of the hemp industry was linked to the availability of slave labor. Although the actual cultivation of both seed and fiber hemp crops was not arduous, hemp grown for its fiber required intensive labor during processing. The tall hemp stalks were cut with a cradle scythe toward the end of the summer and then left to dry on the ground before they were gathered into bundles and stacked. The hemp was spread out again later in the early fall and was not brought in from the fields until it had rotted enough for the fibers to separate more easily from the stems during the breaking process. Most Missouri farmers employed the dew-rotting process rather than the more labor-intensive water-rotting method, which produced higher quality rope but required the hemp to soak in standing water during processing. In both cases, slaves broke the decaying hemp with a manually operated device called a hemp brake, and then dressed and pressed the fibers into bales weighing as much as five hundred pounds in preparation for transportation to market. There were some attempts to mechanize the harvesting, breaking, and baling process, but this early technology satisfied few, and most Missouri farmers continued to rely on manual labor in the years preceding the war. Breaking an expected one hundred pounds of hemp a day—which many slave men surpassed—was a physically demanding task rejected by most white men. W[illiam] M. Paxton of Platte County remembered, "Hemp was the staple product. We became wealthy by its culture. . . . But no machinery ever invented superseded the hand-break in cleaning it. . . . Negroes were, therefore, in demand."[11]

On the eve of the Civil War, Missouri farmers' agricultural practices were in the process of evolving into a fusion of the traditions of both the Upper South and the Old Northwest, an ultimate consequence of the state's border location and the growing presence of migrants from free states. Farmers, especially in the larger slaveholding counties, became increasingly more interested in adopting new agricultural practices that would enhance productivity and improve the quality of their output. Missourians founded a number of agricultural improvement societies, held county fairs, and supported agricultural journals, such as the *Valley Farmer*, which began publication in St. Louis in 1848 and targeted farmers in Missouri, Illinois, and Iowa. Progressive farmers shared information on cultivation techniques, livestock breeding, and agricultural technology through these various venues. Stockbreeders were especially interested in improving the quality of their herds and imported more and more pedigreed breeding animals into the region. Farmers also began to purchase labor-saving mechanical equipment, such as Mc-Cormick Reapers, to aid in the planting and harvesting of grain crops. Local newspapers advertised the new labor-saving devices, and editors urged their adoption, while agents of the manufacturers canvassed the countryside in search of sales. Missourians had invested only $3,984,524 in farm implements and machinery by 1850, but that amount had more than doubled to $8,711,508 by 1860.[12]

Missouri farms were cultivated and rural households were operated by a combination of free—usually family-based—and slave labor. Outside of farmers' access to markets and the quality of their land, agricultural success fundamentally was a result of the number of available workers. In Missouri, a strong correlation existed between the number of slaves owned in a particular county and the rate of production of labor-intensive commercial crops. In outlying areas, with no direct access to the market provided by the rivers, both agricultural productivity and the numbers of slaves employed generally were modest. Although the economic dominance of the river counties began to be challenged on the eve of the Civil War with the construction of both the Hannibal and St. Joseph Railroad and the Pacific Railroad running westward across the state on either side of the Missouri River, it was not until branch lines connected Missouri's hinterlands with the main trunk lines that farmers in outlying areas increased production of market crops. In the years before the railroad's ascent, it was no coincidence that the river counties with the greatest access to distant markets and the largest slave populations boasted the greatest commercial agricultural productivity. Those counties bordering the Missouri and Mississippi Rivers with slave populations that often exceeded 25 percent produced large crops of tobacco and hemp, as well as a substantial amount of the corn and livestock. By 1860, the ten Missouri counties with the largest slave populations produced 27 percent of the state's tobacco, 64 percent of the hemp, 21 percent of the corn, and owned 21 percent of the value of both owned and slaughtered livestock.[13]

Although the benefits of slave labor were apparent, most Missourians chose not to employ large numbers of slaves on substantial agricultural estates. The slave population of the state continued to grow during the antebellum years, and many individual slaveholdings increased in numbers, yet the overall composition of the average Missouri slaveholding changed little over time. Large holdings were rare even in counties with the most sizable slave populations. In Howard County in 1860, for example, the average slaveholding was 7.3, and only 45 out of 801 slaveholders owned 20 or more slaves, and of these only 3 owned 50 or more. In Cooper County the average slaveholding was 5.2, with only 18 slaveholders owning 20 or more slaves. Despite the commercial success of tobacco and hemp, Missouri remained a state of small-slaveholding and yeoman farmers.[14]

Even as agricultural practices in the state became more firmly entrenched in the marketplace, most Missourians continued to employ economic strategies that were deeply rooted in the diversified agricultural heritage of their ancestral homes. As was true of yeomen and small-slaveholding farmers throughout the South, the paramount objective of most white Missourians was to possess unencumbered property—whether land or slaves. Many believed that their rights as republican citizens could be secured only through economic independence. Southerners generally considered it dishonorable to work for someone else, believing that economic dependence on another limited a man's ability to act independently and, most importantly, exercise his free will in civic matters. The average Missourian achieved financial independence through the purchase and improvement of land, the cultivation of both subsistence and cash crops, and occasionally engagement in professional work or business pursuits. In Southerners' view, white men also exercised independence or liberty through the control of the individuals living and working within their households, including their wives, children, and ideally slaves. In a southern white man's ideal world, the household head ruled his dependents as a benevolent paternalist, and those under his charge appreciated his efforts and rewarded him with gratitude and hard work. Although a few engaged in financially risky practices, such as speculating in real estate, the primary goal of most Missouri slaveholders was to maintain their economic independence and mastery of their household while attempting to attain their financial and social goals. White Missourians' decisions about agricultural practices and slave ownership were in large measure influenced by these conservative objectives.[15]

In the end, few Missourians chose to own a large number of slaves or massive tracts of land because diversified agricultural practices did not require them; most instead employed their small number of slaves on moderately sized farms as general farmhands and domestic workers. Missourians were not opposed to using the labor of slaves in pursuits other than agriculture, however. Enslaved skilled artisans, such as black-smiths, bricklayers, carpenters, and the like, were always needed, as were workers for the region's ropewalks and tobacco and hemp factories. Many other Missouri slaves labored in the river trade and in the state's ironworks and mines. Although in outlying parts of the state slaves were few, in the larger slaveholding counties, slaves performed nearly all of the agricultural labor and much of the factory work.

Slaves were in great demand in the Missouri River counties because of a preference for slave labor but also because of a relative scarcity of white laborers in the countryside. Farmers repeatedly complained about the challenge of locating white men to employ as farmhands or overseers. William Napton habitually searched for men to oversee his Arrow Rock farming operations while he served as a Missouri Supreme Court justice. The difficulty of finding white workers was exacerbated in the early 1850s when many local Missouri men were "going off to California." Napton often was forced to rely on a neighbor to check on the progress of his slave men every day or so. William and Melinda Napton employed four overseers during the 1850s, eventually resorting to William's northern-born brother Welling even though Melinda barely tolerated what she described as his "meanness." William likely appreciated the difficulty of finding white men who were willing to work in a dependent position for an extended period of time and eventually relied on a family member in spite of his inadequacies. While on a trip to her father's home in Kentucky, Melinda observed that it would be easier to find an overseer in Virginia where they were as "thick as peas." She thought perhaps it might be better to have a friend send them a Virginia man, rather than hire someone in Missouri.[16]

Nathaniel Leonard had similar difficulties hiring white agricultural laborers to work on his Cooper County farm. He usually oversaw his own farming and livestock operations but wished to employ white laborers so that he might feel free to travel from home on occasion. Yet, Nathaniel incessantly complained to his brother Abiel both about the challenge of finding white laborers and about the quality of their work, observing in 1837, "My two white men haveing no more management than my boys & I am as much compelled to stay at home as if I had nothing but negroes on my farm." In fact, in 1846, he wished to replace a white man with a hired slave, believing that the white man was about half as good a worker as his best slave man. He "would then have the pleasure of telling my white hand that I could do better without him than with him." At one point Nathaniel concluded that he must do without white laborers, as "there are none to be had worth haveing." Instead, he decided to hire additional slave workers for the year and run his farm entirely on slave labor, as Abiel had done for years.[17]

It was not that white Missourians did not engage in manual labor—farmers and their family members labored extensively in their own fields and homes, but it was rather the case that rural whites did not routinely hire their labor to others. In January 1841, L. Hall observed in a letter to his children: "Labour in this country is scarce and high. We have succeeded in getting a boy of 17 years for eighty-five dollars per year. good farm hands were hired from 150 to 160 dollars per year white men seldom hire by the year." In contrast to the eastern states of the Upper South, where land was scarce and expensive, there was still land available for purchase in Missouri—especially in the Ozarks—throughout the antebellum years, and many landowners were willing to lease parcels of land to the landless. The opportunity to work their own land reduced the number of white men willing to work for someone else. The editor of the *Valley Farmer* concurred when he observed in 1850 that in the region "land is cheap, and labor high, and hired labor very scarce and hard to be got at any price; because our young men, instead of hiring out year after year. . . push at once on to the vacant land, open a farm, and thus enrol themselves among the free-holders of the land." White men who boasted of southern heritage had a particular aversion to the dependency of wage labor, often equating it with enslavement. It was one thing for a man to cultivate his own land with the sweat of his brow; it was quite another to labor as another man's dependent. Possessing a worldview representative of many Missourians, Thomas Coleman was appalled when he learned that his younger brother John, who had recently moved to Oregon Territory, had gone to work in a hotel and suggested that he purchase a farm instead and "go at something that is honorable try and make a man of yourself. I would have a higher opinion of myself than to hire as a servant." In truth, there were plenty of opportunities for white workers, especially for those who had mastered a trade, if they were willing to work. Susan Brown asked her mother to pass on word to family and friends in Virginia, including a brickmaker, to migrate to Missouri as "there is no dout about his getting plenty of work the people here say they have to beg and then pay before hand to get there work don there are but few work men here and they have what prices they want." Few white workers chose to pursue these opportunities, however, perhaps fearful of being compared to slaves. J. Calvin Iserman, a New Yorker who lived and worked as a carpenter in the town of Independence near Missouri's western border, was stung by local slaveholders' contemptuous attitude toward him as a Northerner and free laborer: "A person is counted just nobody at all here, unless he owns a lot of niggers and a poor man, and mechanic is looked upon as no better than a slave."[18]

As important as slavery was to the agricultural productivity of Missouri farms, Missourians also valued the labor of slaves within their homes. The domestic operations of a farm household required a tremendous level of labor, and this work by and large was relegated to women. Missouri women spent hours engaged in child care, cooking, washing, cleaning, sewing, gardening, milking, poultry tending, food preservation, and domestic home manufacturing. The amount of home textile production decreased over time as more affluent families began to purchase manufactured cloth, but this change did not translate into less work for women because the ever-expanding consumer culture ultimately encouraged a new understanding among middle-class Americans of what constituted a proper home. These new domestic ideals increased expectations for the furnishings and cleanliness of upper- and middle-class Missourians' homes, the amount and quality of their garments, and the sophistication of the meals placed on their tables.[19]

As with white men, white women's self-identity and how others in their society viewed them was in large measure defined by the type of work in which they engaged. Most rural American women labored at a tremendous amount of housework, and often barnyard work and fieldwork as well. What set slaveholding women apart from other white women was their ability to free themselves from fieldwork and the most physically demanding and undesirable of domestic tasks precisely because they owned slave women to whom they could assign this grueling labor. The work of slaveholding women, or rather those tasks never performed by them, was essential in defining what it meant to be a lady in southern society. Access to the labor of slave women guaranteed white women's elevated social place and freed them to focus their attention on nurturing their children and molding their homes into domestic havens—both fundamental priorities of slaveholding families. In the end, white womanhood and domesticity were purchased at the expense of slave women's toil. Black women were highly valued in Missouri and elsewhere, not only because of their reproductive capabilities, but also because of their flexibility as workers. White Southerners gendered their labor in a way that permitted slave women to work in both homes and fields, and, therefore, it was no accident that white families often purchased or hired slave women or girls before men or boys.[20]

Harrison Trexler, the early twentieth-century historian of Missouri slavery, observed that "[t]hrough tradition, through habit, through necessity," Missourians used, and in fact preferred, "slave labor." Most white Missourians genuinely believed that men and women of African descent were best suited for the dirty and strenuous work of the state's farms, homes, factories, riverboats, and mines, but many also were uncomfortable with the idea of employing white laborers. Even Frank Blair, the eventual leader of the Republican Party and emancipation advocate in Civil War Missouri, once stated that hemp and tobacco could "only be cultivated by slave labor." Others believed that not only were slaves naturally inclined to certain kinds of labor, but they also were preferable and more reliable. William Napton observed to his wife, Melinda, while traveling in the Northeast: "I don't think you would like white servants if you could see as much of them as I do here. It is all a humbug—they stay just as long as they please & when they get time they leave & this they are sure to do whenever any work is to be done." In 1858, Melinda Napton requested that her husband hire an "Irishman" to help in her garden, but she would not tolerate his help inside her house, commenting that it "looks too much like apeing the nobles of Europe." In a perverse way, Napton juxtaposed the European practice of employing servants with American slavery, demonstrating that she firmly recognized that racial subordination was a crucial and desirable component of the southern system of labor. Indeed, as the historian Jonathan Martin has argued, most Southerners chose to hire slaves rather than white workers, "preferring to be masters, not just employers," because they "desire[d] to exert mastery over the laborers they employed." Simply put, employers could order slaves around and discipline them in ways that white hired hands would not tolerate. Southerners by heritage, a majority of Missourians believed that slavery was crucial to the agricultural, manufacturing, and domestic operations of the state both as a system of production and social and labor control. In fact, it was difficult for most Missouri slaveholders to imagine their world without slaves. James Aull, a Lexington merchant, explained to a northern correspondent, "We are the owners of slaves, in this State as well as in other slave holding states you must either have slaves for servants or yourself and family do your own work."[21]

Throughout the antebellum years there was an ongoing demand for slave labor in Missouri that ebbed and flowed in different sections of the state at different times, depending on the stage of settlement and the status of agricultural expansion. The Mississippi Valley in southeastern Missouri and the area surrounding St. Louis were early areas of development; during the first decades after statehood, the Little Dixie region and the northeastern section of the state had tremendous labor needs; and by the late antebellum period, the counties formed from the Platte Purchase in the northwestern corner of the state joined Little Dixie as having the greatest demand for labor. A complex labor system developed to address these shortages and supplement existing slave and family labor that revolved around the hire and sale of slaves, and involved most Missouri slaveholders and many nonslaveholders as well. Although in the decades preceding the Civil War, some northern and immigrant newcomers began to challenge the dominance of this economic system, the slave-based economy remained the preferred system of labor through the antebellum years.[22]

"The hire of my servants is a better business"

Slave hiring was a major means by which white Missourians fulfilled their labor needs. Hiring existed throughout the antebellum South, but it was an especially robust practice in small-slaveholding regions such as Missouri, where diversified agriculture dominated and yet chronic labor shortages existed. Many slaveholders owned more slaves than they could profitably use in the agricultural and domestic operations of their farms, and they willingly hired out some of their bondpeople to individuals who sought to expand their workforce. Throughout the antebellum years there remained a high demand for agricultural and domestic laborers, as well as for those who knew a trade or were suited to work in factories or mines, and because not all Missourians could afford to purchase or chose to own their workforce, a market developed for the hire of slaves of all ages and both genders. Slave hiring became a fundamental component of the labor system in the state and touched the lives of thousands of Missourians both black and white.[23]

Although it is difficult to calculate the number of slaves hired out annually in the state of Missouri, the voluminous references to hiring found in slaveholders' papers, slave narratives, census returns, and Civil War pension records point to the pervasiveness of the practice in the countryside. Most historical sources provide only a qualitative view of how slave hiring operated in Missouri, but selected census returns allow for a quantitative analysis. The efforts of Martin Staley and William Jackson, the conscientious census enumerators from the town of Rocheport in Boone County and the town of Palmyra and rural Liberty Township in Marion County, provide a unique window into the practice of slave hiring in the state's river counties. The individuals employed by the federal government to conduct the 1850 and 1860 slave schedules were instructed to enumerate slaves by where they resided rather than by who owned them. The Census Bureau instructions stipulated, "The person in whose family, or on whose plantation, the slave is found to be employed, is to be considered the owner—the principal object being to get the number of slaves, and not that of masters or owners." In 1860, the enumerators were requested to distinguish owners from employers, but throughout the South few census employees bothered to indicate whether slaves were actually owned or merely employed by the person in whose household they resided. Martin Staley and William Jackson were two of the few Missouri enumerators who followed the instructions to the letter and recorded the employers—and in the case of Jackson, also the owners—of the hired slaves living within their jurisdictions. The implications of this pervasive oversight by most census takers are staggering for scholars attempting to quantify slaveholding rates in the antebellum South. Most enumerators did not reveal their methodology, so it is impossible to know if individual slaveholders were actual owners or merely hirers and whether or not some slaves mistakenly were counted in two different households. Slaveholding rates—both the number of owners and the size of holding—may be significantly affected by this error, especially in regions with a pervasive hiring system.[24]

Staley's and Jackson's work suggests that a large number of slaves living in Boone and Marion Counties were hired out in 1860. The town of Rocheport, which sits along the northern bank of the Missouri River in the central part of the state, boasted a population of 605 free inhabitants and 160 slaves, including 50 slaves (31 percent of the total) who were hired out. The much larger town of Palmyra in northeastern Missouri had a free population of 1,163 and a slave population of 336, including 53 slaves (16 percent of the total) who were living with employers. Hired slaves were a less significant presence in rural Liberty Township, where only 14 of 371 slaves (4 percent of the total) were hired out.[25]

Historians have long known that many slaves were employed in the South's urban areas, especially in manufacturing enterprises, but there has been less focus on the many slaves who worked in the countryside. Hired slaves labored at a variety of tasks, both agricultural and domestic. Nathaniel Leonard repeatedly sought to hire men to work on his Cooper County farm alongside his slaves, and both slaveholding and non-slaveholding Chariton County farmers and manufacturers hired Henry Bruce, a former Chariton County slave who later wrote an autobiography, to work for them. Slave women and older girls frequently were hired to work as domestics in white families' homes and in fact made up the majority of those hired to work in the rural towns of Rocheport and Palmyra. In 1860, Rocheport families hired seventeen women and ten girls from ages eight to fifteen (54 percent of all hired slaves including small children), apparently intending them to labor at housekeeping and child care tasks. The story was similar in Palmyra where eighteen women and fourteen girls (60 percent of all hired slaves, including small children) presumably were hired as domestics. Children as young as eight or ten were taken from their parents' care and hired out to work as nursemaids and at light house- and fieldwork, often rented for a few dollars a year in addition to their upkeep.[26]

Missouri slaves also were hired to work as craftsmen, miners, and in manufacturing, serving a variety of labor needs, especially in the state's towns and cities. William Wells Brown was leased to a number of different St. Louis business owners, including a hotelkeeper, a newspaper printer, and a slave trader. He and many other Missouri slaves and free blacks labored in the river trade, employed on the state's many steamboats and river levees. Stephen Hempstead hired his slave Tom out on a steamboat at a rate of $15 a month in 1828, for example. Men worked as roustabouts, porters, firemen, waiters, cooks, and occasionally as stewards, barbers, and deckhands, on the hundreds of riverboats that plied the waters of the vast river systems of Middle America. Women labored as chambermaids cleaning, preparing laundry, and waiting on the boats' passengers. Although there was limited manufacturing in the Missouri countryside, many slaves were employed in the states' tobacco and hemp factories. Mr. Beasley, who employed around eighty workers in his large Brunswick tobacco factory, hired Henry C. Bruce and his three younger brothers to work for him in 1855. John Crawford, a Rocheport tobacco manufacturer, hired eleven male slaves ranging in age from eighteen to thirty years, as well as a twenty-three-year-old woman and her five-year-old son, to work in his business, and likely his home, in 1860. Slaves who mastered skills or a trade often commanded higher hiring and sale rates than did general workers; therefore, owners frequently hired their slaves to local artisans with the understanding that they would be taught a trade. Abiel Leonard sent his slave Wesley to learn carpentry under the tutelage of a Fayette County man, for example. The payoff for these apprenticeships could be great. Sarah Evalina Lenoir hired out two slave men to work for a Boone County brickmaker for $175 a year, much more than the average slave commanded in the 1830s. Hired slaves also worked in the state's mines and iron industry, such as at the Maramec Iron Works, while others helped construct Missouri's railroads in the decade preceding the Civil War.[27]

Slave hiring interjected flexibility into a labor system that in most ways was immutable. Unlike in a free labor system, slave owners could not easily rid themselves of unproductive laborers, nor could they temporarily adjust the size of their workforce to respond to fluctuations in the market. Slave hiring allowed owners to retain their slave property while generating capital and reducing their operating expenses. Owners could hire out less productive members of their slave force, including children, at the least giving over the responsibility of their maintenance to the hirer and at best collecting a nominal return. Hiring made it possible to turn slaves into "individual units of financial return"; either "labor or as capital," and the practice was especially well suited to areas dominated by small-scale slavery. The historian Keith Barton has asserted that hiring helped to profitably "adapt slavery to an economic system lacking large plantations geared toward staple crop production," since most Missouri slaveholders did not benefit from the economy of scale found on large plantations. Often operating on the economic margins, owners who hired out workers could turn what was often their greatest financial asset into movable capital. Hiring also served as a safety valve by generating economic flexibility and profitability, and ultimately may have resulted in fewer slaves sold. Many owners chose to hire out slaves rather than sell them, allowing them to free up capital, manage the composition of their labor force, and preserve slave property for the future.[28]

The fluid labor market allowed for a unique economic strategy for Missourians who owned more slaves than they could employ on their own farms. Many used the hire of their slaves as a major source of income, sometimes creating a buffer against economic failure and other times simply providing much needed cash. As indicated earlier, after his move to Missouri, Walter Raleigh Lenoir discovered that hiring out his slaves was a reliable source of income. In 1834, he wrote to his brother in Tennessee: "My plan is this, to hire out 9 or 10 negroes which can be done without difficulty immediately in this settlement, fellows at $100 pr [sic] Year and boys and girls in proportion." Lenoir was still hiring out his slaves a year later. Lenoir's wife, Sarah, later explained how she and her husband hired out their slaves and yet maintained the right to use their labor if needed: "We have had ten negroes hired out for some time next week Mr Lenoir intends having three or four at home, to save his Fodder after that, they will return to the same places, where they will work for several months, the hire at this time, amounts to $75 pr [sic] month." Like that of the Lenoirs, Jeremiah Coleman's major source of income during his early years in St. Louis was the money received from the hire of his two slaves. Many others used hiring to manage their labor force for maximum financial return without resorting to selling slaves. Henry Clarkson was one of the largest slaveholders in Boone County with forty-six slaves in 1850 and fifty-seven in 1860. Clarkson frequently ran advertisements in the *Columbia Missouri Statesman* looking for hiring placements for various slaves, many of them young girls. Some set aside hiring income for future needs. Thomas Brown planned to save the money earned from the hire of his slave boys, observing that "I expect to need it someday or other because I am getting old dam fast."[29]

Most Missourians believed that hiring out slaves was a profitable business, and some kept slaves exclusively to lease them. Marie Askin Simpson claimed that her father's master "hired out most of his slaves to white folks that had no slaves and needed work done." Alexander Hitch also "used to hire his slaves out around for wages," and George Jacobs hired out a few of his thirteen adult workers during much of the 1850s. Some slaves were leased out for many years, only rarely living with their owners. Henry Bruce's master hired him out to a series of Chariton County residents from his boyhood until he ran away in his late twenties. Large profits could be made from hiring out slaves. Elizabeth Coleman explained that her husband "would like to have a man he thinks his hire would pay," and after the death of her husband, Sarah Lenoir wrote: "I dont calculate much from the proceeds of my farm, as I keep but 3 hands at home, Old Jess is one of them, the hire of my servants is a better business."[30]

One of the largest sources of slaves for hire was bondpeople who belonged to estates in probate and those owned by widows, orphans, minors, and the elderly. Estates routinely remained in probate for a number of years, and it was common practice to hire out slaves and use their wages to generate revenue for dependents, or to pay down debts. Thirteen slaves from the estate of Benjamin Jones, including a number of small children, were hired to various individuals in 1837 for a total of $447 and in 1838 for $737.50. It was common for estate slaves to remain hired out year after year in order to provide income for widows and minor orphans. Sarah Lenoir continued to farm on a limited basis but chose to hire out a number of male slaves to generate an income to support herself and those children who remained at home. Estate slaves often were not divided or sold until the youngest heir came of age. Testators were especially concerned that the futures of female relatives and young children were secure and saw the steady income from slave hiring as a means to generate the necessary revenue. Slave owners occasionally left directions in their wills, stipulating that executors hire out their slaves to accomplish these various ends. In 1858, Cooper Countian [Weedon] Spenny left his entire estate to his young granddaughter Mary Elizabeth, including the proceeds from the disposal of his real estate, his household furniture, cash, and livestock. In addition, the executors were charged with hiring out his fifteen slaves and using their income for her support until Mary Elizabeth "becomes of lawful age or marries." William Chamber's 1842 will specified that his "slave boy" should be hired out for ten years and his wages used to support his daughter, after which time his slave should be granted his freedom. Other times slaves' wages were used to pay down the debts of the estate rather than forcing the sale of real estate or slave property. George King specified in his 1852 will that his slaves Joe and Sam were to be hired out "untill all my debts be paid if my creditors will wait that long." During the antebellum years, 61 percent of the Boone County estates in probate involved slaves, many of whom were hired out for the year on January 1 at public auction in order to secure the highest rates. Hiring income also was used to maintain elderly slaveholders and their wives. During the last ten years of his life, Stephen Hempstead leased his farm and lived with his grown children for extended stretches of time. No longer needing his slaves to labor on his own farm, he hired them out to people who lived in the St. Louis area.[31]

Slaveholders were well compensated by the hire of their slaves. Harrison Trexler calculated the yearly hiring rate for male slaves as one-seventh to one-eighth of their sale price, whereas female slaves' yearly hiring rates were much less, sometimes as low as one-sixteenth of their value due to the loss of labor and the expense of the care of the small children who oftentimes accompanied them. In 1851, Sarah Lenoir hired out six male slaves for rates ranging from $115 to $175 a year, but hired her "negro woman for $40. having children with her, do not hire for much." Nathaniel Leonard observed that he would rather buy a slave woman than hire one because "hireing negro women & raising their children for other people is poor business." As was suggested by the Rocheport and Palmyra census returns, the hire of women and children was within the means of a broader range of potential employers than was the purchase price of a slave, and, therefore, there remained an active market for less expensive hiring prospects. It became more difficult to hire slaves as rates steadily rose throughout the antebellum years, however, mirroring rising slave sale values during the same period. In 1837 J. R. Bohannon reported that "a boy about the size of your Washington hire for 98 dollars also a girl 9 years of age for $37. Women with 2 or 3 children hire from 30 to 40 dollars." Samuel Smiley leased a slave man named Mose for $12 a month in 1841; by 1859 Phillip Curtis paid nearly double that amount. In contrast, W. H. Bedford hired out his slave woman for $60 a year in 1850. Henry Bruce claimed that his master's slaves were reputed to be such conscientious workers that the men commanded from $250 to $300 a year in the 1850s. Hiring rates had risen so high by the mid-1850s that a Glasgow newspaper editor was concerned that "there is a great danger that the 'institution' will be the means of bankrupting the country at no distant day, without a tumble in prices of at least thirty-three percent."[32]

Rising prices aside, the prospect of hiring other people's slaves remained extremely appealing to many nonslaveholding Missourians. Hiring was an economical way for them to meet their labor needs and enter the slaveholding class—if only tangentially. Many nonslaveholding white families could afford to hire a slave long before they could scrape together the money to buy one. Farmers hired young slave men and boys to work as general farmhands, but those who owned no slaves were more likely to hire women and children who could be employed for a fraction of the cost. Women had the added benefit of providing domestic labor and yet were available to move to the fields when needed. Thirteen nonslaveholders were among those who hired slaves from the estate of John Shock in the years between 1858 and 1863. In addition, nineteen of twenty-four hirers in Rocheport and eleven of twenty-three in Palmyra were nonslaveholders. Henry Bruce was hired to what he described as a "poor white" but "reasonable" man named David Hampton. Nonslaveholders David and Mollie Mendenhall routinely hired slave men and women from their Lafayette County neighbors to work in their home and fields. Those who owned no slaves fulfilled more than their labor needs through the hiring of slaves; they also purchased the social and psychological rewards of mastery—in many cases on the cheap. As Jonathan Martin has argued, "Entrée into the slaveholding ranks brought both cultural and economic rewards; in the South, the luxury of ordering slaves about was a way to enhance both one's social standing and one's production for the market." Foremost, hired slaves alleviated the need of white family members to toil at labor-intensive or undesirable tasks. A hired slave woman could reduce the drudgery of housekeeping or keep white wives and daughters out of the fields at planting and harvesting times. In Rocheport eighteen of the twenty-four households who hired slaves employed only women or older girls, accounting for every nonslaveholding hirer but one, while in Marion County all eleven Palmyra nonslaveholders and the one Liberty Township nonslaveholder employed only women or older girls. The grocers, merchants, attorneys, ministers, doctors, and craftsmen who hired female slaves presumably were interested in lightening the workload for their wives and daughters. Hiring black domestic servants also enhanced these middling families' respectability by giving them a toehold in the slaveholding class as well as allowing them to reach toward achieving the increasingly higher standards of nineteenth-century domesticity.[33]

Yet slaveholders also hired slaves, if they did not choose to or could not afford to invest in additional bondpeople to meet what could be a temporary labor shortage. Only one out of nine hirers in rural Liberty Township owned no slaves, for example. Farmers could tailor their workforces to the necessities of a particular growing season or correct demographic imbalances in their labor forces. William Garner, a seventy-seven-year-old Marion County farmer who owned three adult slave women and four children, hired a thirty-year-old slave man to assist him on his farm; the slave's owners were an elderly slaveholding couple, James and Rebecca Culbertson, who likely did not need the labor of all three of their slave men to run their farm. Nathaniel Leonard often hired slave men to work on his farm, even though he owned a number of slaves. Year after year he asked his brother Abiel to watch for good hiring prospects, usually hiring slave men between January and March for the balance of the year. In 1839, in addition to a request for four male slaves, Nathaniel hoped to find a slave woman to assist his wife with her domestic duties because a long-term houseguest was leaving the Leonard home and taking her slave woman along with her.[34]

The annual slave-hiring fair was usually held on January 1 on the steps of the local county courthouse. It was at these venues that many probate slaves were offered for hire, often with an auction determining the hiring rate. Others made private arrangements beforehand with friends and neighbors, as well as occasionally employed agents—often local attorneys like Abiel Leonard who were familiar with local slaves belonging to estates in probate. Not only did Leonard's extensive legal practice make him particularly well placed to identify potential hiring prospects, but he also lived in a county with one of the state's largest slave populations. When Nathaniel Leonard found it difficult to locate slaves for hire in Cooper County in 1840, he turned to the neighboring county because there were "three negroes in Howard for one in this County." It also was common for agents to manage, on behalf of owners, the hiring careers of slaves employed on riverboats or in industry. They made it their business to find placements that benefited their clients, even if the situation was sometimes at a geographical distance from their homes. Those who made early arrangements may have hoped to better control the hiring process. Owners were anxious to locate desirable employers for their slaves and not leave their placement to the vagaries of the auction. Some wished to place their slaves with employers they knew would treat them well or teach them a skill; others merely hoped to hire their slaves to those who would pay the highest rate. But individuals seeking slaves for hire had concerns as well. They frequently sought out slaves who were reputed to be hard workers, such as the Bruce brothers. Those who waited until hiring day often found it difficult to locate laborers, since, as Nathaniel Leonard found out the hard way, many slaveholders privately negotiated hiring positions for their slaves as the previous year's contract expired. In mid-December of 1847, Mr. Corbyn already was finding it difficult to locate a man and woman to hire for the upcoming year. A correspondent advised at the time that unless he "secures servants very shortly, he will be unable to get any here." In fact, white Missourians often complained that it was challenging to find slaves to hire. In his 1831 letter to his wife still living in Virginia, James R. McDearmon recommended that she purchase a slave woman before her move to Missouri because "it is out of the question to depend upon hiring here."[35]

Not all slave hiring was contracted on an annual basis, however; many Missourians rented slaves to meet their short-term labor concerns. In October 1851, Newton G. Elliott hired a slave boy for seven days at seventy-five cents a day. Stephen Hempstead both rented his slaves to his neighbors, in order to help them with tasks such as mowing or harvesting, and employed his neighbors' slave men to assist him during labor-intensive periods on his own farm and to help build his house. He occasionally sought women to assist his wife with her domestic chores as well. Slave women and girls were frequently employed to aid nonslaveholding women during times of sickness or after they gave birth. As a young girl, Isabelle Henderson was "hired out to the white preacher's family to take care of his children when his wife was sick," and the Strattons' slave woman Dilsy frequently washed laundry for the neighbors, including a white woman who had recently given birth. Other slaveholders used the hire of their slaves as a form of currency and traded their labor for goods and services. Walter Raleigh Lenoir exchanged his bondmen's labor for lumber for building his house, writing to his brother in 1838: "[T]hink that I can have all the materials by next spring without advancing any money. My neighbour who owns the saw-mill owes me for the hire of my hands as much as my bill for sawing will come too [sic]." When the local brickmaker ran out of lime in the middle of the building project, Abiel Leonard offered to send two or three of his men to help him burn more.[36]

Oftentimes, no money changed hands during temporary labor stints, and instead, neighbors simply reciprocated by sending their hands to help at a later date. The Strattons occasionally traded work with others in their New Lebanon neighborhood, especially during the harvest. Edward Bruce, a former slave, explained the ongoing labor exchanges between two Chariton County small-slaveholding farmers: "[Owens] only owned the one family of slaves, my master only owned the one family too and so the Owens' and the Bruces' swapped work at times. I worked or rather was on the Owens plantation often." John Lewis meticulously recorded the number of days neighboring slaves worked on his farm and his reciprocal offers of labor. These informal arrangements were especially common among local slaveholding kin. Stephen Hempstead frequently exchanged slaves with his adult children, sometimes for months at a time.[37]

In addition to paying owners the hiring fee, hirers were usually required to provide room, board, clothing, and medical care for hired slaves. In 1827, Stephen Hempstead contracted with a neighbor who for one year would "board wash and lodge [his slave Tom] and give 1 pair Good Shoes & 1 pair Socks in the time and pay me $100 for his services to be paid quarterly at the opening of the Circuit Court." Another employer agreed to provide a detailed list of clothing, including "a good new janes coat two pare of good new janes pantiloons and vest two pare of good new socks one pare of good new boots too [sic] new shirts one new wool hat . . . and sufficient quantity of Summer cloths." The understanding was that lessees would provide the hired slaves with decent clothing before they left for their next hiring position. Although most lessees held up their end of the contract, a few slaves manipulated the situation by showing up at their next placement in their rattiest clothing. In 1850, Alexander M. Bedford worried that his slave man June would attempt just such a deception in a bid to acquire an extra set of clothes.[38]

The contract terms concerning the health of hired slaves often were more complex and difficult to negotiate. Owners worried that hirers would work hired slaves too hard, possibly in extreme weather conditions, and that they might not seek medical care in a timely manner. As a result, they often negotiated detailed contractual guarantees in an attempt to ensure that employers would protect the health of people who did not belong to them. A sound hiring contract usually stipulated who was responsible for paying for medical care—the owner or the hirer. Once the doctor was called it was important that it was a matter of record who would foot the bill. Mary Rollins contracted the Rollins's slave George to Mr. Lewis, who agreed that he would pay $125 for the hire of George for one year and would "agree to furnish said boy with all suitable and necessary clothing addapted [sic] to the different seasons pay his taxes and doctors bills during the year 1849 and treat him humanely," and in Jackson County in 1856, James Lawrance and W. W. Walker hired a fifteen-year-old slave girl named Nancy for $60 under similar terms, including a "good blanket." Employers might lose money because there was no guarantee that slaves would remain healthy for the duration of their term. Not only could they lose the labor of sick slaves but they often paid a considerable amount in medical bills. Some employers accepted this risk in writing, as did John Ryan who agreed to pay all doctors' bills and "loose [sic] all time" that his hired slave woman was incapacitated. Occasionally leasing agreements specified the acceptable length of time a slave could be out of work due to sickness, such as when Phillip Curtis agreed to allow Henry to remain out for up to two months but expected to be reimbursed for any additional time lost. Most lessees struck less specific agreements and were forced to rely on owners' sense of fairness. In December of 1845, Nathaniel Leonard intended to pay the Widow Davis for the year's hire of her slave Austin but hoped she would consider a deduction for the fortnight he was sick. When the lessee was awarded no compensation, the matter was sometimes taken to court.[39]

Many slaves sought out their own hiring positions even though it had been against Missouri law since the territorial period. A few privileged slaves, often those who knew a trade, were given free rein in making their own employment arrangements and were expected by their owners to turn over most of their wages after paying their expenses and setting a little aside for their own pockets. Henry Bruce's two older brothers were bricklayers, who traveled throughout Chariton and adjoining counties, negotiating their own hiring contracts and collecting their own wages. Some accommodating owners granted their slaves permission to work informally for neighbors during their time off and keep most or all of their wages. The Strattons' Dilsy washed for an elderly neighbor, and Ike cut hay for another farmer, each earning $1 apiece for their labor. Dilsy spent her money on a new linsey petticoat. Not all Missourians were pleased about the liberties allowed self-hired slaves, however. As early as 1824, the *Missouri Republican* supported a statute against self-hire, arguing: "Slaves hiring their own time . . . take upon themselves at once the airs of freemen and often resort to very illicit modes to meet their monthly payments." The editor warned that they would "become unsteady and vicious, and corrupt their associates, and perhaps at length resort to theft as an easier mode of paying their masters." In reality, slaveholders were rarely cited for the offense of allowing their slaves to hire their own time, although some, like Garrett Groomer, a permissive master who two years later freed his slaves in his will, were forced to hire attorneys to defend themselves in the state's cases against them. Most often white defendants were merely fined. Some owners may have flouted the law against self-hiring, reasoning that considerable profit could be made from the wages of their self-hired slaves and believing that the practice barely disrupted the functioning of slavery in the state. At the time, some described the practice of self-hiring as quasi-freedom, and in recent years some scholars have written about it in similar terms. Although it is true that self-hired slaves were granted limited autonomy and could gain some access to capital, in the end, Missouri owners always retained the ultimate power over their slaves and at any time could withhold privileges once freely granted.[40]

Slave hiring was an important factor in the state's labor system because it shored up slavery as a vital economic institution in a region populated by small slaveholders and yeoman farmers. Hiring touched the lives of a large number of white and black Missourians, significantly influencing the everyday experiences of slaves, their owners, and those who hired them by affecting the working relations between slaves and those who controlled their labor. Missouri slaves never shared white Missourians' enthusiasm for hiring, however, because of the hardships the practice imposed on their personal lives.

"It is a bad time to buy, but a first rate time to sell"

The demand for slaves for hire and the economic flexibility that hiring interjected into the labor system may have significantly reduced the number of sales; nonetheless slaves were regularly bought and sold in antebellum Missouri. Indeed, from the beginning, Missouri slaveholders actively engaged in the domestic slave trade. The historical record is littered with references to sales: newspapers were filled with advertisements both for slave sales and for slave traders seeking slaves for purchase; notices of future sales of slaves were posted on courthouse doors and in country stores; slaveholders' private papers include slave bills and references to slave trades; and former Missouri slaves spoke eloquently of the hardships endured as a result of the trade. In Missouri, as elsewhere, slaveholders sold slaves for a variety of reasons, including owners' economic reversals, slaves' disobedience, and to finance purchases of land, household items, or children's educations. Owners also sold slaves simply to pay their debts or equitably settle estates. White Missourians purchased slaves for a myriad of reasons as well; some wished to enhance the productivity of their farms and businesses, whereas others sought to free their wives from domestic toil. Nonslaveholders' initial entrée into the slaveholding class was often acquired on the cheap and at the expense of young children who thereafter were separated from their parents. Whatever the reason, most buyers' forays into the slave market were driven by a desire to transform their lives in ways that they believed would be positive.[41]

Missouri slaveholders often justified their decisions to buy or sell in terms that suited their self-image as paternalists, a particularly salient concern among people who prided themselves on the domestic nature of their slavery. In truth, owners occasionally entered the trade to compensate for losses that were out of their control, but more often sales were a result of poor financial decisions or investments gone sour. Certainly, the economies of Missouri farms did not allow most small slaveholders to keep more laborers than they required or maintain slave families at a financial loss, but more often owners simply prioritized the needs of their own families over those of their slaves. In the end, slaves often were sold to maintain the solvency of slaveholders' households. While many counteracted the financial uncertainties of the slave labor system by hiring out slaves, others chose the immediate gratification of sale rather than the long-term investment of hiring. Owners' decisions to sell often contradicted their paternalistic rhetoric, although they sometimes squared the two in their own minds by arguing that they had no choice but to part with their slaves. Some owners, such as John Bull, seemed genuinely embarrassed and emotionally distressed at the tragedy their insolvency foisted upon their slaves. Bull's slaves, who consisted of three families—two headed by single women—and some individuals, were sold at public auction in 1845. Knowing that families likely would be separated, he wrote of the sale, "I can not be present. The negros will look to me for help & I cannot give it."[42]

For their part, most Missouri slaves understood fully well that slaveholders' economic and personal considerations usually outweighed humanitarian concerns as slaves were sold and families divided. Bill Sims, like many other former Missouri slaves, recounted the harsh realities of small-scale slavery: "A man who owned ten slaves was considered wealthy, and if he got hard up for money, he would advertise and sell some slaves, like my oldest sister was sold on the block with her children. She sold for eleven hundred dollars, a baby in her arms sold for three hundred dollars. Another sold for six hundred dollars and the other for a little less than that." Dr. John Young sold William Wells Brown when he became "hard pressed for money," in spite of a promise to Brown's white father that he would not sell him. Melinda Napton suggested to her husband, William, that he sell their slave woman Nancy and her two youngest children to get their family out of debt so that William might quit his peripatetic legal practice and spend more time at home, although he refrained from taking this course of action. Emma Knight's father was sold simply "'cause de master wanted money to buy something for de house."[43]

Missouri slaveholders often used slave men's and women's disobedience as justification for selling, reasoning that slaves' callous disregard for holding up their end of the paternalistic bargain resulted in a forfeit of their claims to protection, thereby relieving owners of guilt over their decision to sell. George O'Hockaday wrote Abiel Leonard of a slave boy who was sold because he had "be come unmanagable." Rhody Holsell's master told of a man who "was treated mean and they could not do anything with him. The old fellow would play his gourd and de snakes would come 'round. Finally dey sent him down to New Orleans and sold him on de block." In the spring of 1850, William and Melinda Napton corresponded about William's efforts to sell their disruptive slave man Sandy in St. Louis. Napton had hoped to sell Sandy to an interstate trader from whom he might extract a higher price, but there were none in the city at the time and he did not wish to sell locally for less. Napton was concerned that he "may yet have to bring him back to Saline, which will be very disagreeable." The Naptons' overseer Mr. West was dismayed to learn that Sandy might return to the farm and asked Melinda to plead with her husband "not to bring him on the place. He says the boys now here, are obedient and work well, and he does not apprehend any difficulty with them, but if Sandy is brought home again, it will be much worse than if you had never sent him away." Although Sandy wished to return home, Napton decided to hire him out in St. Louis while he awaited a prospective buyer. In November, Napton wrote, "I expect Sandy will prove a dead loss. He is now sick in a negro quarter here & I cant sell him at any price or send him away, whilst in this condition. He has been truly a sore affliction upon me in every point of view." Napton's difficult relationship with his slave ended when he sent Sandy down river to be sold. Conveniently, a doctor had advised him that Sandy's "chance for recovery was better South than here & I could not sell him for any price" in his current state. Napton showed little sign of emotion or guilty conscience as he callously disposed of a slave whom he considered troublesome.[44]

Owners also sold slaves who attempted to run away, thereby both punishing the offenders and offering them up as examples to other slaves. Although he portrayed himself as a reasonable master, Stephen Hempstead expressed no regrets when he sold two of his slaves, Lucy, who had run away earlier, and George, to a slave trader, explaining, "they haveing got uneasey and Said they were free." In 1855, Archibald Hager recorded the runaway attempts of two Perry County slave men, who in turn were sold in St. Louis for $900 a piece, and that same year William Anderson sold two young slave men at $810 cash and $1,075 on six months credit respectively. These slave men sold for a little less than others of their age because "both of the Boys had run off previously, and one of them got as far as Kansas."[45]

Many contemporary Missourians claimed that slaveholders in the state only sold their slaves when forced to by dire economic circumstances or recalcitrant behavior. In reality, however, many sacrificed their slaves to the market simply because so much money could be made by their sale. Slaves were an important and movable financial asset. The *St. Louis Herald* estimated that the value of Missouri's slaves "amount[ed] to the enormous sum of $82,969,000" in the months leading up to the Civil War. Selling slaves was one of the quickest and most lucrative ways for slaveholders to obtain much-needed cash, and during the antebellum years ever-rising slave prices were a temptation even to those not planning to sell. Before 1830 it was unusual for a male slave to sell for more than $500, but the prices given for slaves rose steadily during the three decades preceding the war. William Napton observed in 1847, "Negroes are very high now & rising in price. Men are worth $700. I was told in Boonville. It is a bad time to buy, but a first rate time to sell." That same year, Randolph County slaveholder Jonathan Haines observed after purchasing two bondpeople that "[slaves] are mighty high here and when there is one to sell it apears as if the countrey was full of money I want two or three more if I can get them." In fact, Thomas Hudspeth bought a twenty-seven-year-old slave man named Daniel for $700 two years later. By the 1850s, slave men in their prime regularly sold for over

$1,000, including four male slaves belonging to Thomas Reeves, who sold in Richmond, Missouri, for high prices in 1854—one twenty-three-year-old man for $1,440. Five years later, slaves from the estate of Saline County slaveholder H. Eustace sold for similarly high prices, including four slave women who sold for over $1,000 each.[46]

Many thousands of slaves were sold in Missouri's towns and country-side throughout the antebellum years, but it appears that, as in the South as a whole where two-thirds of sales were local, in most cases the purchasers lived nearby. Many scholars have described the domestic slave trade as the lifeblood of the southern economy, but the local exchange of slaves was particularly important to the fluid transfer of property among neighbors and across generations. Fortunately, the harshest aspects of slave transactions were somewhat ameliorated by local sales. A majority of Missouri slaves who were sold remained in the state—usually within their own counties. This was especially true in the prosperous river counties where the slave population was so heavily concentrated. In general, slaveholders in central and western Missouri preferred to hire out their slaves or sell them locally rather than enter the southern trade. A high demand for slave labor drove many of these exchanges, but the idiosyncrasies of the divisions of small slaveholders' estates were a contributing factor as well. The limited number of slaves owned by smallholders often necessitated the sale of slaves if an equitable division could not be made among the heirs. Occasionally wills stipulated that family slaves should be sold to facilitate the settlement, but often heirs chose to buy those slaves put on the block, both because they were familiar with their work habits and personalities and because they knew that much of the purchase price would come back to them when the sale proceeds were divided among the heirs. The buyers frequently lived nearby; therefore, many estate slaves remained near their original homes. In fact, the historian James McGettigan's examination of probate records and slave bills executed in Boone County between 1820 and 1864 reveals that the residents of the central Missouri county bought 98 percent of those slaves sold as a result of estate settlements. McGettigan argues that the steady growth of the Boone County slave population during these years supports his argument that few slaves were sold out of the county. What's more, slave traders repeatedly advertised in the *Statesman,* the main newspaper for central Missouri, suggesting to him that it was difficult to find owners willing to sell their slaves into the interstate trade.[47]

Many owners instead preferred to buy and sell locally, believing that they were better able to control the process if they were acquainted with their trading partners. Missouri's tight-knit farming communities allowed for a general knowledge of others living in the local neighborhood, including slaves. Buyers usually knew the reputation of the sellers, if not the slaves themselves, and thus reasoned that they were in a more favorable position to strike a good bargain for people whose work habits and personality traits were known—or at the least, could be uncovered by inquiries in the neighborhood. In addition, slaves bought locally could be purchased on terms of credit, often for lower prices, and occasionally in exchange for assets other than cash. It was even possible to purchase slaves on trial. Selling locally also allowed sympathetic owners the opportunity to put their paternalistic impulses into action and keep slaves near their family members and even occasionally monitor the actions of the new owners of their former slaves. Some chose buyers whom they believed would treat their former slaves well, and a few continued to keep tabs on the people who once belonged to them. After Tishey Taylor's old master sold her and her family he defended them to their new owner: "'Old Parker' like mammy and all her people and he tol' 'Old Man Shad' if'n he lashed my mammy and her family he would com' and take us back, 'cause we wus good and didn't need no punishment but that was the only reason that we wusn't lashed like the rest of them."[48]

Although a majority of slave sales were contracted locally, many Missouri slaves nonetheless were sold into the southern trade during the antebellum years. McGettigan acknowledges that in the decades before the Civil War the slave population of the Mississippi River counties decreased, suggesting that owners in eastern Missouri were selling their slaves south. Indeed, the historian Michael Tadman argues that by the 1840s and 1850s eastern Missouri was becoming a slave-exporting region even as the demand for labor remained strong in central and western Missouri. Scores of interstate slave traders operated out of the state in the years before the Civil War. Most large river towns boasted of one or two resident speculators, and itinerant traders scoured the countryside searching for slaves for purchase. Traders were especially active in the state in the late summer and early fall, capitalizing on farmers' willingness to sell laborers after that season's crops were laid by and counting on southern planters' interest in buying their inventory in the late fall and winter after the sale of their cotton crops. St. Louis was the regional center of the trade and the shipping point of slaves down the Mississippi River to southern markets. There were at the fewest thirty speculators working in the city in 1851, many out of permanent trading depots. The Reverend William Greenleaf Eliot, a St. Louis anti-slavery clergyman, wrote: "St. Louis was fast becoming a slave-market, and the supply was increasing with the demand. Often have I seen 'gangs' of negroes hand-cuffed together, two and two, going through the open street like dumb driven cattle, on the way to the steamboat for the South." Marilda Pethy, a former slave, recounted the personal toll on enslaved families that resulted from the interstate trade: "Why, I seen people handcuffed together and driv [sic] 'long de Williamsburg road like cattle. Dey was bought to be took south. I had two brothers and two sisters sold and we never did see dem no more."[49]

There is little doubt that speculators traded freely and openly in the state, yet white Missourians, on both sides of the slavery issue, claimed that public opinion was overwhelmingly against both slave traders and selling slaves to the southern market. Denying the importance of the interstate trade to the state's economy reinforced the belief of many that slavery in Missouri was milder than elsewhere. Captain J. A. Wilson of Lexington relegated slave traders to a lower social level than saloon-keepers, and an antislavery minister claimed that "[s]lave traders and whiskey-sellers were equally hated by many." Henry Bruce concurred in his autobiography: "The sentiment against selling Negroes to traders was quite strong, and there were many who would not sell at all, unless forced by circumstances over which they had no control, and would cry with the Negroes at parting." Others remembered that not all slave speculators were viewed as pariahs, however, arguing that the individual trader's personality, reputation, and often his class status, determined if the community accepted him. J. H. Sallee and J. W. Beatty remembered that although Missourians held some traders in high esteem, other less likable men were held in contempt. In the end, William Greenleaf Eliot agreed that some traders were embraced by white society, observing, "Large fortunes were made by the trade; and some of those who made them . . . were held as fit associates for the best men on 'change.'" Many reasoned that selling slaves was a regrettable reality in antebellum Missouri and, therefore, that slave traders were unfortunate, yet necessary to the workings of the slavery economy.[50]

Despite contemporary Missourians' protestations, scores of speculators operated within the state, and slaves routinely were sold down the Mississippi River to the southern markets. White Missourians generally may have been contemptuous of traders, but their vitriol masked the reality that traders bought their slave inventory from local owners. If the business records of Howard County slave trader John R. White are representative, Missouri slaveholders were all too willing to sell their slaves to professional traders. White purchased hundreds of Missouri slaves, sold them throughout the Upper South and in ports down the Mississippi River, and employed selling agents throughout the Lower South. Traders advertised in Missouri newspapers for slaves available for purchase and many former slaves recalled sales of bondpeople to interstate traders. As was common practice, William Shelby advertised for "fifty likely [n]egroes from five to twenty-five yea[rs] [of] age," while another trader claimed to the readers of the *Columbia Missouri Statesman* that he would pay "[v]ery liberal prices" for forty slaves from ages ten to twenty-five in order "to fill a Southern order." Whereas some speculators set up shop in the region's towns and waited for owners to approach them, others canvassed the countryside in search of potential sellers. While hired out to a slave trader named Mr. Walker, William Wells Brown several times traveled south with gangs of slaves whom he helped prepare for the New Orleans and Memphis slave markets. Walker bought slaves in the interior of Missouri and then transported them down river for sale. In the early years of statehood, Missouri slaves generally were sold into the Mississippi River market, but later they were transported to Texas as well.[51]

Slave speculators' profits lay "between the prices" that they paid sellers in the Upper South and those they could extract from buyers in the Lower South. Ultimately, traders, like White or Walker, would do what was needed to reap the highest profits, including separating slave families when it benefited the bottom line. Certainly slaves' worst indictment of the trade was its destruction of slave families. William Wells Brown movingly wrote of the slave trader as "one who was tearing the husband from the wife, the child from the mother, and the sister from the brother." Although Missouri slaveholders frequently sold slaves in family units, perhaps assuaging their guilt by a hope that their bondpeople would be kept together when sold, most traders did not hesitate to sell slaves individually if it was profitable. Missouri slaveholders placed the blame for family separations on speculators, but in reality they were willing accomplices in the destruction of slave families by their very act of selling to traders. Thousands of Missouri slaves were sold to interstate slave traders, in spite of some owners' reservations about the trade. Henry Bruce suggested that there was an incentive to sell to speculators because they often gave one to three hundred dollars more than local buyers. In addition, traders usually paid cash for slaves rather than the terms of credit used in most local sales.[52]

A few former Missouri slaves believed that some in the state capitalized on the market demand and high prices and bred slaves for the southern market. Hannah Jones spoke of her master's "nigger farm," and W. C. Parson Allen reported that his master "raised hogs, sheep, hemp, and darkies." William Wells Brown wrote in forceful abolitionist rhetoric: "Missouri, though a comparatively new state, is very much engaged in raising slaves to supply the southern market. . . . [T]hose who raise slaves for the market are to be found among all classes, from Thomas H. Benton down to the lowest demagogue, who may be able to purchase a woman for the purpose of raising stock, and from the doctor of divinity down to the most humble lay member in the church." Most white Missourians emphatically denied these charges, however. R. A. Campbell, a former lieutenant governor, observed after slavery's end, "I never heard of any Missourian who consciously raised slaves for the southern market. I feel sure it was never done." There were scattered reports of the practice at the time, such as that of a white woman living in St. Louis who bought slave babies purposely to raise and later sell them, but as was true elsewhere, Missourians generally did not own slaves merely for the purpose of speculation; instead, the priority of most was to efficiently and profitably operate their farms and homes. Keeping slave women only to breed children was not cost effective; too many years of care were required before a return on the investment could be realized. At the time, Missourian W. A. Hall claimed that Missouri slaveholders did not conduct outright breeding operations in the manner of stock farms merely to supply the domestic trade; he argued that the primary motivation for purchasing slaves was to extract their labor. Even Hall recognized that there was some hypocrisy in slaveholders' practices, however; expressing his frustration to Abiel Leonard, Hall complained that they publicly admitted that "the increase of negroes are often a source of great profit. Yet you have the testimony of southern Gentlemen in Congress, who denied in[definitely] the charge that the business of breeding slaves was ever looked upon as a part of the profit."[53]

Missouri slaveholders, like those throughout the western hemisphere, were cognizant of the value of strong, healthy slave women and their offspring. As the historian Jennifer Morgan and others have argued, there was a fundamental "connection between racial slavery and reproduction." Owners clearly understood that a hereditary system of slavery could only be perpetuated through the reproductive labor of slave women. Although the ultimate reason for slavery was the extraction of physical labor from slave bodies, Missouri slaveholders were concerned when women did not or could not add to their workforce through the birth of healthy babies. In February 1858, Paulina Stratton's "prayers [were] answered" when she learned that her often troublesome slave woman Aga was finally pregnant. Aga long had difficulty conceiving and had lost one baby already. The year before, Thomas Stratton had threatened to sell her because "[s]he had got too Smart to have children and she was of no other account." Indeed, the Strattons found little value in their "thrifling" slave woman other than her ability to reproduce. Owners quite frequently manipulated their slaves' sexual lives in an effort to enhance reproduction; marriage and procreation were highly encouraged and often rewarded. They urged their slaves to mate with physically fit partners and conversely discouraged or even forbade them from consorting with those they considered unhealthy or weak. When defending herself against charges of infidelity, one former slave woman explained to the government pension board that her owners had banned her union with a slave man named John because of his "scrofula." A Cooper County slaveholder Thomas Houston took interference in his slaves' personal lives one step further when he planned to invest in young slave boys of similar ages to a number of girls he already owned, explaining: "If I can succeed in buying boys to suit it will increase my male force to 10 or 12 hands, & in a few years, as they & the girls grow up, we may be able to pair them all off in families *at home*." Houston obviously hoped his slaves could make domestic rather than abroad matches, but even he seemed to acknowledge the will of his slaves in such personal matters. In the end, it often was difficult for small slaveholders to dictate the sexual partners of their slaves because most Missouri slaves were unable to find matches on their home farms.[54]

Although most of their concern with fecundity stemmed from a desire to increase their future workforce, there is plenty of evidence that owners recognized the potential for profit represented in the bodies of their slaves. Henry C. Bruce believed that slaveholders actively worked to raise healthy slave children, knowing that their value as adult workers and in the marketplace was dependent on their physical appearance and good health. Enslaved individuals understood fully well that their bodies did not belong to them alone. Many former slaves remembered the monetary value assigned to them at sale, and most recognized that their owners considered them a financial asset—"a person with a price." Even young children feared the wrath of their owners if they sustained bodily injury because of their own negligence; for example, as a child, Henry Bruce and his friends worried that their master would learn that they were treed by wild boars while on an unsanctioned ramble in the woods.

Occasionally this worked to slaves' advantage, however, especially when they reminded their owners that their self-interest would not be served by allowing the gross neglect or abuse of their human property. This issue most often was raised as slaves sought protection from abusive overseers or hirers.[55]

The main objective of most small slaveholders was to develop a slave labor force that they could employ in a drive toward achieving the lifestyle that they imagined for themselves and their families. Missourians used diverse economic strategies to reach their preferred ends, but most engaged in the slave sale or hiring market at some point. Life circumstances, such as economic hardship or death, forced owners into the marketplace, but ultimately, most worked to maintain a slave workforce that, coupled with their family members, could produce enough labor to realize their financial goals.

"Oh Lordee, but I worked hard"

White and black Missourians may have spent some of their time pondering the dynamics of the state's labor market, but most of their waking hours were occupied with work. The small size of most slaveholdings profoundly influenced the relations of labor on Missouri farms. Unlike on plantations where many slaves performed specialized tasks and both men and women made up the ranks of field hands, most Missouri slaves worked at general farming and domestic assignments that ultimately reflected gendered divisions of labor that were more closely aligned with those found within northern farming households.

Each day owners and their slaves worked together to maintain both the agricultural and domestic operations of Missouri's farms and homes. Masters and their sons worked alongside slave men and boys, and together they cleared the land, planted, harvested, and tended the livestock. Meanwhile, slave women and small children worked with mistresses and their daughters at daily housekeeping and child care duties. On smaller holdings, slave women spent a majority of their time laboring at household tasks and generally moved to the fields only during planting and harvesting. While the labor arrangements differed from plantations, white Missourians shared the racial and class prejudices of their southern slaveholding peers. Whatever the work arrangements on individual Missouri farms and plantations, in most cases slaves performed the most arduous tasks and slaveholders merely supervised and assisted this labor. Year after year, the work routines of men and women in rural

FIGURE 5. *Missouri Farmer's Home in 1859.* The origin of this image is unknown, although a later version of the drawing appeared in a gazetteer called *Missouri As It Is in 1867,* by Nathan H. Parker (Philadelphia: J. B. Lippincott, 1867). This drawing by D. H. Huyett depicts the rural home of an affluent Missouri slaveholding family. The bucolic image suggests the layout of Missouri farms, as well as the intimate work relations of small-slaveholding households. Courtesy of the Library of Congress.

Missouri were bound by tradition, predictably following the patterns of agricultural cultivation and changing with the seasons.[56]

Most Missouri masters, unlike southern planters, directly supervised the labor of their slave men, often working alongside them in the barnyards and fields. Overseers were rarely employed on Missouri farms both because white laborers were hard to come by and because the small size of Missouri slaveholdings did not justify them. Slaveholding business and professional men, such as William Napton, whose careers demanded travel, were those most likely to use the services of an overseer. Small slaveholders' engagement in professional occupations such as law, medicine, or business, was often the key to their accumulation of wealth, and many of the state's most prominent and successful slave owners made much of their income through work in addition to farming. Dr.

John Sappington was a Saline County planter, yet his fortune—and that of his adult children—was secured through his extensive antimalarial pill business, and Abiel Leonard operated his Howard County farm with the labor of twelve adult slaves but made most of his income from a successful law practice. Owning slaves certainly freed slaveholding farmers to pursue a nonagricultural career, but it also presented them with a dilemma as to who would manage their slave workers in their absence.[57]

Missouri owners preferred to manage their slaves themselves, but some believed that the circumstances of their particular situation required outside management. Most white Missourians simply thought that slaves would not work hard without constant supervision, whether by slaveholding family members, overseers, hirers, or slave drivers, and if regular monitoring was not possible, they complained that reduced productivity was the consequence. Men especially were concerned that women would not properly oversee agricultural operations, and, indeed, some women felt uncomfortable performing tasks so far outside their prescribed gender roles, whereas others did not wish to assume burdens in addition to their formidable domestic obligations. If no overseer was employed, widows and women whose husbands traveled relied on the occasional assistance of male relatives and neighbors as they managed their slaves and the business of their farms. Abiel Leonard routinely left the supervision of his farm in the hands of his wife, Jeanette, and later his slave man John, while he was away practicing law. Jeanette often observed that work on the farm progressed slowly because of the lack of overseeing, and in 1845, she mused, "[T]he longer I *live*, the more I am convinced that tis folly fer a Lawyer to think of farming." William Napton worried over his hemp crop during one of the many times he left his farm without an overseer in charge. He hoped that a neighbor would check on his crop, believing that "the negroes would let it rot on the ground, unless ordered otherwise." Another time, Melinda Napton was concerned that the slave men broke the hemp too slowly and that they had not filled the icehouse. She wrote, "I have no confidence in their industry tho' when not under an overseer." The Naptons and Leonards were not alone in believing that their slaves required constant supervision in order to maximize their labor potential. Charles Yancey was concerned that his slaves would not attend to harvesting the fruit and fattening the livestock before butchering time. He admonished his wife, Mary, "Make the negroes attend to business while the weather is good, but they wont do anything unless Jerry keeps an eye upon them."[58]

Some owners, such as Abiel Leonard, allowed trusted slave men to manage other enslaved workers. George Bollinger worked as a driver on his owner's farm. "My boss would say, 'George take two men, or maybe three men, and git dat field plowed, or dat woods patch cleared.' And he knowed if he tell me, de work would be done," Bollinger explained. When he grew older, Henry Bruce served in a similar managerial capacity over his own younger brothers. Abiel Leonard and others used incentives, like the task system, to keep their slaves motivated, while others reportedly paid them if they broke more than the required one hundred pounds of hemp a day. Captain J. A. Wilson remembered that some Lexington slaves "made a dollar a day and were paid in silver at Christmas, the negroes keeping accounts on notched sticks and the owner or overseer in his books." A few owners devised creative ways to monitor their slaves when they were not present, such as when Charlie Richardson's master tied a parrot out in the fields to watch his hands while they worked. While the parrot story is quite possibly apocryphal, former Missouri slaves' frequent references to nosy talking birds suggests that they recognized their owners' deep concerns about the possibility of misconduct among unmonitored workers. In the end, most owners reasoned that their bondpeople would be better treated and would work harder if they managed them themselves. Even though Richard Kimmons's master operated more than one small farm, "he seed atter he niggers an' mules heself," because "he didn't want 'em drug 'roun' an' all bruised up."[59]

Most owners took charge of the daily operations of their own farms, however. Slaveholders chose the fields to prepare, the mixture of crops, planting time, the amount of seed to sow, and when to harvest. They also were responsible for the business of the farm, determining what portion of the crops to sell and to whom and how to spend the profits. Most Missouri masters directly supervised their laborers, deciding which hands to employ, whether to enhance or reduce their labor force, and what work was to be done and when, many actually accompanying their workers to the fields. Hattie Matthews's master owned a number of slaves and daily rode his horse out to the fields to monitor their work. In the style of an overseer, he cracked his workers with a horsewhip whenever they slackened their pace. Rhody Holsell claimed that her master knew "every row of corn we would hoe; sometimes we would break de corn off and den we got a whipping with a weed." The composition of the slave force on the farm usually determined whether slaveholding men engaged in physical labor. Farmers who owned only a few slaves, especially if they were women or boys, often worked alongside their slaves at fieldwork. Thomas and Paulina Stratton were accustomed to employing a number of field hands when they lived with Thomas's mother in Virginia but only retained one adult slave man named Ike when they moved to Cooper County. Thomas was physically taxed when he sowed wheat and plowed the family's fields and garden for the first time during his and Paulina's married life. Although slaveholding men, such as Stephen Hempstead and John Lewis, often wrote in their farm journals and letters as if they personally completed the tasks accomplished on their farms, the fact remained that it was usually slaves who engaged in the backbreaking tasks. It often was noted when owners worked at more physically demanding jobs such as preparing new fields, plowing, or hemp breaking. White men who commanded the labor of a large enough workforce could move into a supervisory role and leave the most strenuous physical labor to their slaves.[60]

Seasonal rhythms of agricultural production largely defined the lives of those who tilled Missouri's soil. Over time, the composition of the labor force and the amount of acreage devoted to certain crops may have changed on individual farms, but year after year the nature of the work remained the same, with the same tasks performed during the same time of the year with little alteration. A farm journal kept from 1850 through 1867 by John Lewis, a Howard County slaveholder, is reflective of the work done by many owners and their slaves on Missouri farms. By 1860, John Lewis, his aging father, Henry, and his two younger brothers owned a combined slave force of twenty-three, including nine men of prime working age. The Lewis farming operation was large by Missouri standards, and, in the years preceding the Civil War, the Lewises and their slaves produced as much as sixty thousand pounds of hemp annually. During the early spring of each year, the Lewis slaves traditionally broke new ground in order to increase the amount of productive acreage and then repaired and built fences, plowed, and generally prepared the soil for spring planting. In April and May, they sowed oat, corn, and hemp seed, as well as planted garden vegetables, with an emphasis on potatoes, turnips, cabbages, and pumpkins. Throughout the early summer, they plowed the corn crop again and weeded it and the potatoes. In July, the Lewis hands were engaged in cutting and stacking hay, as well as harvesting the wheat that had been planted the fall before. In August, they cut the hemp. Whenever there were lulls throughout the summer and early fall, the slaves worked at various building improvements around the farm. In October, they spread the hemp on the ground to rot and harvested and stored the corn. Slaves also gathered potatoes and pumpkins, separated hemp seed, plowed the cornfields, and spread manure.

In December and January, the Lewis slaves butchered and processed the many hogs raised on the farm. Throughout the winter months, they collected and chopped firewood, cut ice for the icehouse, and broke thousands of pounds of hemp by hand. The Lewises did not deliver the hemp crop to factors until late spring, well after their enslaved workers had begun planting for the next year's harvest.[61]

John Lewis was rarely specific about which of his hands performed various tasks, although it appears that men more regularly engaged in fieldwork. Missouri slaveholders' decisions about labor assignments were influenced by the small size of most slaveholdings. In many cases, there were not enough slaves to distinguish male and female workers as primarily house servants or field hands. Instead, work assignments varied according to production needs and household demographics, and in many cases the result was a division of labor that fit squarely with white middle-class Americans' gender norms with most men working in the fields and most women working in the homes. The gang system of labor with groups of male and female field workers, so common in the plantation South, generally was used only on the largest Missouri slaveholdings where sizable tobacco and hemp crops were produced. Most slaves rather were employed as general farmhands and domestic workers, laboring at variety of chores throughout the course of the day. Certain tasks were more commonly, although not exclusively, performed by men. Slave men were more likely to clear land for new fields, make rails for building fences, and help white craftsmen with various building projects, such as painting and bricklaying. On most farms, slave men also more often plowed, cut wood and ice, and broke hemp. Slave women only intermittently engaged in fieldwork, although not because white Missourians believed that as women they should not, but because the demands of their many household duties left them little time for this work. Four slaves broke hemp on one slaveholding in the winter of 1841, including a slave woman named Charlotte, for example. The slave men routinely broke well over a hundred pounds daily, whereas Charlotte averaged closer to fifty pounds a day and worked many fewer days, presumably because her domestic work left her less time to assist with hemp processing.[62]

Although slave women worked mainly in their owners' homes, it was, nonetheless, common for women such as Charlotte to move to the fields, especially during planting and harvesting. A few large Missouri slaveholdings included female field hands, but most holdings were too small for exclusive assignments of slave women to fieldwork. Typical was Malinda Discus's mother who "was a fine cook and worked indoors mostly, though she did some work in the fields too." Whether or not slave women spent much time in the fields depended on the demographic makeup of the slave force and the presence of grown sons in the master's family. On the Stratton and Napton farms there were enough slave men, older slave boys, and slaveholding sons to maintain the agriculture enterprises of the farms without much labor from slave women, but on the smallest holdings, the work of slave women in the fields could be crucial. On the farm owned by the master of James Monroe Abbot, the only adult male slave was elderly and, therefore, Abbot's mother worked in the fields rather than the house. As Abbot recalled, "My Muthuh wuz big an' strong . . . dey warn't nothin on de place dat she couldn' do. She cud cut down a big tree en chop off a rail length an' use a wedge an' maul an' make rails as good as anybody."[63]

The ways in which white Missourians understood what constituted proper gender roles and labor assignments influenced the physical mobility of slave men and women as well. Slaveholding men and their male slaves had many opportunities to travel throughout the neighborhood doing the business of the farm. As was true throughout the South, white men frequently left the farm for business purposes, such as patronizing merchants, taking their crops and livestock to mill and market, and pursuing their professions, as well as civic engagements, such as attending county court days, auctions, militia musters, elections, fraternal organizations, and agricultural societies. The customary operations of small-slaveholding farms resulted in liberal mobility for male slaves as well. It was quite common for slaveholders to send their slave men on errands throughout the neighborhood. Abiel Leonard often instructed his men to purchase or transport items to various merchants and tradesmen throughout Howard County, and they also routinely met Leonard family members at the Missouri River when they arrived by steamboat or crossed over by ferry from Boonville. Abiel and Nathaniel Leonard even sent their slaves between their homes in Howard and Cooper Counties— a distance of thirty miles across the river. The Strattons' slave men and boys also traveled throughout Cooper County on farm errands or to the local mill. Slave men, more so than women, temporarily were hired out or loaned to neighbors to work. In addition, it was slave men, rather than women, who traveled to visit their spouses and children who lived on other farms in the neighborhood. Women in general—both white and black—had fewer opportunities to venture from home, with the exception of attending church services, occasional social events, visits to family and neighbors, or in the case of slave women, hiring assignments.

Slaveholding women's mobility was severely circumscribed by social customs that dictated that they must be accompanied by men when traveling from home, whereas slave women were kept on the farm by the relentless demands of their work, as well as their owners' restrictions on their movement. Most of black and white women's days were spent working together in the home, giving them limited time to interact with others outside of their own house and barnyard.[64]

In Missouri, the labor of both mistresses and slave women by and large revolved around domestic concerns, and, as on plantations, the mistress's role as supervisor of these activities was crucial to the economic well-being of the household. Slaveholding women's sphere of influence included cooking, cleaning, sewing, child care, and maintaining the barnyard and kitchen garden. Due to small slave workforces, Missouri mistresses engaged in more actual labor and were less involved in leisure pursuits than were their plantation counterparts. Slaveholding women supervised and augmented the labor of their slave women, who performed the most grueling of household tasks, while mistresses devoted much of their time to child care and needlework.[65]

Women and girls exerted tremendous labor as they worked to maintain the domestic operations of rural households in the years before the adoption of labor-saving household devices. Certain tasks, especially those involving the cultivation, processing, and preservation of food, were bound to distinct seasons, but chores such as cooking, cleaning, washing, and child care were daily and weekly concerns. Throughout the years, Paulina Stratton chronicled the seemingly endless domestic work performed on her Cooper County farm. As was the case in most rural households, much of the Stratton women's time revolved around the production and preparation of food. They cultivated a kitchen garden, raised poultry, sheep, and hogs, and milked cows through the combined efforts of Stratton, her two oldest daughters, and her two slave women, Aga and Dilsy. The women put up vegetables and dried fruit for the winter, processed meat after the early winter butchering, and made cider, molasses, soap, and butter. Everyday meal preparation was an unrelenting chore, which was compounded by the fact that the Strattons' kitchen, like those on most Missouri farms, was a separate building located a short distance from the big house and was likely equipped with a large kitchen fireplace rather than a free-standing stove. Slave women constantly minded the kitchen fire, occasionally with some help from men and boys to fill the woodpile, and daily "had to burn [their] faces cookin' over de fireplace." Stratton, like most mistresses, allocated food resources within the household but left it to Aga to get the family's meals to the table. Aga and Dilsy were in charge of the wash also, hauling the laundry over a mile to a nearby creek during times of drought. Stratton engaged in less spinning and weaving after her move to Missouri, although she continued to spend hours cutting out and sewing clothing for all members of her household. Interestingly, she never made much mention of housecleaning, perhaps because the constant and demanding labor of farm life limited the appeal of outfitting her home to the domestic standards of the day. Town-dwelling slaveholding women, such as Elvira Scott and Mary Belt, were more likely to furnish their homes to middle-class tastes, expecting their slave women to keep their draperies, furniture, and knickknacks tidy.[66]

It was oftentimes unclear in white women's accountings of domestic labor as to who actually did the work, but it appears that most often slave women labored as cooks, housekeepers, and laundresses and assisted the mistress with cloth production, sewing, and child care when their primary chores were done. Marilda Pethy, a former slave, related that her mother "done everything . . . all kinds of work," and Mollie Renfro Sides, another former slave, said of her mother, "Mah mammy done de cookin' an' 'twen time she he'p weave on de loom, an' spin an' knit." Most slaveholders recognized the important contributions that slave women made toward maintaining the small-slaveholding household. Nathaniel Leonard, for example, refused to make any major expenditure while still in debt with the one exception of the purchase of a slave woman, whom he deemed crucial to the domestic operations of the household. The fact that nonslaveholders chose to hire slave women before men suggests the premium that middle- and upper-class Missourians placed on providing white women with domestic help and relieving them of fieldwork. The mistress of Sarah Waggoner never allowed her to work in the fields, believing that her labor was much more valuable in the home. "Oh Lordee, but I worked hard since I was twelve years old. But not in de fields. Old Miss she say dere was plenty for me to do in de house, and dere was, sure 'nough," Waggoner stated. Much of slave women's time was spent laboring at tasks that made their owners' or employers' lives more comfortable or enhanced the economic viability of their farms, leaving them little time to engage in reproductive labor for their own families.[67]

Employing domestic workers was considered a sign of gentility; however, white Missourians never expected that domestic help would free white women from housework. Although slave women performed most domestic tasks, Missouri slaveholders usually owned few female slaves, making the labor of mistresses necessary. Even though a plantation mistress's role was largely supervisory, small-slaveholding women were unable to keep from getting their hands dirty. Nicholas Patterson observed of Missouri settler women as early as 1818: "Many of the females are modest, tidy and industrious. All perform domestic labor, even when they have servants. I have found but few exceptions in all this 'range.'" Most mistresses merely managed slave women as they cooked, cleaned, and washed, however, laboring at these strenuous chores only while slave women recovered from sickness and childbirth. Willard Mendenhall observed that his wife, Mollie, and his mother-in-law, Margaret Kavanaugh, worked hard at "house work," but that their hired slave woman, Caroline, performed "the drudgery." In fact, mistresses so rarely engaged in the dirtiest and most arduous of household labor that when they did it elicited special remarks in their diaries and letters. Elvira Weir Scott, the wife of a Miami, Missouri, merchant, wrote that she did "the cooking & most of the housework for a family of 10" for two weeks while her only slave woman, Margaret, recovered from childbirth, and Paulina Stratton cooked while her slave cook Aga suffered from the chills. The amount of housework performed by small-slaveholding women depended on the household size and circumstances, including factors such as the number of female slaves owned by the family, the number of children in the family, the point in the life cycle of the slaveholding family, the employment of husbands, and whether the family lived on a farm or in town. However much mistresses and their daughters labored in homes and barnyards, small-slaveholding women did not toil in the fields as did slave women and the wives and daughters of many nonslaveholding farmers. Slaveholders considered fieldwork to be well beneath the dignity of a proper southern white lady. Owning slaves protected small-slaveholding women, such as Paulina Stratton, from this type of labor. It was only after emancipation that Stratton and her young children worked in the fields, for example.[68]

As with housework, mistresses' participation in the maintenance of the dairy, poultry, and kitchen gardens largely depended on the number of potential laborers living in the household at any given time. Paulina Stratton, who had only two slave women, assigned the care of the chickens to her teenage daughters, whereas Melinda Napton, who had more slaves, assigned this task to a slave woman. But even Napton depended on the labor of her young sons to cultivate the family's garden. In fact, she worried about who would help her with gardening if her sons attended school rather than were tutored at home. Few slaveholding women complained about this outside work, however, finding it welcome relief from more tedious indoor tasks such as needlework.[69]

Most Missouri mistresses spent hours in the production of cloth and in sewing for both the white family and their slaves. Although by the middle of the nineteenth-century women in many parts of the United States bought their material rather than produced homespun, much cloth was still woven on Missouri farms. Slave women frequently assisted mistresses in the production of homespun, which was often used for slave clothing. Paulina Stratton and other slaveholding women wrote of making carpets, usually for their families' use, but also for sale to neighbors. Although a number of former slaves remembered their mothers sewing, the records indicate that it was often mistresses who engaged in the bulk of the needlework for all members of the household. Melinda Napton constantly complained about her many hours of sewing, claiming that she barely had time to write her absent husband a letter. Abiel Leonard was concerned that the voluminous amount of sewing was overtaxing his wife, Jeanette. He told her that he would rather pay someone to sew for her than have her "killing yourself and putting out your eyes with work." One of Paulina Stratton's primary occupations was preparing clothing for the members of her household. Rather than use the labor of her slave women, Stratton invited her neighbors to a "sewing" to assist her with the preparation of the slaves' clothing. Although they also engaged in sewing for their households, plantation mistresses delegated more of this work to slave seamstresses than did the mistresses on Missouri's farms.[70]

The most time-consuming job of small-slaveholding women—although perhaps most rewarding for many—was the care of their children. Slave nurses occasionally assisted slaveholding mothers with child care, but most women did not own enough slaves to assign a slave woman to this specific task. In some households, the only nurse was a young slave child. In addition, in a state with scanty opportunities for public education, many women, such as Melinda Napton and Mary Ann Kendley, spent hours overseeing the education of their children. Although the record is largely silent on the issue, some mistresses watched over slave children while their mothers worked.[71]

Most Missouri slaveholding women were left with little time for leisure pursuits, and the amount of free time they enjoyed largely depended on their position in the life cycle, the number of slaves owned, and whether they lived in town or on a farm. Melinda Napton spent a few precious minutes each day reading and writing to her husband, who worked as an attorney and judge and was often away, but only after her children had gone to bed. Paulina Stratton began to socialize more with her neighbors, became more involved in her church, and wrote more frequently in her journal, as her children grew older. Elvira Scott was unique in describing a great deal of leisure time. She often spent up to two hours a day practicing the piano. Scott, however, lived in the town of Miami, was married to a successful merchant, and had only two daughters. In addition, she owned an extremely capable female slave named Margaret, who apparently kept the household running smoothly. Slave women had virtually no time for leisure due to the overwhelming demands of their productive and reproductive responsibilities—both in their owners' homes and fields and in their own cabins and provision grounds.[72]

Children also worked on Missouri farms, although slave children generally worked much harder than their slaveholding peers. Most of the individuals interviewed by the Federal Writers Project, usually referred to as the WPA, were children at the time of emancipation; therefore, the narratives are filled with stories of the work experiences of slave children. Young Missouri slaves engaged in a number of jobs that were usually located within the big house or barnyard. Slave children, such as James Goings, were often employed carrying wood and water. Charlie Richardson and Malinda Discus ran errands for their mothers and helped with their chores. Mary Bell rode a pony to the field to call the hands to dinner and assisted in the kitchen with cleanup. Sarah Waggoner milked eight cows, and Peter Corn drove the cows to the barn for milking every day. Like many young slave girls, Margaret Nickens and Isabelle Henderson served as nurses for white children, while others, such as Malinda Discus and Louis Hamilton's older sister, minded their own siblings. Eventually slave children graduated to more physically demanding labor, following in the footsteps of their parents. As a small boy, Lewis Mundy rode an ox as the fields were harrowed, but when he was ten or eleven he learned to walk behind the plow with the oxen team. Madison Frederick Ross was proud of himself when he finally was allowed to plow for the first time.[73]

The work of slave children generally was not difficult, although they usually were kept busy. Emma Knight observed of her childhood, "We didn't have to work none too hard, 'cause we was so young, I guess." She worked in the garden weeding and hoeing and fed the livestock. Louis Hill agreed, "We always had ta be doin' somethin', even if it war pickin' up kindlin'." Marie Askin Simpson also recalled, "I was just a little girl but I can remember how they kept me busy waiting on them. Carrying water from the spring, hunting eggs and a lot of other little things." And Malinda Murphy remembered as a four-year-old picking up feathers in the field under the supervision of her mistress. Many children chafed under these constraints, however, understandably preferring to spend their time in play. As a small boy, James Monroe Abbot was asked to spend his entire summer brushing the flies off of his sick master. He was happy when his master died because he could finally go outside and play. When he was ten years old, Henry Bruce was hired out to work in a tobacco factory, and he remembered, "I was kept busy every minute from sunrise to sunset, without being allowed to speak a word to anyone. I was too young then to be kept in such close confinement."[74]

In contrast to their counterparts on plantations, small-slaveholding children often worked on their parents' farms. Daughters frequently produced textiles and sewed, although they occasionally were reluctant workers. Abiel Leonard implored his daughters to spare their mother by making their own clothes, and Manie Kendley remembered seeing her mother, Mary Ann Kendley, exhausted from sewing, asleep in her chair with garments scattered around her on the floor. The young Kendley felt guilty that she had hidden her needle skills from her mother in order to keep from spending hours in a dark room assisting her with the loathsome task. Mary Agnes Stratton helped her mother make carpets and weave cloth that they then sold to neighbors. Sons often assisted their fathers and their slaves in the gardens, fields, and barnyard. The Naptons' many sons plowed, helped in the garden, cleared new land, and chopped firewood. Melinda Napton complained that her older sons were more interested in farming than their schoolwork, observing of her son Billy, "I really believe he hates the sight of a book, but he drives the oxen for the plough very willingly." A few weeks later she wrote, "The heir apparent is behind a plough & pair of steers this morning—he thinks himself a farmer, in truth now." Some slaveholders were dependent on the work of their children to maintain their farms and homes. Nathaniel Leonard required the work of his children in 1851, reportedly declaring, "Next year they may go to School & learn as much as they please but *this* year they must work." Slaveholding children assisted their parents with light chores around the house and farm, but they did not work as steadily, diligently, or as hard as slave children. As was true of their mothers, slaveholding children who lived in town were much less likely to engage in manual labor. The primary concern of most slaveholding parents was the education of their children. White children spent many hours with their studies, whether at the neighborhood one-room schoolhouse, at the local academy or college, or at home with their parents or a hired tutor. Schoolwork left slaveholding children less time for work, a privilege not shared by slave children, who quickly recognized the wide gulf between their own lot in life and that of the white children whom they frequently escorted to and from school. Mark Discus responded when asked whether he attended school: "Lawsy no, chile. I just worked. I don't know nothin' bout larnin. When I was nine years old I cut all the corn stalks offen a forty-acre field with a hoe. We had to work from sun up 'til dark too."[75]

With the exception of the youngest children, most members of Missouri's small-slaveholding households worked hard, but slaves worked the hardest. "Lord, when I thinks of de way we used to work. Out in de field before day and work till plumb dark," George Bollinger, a former Cape Girardeau County slave, recalled. Another Missouri slave described slaves on her owners' farm as working "from daylight ta' dark, and on good light nights it wus way up in the night." Henry Dant, formerly enslaved in Ralls County, claimed that since he was the only slave man on his master's farm, he "worked hard . . . cradled wheat and plowed often till midnight." Sarah Graves's master always found some kind of work for his bondpeople, wishing for none to remain idle, and Charlie Richardson recalled that the slaves on his master's farm worked from four in the morning until eleven at night seven days a week. Most Missouri slaves worked these long hours six days a week from Monday through Saturday, however, and were traditionally given Sunday as a day free from fieldwork. Tishey Taylor claimed that she did not know "Sunday from Monday" except that she did not work in the fields on Sunday and attended worship instead. Some slaveholders gave their slaves additional time off, such as the Lewises who granted their slaves a "holiday" on the fourth of July, the day before Easter, and an occasional Saturday afternoon. But most days—year in and year out—slaves worked long hours for their owners, in all kinds of conditions.[76]

Both by tradition and choice, Missouri farmers employed slaves to work in their homes and fields. Slaves performed the most difficult tasks, but unlike on most plantations, masters, mistresses, and children daily lived and worked alongside the slave men, women, and children with whom they shared their households. The daily labor of slaveholders and slaves defined their days, but as crucial to the quality of their lives was the nature of their relationships with one another. Working and living so closely together fostered personal interactions between owners and slaves and allowed them the extraordinary power to influence one another's lives. It was in these homes and fields that black and white Missourians stridently contested the terms of their relations and labor and ultimately determined their experience of life on slavery's border.

4 / "May we as one family live in peace and harmony": Small-Slaveholding Household Relations

One autumn day in 1852 while still living in western Virginia, Paulina Stratton incurred the displeasure of all the slaves on the farm after she whipped a young slave boy for an unspecified infraction. The boy's mother, Dilsy, "got angry jawed a great deal" about what she considered unjust punishment. When he returned home later that day, Thomas Stratton whipped Dilsy for her impudence. In reaction to the whipping, the other bondpeople on the farm retaliated by engaging in a work strike of sorts, protesting for over a month by feigning sickness, "pouting," and generally remaining in a "bad humour." At one point during the ongoing strife, Thomas confronted his slave man Sam with gun in hand in a futile attempt to force the household relations back on course. After weeks of conflict between the slave and slaveholding members of her household, Paulina finally admitted in her diary that she felt "badly" about her part in initiating the conflict, yet she reasoned that she could not confess her regrets to her slaves because "while we have them they must be kept to their place." She sincerely believed that she had "tried to do what was right in all respect but they blame me with all," and she defiantly refused to speak to all those who faulted her. Exasperated after weeks of discord, she pleaded to God in her diary, "[M]ay we as Christians forgive one another and as one family live in peace and harmony."[1]

During this episode Paulina Stratton described her family as including both white and black members, as did many slaveholding Southerners, yet her words suggest a more personal system of economic and social relations on small-slaveholding farms than that which existed on the

South's plantations. Such a description would have rung true
of her contemporaries, for many in Missouri sincerely believed .
slavery in the state was more humane, and they publicly congratulated
one another that they had perfected a milder system of bondage. This
positive portrayal was partly an informal public relations campaign to
enhance the reputation of Missouri's domestic institutions in the light
of perceived outside attacks, but it also spoke to slaveholders' image of
themselves as paternalistic masters and mistresses. Interestingly, some
Missouri slaves bought into aspects of this rhetoric, expressing fears of
the possibility of being sold farther south where they would be separated
from family and friends and might endure less favorable work conditions in a harsher climate. While they would never consent that Missouri
slavery was mild, they might reason that their circumstances could be
far worse in the cotton and sugar fields of the Deep South.[2]

Indeed, the conditions of life on Missouri's small slaveholdings appeared to be a more "domestic" form of slavery to many. The everyday
work routines and "social habits were those of the farm and not the
plantation," as John G. Haskell explained. Slaves and owners on most
Missouri holdings intimately interacted as they conducted the daily
business of the farm, and what's more, when the working day was done,
they very often resided in close proximity to one another, either in the
same house or in nearby domiciles. White Missourians argued that this
familiarity ultimately led to better treatment of the state's slaves. Indeed,
the portrait of mild slavery painted by many Missourians would appear
to be the ultimate expression of the paternalistic relations promoted by
southern slaveholders.[3]

Historians of slavery have argued that many American slaveholders
believed that excessive abusive or exploitation would not result in highly
productive plantations and farms, and, therefore, they often responded
positively to slaves' attempts to shape their lives in an effort to encourage compliancy and productivity. In an ideal iteration of paternalistic
relations, slaveholders and slaves reached a consensus on the smooth
maintenance of the household through the intricate give-and-take of negotiation and reciprocal obligations. Within this seemingly intractable
system of dominance, bondpeople navigated their enslavement by walking a tightrope of accommodation and resistance, using various tactics
to negotiate the terms of their labor and living conditions. Owners anticipated a certain level of conflict and willingly made concessions in order
to ward off more serious infractions and keep the level of productivity
high. Many gave their bondmen and women a limited autonomy over

their work and family lives, believing that if content they would be more industrious. Slaveholders hoped that if they lived up to their obligations to their slaves, they might reward them with respect, obedience, hard work, and possibly even affection, and if relations ran smoothly it would confirm their views of themselves as benevolent paternalists.[4]

Eugene Genovese and others have argued that in the American South, unlike in the Caribbean where absentee ownership prevailed, paternalistic relations were reinforced by the fact that most owners lived in residence on their plantations. Those planters who resided in close physical proximity to their slaves gained a familiarity with their workers that sometimes translated into improvement in their treatment and labor situations. The closing of the international slave trade in 1808 also encouraged American owners to improve their slaves' conditions in order to encourage the natural increase of the slave population. These factors, coupled with increasing outside pressure from antislavery forces, led many white Southerners to embrace a philosophy of paternalism.[5]

In theory, Missouri farms, with their intimate living and working conditions, should have been the epicenter for paternalistic relations, but the brutal realities of slavery rarely favored small slaveholders' attempts at paternalism. In Missouri, as elsewhere, slavery was slavery. At its foundation, slavery was a system of labor exploitation and social and racial control in which the master class wielded ultimate and often brutal power over those it owned. Enslaved people resisted the control that slaveholders attempted to exert over them and worked to influence both the terms of their labor and their family and community lives. Scholars have found this to be the case on the South's plantations, but this tendency was exacerbated in a place such as Missouri, where the state's unique geography and the resulting preponderance of small slaveholdings resulted in significant differences from those found on plantations in daily living and working conditions for slaveholding families and their slaves. For paternalism to operate smoothly, lines of power had to be clearly drawn, but in Missouri, slaves' and owners' intimate knowledge of one another granted them the extraordinary power to influence the quality of one another's lives in profound ways. The close proximity in which black and white members of the household lived and worked sometimes led to improved material conditions and physical care for slaves because their owners were so intimately aware of their daily circumstances, yet small-scale slavery exposed many others to the worst forms of abuse. In many ways the relationships between Missouri slaves and their owners were similar to those between planters and their slaves working within a big house, but systemic factors inherent in Missouri slavery compounded many of the effects of these intimate living and working conditions and frequently resulted in personally charged and often violent interactions between slaves and owners. The complexities of these interactions were intensified among women, who were confined to the often cramped quarters of small slaveholders' homes and lacked the space provided men in the fields and greater community.

The circumstances found on most Missouri farms afforded slaves tremendous opportunities to effectively resist their enslavement, and ultimately eroded the power of their owners, through passive acts of resistance, such as work slowdowns, theft, and verbal retorts. Slaves also took great risks to escape slavery or violently defy their owners' authority. In the end, the ways in which Missouri slaves contested their enslavement were not unique, but the atmosphere in which the resistance occurred was often more emotionally charged because of the intimate relations between the two parties. Ultimately, the circumstances of small-scale slavery led to a continuum of treatment from "kindness" to depraved cruelty. The fact that slaves and owners found it difficult not to take the conflict personally was precisely why the situation frequently ended in violence. Although Missouri slavery was small in scale, slaves' resentment of their exploitation, and often their owners, was as intense as anyplace.

"Massa was mighty good to his cullud folks"

A few Missouri slaves' experience of their enslavement approached the domestic ideal so enthusiastically touted by the boosters of the system, and they actually remembered their treatment at the hands of their owners in a positive light. Some scholars have questioned whether these memories of slavery say more about the problems of the WPA evidence than the actual conditions during slavery; however, the nature of the relationships between slaves and owners on small holdings allowed for a variety of possible interactions and treatments, ranging from moments of empathy to excessive violence. It appears that some Missouri owners treated their slaves as kindly as possible within the obvious confines of the system. If individual slaveholders were inclined to kindness, the intimacy of small-slaveholding households may have increased the possibility of better treatment. Some owners expressed a sincere and profound interest in their slaves and treated them well. They went beyond caring for the sick and supplying basic needs, and recognized their slaves' humanity.[6]

A few former slaves remembered their owners in an extremely favorable light, describing them as models of benevolent slave ownership. "Everybody called us 'free niggahs'—cause Higgerson slaves was treated so good," Joseph Higgerson recalled in language that reflected both recognition that his situation was better than most other slaves and that Higgerson's neighbors might not have appreciated his liberal approach to mastery. Steve Brown, another former slave, reported of his Cape Girardeau County owner: "Massa was mighty good to his cullud folks. He never 'lowed none of 'em to be sold and I don't recollect ever seeing anyone getting whupped." A WPA interviewer reported that the slaveholder Erskine Danforth was extremely kind to his slaves and for that reason Nelson Danforth took his master's name on freedom rather than that of his father. Erskine Danforth even bought abused neighborhood slaves. In all cases, those who were kindly treated did not translate these favorable experiences into a defense of slavery but instead simply acknowledged that their situation was better than that of many Missouri slaves.[7]

The intimacy of everyday life on Missouri farms led some owners to favor particular slaves, who in turn were able to translate this affection and concern into benefits and personal privileges. Emily Johnson fondly remembered her father's slave woman Jane as "a favorite house servant and a good woman and almost seems like one of the family to me." Some owners held individual slaves in such high esteem that they bestowed rewards and privileges on them. Abiel Leonard's daughter petitioned him on behalf of a slave woman named Ann to grant her request for a closet in her newly constructed cabin, and Joseph Abernathy sent his slave man Robert to California in search of gold in 1850, and two-and-a-half years later, he returned with enough money to purchase his wife, Mahala.[8]

Occasionally, slaveholders developed genuinely positive relationships with individual slaves. Abiel and Jeanette Leonard were faced with replacing their valuable slave man Willis after he died in 1843. The Leonards required a trustworthy slave man who could run the farm under Jeanette's supervision while Abiel was away practicing law. In July 1845, for only $450 the Leonards purchased a forty-three-year-old slave man named John from Jeanette's father, Benjamin Reeves, who considered him to be "faithful" and a "great favourite" among his servants. "Papa's John is very anxious for you to buy him & Pa is willing for you to have him. What say you do you think you can do better," Jeanette wrote to her husband of the generous offer. There is nothing in the records to indicate why John wished to come to Missouri from Reeves's Kentucky plantation, although it is easy to speculate that his family members were among slaves Reeves earlier had given to his daughter. The Leonards quickly found that they could not have found a "better," more faithful, or harder worker than John. Throughout the years, John managed the Leonard farm in a manner that greatly pleased his master and mistress, following the often copious farming instructions relayed to him in Abiel's many letters to his wife and daughters. He also supervised the younger slave men, as together they tended to the cornfields, gardens, and livestock, as well as kept the icehouse filled and the white family supplied with wood. The men also repaired fences and buildings, cleared fields, and assisted white carpenters with various construction projects. There is no way to know John's motivation for his faithful service, but it appears that his hard work, loyalty, and congeniality may have led to extra autonomy and some measure of respect within the Leonard household. As the years passed, it became apparent that Abiel encouraged John to make his own management decisions, submitting much to "his judgement" and trusting him to traverse the countryside, conducting business on his behalf. He once instructed John to purchase a scythe and "examine and see where he can get it best & cheapest." John apparently felt comfortable enough with his place in the Leonard household to voice his opinions about the farming business and occasionally even articulate negative feelings about his circumstances. In March of 1850, for example, John was discouraged when a fence washed out during a rainstorm and reportedly complained, "Says it is work, work all the time & never get anything done."[9]

Slaveholders routinely sent greetings to favored slaves in their letters, albeit often as an afterthought in the postscript. The Glasgow and Lane families lived in St. Louis, but the contents of their letters reveal the close relationships that sometimes existed between slaves and slaveholders in households with few servants. Sarah Lane Glasgow was separated from her husband and children when she traveled to Hot Springs, Arkansas, for her health. Two of the family's slaves accompanied her, resulting in a series of letters in which major portions were written to or about these individuals. At one point a Glasgow child teased: "Give [my] love to Aunt Caroline and Joe and tell them not to fall in love with Arkansas so as to want to be hired on one of the Cotton farms for we want them at home." The white child clearly signaled the difference between what she imagined was her family's kind treatment of their servants and the harsh treatment of Arkansas plantation slaves. Caroline made the distinction herself, reportedly observing, "[W]e have come to a land of heathens where they think no more of niggers than of dogs indeed not so much."

Other slaveholding families, such as the Leonards and the Naptons, also sent cheerful greetings to their bondpeople.[10]

Some owners extended their kindness to slave children as well. When slave mothers and children were separated through sale or death, motherless children sometimes were left without adequate care if there were no other slaves on the farm to tend to their needs. On smaller holdings, orphaned children oftentimes were raised in the homes of their white masters and mistresses. Mary Armstrong called her master and mistress "'pappy' an' 'mammy', 'cause they raises me up from the little girl," and Mary Estes Peters reported that her owners fed and clothed her the same as their own children. Although economic considerations clearly played an important role in the care of orphaned children, occasionally the level of attention suggests greater depths of concern and affection. Peter Corn, who had been a slave in Ste. Genevieve County, spoke fondly of his old mistress, saying, "I can't say a hard word about her. Before I was borned she was left a widow and she treated us almost like white folks. She took care of us and raised us up. Mother died after she had six children and we was left in de care of dis old mistress." While in this particular case the outcome was largely positive, it is important to note that Corn's mistress treated him and his siblings "almost" but not exactly "like white folks." Few slave children would have mistaken their position in the household with that of white family members. Regardless of favorable treatment, separation from their kin and community likely extracted a great toll on enslaved children. In a worst-case scenario, this isolation within white households presented slaveholders with opportunities to abuse their charges.[11]

A few owners showed genuine concern for the welfare of slaves even when they no longer had economic motivation, extending their kindness after their deaths by specifying in their wills that certain slaves be kept within the family or emancipated. In 1836, Sylvestre Labbadie freed his twenty-nine-year-old slave man Celestin upon his deceased daughter's request that he be emancipated for "his kindness to herself and to the family & for his faithfulness." Garrett Groomer's 1859 will emancipated all of his slaves. Groomer was the permissive master, who two years earlier had been fined five dollars for allowing a slave to search for his own hire position. Nelly Read manumitted her slaves in her will and set aside $100 in trust to care for them in their old age. Hugh Rogers stipulated in his will that his slaves be distributed among his children regardless of whether greater profit could be made by their sale in the open market. In the event that the heirs did not want them, Rogers instructed that his slaves be placed with owners they found satisfactory. William Spud also demanded that his slaves' "future happiness" rather than price be the driving consideration if they were sold. A few owners attempted to extend their mastery from beyond the grave by placing conditions upon those they intended to emancipate, just as was the case with parents who attempted to control the behavior of their children through the terms of their wills. John Lacy, a Cooper County resident, specified in his 1855 will that his one slave man, Adlai, be set free upon the death of his wife, Susan, but only if "during her lifetime . . . he conduct himself well and not become guilty of, any bad practices such as lying, stealing, drunkenness, gambling or fighting or quarrelling with other negroes." Bill Messersmith's father divided his slaves among his heirs in his will, but indicated that he wished to provide them with the opportunity to earn their own freedom. Each slave would be hired out to work until he or she earned $800. Gus Smith, a former slave, remembered of the elder Mr. Messersmith: "He did not believe it was right to keep dem in slavery all their lives. But de war came and dey were free without having to work it out." Oftentimes, slaveholders' heirs blatantly disregarded these posthumous acts of kindness toward slaves. John Copeland of Boone County liberated his slaves in his will, but his daughters disputed it, contending that he was incompetent at the time it was drafted. When Copeland's son-in-law William Rowland kidnapped one of those emancipated, members of the community signed a petition asking that the legal charges against him be dismissed.[12]

In many ways the actions of Missouri's small slaveholders were similar to those of plantation masters and mistresses toward their favored house servants. On small holdings, owners knew all of their slaves well, as they daily lived and worked with them, and this intimacy created situations where some owners recognized their slaves' humanity and as a result felt some obligation toward improving their lot in life. Although a few Missouri owners manumitted those they favored, in most cases this dramatic step was not taken until after the slaveholder's death, suggesting that freedom was granted in recognition of faithful service and affection for individual slaves rather than as a result of a wholesale rejection of slavery. In most cases, favored slaves were rewarded with nominal tokens and kindnesses and not with the true gift of freedom.[13]

The Material Conditions of Life

In addition to acts of kindness from individual slaveholders, there is evidence to suggest that the circumstances of small-scale slavery resulted in better material circumstances for some Missouri slaves. In many cases, formerly enslaved Missourians reported the quality of their food, clothing, and shelter in reasonably favorable terms. This appears to be the case despite the fact that many small-slaveholding farms operated on slim economic margins. Enslaved Missourians' positive reflections confirm Stephen Crawford's findings in his quantitative analysis of the interviews of former slaves conducted by the WPA that the size of slaveholdings was a major determining factor in descriptions of the material conditions of slavery. A myriad of factors likely contributed to better material conditions for Missouri slaves, including the fact that the state's farmers grew a variety of food crops in addition to cash crops and encouraged their slaves to supplement their food supplies through cultivating gardens and raising livestock. Pragmatism also may have played a role in small slaveholders' decisions to provide materially for their slaves, as it was in their economic best interest to keep their few workers healthy and working. Just as significant, the fact that owners lived and worked so closely with their slaves made them more aware of their physical needs and may have resulted in some owners providing more generously for them.[14]

Although most owners simply met slaves' basic needs, some went so far as to share what they had with their bondpeople. "Our white folks was good to us an' treated us like we was w'ite as dey was. Ef dey had flour, meal, coffee or sugar we had some too," Richard Kimmons claimed. Generous provisioning was not offered unselfishly, of course. On farms, the labor of all hands was vital, and, therefore, it was important that workers remain physically fit. Owners believed that well cared for slaves were in better health, willingly worked harder, and would command higher sale or hiring prices. Mahala Prewitt remembered her experience as a Missouri slave: "We ate just what the family ate and was provided with plenty of clothes by our master but we had to work."[15]

Former Missouri slaves overwhelmingly reported satisfaction with the quantity of their food, and in fact many who lived on smaller holdings were given the same fare as the slaveholding family. Rachal Goings, her mother, and her siblings were the only bondpeople owned by her master and mistress, and her mother served as the cook for the slaveholding family. "We allus had plenty good things to eat. De white folks would set down en eat, en when dey's through we'd sit down at de same table," Goings recalled. Hannah Allen also sat at the same table with her owners. Like Goings's mother, Fil Hancock's grandmother was the cook, so "[w]e got to eat what de white folk did." Enslaved people living on small holdings often ate the same food as their owners, but they frequently were allowed to partake only after the white family had their fill. "When de white folks was through eatin', I got a pan and got de grub, and set on de floor and et it," Sarah Waggoner remembered. Hattie Matthews and her fellow slaves also ate from the master's table, but as a child her repast was less substantial. The adult slaves ate the leftovers from a communal pot, and once they were finished the children drank the "pot liquor" at the bottom of the kettle.[16]

Other former Missouri slaves reported cooking in their own cabins, especially their morning and evening meals. Those living on larger holdings were the most likely to prepare their own food separately from that of the slaveholding family. The foundation of their diet often consisted of the rations doled out by the owners. Charlie Richardson's fellow slaves cooked in their cabins and regularly ate hoecakes made from corn meal. Smokey Eulenberg claimed that there was plenty of food on his master's plantation, but every morning when a slave woman went to the smoke house to cut the meat for the day the slave children gathered around her hoping for something extra. Tishey Taylor remembered eating three times a day on her master's plantation, although she observed, "Some them slaves cooks in their cabin, not what they wanted but what 'Marse' gibd 'em, most times wus beans an' 'tators and corn bred and milk, and some times 'round hog killin' time he pass out the 'jowl meat.'" Slaves on one Missouri slaveholding ate "salt meat, cabbage, 'taters, and shortnin' bread three times a day."[17]

Although the quantity of food was sufficient in a majority of the reported cases, the variety of the fare was often far from adequate and nutritionally insufficient by modern standards. Mark Discus put it best, "We had 'nough of what we got, but hit was just course grub." Missouri slaveholders routinely allowed, and often expected, their slaves to supplement their mundane diets by raising their own vegetables, tending their own livestock, hunting, and fishing. In the end, enslaved Missourians' favorable memories of food were partly due to their own efforts to procure it.[18]

A few Missouri slaves complained of inadequate sustenance, such as Harriet Casey, who described the conditions on her rich but cruel mistress's farm: "To eat we had corn meal and fried meat dat had been eaten by bugs. We had some gravy and all ate 'round de pans like pigs eating slop. And we had a tin cup of sour milk to drink." It was a real treat when Casey was given gingerbread twice a year. Slave children often suffered the most because many owners skimped on their food allowances, believing that the youngsters did not deserve as much since they could not yet labor like adults. Louis Hill, who had been a slave in St. Francois County, told of the desperate scramble for food among the children on his owner's farm: "All us kids ate on da flo frum da same plate an da biggest dog got da mos."[19]

Missouri slaves who praised their food vastly outnumbered those who complained, although it is difficult to know how many WPA interviewees fondly remembered the security of slavery in the light of Great Depression poverty or altered their testimony in an attempt to ingratiate themselves with white interviewers. A few specified that their diet in slavery days was better than in freedom. "[W]e had good livin' dar. Ole 'Massa an' Missus Patsy wuz mighty good to us. Eatin's? Lawd we had everythin'—not de mess we has to make out wid now," Emily Camster Green remembered. Harry Johnson agreed with Green's assessment, observing, "Times was much better dan dey are now." Perry Sheppard's owners provided him with plenty of meat, and he stated, seemingly without reservation, "I think slavery was a good thing. I never suffered for nothin'."[20]

Slaves generally did not remember their clothing in such glowing terms, however. Owners typically distributed only one or two sets of coarse clothing per season, and these garments often were made from homespun that had been produced within the household, although in the later antebellum years, some material was store-bought. The situation differed from the plantation South where many planters turned to readymade garments in the years before the Civil War. Missouri slaveholding women, such as Sarah Chandler, Mary Hardin, and Paulina Stratton, spent hours producing both fabric and garments for their slaves, although slave women and girls played a significant role in the process as well. Sarah Graves described how she helped to make clothing; gathering wool, carding, spinning, weaving, coloring, and sewing the garments. "I jes' had two dresses. De best one was made out of plain, white muslin. I went out in de woods and got walnut bark to color it brown," Sarah Waggoner reported. Malinda Murphy remembered dresses made from linsey, a coarse woolen and cotton or linen blend. A runaway slave woman named Rachel was captured wearing "a Dark Linsey Dress and a white Dress Coat made for a man over it." Rachel traveled with a slave man who wore "an old fur cap Blue Jeans Coat" and "casinet Pantaloons." A number of men remembered the dresses or shirttails that they wore as young boys. Lewis Mundy wore a knee-length wool shirt until he was twelve or fourteen years old, and Mark Discus described his shift as being of the "coarsest of cotton stuff an' had no collar." In fact, Louis Hill claimed that the boys were all naked under their long shirts. As was the case with plantation house servants, slaves on small holdings occasionally were given the worn-out garments of white family members. Paulina Stratton passed on her husband's old pants to her slave Griffin, and Mark Discus recollected that he was given old clothing to wear in the wintertime. The only "fancy" clothes worn by Hattie Matthews's grandmother were those discarded by her mistress. Oftentimes these garments were at the end of their useful life, and, therefore, the gift may have been one more of economy than favoritism. Indeed, John Woods observed of his slave Wert: "[H]e has no clothes pants or shirts worth anything I have had him wearing out my old pants and he is nearly through them."[21]

The quality of Missouri slaves' clothing was generally poor, and although most reported that their basic needs were met, an overwhelming number complained about the lack of adequate footwear. Many went barefoot for most of the year and were given a pair of ill-fitting and poor quality shoes to wear exclusively during the frequently harsh Missouri winters. "Only in the coldest of weather we had split leather shoes without any linin'. I have had my feet freeze and crack open on the heels and bleed. Didn't do us no good to complain neither," Mark Discus remembered. Steve Brown and Madison Frederick Ross claimed that their shoes were homemade on their owners' farms, but slaveholders' accounts reveal that footwear more frequently was purchased from local merchants. Many slaves reported that they either received their shoes too late in the winter or not at all. Emma Knight said of her childhood: "We went barefoot until it got real cold. Our feet would crack open from de cold and bleed. We would sit down and bawl and cry because it hurt so." Knight's mother made moccasins from old pants to protect her feet. Rhody Holsell remembered waiting in the cold for a wagon to bring her back from the field. She wrapped her shoeless feet in her dress to keep them warm. "Man, I don't know how I'm here today," she observed. Malinda Murphy left "tracks of blood in de snow" from her cracked bare feet. Lack of shoes sometimes affected the quality of work done by slaves. In February 1835, Jeanette Leonard informed her absent husband that their slave man Willis was loitering around the farm, claiming that he could not work without shoes. Jeanette desperately attempted to find him a quality pair in the local stores.[22]

Rachal Goings's stepfather certainly understood the value of a good pair of shoes. A slave neighbor gave Rachal her first pair when he found that the shoes he had purchased for his own little girl were too small, but they were uncomfortably big for Rachal so she threw them out after wearing them only a short time. When her stepfather found that she had discarded the highly valued commodity, he whipped her, retrieved the shoes, and made her wear them the rest of the winter. Children, like Rachal, went shoeless even in winter because many owners were unwilling to go to the expense to buy them footwear. "In dem days no nigger got boots till he was big and able to work for 'em," Fil Hancock explained, although his mistress spoiled him as a boy by giving him a pair of red high-top boots for Christmas one year.[23]

Missouri slaves were housed in a variety of domiciles, but most resided in slave cabins a short distance from their owners' homes. Oftentimes, married slaves—whether resident or abroad—were given their own cabin in which to raise their families. Single slaves frequently lived in cabins together with other unmarried slaves of the same sex, with their parents, or in their owners' homes. Some slave cabins were well made of hewn logs, clapboard, or brick; others were shoddily constructed. A few had puncheon floors and glass or shuttered windows, but more often they had only dirt floors and openings for windows. The cabins usually consisted of one or two rooms, contained a fireplace for cooking and heating, and were sparsely furnished with only a couple of pieces of furniture, a few personal effects, and cooking utensils. Susan Duncan's cabin was described in a Civil War pension claim as including "beds and beddings, cooking utensils and such household articles as are usually found in the cabins of negroes in her condition." Slaves slept on a variety of beds from rope hammocks to cornhusk and occasionally even feather-stuffed mattresses. Tishey Taylor remembered that "our beds wus poor stuff, but mammy said she wus allays 'dog tired' and could 'a slep on the ground."[24]

The number of slaves on the farm usually determined the location of slaves' lodgings. Cabins sometimes were arranged like a small slave quarter on Missouri's few larger holdings, but on most farms the one or two slave cabins were located directly behind the main house. On the smallest holdings, it was not unusual for women and children to live within their owners' homes. Sarah Graves and her parents lived in a log cabin kitchen that was attached to her owners' modest home. Hannah Allen and Lucinda Patterson both slept on the floor in the bedrooms of the big house or in the kitchen. Sarah Waggoner and her brother lived in the main house, sleeping in the kitchen on a trundle bed in the summer and on a pallet by the fireplace in the winter. "Old Pap was good to us," she said of her master. "He kept up a fire all night when it was cold."[25]

Not only did most Missouri slaveholders provide adequate material comforts for their slaves, but it was in their best interest to tend to their health as well. The papers of slaveholders and physicians are filled with discussions of steps taken to save slaves and the expense of medical treatment. Some owners exhibited humanitarian concern, although they likely were more motivated by preserving valuable property and keeping workers healthy. Missourians were preoccupied with sickness and death, frequently chronicling the health of their family members and their neighbors both black and white. Over the course of twenty-six years, Archibald Little Hager kept a detailed diary in which he recorded the illnesses and deaths of those in his Perry County, Missouri, neighborhood. Many others reported epidemics in the neighborhood, exposing their fears that they, their loved ones, or slaves would also succumb to sickness.[26]

Most owners first tended to their sick slaves at home, hoping to delay the expense of medical care for as long as possible. Many educated themselves on the diagnosis and treatment of common illnesses and maintained a store of commonly prescribed medications and home remedies. Both white and black women took an especially large role in caring for the sick members of their households, as well as helping others in the neighborhood. Rhody Holsell's mistress was gone for days at a time tending to sick people in the neighborhood and George Bollinger's mistress and his mother together doctored the sick with a bag of medicinal herbs that always hung from the big house porch. Missouri owners also enlisted the assistance of local slaves known for their medical or midwifery skills; a course that generally met with the approval of their bondpeople, who appreciated slave healers' attention to both bodily and spiritual matters. Gus Smith's grandfather was an herb doctor, who had the confidence of many in the neighborhood, including the white people, and Smith believed that his grandfather "could cure anything." The task of keeping household members well was oftentimes discouraging, as it seemed that someone was always sick. Nathaniel Leonard lamented, "It seems hardly worth while to cure them they get sick so soon again. For my part I am tired of making & giveing quinine pills."[27]

Some slaveholders took preventative steps to ensure the health of their slaves, vaccinating both white and black household members and attempting to protect slaves from unhealthy work conditions, occasionally refusing to hire them out in areas with reported outbreaks of disease. Others expressed concerns that their slaves would contract illnesses by performing particular tasks, although in the end they rarely kept their bonded laborers from their work. Nathaniel Leonard was reluctant to start butchering his 320 hogs, fearing that laboring at such a difficult and wet job in harsh weather would make his slaves sick, although there is little doubt that the butchering was completed that winter.[28]

Slaveholders ultimately were most concerned about permanently losing their slaves to death, but they worried about disrupting the work regime of their farms and plantations as well. One or two incapacitated workers could seriously undermine the ability of small slaveholders to operate their farms, businesses, and homes effectively. Jeanette Leonard and her daughters repeatedly wrote of the difficulties of maintaining suitable standards of housekeeping and hospitality when their slave women were sick: "Our *lady* servants have all been sick Aunt Lydia is confined to the cabin now so you see it is very well we have had no company." Workers who were incapacitated during periods of heavy labor could severely affect the financial bottom line. In May 1848, Nathaniel Leonard hoped to begin his plows in another day and observed, "We are all well but Westly who is laid up with a pain in his side. If he will be fit for duty day after tomorrow I shall think he selected an admirable time to be sick." Both Abiel and Nathaniel Leonard owned and hired a number of slave men to maintain their farming operations. If one of the workers was sick, another usually was able to pick up the slack, but for those with fewer slaves, white family members were required to step in during times of sickness. It was Elvira Scott who maintained the domestic operations of her home while her only slave woman, Margaret, recovered from childbirth.[29]

As was often the case even with white family members, slaveholders usually called in doctors only if the sick did not improve with home care, although oftentimes this step was not taken until slaves already were gravely ill. Payments to doctors for their services were recorded in slaveholders' letters and accounts, as well as in physicians' ledgers. Engaging the services of a doctor was no guarantee of a return to health, however, since nineteenth-century medicine was less than effective and the heroic measures undertaken by physicians sometimes actually made patients sicker. Justina Woods wrote that her mother reluctantly sent for a doctor when a family member was sick: "Ma was afraid to send for fear they would kill him, till she could do no more. She thought it would never do to let him die without a Doctor." Slaveholders hoped that by calling in a physician they might improve the chances of sick patients, as well as feel confident that they had exhausted every effort to save the patient's life.[30]

When slaveholders provided for the well-being of their slaves it is oftentimes difficult to determine whether their interest was of a personal or economic nature, but this was particularly the case on Missouri's small holdings where owners and slaves associated so intimately. Missouri owners expressed concern for their sick and dying slaves in their diaries and correspondences, although it was often apparent from their language that they considered their loss more financial than personal. The Leonards appear to have grieved when their slave man Willis died, and extended family members and friends offered their condolences at the loss of such a trusted and valued servant. The Leonards missed Willis because of their relationship with him, but they also were deeply concerned about who would run the farm in his stead. William Napton was sorry to hear of the illness of his slave woman Nancy after she gave birth in the fall of 1858 and wrote, "I cannot think off very gloomy feelings in thinking of the death of one who has been so long a member of my family & whose presence has become so familiar." He suggested that his wife would also miss Nancy "notwithstanding all her faults." When Nancy actually died a few days later, Melinda Napton expressed regrets about the inadequate medical care provided by local doctors and worried about raising Nancy's three-week-old baby. Melinda would miss Nancy, yet she observed: "She was a servant who gave great dissatisfaction on this farm." In fact, she was the same slave woman whom Melinda earlier had suggested that her husband sell to pay off the family's debts.[31]

The relationships forged between mistresses and slave women on small slaveholdings demonstrate the great tension that existed between familiarity and economic pragmatism. Black and white women were more likely to become enmeshed in one another's lives because of the confined conditions in which they daily lived and worked. Small-slaveholding women's interest in the health of slave women and their babies is an excellent example of this ambiguity. Female relatives, friends, and mistresses usually surrounded new slave mothers when they gave birth. Slave midwives routinely delivered slave babies, although during the years before the Civil War, it became more common to call in doctors for complicated cases. Mistresses attended these births for a number of practical reasons, including accounting for new property and an interest in preserving the health of mothers and babies, but occasionally white women's concerns ran deeper than economic self-interest. Paulina Stratton often attended the births of slave children along with a local slave midwife, but she became more interested in the welfare of babies and their mothers after the death of her own baby daughter Lena in 1852. Former mistress Eliza Cochran remembered being present at the births of Dilsy Lewis's children, "aiding and assisting the mother as a friend and nurse, being interested in her welfare." Former mistress Elizabeth Griffen accounted for her presence at the birth of her slave Mary's child, Ann Eliza, on November 3, 1862, by explaining that she was "interested in the safety and welfare of said Mary, waited on her and assisted her in her confinement and sickness as a friend and nurse." Some mistresses clearly felt connected to slave women through the shared experience of childbirth, although the women never indicated how they felt about the presence—and possible interference—of white women as they delivered their babies.[32]

Similar stories told by three different women—two mistresses and one former slave woman—profoundly suggest the ambiguities and tensions that accompanied the interaction of slave women and mistresses on small holdings. Paulina Stratton, Melinda Napton, and Sarah Graves's mistress, Emily Crowdes, nursed slave babies alongside their own children. Stratton nursed a slave infant because she rejected her mother's milk; Napton nursed a slave baby whose mother was dying; and Crowdes nursed Graves so that her mother could continue working in the fields. All three white women nursed the babies because no slave women were lactating on their farms at the time. Economic considerations clearly played a role in the women's decisions, but Paulina Stratton's diary suggests additional motivations. Understanding the heartache of losing a child, Stratton indicated that she wished to spare the baby's mother similar pain. A fusion of demographics and personal relations led white women to nurse slave babies, something that would likely only happen on small holdings where there was no other alternative. There were, nonetheless, limits to these white women's compassion. Melinda Napton put Nancy's baby on a bottle when she realized that it was too physically straining to nurse both her own baby and the slave infant; Sarah Graves's mother made the decision to take Sarah to the fields when it became clear that Crowdes was too inattentive; and when a white family member became gravely ill and needed care, Stratton stopped nursing the slave child, who died soon after. Clearly these white women prioritized their needs and those of their own families over those of slave infants and mothers. Slave women were never allowed to make that choice, however. They commonly acted as wet nurses to both black and white infants, serving the vitally important role of nourishing other women's babies at the expense of the time and milk that should have been extended to their own children.[33]

Whereas some acts were purely altruistic, more complex motivations inclined most masters and mistresses toward what they perceived as acts

FIGURE 6. Louisa and Harry E. Hayward. Ambrotype. Circa 1858. Louisa was the slave nurse for Harry E. Hayward (c. 1857–1933), who was seated on her lap. George A. Hayward, a St. Louis businessman and investor in New Mexico copper mines, purchased Louisa in 1858 perhaps for the purpose of assisting his wife, Ellen, in caring for their young son. The image suggests the intimate relations that existed between slaveholding family members and their slaves within Missouri's small-slaveholding households, yet it also suggests their complex nature. Courtesy of the Missouri History Museum Photographs and Prints Collections, St. Louis.

of benevolence. Certainly many Missouri slaveholders understood that in their situation kindness was more pragmatic than cruelty. They knew that it was not in their best interest to exploit or abuse their slaves to the extent that they were no longer productive, and, in fact, an appropriate level of attentiveness might ultimately increase the bottom line. Owners also reasoned that slaves worked harder when treated humanely and were less susceptible to rebellion or flight. This simple calculus benefited the master of the former slave Will Daily, who explained that his owner believed that his slaves "was human, wid human feelin's. . . . Course we had to do de right thing but jes' some how did, mos' of de time 'cause he was good to us."[34]

"Mose as usual finds it convenient to cut up some shines"

Although it often proved a double-edged sword, the close proximity in which Missouri slaves and their owners lived and worked at times benefited slaves. Small-scale slavery provided slaves with the tools to shape their relationships with their owners in ways that generally were not possible for the average plantation slave. By virtue of their close daily relations, slaves were well placed to study their owners' personalities and used this knowledge to their advantage, notably by exploiting their masters' and mistresses' personal weaknesses in order to gain greater control over their circumstances. Slaves throughout the South used resistance as a means of negotiating their situation, but these efforts were especially effective on small slaveholdings because they were directed at the individuals with whom slaves shared such a great part of their lives.

The case of Paulina and Thomas Stratton dramatically reveals the masterful strategies slaves employed to gain an upper hand in the small-slaveholding farm's power structure and the effects of this struggle on the relations among the slaveholding and slave members of the household. The Strattons migrated to Cooper County, Missouri, from western Virginia in 1855 with their four children and their eleven slaves. Long before the move to Missouri, the contentious personal relations among the white family members had seriously undermined authority within the Stratton household. During the early years of Paulina's and Thomas's married life, while still living with Thomas's mother, Mary Ann Stratton, a power struggle developed between the two women over control of the household that eventually undermined Paulina's authority over the family's slaves. Paulina claimed that her mother-in-law purposely cultivated this discord, thereby creating a power vacuum that affected her relationships with her servants. Mary Stratton went so far as to disagree with Paulina over the treatment of slaves in front of them. "[G]ave Aga a little whipping about knitting the old lady got very angry allowed I would make a fool of her and said a good many hard things hurt my feelings very much," Paulina once lamented. "It is not the first time she has found fault and taken her part just before her."[35]

The Stratton slaves manipulated the strained relations among white family members to gain personal advantage. During Mary Stratton's lifetime, they understood that there were two mistresses, often with conflicting ideas about running a household and managing slaves, and frequently they played one white women off the other. The slave women became especially adept at telling one mistress stories about the other in order to create conflict. Paulina recorded one such incident: "Patience spun the two days it rained and as usual told stories enough to keep her Mrs in hot water the rest of the week." Paulina concluded that she could better manage her slaves and household affairs if she did not live with her mother-in-law, but her dream of improving her household relations when she and her husband finally secured a home of their own proved naive. Her influence over her slaves, already irreversibly damaged, as was so dramatically exposed when they joined together in common cause against her in Virginia, continued to decline well after Mary Stratton's death and the family's move to Missouri. Thomas also constantly undermined her, which did little to bolster her authority in the household. Capitalizing on their mistress's weaknesses, the Stratton slaves used resistance to register their displeasure and occasionally to improve their circumstances. Paulina reported throughout the years that they often were insolent and disobedient and occasionally even verbally threatened their owners. Despite Paulina's self-professed best efforts, never were the relations within the Stratton household harmonious.[36]

The Stratton slaves were not alone in using the intimate conditions found on Missouri's small holdings as a tool to negotiate power relations within households. Many slaveholders echoed the Strattons' complaints about the verbal resistance of their slaves. The personal interaction between owners and slaves often resulted in a breakdown in deference and moments of defiance of masters' and mistresses' authority. Some slaves subtly, yet effectively, resisted their owners through various forms of deception. The slave trader John White warned his associate to use caution when retrieving a captured runaway slave man, "[He] is exceedingly Smart. he is mild and Smooth and will deceive you if possible.

Place no confidence in him whatever." Other bondpeople outwardly revealed their contempt for their owners' authority, leaving little question in slaveholders' minds as to where they stood with their slaves. Sallie Bedford described the slaves on her mother's farm as acting as if they were "entirely without a master, and serve us through their own good or bad will." Slaves frequently challenged their subservience by verbally expressing to their owners what was on their minds. When the mistress threatened to sell her mother down the river for not performing a task correctly, Lucy Delaney's mother responded that she did not care to live there anyway. The son of James Monroe Abbot's master demanded of the slaves, whom he had recently acquired upon his father's death, that they call him "Mastuh" and his wife "Missus." Abbot's mother publicly humiliated her new master, proclaiming, "I know'd yuh all dese year as Joe an' her as Jane, an' I aint gonna start now callin' you Mastuh or Missus. I'll call you Joe an' Jane like I allus done." Melinda Napton's elderly slave woman Jinney even saucily challenged Napton's right to her labor, stating that she had never wished to be brought to Missouri from the Tennessee home of Napton's father and that the Naptons "required work of her that she was unable to do." Jinney further claimed that she and her children were actually free people. Napton was so appalled by what she believed was the slave woman's impudent behavior that she wrote her husband: "I will not be imposed upon by her any longer, and Papa must either give me another or consent for her to be sold." Jeanette Leonard felt similarly about her slave woman Sally and hoped that her husband would make a deal to sell her, "for I really would give Sally away—before I would be obliged to keep her about me." Slaves may not have actually improved their conditions through these exchanges, but at the very least, they may have served as a way to release pent-up hostilities, providing some satisfaction through the act of confrontation.[37]

The close interaction between owners and slaves appears to have led a few bondpeople to reckon that they had a stake in decisions that affected them and, therefore, had a right to express their opinions. Some successfully altered their circumstances by openly making demands or asking for intercession on their behalf. In the account of his life, Henry Bruce repeatedly described situations when his willingness to speak up altered his situation in a favorable way. Bruce's boasts of his own power to influence his destiny clearly were meant to reinforce his portrayal of himself as a self-made man, but it is not unrealistic to believe that the intimate relations of small-slaveholding households provided the space for negotiation. While his owner was settling the terms of his employment at a Brunswick tobacco factory, Bruce informed his prospective employer that he did not wish to work for him because he had "heard that he was a hard man to please." Bruce took over the negotiations and reached an agreement with Mr. Beasley, while his owner remained silent. Although later chastised by his master for his impertinence, Bruce always believed that he had influenced his employment situation in a positive way. He also claimed that his master acquiesced to his and his brothers' wish to remain in Missouri when he was contemplating migration to Texas.[38]

Some Missouri slaves even attempted to influence the outcome of their own sales. When Smokey Eulenberg's mother refused to leave with a new mistress who had purchased her, her mistress called off the sale. Lucinda Patterson also took control of her fate when she was placed on the auction block at the Cooper County Courthouse. When a reputably cruel man entered the bidding, she spoke up: "Old Judge Miller don't you bid for me, 'cause if you do, I would not live on your plantation, I will take a knife and cut my own throat from ear to ear before I would be owned by you." The man who owned Patterson's father had come to the sale hoping to purchase her but decided against buying such a "sassy" slave girl. Jonathan Ramsay of Callaway County wished to sell his slave man Gery to Abiel Leonard who lived approximately forty miles away in Howard County but was concerned that he would resist the sale. Ramsay did not think Gery would run away, yet he felt "equally confident he will not agree to live with any one at a considerable distance from his wife." Leonard did not buy Gery for this reason; however, there is no record of whether or not he remained near his wife.[39]

As in the case of the Strattons, it was especially common for slaves to use knowledge of the dynamics of the white family relations to manipulate situations by blackmailing their owners or simply enacting vengeance against those who had wronged them. The close living and working situations made it extremely difficult for slaveholders to keep personal information from their slaves, who often used the knowledge gained to their advantage. Lucinda Patterson struck back at her difficult mistress when her master returned from an extended journey. Before he left, the master asked Patterson to report to him if his in-laws, whom he disliked, came to visit in his absence. Patterson was disgruntled with waiting on the mistress's many relatives and tattled on her to the master. Esther Easter took revenge on her master and mistress, both of whom she considered cruel. When her master returned on a furlough during the Civil War, Easter informed him that she had witnessed his wife engaging in sexual relations with a neighbor man through a crack in the wall. Easter believed that the master would have beaten his wife to death upon learning of her betrayal had a relative not stopped by.[40]

Slaves were especially adept at resisting the authority of mistresses because they inherently understood that white women held a weaker position in the power structure of the slaveholding household. Mistresses throughout the South lived with the problem of slave resistance, but structural aspects of small-scale slavery exacerbated the negative effects on white women's authority. Slave men most often tested their mistresses' power, knowing that their ability to physically punish them was circumscribed. Resistance was particularly acute when slaveholding men left the farm on business, whether for a few hours or for days; the scarcity of overseers in Missouri often left the mistress as the sole and final authority in her husband's absence. Judge Charles Yancey frequently traveled, leaving the management of the farm in the hands of his capable wife, Mary, whose letters to her husband chronicled constant struggles with their servants, particularly a man named Mose. As Charles Yancey observed, "Mose as usual finds it convenient to cut up some shines whenever I leave home." When Thomas Stratton was away from the farm, the family's one slave man, Ike, frequently used the opportunity to challenge Paulina's weak authority. Jeanette Leonard and the family slaves successfully operated the farm when her husband, Abiel, was away tending to his legal practice, yet she frequently observed that the slaves did not work as hard as they might have if better supervised. In spite of the fact that most men could physically overpower their mistresses, most slave men shrewdly recognized that they must limit their resistance to more benign acts, such as verbal insolence or neglect of their work. The consequences for attacking a white woman could be grave. Henry Bruce physically resisted punishment at the hands of David Hampton, the nonslaveholding white man who hired him, but recognized that he could not afford to physically engage Hampton's wife when she inflicted a hickory switching upon him. Slave women, like Melinda Napton's Jinney, who claimed she was not legitimately owned by the Naptons, were just as likely to test their mistresses when their masters were away and unable to reinforce the white women's authority, however.[41]

"He will not work but trifles about his business"

The intimacy found in small-slaveholding households was the primary influence on the quality of the relations between owners and their slaves; however, systemic aspects of Missouri slavery provided bondmen and women with additional opportunities for resistance. The tactics slaves used to sabotage the smooth functioning and economic profitability of Missouri farms did not differ significantly from those used in the plantation South, although the impact of this resistance often was greater. On a large plantation, one slave's slow performance, truancy, or theft did not substantially affect the enterprises' overall economic stability. Missouri slaves recognized the immediate and destructive consequences of their resistance to small slaveholders' financial bottom lines, however, and many became expert at undermining the economy of the farms through behavior ranging from theft and work slowdowns to running away and violently resisting their owners' authority. Although the impact of this resistance was mainly financial, Missouri masters and mistresses often were surprised and disappointed when their bondpeople betrayed their trust by engaging in these disruptive activities. The fact that slaves and owners lived and worked so intimately led owners to consider this resistance a personal affront.[42]

Missouri slaves understood that they could severely cripple the smooth operation of the farm by undermining the effectiveness of their labor. They regularly demonstrated their disgruntlement with the daily work regime by performing their tasks in a less than efficient manner, often working slowly or carelessly. As historians have documented elsewhere, slaves meant this economic resistance to signal to their owners that they were dissatisfied with the terms of their labor. Instead, owners often saw this behavior as either a character flaw or a personal slight. Most simply were too close to the situation to step back and see that their people were sending a message about their dissatisfaction with their circumstances. Many slaveholders, like Paulina Stratton and Melinda Napton, interpreted slaves' behavior as laziness rather than resistance. "Aga is very troublesome she is so careless and slovenly we have helped her milk ever since Dilsy was confined," Stratton criticized. Throughout the years Stratton continued to complain about Aga and her fellow slaves' unsatisfactory work habits. She was disgusted that Aga would not maintain her own household economy and neglected to knit her husband, Ike, a pair of winter stockings, work Stratton was forced to complete. At the time, she lamented that working together, all of their slaves "do not do as much work as two ought to do, but I will try and not mind it and take things more as they come." Stratton never considered that Aga might believe that her mistress owed Ike those socks in exchange for his hard labor. The Leonards also faced difficulties with less than diligent workers. In September 1837, they received a letter from F. F. Peake, who with his wife was tending to the Leonards' children and farm while they visited Abiel's family in New York, in which Peake observed of the Leonards' slave man Willis that he "seems to be always engaged—but some how or other he has a wonderful faculty of making 'much ado about nothing' more than any other man of his size I ever knew." Jeanette Leonard often reported to her husband that work on the farm progressed slowly, yet the slave men "seem to be busy all the time."[43]

The consequences of slaves' economic resistance could be profound. Slaves directly assaulted their owners' bottom line when they "stole" supplies from their owners, thereby compromising their carefully guarded and managed food supplies. Slaves likely reasoned that they were entitled to the fruits of their own labor, but the routine theft of food also suggests inadequacies in the diets of many Missouri slaves. Most often slaves sought additional meat, since access to this important dietary element usually was stringently regulated and rationed. Missouri owners, like those elsewhere, were cognizant of the possibility of theft and locked up provisions, especially the meat stored in the smokehouse. At one point, William Napton was concerned that his meat was too rapidly disappearing, and he questioned his wife about the reason for "the failure of the smoke house—do you think the meat has been stolen, or not enough put up?" Eliza Overton stole and killed her master's hog, but before she could boil the water for it, a fellow slave took it from her. She simply went to take another, believing her owner had so many he would not miss it. Overton also frequently purloined the keys to the smokehouse in order to acquire meat. Overton was correct in reasoning that her owner, John Coffman of Ste. Genevieve County, could make do with less. He was a large planter by Missouri standards, who owned eighty-three slaves in 1860. The loss of material resources could be a significant issue on smaller holdings, however. Some slaves chose to demand more provisions rather than take them from their owners. When the Strattons' Ike complained to his mistress that he did not receive enough meat, Paulina acquiesced and gave him and the others more, all the while fearing that her supply would run out. Slaves also took provisions from their owners in order to enhance the variety of their often stark fare. Charlie Richardson's mother cooked flapjacks made from mixings stolen from the big house. She hid the cooked pancakes under a seat cushion when the mistress came to visit her cabin and claimed that the mistress's parrot alerted her to the contraband treat. Another Missouri slave woman's mother told a similar story, but in this case the slaves took revenge on the tattling parrot by attempting to wring its neck. Richardson also revealed that the cook would purposefully burn the master's coffee, knowing he would give the ruined brew to the slaves for their own use.[44]

Legitimate illnesses were quite common in antebellum Missouri, yet it appears that slaves sometimes used sickness as an excuse to absent themselves from their assigned work. Slaveholders often believed that their slaves' physical complaints were exaggerated or faked, but most were reluctant to ignore them in case the illness was indeed legitimate. The fact that the sick individual was often one of only a few adult workers exacerbated slaveholders' concerns about health but of course also made the loss of their labor an even greater hardship. In the end, a few days' less work was preferable to the death of a valuable slave. Bondmen and women likely capitalized on owners' concerns, thereby making feigned illness a particularly effective form of resistance. When Mary Rollins's slave George was bedridden for ten days as the result of an ice-cutting accident, the family doctor informed her that George was feigning his injuries as "an excuse to remain in out of the cold." Abiel Leonard's slave Wesley complained of illness while Leonard was away, but quickly recovered when his master returned. Leonard observed that Wesley was "as lazy as usual" after his speedy recovery and resumption of work. Slave women also perfected behavior that allowed them a brief respite from labor. It was Melinda Napton's inquiry into a feigned illness that precipitated the previously described hostile encounter with her slave Jinney.[45]

Missouri slaveholders' problems with labor discipline were exacerbated by the unique circumstances of small-scale slavery and diversified farming. Owners often gave their slaves, especially the men, considerable responsibility and allowed them liberal freedom of movement in order to run their farms successfully and accommodate the creation and maintenance of abroad slave families. Many men likely recognized their vital importance to the economic success of Missouri's small-slaveholding farms and manipulated the situation to their own benefit. Paulina Stratton, for example, believed that her husband had entrusted Ike with too much responsibility and wrote: "we have lost so much by trusting to Ike that I dread the consequences." Eight months later she complained again: "Ike does not do as he ought his master trusts him and he is not faithful he will not work but trifles about his business." Paulina believed that her husband's faith in Ike was proving to be an economic liability and that the slave man acted as if he thought that he was in charge of the farm. She suggested that Ike appointed himself driver on the Stratton farm—a leadership role accepted by neither her nor, it appears, the other slaves. At one point Ike took it upon himself to whip a fellow bondwoman's two young boys when they misbehaved and the boys' mother threatened to thrash him for his presumptiveness.[46]

Other systemic aspects of Missouri slavery contributed to the difficulties that some owners had managing their slaves. Hiring was perhaps one of the greatest challenges to the maintenance of labor order on Missouri farms, but the situation was even more dire for those who employed slaves. Hiring demanded that bondpeople recognize the authority of two masters, yet hirers were unable to command the same respect—both under the law and in practice—as could owners. Hired slaves used this "dual mastery" to their advantage, as they frequently resisted the authority of the men and women who only temporarily employed them. Hired slaves occasionally sought the protection of their owners if they suffered abuse at the hands of their hirers, playing on owners' suspicions that employers would not have an incentive to protect property that they did not own. As the historian Jonathan Martin has argued, slaves understood their intrinsic value and often gambled that their master or mistress would intervene if they believed they were in danger of physical harm. Some hired slaves ran away to their owners when they felt threatened, although this course was not taken without risk. Hirers apprehended some runaways on the road home, while owners returned others, like William Wells Brown, to their employers. After Betty Abernathy's two brothers ran away from the cruel man who had hired them, their master came to their mother's cabin to send them back. The master beat the boys' mother to force her to reveal where they were hidden. Occasionally slaves' gamble paid off and owners intervened to protect them. Hirers wished to exert mastery over those they hired and were not pleased when their authority was undermined either by hired slaves or their owners. It was not unheard of for disputes to lead to lawsuits and occasionally even violence between hirers and owners. In one case, a Missouri slave woman ran away from an abusive hirer and sought refuge at the home of her mistress, Alvira West. The employer caught up with the slave woman in the front yard of her owner's home and began to severely beat her with a cowhide whip. West, who had recently given birth, heard her slave woman's cries of distress and attempted to usher her into the house. The hirer did not arrest his brutal whipping even though he inevitably struck the white woman in the process. When the two women challenged his masterly prerogative, he became so enraged that he knowingly abused an unrelated white woman—an act that landed him in legal jeopardy.[47]

Dual mastery worked to the advantage of some slaves as they negotiated their relationships with hirers and presented them with opportunities to undermine the authority of their owners after the hiring stint ended. Returning slaves occasionally became management problems for their owners, especially if the lessee was more permissive than the owner. Some hired slaves were given more freedom of movement than their associates who remained at home, and it was often difficult to force recently returned slaves back into the labor routine of the farm. The Leonards became increasingly frustrated by the behavior of their slave man Wesley and blamed it on the liberal mobility granted him by his hirer, carpenter D[aniel] D. Buie. Wesley was leased for the entire year of 1855, but when work slowed in July, Buie allowed Wesley to pay him one dollar a day for time off and granted him permission to travel home to the Leonard farm for his work holiday. Wesley apparently had saved enough money to pay for this privilege. Jeanette Leonard was concerned that the other slave men on the farm were "a little discontented to see him stepping about taking his pleasure, while they are at work," and she threatened to put Wesley to work cutting grass if he stayed much longer. In January 1856, Leonard's brother-in-law William A. Wilson wrote Leonard that many around Marshall considered Wesley to be a "rascal." He had stolen a silk vest worth five dollars from a local merchant, and he and another slave had taken "a spree" to Boonville when Wilson gave him a pass to return to the Leonard farm. Wilson, like many others, was concerned about the many "temptations" for slaves living in a town or city and advised Leonard to hire out Wesley in the country. He also recommended that Leonard find a stricter employer than Buie, observing that "Wesley must have a *master soon* or it will be *too late*." Although Buie wished to hire Wesley again, Leonard decided to lease the slave man to Captain Swinney for the following year, believing that Wesley would benefit from a more structured situation and perhaps a stricter master. Wesley complained of sickness on the eve of his departure, but when the doctor determined that there was little wrong with him Jeanette's suspicions were confirmed that "Wesley's disease was more of the mind than body." Already incensed by his slave man's behavior over the Christmas holiday, Leonard asked his wife to warn Wesley that he had better obey Swinney or "it will be his own fault, and he must submit to the consequences." Apparently Wesley heeded the warning—or perhaps Swinney broke him—because he returned to this same hiring situation for a number of years thereafter.[48]

Some Missouri slaveholders punished slaves for less serious infractions, but resistance was often so relentless that they occasionally ignored subtle offenses or chalked the behavior up to laziness or ineptitude. Few could admit to themselves that their workers were acting out against them, for if they faced this reality it would shatter their belief that they were content in their enslavement. A few implicitly understood that resistance was bondpeople's only means to shape their lives, however, and they recognized that it was in their best interest to compromise with their workers in order to keep them reasonably content and productive. Slaveholders' willingness to negotiate the terms of slaves' labor was vital to the smooth functioning of the small and more vulnerable slaveholdings of Missouri.

"They will not appreciate my motives"

The close interaction between slaves and owners on smaller holdings heightened slaveholders' need to be liked by their slaves and to have their acts of kindness acknowledged and appreciated. The rituals and rhetoric of paternalism were developed not only to help slavery operate smoothly but also to preserve slaveholders' self-image as benevolent Christians and portray them in a positive light to the outside world. Slaveholders were interested in receiving deference and respect from those they owned. Most could not recognize that their slaves never fully bought into paternalism, understanding that it was often more rhetoric than reality. Smallholders lived too closely with and were too emotionally invested in their enslaved people to see this and instead mistakenly believed that they were engaged in relationships based on mutual affection. The very nature of the intimacy found on small-slaveholding farms made it unlikely that the relations between owners and slaves would be anything but fraught with tensions, however. Many slaveholders, such as Paulina Stratton and Priscilla Patton, were disappointed to receive indifference or contempt rather than gratitude from their slaves. Stratton took personally her slaves' acts of resistance and never understood why they did not like her better when she, in her own opinion, had done so much for them. "Negros are the bane of my life," Patton complained in 1855. "I wish to be kind and do right with them but they will not let me they will not appreciate my motives."[49]

The close living and working conditions found among black and white women within small-slaveholding households heightened these tendencies and ultimately led some slaveholding women to express extreme consternation with their circumstances. Mistresses particularly found the responsibility of managing slaves so trying and their relationships with slaves so acrimonious that some claimed that they would prefer to own none. Elizabeth Coleman wrote to her parents that she would rather make do with her daughters' help than with that of her family's two unreliable slave women, but unfortunately "Mr Coleman has a thirst for them." Occasionally these thoughts arose from fear, as when Jeanette Leonard learned that her father's slaves had attempted to poison the family with hemlock root. Her father sold the two likely culprits but was uncertain that he had rid his household of the perpetrators. Although the incident occurred in Kentucky, Leonard was unsettled by the experience, claiming that she would "rather not have a slave at all" than live in constant fear. More typically, slaveholding women simply expressed their frustration with uncooperative slaves. Priscilla Patton hoped to convince her husband to move to the North and free their slaves because "constant worry with the servants" annoyed her. "I do want to free them and move away from them I've thought much on this subject and I know I shall never be happy until I am freed from the responsibility," she wrote in her diary in 1855. "I have hopes of being released from *my bondage* soon My constant thought is to move North where the negro is not held a slave. . . . It has caused me more unhappiness than every thing else in this world. I will get away from it." It is interesting to note that Patton could only envision a slave-free household if she moved outside of the slave states. Although these protestations sound similar to those of plantation mistresses, the impact of resistance was greater on small-slaveholding women whose lives were defined by slaves with whom they shared so much. It was difficult for mistresses, like Paulina Stratton, not to take personally the resistance they encountered rather than recognize that much of it was due to the unique circumstances of small slaveholdings. They instead interpreted resistance as acts of betrayal by people who they believed they knew intimately.[50]

Missourians were extremely sensitive about outsiders' perceptions of their domestic institutions as well. As the historian Melton McLaurin has argued, they understood that the eyes of the nation rested on them once they became embroiled in the dispute over the status of slavery in Territorial Kansas during the 1850s. Missourians not only generally promoted the institution of slavery, but they also wished to represent slavery in their state as especially benign. Missouri slaveholders found it easy to make this case within the state because many people sincerely believed it to be true. Concerns that outsiders would not buy into this rhetoric about milder border-state slavery likely caused some Missourians to put social pressure on those who they deemed had stepped over the line of what was considered acceptable behavior toward their slaves. This public monitoring of the treatment of slaves may have improved conditions for some. In the decades preceding the Civil War, fearing for the stability of slavery, Missourians, like the South's planters, monitored their neighbors' treatment of slaves in order to maintain at least the appearance of humane conditions. They wished for slavery to appear benign to their enemies both inside and outside the state—to free-soilers in Kansas, to abolitionists in the East, and to the increasing number of newly arrived northern migrants. The relatively small size of farms placed slaveholders in close proximity to their neighbors, and, therefore, both black and white Missourians often were aware of how others treated their slaves— whether for good or ill. At one extreme, the neighbors of Gus Smith's master would not allow their slaves to associate with his slaves "for fear we would put devilment in their heads" because they were so well treated and had so much freedom. At the other extreme, a Cooper County slaveholder named Judge Miller developed a reputation in his neighborhood as a brutal master. "He was so cruel all the slaves and many owners hated him because of it," Lucinda Patterson remembered.[51]

Some white Missourians believed that this avid interest in others' business actually resulted in better treatment of slaves. St. Louis antislavery advocate William Greenleaf Eliot claimed that all "cruelty or 'unnecessary' severity was frowned upon by the whole community. The general feeling was against it." He argued that Missouri slavery was comparatively humane and that public opinion supported a milder form of slavery, although he later qualified his statement when he acknowledged that brutalities did exist and were not always openly censured. William Schrader, another white Missourian, agreed: "As a general thing the slaves in our section of Missouri were well treated. I can remember but one instance where an owner gave his slave, a girl about sixteen, unusual punishment, and for this he was cautioned by his slave owning neighbors that it must not occur again." In 1839, Mr. Eustace sued the slave trader John White over the unsound condition of a slave girl bought from him. Eustace's general reputation for inhumane treatment of his slaves was used against him in court, as White's attorney, Abiel Leonard, attempted to prove that it was Eustace's abuse and neglect that led to the girl's death. Occasionally sanctions were brought against offending slaveholders, such as when the Lexington Presbyterian Church suspended William Rowe for cruelty to his slaves or when the state of Missouri indicted Conrad Carpenter for having his slave woman Minerva whipped to death. After admitting his guilt and promising not to repeat the offense, Rowe was reinstated; Carpenter jumped bail and fled. Unfortunately for slaves, public opinion typically censured owners only after the act of cruelty had already been committed. Although the threat of social ostracism may have led some owners to treat their slaves more humanely, more often it only slightly tempered their behavior or caused the offenders to act more secretively. In fact, the legal historian Harriet Frazier believes that in the end this social pressure had little tangible effect. She followed the cases of a number of individuals accused of grossly abusing their slaves, including William S. Harney's infamous murder of his slave woman, and found that while there often was an initial uproar over the incidents, eventually the cruel owners were accepted back into their communities.[52]

"Keep on running away until he made de free state land"

When slaves' and owners' expectations of one another were disappointed and more traditional avenues of negotiation and resistance failed, Missouri's small-slaveholding households occasionally erupted into violence. Southern slavery was fundamentally undergirded by violence; although not all owners maintained their mastery through brutality, the threat of physical abuse was always present. Slaveholders in Missouri, like elsewhere in the South, used this possibility to their advantage as they worked to control the behavior of their bondpeople. Owners also recognized that their slaves could likewise respond to them with physical force. The potential for bloodshed led Missourians to closely monitor the movements and actions of the state's bondpeople, but the threat of slave rebellion also occasionally worked to temper some slaveholders' treatment of their slaves in order to minimize the probability. In the end, most black and white Missourians sought to negotiate the terms of their relationships in order to minimize violent outcomes. That Missouri slaves and owners interacted so intimately made these contestations of household power relations particularly intense, and inevitably these conflicts sometimes disintegrated into extreme responses by one party or the other.[53]

Missouri slaves occasionally resisted their enslavement through dramatic, and even violent, acts of resistance, such as running away, physical confrontations, and murder. The intimacy fostered within small-slaveholding households made these forms of resistance particularly odious to slaveholders and, therefore, more effective than might have been the case on larger holdings. In addition, systemic factors of border-state slavery also played a role in some Missourians' successful struggles against their enslavement. Slaveholders generally felt much more vulnerable to forms of resistance like running away, knowing that their slaves had a much greater chance of making good on their threats.

As was true throughout the South, both men and women engaged in truancy as a means of challenging their enslavement. They routinely responded to unacceptable work conditions or traumatic events by leaving their farms or plantations for short periods—sometimes as a spontaneous response to real or perceived threats of punishment or sale and sometimes in a calculated effort to influence the actions of their owners. Records from southern plantations reveal that incidents of truancy were especially common during the harvest when the work pace, and oftentimes the brutality, of slavery increased. This was true for Missouri slaves as well. Most runaways hid in nearby woods or at a friend's or relative's cabin and returned later to face the consequences, such as when Daniel Abernathy's two slave men came back within a matter of days. The Strattons' Green so feared punishment after he was sent to the mill and came home late that he hid in the stable loft for two days. A former Greene County woman recalled that as a small child she was cared for by a slave woman while her parents were away on a trip. In this somewhat apocryphal tale, the slave woman took the white child and ran away when the man who had been left to manage the farm demanded that she work in the fields rather than watch her white charge as her owners had instructed. The pair remained at large for some time with the assistance of other slaves living in the neighborhood. Mary Anne Phelps Montgomery intended the story as proof of her slave mammy's devotion, but the incident suggests how one slave woman effectively used truancy as a means to resist the authority of a man who was not her owner. The decision to engage in truancy was not made lightly because the consequences could be grave; whippings and occasionally even sale greeted many when they returned from their time at large, although in the end, some owners overlooked these infractions in the interest of putting their absent hands back to work. Lucinda Patterson was angry enough to hide in the woods for several days after her mistress hit her with a hairbrush. Her master sent word out to her that she would not be punished if she returned.[54]

Some, such as Cynthy Logan, were able to influence their treatment through these temporary acts of truancy. Logan's daughter described her mother as half Cherokee, and as always "mad and had a mean look in her eye. When she got her Indian up de white folks let her alone. She usta run off to de woods till she git over it. One time she tuk me and went to de woods an' it was nigh a month fore dey found her." Madison Frederick Ross also used Native American heritage as an explanation for the effectiveness of his grandfather's resistance, claiming that he "was mos'ly Indian an he usta go out into the woods an' stay for days at a time." These Missouri slaves apparently embraced what they believed to be positive Native American attributes, especially the ability to live off of the land while at large. Historians of Native American and African American interaction have shown that black Americans frequently imagined "Indian Country" as a place of freedom, and perhaps they believed that connecting themselves with what they considered effective resistance traits was a step toward freedom.[55]

Following patterns similar to elsewhere in the South, Missouri slave women more frequently opted for truancy rather than risk a true runaway attempt. Historians of American slavery often have described truancy and running away in gendered terms, arguing that men more frequently and successfully sought their freedom through running away, while women usually were constrained by restricted mobility and motherhood. Despite Missouri slave women's close proximity to the free states, the odds of successful flight were not great because women often had their children in tow. It also was less common to see women traveling the countryside unaccompanied, and the presence of children made fugitives even more conspicuous. In addition, Missouri slave women's work generally tied them to home, and, therefore, they had less extensive knowledge than men of local roads and byways, while conversely they were extremely familiar with nearby woods and the location of enslaved neighbors' homes—both potential shelters for truants. Cultural expectations within the slave community also made it unlikely that women would choose to leave their children behind if they attempted permanent escape. All of these considerations led to greater rates of truancy than fugitive status among slave women.[56]

In contrast to many scholars' descriptions of truancy and runaway attempts elsewhere, in Missouri men still were more likely to strike out for permanent freedom, but both men and women routinely engaged in truancy as a means of challenging the conditions of their enslavement. These high levels of truancy were primarily a consequence of the liberal mobility that resulted from small-scale slavery. Missouri slave men had an understanding of the local geography because their owners allowed them to move about for work, family, and social reasons, and they used their knowledge of the terrain, as well as the fact that white Missourians were used to seeing enslaved men on the roads, to their advantage when attempting to run away either temporarily or permanently. Women also moved about in Missouri, but were relatively more constrained than men, thus raising more suspicions if they were observed away from home. Similar patterns likely existed in other small-slaveholding regions.[57]

Even though most enslaved Missourians remained in their local neighborhoods when they absconded, many slaveholders believed that their bondpeople would leave the state in search of their freedom. As the antebellum years progressed, slaveholders increasingly feared that the precarious location of the state, coupled with the threat of antislavery agitators, would influence their slaves to flee. Free states or territories surrounded Missouri on three sides, foreign-born and northern immigrants flooded into the state after the 1830s, and the political crisis in Kansas during the 1850s all concerned slaveholders. Missourians were particularly alarmed by the unobstructed border between Missouri and Kansas south of the great bend in the Missouri River, especially after Kansas Territory was opened for settlement in 1854 and opponents of slavery flooded into the new land.[58]

Missouri slaveholders' worst fears were confirmed by the infamous 1841 slave-stealing case of Alason Work, a Quincy, Illinois, divinity professor and his two students, James Burr and George Thompson, who were convicted of enticing Marion County, Missouri, slaves to escape. The men's imprisonment created a stir in antislavery circles; letters and petitions flooded into the Missouri governor's office pressing for their release, and none in fact served his full sentence. Harriet Frazier has determined that forty-two individuals served time in the Missouri State Penitentiary between 1837 and 1865 for the crime of slave stealing. In May 1846 Mr. Whitman, possibly a member of a traveling circus, was arrested in Perry County and served two years for attempting to steal a slave, for example. Perhaps the most notorious and successful slave-stealing incident occurred in late December 1858 when John Brown and a group of Kansas free-soilers liberated eleven Bates County slaves, killing a white man in the process. Brown escorted the runaways through Kansas, northward up the Lane Trail, which was named after free-soil politician James Lane, through Nebraska, Iowa, Illinois, and eventually into Canada. It was after this trip that Brown began to actively plan his raid on Harper's Ferry. Early the following year, Platte County slaveholders captured a large group of runaway Missouri slaves in Kansas Territory. Three white men, including New Yorker John Doy, were found in the company of the fugitives and were charged with slave stealing in the state of Missouri. After a mistrial and a change of venue, only Doy was tried and convicted of enticing a Platte County slave to flee, although soon after the verdict was rendered, three of Doy's friends broke him out of the Buchanan County jail. In 1859, the citizens of one Mississippi River county petitioned the county court for the creation of a patrol to protect their slaves from abduction by what they described as a gang of free blacks and abolitionists from Illinois. Missourians commonly focused on the nefarious activities of outside agitators both within the state and on its borders rather than face the reality that slaves most often made their own decisions to seek freedom without any outside encouragement. In most cases, abolitionists rendered assistance only after Missouri slaves had successfully escaped onto free soil.[59]

Slaveholders' fears were grounded in some sense of reality, however, since over the years a number of Missouri slaves successfully achieved their liberty in the free states and Canada. Contemporary newspapers were filled with advertisements for runaways, and references to escapes were scattered throughout former slaves' accounts and slaveholders' papers. For those who did run away, the chances of success, at least compared with bondpeople in the Deep South, were increased by the state's geography. Mark Twain's *Huckleberry Finn* is a fictional account, yet it realistically portrays the possibilities the rivers held for escape. Although Jim and Huck hoped to ride the Mississippi River to freedom, real Missouri slaves preferred simply crossing over the river to freedom in Illinois. In 1847 an entire family, including three children ages four through twelve, escaped in this manner, likely traveling in a covered wagon in the company of a white man. Richard Graham of St. Louis County in 1854 petitioned the court for permission to retrieve four escaped slave men in Illinois, while that same year, A. King advertised a reward for the capture of his twenty-year-old slave girl, Ann. In the 1850s, the beacon of freedom shone brightest in Kansas, where many western Missouri slaves believed they would receive assistance from the antislavery settlers who were pouring into the territory. Some northwest Missouri slaves, such as the man Doy was convicted of enticing to freedom, escaped into Kansas Territory by commandeering small boats or simply walking across the frozen Missouri River in wintertime.[60]

The active commercial river trade provided additional opportunities for slaves who sought their freedom. The unique circumstances of slaveholders who hired slaves out as riverboat crewmen provide excellent examples of how the state's geography enhanced the possibility of successful escape. Missouri court records are filled with cases of slaveholders who filed suits against boat owners for recovery of the value of the bondpeople who they often accidently transported to free soil. In some cases, slaves stowed away on vessels, and in others, boat owners accepted

$100 REWARD:

R AN AWAY from the subscriber, living in Boone county, Mo. on Friday the 13th June,

THREE NEGROES,

VIZ DAVE, and JUDY his wife; and JOHN, their son. Dave is about 2 years of age, light color for a full blooded negro— is a good boot and shoe maker by trade : is also a good farm hand. He is about 5 feet 10 or 11 inches high, stout made, and quite an artful, sensible fellow. Had on when he went away, coat and pantaloons of brown woollen jeans, shirt of home made flax linen, and a pair of welted shoes. Judy is rather slender made, about 28 years old, has a very light complexion for a negro ; had on a dress made of flax linen, striped with copperas and blue ; is a first rate house servant and seamstress, and a good spinner, and is very full of affectation when spoken to. John is 9 years old, very likely and well grown ; is remarkably light colored for a negro, and is cross-eyed. Had on a pair of brown jeans pantaloons, bleached flax linen shirt, and red flannel one under it, and a new straw hat.

I will give the above reward and all reasonable expenses, if secured any where out of the State, so that I can get them again, or $50 if taken within the State—$30 for Dave alone, and $20 for Judy and John, and the same in proportion out of the state. The above mentioned clothing was all they took with them from home, but it is supposed he had $30 or $40 in cash with him, so that he may buy and exchange their clothing.

WILLIAM LIENTZ.

Boone county, Mo. June 17, 1834:   52-2

the word of slaves who represented themselves as free people. A number of owners sued for the loss of individuals hired out to work on riverboats, although these suits generally met with little success. When one owner of an escaped slave sued a riverboat captain for damages, the Supreme Court of Missouri considered the precariously close location of Missouri to the free states and the difficulty of "retaining negroes in slavery" in deciding the case. The court argued that slaveholders accepted the risk for escape when they hired out their slaves on riverboats. Indeed, William Wells Brown took advantage of a riverboat trip up the Ohio River with his master to successfully escape. In the years before and during the Civil War, slaves also took advantage of the recently built railroads for their runaway attempts.[61]

There is no question that many Missouri slaves attempted to run away to free states and territories, and a number were successful. George Bollinger's father ran away when he learned that his owner planned to sell him to a slave trader and financed his flight with the money that he had saved from making baskets at night. "I ain't never seed my 'pappy' since. Las' I hurd a' him he was in 'Indiana,'" his son later explained. Madison Frederick Ross's grandfather crossed the Mississippi River from Scott County in southeastern Missouri and eventually escaped to Canada. Ross remembered that his grandfather "usta write tuh Old Mastuh an' he'd read the lettuhs tuh us." In December 1845, Beverly and Rachel, two slaves belonging to Captain W. D. Swinney, were captured in Franklin County and held in the Gasconade County jail about sixty miles down the Missouri River from their Howard County home. A few days later,

FIGURE 7 (opposite page). Fugitive slave advertisement. *Columbia Missouri Intelligencer,* June 21, 1834. William Leintz, a Boone County slaveholder, advertised for the return of his three slaves in the *Missouri Intelligencer,* a newspaper that served the residents of central Missouri. Although it was most common for slave men to run away unaccompanied by women and children, in this case a husband and wife absconded with their young son. The advertisement suggests both the type of work done by Missouri slaves and the clothing that they wore. The 1830 federal census indicates that Leintz was a substantial slaveholder by Missouri standards; he owned nineteen slaves in 1830 and twenty-six in 1840. It is unknown whether Leintz captured his slaves, although there was no adult slave man listed in 1840. If Dave, Judy, and John were captured—as was most often the case in Missouri—Leintz may have sold them away as punishment. Courtesy of the State Historical Society of Missouri.

they broke jail and were presumed on their way to St. Louis. Other fugitives ran toward loved ones rather than the free states. A St. Louis slaveholding woman Anne Lane was distressed that a favored slave man named Pompey had "gone coon," yet she approved of his reasons for absconding, musing: "Poor Pompey! I am glad he had so good a reason for running away most men run *from* instead of *to* their wives." There is no indication in her future correspondence that Pompey ever returned.[62]

Accounts of successful runaways, especially those spirited away by abolitionists, were greatly exaggerated, however. As in the rest of the South, most runaway attempts proved futile. In fact, most fugitives were caught before they left the state, often even before they left their own neighborhoods. Owners raised the alarm locally and frequently took out advertisements in regional newspapers. It was difficult for runaway slaves to travel through the state undetected because most white Missourians were suspicious of unfamiliar black travelers and presumed they were on the run. Twice Stephen Hempstead wrote of his slaves running away from his home near St. Louis; both were caught and eventually sold south to New Orleans. Nonslaveholder Archibald Hager also repeatedly wrote of Perry County masters searching for their runaway slaves. Hager captured Joseph Abernathy's Miles only for the slave man to run away again three weeks later, and Hager's neighbor "Ciron Abernathy caught Mr Minsters negrow man that has bin runaway for along time." Missouri citizens were encouraged to apprehend fugitive slaves both by a financial incentive stipulated by state law and reward money offered by individual owners. These attempts to capture runaways were made at some risk to the pursuer as well as to the fugitive. Seneca T. P. Digges, a Howard County slaveholder, continued to chase a suspected runaway named John Anderson even after he brandished a dagger. Once cornered, Anderson administered stab wounds that eventually led to Digges's death, while the slave man successfully escaped to freedom in Canada.[63]

Runaway Missouri slaves were just as likely to be captured in bordering free states and territories, especially after the passage of the 1850 Fugitive Slave Law. Not only did owners hunt their runaways—or employ others to do so—but many citizens of Illinois, Iowa, and Kansas happily collected payment for their efforts. During his first escape attempt, William Wells Brown and his mother crossed the Mississippi on a stolen raft into Illinois, where they quickly were captured. The separate escapes of two Boone County slaves in 1857 were reported in letters exchanged between James and Mary Rollins and their son Jim who attended West Point. One slave man was retrieved from St. Joseph, Missouri, and the other from Springfield, Illinois. William Schrader told of the unsuccessful escape from Chariton County of his slave acquaintance Abe Sportsman. The slave man and two others sought safety in Iowa, but instead, a farmer, to whom they appealed for food, chased, captured, and returned them for expected compensation. Occasionally runaway attempts ended tragically, such as when Charlie Lewis tried to escape sale south by crossing the Mississippi River into Illinois. Lewis's wife, Floretta Castleman, was informed that her husband was injured and died while crossing the river. She always believed that he had perished as reported; however, this interesting story raises the question as to whether the cause of Lewis's death was as accidental as described.[64]

In reality, slaveholders' fears should have been calmed by the active presence of slave patrols throughout the state. In 1825 the Missouri General Assembly enacted a statute to establish slave patrols to regulate the local slave population. White men actively participated in maintaining Missouri's slavery regime, often through community-sanctioned intimidation and violence, by their service on their neighborhood slave patrol. Controlling the movement of slaves was the primary purpose of patrollers, although they were also on the lookout for signs of illegal activities, such as buying and selling goods, and unsanctioned gatherings of bondpeople. Patrollers generally worked to maintain labor discipline and thwart rebellion, but they also captured runaway slaves. Although generally not officially employed as slave catchers, patrollers were familiar with local slaves and often were enlisted to keep an eye out for those who had absconded. Sam Ralston, writing from Missouri's western border in 1844, encouraged friends to move there, arguing that they need not be concerned about the safety of their slave property: "The Negroes that ran away last fall have all been taken, and their owners have sent them to N. Orleans, this will deter others from a similar movement, we have had an active patrol established, these together will ensure perfect safety to the owners of Negroes, and will encourage many persons to become citizens of our county who hitherto have been afraid in consequence of our border location."[65]

As suggested by Ralston, many slaves did not run because they inherently understood that success was unlikely and they feared the potential consequences of an unsuccessful attempt. Slaveholders throughout Missouri made slaves fully aware of what might happen to them if they failed, and most heeded these warnings. "Mistress always told us dat if we run away somebody would catch us and kill us. We was always scared when somebody strange come," Emma Knight remembered of her childhood.

Certainly slaves' fears of punishment if they were captured were not unfounded. They understood that they were likely to suffer violence at the hands of those who caught them and yet again when they were returned to their owners. Mary Martha Bolden witnessed her master and two other men unmercifully whip three male slaves for running away. Esther Easter also recalled the example made of one runaway slave from a neighboring farm: "[T]here was a public whipping, so's the slaves could see what happens when they tries to get away. The runaway was chained to the whipping post, and I was full of misery when I see the lash cutting deep into the boy's skin. He swell up like a dead horse, but he gets over it, only he was never no count for work no more." The experience made a lasting impression on Easter. She claimed that when she threatened her master soon after that she would run away, he ignored her act of defiance knowing that she would not "run away 'cause of the whips." Whether or not they received physical punishment, unsuccessful fugitives knew that they, like Hempstead's slaves, risked sale away from family and friends. William Anderson told of two young slave men who were auctioned off for sale in Lexington, Missouri, "[b]oth of the Boys had run off previously and one of them got as far as Kansas."[66]

Many Missouri slaveholders held on to the belief that their slaves might be tempted to flee even though not that many slaves actually ran away to surrounding free soil. The fear, bordering on hysteria for some, played a large role in Missourians' desire to secure Kansas for slavery, especially after it became clear that a number of antislavery settlers were moving into the territory. Some Missouri slaves brazenly exploited this paranoia. John Woods's young slave man Wert tested his master's authority by bragging to his fellow slaves that if Woods punished him he would run away. Wert gambled that he could ensure better treatment for a while, although he eventually made good on his threat to run. Spotswood Rice's master acted so cruelly toward him that he asked to be sold to a slave trader. When the master would not sell him, Rice told him "dat if he whipped him again, he would run away again, and keep on running away until he made de free state land." The master so valued Rice as a worker that he treated him better thereafter in an effort to keep him from fleeing. When Missouri slaves threatened to run, slaveholders took the threat seriously, and some appear to have been more careful about provoking slaves that they considered a flight risk.[67]

Missouri slaves lashed out against their enslavement in more dramatic and violent ways than simply fleeing. The intimacy of small slaveholdings had the potential to lead to volatile relations between owners and slaves, and when the tensions between Missouri slaves and their owners became too great, the situation could rapidly deteriorate. Although it was most often slaveholders who physically abused their slaves—sometimes with measured forethought and sometimes in the heat of passion—Missouri bondpeople occasionally violently lashed out at their owners as well.

Although physical punishment was routinely used as a method of slave discipline, emotions often were so raw within small-slaveholding households that everyday interactions frequently turned violent. Paulina Stratton cracked Aga with a stick when she refused to do work requested of her, and the angry slave woman, who believed she had been unfairly disciplined, physically resisted her mistress. Stratton recounted the altercation from her perspective: "[Aga] caught hold of the stick and would not let it go I then picked up the poker and we had a scuffle for It and She either hit her Temple against the house or I hit her I do not know but she got a good knock and a black eye and let the Poker go." Stratton regretted the incident, not because Aga was hurt or because her actions were unbecoming for a Christian, but because she "was wrong in contending with her she had double my strength and might have hurt me." It is not surprising that slaves attempted to physically assault owners of the same gender or age, but they occasionally were emboldened to act out against those who presumably were more physically powerful than themselves. James Monroe Abbot's mother dramatically showed her contempt for her owner one day as she chewed a plug of tobacco while hoeing a field of corn. When her master demanded that she swallow the tobacco, she asked him why he did not swallow his own, and he responded by whacking her with a doubled-up rope. "Den she grab huh fingers roun' his throat, an his face wuh all black es my own fore dey pulls her offen him," Abbot explained. Even children sometimes responded with violence when slaveholding family members abused them. Mary Armstrong's cruel master and mistress gave her as a gift to their kind daughter when she married. When the former mistress attempted to whip her, Armstrong picked up a rock and hit her in the eye. Mary's new mistress expressed the opinion that her mother had gotten what she deserved.[68]

The threat of extreme punishment was the most common trigger for slaves' physical resistance to their owners. Fil Hancock's uncle fought back when his master attempted to whip him, and Hattie Matthews's "grandmuthuh got whipp'd only onc't an de master wuz sorry cause she fought back." Some vigorously defended themselves, especially when whipped for the first time. Samuel Ralston wrote of the difficulty he faced when he attempted to punish his slaves Sam and Dill: "Last night they gave me a great deal of impertinence they told me they did not want to live with me. I undertook to whip them and they ran away." Ralston found the slave men back at work the next morning and tried to punish them with the assistance of a man named Mr. Hill, but Sam defended himself with both an ax and a butcher knife. Brandishing a pistol, Ralston and Hill eventually overpowered Sam and another slave Riley but not before Dill ran away. "I corrected Sam & Riley, and made the former say that he would never do it again," Ralston reported. "This is the first time that I whipped any of them, and they began to think that I dare not do it, and were very saucy." William Wells Brown remembered a local slave man named Randall who repeatedly boasted that he would rather die than be whipped by a white man. When the master was away serving in the state legislature, the overseer unsuccessfully attempted to whip Randall and had to call in three white men to assist him. In the end, they shot Randall in order to subdue him enough to administer the whipping. Violent resistance mounted by slaves such as Randall and Hattie Matthews's grandmother may have led some owners to think twice about physically disciplining their slaves.[69]

The ultimate form of resistance was when slaves took a life; some deprived owners of their human property through abortion, suicide, or infanticide, while others murdered members of the slaveholding family. Slaves were most likely to resort to these desperate acts when they felt threatened, and frequently they turned this violence on themselves. Despondency over separation from loved ones and fear of the unknown—especially if propelled into the interstate slave trade—led a number of slaves to take their own lives. James Fenton sued to recoup his losses when his newly purchased slave girl hanged herself before he could take possession of her. William Wells Brown witnessed a slave woman who leaped to her death from a steamboat rather than be taken south, and another young slave man, en route to the Deep South, jumped overboard and was killed when struck by the boat's paddle wheel. Other bondmen and women chose death over continued physical or sexual abuse. A St. Joseph slave woman broke free from a beating administered by her master and plunged into and drowned in the Missouri River. Henry Bruce told of another slave woman who drowned herself in the river rather than face the public humiliation of an out-of-wedlock pregnancy. Bruce attributed the suicide to the girl's sense of honor and propriety, although the general tolerance of premarital pregnancy in the slave community suggests that a white man may have been the father. The rivers figure prominently in enslaved Missourians' stories of escape from bondage, but in these cases, the waters beckoned bondpeople to a permanent and tragic form of freedom. Occasionally suicides were reported without any explanation of a trigger, as when Samuel Sutherland received news in a letter that "Robt Gardner's negro man hung himself last Saturday Morning the cause I do not know."[70]

Although infanticide was uncommon among slaves, there were a small number of cases of slave women who killed their own children. A Callaway County woman named Jane gave her child a high dose of laudanum and then smothered her. Jane's motive remains unknown, although she may have been unwilling to raise her child in bondage. A Marion County woman's motive for murdering her children is starkly clear, however. When she learned that her three sons were sold away from her, she struck them down with an ax and then turned the weapon on herself.[71]

White Missourians always knew that there was a possibility that their slaves might violently turn against them; however, they only rarely gave voice to these fears, perhaps suggesting their reluctance to acknowledge the flaws in their system of racial and class subjugation. A few Missouri slaves murdered members of the slaveholding household, most often in self-defense, retaliation for abuse, or in response to a stressful or threatening situation. A faithful and trusted middle-aged slave man named George refused to assist in disciplining another slave man, and the mistress threatened to have him sold when her husband returned from a trip to St. Louis. George murdered his mistress with an ax a few days later. Believing he had fled, the citizens of Monroe County searched for George and eventually found him with a self-inflicted gunshot wound to the head. When those accused of murder were caught, they usually were summarily tried, convicted, and executed for their crimes, as was the case of the sixteen-year-old slave boy Henry, who shot his owner to protect himself from a whipping, and the well-documented case of the sexually abused slave woman Celia, who murdered her master. If no confession was forthcoming, interrogators routinely threatened the accused or their friends and family in order to extract testimony favorable to conviction. Such was the case of a Lincoln County slave boy named Ellick, who, under threat of hanging, fingered his mother, Fanny, as the person who murdered the white neighbor's children.[72]

Occasionally slaves banded together to murder white Missourians, as was the case in Boone County in 1843, when three male and two female slaves murdered their master with an ax—seemingly a weapon of choice among the enslaved. In the late 1850s, two Randolph County slave men allegedly attacked their owner with a poker and a shovel while he slept. Slaves killed relatively few whites, but these crimes were so sensationalized that many slaveholders feared they too might fall victim to violence at the hands of their bondmen and women. Most frightening was the notion that the assault could come at any time and from those with whom they lived and worked so closely. The *Liberty Tribune* published a story in 1850 decrying the fact that "a family cannot sit down to partake at their own table with impunity; or retire to their own beds without being made a victim to the murderous and vindictive slaves." This editorial outrage was the result of two reported cases of poisoning; one in which a gentry woman was poisoned in her bed by her house servant and another in which an entire family was made ill by arsenic-laced coffee. The family's slave woman had scraped up the poison that was "spread beneath the kitchen floor."[73]

Along with enslaved people killing those who owned them, white Missourians feared the possibility of larger, organized slave revolts. Incidents of slave insurrection were rare in the state, but as was the case throughout the South, white Missourians were concerned about the potential for unrest among the local slave population. An aborted slave insurrection plot was reported in the Fulton area in 1842, and a group of slaves successfully attacked their owners, resulting in the death of one white man, near Bolivar in late 1859. The hysterical response to this 1859 revolt likely had more to do with the climate of fear that reigned throughout the South in the aftermath of John Brown's Raid than any real danger of insurrection. The threat appeared real in 1849, however, when a group of approximately thirty Lewis County slave men and women belonging to four different owners armed themselves with an assortment of weapons, including three guns, and attempted to make their way to freedom. They initially stood their ground when confronted by their pursuers, but after one runaway man was shot, the others eventually surrendered. Sale in the St. Louis slave market was the fate of most of the rebellious Canton slaves. It was noted at the time that other local slaves had fled, leading many whites to conclude that "it was intended to be a general insurrection, and, to that end, it is believed that nearly all the slaves in the county had notice." Acknowledging the potential for collective violence, Missourians enacted laws that made it illegal for slaves to congregate without a white person present, organized neighborhood slave patrols, and vigilantly watched for signs of trouble.[74]

"Some masters was good an' some was bad"

The intimacies of small-slaveholding households in some cases resulted in better material conditions and undoubtedly allowed slaves increased latitude in altering their relationships with their owners through resistance, yet this intimacy by and large had profoundly negative consequences for Missouri slaves. Nothing changed the fact that slaves were the property of their owners, and even if complete domination was not possible, slaveholders controlled vital aspects of slaves' lives. A cruel master or mistress could inflict devastating blows, and there were few, if any, checks on slaveholder abuses. Many owners pushed slaves to their physical limits in order to extract the most work out of them, especially since each laborer was crucial to the economic well-being of most Missouri farms, and the give-and-take of the relations of farm life regularly exploded into violence, frequently leading to exploitation, neglect, and physical abuse.

On balance, the close living and working conditions were at the least a nuisance for slaves, who had little time free from the watchful gaze of the owners who worked alongside them. The close quarters in which black and white Missourians lived also left enslaved families little time alone together. Worse, many masters and mistresses believed that they had the right to interfere directly in their bondpeople's personal lives. The fact that slaveholders felt a sense of intimacy with their slaves, which they oftentimes naively believed was reciprocated, exacerbated this tendency. Paulina Stratton constantly attempted to convert her slaves to her evangelical faith and closely monitored their moral behavior, even confronting her slave woman Aga about her extramarital sexual activities, for example. Similarly, William Wells Brown's mistress hoped to romantically match him with a woman of her choosing rather than his own. When she realized that he loved another woman, she attempted to buy her for him, despite his wish not to marry while still enslaved.[75]

On farms, as in plantation households, intimacy at its worst led to the sexual abuse of slave women by white men: the close living and working conditions increased the chances that slave women would attract the attention of those men residing in the household. Scattered throughout the historical record are references to interracial relationships. A number of former Missouri slaves claimed that their fathers were members of the white family, and many others spoke of parents and grandparents who were the result of such unions. The historian Paul Escott calculated that throughout the South as a whole 6 percent of former slaves interviewed by the WPA claimed that their fathers were white, but members of the slaveholding family accounted for nearly 12 percent of the fathers of the former Missouri slaves interviewed. And although the racial classifications recorded by the census enumerators were highly subjective, 14 percent of Chariton, Clay, Cooper, Marion, and Ste. Genevieve County slaves in 1850 were listed as "mulatto," and in 1860 that number had increased to 18 percent. The intimacy of small slaveholding resulted in a variety of possible relationships between slaveholding men and slave women—ranging from violent rapes to something resembling more consensual relationships. In Missouri, there were fewer slave women living on each slaveholding, and, thus, individual women were statistically more likely to experience sexual pressure or abuse from the white men residing within their households than was the case on larger slaveholdings. Yet, the confines of small-slaveholding households also created the possibility that genuine bonds of love and affection might occasionally develop across the color line.[76]

As was the case on plantations, a few slave women pragmatically entered into long-term sexual liaisons with their masters, perhaps gambling that the relationship would improve both their own and their children's lives. Indeed, a few women and children were better cared for and spared physical punishment or sale. "My mother was the house-girl in a way she was the mistress of her master because he was the father of all my brothers and sisters," Phannie Corneal recalled. "He freed her before the Civil War and her and us children was treated better than the other slaves on the place. She continued to stay there after her freedom." Charles Younger sent his racially mixed son, Sim, to school at Oberlin College in Ohio, and both Alice Freeman and Mrs. James O'Donnel claimed that their white fathers gave them money or land at emancipation.[77]

In 1850, Eli Keen, a resident of St. Charles County, and his slave Phoebe entered into what was by all accounts a loving relationship that produced eight children and lasted for thirty-five years. The historian Kimberly Schreck and others have argued that families such as the Keens managed to successfully merge family and slavery precisely because of the power that southern white men wielded in southern society. Although not everyone in the neighborhood approved of interracial families, few people, including southern judges and juries, disputed the right of white men to establish these unconventional conjugal arrangements within their own households. In the case of Eli Keen and his family, it was not until after his death in 1901—well after slavery's end—that his right to treat his mixed-race children as family was disputed. Keen left his St. Charles

County property to his "beloved children" in his will, a bequest success-fully overturned by the white woman whom he had married when his common law marriage with Phoebe ended.[78]

The decision to acquiesce to sexual relations with a white man was made at some risk, however. These encounters were a result of vastly un-equal relationships of power that at their foundation rested on the threat of violence and, therefore, could never by truly consensual. The fact re-mained that as white men and masters they held ultimate control over enslaved women's destinies. Promises made by masters to slave women were easily broken if their feelings changed or if they were faced with pressure from white family members. Heirs routinely contested wills made by white men with good intentions toward slave lovers and their mixed-race children. Other white fathers were never kind to their slave children, in some cases ignoring their existence and in others selling them away in order to maintain peace within the white family or hide visible evidence of their indiscretions. Annie Bridges, a former slave, re-membered "a white man who had a child by one ob his slaves an' den sold de chil' as a slave. Was'nt dat tarrible, sellin' his own son?" The white father of Harriet Casey's uncle also sold him.[79]

A much larger number of slave women entered into long-term sexual relationships with white men because of threats, coercion, and even bru-tal force. William Wells Brown wrote that a "quadroon" named Cyn-thia was presented with two equally horrible choices: become the sexual partner of the slave trader Mr. Walker or be sold south; in the end she chose Walker. A few women successfully repelled the advances of their owners, but most often the consequences of resistance were dire. William Greenleaf Eliot witnessed a young slave woman "tied up to the joist by her thumbs, so that her feet scarcely touched the ground, stripped from her shoulders to the hips, and a man standing by her with cowhide-whip in hand." The woman was beaten for failing to "'submit to the wishes' of her master." Some women eventually gave in rather than continue to face physical and psychological abuse. Either way, slave women were forced to suffer the brutality of sexual acts to which they did not freely consent. A case in point is the awful experience of the fourteen-year-old slave girl named Celia, mentioned earlier, who was raped by her new owner, Robert Newsom, on his return trip from purchasing her. Likely seeing no alternative, Celia continued to engage in sexual relations with the widower Newsom and bore him two children over the next five years. She eventually attempted to extricate herself from the situation after she became romantically involved with a fellow slave man, but breaking off a relationship with an unwilling white man was virtually impossible. Newsom tried to force himself on Celia after she unequivocally told him that she would no longer sleep with him, and she defended herself when he lunged at her by twice hitting him over the head with a large stick, killing him instantly. She later disposed of his body in her burning fireplace. After lengthy legal wrangling, including a plea of self-defense, Celia eventually was convicted and executed for the killing. A number of Missouri slave women were brutally assaulted and raped by white men, including Mary Estes Peters's mother, who experienced an especially horrific rape at the hands of her mistress's three teenage sons. "While she was alone, the boys came in and threw her down on the floor and tied her down so she couldn't struggle, and one after the other used her as long as they wanted for the whole afternoon . . . that's the way I came to be here," Peters explained.[80]

Ruth Allen succinctly described the limited control that slave women had over their own bodies and sexuality: "My mother was a slave, an' me daddy, the ol' devil was her ol' white master. My mammy didin' have any more to say about what they did with her than the rest of the slaves in them days." George Jackson Simpson agreed: "What was done in slavery days, was simply done and not much thought of it." Simpson's choice of words is curious. It seems highly unlikely that slave victims of sexual abuse did not think about what had happened to them. What was more likely is that they did not feel free to express their feelings about their abuse to either those who victimized them or within their own families and communities. White men's access to slave women's bodies took a large toll on slave men as well. Many could not tolerate the thought of their wives or lovers with another man—even though the women generally had no choice in the matter. That white men took sexual liberties with black women was considered a galling affront to black men's already bruised sense of their masculinity. Unfortunately, as with white women, black men sometimes blamed the victims. Lewis Washington separated from his first wife, Phebe, because "a white man got between him and her and he just quit her right there." Celia's desperate attempt to break off her relationship with Newsom was instigated by her slave lover's unrealistic demand that she end it, and his ultimatum ultimately led to Newsom's death, as well as her own.[81]

White men's sexual relations with slave women placed terrible strains on their own families as well. The acknowledgment of these relationships might cause tremendous discord within white families, although slave women and children in most cases paid a greater price than the white perpetrators. Mary Estes Peters wrote of how threatened her white family felt by her existence: "[T]hey didn't like my mother and me—on account of my color. They would talk about it. They tell their children that when I got big enough, I would think I was good as they was. I couldn't help my color. My mother couldn't either." Ruth Allen told of a master who deeply regarded his slave woman and their five children. After both his wife and his lover died, he gave each of his nine white and mixed-race children farms; however, his white children "never had nothin' to do with the others, 'though they wan no better. All o' the colored ones was fair." Ruth Allen may have had strong feelings about what she saw as the unfair nature of whites' strict racial code, particularly focusing on the value that white people placed on appearances, because she was herself the child of a slave woman and her master. Three-year-old Allen and her mother were sold when her father "saw I was goan 'a be much whiter and even better lookin' than his chilern by his own wife, they . . . got rid of us for good." Often white wives felt anguish and embarrassment when they discovered that their husbands had broken their marriage vows. Rachal Goings reported the tragic consequences of her master's apparent sexual relationship with her mother: "[I] didden' know de ole Missus. Dey tole me she went crazy and kilt herself shortly after [I] wuz borned 'cause she though[t] I was white."[82]

White family members commonly refused to acknowledge their genetic ties to the slave children who were the result of these unions. In some cases, they took out their frustrations on the black women and children who were victimized rather than confront their male kin who were truly at fault. In reality, even if white women chose to confront their men they were largely powerless to stop their behavior, primarily because they also were subordinates in small-slaveholding households, economically and socially dependent on male family members. Robert Newsom shared his home with his two grown daughters and four grandchildren, and the historian Melton McLaurin rightly suggests that his two daughters likely knew of his relationship with Celia but may have felt powerless to intervene on her behalf. It is possible that the Newsom women felt sympathy for Celia, but they were both financially dependent on their father and, therefore, unlikely to side with a slave woman over him. A few white women acted admirably, however, as when Mary Estes Peters's mistress whipped her three teenage sons for their cruelty when she returned and found her brutally raped slave woman; it was permissible for a white woman to discipline her male children, but it was yet another matter for a woman to confront her husband or father. There is one tantalizing bit of evidence of the assertiveness of a wronged white woman, however. Justina Woods wrote about a local white woman who found her husband in a compromising position with a woman who appears to have been a slave: "Mary Evans and Jess had a perfect rippet not long ago. Mary caught him and Charity, it is said she beat them both with the broom and gathered up her clothes to leave and the women in town went and persuaded her to stay, if I was her I would kill him."[83]

Although the historical evidence is limited, it appears that some white women may have used the intimate circumstances of small-slaveholding households to pursue illicit sexual activities with slave men. During the Civil War, Captain Richard J. Hinton of the Union army provided intriguing testimony to the American Freedmen's Commission about the circumstances of contraband slaves who had fled guerrilla violence in western Missouri for safety in eastern Kansas. Conversations with formerly enslaved men led him to believe that there was "a large amount of intercourse between white women and colored men" in western Missouri. He claimed that he knew of a number of cases in which "bright looking" slave men were "compelled, either by his mistress, or by white women of the same class, to have connections with them." A Leavenworth physician pointed to the intimacy of small slaveholdings as the reason for this activity, arguing "that a very large number of white women, especially the daughters of smaller planters, who were brought into more direct relations with the negro, had compelled some one of the men to have something to do with them." Hinton told the story of a forty-year-old widow who "ordered" her slave man to sleep with her ten months after the death of her husband. The white woman "procured some of those French articles, that are used to prevent the consequences of sexual intercourse" to keep her interracial tryst a secret. The consequences of public exposure were grave for both parties. The daughter of a Platte County planter was unable to protect her secret slave lover when she gave birth to a mixed-race baby. She was induced under threat to reveal the name of her baby's father, but before action could be taken against him, the slave man escaped into Kansas. The baby reportedly died, although its father always believed that it had been murdered. Although some mistresses initiated sexual contact with kindness, others compelled it through coercion or threats. Hinton reported that another white girl enticed a slave man into the woods and then threatened to cry rape if he would not have sex with her.[84]

Hinton claimed that his information came from reliable sources, although his testimony suggests the prejudices that he harbored against

Missouri slaveholding women as a result both of his abolitionist lean-
ings and his Union military service on the Kansas and Missouri border.
He judged Missouri slaveholders as not of the best class of people and
criticized them for providing their children with "flashy" rather than
substantive educations. He also accused slaveholders' daughters of being
envious of the sexual liberties that their brothers took in the slave quarters and as wishing to "give loose to their passions" with men who would
not betray them as white men might. The hostility that many secessionist
women showed toward Union troops led him to believe that they generally were demoralized. Wartime prejudices clearly were a factor in Hinton's willingness to believe these stories of southern slaveholding sirens;
however, his suggestion that these interracial relationships might emerge
out of the intimacies of small-slaveholding households rings true.[85]

The social relations within small-slaveholding households were not
the only aspect of Missouri slavery that placed slaves at risk. Missouri's
pervasive hiring system also exposed slaves to exploitation and abuse.
Most hiring contracts dictated that the employer provide clothing and
medical care for hired slaves, but in reality slaves were more vulnerable
to cruelty because those who hired them had less economic incentive to
protect their health than did their owners. Although concerns over reper-
cussions from owners usually precluded extreme exploitation or abuse,
evidence indicates that many slaves were driven harder and treated more
cruelly by those who hired them than by their owners. Slaveholders were
aware of this potential, and pragmatic owners often attempted to place
their slaves with people who they believed would safeguard their property. Preston Reed sought to hire out his slave Dick for the entire year:
"[I] will endeavour to see that he is placed in hands entirely safe. I shall at
least use every precaution calculated to effect that end." Ultimately, unless it was clearly visible that a lessee had physically abused a slave, it was
difficult for an owner to prove it. Charles Baker, the son of former slave
Jane Baker, said, "Ma muther say dat de worse side ob slabery wuz when
de slabes war 'farmed out.' . . . De man who rented de slabes wud treat
den jus lik animals." The truth is that some owners were little concerned
about how their slaves were treated as long as they were paid. When William Wells Brown complained to his master of the terrible treatment he
received from the man who hired him, his master "cared nothing about
it, so long as he received the money for my labor."[86]

Slave children were especially vulnerable to abuse at the hands of hirers. As the Rocheport and Hannibal census roles indicate, it was common for nonslaveholders to hire children to work as domestic laborers

in their homes. Children frequently were separated from their parents, and sometimes even other bondpeople, during long-term hiring assignments. The practice not only forced children to grow up fast, but it also potentially exposed them to physical and sexual abuse at the hands of those who hired them. William Black's sister was hired out to a man who when drunk was "awful mean" and who actually struck at her when she wished him a "merry Christmas."[87]

In Missouri, as elsewhere, physical punishments were often unfairly and cruelly administered by slaveholders. Ultimately, no form of discipline was "fair" in a system of unfree labor, but slaves anticipated the likelihood of punishment if they knowingly broke their owners' rules or publicly flouted the racial code. In some cases, they willingly took a gamble and hoped for a positive outcome. They understood that a whipping or sale might be the result of a failed runaway attempt, for example, but many took the risk anyway. Slaves found violence particularly intolerable when it was arbitrarily administered or when they had not broken the rules, especially when it came at the hands of people with whom they interacted so intimately. Mary Bell's father ran away after he received a particularly harsh whipping that he believed was unwarranted, and William Wells Brown witnessed the whipping of his mother simply because she was late to the field one morning. Slave children were especially vulnerable to abuse; they could not easily fight back or effectively resist their owners. James Monroe Abbot spent his seventh summer in his master's sick room fanning flies and remembered his tortured existence, "Co'se I'd sleep sumtimes wen he wuz sleepin'. Sumtimes when I'd doze, my bresh ud fall on he's face, den he'd take he's stick an' whack me a few across de haid an' he'd say, 'Now I dare you to cry.' I cried, but he didden see me do it." A neighbor woman gave Harriet Casey a gift of a goose egg on her way back from taking the cows to pasture, but when she returned home later than usual, Casey's mistress kicked and beat her, in the process breaking her treasured egg. "Did'n mind de whipping but sure hated to break my egg," she recalled. Peter Corn was wantonly beaten by his master for not lowering all the fence rails while letting the cows through.[88]

Slaves were most devastated by masters and mistresses who were sadistic. The mistress of Louis Hill was nicknamed "Whip" because "[s]he beat da ole folks mor'n tha kids. She used tha cowhide an we got a lickin' whether we did any thin' or not." Mark Discus was beaten "'til the blood run offen [his] heels for breakin' an axe handle," and he recalled of his master, "We knowed to step when he yelled at us." M. P. Cayce whipped his elderly slave man "every Monday mornin' 'til his back bled. Den he tuk salt an' put hit in de gashes." Gus Smith spoke of Mr. Thornton, the neighboring master who beat his son to death and who also was "mean to his slaves. He whupped dem all de time. I've seen their clothes sticking to their backs, from blood and scabs, being cut up with de cowhide. He just whupped dem because he could." Thornton starved his slaves, and when an elderly woman stole a chicken to satiate her hunger he confronted her and forced her to eat every bite of the scalding food. "She died right away, her insides were burned," Smith remembered. A Saline County slave man froze to death when his master chained him to a hemp brake as punishment one frigid night. Charlie Richardson generally observed that slaves were not punished in jails: "Your back was the jail"; Tishey Taylor concurred, "If they wus jails then fo us slaves I never seed one, jes whippin' fo' punishin', some one wus gittin' it all the time."[89]

Mistresses commanded limited power in Missouri slaveholding society, yet many women used what little authority they had against the subordinates living and working within their household. The historian Thavolia Glymph argues that scholars of American slavery have often downplayed the violence that white mistresses perpetrated against their slaves. Whereas some historians have argued that mistresses developed an affinity with their slave women based on gender, others have described female violence against slaves as sporadic and personal, originating from the heat of the moment rather than as part of a sustained system of violence. Glymph believes that violent mistresses have been considered an anomaly both because the powerful and persistent construct of white womanhood leaves little room for the possibility of systemic female violence and because the homes in which this abuse often occurred have been viewed as domestic spaces. She instead argues that big houses, where violent interactions between owners and slaves occurred, should be seen as sites of work; places where the terms of labor often were hotly and sometimes violently contested. What's more, white mistresses' violence was not occasional or the result of temporary passions but instead was a vital component of the maintenance of labor discipline on the South's farms and plantations. Some Missouri mistresses, like others throughout the South, actively participated in upholding the slavery regime through the sustained use of violence. As is sometimes the case, greatest cruelty often comes from those less powerful. Most mistresses could not whip a grown slave man, but many routinely took out their frustrations on the slave women and children who lived and worked within their households. Emma Knight remembered that her master treated the slaves better than her mistress, and Margaret Nick-ens's mistress treated her so poorly that she did not wish to meet her "in either hell or heaven." Mary Armstrong claimed that her cruel mistress whipped to death her nine-month-old baby sister when she tired of her persistent crying. A number of slaves, such as Esther Easter, spoke of the whippings received from their mistresses. "Master Jim's wife was a demon, just like her husband," Easter remembered. "Used the whip all the time, and every time Master Jim come home he whip me 'cause the Mistress say I been mean." Mary Estes Peters said that her mother had "one big scar on the side of her head. The hair never did grow back on that place." When she was a girl her mistress "took one of the skillets and bust her over the head with it—trying to kill her, I reckon."[90]

Although mistresses could be extremely cruel, masters usually perpe-trated the worst cases of physical abuse against both women and men. Eliza Overton's children recalled her master's abuse: "They whoop'd with a rawhide whop an' trace chains. Wilson Harris wuz whooped at a tree onc't an' when dey got thro' he say he wud fight. They whop him some mor' 'til he wuz weak an' bleedin'. The other slaves had to grease his shirt ta take it off his back ta keep frum tearin' off de flesh." Sarah Graves's master whipped his slaves with a cat-o-nine-tails, and she re-membered, "He'd say to me, 'You ain't had a curryin' down for some time. Come here!!!' Then he whipped me with the cat. The cat was made of nine strips of leather fastened onto the end of a whip. Lots of times when he hit me, the cat left nine stripes of blood on my back." Hannah Allen told of the punishment meted out to one slave woman: "De master took two boards and tied one to de feet and another to de hands and tied her back with ropes and whipped her with a cat-o-nine tails till she bled and den took salt and pepper and then put in de gashes." Marilda Pethy also recalled, "I seen people turned across barrels and whipped. Dey was whipped 'cause de white people was mean. Sometimes dey tied dem to trees and whipped 'em. Dey didn't have no clothes on at all—dey was just like dey come into de world! Dey used a cowhide as big as my finger. . . . De master whipped when he could. When he couldn't do it, he called in de neighbors 'til you'd think dere was a meetin'. De poor darkies had a hard time!" William Wells Brown scoffed at the supposed mildness of Missouri slavery, relating the aforementioned St. Louis inci-dent in which Colonel William Harney whipped a slave woman to death. A friend of William Greenleaf Eliot wrote to him of the Harney incident several years after it occurred and discussed how many Missourians believed slavery to be milder in the state: "Several years afterwards, in conversing with a lady . . . about 'Uncle Tom's Cabin,' I said, 'You and I know parallel cases to every one in that book'. She said, 'Yes, except the case of Legree.'—'Ah, madam,' I said, 'you forget' . . . and she assented."[91]

Despite evidence to the contrary, many Missouri slaveholders continued to believe that slavery in their state was milder and more domestic than that which prevailed in the plantation South. This rhetoric was vital to the self-identity of small slaveholders who interacted with slaves on such an intimate level. Slaveholders such as Paulina Stratton could never understand why their slaves did not respond to them with the same respect and affection found within families. Slaves understood the limitations of this rhetoric fully well, however, realizing that the existence of a more paternalistic or "domestic" slavery in Missouri was more rhetorical than otherwise. In Missouri, slave owners and their slaves were in a unique position to recognize the humanity of one another, but more often than not, the more personal nature of small slaveholding fostered enmity rather than empathy. Slaves were better able to resist and negotiate, but positive effects notwithstanding, the circumstances of small-scale slavery negatively affected their lives. Most were afforded less individual autonomy, were more likely to be sexually exploited by their masters, and, as will be seen in the following chapters, were more often separated from their spouses and fathers and received less support from the slave community. In the end, the quality of individual slaves' lives was profoundly affected by their treatment at the hands of their mistresses and masters. The circumstances of small slaveholding left Missouri slaves particularly vulnerable to the whims of the white individuals with whom they shared their lives. As Sarah Graves succinctly put it, "Some masters was good an' some was bad." While this was true throughout the South, in a place like Missouri, where slavery consisted overwhelmingly of small holdings, this adage took on increased significance.[92]

5 / "Mah pappy belong to a neighbor": Marriage and Family among Missouri Slaves

Mary Bell, a former slave, remembered life during slavery as extremely difficult for her parents, Spotswood and Orry Rice. The Howard County, Missouri, couple began their marriage in 1852, but spent the first twelve years of it living on separate slaveholdings. Benjamin W. Lewis, a large tobacco planter and manufacturer who commanded sixty-five slaves in 1860, owned Spotswood Rice, and a forty-three-year-old small-slave-holding spinster named Kittey Diggs owned Orry and their children. Mary Bell described her parents as helping one another endure the "hard times" of slavery. Spotswood was allowed to visit his wife and children "two nights a week"—on Wednesdays and Saturdays. Her father often came to them bloodied from beatings he had received at the hands of the slave driver on his master's plantation. Orry would tend to his wounds, wash his clothes, and send him back to suffer more abuse. After a particularly severe beating, Spotswood ran away and hid near his family's cabin while watching for a chance to escape to freedom. Mary's mother begged him not to leave in spite of the violence he continually suffered and the emotional toll that separation was taking on the family. The local slave patrol thwarted Spotswood's attempts to make good on his escape, and he eventually turned himself over to a local slave trader hoping that he might help him secure a kinder owner. The man promptly returned Spotswood to his master, although he gained freedom through enlistment in the Union army six months later.[1]

Spotswood Rice remained devoted to his wife and children throughout his many years of tribulation, and his dedicated pursuit of their best interests did not falter once he achieved his freedom. Like many other recently enslaved soldiers, he focused his energies on bringing his wife and children out of bondage. He arranged for Orry and most of the children to come to St. Louis, where he served as a military nurse at Benton Barracks. After their arrival, Orry labored as a laundress and the children attended school for the first time. Spotswood, who was literate, became licensed as a preacher in the African Methodist Church and over the years served a number of congregations throughout Missouri and Kansas. The former slave couple, who began their long partnership living apart, boosted their family into the black middle class through education, hard work, and sheer force of will.[2]

The story of Mary Bell's family differs in significance ways from how historians typically have described enslaved families. Since the 1970s, scholars have devoted considerable attention to understanding slave family and household structures. Some of the earliest scholarship focused on the experiences of slaves living on plantations and pointed to the family, the slave quarter community, and religion as the three most important factors that mitigated the harshest aspects of slavery. Many of these early studies emphasized the agency of slaves with less attention to the ravages that slavery inflicted on individuals, families, and communities. Some suggested that a majority of American slaves spent much of their childhood living in stable two-parent households and benefited from the support of a slave quarter community as they struggled to maintain these crucial social ties. Historians have muddied the picture presented in the early scholarship by examining the diverse experiences of American slave families, recognizing that region and demographics often influenced the structure of families and households. Although the two-parent resident family was the preferred type, the percentage of families living together differed according to place and changed over time. For example, as Louisiana's slave society matured and stabilized in the decades before the Civil War, the two-parent resident family emerged as the dominant structure of slave households, while during this same period, families in Appalachia faced devastating dislocation from the ravages of the interstate slave trade and the depravations that resulted from the marginal economics of many mountain slaveholdings. Historians also have enriched and expanded the understanding of slave families and communities by exploring slaves' marriages, mobility, gendered work patterns, household structures and economies, ownership of property, and political activities. There is still no consensus on the composition and strength of antebellum slave families, but some scholars have made a concerted effort to strike a balance between the power wielded by slaveholders and the agency of slaves when describing slave families and communities. There has been less focus on how size of holding and region influenced the family lives of American slaves, however.[3]

The social relations of slaves were profoundly affected by the unique demographics and history of Missouri slavery. The demand for labor in Missouri resulted in a small number of slaves who were sold out of the state. The outcome was that even during the last decades of the antebellum era, when interstate slave sales accelerated, the male-female ratio—both of the entire slave population and of adult slaves—was virtually even. This demographic equity supported the creation of families, although the small size of holdings caused these households to be in a variety of forms. Stephen Crawford, in his important quantitative analysis of the WPA narratives, argues that the size of holding was the major determining factor in the composition of slave households, finding many more abroad marriages on smaller holdings. This certainly was the case in Missouri, where the average slaveholding was just five slaves even in areas with the largest concentrations of slaves and slaveholders. The small number of slaves held on individual farms forced men and women to look elsewhere for romantic partners. Abroad marriages, like that of Spotswood and Orry Rice, were by far the norm in Missouri, where the typical slave family consisted of a mother and her children with a husband and father who lived on another farm (see table 3).[4]

Abroad marriages existed throughout the South, yet the importance of these unions has been de-emphasized, overshadowed by concentration on the resident marriages of most plantation slaves. In fact, some scholars have dismissed abroad families as at best ineffective and at worst dysfunctional. Abroad marriages existed in all regions of the South and on all sizes of slaveholdings, but were especially prevalent in regions where small-scale slavery forced individuals to find spouses on other slaveholdings. Paul Escott first estimated in his 1979 analysis of the slave narratives that in the South as a whole 27.5 percent of slave marriages were abroad unions, while the historian Emily West later claimed that even in the large-slaveholding state of South Carolina 33.5 percent of slave families were abroad. People living on plantations often chose abroad matches even when partners were available on their home place, suggesting that they were not motivated by demographics alone. Rules of exogamy, with roots in African cultures, made it taboo to marry closely related blood kin such as first cousins, drastically reducing the number of suitable, unrelated, potential spouses even on plantations. Men and women also exercised limited self-determination when they chose abroad partners, and men enjoyed the expansion of their social world and a break in their routine as they traveled to visit their spouses on the weekends. Men also may have chosen women who lived elsewhere so as not to witness the abuse of their wives and children at the hands of their owners. A number of historians have pointed to the numerical significance of this household structure as an important reason to study abroad families in a more critical light.[5]

A quantitative analysis of the WPA narratives and Civil War pension claims filed by the dependents of formerly enslaved soldiers reveal that a full 57 percent of Missouri slave marriages were between men and women who lived on different holdings, a significantly higher percentage than was found in other regions. The two types of evidence provide a slightly different picture of slave marriages in Missouri, but both establish that an overwhelming number of couples participated in abroad unions (see table 4). Abroad marriages altered the ways in which most Missouri men, women, and children experienced slavery from that documented on plantations. The limited presence of abroad men in their families' daily lives had profound implications for women and children. They were unable to draw on the same level of emotional, physical, and economic support afforded resident families, and various systemic factors inherent to small slaveholding further compromised these families. Although daily contact with spouses might have been more satisfying and two-parent resident households the ideal, living together was not an option for most Missouri slaves. The devastating effects of slaveholder interference had long ago forced them to accept alternative family compositions and household structures. Faced with little choice, Missouri slaves adapted and fashioned strong bonds of family and kinship despite the limitations of their separate living situations. Many of these relationships proved remarkably stable, surviving for many years during both slavery and freedom. Missouri slaves embraced their abroad families as an important aspect of their lives over which they exercised some control and as a source of personal fulfillment.[6]

"Mah daddy come tuh see us on Satudays"

As in all parts of the South, the formation of slave families greatly depended on the will of Missouri slaveholders. Slaves were never allowed to fully control vital aspects of their personal lives, including their relations with family members and friends, but instead were forced to gain their owners' permission to interact socially with other enslaved people. Most owners gladly sanctioned their slaves' romantic attachments with bondmen and women living on other holdings because they recognized that, at the very least, their economic interests depended on it. Slaveholders undoubtedly would have preferred their slaves to marry on their own farms, but most did not own enough bondpeople to provide suitable, unrelated potential spouses. On the most basic level, owners of women accepted abroad families out of necessity if they hoped to increase their holdings through the birth of children. Owners generally allowed the abroad unions of their men as well even though they forfeited some of their work time and suffered the consequences of the sense of independence they gained from increased mobility. Despite the disadvantages, owners accepted the abroad marriages of their slave men even though they suffered most of the inconveniences and did not reap the benefits of the family's reproduction. Some owners may have reasoned that men who forged ties to women and children would be more content in their enslavement and less likely to flee, and consequently they often granted or withheld visitation privileges as a mechanism to ensure good behavior. In addition, slaveholders permitted men to take wives on nearby farms and plantations as a favor to their neighbors who owned slave women. In fact, an owner of an abroad husband might also own women who were involved in abroad marriages, and they expected their slaveholding neighbors to extend visitation privileges to the husbands of these women. In the final analysis, slaveholders consented to these unions because they recognized that the fate of the entire Missouri slavery system depended on cross-farm families. Owners of both male and female slaves recognized these unconventional marriages as legitimate by sanctioning weddings and permitting regular visiting.[7]

Most Missouri owners allowed their slaves to socialize with others in the greater community, acknowledging that they needed opportunities to meet and court their future spouses. Slaves knew other enslaved people well, frequently meeting them at the many social events that occurred in their neighborhoods. Many former slaves spoke of dances and suppers, which were held in conjunction with slave weddings; others met at cornhuskings and quilting parties organized by local slave owners. They also recalled meeting slave neighbors at churches and camp meetings. Men and women recognized these many social opportunities as times to identify and court prospective partners. Before his marriage, Alfred Smith spent most Saturday nights attending dances and wooing women, and Benjamin Hubbard was described as a young man who "was courting around among the women considerably." Men also met women living on neighborhood farms during the course of their daily work routines, frequently visiting with their neighbors on their way to and from running errands for their owners. The pervasive practices of hiring slaves and exchanging slave workers with slaveholding neighbors and relatives also provided them with increased opportunities to meet others in the community. Susan Scott met her future husband and married him while she was temporarily hired to work on his master's farm.[8]

The demographics of small-scale slavery made it difficult for owners to manipulate romantic matches because frequently no suitable candidates were available on their home farms. Most owners permitted men and women to choose their own partners in the greater neighborhood. Even so, Bill Sims claimed that some owners tried to influence their bondpeople's choices: "If a man was a big strong man, neighboring plantation owners would ask him to come over and see his gals, hoping that he might marry one of them, but if a Negro was a small man he was not cared for as a husband, as they valued their slaves as only for what they could do, just like they would horses. When they were married and if they had children they belonged to the man who owned the woman." As in other parts of the South, the formation of slave families greatly depended on the blessing of the couple's owners. The white community acknowledged the legitimacy, if not the legality, of a marriage only after the man and woman involved gained the consent of both of their owners and often the parents of the prospective bride. Harre Quarls, a former slave, described the courting process: "I'd ask massa could I have a gal, if she 'long to 'nother massa, and she ask her massa could I come see her. If dey say yes, I goes see her once de week with pass." Peter Corn agreed: "I would choose who I wanted to marry but I had to talk to my master about it. Den him and de owner of de girl I wanted get together and talk it over." Some couples thwarted their owners' wishes and engaged in conjugal relations without permission, but these clandestine relationships were risky and difficult to sustain.[9]

Although largely silent on the issue, Missouri slaves likely were pleased to have some choice in such an important and intimate matter. Slaves living near Natchez, Mississippi, apparently classified men's and women's romantic relationships on a continuum from casual couplings with little or no commitment to those who lived together in stable relations to marriages sanctified by formal vows. In contrast, it appears that in most cases Missouri couples embraced the promises of fidelity and mutual support that came with marriage, even in the absence of legal unions. Since a majority of couples were unable to live in the same household on a daily basis—a traditional signifier of married status, men and women placed an even greater premium on legitimizing and sanctifying their abroad marriages in the eyes of both their owners and their slave neighbors through public rituals and festivities. Their vigorous commitment to formalizing marriages may have stemmed from the tenuous nature of relationships that were built on the shaky foundation of the consent of two different owners. The pension bureau did not require a wedding ceremony as proof of slave marriages; instead cohabitation was enough to successfully gain a pension. Thus, the fact that so many widows testified to ceremonies suggests that they were not altering their past to fit the federal government's expectations of proper marriages but rather were describing rituals that they considered important to their identity as a married couple, both personally and in the eyes of their owners, kin, and neighbors. An associate described the strong bonds of one formerly enslaved couple, "[T]hey lived together and the marriage relation was as sacredly observed between them as between persons who were lawfully married."[10]

Many years after slavery's end, people remembered celebrating their unions with wedding ceremonies and parties. Couples invited friends, relatives, and owners to bear witness to their vows to join their lives as one. Slave preachers, county officials, white ministers, or masters married some couples, but others, like Hattie Matthews's grandparents, merely "jumped the broomstick," a folk ritual in which the couple literally jumped over a broomstick to signify their marriage. In most cases, the bride's owner officiated at the wedding ceremony. Peter Corn described the words used by many owners: "When de master first married us he would say in de ceremony something like dis. 'Now, by God, if you ain't treatin' her right, by God, I'll take you up and whip you.' The girl's mistress would chastise her de same way." In order to please a slave woman and her new husband, another owner performed a makeshift ceremony at which he also provided a "word of advice." One former slave explained that illiterate slaves had no way of knowing from what book the master read: "When dey married de master could pick up any old kind of paper and call it lawfully married. An almanac or anything would do." Countless other abroad couples, such as Isaac and Mathilda Smith and William and Millie Miller, were married by slave preachers. Hannah Morton, a former slave, described the way a literate fellow slave named Isom Giles officiated at the marriage of Alfred and Clarinda Smith: "He had them stand up and join right hands and he said something to them but I can't tell you what he said." Priests even married some couples in the Catholic Church.[11]

Many slaveholders provided couples with traditional wedding feasts following the ceremony. William Silvy recalled his slave woman Harriet's marriage to Asbury Warden on his Howard County farm in April 1851: "[T]here was quiet [sic] a gathering and supper on this occasion so much so that it was considered by all as a regular formal marriage." Slaveholding women often were involved in the preparations for the festivities. John Davis, a former slaveholder, remembered that his wife allowed "what was called a big wedding" between his slave woman Fanny and her abroad husband, Peter Woods. Favored slaves, who were often female domestic servants, sometimes were provided elaborate weddings. Emily Johnson, the daughter of a slaveholder, remembered the preparations for a favorite woman's wedding: "I helped to fix her, dress her & prepare the wedding supper. She was married in Mother's dining room." Many nuptials, like those of Emanuel and Elizabeth Gatewood, took place in the owner's home, often in the dining room. Historians have documented slave wedding ceremonies throughout the South, but the level of involvement of Missouri slaveholders and the number of wedding parties thrown suggests that the intimacy of small-scale slavery increased the likelihood of a more formal celebration. Small slaveholders knew their slaves well and, therefore, may have been more compelled to sanction these wedding parties. What is not revealed is how slave women felt about their mistresses' involvement in their special day. As was often the case, white women may well have interjected too much of themselves into the festivities, falsely believing that the intimacy of their relationship with the slave couple compelled this interference. Quite possibly, slave women and men were simply happy to have a party thrown in their honor, even if it did come with strings attached.[12]

Weddings were much-talked-about social activities in slave neighborhoods, and former slaves remembered them as important community events that were usually attended by friends and relatives, as well as representatives from both slaveholding families. Likely at the request of owners, these celebrations often coincided with lulls in the agricultural work schedule, such as in the weeks following Christmas. Richard Kimmons told of the many "suppers an' all-night dances" he attended when Lawrence County slaves were married. Both white and black guests enjoyed the feasting and excellent fiddling at Kimmons's own wedding, to which he wore a suit of dark homespun, and his bride wore a white dress and a veil given to her by her owners. George Posten, a former slave, played the fiddle at the dance that followed the wedding of Henry and Martha Berry. Even pious slaves such as Floretta Castleman were accommodated on their special day. Following her marriage ceremony to Washington Castleman they "had no dance, as I belonged to the church but we had a little party with refreshments."[13]

Custom dictated that husbands could regularly visit their wives, but couples relied on their owners to recognize these rights. Men and women frequently began their married life when the bride's owner acknowledged their status as a family by providing them with their own cabin. Men usually were given passes to see their wives and children once on the weekend and occasionally once during the week. Depending on the distance traveled, slave men typically arrived for visits on Saturday evening and left before sunrise on Monday morning. Bill Sims described the living and visiting arrangements of Missouri slave husbands and wives: "Back in Missouri, if a slave wanted to marry a woman on another plantation he had to ask the master, and if both masters agreed they were married. The man stayed at his owners, and the wife at her owners. He could go to see her on Saturday night and Sunday. Sometimes only every two weeks." Matthew Carroll and his wife were just such an abroad couple; when Matthew "was well he always went to her house on Saturday night and remained until Monday Morning." Mollie Renfro Sides, a former slave in Cape Girardeau County, reported the visiting arrangements of her parents: "'Massa' English wouldn't sell us, an' 'Massa' Renfro woun' sell mah daddy, so dey jes' let mah daddy come tuh see us on Satudays."[14]

Couples usually lived within a few miles of one another, although some men journeyed a much greater distance, usually on foot, to spend a few short hours with their families. The time needed to travel between the two homes often determined how frequently husbands were allowed to visit. George Madison lived only a mile from his wife, Anna, and saw her nearly every night, and Washington and Floretta Castleman, who both lived in the town of Potosi, also spent every night together. Even Isaac Davis who lived a few miles from his wife, Mary, managed to spend most evenings with his family. Abroad husbands at greater distances came much less often than even the traditional weekly visit. Benjamin Madis lived three miles away from his family and visited only "about once a month and sometimes oftner." John Gunn "only saw his wife occasionally, as his master lived at a distance" from the owner of his wife and child. The formidable distance of twelve miles separated Thomas Jackson and his family; however, the dedicated husband and father managed to make the journey about once a week.[15]

Occasionally, the right to visit a spouse was made part of a sale or hiring agreement. When the slaveholder Sallie Gaines purchased Asbury Warden from her brother, she agreed that she would provide Warden with "certain time to go and see his wife and family," and she later claimed, "I kept my promise and not only permitted him to see his said wife Harriet, but I also furnished him a horse to ride when he went to see his said wife." Charles Elliot was lent his owner's horse to ride the eight miles to visit his wife, Ellen, every other Saturday night and Sunday. In the end, the frequency of visits was left to the discretion of the man's owner, unless the abroad husband was willing to risk traveling without a pass. Even with a pass in hand there existed the possibility that abroad men would run into trouble with local patrollers. Despite the risks and potential roadblocks, on the weekends Missouri roads were alive with slave men coming and going from visiting their lovers, wives, and children. Clarinda Smith remembered her abroad husband's devotion: "My husband worked and continued to live on the Smith farm 3 or 4 miles away and came to see me about twice a week—as often as the slave times would allow."[16]

"He never stayed wif us in our cabin . . . we never knowed him much"

Fragmented Missouri families were allowed to come together briefly, but for most of the week a majority of women and children lacked the regular presence and support of husbands and fathers. Although slave men in general, even those with resident wives, struggled to protect and support their families in light of the power that slaveholders held over their lives, abroad men found it especially challenging to contribute to the well-being of their families. They could provide their wives and children with only limited economic assistance, physical protection, and emotional support because they spent so little time with them.[17]

Scholars have pointed to the importance of slaves' contributions to the creation and protection of stable families. Slave men and women were responsible for tending to their own families' needs once work for their owners was done. The small number of bondpeople who resided on most Missouri farms made this work even more an individual family effort. On large plantations, noontime meals and child care during work hours sometimes were provided on a communal basis. In contrast, slave parents living on smaller holdings often were forced to squeeze reproductive labor in between work for their owners. Women sprung into action, oftentimes after the sun went down, cooking their families' evening meals, tending to the needs of their children, and completing chores around their cabins. Men cut firewood, hunted, and fished, and the whole family cultivated family garden patches and cared for livestock. The hours spent tending to their own families' needs often were physically demanding and stole their sleep, but this labor held emotional value that work for their owners could never match.[18]

One of the greatest challenges facing Missouri slave families was providing quality, and oftentimes even adequate, care for their young children. The small number of adult workers on most Missouri slaveholdings made it difficult for owners to assign someone specifically to child-care duties. In many cases, women were asked to care for their children while they worked. It was common practice for nursing mothers to keep their infants with them throughout the day. Justina Woods wrote of one small-slaveholding mistress's expectations: "She makes Old Darkey take her young babe out to the field and work, she says it wont pay to keep negroes and them not work." The mothers of Sarah Graves and Annie Bridges left their babies at the edge of the field while they plowed. Hattie Matthews described the dilemma faced by mothers who had to choose between immediately responding to their crying infants or incurring the wrath of their watchful masters: "De master ud ride his hoss in de fiel an had a horse whip dat wuz platted, an he ud cut slabes with dis whip wen de slabes slack'd hup. If de babies cried de muthuh had ta get de master's permishun fore she cud pick up their baby." It was even more difficult to work while caring for mobile infants and toddlers. Mattie Jackson's mistress demanded that her mother keep her baby brother in a box so that she would not have to tend to him while she worked in the house. The two-year-old boy was unable to walk for want of exercise and eventually died. Small-slaveholding mistresses occasionally cared for slave children, but, already distracted by household duties and care for their own children, watching slave children was a low priority for most. Sarah Graves's mother chose to take her to the field rather than leave her under the careless supervision of her mistress, Emily Crowdes. The decision was reached after Graves was nearly burned by a curtain that had caught fire near where she lay. The most common child-care solution was to enlist older children, who often were only a few years senior, in the care of younger siblings. These youngsters were often less than vigilant, and the results were sometimes tragic, such as when Louis Hamilton's sister fell asleep while rocking him and he rolled off her lap into the fireplace.

Four of Hamilton's fingers were permanently deformed as a result of the burns. Slave children routinely were left to their own devices at the tender age of three or four. Tishey Taylor and her siblings were without adult supervision while their mother labored for her owners, but she periodically stole away from her work to check on them.[19]

Most slave men and women struggled to improve the material circumstances of their families beyond the requirements of basic care, and they devoted much of their little free time to working for their own families. Some owners promoted and aided their initiatives by providing them with the resources and time to improve their families' circumstances. On the surface, these arrangements appear to stem from kindness or generosity on the part of owners, but in most cases, practicality and self-interest drove most slaveholders' decisions to allow slaves' self-work and provisioning. Slaveholders could reallocate resources slated for basic needs if they encouraged their bondpeople to supplement the food and clothing apportioned to their families. Slaves' efforts on behalf of their own families especially benefited small slaveholders, many of whom were already operating their farms on slim economic margins.[20]

Slaveholders in Missouri, as in other parts of the South, frequently gave their bondpeople a piece of land on which to plant a garden and then allotted some time to cultivate it. In 1831, Stephen Hempstead noted: "One acre I give to Thos & pierre the produce at harvest for themselves & if they make good prudent use of it . . . they always Should have as much or more & tend the piece together in my time as I had thereby give them time to work their Corn." Slave families generally used produce from their gardens to supplement their diets; such was the use of the garden tended by William Nelson's mother. John Carter permitted his slaves to grow crops on land they had cleared the previous year, as well as raise hogs. Carter furnished his slaves with meat only once a day, and they supplemented their protein intake by raising their own hogs. Others hunted and fished in order to increase the variety of their families' fare. Gus Smith told of the wild game that was abundant in many parts of Missouri: "I remember my father shooting so many pigeons at once that my mother just fed dem to de hogs. Just shoot the game from our back yard. . . . Ducks and geese de same way. We could kill dem by tow sacks full, with clubs." Former slave men fondly recalled the pleasure they took from days spent fishing. "De Bes' times we-ens had wuz going fishing, an' man! did we like to fish. Allus we had Saturday afternoon off, 'lessen it war wheat harvest 'er sumthin' special like. 'En Sunday's we allus fished all day long," George Bollinger reported.[21]

Some slaves earned money by working for their owners and neighbors during their off time or by cultivating cash and garden crops for sale in the marketplace. The practice of slaves growing cash crops such as tobacco worried some white Missourians because they feared that they might steal from their owners or other farmers and then claim the harvest as their own. Despite these concerns, it was common practice for Missouri slaves to grow their own crops of tobacco. Many bondpeople were highly motivated by the opportunity to earn a little cash and willingly cultivated their fields late at night and on the weekend. Sarah Graves explained that her mother and stepfather "often tended their own tobacco and grain in the moonlight. This they could sell and have the money." Henry Bruce remembered Chariton County slaveholders who allowed their people to grow tobacco "after sundown, and without plowing." Over time slaves were able to accumulate considerable resources for their families through their dedicated labor. John Carter, a former slave in Lincoln County, worked nights, holidays, and Saturdays, earning up to $250 a year, by cultivating his own tobacco crop and by making rails and cutting wood for neighboring farmers. Gus Smith's master allowed his slaves to work for neighbors when they had finished their work at home. "[W]e kept our money we earned, and spent it to suit ourselves," he boasted. Another former slave Squire Burns explained, "We folks used to get paid for the work that we done after night on Sunday or during the Hollidays Christmas and New Years." Clarissa Combs's sons provided for her needs with money that they earned "by doing chores or errands, or odd jobs."[22]

Missouri slaves' strategies for improving the lives of their family members are suggested by the way they chose to use the resources accrued through extra work. They routinely purchased livestock, coffee, and sugar, simple household goods, and material for clothing and bedding with their earnings. Others saved the proceeds of their labor with the intention of buying themselves or family members from slavery. Some instead chose to invest in livestock so that they might breed and sell them or use them as draft animals. Stephen Hempstead wrote of the importance his slave man Pierre placed on his mule: "[P]ierre unwell hath not been here this morning to take care of his mule which is his Idol." Hempstead cared for the mule during Pierre's sickness. Through a letter to her husband, Mary Rollins asked an absent slave named Hamilton about the number of chickens that he owned. Some purchases were meant to provide personal pleasure rather than fill a vital need for the family, however. Dilsy earned a dollar washing for a neighbor and bought a linsey petticoat with it. Like Dilsy, many other bondpeople used the money they earned to buy additional clothing. In 1859, Ike bought his wife, Aga, a new dress. "[Slaves] would get paid for working for others and den buy clothes. Dey had de finest boots," Hannah Allen recounted. Enslaved people throughout the South placed a premium on buying or making nice clothing for special occasions. Henry Bruce noted that many Missouri slaves spent the little money that they earned on "fine clothes" in order to wear them to church services and parties. A fair amount of women's free time was devoted to fashioning this special clothing for family members. Not all purchases benefited the family, however. Missouri court records are filled with the prosecutions of white men who illegally sold liquor to slaves.[23]

Owners frequently purchased material goods on behalf of their slaves, oftentimes running the enterprise like a company store. Sarah Graves described these transactions: "The Masters had stores and you had to go to that store and get your needs and when the month was up you had nothing as it took all you earned to pay your bill." It was not uncommon for bondpeople to deal directly with local merchants, however. Eliza Overton's husband was allowed to work as a teamster and frequently traveled to a nearby town as part of his job. "He'ud bring bak things frum Ste. Genevieve that war hard ta git. Salt wuz hard ta git at this time," Overton remembered. The fact that Overton's husband could purchase incidental items on behalf of friends was not surprising given the liberal mobility of many Missouri slave men.[24]

The material quality of life enjoyed by slave women and children was directly influenced by the contributions of all members of the household. Families often structured the labor of those living within their households in order to work toward realizing their goals, but the priorities of their owners had a tremendous impact on slaves' ability to improve their economic situation. The abroad structure of so many Missouri slave households is a prime example of the limitations imposed on slave families. It was clearly more difficult for abroad men to labor for their families. They were not at their families' cabins long enough to be of much assistance with basic household chores, such as chopping firewood, nor could they spend much time hunting and fishing or assisting their wives in the cultivation of garden patches and cash crops. They also did not have as many free hours in which to earn money through hiring out their own labor. Much of the free time and energy of abroad men was consumed in travel to visit their families. Abroad wives often were forced to make up for what their husbands could not furnish, struggling to improve the quality of life for their children in what were reduced material circumstances. The reproductive labor of slave households already burdened women; cooking, child care, cloth and garment production, the cultivation of gardens, and the care of poultry kept them occupied until late in the evening. The historical records provide little indication as to how abroad women felt about their added responsibilities. Although they may have taken pride in their ability to cope with their circumstances, there is no sign that they preferred the situation.[25]

The lack of resident husbands on some Missouri farms exacerbated another problem faced by many women. Abroad women endured slavery with little chance of protection from physical and sexual abuse at the hands of their owners. The power wielded by small-slaveholding men within their households and their ample access to the slave women living and working within them were the primary reasons for the increased vulnerability of slave women to sexual exploitation, but the absence of abroad husbands likely was a contributing factor. The power dynamics of slavery left slave men virtually powerless to protect their wives from white men, but their physical presence may have served as a deterrent for some abusers. Slaveholders understood that there was always the potential for slave men to defend their wives through violent means, such as when Moses shot and killed his master after he learned that he had attacked his wife. White men may have viewed women in abroad marriages as easier targets, ultimately enhancing the likelihood that slave women residing on small slaveholdings would become victims of sexual exploitation.[26]

In addition, the emotional lives of abroad family members were compromised by the limited presence of husbands and fathers. When interviewed by the WPA many years after slavery had ended, the memories of most former slaves focused on mothers, and many merely reported in passing that their fathers lived elsewhere. The brief nature of fathers' visits made it difficult for some children to become emotionally attached to their fathers. Tishey Taylor explained, "Mah mammy's name was 'Katie'; Katie-Cherry, an ma father wus William Walturf, er somethin' like 'at, never did know good 'cause he never stayed wif us in our cabin no how and we never knowed him much." Mary Armstrong's father lived on a different farm, and she was never close to him: "Then I hears my papa is sold some place I don't know where. 'Course, I didn't much know him so well, jes' what mama done told me, so that didn't worry me like mamma being took so far away."[27]

Former slaves primarily told stories of their mothers because it was their mothers who tended to their physical and emotional needs on a daily basis. Many remembered their mothers as strict disciplinarians and almost exclusively focused on mothers when describing the discipline doled out by their parents. As was true with many parents of the time, corporal punishment was viewed as an essential and effective tool in the training of children. That slave parents turned to physical discipline was not surprising in a society that rested on violence as a means of control. In most cases, former slaves did not chafe under the memory of punishment from their parents but instead viewed it as necessary to their proper upbringing. Lewis Mundy explained, "Our master and mistress was good to us, but of course my own mother had to whip me often. She used a whip made from twisted buckbrush twigs and did it sting!" And Harry Johnson reported, "De worst whippin' I ever got, my mother whipped me." Fil Hancock's mother managed to whip him with a razor strap even though she suffered from tuberculosis. She was so incapacitated by her illness that she could not physically hold her children to punish them and instead asked one of their siblings to "push de other up to her bed while she whipped" them. Hancock believed that his mother punished her children because "she loved us and wanted us to do right. We never got a whipping 'ceptin' we needed it." Many parents commanded their children's attention through the use of physical discipline, punishing them in order to better teach them the skills needed to successfully negotiate their enslavement, but parents, such as Tishey Taylor's mother, also schooled their children in effective resistance strategies through example. Taylor's mother habitually hid in her cabin and feigned sleep so that she could spend the evenings with her children.[28]

Some women may have found it daunting to raise their children without daily emotional support or help from their partners. Mothers had to both discipline their children and teach them survival strategies because most fathers were not around to assist with these tasks. Former slaves rarely spoke of their fathers in the role of disciplinarian. Abroad fathers spent so little time with their children that many may have wished to enjoy these few hours engaged in pleasant activities, such as fishing, rather than focus on everyday child-rearing tasks or discipline. As a result, it may be that some children perceived of their mothers as the heads of their households and saw their fathers more as occasional visitors.

The difficulties of sustaining a long-distance relationship also appear to have strained some marriages. Abroad living arrangements made women more susceptible to heartbreaking deception by their frequently absent spouses. Evidence from the pension records suggests that it was not uncommon for abroad men to become sexually involved with, and even married to, two women simultaneously. Some men abandoned their wives for another woman, but many continued to visit both women. The circumstances of abroad marriages increased opportunities for those who wished to stray because the sporadic visiting habits of some abroad spouses easily concealed these relationships. There generally was an expectation of fidelity among committed couples, especially those who were promised to one another in a marriage ceremony, but the existence of plural marriages suggests that not everyone lived up to this ideal. Clay Taylor was not surprised to discover that his former slave Henry Pratt had two families, claiming that he knew a number of such cases. Separations due to the deprivations of slavery led some to marry again, but it appears that some men chose another woman even when their first marriage remained intact. Henry Berry's friend explained that Berry was seeing a woman named Nisa Kurd at the same time that he was married to Martha Johnson. He excused his friend Henry's actions by stating, "The truth is all we slaves 'Sweethearted' a little." Some men apparently used their inability to form legal unions and the prevalence of abroad marriages to their advantage as they formed romantic partnerships with multiple women. Hannah Jones reported that her father was married to more than one woman and claimed that slave men often "had three or four wifes before de war, as many as dey could bear chillun by. But after de war de had to take one woman and marry her. My mother had three chillun by him and de odder wifes had three and four chillun too." Harre Quarls reported that he maintained three wives simultaneously by merely receiving permission from the women's owners for weekly visits. "When I's sot free dey wouldn't let me live with but one. Captain, that ain't right, 'cause I wants all three," he lamented. Clearly, some men chose to maintain more than one wife and family. A few abroad women likely also took up with other men; however, only one such case was found in the Missouri evidence. The Stratton slaves Ike and Aga lived apart from each other for the first time in their married life after Aga was given to the Strattons' eldest daughter, Mary Agnes, upon her marriage. Paulina Stratton reported in her diary: "[Ike] went down last week and Aga told him that Lauda slept with her, Ike has not been since. She is such a fool." Months later, Stratton commented that Ike still had not accepted Aga back into their cabin. Rather than pointing to personal failures and indiscretions, William Cheatham blamed dual relationships and the instability of some slave families on the fragile nature of marriages that were allowed no legal foundation by white Missourians. "The way the slaves married at that time was that they simply went to living together and stayed together as long as they wished and then took some other partner," Cheatham explained.[29]

Civil War pension files are filled with examples of two wives claiming to be the sole legitimate heir to a deceased soldier's pension. Asbury and Harriet Warden maintained an abroad marriage and were the parents of five children before he enlisted in the Union army. After his death, both Harriet and another woman named Emma Warden filed a claim as Asbury's widow. Emma testified that Sandy Bruce, a slave minister and the brother of Blanche and Henry Bruce, officiated at her marriage to Asbury Warden on her master's farm in September 1862. The couple had a baby boy soon after. Apparently, Asbury Warden applied to his mistress, Sallie Gaines, for her consent to marry Emma, who lived nearby. Gaines explained, "I refused to give him permit to marry said Emma Borum as his wife Harriet had been living with him as husband and wife for such a long time and had always treated him nicely, and had a good character, that I considered it wrong for him to abandon her then." The evidence indicates that Asbury arranged the second marriage without his mistress's permission. Sallie Gaines supported Harriet's claim by pointing out to the pension board that whether or not a wedding took place, in her opinion the marriage was not legitimate without her consent.[30]

The historian Brenda Stevenson found that in Loudoun County, Virginia, many slave men also kept two wives; she described these relationships as polygynous. Stevenson argues that the plural marriages stemmed both from African traditions and a reduced number of young slave men due to the domestic slave trade. In contrast, Missouri slave women never described themselves as polygamists, nor was there a demographic need for plural marriages. Although some women may have knowingly and willingly participated in polygyny, in all the reported pension cases the two wives lived on separate holdings and did not associate with each other. There is little indication that the first wives accepted the second wives as part of a plural marriage; instead the second marriages often were without the first wives' knowledge and consent. It appears that in some instances the bureaucrats in the pension office were the first to put together the pieces of men's romantic lives only after two women filed claims as the widow of the same soldier. Most first wives indicated that they either were unaware of the second wives altogether or that they knew their husbands were seeing other women but that they had never legitimately married them. Conversely, second wives often were aware of their partners' previous relationships and wished for their husbands to sever their ties to their first families. Of course, the purpose of pension cases potentially colored the evidence since it was in the financial interest of claimants to deny participation in plural marriages. Certainly, those submitting claims understood that the pension bureau expected them to mold their family relations to emulate middle-class white norms. The vagaries of slavery and the misconduct of some men made it difficult for some couples to maintain their relationships long term, yet these dual marriage cases suggest that many slaves, especially women, strove for monogamous marriages that would last a lifetime. Each claimant clearly regarded herself as the sole wife, and jealousies and hostilities existed years after slavery had ended.[31]

The pension board discovered that Henry Pratt had maintained two families at the same time. Millie Pratt testified that "Henry and I had considerable trouble" about his occasional visits to his first wife and family but claimed that she was powerless to stop him. Although there is little indication of the motives of polygynous husbands, second marriages often occurred when slave men established relationships with women who lived in closer proximity than their abroad wives. Caleb Jones married Eliza in 1856, and the couple had three children. Around 1861, Jones married a second woman named Susan after she was hired to work for his master. Martha Banks reportedly separated from her abroad husband Reuben after he engaged in an intimate relationship with a woman who lived on a farm adjoining that of his owner. In many cases, the men's relationships appear more serial than polygynous. Discarded first wives may have decided to lay their claim as the sole legitimate spouse only when there was the potential for financial gain.[32]

"We pray that none of us will go down the river"

Systemic aspects of small-scale slavery had the potential to compromise the integrity of slave families in additional ways. Abroad families ultimately were more vulnerable to separation through hiring, migration, estate divisions, and sales than were their plantation counterparts because they were dependent on the life circumstances and temperaments of two owners. The often tenuous finances of small-slaveholding families might threaten the economic independence of their household and lead them to part slave families through hiring or sale.

Missouri's pervasive system of hiring resulted in the separation of a great number of Missouri slave families, even if the arrangement was not always permanent. There was no guarantee that families would remain living together even if they were owned by the same master. Hiring created abroad families where they might not originally have existed. Mary Rollins's slave "George objected to going to Glasgow because he would be separated from his wife." Rollins wished that George's wife could be hired with him, "for she requires more waiting on than her services amount to." Children also were routinely hired away from their parents and siblings. Although small children frequently accompanied their mothers to their hiring placements, many older children were hired out on their own. Slave girls, like those employed by the Rocheport businessmen, were put out at extremely young ages to serve as domestics and nursemaids. Mary Bell remembered, "Slavery was a mighty hard life. Kitty Diggs hired me out to a Presbyterian minister when I was seven years old, to take care of three children." Many children were placed in households where they were the only enslaved person, thus forcing them to fend for themselves without the assistance of fellow bondpeople. Although there was the possibility of visits, the emotional toll of these separations on parents and children likely was great. Most Missouri slaves were hired locally; however, in some cases, hired slaves, like those who worked on riverboats, were removed at such a great distance that it was no longer possible to regularly visit their families. Even though many slaves maintained at least some contact with kin, most viewed hiring as highly detrimental to family life. Sarah Graves commented, "My mama was sold only once, but she was hired out many times," making "a lot of grief for the slaves." Not only did employers have less economic incentive to treat those they hired humanely, but they sometimes were less inclined to allow visits to family members.[33]

Abroad families were also vulnerable to separation when their owners migrated. Parting was most common when owners first moved to Missouri. As described earlier, countless former Missouri slaves reported forcible separations from loved ones who were left in eastern homes. Not as many families were parted by migration out of Missouri, however. As a western state largely settled during the antebellum years, there were few slaveholders who moved from Missouri, with the exception of a fairly sizable migration to Texas in the years directly before and during the Civil War. J. W. King's father, Egeton Bolton, was left in Missouri when his mother and siblings were sold to a man who moved to Texas, for example. King remembered, "Fathaw, so I'se told, was Egeton Bolton but I couldn't tell yo' mo'e about him dan yo' kin. Fathaw wasn't brought by de Texas man, and he had to stay up in Missouri. We never did see him again." Levi Wilson remarried after his master moved him to Texas.

When he visited his first wife after emancipation, she told him to remain with his new wife and children since they had no children of their own.[34]

Owners' deaths were moments of extreme anxiety for Missouri slave families because so many were separated from loved ones at this time. There were many points in the probate process when family divisions might occur. Administrators routinely hired out slaves while estates were in probate in order to pay down debts or generate income for heirs, but the final settlement of small slaveholders' estates oftentimes resulted in the dismantling of slave families. Occasionally all of the white family's slaves were left directly to the slaveholder's widow, but often, they were dispersed among many heirs. In many cases, slaves were divided according to their value with little regard for maintaining family ties, and these divisions often physically separated slave family members from one another. Samuel Smiley's 1843 will requested that after his wife, Emily, received her dower portion of the estate, his slave property was to be equally divided among the many Smiley children. Smiley hoped that his oldest children would receive the oldest slaves, but if they could not be evenly divided, individual slaves should be sold to the highest bidder among his heirs. George King specified in his will that two slave men should be hired out to pay the debts of his estate. He left the two men and seven other slaves to his wife, and divided six additional slaves among three of his children. Earlier, he had given nine slaves to five of his other children. Slave birth records indicate that many of those bequeathed before and after King's death were young children and, therefore, were likely separated from their parents and siblings.[35]

If equitable divisions of the estates could not be made among the heirs, slaves often were sold, frequently auctioned off individually rather than as family units. Family ties generally were ignored when the financial interests of the heirs were at stake. All of the slaves belonging to Stephen Hempstead's son-in-law and his son were sold at public auctions after the men died, for example. Often members of the white family purchased the deceased's slaves, as was the case with the Smiley estate. The heirs received their portion of the proceeds of the sale and, therefore, saw the sale as an opportunity to acquire slave property on the cheap. At the most, slaveholders requested in their wills that slaves should be kept within the white family or occasionally that married couples or mothers and small children should be allowed to remain together. A few owners successfully engineered sales to the benefit of their slaves, such as when Hiram Sloan's widow convinced her neighbors to buy her twenty-two bondpeople in order to keep them near their family members. Most often the priorities of white families usurped any concerns about slaves' lives, and it was not uncommon for heirs to ignore directives in the interest of higher sale prices. Samuel Hannah instructed his trustees to "sell said slaves at private sale, to enable my executor to sell them to those who he may think would treat them humanely," but the Hannah slaves instead were sold to the highest bidder at a public auction. Even when heirs wished to purchase family slaves, limited personal finances sometimes overruled sentiment. Elizabeth Coleman hoped to purchase family slaves at the Fayette auction of her late father's property but was advised by her brother-in-law "to let them all go, rather than give an exorbitant price for any of them." There were few advantages to slaves if white family members purchased them. It might be helpful to have prior knowledge of the temperament of new owners, and sale to a white family member could result in future reunions with family members; nonetheless, slaves frequently were separated from their loved ones, occasionally by hundreds of miles, when slaveholding family members returned to their homes.[36]

Bondpeople commonly were loaned or given to slaveholders' children—often upon their marriages—well before the death of the owner. Thomas and Paulina Stratton presented to their daughter Agnes, upon her marriage, "Aga and two ca[l]ves," thus creating an abroad marriage between the slave woman and her husband, Ike. The new living arrangement was likely one of the factors that led to Aga's affair with another man. Parents also sold slaves to their children on extremely favorable terms, such as in 1858, when Eliza Williams sold her eleven-year-old slave girl Celia to her daughter Margaret Dorsey for the sum of $5, although she was valued at around $500, or in 1854 when Betsey Rutter sold her son Edmond a twenty-five-year-old slave man for merely $25. Gifting slaves, especially slave children, sometimes led to devastating separations of families. Eight-year-old Margaret Nickens was given to her owner's daughter and her husband and was taken across the state: "My mother had to stand dere like I wasn't her's and all she could say was, 'Be a good girl, Margaret.'"[37]

Slave families understood that the odds were against their staying together when estates were divided and slaves sold. Occasionally slaveholders sold their slaves with at least part of the family unit intact; women and their youngest children were frequently sold together, for example. Such was the case when William Melton sold his slave woman and her two children together in 1829. Malinda Discus also was sold with her mother when she was a tiny baby. Unlike mothers and babies, older children were frequently torn away from their mothers by sale. The emotional trauma of auction day was imprinted in Will Daily's memory years later: "I seen some slaves sold off dat big auction block and de little chillun sho' would be a cryin' when dey takes dere mothers way from dem." Annie Bridges's mother passed down stories of small children who were sold "fum de breast's ob der muthuh's." Although the WPA interviews contain few cases, other historical sources, such as newspapers and runaway slave narratives, reveal that young children routinely were sold individually. In 1859 Daniel Jones bought an eleven-year-old girl named Diana for $800, and in 1853 five-year-old Addelline was sold for $300. Robert Davis bought a three-month-old slave child intending for his wife to raise the girl along with their own child who was about the same age. William Wells Brown observed a particularly disturbing incident when the slave trader by whom he was employed gave a month-old baby to a white acquaintance simply because he had tired of the infant's cries. Brown was forever haunted by the plaintive wails of the child's mother. William B. Lenoir wrote that his father, Walter Raleigh Lenoir, had "sold Emma for $650 kept her child which is a promising looking Boy. I have the money loaned out in good hands at 10 pr [sic] ct." Lenoir had divided a slave child from his mother purely because it was profitable.[38]

Owners rarely placed the concerns of slave families over their own families' economic interests, and the result was that most recorded transactions of sales involved individual bondpeople. Since many of those sold were in their late teens through their thirties—the ages at which slaves were valued the highest—it is probable that a majority were sold away from spouses, parents, or children. William Wells Brown's mother and siblings were all sold to different owners, and George Johnson, a former slave, reported that all of his grandmother's twenty-one children were sold away from her. Slave families were especially vulnerable to separation if sold at auction or to interstate traders. Marilda Pethy was sold locally with her mother when she was only six weeks old, but her four siblings were sold south at the same time. "I had two brothers and two sisters sold and we never did see dem no more," Pethy lamented. Emily Camster Green told a heart-wrenching story of an owner who secretly sold off a man's wife and child without his knowledge, possibly in an attempt to avert an unsettling emotional scene. When the husband and father came in from work in the evening and discovered his wife and child gone he "fell down on he's knees an' he begin prayin' an he pray an' he holler 'Oh! nobody know but Jesus! Nobody know but Jesus!'" Chloe Marshall and her husband, Henry Jackson, had four children together before Henry's master sold him south. Marshall was so sure of her husband's devotion that she was convinced that he must have died because "he would have come back after the colored people had been made free if he had been living." At the age of four, Mark Discus was put on a stump and auctioned off. Even as an old man he remembered the pain and emotional trauma of that day, "I remember my Mammy cryin' and I was scared." All nine of his brothers and sisters were separated from him at this time, although he occasionally saw them since they all were sold locally. In contrast, his mother "was sold down South and I never seen her again 'til after the war was over."[39]

The fact that Missouri slaves did not enter the domestic trade in as large numbers as those from other states in the Upper South did not dampen the serious psychological effects of the trade on individuals. Former Missouri slaves frequently recounted both the emotional impact of actual sales as well as the psychological weight of the fear of sale in the future. Henry Bruce wrote that Chariton County slaves were frightened when they heard that the slave trader John White was operating in the area. Local slaveholders frequently threatened the destruction of personal ties through sale to speculators, like White, as a way to intimidate their slaves into submission. Bruce claimed that this method worked effectively because "the slave dreaded being sold South, worse than the Russians to banishment to Siberia." Even though they feared the harsher conditions of slavery in the cotton and sugar regions, Missouri slaves were most concerned by the thought of permanent separation from family and friends. Even when masters and mistresses respected the sanctity of their slave families, circumstances might change—especially if owners died—that would necessitate sale. Before Hiram Sloan's widow arranged for local purchasers, the Sloan slaves had been worried that they would be sold to speculators, especially after they learned that strange men from downriver had arrived in town. The morning of the sale, fifty-year-old Uncle Nelson prayed in the slave cabins: "Some of us may go nawth, some of us will go west, but, Good Lord, we pray that none of us will go down the river, where black folks ain't held much account." Malinda Discus's mother was emotionally scarred by separation from her parents when she was brought from Tennessee to Missouri as an eleven-year-old girl, and impressed these anxieties onto the next generation. "[M]y mother use to gather us children around her and pray that we would not be separated," Discus remembered. Her fears were realized when one of her sons was sold south. Charlie Richardson expressed the feelings of many former slaves when he spoke of the sale of his stepfather:

"Like to broke my Mammy up, but that's the way we slaves had it. We didn't let ourselves feel too bad, cause we knowed it would come that way some time. But my Ma she liked that Charlie and she feeled it mos.'"[40]

A few individuals who were sold away managed to maintain contact with family members over long distances. In 1859, the Texas slaveholder T. T. Bradley wrote a letter for his newly purchased slave man Dave to his father and mother remaining in Missouri. Dave professed to be pleased with his new Texas home, although "I would like to se [sic] you and Mother and my Sisters and Brothers but we are two fur a part to think a bout that . . . now father you and mother content your selves a bout me the best you can." Bradley included his own note to the slave father saying that he was pleased with Dave and inclined to "keep him as long as we Both live and I will treat him well." The promise of good treatment and continued written contact with their son was the best for which Gabe and his wife could hope. Some fortunate families, like that of Mark Discus, were able to reunite after emancipation. Unaware that freedom was in their future, however, most bondpeople at the time believed that they would never see their loved ones again.[41]

Fortunately, a majority of those who were sold or divided in estate settlements remained within the state of Missouri, many within their own home counties. Missouri slave narratives and pension claims are filled with examples of slaves sold, often multiple times, within their local area. The story of Alcy Smith Carroll is indicative of the experiences of many Missouri slaves. When Alcy Carroll was five years old her master transported her from Kentucky to Ralls County in northeastern Missouri, where she lived for the next sixteen years before her owners moved a few miles north to the town of Hannibal. After the death of her master, Alcy's mistress settled on Buffalo Creek, a few miles to the south in Pike County. It was there that Alcy met and married her husband, Matthew Carroll. Soon after, Alcy Carroll was sold and relocated within the county twice, eventually landing in Clarkville, where she lived until she was freed during the Civil War. Like Alcy, Matthew also was transferred within the county when he and his brother were given to their master's son. Despite their many owners and residences Alcy and Matthew Carroll were able to sustain their marriage because they always remained in close proximity to each other. Many other Missouri slaves shared similar experiences.[42]

When migrating, dividing estates, or selling slaves, some sympathetic owners attempted to keep abroad family members close to one another. Masters and mistresses occasionally responded to the requests of slaves, who tirelessly advocated for maintaining their own family ties. A Saline County woman pleaded with Mary Leonard Everett to buy her so that she would not be separated from her husband, children, and mother when her master moved to Arkansas. Recognizing the depth of her feelings, Everett sympathized with the slave woman and asked her husband to make a deal with her owner. Susan and Ersey, the slaves of absentee master Beverley Tucker, also begged their owner to sell them rather than to allow their transfer to Texas. They explained, "to be separated from our husbands forever in this world would make us unhappy for life." When Callaway County slave Martha Wisely's master died, she was taken miles away to the Pettis County home of her new owner; however, she was eventually hired out in her home county upon her request that she be placed near her husband, William. A few owners purchased their slaves' spouses in order to unite families on the same farm or at the very least move them closer to their loved ones. Frank Cochran's and Frank Duncan's masters both bought their abroad wives soon after their marriages. Jonathan Ramsay hoped to honor the request of a slave man to be sold to an owner near where his wife lived, and William Carr Lane sold his slave Melinda because "she was anxious to go up and live near her husband." Thomas Delaney sold Archer Alexander to his wife's master before he moved from Missouri in order to keep the couple together, and when Thomas Vaughn's master moved away from Howard County, his wife's master bought him "so that the family would not be broken up."[43]

Other Missouri owners worked hard to keep families together if they believed that circumstances necessitated their sale. Judge Hays of Marshall insisted on keeping a family together when he sold his slaves in 1852 before moving to Oregon. Knowing he was in the market for slaves, W. A. Wilson reported to Abiel Leonard that Hays had "a favorite family that he wished to sell to gether—a man & his wife & 2 children . . . the man he speaks highly of and of the woman, he says she is a first rate cook and can make a coat, & sew as well as any white woman—he wont separate them." It is not known whether the family was indeed sold together, however. Like Hays, Leonard also sought to accommodate the domestic relations of his slaves. In 1846, he sold his slave woman Sally and her child to the man who had bought Sally's husband. Leonard recorded in his account book that she had been "sold at her desire, in order to go with Luke her husband." That same year, Abiel Leonard chose to sell his slave Sam rather than Sanford because "Sandford did not wish to leave his wife." The situation did not end happily for the Leonards' slave woman Ann, however. She asked Leonard to purchase her husband, William,

FIGURE 8. Archer Alexander. Archer Alexander (c. 1810–1879) escaped slavery in St. Charles County in 1863 and made his way to St. Louis, where he found employment with anti-slavery advocate William Greenleaf Eliot, who later chronicled his story. Eliot was a driving force in the effort of former slaves to commission a statue of Abraham Lincoln to honor his role in ending slavery. This photograph of Alexander was taken as a study for the slave man kneeling at Lincoln's feet in Charles Ball's well-known and controversial *Freedom Monument*, which still stands in Washington, D.C. Photo by J. A. Scholten; Missouri History Museum Photographs and Prints Collections, St. Louis.

so that he would not be sold away. Leonard determined that he could not afford to buy William without selling another of his slaves. Before Leonard could find the means to purchase him, William "was carried & sold south." Even though Ann was a great favorite of the Leonard family, this consideration did not result in the acquisition of what she most desired—an intact family. Leonard's paternalistic inclinations would not allow him to trade one slave for the happiness of another. As much as he appeared to want to accommodate Ann, be believed that his finances would not allow it.[44]

A few owners considered the needs of abroad couples when they sold slaves, divided estates, or migrated, but practically, most were unwilling or financially unable to purchase slaves in order to unite families. If the new distance between households could not be traveled in a few hours, the separation was "tantamount to a divorce" in the eyes of both white and black communities. Although it is not clear what actually transpired, it appears that the marriage of John Ewing's parents was dissolved when his father was sold. Interestingly, the records indicate that in 1860 Ewing's father died in the same county in which his family still lived. His father possibly was sold just far enough away that it became impractical to visit his wife and family. Sales that moved men and women at greater distances were certain to destroy marriages. Henry Smith explained that he did not voluntarily separate from his first wife, Martha, "[T]he white people divorced us—sold her off."[45]

Slaves praised owners they believed had acted to keep families together. One former slave reported that her mother's owner treated her family favorably and specifically pointed to the fact that the mistress did not sell her slaves as proof of her kindness. Three former bondpeople claimed that either the mistress or white children intervened to stop the sale of a favored individual. Assurances from owners that they would protect the sanctity of families might work to the benefit of slaveholders, as slaves often rewarded these efforts with loyalty. Gus Smith's situation was a case in point: "Our master would not sell any of us. He did not believe in separating us, and tried to keep us together. He didn't have any trouble with his slaves at all. He was as good a man as ever lived and we did pretty much as we pleased."[46]

In a strange twist, abroad marriages had the potential to work to the advantage of slaves because they possessed a unique flexibility that protected some from permanent separation from family members. Relationships often were little disturbed by estate divisions or sales if slaves were transferred to local owners, as was most often the case in Missouri. Slave husbands, such as Matthew Carroll, merely continued their visits to their wives. Malinda Discus claimed that her parents' abroad marriage survived a series of sales and estate divisions. Remarkably, the couple ended by living together on the same farm when the widow of her father's master married the eventual owner of her mother and siblings. Abroad couples certainly understood the limitations of their separate existences, yet these marriages were so common in Missouri that slaves may have accepted the arrangements as normative. A former neighbor explained that despite the sale of Mary Brown and her first child, Mary and her husband, Jesse, "continued to live together as husband and wife, as much as slaves belonging to different masters could." Local sales rarely

destroyed slave marriages. The distance traveled to visit loved ones may
have become more formidable, but most slave men believed it worth the
effort to spend a little time with their families. But even nearby separations of young slave children from their mothers would have been a
considerable hardship.[47]

The many destructive effects of abroad marriages and divided families were somewhat tempered by the fact that many men, women, and
children did not face the challenges of slavery alone. Many bondpeople,
although daily separated from their husbands or wives, lived on their
owners' farms with other slave men and women, who often were their kin.
The ravages of sale and death, as well as the realities of abroad families,
resulted in the construction of household forms that were alternatives to
the nuclear family. Slaves made the best of the situations in which their
owners had placed them and forged ties with other bondpeople living on
their holdings in order to help ease the burdens of slavery. Sometimes
housemates were extended family members, but in other cases Missouri
slaves lived with unrelated individuals who were embraced as family.
Composite households existed throughout the South and were due to
many factors, including death and the slave trade, but in Missouri they
were most frequently a result of the prevalence of abroad marriages.[48]

In the five counties studied, only 28 percent of slaveholdings in 1850
and 27 percent in 1860 comprised just slave women or slave women and
children alone. In fact, a full 47 percent of slaveholdings in 1850 and 50
percent of slaveholdings in 1860 had in residence both male and female
adults. Slave men were even less likely to live without slave women. Only
10 percent of slaveholdings in 1850 and 11 percent of slaveholdings in
1860 had in residence just men or men and children alone. If half of slaveholdings consisted of both male and female adults and only one-quarter
of slave couples were part of resident marriages, it can be concluded that
a great number of abroad and single women resided on slaveholdings
with slave men who were not their husbands. Many of the men living
with abroad women may have been related in ways other than marriage;
they were fathers, brothers, and sons. While it was common for young
adult sons to contribute to the support of their aging parents, younger
slave women also were assisted and protected by male relatives and occasionally even unrelated men, who may have been engaged in abroad
unions as well. In the face of limited assistance from husbands, consan-
guineous ties were especially important to abroad women. For their part,
female relatives may have assisted men whose wives lived abroad with
daily tasks such as cooking meals and cleaning cabins. In the absence of

FIGURE 9. Slave cabin at the Cedars. This Jefferson County, Missouri, slave cabin is typical of the double pen cabins with an enclosed dogtrot that were common in the Missouri countryside during the early days of settlement. Slaveholders initially lived in log cabins and often turned them over to their slaves after they constructed finer homes. It is likely that this large cabin housed two slave families. Courtesy of the Historical American Building Survey, Library of Congress.

daily support from spouses, abroad men and women sought assistance from those with whom they lived whether or not they were related (see table 5).[49]

It appears that many abroad wives did not live alone with their children in their own cabins. In 1860 an average of five to six slaves lived in a cabin together—two or three of whom were adults sixteen years or older. Two abroad wives and their children occasionally shared a cabin. Maria Bayne reported that she saw David Price weekly when he came to visit his wife, with whom she shared a home. Other abroad men and women continued to live in the same cabins as their parents. In fact, 13 percent of slaveholdings in 1850 and 16 percent of slaveholdings in 1860 were intergenerational in nature; many of these were made up of parents living with their adult children. Clarinda Smith's mother and siblings testified that they lived together with Clarinda in a two-room cabin and often saw her sleeping in bed with her abroad husband, Alfred Smith. The priority of most slaves was to configure their households in ways that helped to elevate the circumstances of those who lived within, but even if they did not reside in the same cabin, they could choose to mutually support one another. Forging ties to other bondpeople especially was crucial to the well-being of abroad families. Abroad women likely welcomed assistance from relatives and friends living with them on their home farms; however, this help could not entirely substitute for the important daily role of a resident husband and father.[50]

"He lived happy only when with his wife and children"

Most abroad couples did not have the luxury of daily contact, but many, such as Spotswood and Orry Rice, created long-lasting relationships regardless of the difficulties facing them. Historical sources, including the WPA narratives and pension records, reveal the existence of strong bonds of marriage and family among many Missouri slaves. Many couples maintained long-term relationships, including those of abroad couples, which lasted long after slavery ended and were broken only by death. Of course, the success of widows' and orphans' claims was dependent on evidence of strong marriages between the claimants and the soldiers, a positive portrayal frequently corroborated by affidavits from friends, family, and former owners.

In the 1890s, Isaac and Mary Fowler, former Missouri slaves, filed a pension claim as the aging parents of Henry S. Fowler. Henry, who was their second child, died in March 1864 at the age of eighteen at Benton Barracks. In an effort to prove their relationship to their son, the Fowlers enlisted the testimony of a bevy of relatives, friends, and former owners. The pension board was presented with the story of a deeply devoted couple who, in nearly fifty years of marriage, saw the birth of fourteen children, watched most of them die, survived both slavery and the turmoil of the Civil War, and made a life together following emancipation. Their extraordinary partnership started with both of their owners consenting to their marriage in 1844. For the first twenty years of their married life, the two lived on separate farms, and Isaac was allowed to visit his family only on Saturdays and occasionally once more during the week. By all accounts, both white and black neighbors recognized the marriage and the children from it as legitimate despite the fact that Isaac and Mary did not live together. Isaac may not have spent much actual time with his children, but it was reported that he was extremely attentive when he was with them.[51]

The Fowlers were by no means unique. As in other parts of the South, Missouri slaves demonstrated an amazing ability to adapt to their circumstances. Given the alternative of isolation, most men, women, and children accepted the limitations of abroad families and relished the little time they spent with one another. Although these relationships were challenging to maintain, vital emotional ties existed between many men and women and between children and their fathers regardless of the distance that often physically separated them. They tenaciously made these truncated families work for long periods of time. The WPA interviews confirm that, in the face of high mortality and the deprivations of slavery, abroad marriages were remarkably resilient. Death, sale, or flight severed only 24 percent of abroad marriages. Pension claims also point to the longevity of many Missouri slave marriages. There are few fifty-year-long marriages, like that of the Fowlers, found in the pension records because most of the young and middle-aged soldier husbands died during the war. There were a great number of marriages, however, that lasted fifteen or twenty years and produced many children: 57 percent of those pensioners who recorded their wedding dates were married ten years or more; 32 percent of couples were married fifteen years or longer; and 14 percent were married twenty years or longer. Following the war, Missouri's former slaves were required by law to legitimize their marriages through legal ceremonies and registration, and thousands of men and women were remarried under this 1865 statute. The marriage records generally provide no date of the couple's original marriage, but they do list their children. Many reported a large number of offspring, suggesting that their marriage during slavery was long-lasting. Of the 269 couples who registered in 1865 and 1866 in Boone and Chariton Counties, 54 percent had been together for close to ten years, and 20 percent of these unions were approximately fifteen years or longer. Not only had these relationships survived slavery, but the couples chose to remain together after emancipation. There is no way to confirm their living arrangements, but it can be assumed that abroad marriages occurred at equal rates to those in the WPA narratives and pension claims. Therefore, over one-half of these unions were likely abroad marriages (see table 6).[52]

Many abroad couples demonstrated considerable affection for each other. Former slaveholding family members testified to how well Jane Washington's husband, Lewis, treated her and how devoted he was to his family. Lewis apparently never missed a weekly visit to his wife and three children. A former white neighbor complimented the Lewises in a somewhat backhanded manner: "They appeared to be quite devoted and lived more harmoniously than most darkeys." Thomas and Mary Vaughn had many children together and were described by Juliet Halliburton, the daughter of their former owner, as "the most exemplary couple of negroes I ever knew." Emanuel and Elizabeth Gatewood married in August 1846 and had nine children in the following years. A family friend lauded him as "was one of the best man [sic] that ever lived and he lived happy only when with his wife and children." While serving in the army, Emanuel wrote a loving letter to "My Dear Wife," asking her "to take care of yourself and the children for my sake." He reported that he frequently awoke in the middle of the night and thought about them. When Emanuel left to join the army, he asked his wife's master and mistress to care for his family until he returned. Tragically, death parted Emanuel Gatewood from his family.[53]

Like Clara McNeely Harrell, whose "pappy . . . belong [sic] to a neighbor," a majority of Missouri slave women and children faced their enslavement without the daily support of husbands and fathers. For most hours in the week, mothers were forced to meet the emotional, physical, and economic needs of their children without the assistance of their husbands. Often visiting during the dark of night, slave men spent little time with their families. It is no wonder then that some children had few memories of their fathers and gave limited weight to their importance in the household. Despite the many limitations, abroad marriages were extremely important to Missouri slaves. The fact that the men and women chose one another was crucial to their sense of self and gave them some measure of control over their lives. Enslaved Missourians demonstrated their adaptability as they worked diligently to create and maintain family, kinship, and community ties despite the many challenges facing them. Although physical distance limited the role of these relationships in their everyday lives, Missouri men, women, and children tenaciously fashioned families that enabled them to survive their enslavement, minimize their feelings of isolation, and create some happiness in their lives.[54]

6 / "We all lived neighbors": Sociability in Small-Slaveholding Neighborhoods

Archibald Little Hager was an astute observer of the many happenings in his Perry County neighborhood; for twenty-six years he faithfully chronicled weddings, births, sicknesses, deaths, sales of land and slaves, and even beatings and shootings involving his kin and neighbors. Hager was not a slaveholder, yet he maintained close relationships with many who were. He described a community where people knew their neighbors well and often cultivated their associations through mutual aid and sociability. His detailed journal reveals that the residents of Perry County, both slave and free, were inextricably connected to one another through the course of their everyday work and social interactions.[1]

Archibald Hager described his Perry County neighborhood as expansive, encompassing local residents who shared similar backgrounds and experiences. Sites of sociability allowed people to connect with one another, but they also excluded those who were considered outsiders. White and black residents of Perry County did not share all social spaces, and for that matter, all white people did not socialize with one another. Instead, neighborhoods often were created within neighborhoods. Hager clearly excluded from his definition of neighbor a large group of German Saxon immigrants—people with a different language, customs, and faith—who had recently settled on the eastern margins of the county. Hager also suggests that there were many instances in which his neighbors were segregated by age, gender, and race. Men and women engaged in some social activities together, although just as often they socialized apart. Enslaved Missourians were especially effective at developing their own social networks—often hidden—within the framework of the large whole.[2]

Approximately 150 miles to the north of Perry County, a slave man named Alfred Smith forged vital connections with other bondpeople living throughout his Pike County neighborhood. Soon after the Civil War, both Esther Smith and Clarinda Morton filed claims with the federal government for the military pension of Alfred Smith. Esther Smith disputed Clarinda Morton's assertion that she was Alfred's wife and argued that as the soldier's mother she was entitled to her deceased son's pension. Morton defended her claim by asking her relatives and friends to testify that she had married and cohabitated with Alfred Smith in the years before his enlistment. Although her main objective was to prove the validity of her abroad marriage, a fortunate and unintended consequence of the resulting paper trail is a detailed description of the complex relationships that existed between slaves living on the farms of Pike County. The picture that emerges from the pages of Alfred Smith's pension file, and those of hundreds of other Missouri soldiers, is one of strong bonds of family and friendship forged within rural neighborhoods where bondpeople knew one another well and were interconnected through their families, owners, work, and play.[3]

Archibald Hager and Alfred Smith's friends and family described close-knit communities in which neighbors interacted with one another as they conducted business, provided mutual aid, and gathered socially. Most white Missourians owned small to medium-sized farms—there were more farms under one hundred acres than over; therefore, neighbors' homes frequently were located a short distance from one another. The immediate neighborhood was the site of the most intense and frequent socializing as neighbors regularly exchanged social calls and lent aid to one another. Neighbors both black and white knew the business of those who lived within "hallooing distance." They associated as they sat at one another's firesides, passed by neighbors' farms on the way home, labored in close proximity in the fields abutting property lines, and ran into one another while rambling, hunting, or working in nearby woods. Neighbors figured prominently in Missourians' accountings of their lives, no matter their social standing.[4]

Rural Missourians' social circles also radiated outward from their home farms and neighborhoods; however, the extent of this social interaction was dependent on an individual's place within his or her household and society. White youngsters often walked to the local one-room schoolhouses where they met neighborhood children, thus connecting their families to those of their fellow students. White men rode to the nearest town to purchase goods at mercantile establishments and haul crops to mill and market, and they periodically attended court sessions and conducted legal business at the county seat. White women's social activities were more constrained; most regularly traveled only as far as the local church and to friends' and relative's homes for occasional social calls or to lend a hand to those in need. The small size of most slavehold-ings and the nature of Missouri farming required slaves to forge social connections beyond their home farms as well. Rural roads and byways were alive with slave men who conducted their owners' business during the week and visited their abroad families on the weekends. These travels often took them far afield from their home places, and they frequently paused in their journey to stop and chat with other bondpeople who lived along the way. As with white women, slave women's mobility was more circumscribed, although they too worshipped at local churches on Sundays and attended work frolics and wedding feasts on Saturday evenings. Slave children played with neighborhood children—both black and white. Most white Missourians gave their blessings to these types of social interactions among slaves, yet clandestine socializing also oc-curred behind the closed doors of slave cabins or in abandoned buildings and clearings in the woods.

Since the 1970s, historians have raised many questions about the na-ture of southern communities. They have explored the ways in which people related socially with one another, with a special focus on the relations between planters and yeomen and how slaves' relationships with others living in plantation slave quarters helped them survive their enslavement. They have also examined how women's social experiences differed from those of men and how slaves and poor white neighbors forged connections with others in the neighborhood through economic exchanges, social interaction, and intimate relations. Nearly all these studies have focused on the plantation regions of the South, however, with only limited study of the southern backcountry or borderlands such as Missouri.[5]

Demographics, farm and slaveholding sizes, and settlement patterns altered the nature of social interactions among rural Missourians from those found in the plantation South. Residents of Missouri neighbor-hoods—slaveholders, yeomen, and slaves alike—knew one another well and were interconnected through the activities of their everyday lives. Relationships were forged on the church lawn after Sunday services, in town on county court day, in local schoolhouses and mercantile establishments, and at frolics or in neighbors' kitchens and parlors. Black and white Missourians shared significant community spaces, especially in their churches; however, they just as often segregated themselves according to race, class, and gender.

"[C]itizens of this County are nearer on an equality . . . than in any place"

During the first decades after statehood, there was little question that Missouri was a slave society, with slavery placed firmly at the center of the state's economy, politics, and social relations. The slaveholding culture that emerged in Missouri was not unlike that in the rest of the South, but in the absence of a large planter class, small slaveholders dominated during the antebellum years. This was despite the fact that the slaveholding class on average owned fewer slaves and accounted for a much smaller percentage of the total free population of the state than in the rest of the South. Slaveholders made up 18.4 percent of Missouri's free population in 1850 but only 12.5 percent in 1860. In southern states as a whole, slaveholders constituted a little more than one-fourth of the free white population in 1860. Yet, slaveholders were the upper echelon of Missouri society, commanding the greatest wealth through their ownership of land and slaves. In New Lebanon Township in Cooper County, slaveholders disproportionately held a greater percentage of property, for example. In 1860, slaveholders accounted for 17 percent of the households in the township, yet they owned 46 percent of the real estate and 57 percent of the personal property, which included slaves. Up until the Civil War, slaveholding politicians—many of them from the largest slaveholding counties—controlled statewide politics. Initially strong supporters of Democratic Senator Thomas Hart Benton, members of the "Central Clique" routinely placed agrarian issues, such as support for hard currency, over the commercial interests of St. Louis merchants.[6]

Yet, Missouri society was more socially fluid than in the plantation regions—at least it appeared that way to slaveholders. On arriving in Boone County in 1834, Walter Raleigh Lenoir was pleased to find that the "citizens of this County are nearer on an equality as respects property than in any place I ever was in. They own good land and a few slaves, and appear contented with what they have and care not who possesses more." Indeed, landownership was widespread in rural Missouri, although a few wealthier Missourians, like Abiel Leonard, owned large tracts of land that they leased to tenants. Even so, young men and newcomers often rented land with the idea that they would save enough to eventually purchase their own farms and possibly even slaves.[7]

Slaveholders and nonslaveholders were interconnected in many ways. Although slaveholders on average owned larger farms and produced more, nonslaveholders grew similar crops and also raised livestock. Missouri farms typically were not large, and white Missourians frequently traveled throughout their neighborhoods conducting business and visiting one another. Slaveholders and yeomen bought land next to one another and they patronized the same merchants and millers. They attended Sunday services together and their children sat side by side at the local subscription schools. Slaveholding men served on juries and attended militia musters with their nonslaveholding peers, as well as gambled, drank, and watched horse races together. Slaveholding and nonslaveholding men, women, and children visited one another and attended parties, dances, and weddings. They jointly partook of amusements such as political speeches, agricultural fairs, traveling circuses, and Fourth of July festivities. Few Missouri slaveholders owned so many slaves that they believed that they were too superior to socialize with their hardworking, like-minded neighbors, especially if they or their kin also hailed from Upper South states such as Kentucky or Virginia.

Affluent slaveholders had access to some institutions that their less wealthy neighbors could not afford, however. Many sent their older children to institutions of higher learning such as the Kemper School, Clay Seminary, Howard Female College, William Jewell College, or the University of Missouri. While in attendance at these schools many students joined collegiate literary societies, such as the Erodelphian Literary Society of Lexington's Masonic College or the Eunomian Literary Society of Liberty's Clay Seminary. Slaveholders' sons and daughters forged friendships with other young people from the slaveholding and business or professional class who hailed from throughout Missouri and nearby states. Many educated and socially connected adults also participated in voluntary associations, such as agricultural improvement societies, fraternal orders, temperance organizations, and literary and debating societies, which allowed them to socialize with others who shared similar views. But although both slaveholders and nonslaveholders held offices in the churches and local governments, slaveholders remained more politically powerful at the state and national level.[8]

Gender was perhaps the greatest factor determining the nature of so-cial interactions among rural white Missourians. Men had more oppor-tunities to travel the neighborhood in the course of their work and civic duties. They rode into the local towns and hamlets to purchase goods and to county seats to attend circuit court proceedings and sheriffs' sales. A Jefferson City newspaper described a scene that many Missourians would have found familiar; it was reported that at a local slave sale "a large number of persons were in attendance from all parts of the coun-try, and the bidding was unusually spirited." Although some women, and even slaves, attended these sites of civic engagement, white men dominated these social spaces. The events often were marked by political speeches, male camaraderie, and the consumption of large amounts of alcohol, as is so well depicted in the electoral paintings of the Missouri artist George Caleb Bingham. White men, regardless of their social sta-tus, were bound together by these rites of citizenship; the most socially affluent usually commanded center stage in these civic displays, yet all white men were included in the proceedings, while dependents, such as women, children, and slaves, were symbolically pushed to the periphery. As the historian Harry S. Laver has observed, gendered civic ceremonies, like militia musters, "bridged class differences with out threatening their hierarchical order." These public rituals served to remind white men from across the social spectrum that they were equals by virtue of their gender and race, as well as demonstrated to their dependents that they were the masters of both their households and their society. Perhaps no activity, outside of voting and the militia, united white men in common cause more than service on the neighborhood slave patrol. Local white men banded together to maintain the slavery regime through vigilant, and oftentimes violent, enforcement of restrictions on slaves' mobility and attempts to assemble.[9]

White Missourians living in the countryside overwhelmingly sup-ported slavery even though most did not own slaves. They recognized that slaves were a primary source of labor in rural Missouri; a large num-ber, like the professionals and businessmen of Rocheport and Palmyra, became de facto slaveholders when they hired slaves, and many aspired to slave ownership in the future. Some, such as Willard and Mollie Men-denhall, nearly always had other people's slaves in their employment. It is not surprising that many nonslaveholding Missourians supported slavery given their widespread involvement with the system and their historic ties to the Upper South.[10]

A few slaveholding men also traveled into the greater world in the course

FIGURE 10. *The County Election.* 1852. The Missouri artist George Caleb
Bingham (1811–1879) illustrates the workings of frontier democracy in his
1852 election day painting. A sometime Whig politician, Bingham's strong
feelings about the strengths and weaknesses of the American democratic
process are clearly suggested in his paintings. An astute observer of life in
early Missouri, Bingham captures the essence of these male-dominated civic
gatherings. White men of all social classes gathered on equal terms to cast
their votes, while women are nonexistent and the sole black man is relegated
to serving liquor to the drunken crowd of citizens. Bingham mass-produced
and sold his images of American frontier and political life to a public audience. The original painting is in the collection of the St. Louis Art Museum.
Courtesy of the State Historical Society of Missouri.

of their work, broadening their experiences and social connections beyond the local neighborhood. While serving as a Missouri Supreme Court justice, William Napton spent much of his year in Jefferson City and St. Louis, where he engaged in boarding-house culture and attended lectures and theater productions. Merchants such as Silas McDonald made annual buying trips to St. Louis and sometimes even New York or Philadelphia.[11]

Social opportunities were more limited for white women because class-bound gender conventions and rural settlement patterns circumscribed their mobility. As in the South, it was expected that slaveholding women would not travel any distance without a male accompanying them, and as a consequence most white women were not as familiar with the local landscape or roads. Paulina Stratton often complained that her husband, Thomas, would not take her to church or to visit friends. In one instance, fearing that he would forbid her to go, she took her daughter and attempted to walk a distance to a friend's home but got lost along the way. Rural women occasionally accompanied their husbands to town on business or to attend community events like picnics and civic celebrations, but by and large their social circle remained their neighbors and kin. As time progressed, these webs of social relations became increasingly dense as slaveholders married others from their class, thereby connecting families to one another. Extended family members frequently lived near one another, but it was not unusual for more affluent women to travel many miles to visit relatives, often staying for months at a time. Abiel Leonard's nieces lived with his family for a long period of time so that they could attend school in Fayette, and Melinda Napton made a number of trips to her parents' home in Tennessee. Women living in town had increased opportunities for social interaction. Not only were cultural events, such as literary societies and theatrical performances, available, but women also traveled more freely throughout town as they patronized stores and visited friends' homes. Elvira Scott spent much of her time playing the piano, entertaining guests, and making social calls.[12]

Paulina Stratton vividly described the interactions among the residents of her Little Dixie neighborhood. Within five years of their move from Virginia in 1855, the Strattons were among the twelve wealthiest householders in the New Lebanon Township and among the nine largest slaveholders. They owned five hundred acres of farmland valued at $6,000 and had $8,000 worth of personal property, which included eleven slaves at a time when the average number of slaves per New Lebanon slaveholding household was only two. It is no wonder then that the family was so easily accepted into New Lebanon society. Despite their economic prominence, the Strattons did not set themselves apart from their less affluent neighbors and instead were friendly with both slaveholders and nonslaveholders alike. In fact, the Strattons counted among their closest friends and neighbors the Shacklefords and the Manns—neither of whom owned slaves. The Strattons socialized with people of all classes; neighbors aided one another when household members were sick, and they routinely exchanged goods and labor. Although slave ownership was not a criterion for friendship, the Strattons associated almost exclusively with other property owners who also hailed from the Upper South. Records from New Lebanon churches and schools also suggest the relatively egalitarian nature of the community with slaveholders and non-slaveholders both serving in leadership positions in these institutions.[13]

This freewheeling sociability went only so far, however. Like Hager, Paulina rarely mentioned the many German immigrants who lived in Cooper County in 1860, although a large number resided near Boonville, where they established German cultural institutions such as the Turn and Gesang Verein in the 1850s and a German-language newspaper after the Civil War. Similarly, she did not acknowledge the hundreds of Irish immigrants who lived only a few miles from her home while constructing the Pacific Railroad line. In fact, 14 percent of the county's white residents were foreign born in 1860. It is interesting to note that the Strattons never engaged in activities that were sponsored by the county's social elite either. They did not send their children to private academies, nor did they patronize programs at the newly constructed Thespian Hall in Boonville. Instead, Paulina socialized with her neighbors at local church services or during visits to their homes, while Thomas frequently attended auctions and journeyed into town on business or to patronize mercantile establishments. As they grew older, it was the Stratton children who traversed the neighborhood in a flurry of visits and party going. It is noteworthy that despite the Strattons' inclusive social circle, the three eldest children all married young men and women from local slaveholding families. All the while the Strattons were integrating themselves into the New Lebanon neighborhood, the Stratton slaves were forging relationships with local bondpeople as well.[14]

Slave Neighborhoods

Historians have identified the slave community found within the plantation slave quarters, with its vital religious and cultural heritage, as one of the most important mitigating factors for southern slaves. Since the 1990s, scholars have enriched and expanded the understanding of plantation slavery by exploring slaves' relationships with those living on adjoining plantations, as well as slaves' medical practices, ownership of property, and political activities. Yet few have described the ways slaves socialized in the many small-slaveholding regions outside of the plantation South. Most enslaved Missourians lived on small slaveholdings and, therefore, were deprived of the opportunity to engage with a plantation slave-quarter community. For most hours of the week, they toiled together with only the few other bondmen and women living with them and with members of the slaveholding family. In fact, some Missouri slaves had more daily contact with their owners than with fellow slaves.[15]

Some historians of slavery have argued that slaves on smaller holdings lacked participation in any meaningful slave community with its many benefits of psychological, physical, and economic support. Indeed, a few Missouri owners attempted to socially sequester their slaves. Robert Newsom denied his slave woman Celia's engagement with the greater slave community, and Eda Hickman was so isolated that her owners reportedly kept her unaware of emancipation. George Bollinger, a former slave from southeastern Missouri, observed that some slaveholders did not encourage their slaves to socialize. "Dey wuz a church, but we didden go much, 'en we never had no kind 'er gatherin's. Dey wouldn' let de cullered folks congregate—no, shu, why; even de man over at de store wouldn't let mo' dan two cullud folks come in at a time," he remembered. A minority of Missouri slaves, especially those living in the Ozarks and northern Missouri, lived in virtual isolation because the local slave population was so sparse. Sarah Waggoner reported that she often was the only black person in attendance at the church in her northwestern Missouri neighborhood.[16]

Scholars have argued that plantation slaves routinely forged relationships—often without their owners' consent—with individuals on nearby plantations. Missouri slaves resisted isolation as well by moving beyond their home farms to fashion cross-farm slave communities and kinship networks within the state's small-slaveholding districts. The work requirements of diversified agriculture and the conditions of small-scale slavery encouraged owner-sanctioned social interaction among bondpeople in the greater neighborhood. Slaves roamed the countryside doing their owners' business and participating in the extensive slave hiring system found in the state. Slaveholders also generally supported their slaves' engagement in social activities, such as work frolics and church services, which promoted their economic and management goals. But most important, slaveholders allowed liberal slave mobility in order to accommodate the many slave couples who lived on separate farms. Slaves required opportunities to meet and court their future spouses and to visit their families after they wed. Slaveholders inherently understood that the natural increase of Missouri's slave population was dependent on the creation of abroad slave families; therefore, they could not afford for their slaves to live in social isolation.[17]

Slaves knew other slaves within their neighborhoods well, frequently meeting at church services, family events, and community gatherings. The Civil War pension files of former slave soldiers and the WPA slave narratives shed new light on the vitality of bondpeople's social networks in small-slaveholding regions and reveal the ways in which they associated with one another. The records are filled with affidavits from fellow slaves testifying that they were present at the weddings, births, and funerals of their friends and relatives. Former Missouri slaves described in great detail their relationships with those who lived as their "near neighbors."[18]

Both slaveholding and nonslaveholding Missourians were quite familiar with local bondpeople. They met slaves as they conducted business for their owners, attended church, visited their abroad families, or were hired out. White Missourians occasionally testified in the pension records to acquaintances with slaves whom they did not own. For example, J. T. Anderson, a miller in Pike County, remembered Matthew Carroll well: "I have rolled logs and worked with Matthew and have Danced after his playing the Fiddle all night and knew as much about Matthew as I did about any black man." T. M. Rhea, a merchant, also knew Carroll from trading with him before and after the war. In another case, white Missourian Levi Dodd explained to the pension board that he knew Anna Priest well because he had "worked with her many a night when she was owned by Wm Priest at shucking corn, and other things."[19]

Missouri slaves, especially adult men, were constantly on the move throughout the countryside. Men frequently visited with inhabitants of other farms, especially slave associates, while running errands for their owners. Pleasant Smith could date the birth of Thomas Vaughn's son because he remembered stopping at a neighbor's farm to relay news of the baby's birth. Smith had been sent to Vaughn's master for ice and was whipped when he returned home because he allowed it to melt while he socialized. Garrett Williams was acquainted with Thomas Vaughn as well and remembered seeing him for the last time about a month before his enlistment when he stopped by his house on the way to town. Men also socialized with neighbors on their way to visit their abroad wives. Both Charles Elliot and Scott Merriwether stopped to chat with friends as they traveled to stay with their families each weekend. The pervasive practices of hiring slaves and exchanging them with slaveholding neighbors and relatives during periods of peak agricultural intensity also provided bondpeople with opportunities to meet others in the neighborhood. Slave women typically were not granted as much mobility as slave men; gendered work practices, unbalanced domestic and child care responsibilities within slave households, and customary ideas of abroad marriage visiting arrangements privileged the mobility of men. Men and women both sought out opportunities to spend time with other bondpeople, however, when they attended parties and church services and visited with kin.[20]

"We went to the same church and saw each other often"

Black and white Missourians were not entirely isolated from one another but instead shared significant social spaces. Slave, slaveholder, and yeomen neighbors regularly met one another in church buildings and revival grounds, on town streets and local roads, and at neighborhood farms and plantations for work frolics and wedding parties. An individual Missourian's experience of these social exchanges had everything to do with his or her position in the social order, however. A hallmark of slavery was slaveholders' desire to control the mobility and associations of enslaved people. Owners regularly monitored slaves' relations with both their white and black neighbors and used management of their sociability as an instrument of racial and labor control. Rules of deportment, dress, uses of space, and interpersonal relations all focused on these goals. On a fundamental level, slavery was a system of constraint; slaveholders sought to literally control the bodies—and ultimately they hoped the minds—of their slaves. Of course, neither goal could be fully realized. Even when owners co-opted their bondpeople's social occasions by inserting themselves into them, there was no guarantee that slaves experienced these moments of social integration in the ways intended by their owners.[21]

Missouri slaveholders diligently worked to dictate the terms of their slaves' social connections with others in the neighborhood. Owners willingly allowed their slaves to interact socially, yet they wished to regulate these activities and the physical spaces in which they occurred.

Slaveholders directly engaged in the social lives of their slaves by sponsoring social events. In this way, they promoted productivity and labor control, as well as demonstrated their mastery. In addition, slaveholders sincerely believed that granting their slaves permission to attend church services or to throw a wedding party or work frolic was an expression of their paternalistic benevolence. For their part, slaves were grateful for the chance to congregate with their neighbors, even though they understood the limitations of this owner-controlled sociability.

The most important shared social space was the local church; the epicenter of social life for many rural Missourians. During the early years of settlement, there were few churches and limited denominational diversity in the Missouri countryside. As late as the 1830s, Jacob Lanius, an itinerant Methodist minister, observed that in western Missouri "the people seem to have no relish for devine things. they will no[t] assemble even on the Sabbath, but are in the habit of spending this holy day in settling accounts, hunting, etc." Frontier church services often were held in congregants' homes until the funds could be raised to construct a church building. Lanius and other ministers rode circuits and preached to each congregation every four to six weeks. By the Civil War, however, Baptist, Methodist, Presbyterian, and, occasionally, Catholic churches were scattered throughout the countryside, and most bigger towns boasted a number of churches. Some neighborhoods, such as New Lebanon Township in Cooper County, developed around a church. The Reverend Finis Ewing and his congregation migrated together from southwestern Kentucky to central Missouri and made Cooper County the western center of the Cumberland Presbyterian Church. These Cumberland faithful and their descendents made up the core of New Lebanon and the surrounding area. By the time Paulina and Thomas Stratton moved to Cooper County in 1855, the neighborhood was well established and the New Lebanon Presbyterian Church, with its sizable congregation, stood at its social center.[22]

Outside of kinship networks, the social lives of many white Missourians revolved around their local church. This was especially true for women who, unlike men, did not generally attend local civic events. Sunday services gave rural people the opportunity to mingle with others with whom they shared similar beliefs. Paulina Stratton and other Missouri women frequently wrote about the many church services they attended and the sermons they heard. The Strattons were Presbyterians, but they also attended the services or camp meetings of other religious denominations. Reverend Lanius repeatedly commented about the hostility that existed between the various evangelical denominations and described his work to win converts from other churches, but, in the case of the Strattons and many others, the opportunity to associate with Christian neighbors and hear a good sermon trumped denominational allegiances. Attending Sunday services was the highlight of Paulina Stratton's week.[23]

Most antebellum Missouri churches, especially those located in counties with large slave populations, welcomed slave congregants, who often accounted for a third of the membership. White church members may have recognized slaves as their brothers and sisters in Christ, but they rarely treated them equally in the worldly matters of the church. Slaves could not hold church leadership positions, and most congregations created segregated seating for them. White women, who generally lacked authority within churches, in many cases also had their own seating area, separate from that of men. Holding positions of authority within Missouri churches was yet another avenue for white men to share common bonds, as well as exercise their mastery. Black and white members might stand equally before God, but the physical segregation of slaves and women in the pews of Missouri churches signified their unequal place in society. Malinda Discus attended church with her master, but was required to sit in a corner with fellow bondpeople. Isabelle Henderson described the local church as having "a gallery for the slaves." She recalled the reaction of white church members when an elderly slave woman named Cindy became so infused with the spirit that "she got 'happy' and commenced shoutin' and throwin' herself about." People sitting below scurried to get out of the way lest Cindy lose her balance and tumble over the balcony railing.[24]

Not only were churches the social hubs of rural neighborhoods, but many evangelical sects attempted to set community standards for morality as well. Ecclesiastical church trials were used to discipline both white and black congregants for "disorderly conduct" and various other infractions. Members were tried for moral lapses such as adultery, drunkenness, dancing, and failing to attend Sunday services. Tribunals were convened to meet with the accused and investigate the validity of the charges. If the offense was minor and the wayward member repentant, he or she was graciously accepted back into church fellowship. Membership was severed only if the fallen brother or sister did not seek forgiveness or the moral lapse was especially egregious. Evidence about black and white members' relationships within the walls of the church is scanty, but these trials suggest the racial hierarchy that existed in Missouri churches. In most cases, white church members, rather than fellow slaves, "visited" slaves accused of immorality. It is unclear whether slave members were allowed to vote on exclusion cases, but it is unlikely that they were given this privilege. Discipline cases also rarely addressed issues related to slavery, although in 1845 the Lexington Presbyterian Church cited Bother William Rowe for "cruelty in the treatment of his servants." He was simply reprimanded for the abuse and allowed to remain in the church.[25]

The ecclesiastical trials of Cooper County's Mount Nebo Baptist Church—a church attended by many of Paulina Stratton's neighbors—provides valuable insight into the ways in which congregations regulated the behavior of the faithful. Mount Nebo members frequently were cited for routine infractions, such as drunkenness, dancing, and card playing, and, as was true elsewhere, wayward members were usually accepted back into the fold if they were contrite and asked for forgiveness. Occasionally, members requested exclusion from the fellowship of the church if they acknowledged their unwillingness to reform. Mount Nebo congregants also used the church court to mitigate personal and business disputes among members and even to resolve marital problems. Oftentimes, the individuals involved settled their disagreements before the congregation could act on their cases. Discipline cases overwhelmingly were brought against white church members. Few slave members were charged, perhaps suggesting a lack of interest in slaves' personal lives, a racialized belief that slaves would be unable to adhere to strict evangelical moral standards, or a recognition that slave discipline was the purview of owners rather than the church. In the few cases of immoral conduct brought against enslaved members, the congregation most often voted for exclusion. In 1836 the Mount Nebo congregation demonstrated some concern for slaves when they excluded William Lowry for "buying and selling slaves for the [lower] market," however. There is no way to know if the church only became involved when Lowry sold Mount Nebo congregants south, or if the case reflected a negative opinion of the interstate slave trade in general.[26]

Missouri churches also aided slaveholders as they worked to control the behavior of their slaves. As in the rest of the South, many slaveholders encouraged their bondpeople to embrace Christianity and join the church, hoping that once converted they would internalize evangelical values of obedience, sobriety, frugality, and hard work. It was commonly believed that Christian slaves would be more content in their enslavement and less likely to rebel or flee. Slaveholders' concerns about the ways in which small-scale slavery compromised their authority especially may have motivated them to encourage their slaves' conversion

FIGURE 11. Mount Nebo Baptist Church. The Mount Nebo Baptist Church was founded near Pilot Grove, Missouri, in Cooper County, in 1820. The congregation began construction of the extant church building in 1856, and the first services were held in August 1857. A partition ran down the middle of the sanctuary to separate men's and women's seating; each section had its own entrance. Enslaved congregants were segregated in a balcony. The design of the church was typical of rural Missouri churches of the time. Courtesy of the Historical American Building Survey, Library of Congress.

so that discipline might be internalized rather than outwardly imposed. The few slaves on most Missouri holdings made it less practical for owners to organize special slave churches or services, and in most cases owners expected their slaves to accompany them to the "Boss' Church." Steve Brown's master went out of his way to make sure that his slaves regularly attended church, and Brown recalled, "Massa had a fine big carriage and one Sunday he'd take all de white folks to church and de next Sunday, he put de cullud folks in de carriage and send dem to church. Dat's how come us to be Catholics." Other owners did not care if their slaves belonged to the same congregation as long as they attended services. Lewis Mundy was a member of the Baptist Church, and his mistress was a member of the Christian Church, while Paulina Stratton's slave man Ike was baptized at Mount Nebo Baptist Church rather than New Lebanon Cumberland Presbyterian. Other owners provided religious instruction within their homes. Robert Bryant's mistress "would read de Bible every night at 9 o'clock and she would 'splain it to me. If she was not able, her daughter read it." A prominent southeastern Missouri slaveholder also led his slaves in evening prayers.[27]

Many masters and mistresses, such as Paulina Stratton, believed that God charged them to evangelize among all those living in their households, including their slaves. Stratton did not wish to convert her slaves purely for reasons of control, but her personal and religious beliefs aligned with her economic and practical concerns, as was the case with many others. She sincerely believed that her personal salvation was jeopardized by her slaves' unconverted state. They often acted toward her in a manner she considered unbefitting of a Christian, and she frequently gave in to the temptation to respond to them in a like manner. At times she admitted that it was her personal failings that caused her to govern her slaves poorly; most often, however, she blamed the loss of her temper on their inability to behave right. She thought the best way to ensure their proper conduct was to convert them to her evangelical faith. Stratton was not unlike many slaveholders in hoping that evangelical conversion would be the solution to her servant problems. If they were Christians, her slaves would accept their servitude and acknowledge her authority as God's worldly representative. Stratton's attempts to read to and instruct her slaves in religious doctrines were of little avail, with the exception of Ike, but in spite of their apparent lack of interest in her faith, she continued to pray for their conversion.[28]

Some ministers, like the Methodist circuit rider Jacob Lanius, appeared to be genuinely concerned about the religious state of the slave population. During his preaching career, Lanius was particularly interested in converting Missouri slaves to evangelical Christianity. In an 1834 journal entry, Lanius observed that missionaries were sent to the far corners of the earth and yet the church largely ignored the plight of American slaves. He lamented that the church members' homes where he held his services were too small to accommodate both white and black worshippers. He solved the problem by establishing separate meetings for his slave congregants, arguing that they could not relate as well to the spiritual messages that he delivered to whites. Lanius's own preaching was invigorated by the religious enthusiasm of his black parishioners. He wrote in the winter of 1837, "On Sabbath my own soul rejoiced in the Lord while administering the Holy Supper and engaged in worship with the negroes. To [sic] joined the church the one a young lady and the other an african exhorter of the baptist church." Lanius's uplifting experiences preaching to slaves and his success among them encouraged him to continue his evangelical mission. Yet, Lanius was still bound by the racial prejudices of his time despite his apparently sincere concern for slaves' souls. Lanius may have referred to the converted slave woman as a lady, but unlike his white church members, he never once listed slaves' names at their conversion. Saving slaves was an important missionary project for Lanius, but he never got too close to those he believed he was helping. In addition, it was unclear whether he tailored his spiritual messages to accommodate the actual needs of his enslaved listeners or because of race-based assumptions about appropriate lessons for those who were held in bondage. Lanius's involvement in Missouri's Colonization Movement suggests that he may have been most comfortable if his congregants had been freed and transported to Africa.[29]

Jacob Lanius boasted about the sizable slave congregations on his circuit. Apparently slaveholders were comfortable with the messages he preached and allowed their people to attend his meetings, perhaps suggesting that he encouraged slaves to be submissive to the laws of both God and man. As elsewhere in the South, white ministers taught spiritual lessons to slaves that strengthened the authority of their owners. It was no coincidence that slaveholders often encouraged ministers to preach to bondpeople at separate services, believing that the message could be better tailored for them. "In the county where I was raised de white people went to church in de morning and de slaves went in de afternoon," Mary Bell remembered. A few larger slaveholders, such as Tishey Taylor's New Madrid County master, Shapley Phillips, invited ministers to their plantations to preach directly to their slaves. While some slaveholders were concerned with their slaves' souls, many masters and mistresses merely wished for them to learn to be good servants. Tishey Taylor provided an excellent example of the "Christian" message that her minister preached to slaves: "I 'member every 'preach day' he say, 'Mind you not to steal from Missis or Marster.' He was plenty strong on that part." W. C. Parson Allen's "white preacher always read a special text to de darkies, and it was this, 'Servants, obey your master.'" Some Missouri slaves had access to black preachers, and a few could read the Bible for themselves, but a majority were forced to rely on the questionable spiritual messages promoted by white ministers.[30]

Most slaves fully understood the contradictions inherent in the messages of slaveholders' Christianity, however. "Yes, our Master took his

slaves to meetin' with him," Malinda Discus observed. "There was always something about that I couldn't understand. They treated the colored folks like animals and would not hesitate to sell and separate them,
yet they seemed to think they had souls and tried to make christians of
them." Harriet Casey also commented on the disparity between words
and deeds: "De mistress would take a couple of us young ones to church
but when we got home things were different." While sitting together in
the gallery or in pews at the back of the church enslaved Christians often
were skeptical listeners; rejecting what they believed were hypocritical or
self-serving messages endorsed by Missouri slaveholders. All the while,
Missouri slaves took away spiritual messages never intended by their
owners and embraced the liberating potential of Christianity instead.[31]

Slaves enjoyed socializing with one another at Sunday services
whether or not they embraced their owners' theology. Former slaves repeatedly recalled seeing their friends and relatives at church. Fleming
Robertson testified that he "knew Thomas and Mary [Vaughn] very well.
We used to visit each other often, went to the same church and saw each
other often in slave times." Beverly Givens was friendly with Millie Williams, "having been members of the same church and being fellow slaves
having frequent intercourse with each other both before and after the
war of 1861." Carrie Washington became well acquainted with Matthew
Carroll because she saw "him at Church nearly every Sabbath before the
war." Church attendance was a social outlet for slaves to which few slaveholders could find objections.[32]

In the late summer and early fall, white and black Missourians alike
looked forward to attending the many religious revival camp meetings
held throughout the countryside. These meetings often lasted for a number
of days and were held in the open air or under tents. People flocked to these
popular community events no matter which denomination sponsored the
meeting. Mark Discus remembered both white and black neighbors attending the camp meetings together "in the fall, after the crops was laid
by." Usually more than one minister preached at these events. Reverend Jacob Lanius presided at camp revivals throughout his career and saw them
as prime opportunities to increase the number of converts to the faith,
recording the conversion of around 150 individuals at one camp meeting
in his circuit. Many of the attendees chose to camp near the sites of these
meetings; therefore, the revivals served a social as well as a religious purpose. Paulina Stratton and her children frequently traveled to camp meetings near their home in Cooper County, and Carrie Washington first met
her fellow bondperson Matthew Carroll at a camp meeting soon after she

arrived in Missouri. Apparently, God was not the only thing on worshippers' minds; the behavior of those attending the meetings was often far from wholesome. Lanius reported that a number of campers engaged in numerous vices at a northern Missouri Cumberland Presbyterian camp meeting, although he may have been merely wishing to draw a sharp contrast between the Methodist faithful and his Presbyterian rivals.[33]

Church was not the only social space shared by rural Missourians. Slaveholders and their slaves associated with one another at parties and dances that were held throughout the neighborhood on many Saturday evenings. These festivities frequently were in conjunction with work-related activities, such as house and barn raisings, grubbings, cornhuskings, and quilting parties. Archibald Hager chronicled the many "work frolics" held in his Perry County neighborhood. Owners frequently combined their small slave workforces to complete large jobs quickly and efficiently; neighboring slaves worked with the hosts' slaves to finish the task at hand. William Black, a former slave, explained that slaves had a "good time" at the local corn shuckings, "but we always shucked a lot of dat corn." Slaveholders and slaves often attended work frolics together, but slaves did most of the work. Hosts sometimes provided alcohol to quicken the work pace, as well as a dinner and often a dance, after the work was completed, although some evangelical slaveholders and slaves frowned on these practices. Slave fiddlers played for parties and were often paid for their services. Slaves typically ate and danced separately from their owners and guests, although white guests frequently stayed to observe the dancing feats of slaves—often through a lens of racial superiority. As the night wore on, slave guests usually were free to socialize separately, but the hosting master usually kept abreast of the activities in his barn and slave cabins.[34]

Slaves and slaveholders attended slave couples' weddings as well, often with dinner and dancing following the ceremony. The owners of both the bride and the groom were customarily present at these weddings, witnessing the vows and sometimes even administering them. Slaveholding family members and their friends usually ate the wedding supper first and then the bridal party and their guests were allowed to dine. White and black Missourians rarely ate together publicly; therefore, the neighbors gossiped when Edward Wingfield sat at the dining room table with his slaves during the wedding feast of his slave woman Elizabeth.[35]

Work frolics and weddings were well-attended, important neighborhood events, where slaves were allowed to meet and socialize with one another, often celebrating late into the night. Sarah Waggoner told of the "good times" she had at the neighborhood dances: "I liked to dance. . . . I was a regular king ruler at de dances. Many a time I danced till broad daylight, and den when I worked I was so sleepy, I'd nod, and nod." Sarah's permissive master sometimes allowed her to leave work in order to rest the day after she attended one of these local events. Owners occasionally allowed their slaves to organize parties, even when there was no need for the guests' labor. Tishey Taylor remembered that "maybe once week or more some one get 'mission' from his Marster and gib a 'hoe down'" and invited slaves from the neighborhood. Bondpeople of all ages might attend neighborhood frolics, although these events were especially the domain of the young. Slave men and women often used these gatherings as opportunities to form romantic attachments. In addition, parties were places where slaves felt greater freedom to express themselves personally as well as culturally. African American cultural traditions, such as music and dance, were disseminated during these social occasions. Slaves often attended church services, weddings, and dances wearing their Sunday finery. Henry C. Bruce claimed that his neighbors "were dressed almost as nicely as their owners, at any rate they looked as well as I have seen them on like occasions since they have been free." Enslaved Missourians valued the little time they were allowed to spend at neighborhood gatherings because these events presented opportunities for individuals to express themselves through the ways they adorned and moved their bodies, as well as the bonds of love and friendship formed and the words spoken and sung.[36]

The week between Christmas and New Year's Day was often the highlight of the neighborhood social scene and a time when Missouri slaveholders customarily lessened slaves' work burdens. Hired slaves traditionally came home from their yearly assignments during this time and awaited their placements for the following year. Since they were allowed only limited contact with kin during the year, they used this extended, and often unrestricted, downtime to socialize with friends and family. Some owners provided their slaves with extra food and alcohol for their celebrations and reunions. Louis Hamilton remembered that his owners "treated us with fun" during the Christmas holiday. Others gave their bondpeople presents, like the new clothes or candy received from the owners of Eliza Madison and Malinda Discus. Slaves were permitted to travel throughout the neighborhood—occasionally at great distances—to visit their family and friends. Gus Smith claimed that Osage County slaves were given the month of January to "go and come as much as we pleased and go for miles as far as we wanted to, but we had better be back by de first of February." Abiel Leonard allowed his slave man Wesley to cross the Missouri River to visit his relatives over the holiday week in 1850. Nathaniel Leonard was charged with keeping tabs on Wesley, although he reported to his brother that the slave man was out visiting in the neighborhood and he had not seen him since his arrival. A week later, Wesley had not yet returned home because bad weather made the river impassable. Most owners accepted that their slaves' social lives would take precedent over farm chores during the holiday season. In a letter dated December 20, 1849, Abiel Leonard asked that his trusted slave man, John, be responsible for the care of the livestock over the Christmas holiday because he was concerned that the other men would be inattentive to their work. During Christmastime 1863, Missouri slave men took advantage of this laxity and ran away to enlist in the Union army in large numbers.[37]

As with the churches, slaves often used the social opportunities sanctioned by their owners and transformed them to suit their own needs. Slaveholders tolerated these social gatherings primarily because they recognized that they gained economic and time-management benefits from them. They could tackle large work projects with the labor of their neighbors' slaves for the small cost of throwing a party. In addition, they celebrated slaves' marriages as a way to promote families and encourage fecundity. At the same time, they hoped to control their slaves' associations and the expression of their sociability through their physical presence at these social events. In the end, hosting frolics and weddings was crucial to masters' and mistresses' self-identity as paternalists and to the image they wanted to project to their slaves. Owners wanted bondpeople to both recognize their benevolence and simultaneously acknowledge their mastery. They could graciously provide a wedding feast for a bride and groom yet all the while remind them that they controlled even the most intimate aspects of their lives.

"De colored men would slip out at night sometimes for a little pleasure"

Missouri slaves were not altogether satisfied with owner-sanctioned gatherings, and instead many yearned for social spaces free from whites' gaze. They frequently socialized with their relatives and friends in more intimate and slave-centered gatherings, as well as congregated in clandestine locations, where their associations and social expressions were unconstrained. These underground activities gave them the space to associate in meaningful ways, freely sharing with one another and expressing themselves as they saw fit.

In small-slaveholding regions, extended family members frequently were scattered among slaveholdings and separated by many miles. Even immediate families were routinely divided when estates were settled, or when slaves were given to slaveholders' adult children. Others were sold locally or were temporarily hired away from their kin. The situation was not ideal, yet many bondpeople maintained rich relationships with their family members even though they did not live together. Given the local custom of liberal mobility, it is not surprising that some owners allowed their slaves to visit kin who lived nearby. Abiel Leonard sometimes granted Wesley permission to visit his mother, and in October of 1847, Jeanette Leonard reported, "Wesley's feeling were so much hurt—that he did not get to see his Mother—that he could not work any, for a day or two after you left." As a child, Fil Hancock visited his aunt one half mile down the road to show off his new red boots. Since slave families were often separated among slaveholding family members, accompanying and assisting owners on visits to their relatives allowed some bondpeople to maintain ties with their kin. Silas Morehead claimed that he saw his relatives every two or three weeks in spite of the fifteen miles separating them. His family members belonged to relatives of his owner, and they were constantly sent back and forth between the two households on errands. Others developed close kinship-like relationships with nonrelated individuals belonging to their owners' relatives. Maria Bruce knew Easter Vaughn well because "[s]he belonged to old Col. Owens and I to the Pages and those two familys were related so that Easter and I were practically raised in the same family." Bruce lived with her owner in Howard County and often visited the Owens farm in neighboring Chariton County. Martha Washington explained that she was well acquainted with John Fultz because "his White folks and our White folks were cousins." Although not blood relatives, Missouri slaves often fashioned relationships with others in their neighborhood into fictive bonds of kinship. Ultimately, these relationships could not provide the daily emotional and physical support that scholars have identified in plantation slave quarters, yet, as was the case with abroad marriages, enslaved Missourians reached out to form human connections in any way possible.[38]

The pension claims point to the rich relationships that many bondpeople maintained with their parents, siblings, grandparents, aunts, uncles, and cousins. Owners routinely attempted to co-opt significant events in slaves' lives, such as weddings, funerals, and births, but slaves rejected their proclivity to focus these important personal and family moments on their mastery. Slave neighbors and kin resisted these intrusions and gathered to collectively rejoice or mourn loved ones and friends, turning life events into celebrations of kinship and community instead. On behalf of would-be pensioners, former slaves frequently testified to their presence at the weddings, births, and funerals of relatives and neighbors. A successful pension claim required proof of conjugal unions and paternity, as well as the birth dates of children. Widows who were wed during slavery could not produce a marriage license; therefore, they asked their friends, relatives, and occasionally former owners, to testify to their marriages, or at the least, their "cohabitation" with the deceased soldiers. Those who were asked generally complied, describing their presence at the wedding celebrations of slave couples. Many others provided the birth dates of the soldiers' orphans. Pinpointing birth dates was crucial because only those children under the age of sixteen were entitled to a pension. Occasionally midwives and former mistresses testified that they witnessed a child's birth, but former slave women repeatedly claimed that they were present at the births of a grandchild or niece or nephew who lived in the neighborhood. Funerals were also well-attended community events, especially the funeral sermons that were often preached during a church service some time after the burial.[39]

For the most part, slaveholders were tolerant of their bondpeople's social involvement with others in the neighborhood. Henry Bruce observed that Chariton County slaveholders were quite lenient when it came to the social lives and mobility of their slaves. Bruce traveled unmolested throughout the countryside, often on his master's borrowed horse, with a pass in his pocket. He observed that not all masters were as permissive as his, but he blamed the curtailment of the "liberties of their slaves" on the fact that they had not been in Missouri long enough to adopt the more lenient, local customs.[40]

Slaves generally were unable to pursue their social interactions purely on their own terms, however. A few owners attempted to isolate their slaves by forbidding their involvement in the greater slave community, but most sought to control and limit their participation instead. Whether at a slave wedding or at a shucking party, a white person was usually within earshot. Slaveholders strongly discouraged gatherings of slaves without some supervision, worrying that unmonitored bondpeople might commit crimes or at worst plot insurrection. They also sought to limit connections between slaves and poor white people living in the neighborhood. A series of laws targeted the illicit trade in goods and alcohol that commonly occurred among people at the lower end of the social stratum, stemming from concerns that these exchanges might encourage theft of property and unsanctioned social gatherings. Missouri slaveholders were particularly wary of strangers, such as northern travelers or slave or free black riverboat workers, who they believed might foment rebellion or entice slaves to flee. In 1858, the *Marshall Democrat* advised its readers to watch "the itinerant population . . . [e]very one found talking with the slaves should be spotted and their movements closely watched." Owners especially worried that radical ideas might be transmitted between boat workers and local slaves laboring on landings, thereby connecting Missouri slaves to the Mississippi world and beyond. In 1842, Missouri lawmakers passed legislation banning riverboat workers from disembarking at the state's ports after four free black men with ties to the river world killed two St. Louis bank clerks during a robbery.[41]

Owners understood that slaves could communicate information to one another during unsupervised gatherings. Henry Bruce suggested as much when he observed that "[s]laves were much truer to one another in those days than they have been since made free." People were always listening to their owners' conversations about politics or the fate of fellow slaves, and first chance, they would steal away to report the news or offer warnings to their kin and neighbors. Slaves used this purloined information to their advantage, as they decided how to interpret local or national news or to respond to threats of sale or punishment. Slaveholders' fears about slave communication networks were compounded during the Civil War when enslaved Missourians shared news of Union victories and circulated rumors of imminent emancipation.[42]

Slaveholders attempted to control slaves' social interactions by requiring them to seek permission and a pass before they ventured off their home places. Henry Bruce observed that some owners limited the number of passes allowed, preferring their workers to rest rather than gallivant around at night. In spite of attempts to restrict their movement and associations, it appears that slave men and women roamed the Missouri countryside in great numbers—especially on the weekends, most traveling with passes or else risking punishment. George Bollinger observed: "[D]e darkies had better not congregate; cause day shore take 'em out an' flag 'em. If dey kotch you at a neighbor's house atter dark, you shore better have a pass fum yo' 'Massa.'" Any white person could demand that a slave present his or her pass, but slaves most feared harassment from the local slave patrol.[43]

Many Missouri counties established patrols in order to watch for run-aways and monitor the movement of local slaves. The number of slave patrols increased in the decade preceding the Civil War when the po-litical situation in Kansas heightened Missourians' concerns about abo-litionist influences both within the state and along its western border. Slave-stealing forays, such as those led by John Brown and John Doy, and an increased number of runaway attempts caused great alarm among white Missourians, especially those living in close proximity to Kansas, leading them to make it a priority to work together to keep their neigh-borhood slaves under control. "There was a tough gang called patrollers. Dey would scare de Negroes and would keep dem always afraid," Har-riet Casey observed. Marilda Pethy described the brutality of these local police forces: "De patrollers used blacksnake whips. Dey was a lot of de neighbors dat were patrollers. When dey would meet de colored men out at night, dey would ask dem if dey had a pass. If dey didn't, de patrollers would get off de horses and whip dem." Henry Bruce remembered that the patrols often were made up of "poor whites, who took great pride in the whipping of a slave." Some slaves tried to deceive illiterate whites, who often served as patrollers, by giving them "a portion of a letter picked up and palm it off on them as a pass." Literate slaves erased the dates in passes in order to recycle them, while others asked slavehold-ing children to write them passes. According to Bruce, Missouri slaves found it particularly gratifying to trick these poor white men, whom they held in such contempt.[44]

Despite their best efforts, slaveholders could not always regulate their slaves' social interactions. Even when they sanctioned their attendance at local parties and weddings, white Missourians could not control bondpeople's every movement and conversation. Not satisfied with the constraints of owner-sanctioned social interaction, many people craved more slave-centered sites of sociability. Slave men and women frequently left their cabins at night in search of social opportunities. Some ven-tured out to local gatherings without the permission of their owners or remained out past their curfews. In most cases, Missouri slaves lived in such close proximity to their owners' homes that it was difficult to meet quietly in their own cabins and they instead chose to gather in what the historian Stephanie Camp and others have called "rival geographies." Abandoned buildings and clearings in the woods often served as the sites of their clandestine gatherings.[45]

Slaves took great risks to attend neighborhood dances. A local slave-holder might host a party, but there was no guarantee that owners would grant their bondpeople permission to attend; so many chose to venture out without passes. Eliza Madison remembered that one fellow slave routinely traveled to dances and did not return until morning for which "he would get a whippin'." Tishey Taylor's master, Shap Phillips, allowed his slaves to attend social functions if they returned before their curfew. Taylor's mother, Katie Cherry, encouraged Taylor's sister to stay home from these parties if she thought she could not return home on time. Taylor explained that those who did not follow the master's rules "got 'it', and plenty of it." Marilda Pethy claimed that many of "[d]e colored men would slip out at night sometimes for a little pleasure." The slaves on Sam Biggs's farm were so anxious to host a party that they held one without their master's permission. William Black fondly remembered his master, Sam Biggs: "I guess de master knowed we was going to have one, 'cause dat night, when we was all having a good time, my sister said to me, 'Bill, over dere is old master Sam.' He had dressed up to look like us and see what we was up to. Master Sam didn't do anything to us dat time 'cause he had too good a time hisself."[46]

Henry Bruce remembered that patrollers often targeted the partygoers at the many dances he attended in Chariton County, although slaves with passes usually went unmolested. Men often were given general passes for work purposes or to visit their abroad families, but they were not adverse to using them to attend unsanctioned social engagements. In contrast, it was extremely difficult for women to procure passes for parties because they customarily did not travel on the business of their owners or to visit their families, and they, therefore, often were forced to attend these gatherings without permission. Women knew that the consequences of running afoul of patrollers could be grave, as they might suffer both physical and sexual abuse at the hands of these roaming bands of white men. At one dance in 1859, Bruce recalled that the patrollers found four young slave women in attendance without passes. The white men planned "to whip the four girls . . . right there in the presence of their beaux, who were powerless to protect them." A young slave man offered to take the lash in their stead, but after the girls were released, the man bolted and ran home to the protection of his master. When a group of local white "roughs" harassed slaves without passes attending a dance at a Chariton County mill, someone extinguished the lights and threw burning coals at the patrollers allowing everyone to escape. Many young slaves apparently believed that a few hours socializing with neighborhood friends were worth the risk of incurring the wrath of their owners or the local patrol.[47]

Slaves attended other kinds of activities that were either against the wishes of their owners or were simply illegal. There is ample evidence that many Missouri slaves—especially men—consumed alcohol. Owners routinely treated slaves to alcohol at the parties they hosted, as well as during holidays and special occasions, but they wished to limit the amount consumed, reasoning that intemperate workers were less productive and might injure their health. Some bondpeople gained access to alcohol despite their owners' attempts to control their drinking. George Farris was remembered as a heavy drinker who eventually went blind, and Annie Bridges's stepgrandfather drank himself to death. P. R. Hayden explained that the deaths of two neighborhood slave men from cholera were not surprising because they had contracted and died from the disease after neglecting their health and drinking too much. In 1850, Margarett Hughes sued three defendants in the Platte County Circuit Court and won a verdict of $850 because they "sold to a slave of mine, whisky without leave, which so much intoxicated the boy that he was unable to reach home, lay out all night—was very much frozed & consequently died." The clerk at a local store sold the alcohol to Willis, and he took it down the road to drink with the "white hands" at the local mill. Slaves could not legally purchase liquor without the consent of their owners, but there were many white people who were willing to sell to, and sometimes drink with, slaves. Although some slaves imbibed in solitude, many more drank when they congregated. Often these gatherings were small, informal, and usually without the consent of their owners. Alfred Smith frequently met fellow slave men at a cabin where they spent the night gambling and most likely drinking. Alcohol may have held an appeal in addition to lubricating slaves' festivities. Intoxication allowed bondmen—and occasionally women—to enter an altogether different kind of rival geography.[48]

Slaves also met with one another during informal religious gatherings led by slave preachers. Worshippers congregated "in the cab'ns an' out under the arbors on Saturday nights an' Sunday." Fil Hancock reported that as a child he knew nothing about formal church but instead relied on older slaves to take him to slave "churches out in de brash, under de shade trees. I kin 'member one of my cousins carryin' me pick-a-back, one time, three miles to church." He remembered that these meetings were held in the woods only during the summer months. It was in these settings that enslaved Missourians could worship as they pleased, free from the interference and self-serving theological messages of the local white churches. Bondpeople were able to express the liberating and egalitarian potential of Christianity, as well as participate in rituals that merged evangelical Christianity with African spirituality. In these gatherings, they could use their faith as a means to resist their enslavement both collectively and as individuals, turning religious worship into a political act.[49]

Other Missouri slaves practiced hoodoo and slave medicine. George Bollinger claimed that his father "had de power" and could break "Hoodoo" spells, and Tishey Taylor remembered Uncle John and Uncle Jake who came to "conjure" slaves when they were ill. Henry Bruce had a low opinion of conjurers, believing that they merely duped and fleeced gullible fellow bondpeople. These men and women claimed they could influence the actions of masters and slaves alike—conjuring masters to "be kind to a slave, to prevent him from selling one, even if he desired to do so, to make a girl love a man, whether she desired him or not, to make a man love and even marry a woman if she desired him." Individuals who believed in conjurers' powers willingly paid for their services. Bruce described them as wielding tremendous power among his neighbors. Many people refused to interfere with or dispute conjurers because they feared they might turn their reputed powers against them. Missouri slaveholders often disliked slaves gathering to listen to slave preachers or conjurers, worrying that these leaders within the slave community might communicate messages that would undermine their authority.[50]

Slaveholders sought to constrain not only the bodies but also the minds of their slaves. Most owners supported the law that banned teaching enslaved people to read and write, reasoning that they might forge passes or read abolitionist literature and, thereby, gain exposure to ideas that would make them unsatisfied with, or cause them to strike out against, their enslavement. Slaveholders were right to be alarmed by the subversive nature of literacy. Mary Bell's father stirred up trouble on his owner's plantation when he read news of the Civil War to his fellow slaves, for example. Chariton County slaves stole newspapers and carried them miles to people who they knew could read. During the election of 1856, they kept abreast of political news and expected to be freed if Republican John C. Frémont won.[51]

Most Missouri slaves were illiterate, although a few surreptitiously learned to read and write in spite of the law and their owners' restrictions. Young masters and mistresses taught some slaves to read and write, perhaps showing off their new literacy skills to slave children and adults with whom they associated so intimately. Madison Frederick Ross claimed that he progressed as far as the fourth grade under his young master's tutelage, and the white children took Lucinda Patterson's father to the basement and taught "him to read in a blue back spelling book." Often slaveholding children taught slaves without the knowledge of their parents. One man's master "would not allow him to have any books, but de master's son would steal a book and when dey was in de mines working . . . would go off in one side of de mine and dere learn to read and write." Henry Bruce and his siblings all learned to read and write well before emancipation—the older Bruce siblings taught the younger ones. Most slaves hid their literacy skills from their owners, fearing punishment. Charlie Richardson remembered, "We had to be mighty careful we didn't use a pencil or any paper or read out where the Marster could see us. He would sure lick us fer that." It was only on the eve of freedom that Sarah Waggoner's paternalistic master taught her "to count and learn about money so's de white folks couldn't cheat me after I was free." A few liberal owners taught their slaves themselves or allowed others to teach them. Smokey Eulenberg's mistress permitted her child's tutor to teach "some of de cullud children to read and write." Henry Bruce argued that Missourians were more permissive about literacy than elsewhere: "Slavery in some portions of Missouri was not what it was in Virginia, or in the extreme South, because we could buy any book wanted if we had the money to pay for it, and masters seemed not to care about it, especially ours, but of course there were exceptions to the rule."[52]

Many white Missourians worried that if slaves congregated unsupervised or had access to print materials it ultimately might lead to the commission of crimes, such as theft, rape, murder, or at worst insurrection. Owners understood that it was not practical to forbid their slaves' relationships with others in their neighborhood, however; farm work and maintenance of abroad marriages required mobility and sociability. They instead tried to manage their slaves' minds and bodies, but in the end they could not always monitor the movements, associations, or thoughts of their slaves.[53]

"We all lived neighbors, and I know the family as well as my own"

Whether meeting one another at churches, frolics, while visiting family, or clandestinely at night, Missouri slaves were all the while forming vital connections with other slaves in their neighborhoods. In the pension depositions, former Missouri slaves, or those who recorded their testimony, used the words "near neighbors" when describing other bondpeople in their communities. One former slave testified that he was well acquainted with Polly Beasley because he "lived a near neighbor to her all of the time." Slaves knew their "neighbors" well, establishing large networks of friends throughout the countryside. By 1866, Philander Draper had lived in Pike County for twenty-one years and claimed that he had "an extensive acquaintance in said county."[54]

Slaves living in close proximity often knew one another well. Flem Robertson and Thomas Vaughn lived on bordering farms and visited "each other weekly for years," and Susan Santafee had known Henry Whitson since her childhood because their masters lived on adjoining farms in Franklin County. James Wells and John Turner each lived on either side of the farm on which Emily Miller resided. Wells lived within sight of the "Miller place" and was "acquainted with the slaves on that farm very well." Missouri farms were small, and it was not unusual for slaves to live within shouting distance of those living on their neighbor's place. The owners of Burgess Harrison and Alfred Smith lived near one another, and Harrison recalled, "The house [sic] on the Wigginton and Smith farms were close together and we were in hallooing distance of each other for the 6 years that I lived there." Slaves lived close enough to be aware of both the work habits and the abuse suffered by their next-door neighbors. Henry Bruce knew much of what transpired on the farm bordering that of his owner. He recalled the circumstances that led to the whipping of four men belonging to the neighbor Mr. Cabel. Bruce, his brother, and the Cabel slaves were all making rails near one another in the woods between the farms. Mr. Cabel became infuriated by his slaves' lack of effort when he learned that the two Bruce brothers had made more rails than his four workers combined.[55]

Even slaves who lived miles apart were able to form relationships with one another because they frequently met in the course of their daily lives and at church and social occasions. Eliza Cochran lived about five miles from Frank Cochran, yet the two "often met each other, as neighbors, at gatherings and I was well acquainted with him for several years before he was married to Fannie Watkins." Moses Jones lived within a mile or two of David and Mary Cheatham and was "constant[ly] meeting and associating with them." James Wallace lived close to four miles from James Whittenbury, yet he "knew him well from the time he was five years old until he died" and "saw him every few days for years and knew him as well as any person in the world." Waylard Green could testify to the marriage of one slave couple because he was "raised in the same neighbor hood" and had known the man and woman his entire life. Milly Wells knew Sandy and Mary Farrer since her childhood because "they all grew up together in same settlement."[56]

Former slaves also testified to lifelong friendships with neighbors. Aaron Herryford and Benjamin Hubbard knew each other all their lives and "played as boys together." Andrew Jackson Ming and David Cheatham lived within one mile of each other when they were boys, played together, and later enlisted together. William Bosley lived less than a mile from Anna Priest and her son Jacob, and he had been friendly with her husband, George, since their childhood. Bosley explained to the pension board: "We all lived neighbors, and I know the family as well as my own." Slave children welcomed the opportunity to socialize with one another on Sundays. Katy Johnson remembered her friend Clarissa Combs: "Her children and mine were almost like they belonged to the same family. We lived not two miles apart, and our children were together every Sunday." Slave children sometimes played together on days other than the Sabbath. Samuel Burns lived on a farm that was within two and a half miles of the home of Matthew Carroll, and he remembered his childhood friend well: "From our boy hood up through our early man hood, we run and raced together, 'Fit' played 'Marvels' and played in all manner together. I knew Matthew Carroll at the begining [sic] of the late war as well and intimately as any man." George Hale also remembered playing marbles with John Jackson when they were both boys.[57]

Missouri's interfarm slave communities did not provide the daily support found in plantation slave quarters, but most Missouri slaves did not view their relationships as lacking. The many risks that they took and the great lengths that they went to in order to maintain friendships and extended family ties demonstrate the importance of these relationships to enslaved Missourians. Interfarm slave neighborhoods functioned differently than plantation quarters, yet slaves were able to lend a degree of emotional support and mutual assistance to one another just the same. They still were able to enjoy the company of fellow bondpeople and participate in the rich African American cultural heritage. This is not to suggest that all relationships among enslaved people were harmonious. As is the case in any neighborhood, their associations represented the full range of possibilities—from friends and lovers to foes and rivals. Nonetheless, these human connections forged across farm boundaries were vital to slaves' self-identity and to their ability to survive enslavement. Slaves also communicated vital information throughout their neighborhoods, linking individuals together and connecting them to the greater world. The friendships forged and the lessons learned from years of socializing throughout the countryside served enslaved Missourians well as they approached the revolutionary moment of emancipation.

Fractured Neighborhoods

Slave neighborhoods began to coalesce during the later antebellum years as the slave population of many Missouri River counties approached, and sometimes exceeded, 25 percent of the total population. Yet, during these same decades, Missouri's white communities began to fracture, as the state was convulsed by dramatic demographic and political changes. By the onset of the Civil War, white Missourians were increasingly divided over political issues revolving around the status of slavery in Kansas and the question of disunion. Although Missourians vigorously debated politics, only a small minority of people actually opposed slavery, and most of them lived in St. Louis. The vast majority of white Missourians, especially in the countryside, continued to support a racial and social code in which racial lines were clearly drawn and whites remained dominant, and when political circumstances made it appear that slavery was threatened, slaveholders and nonslaveholders alike reacted by clamping down on any fissures that they perceived in the system.[58]

Southern migrants overwhelmingly settled Missouri during the first two decades following statehood, but in the thirty years preceding the Civil War the demographics of the state shifted dramatically. By 1860, a majority of Missourians still had ancestral roots in the Upper South, but the population of the state increasingly was becoming more diverse. Although migrants continued to come from Kentucky, Tennessee, North Carolina, and Virginia in great numbers, many of the newcomers hailed from the states of the Old Northwest, and even New England, and settled the prairie lands of northern Missouri. By 1860, nearly 15 percent of white Missourians were born in free states. German immigrants also flooded into the state during these same years, settling along the Missouri and Mississippi Rivers directly west and south of St. Louis and even venturing as far as western Missouri. By 1860, the foreign-born population of Missouri reached 12 percent; as early as 1850 half of St. Louis residents were immigrants, mostly German and Irish. On the eve of the Civil War, nearly 17 percent of state legislators were natives of northern states or foreign countries, more so than in any other slaveholding state. This influx of nonslaveholding settlers resulted in a decrease in the slave population as a percentage of the total population. Slaves constituted 18 percent of Missouri's population in 1830, yet by 1860 they accounted for less than 10 percent. Even though the slave population grew eleven-fold since statehood, the white population multiplied by a much more dramatic eighteen times.[59]

In the 1850s, Missourians again found themselves in the midst of a national political crisis. Illinois Senator Stephen A. Douglas put forth legislation to organize the territory west of Missouri in order to build a transcontinental railroad, and in 1854 President Franklin Pierce signed the Kansas-Nebraska Act into law, repealing the Missouri Compromise and allowing the citizens of the new territories to decide the fate of slavery in their jurisdictions. Emigrant Aid Companies were established in northern states to provide financial backing for free-soil settlers to Kansas. The ambiguous status of slavery in Kansas created turmoil across the border in Missouri where politicians were deeply divided on how to confront the issue. Although Senator Thomas Hart Benton was opposed to the extension of slavery into Kansas, many others, including Senator David Rice Atchison and future governor Claiborne Fox Jackson, believed that slavery in Missouri could not survive if Kansas became a free state. One Missourian wrote from Boonville in 1854 that locally it was the "prevailing opinion" that if slavery was prohibited in Kansas Territory "slaves will almost be value less in Missouri." Most Missouri slaveholders agreed that the extension of slavery into Kansas was desirable, but they differed sharply over how best to achieve that goal. Proslavery conventions and vigilante committees were organized throughout the state. In the end, a number of Missourians took matters into their own hands when they crossed the border into Kansas to vote in the 1855 territorial election. Soon after, the Missouri/Kansas border dissolved into violence.[60]

During the 1850s, Missouri slaveholders were preoccupied with the situation in Kansas and, as a result, believed that antislavery forces, both external and internal, threatened slavery in their state. Modest dissent on the issue of slavery was acceptable in earlier days, but after Kansas, Missouri slaveholders no longer tolerated advocates of abolition or colonization. Yet, at the same time, some of the newest citizens of Missouri, especially the Germans and Northerners who lived in St. Louis, were beginning to voice opposition to slavery. In the slaveholding rural areas, those individuals who did not enthusiastically support slavery often were intimidated by proslavery groups, such as the Platte County Self

Defensive Association, which were organized to protect the slave property of Missouri slaveholders from Kansas free-soil settlers, who they
believed were slave-stealing abolitionists. Vigilante forces attacked the
presses of newspapermen, such as George Parks and W. J. Patterson of
Platte County, who either spoke out against slavery or the actions of
proslavery Missourians in Kansas. Proslavery supporters also worked to
bully into silence preachers who they believed were not safely on their
side, while other vocal clergymen, such as the Reverend Frederick Starr,
a New York native, were forced to flee the state in order to ensure their
own and their families' safety. Although their fears were greatly exaggerated, many slaveholders worried that the "Yankee abolitionists &
German radicals" had overtaken St. Louis and would soon spread their
abolitionist and free-soil influence throughout the state. Interestingly,
newspapermen in the South also were apprehensive about the future of
slavery in Missouri, especially after the Republican Party made gains in
the St. Louis elections. In 1858, the *New Orleans Crescent* expressed its
concerns: "We had thought it would take ten years to bring about abolition in Missouri, but the St. Louis Democrat is of the confident belief that
it can be accomplished 'within two or three years.'"[61]

Missouri slaveholders raised the alarm that the dangerous ideas promoted by antislavery enemies along the state's border, and even possibly
within it, would foment rebellion among the slave population. These
concerns seemed to come to fruition in the summer of 1859 when there
was a series of crimes purportedly committed by Saline County slaves
against white residents. The trouble began in May with the murder of
Benjamin Hinton, the owner of a riverboat woodlot near Miami, Missouri. A slave man named John, who belonged to Hinton's business
partner, was arrested and eventually confessed to the brutal killing. The
following month a white man attempted to discipline a local slave man
named Holman, who slashed him with a knife in self-defense. A few
weeks later a slave man named Jim was arrested for breaking into Mary
Habecot's home and attempting to rape her. Although his guilt remains
unclear, Habecot and her sister identified Jim as the man who assaulted
her. The final outrage occurred when a naked slave man brutally raped a
young white girl, who was picking blackberries with some other children
in the woods near Arrow Rock. After the children fingered the attacker,
a vigilante mob of close to a thousand local citizens apprehended the
man, tried, and hanged him. The next day, despite the efforts of a local judge to move forward with legal proceedings, the citizens of Saline

County seized the other three slave men from the Marshall jail, burning John alive and hanging Jim and Holman. The historian Thomas Dyer argues that the actions of the Saline County lynch mob were emblematic of "a tense society enmeshed in slavery, wearied by years of border warfare, and apprehensive that the established legal system would yield to a powerful, perhaps protracted, vigilante impulse." Although a few Saline County citizens feebly objected to the mob's rejection of the rule of law, most whites defended its actions, believing that the state's legal code was insufficient to protect the county's white women and girls from the actions of rapacious slave men. Indeed, it was a nonslaveholding man, James Shackleford, who reportedly led the mob and later eloquently defended its actions by employing proslavery rhetoric to rival that espoused by any Missouri slaveholder. These outrageous and brutal acts ultimately reveal the extent to which rural white Missourians were allied in the defense of border slavery.[62]

White Missourians by and large advocated slavery and its extension, but most supported the preservation of the Union as well. Their experiences of living in the "middle ground" between the North and the South led most to move cautiously when it came to questions of disunion. Missourians understood that the state was increasingly tied economically to the northeastern marketplace through the construction of the railroads, yet at the same time, their tradition of diversified agriculture and the growing mixture of slave and free labor linked them to both geographic sections. Ultimately, some Missourians believed that they had more in common with the farmers of southern Illinois or Indiana than with the firebrand secessionists of South Carolina. In addition, they feared that Missouri's exposed geographic position left the state particularly vulnerable should it side with the South in the cause of secession. In the end, many people reasoned that slavery was best protected if Missouri remained part of the Union. In the election of 1860, a number of slaveholders threw their support behind John Bell of the Constitutional Union Party, although Stephen Douglas won the state as a whole, reflecting the commitment of most Missourians to preserving the Union. In fact, still not wavering in their support for both slavery and Union, the state's residents voted overwhelmingly against secession a few months later. There was a minority group, however, most of them slaveholders, who supported the goals of the secessionists.[63]

Missouri Supreme Court Justice William Napton observed in 1857 that Missouri slaveholders should not fear that non-southern settlers would disrupt their social, economic, and political supremacy, believing that they had "wealth, the population, the intelligence & consequently the power, & until this power is turned against us, we may rest secure." Feeling confident in the dominance of the slaveholding class, Napton did not foresee that many Missourians would indeed turn against slaveholders during the violent years of the Civil War. Missouri was plunged into chaos as its citizens took sides and neighbors literally fought against neighbors. Even Missouri's slaveholders were divided in their support for the Union and the Confederacy. President Abraham Lincoln sought to keep Missouri in the Union by protecting slave property, but slavery began to erode from within as slaves secured their own freedom. By the time enslaved Missourians were officially emancipated in January of 1865, most were already effectively free.[64]

7 / The War Within: The Passing of Border Slavery

In September of 1864 while stationed at Benton Barracks in St. Louis, Spotswood Rice penned two letters regarding the welfare of his children, who remained enslaved in Howard County. Rice explained to his daughters Corra and Mary that they should not despair that they had not yet gained their freedom, but instead "be assured that I will have you if it cost me my life." He expected to march to Howard with a combined Union military force of black and white soldiers and intended to use the full power of the government to liberate his children from their owners, who, he believed, were working against the laws of God in keeping them. Rice had heard that Kittey Diggs had accused him of trying to steal his child away from her, and he proclaimed that "She is the frist [sic] Christian that I ever hard say that aman [sic] could Steal his own children especially out of human bondage." In another letter written to Diggs that same day, Rice damned his daughter's mistress to hell and threatened her: "[N]ow you call my children your pro[per]ty not so with me my Children is my own and I except to get them and when I get ready to come after mary I will have bout a powrer and autherity to bring hear away and to exacute vengencens on them that holds my Child." In case Diggs did not understand that the federal government would back him in his claims to his children, he assured her that "I have no fears about geting mary out of your hands this whole Government gives chear to me and you cannot help your self."[1]

By the time Spotswood Rice wrote these letters in September 1864, the world of Missouri slaves and slaveholders had been turned on end.

Clearly, the prerogatives of mastery were eroding as a result of the experience of war. As a single woman, Kittey Diggs engaged the assistance of her brother F. W. Diggs in her efforts to respond to Rice's threats. Like Rice, F. W. Diggs recognized the Union military as the only legitimate source of power in the war-torn state. He sent a letter directly to General William Rosecrans, commander of the Department of the Missouri, regarding the case, in which he asserted his and his sister's loyalty to the Union "from the commencement of this wicked rebellion" and assured him that they cast their lot knowing that it likely meant the end of slavery. Diggs had allowed his slave men to enlist and claimed that his sister had permitted Rice's wife and most of their children to join him in St. Louis. Mary was detained temporarily because the man who hired her would not agree to break their contract. Given their loyalty, F. W. and Kittey Diggs were profoundly "insulted by such a black scoundrel" and demanded that Rosecrans send Rice out of the state.[2]

The altercation between a man, who had been enslaved only months earlier, and slaveholders, who had not adapted well to the erosion of their power, starkly reveals the social and political turmoil of the moment of emancipation. The dramatic exchange between Rice and Diggs is representative of the response of many Missourians to the revolutionary changes that were convulsing their world. Most Missouri slaveholders desperately held onto the authority they once commanded, while enslaved Missourians used all the resources at their deposal to secure their freedom and assert what they believed to be their rights as citizens. Decades after slavery's end, Rice's daughter Mary Bell articulated the lessons that she had learned as a child of the Civil War when she proclaimed, "I love a man who will fight for his rights, and any person that wants to be something."[3]

No period in Missouri's history better exposes the many tensions of border-state slavery than the tumultuous years of the Civil War. In many parts of the South, the unity of the white population in support of the war and the distance of plantations from the center of fighting kept discord under the surface for much of the war. In contrast, Missouri straddled the border between the North and the South, and, therefore, quarrels that once simmered beneath the surface dramatically erupted in the early days of the conflict. The divisiveness of wartime politics fractured a white community that once had been virtually united in support of slavery, and the fabric of Missouri society was irrevocably rent by the internecine bloodshed that scourged the state during the war years. The ambiguities and conflicts that plagued the interactions between the slaveholders and slaves who lived on the state's farms before the war were exacerbated by the uncertainty and violence during the war. Although always compromised by the realities of life on slavery's border, enslaved Missourians' families and communities were further complicated by the deprivations and dislocations brought about by the fighting. As the war progressed, many of Missouri's nearly 115,000 slaves took advantage of the chaos and struck a blow for their own freedom.

"[N]o one escapes the ravages of one party or the other"

Missouri's precarious border location and increasingly diverse demographics resulted in an overwhelmingly large pro-Union vote for delegates to the state's secession convention in February 1861. Missouri's newest residents were by and large Unionists, but many slaveholders initially supported a conservative Unionist position as well. Their political philosophy was born out of the experience of living in a border state with economic and social ties to both the North and the South. Most Missourians had long been suspicious of the motivations of southern secessionists, and although they also wished to defend slavery, they did not see secession as the preferred option. Many did not view Lincoln's election as a reason to abandon historical ties to the Union and instead chose to wait and see how events would transpire. Ultimately, the political compromises made by Missouri Unionists were rooted in a conservative wish to maintain the status quo, especially regarding slavery. Many slaveholders sincerely believed that they could best protect their slave property by remaining in the Union, fearing if Missouri seceded it would lead to armed conflict in their border state. At the same time, many of those of southern heritage were ambivalent about their political loyalties and hoped to avert engagement in the conflict altogether.[4]

Although initially publicly supporting a conservative Unionist position like many of his fellow Missourians, the newly elected governor, Claiborne Fox Jackson, and members of his administration became increasingly sympathetic to the South after Abraham Lincoln's election, the secession of the Deep South states, and a growing presence of federal troops in St. Louis. Likely in an effort to provoke Union forces and catapult Missouri out of the Union, Governor Jackson organized pro-secession state militiamen to establish a base near St. Louis from which to attack the federal arsenal located there. When Captain Nathaniel Lyon, the temporary commander of the federal army in St. Louis, learned in May 1861 that the Confederate government had armed Missouri troops, he captured "Fort Jackson" with a force of locally recruited German Home Guard soldiers. Pro-secessionist civilians taunted the Union troops as they marched the captured men through the streets of St. Louis, and when a soldier was shot and killed by someone in the crowd, the Home Guard returned fire, killing twenty-eight civilians. Governor Jackson responded by calling for fifty thousand volunteers for the Missouri State Guard and easily convinced the southern-leaning state legislature to authorize funds to finance them.[5]

Newly promoted Brigadier General Lyon moved to capture the secessionist government in Jefferson City in mid-June, and by the end of the summer, Governor Jackson and his followers were driven to the southwestern corner of the state. The pro-southern, but duly elected, state government operated an exile administration, recognized by the Confederacy, for the duration of the war. The state convention reconvened in July and, after some dissension from pro-southern delegates, voted to depose the secessionist government and install a provisional government headed by Hamilton R. Gamble in its place. Large portions of Missouri were essentially under Union military rule from this point until the fighting ceased in 1865. In addition, the unconditional Unionists, based in St. Louis and under the control of Abraham Lincoln's associate Frank Blair, eventually wrested political power from the more conservative Unionists who had dominated the state secession convention of 1861.[6]

Many Missourians threw their support to the Confederacy in the summer of 1861 after the Union military enacted a series of policies that alienated southern-leaning people. In August 1861, Union General John C. Frémont, the next in a long line of Union commanders, agitated Missouri slaveholders when he instituted martial law and ordered the seizure of secessionists' property and slaves. Although President Lincoln quickly reversed Frémont's premature emancipation proclamation in order to keep Missouri—with the largest white population of any slave state—in the Union, the damage was already done. Plundering by Union troops and home guard units as they confiscated food and livestock from civilians further angered Missourians. In addition, as the historian Mark Geiger discovered, some pro-Confederate Missourians lost their land in 1862 and 1863 as a result of an ill-conceived financial scheme to equip pro-southern troops during the early days of the war. Leading secessionists and their neighbors and kin took out loans from local banks to finance southern troops with the belief that the Confederate or Missouri state government would later repay them. The reimbursement was not forthcoming after federal forces took over the state and the provisional state government was put into place. The banks, now run by citizens loyal to the Union, called in the notes. The result was that local county courts, also controlled by Unionists, forced the sale of the land of hundreds of secessionists in order to pay their debts. Geiger argues that the dispossession of their land led a great number of Missourians, many of them slaveholders, to virulently oppose federal rule in the state. In fact, many young men from these families took to the bush as rebel guerrillas. Some slaveholders continued to support both slavery and the Union, however, in spite of their sympathies with their natal region and their many grievances with federal occupation. At the very least, they hoped that they could remain out of the fight, but the possibility of neutrality became increasingly less feasible as violence escalated in the state.[7]

Federal troops overran Missouri during the first months of the war, but after they drove Confederate forces and the secessionist government out of the state in early 1862, most regiments were sent east to fight. There remained a strong federal military presence near St. Louis for the duration of the war, but Union troops were less in control of the countryside, where Missouri State Militia and Home Guard units augmented smaller federal forces. With the exception of Sterling Price's raid in the fall of 1864, most of the fighting in Missouri was between Union soldiers and Confederate guerrillas, commonly called bushwhackers. A good number of Missouri men joined the regular Confederate army early in the war, but as time progressed many secessionists found themselves hundreds of miles inside federal lines. Some of these men preferred to join guerrilla bands, both because it was difficult to access legitimate Confederate forces and because they believed that they could better defend their state, homes, families, and slaves if they joined these irregular forces. Deprivations occurred throughout the state, but Kansas Jayhawkers and secessionist bushwhackers perpetuated some of the worst atrocities along the border of Missouri and Kansas, where there were still strong memories of the earlier violence. Kansas Union troops, led by border war veterans James Lane and Charles Jennison and derisively called Jayhawkers by Missourians, frequently made forays across the state line, and bands of pro-southern Missouri bushwhackers, led by men such as William Quantrill and "Bloody" Bill Anderson, responded in kind.[8]

Certain areas of the state were Unionist strongholds—for example, St. Louis and northern Missouri—but most of the countryside was a toxic mixture of people with divided loyalties. Many slaveholders in the river counties leaned toward support for the Confederacy, but slaveholding did not necessarily determine a person's political allegiances, as some continued to support the Union on conservative terms. Missourians of German descent and free-state origins swelled Unionist ranks in many of these same counties. As a result, neighbor often literally fought against neighbor, and even families occasionally were divided in their loyalties. People were not always truthful about their politics, and it was sometimes difficult to know whom to trust.[9]

Missourians on both sides of the conflict lived in fear of the violence that escalated after the autumn of 1861. Marauding gangs of men from both sides roamed the countryside, pillaging, burning, and killing. There were countless incidents of guerrillas or federal soldiers demanding food at rural homes, although Missouri women often were happy to serve men whom they knew personally or with whom they shared political sentiments. In fact, secessionist women were crucial to supplying guerrillas with food and clothing throughout the war. It also might be the enemy who knocked on the door, however, and women, such as Elvira Scott of Saline County, knew that it was best to comply with armed men's requests. Although she was strongly sympathetic to the South, Scott and her daughter frequently played their piano for the Union soldiers stationed in her town. Both soldiers and guerrillas routinely helped themselves to the fruits of Missourians' labors, scouring the countryside looking for crops and livestock to confiscate. Henry Bruce's master was stripped of his livestock and horses by the end of the war, and the residents of Buchanan County near the Kansas border actually bought inexpensive cattle and horses expressly for the raiders to steal while their higher-quality stock remained hidden. Hundreds of Missouri homes were looted of everything from clothing to guns, and many were ultimately ransacked and burned. Lizzie Brannock described the situation in western Missouri: "Our country is desolate, indeed almost entirely a wilderness, robbery is an every day affair so long as their [sic] was anything to take our farms are all burned up, fences gone, crops destroyed no one escapes the ravages of one party or the other." In 1862, Willard Mendenhall recorded Nancy Pitcher's description of the violent attacks on the residents of Jackson County by Jennison's Kansas Jayhawkers: "Several of her relations have had thare houses burned by them, thare negros, hoares and everything they had taken from them. They have taken the lives of boys ten years old."[10]

Acts of violence committed against men and teenage boys were the most frightening aspect of the wartime experience for Missourians, and fearing for their lives, many took to the woods at the sight of soldiers or guerrillas. Perry County slave James Monroe Abbot remembered that his young master attempted to avoid military service: "[W]henever de sojers cum round' Mastuh Joe couldn' nevuh be foun'." Marilda Pethy concurred, "When de soldiers come de men folks just got up and flew. Dey taken to de woods." Both white and black Bollinger County residents attended a wartime husking party, and many of the white men stayed the night. When soldiers came to the farm the next morning, the visitors hid in the pile of cornhusks and came out only when the commander ordered his men to ride their horses through the husks. Paulina Stratton was terrified when two men in Union uniforms came to her door in the middle of the night, roughed up her nephew, and demanded the family's firearms. She wrote soon after, "I was so uneasy to-night and indeed every night." It was not unreasonable for Stratton to be fearful in wartime Missouri. She had only to reflect on the many deaths of Cooper County men of both persuasions at the hands of bushwhackers and Union soldiers. Men were taken from their homes at night and killed, and her own son-in-law was shot at as he returned from registering his loyalties with the South. Stratton's most horrifying experience occurred when she went to her neighbor's farm and found the two Koontz brothers lying dead in the front yard.[11]

Elvira Scott also told of an old secessionist judge who left his home in western Missouri and fled to the town of Miami in Saline County to wait out the war. Scott's slaves and neighbors witnessed Union soldiers chase down and kill the unarmed old man for the offense of harboring bushwhackers. Willard Mendenhall repeatedly wrote of the many atrocities committed by secessionist guerrillas and Union soldiers in his Lafayette County neighborhood, and in July 1862, he reported, "We hear of acquaintances being shot every few days, by both parties." Elvira Scott observed that the deprivations occurred "all the time, & men here become so paralyzed with fear that they are submitting to every indignity."[12]

What was most frightening to Missourians was that the violence was sometimes indiscriminate, especially since it was often difficult to distinguish one side from the other. Elvira Scott told the story of an old man who believed that bushwhackers were federal soldiers, and telling them what he thought they wanted to hear, he indicated that his two sons planned to enlist in the Union army. In response to this information, the Confederate guerrillas shot and killed both boys. In fact, guerrillas frequently donned the uniforms of their enemies in an effort to ferret out traitors to the southern cause.[13]

Some Missourians, such as Peter Burns, attempted to remain neutral, or at the very least not publicly declare their political allegiances. Burns shrewdly and successfully maintained his neutrality, and his former slave Wes Lee remembered: "[W]hen de Rebel sojers come by our place old mastuh had de table set for 'em, and treat 'em fine—'cause he's a rebel—den when de 'Yankee's come along he give dem de bes' he had, and treat 'em fine 'cause he's a 'Yankee'. . . . In a way I guess old mastuh was right for none of de sojers never bother nuthin' on de place." The historian Michael Fellman argues that the key to maintaining a neutral stance was to remain unobtrusive and not to volunteer personal opinions about the war. The Strattons were able to make it through the war with little harassment from the warring parties in just such a manner. They generally complied with the demands of the federal troops stationed nearby, and they kept a low profile by not outwardly aligning themselves with one side or the other. In addition, there were no men in the Stratton household who were of military age, making it easier to stay out of the fray.[14]

As civil institutions, such as the court system, broke down in many locations, Missourians increasingly turned to the Union army to maintain law and order in the countryside. The adjutant general's office appointed a special provost marshal to preside over the state in September 1862, but by 1863, the military court system was reorganized to include an assistant provost marshal general who had jurisdiction over the entire state from his headquarters in St. Louis, provost marshals for congressional districts, and deputy provost marshals in every county. Provost marshals primarily were charged with maintaining troop discipline, but they also were asked to preserve order among the civilian population and prosecute cases of disloyalty. They essentially operated as magistrates, hearing complaints brought by Missourians against both the army and fellow citizens, oftentimes handling cases that would have been civil matters in peacetime. The provost marshals also granted passes for movement within and out of the state, maintained labor discipline, and were actively engaged in questions of freedom. Both black and white Missourians relied on the provost marshals and other local military officers to act on their grievances in the midst of civil disorder. As one Missourian put it, "If not to the military to whom shall I look for protection?"[15]

The Civil War turned Missouri slaveholders' lives on end no matter which side they supported. Unionists were required to sign loyalty oaths, and southern sympathizers had to register their allegiances, relinquish their firearms, and swear that they would not aid the rebellion. Many Missouri men, including some who had recently returned from

Confederate service, took the oath and joined the Missouri State Militia or the Enrolled Missouri Militia, often in an attempt to avoid the draft and service in the regular Union army. Others with stronger pro-southern sentiments chose to leave the state or took to the bush as guerrillas. German immigrants and other newly arrived Missourians were placed in civil and military leadership roles in the militia because of their alignment with the Union military and political powers. Secessionist slaveholders, such as Elvira Scott, were outraged by this upheaval of the prewar social order that long had been dominated by the slaveholding class. She was contemptuous of the "Dutch and Irish" Union recruits, believing that these men enlisted out of class envy and purposefully to "prey upon their neighbors, or jayhawk. Generally they have a malicious, envious feeling toward their neighbors who by honest industry have surrounded themselves by the comforts of life." While insinuating that the Germans and Irish lacked industry and were overwhelmingly inferior as a people, Scott utterly failed to acknowledge that slaves provided a good part of the "honest labor" of Missouri slaveholders. Priscilla Patton, and many other pro-southern Missourians, shared Scott's prejudices: "The Union Army of Home Guards wer[e] made up of the lowest, poorist, and most illitterate class of persons. Who took this oppertunity of persecuting those who were their superiors, which they did by being armed and protected by those in autherity." Elvira Scott sincerely believed that these "poor & vicious" armed men would rob more affluent slaveholding Missourians and bring about a social "levelling process." Secessionist women, such as Scott and Patton, may have disparaged German Missourians verbally and in their writing, but Confederate guerrillas actually targeted much of their violence against this despised group.[16]

Many people found the social turmoil of wartime Missouri to be unsettling, as their old way of life began to slip away. "It seems a terrible state of affairs when all substantial, worthy men must be fettered down from a free expression of opinion, deprived of arms, deprived of the privilege of voting & kept under subjection by the lowest most unprincipled Dutch, with a very few American hirelings," Elvira Scott lamented in 1862. "This is what the Federal government is doing now. Gentlemen of the highest social &—a year ago—political position are hunted down & shot like dogs if they do not come forward & take the Oath to support these usurpations. A little moral courage in these days of terror is certain to bring ruin on a man." Union forces instituted martial law in large parts of the state and as a result confiscated disloyal citizens' mail, seized their property, and silenced pro-secessionist newspapers. Countless Missourians were arrested and held by federal troops because they either aided the southern cause or simply stated their support for it. The historian Mark Neely has calculated that Union officials detained, arrested, and tried by military commission more civilians for disloyalty in Missouri than in any other state. These actions in large measure were in response to the ongoing guerrilla warfare, but they also were meant to suppress political dissent. Willard Mendenhall claimed that 355 suspected Lafayette County secessionists were arrested in November 1862 in order to "keep them from voteing thare sentiments on Tuesday last." The men were released directly after the election. John Scott was twice arrested and held by Union soldiers, and although the Strattons attempted to remain neutral, federal soldiers also arrested Thomas Stratton early in the war. Missouri men were temporarily incarcerated at army encampments throughout the state, but many eventually were transferred to military prisons, such as the Gratiot Street facility, in and near St. Louis. Neely has calculated that "well over one out of every 100 males in the state of Missouri" was incarcerated in the Gratiot Street Prison during the course of the war.[17]

Missouri society was in such a state of upheaval during the war years that even traditional gender norms were placed in flux as women increasingly became involved in the war effort and wartime politics. Throughout the state, federal officials cited or arrested a number of secessionist women for political crimes against the Union. Lieutenant Adam Bax, the commanding Union officer at Miami, charged Elvira Scott and some female neighbors with "treasonable language" and placed them under military house arrest. Bax used the arrest warrant to chastise Scott for stepping outside of her proper womanly role: "A Ladies place is to fulfill her household duties, and not to spread treason and excite men to rebellion." Scott was warned that if she could not "behave yourself as a Lady Ought," she could expect the transfer of her husband to military prison. John Scott indeed was arrested when a local acquaintance reported that he had "called it most damned disrespectful for a military officer to tell a lady in such a document that she did not attend to her household duties." Scott's and her friends' gender afforded them at least limited protection to express their political views; secessionist men could not risk such public confrontations with local Unionists or federal military forces. A wrong move could cost them time in military prison and even their lives. In fact, John Scott was released only after his wife and the other women went to Lieutenant Bax to plead his case and promised to refrain from outwardly expressing pro-southern sentiments.[18]

The disloyal Miami women were not alone as they stepped outside of traditional gender roles and actively engaged in the politics of war. Secessionist women were the backbone of the guerrilla insurgency, supplying their men with food, clothing, and shelter in order that they might continue the fight, and women on both sides of the conflict were left to care for their families and manage their slaves after their men marched off to war, took to the bush, were imprisoned, or fled the state. Elvira Scott remained in Miami for months after her husband fled to St. Louis, and Priscilla Patton stayed in Rocheport with her children after her husband joined the Confederate army as a physician.[19]

Distinctions between the public world and the private household broke down as women increasingly were drawn into, and in fact often actively engaged in, the conflict. As much as they articulated a philosophy of honoring women, Confederate guerrillas did not spare Unionist women and children when they made their attacks. White women generally did not suffer serious physical violence at the hands of guerrillas, but they often witnessed the deaths of their husbands, fathers, and sons, as well as suffered a reduction in their circumstances, as their homes were ransacked and burned and their property and livestock stolen. The Union military authorities were no better at honoring women or the sanctity of the home. Women, who before the war by and large were considered outside the realm of politics, were suddenly held accountable for their personal political views and activities and were occasionally harassed, fined, or arrested. One of the greatest tragedies of the Civil War occurred on the heels of the arrest of secessionist women who were accused of aiding Confederate guerrillas. In 1863, four female relatives of rebel guerrillas were killed, and a number severely injured, when the makeshift Kansas City jail in which they were incarcerated collapsed. William Quantrill and his band of bushwhackers used the deaths of the women as the justification for their bloody raid on Lawrence, Kansas, during which they killed more than 150 men and boys, most of them civilians.[20]

General Thomas Ewing, the commander of the Western District of Missouri, understood that a network of civilian households—made up of guerrillas' friends and family—supplied these irregular forces. He reasoned that the only way to stop the violence was to root out the guerrillas' supporters and supply lines. Partly in response to Quantrill's infamous raid on Lawrence, but mostly because of his concerns about civilians' support for guerrillas, Ewing issued General Order Number 11 in August 1863 to virtually depopulate the four Missouri counties bordering Kansas south of the Missouri River. This extremely unpopular measure did little to stop the violence and only served to turn thousands of women, children, and the elderly, into refugees.[21]

Missouri became such an unpredictable and violent place that many residents fled their homes altogether. Families on both sides of the conflict sold out and moved west to Oregon and California. Nan Cooper and her family moved from Lawrence County in southwestern Missouri to Oregon in 1863. She explained that nonslaveholding Unionists left their home because "[a]t that time we had no thought of being abolitionists, but the rebels treated us as such." The Coopers could not even escape Missouri's troubles on the trail west. When their Unionist wagon train joined with a secessionist one to strengthen their numbers against Indian attack, the relations between the two groups were nearly as rancorous as if they had remained in Missouri. Men also left in large numbers for places such as Colorado or Montana because they either feared for their lives or wished to evade military service. The Strattons' son-in-law John Starke left Missouri in 1863 for the western plains in order to avoid fighting against his southern relatives and neighbors, but he eventually returned and served in the Missouri Infantry. Large numbers of Missourians fled to their relatives' homes in eastern states, often leaving most of their belongings behind. Mrs. Silliman observed that many of the western Missouri women whose husbands were in military service were "going back to other States to their relatives, some on foot carrying their little children, the others following with their bundles in their hands, women driving an ox team, with what little furniture they dare [sic] to stop long enough to tumble in, to flee for their lives from the bushwhackers." Priscilla Patton and her physician husband permanently relocated to Vincennes, Indiana, during the war, because of the large number of southern sympathizers living there. The Scotts and others waited out the war in safer locations, such as St. Louis, and came home after the fighting had ceased, but many rural Missourians, especially those who hailed from the burned-over district along the Kansas border, never returned.[22]

"They go in droves every night"

Missouri slaveholders were devastated by what the war had wrought; violence, death, and destruction touched the lives of many, and all experienced the upheaval of the prewar social order. As much as they were discouraged by the turn of events, perhaps most distressing was the realization that their long-term fears about the stability of slavery suddenly

FIGURE 12. *Martial Law or Order Number 11.* The Missouri painter George Caleb Bingham (1811–1879) was appalled by the Union General Thomas Ewing's order to depopulate the Missouri border counties, so he painted *Martial Law* in an attempt to discredit him. Bingham felt personally connected to the incident because he owned the Kansas City building in which the Union military housed the arrested secessionist women. Bingham's painting has become the quintessential visual image of Order Number 11; however, his highly dramatic depiction of the event did not represent historical reality. Unlike in the painting, in most cases young men of southern persuasion who lived along the border had either left the area or had gone to the bush, leaving women, children, and elderly men behind. In addition, few enslaved Missourians would have been so emotionally devastated by their liberation at the hands of the Kansas Jayhawkers, who were also called Red Legs because of their distinctive red stockings. There are two extant copies of *Martial Law*—one owned by the Cincinnati Museum of Art (1868) and the other by the State Historical Society of Missouri (1870). Courtesy of the Library of Congress.

were realized. Many of the political decisions made by Missourians in the first years of the war were in the interest of defending the institution of slavery. During these early days, a good number maintained loyalty to the Union under the belief that the federal government would protect slavery. Certainly, President Lincoln had given every indication that he intended to cater to the conservative Unionists who had worked so hard to keep Missouri in the Union. Enslaved Missourians did not see things this way, however. As Union troops occupied the state, slaves recognized the soldiers as harbingers of their freedom and "believed, deep down in their souls, that the government was fighting for their freedom, and it was useless for masters to tell them differently."[23]

It was nearly impossible to isolate slaves from the political discussions of the day. William Greenleaf Eliot remembered that in the years before the war, enslaved Missourians understood the potential implications of the sectional conflict: "Even on the best-managed farms a sense of un-easiness began to prevail, and the uncertainty of slave property to be felt. The slaves felt it no less than their masters." St. Louis resident Mattie Jackson and her mother, Ellen, collected information about the progress of the war by eavesdropping on their owners' conversations and reading newspapers tossed over the fence to them by the Union soldiers who occupied the city. Ellen well understood the possible implications of Union victory and quietly showed her support by posting a newspaper picture of Abraham Lincoln on her bedroom wall, an act for which she received a brutal beating. On the other side of the state, Chariton County slaves, according to Henry Bruce, had long paid attention to local and national politics but became especially attentive during the election of 1860 when they believed that their destiny lay in the balance. They talked about the progress of the war whenever they met and "understood the war to be for their freedom solely, and prayed earnestly and often for the success of the Union cause." They celebrated Union victories and were disheartened "when they saw their masters rejoicing." Literate men and women gained access to newspapers and passed the "latest news" to their neighbors, and "from mouth to ear the news was carried from farm to farm, without the knowledge of masters." Missouri slaves took advantage of the intricate web of social relations that they had so carefully cultivated during slavery, putting their associations and knowledge of the local geography to good use as they prepared for freedom. They were focused on the possibilities introduced by the chaos of war and worked together to collect and share information because they understood that the stakes were high. "There were no Judases among them during those exciting times," Bruce remembered.[24]

Slaves heard rumors of their coming freedom from the earliest days of the war and events seemed to confirm that eventuality. Their first glimpse of freedom was General Frémont's premature emancipation proclamation in August 1861, and around that time Missouri slaves began to flee from their owners. By midway through the war, the institution of slavery had been seriously compromised by the wartime experiences of Missourians—both slave and free. William Greenleaf Eliot remembered that by 1863: "The events of the previous years in Missouri had shaken society to its centre . . . the bitterness of war was everywhere felt. On every farm and in every household the possibility of emancipation was discussed, and its almost certainty began to appear . . . unsettled, revolutionary, with nothing clearly defined, neither slave nor slaveholder having any rights which they felt bound mutually to respect." In order to accommodate Unionist slaveholders, Lincoln specifically excluded Missouri and other areas of the South under Union military control from his January 1863 Emancipation Proclamation; nonetheless, slaves understood the implications for their freedom. Spotswood Rice "read de emancipation for freedom to de other slaves, and it made dem so happy, dey could not work well, and dey got so no one could manage dem, when dey found out dey were to be freed in such a short time." In the summer of 1863, the state convention reconvened, minus pro-secession delegates, and recognized this reality when they passed a compensated and gradual emancipation plan that would go into effect in 1870.[25]

The tensions and ambiguities that had always existed in the relations between Missouri owners and slaves became more pronounced during the war years as bondpeople became emboldened by the increased likelihood of imminent emancipation. The circumstances of small-slaveholding households had always enhanced the effectiveness of slaves' resistance, but the turbulence of wartime Missouri presented additional opportunities. Missouri slaveholders complained more and more in their letters and diaries about their slaves' behavior and work habits. Elvira Scott criticized her trusted slave woman Margaret's "careless & impertinent" behavior for the first time in 1862, and, like many other small slaveholders, she felt personally slighted by what she saw as Margaret's disaffection, never acknowledging that she was asserting her independence as freedom neared. As was also true with planters and their house servants, Missouri slaveholders lived and worked so closely with their slaves that they often sincerely believed that they shared bonds of affection; therefore, many were shocked when their bondpeople began to lash out at their enslavement during the war. Slaves simply had less incentive to work hard for their owners as labor discipline eroded and as emancipation appeared more certain. Henry Bruce observed: "Work, such as had usually been performed, almost ceased; slaves worked as they pleased, and their masters were powerless to force them." He attributed this to the fact that they knew they could leave their owners to work for Unionists for pay, but the absence of white men on many farms and the confusion caused by wartime violence were contributing factors as well.[26]

Slaveholders were concerned about recalcitrant behavior, but they recognized that the greatest threat to slavery was that their slaves would simply leave. Since the state's inception, slaveholders had worried about the possibilities that Missouri's geography presented for successful escape, a concern that intensified during the Kansas conflict, but as the war progressed, enslaved Missourians capitalized on the presence of the Union military and the political divisions among the white population and left their owners by the thousands. Initially, many slaveholders could not accept that their bondpeople were making their own decisions to flee and instead accused federal soldiers of encouraging their "loyal" servants' defection. Mrs. Silliman of western Missouri claimed that her slave woman was enticed by soldiers: "[T]hey encamped on our premises, were constantly round our door, & from the time they first came, they never ceased importuning her to go to Kansas, till 2 months ago she ran off. She came back in a few days, but she was so demoralised that I would not take her." Secessionist slaveholders, such as Elvira Scott, reported that Union soldiers actually stole Missouri slaves, and indeed federal forces were collecting scores of slaves on their sweeps into Missouri from Kansas. Scott complained of federal hypocrisy in 1862, asking: "If they do not intend to interfere with slavery why have Federal soldiers stolen thousands of slaves from their masters?"[27]

While soldiers, such as Jennison's Jayhawkers, did "steal" some Missouri slaves, most often slaves recognized the presence of soldiers as an opportunity to seek their own freedom. Mrs. Waller of western Missouri wrote to her friend in 1863: "We have had a very troublesome time her[e] in Mo, in the last two years, Missouri is in possession of the federals, and we have had several head of horses, and mules, taken from us, but our blacks all stay with us yet, while last winter, a large number around her[e] ran off, but we have had no trouble with them yet, we hear of some running away every week, and we do not know when they may all go."

Wylie Miller's mother and a fellow slave man ran off after soldiers came by their master's farm, and Paulina Stratton frequently wrote of New Lebanon slaves leaving their owners for the protection of federal troops stationed in nearby towns along the Pacific Railroad line. Slave men, women, and children flocked to the nearest military encampments seeking their freedom.[28]

Early in the war it was the policy of the military to return runaway slaves to their owners, and in January 1862, Willard Mendenhall reported: "Several negros that ran away and sought protection from thare masters with the soldiers were given up to those owners today by order of Col. Dietzler." As the war progressed, slaveholders were less likely to reclaim their slave property, and by mid-1862, Mendenhall reported that soldiers were flagrantly assisting Lafayette County slaves in fleeing from their owners. Missouri slaveholders told stories of federal soldiers who aided runaway slave men as they hoped to liberate their wives and children who remained in bondage. Mendenhall wrote of his wife's Saline County relatives: "One of thare negroes (Bob) that ran off some time ago, went home one night last week, took a squad of white men with him and took his wife and two children away, stole two hoarses from his master at the same time." The image of white and black men, who were both wearing the blue uniform, working in concert to free Missouri slaves must have been a frightening prospect for many slaveholders. In November 1862, a Cooper County man observed that the Union commander at Tipton had with him seventy-five slaves that he "had taken from the secesh" near Arrow Rock in Saline County. The number of slaves leaving their owners grew as the war progressed. A few months later, Mendenhall mused, "All the negroes in this country will run off, they go in droves every night." By the summer of 1863 there was a veritable "stampede" of slaves leaving their owners.[29]

Just as in the eastern theater of the war, there was tremendous confusion within the Union army regarding fugitive slaves, who were oftentimes referred to as "contrabands" because it was assumed that they had been owned by the enemy and, therefore, were considered contraband of war. From the war's beginning, army officers at both the departmental and local level developed policy as circumstances unfolded. At first, concerns about maintaining the loyalty of Missouri Unionists resulted in the return of fugitive slaves to their owners, but enforcement was sporadic and largely dependent on the discretion of individual soldiers and officers. Commanders in rural districts bombarded general headquarters with inquiries about what to do with the many people who were flooding into their posts. Initially, General Henry Halleck, who became commander of the Department of the Missouri in October 1861, issued General Order 3, which barred fugitive slaves from military camps in order to spare officers the confusion of determining their status, but the force of events made this order impractical as the number of people leaving their owners multiplied. Some officers, like the federal commander in Willard Mendenhall's county, returned runaway slaves to their owners, but others granted protection to those who had been used in the Confederate war effort or were threatened by their former owners because they had provided military intelligence to the federal army. Many of these sympathetic officers commanded regiments from free states and put fugitives to work within their camps rather than return "the slaves of traitors while the secessionists are robbing & plundering loyal men." Loyal slaveholders viewed this disregard of Lincoln's promise to protect slavery with particular dismay and argued that it undermined Missourians' support for the Union.[30]

The Second Confiscation Act, passed by Congress in July 1862, stipulated that the military could seize the property—including the slaves—of those disloyal to the Union. The passage of this act further complicated the situation, as it was often difficult to determine the true loyalties of Missouri slaveholders. The general confusion over the issue and the vast number of slaves who sought refuge at Union military encampments led some soldiers to determine their own course. There was no consensus on the issue, especially after the vast majority of federal troops were sent east in the spring of 1862, and Missouri State Militia and Enrolled Missouri Militia soldiers, who often were sympathetic to slavery, were put in their place. Still, as time progressed, slaveholders—no matter their loyalty—were less likely to reclaim their slaves, as soldiers increasingly saw the benefits of employing them in their camps. In December 1862, General Samuel Curtis, the new commanding officer of the Department of the Missouri, issued an order that authorized the provost marshals to grant freedom papers to the slaves of secessionist slaveholders who came within military lines. Few soldiers questioned fugitive slaves' veracity when they declared that their owners were disloyal, and, indeed, many were inclined to believe that most white Missourians—especially slaveholders—were on the wrong side of the war. During the final years of the conflict, the military no longer debated whether Missouri slaves should be liberated but rather what to do with the many who already were free.[31]

As more slaves fled, Missouri slaveholders, both loyal and disloyal alike, became extremely anxious about protecting and maintaining their

slave property. The loss of even one slave had tremendous economic consequences for small slaveholders because most owned only a few adult
slaves, but the extreme emotional response of many suggests that they
had a significant social stake in slavery as well. Not only did losing their
slave property potentially compromise their plans for their own families'
futures, but it also disrupted the social and racial hierarchy that Missouri slaveholders had created within their own households and in society at large. Many Missouri slaveholders' initial response was to exhaust
all options in order to bring their runaway slaves home in an ill-fated
attempt to reconstitute the world that they had created for themselves
on slavery's border. Morgan County slaveholder John R. Moore pleaded
with military officials for the return of two of his slave men, complaining that "a large part of the hard earnings of my laborious life, is in my
Negro property, to all of which a death blow has been struck & lastly I
ask it because I raised those Boys am greatly attached to them." Soldiers
physically assaulted Moore and his son when they attempted to retrieve
the slave men, but Moore chose to tenaciously work through proper military and government channels in a futile attempt to reclaim his property.
There is no way to know if Moore's emotional attachment to his slaves
was indeed sincere, but it is possible that the experience of small-scale
slavery had led him to regard them with affection. His slave men clearly
did not see the relationship in the same light, however.[32]

Charles Jones, a Franklin County Unionist slaveholder, appealed directly to President Lincoln after his slaves ran away to a local military
encampment: "I have a large family, of helpless little children to support,
& have got a farm to support them on, & if I cant cultivate it, it will be valueless to me." Jones reasoned, in a second letter to General Davidson, that
his slaves should be returned because of his loyalty to the Union: "I trust
that my Government which I have always delighted to obey, will not suffer me to be sacrificed." Unlike Moore, Jones revealed that his motivation
for reclaiming his human property was more for the benefit of his own
family rather than from any concern for his slaves, as was the case with
slaveholders throughout time. Loyal Missourians at least had the satisfaction of appealing to higher authorities, whereas those who supported the
Confederacy had no possibility of a hearing. Missouri slaveholders became
increasingly angry and desperate as their world began to slip through their
fingers. A prime target of frustration for secessionist slaveholders was the
federal presence in their communities, which not only escalated the violence on both sides but also destabilized slavery as slaves fled to military
encampments. Many Missouri Unionists were deeply disillusioned when

the aims of the war changed from preserving the Union to the emancipation of slaves. The situation presented a complex dilemma for loyal slaveholders; although maintaining the institution was in their personal best interest, many Union politicians and military officials argued that slavery was not in the best interest of the Union cause. Despite their support for the Union, a great number of loyal slaveholders joined their secessionist foes in an attempt to maintain slavery in the state.[33]

Many Missouri owners directed their anger at their slaves. Slaveholders—Confederates and Unionists alike—unleashed a reign of terror as they frantically tried to maintain Missouri's slavery regime. Fugitives reported violent abuse at the hands of owners who desperately worked to control their slaves in the face of the institution's demise. "Nearer time for us to be freed, the owners got meaner all the time," Tishey Taylor remembered. The fact that Missouri owners lived and worked so intimately with their slaves likely made their disaffection feel even more personal. The primary focus of the violent reprisals and intimidation was slaveholders' desire to keep slaves working on their farms, however. They especially wished to discourage the trend of Unionist farmers who were employing escaped slaves as paid laborers. Colonel Samuel M. Wirt reported the efforts of Knox County guerrillas to terrorize local citizens who hired former slaves, threatening to drive both the employers and employees from the area. As slaveholders tightened their grip and increased their violence, many Missouri slaves became even more motivated to run.[34]

Some slaveholders took their slaves south to wait out the war in a desperate bid to secure their property. Richard Kimmons's master feared that federal soldiers would confiscate his slaves and so sent them to his son living in Texas, leaving his crops standing in the fields. Kimmons explained that the soldiers had been around all summer and "dey nebber boddered us, de w'ite folks jus' got talkin' 'round an' got scared." On the road south, he saw another group of slaves chained together and forcibly marched to Texas.[35]

Believing that emancipation was imminent, other Missouri owners merely cut their losses and sold their slaves in Texas or Kentucky where they commanded higher prices. Union military officials calculated that as many as a thousand Missouri slaves were sold in Lexington, Kentucky, in the autumn of 1862. In fact, Charles Jones, who wrote the distressed letter of appeal to Lincoln, attempted to arrest his economic hemorrhaging by selling six of his slaves to a man who transported them to Louisville. Esther Easter was sold to a woman in Bonham, Texas, and

Shap Phillips's slave woman Phebe was taken south and never heard from again. Mark Discus's story turned out better than that of many other Missouri slaves. His master wished to set his slaves free "when he saw how things was goin'," but the master's oldest son had other plans. "[Y]oung master loaded me and four others of the best slaves in a wagon and linked our hands together and started South with us to sell us," Discus recalled. Union soldiers encountered the group close to the Texas state line and freed the slaves: "That made young master mad as a hornet, but he let us go right there and then."[36]

Missouri neighborhoods increased the presence of slave patrols in an effort to maintain labor discipline and control the mobility of the local slave population. Willard Mendenhall wrote in late 1862: "The Patrole in the country are arresting negros every night. It will put a stop to thare running abought at night." Elvira Scott observed in Saline County that same month: "People seem apprehensive of trouble with the Negroes. The patrol is out every night. They have searched for arms in every cabin; several pistols were found. Many Negroes have run off, & many returned home. They are regarded with suspicion." Slaveholders feared their slaves, but slaves had much greater reason to fear patrollers. William Black remembered the brutality of wartime patrollers: "Durin' de war we could not leave de master's house to go to de neighbors without a pass. If we didn't have a pass de paddyrollers would get us and kill us or take us away." Patrollers had always brutalized slaves, but on the eve of emancipation there now was little expectation of restraint because owners had little to lose if their bondpeople were maimed or killed. Henry Bruce reported that the Chariton County slave patrol disintegrated in the face of Union military occupation. It is not surprising that civil unrest led to the breakdown of official slave patrols in some locations, but what was once an arm of local governments was fast becoming the bailiwick of secessionist guerrillas.[37]

In fact, many Civil War–era "patrollers" were indeed secessionist guerrillas, who were encouraged by pro-southern slaveholders to preserve the slavery regime through a campaign of intimidation, violence, and murder. General Thomas Ewing, commander of the District of the Border, believed that Missouri slaveholders fed and supplied guerrillas in exchange for their services in helping to maintain slavery. Guerrillas harassed local slaves, threatened white Missourians who hired former bondmen and women for pay, and later intimidated slave men to keep them from enlisting in the Union army. Guerrillas also terrorized slave women through violence and brutal sexual assaults, such as when Frances Kean's slave woman was gang-raped by bushwhackers. Others were kidnapped by Confederate soldiers and bushwhackers, taken south, and sold. Harry Johnson was stolen from his master's house during a Confederate raid and sold in Arkansas, and rebel soldiers took the slave men living in Cape Girardeau County, leaving the women and children behind. Eliza Madison and her fellow slave women hid under the staircase to keep from being stolen: "De soldiers took some of de slaves south and sold them somewhar' and we never heard from them again."[38]

Missouri slaveholders were not only concerned with those slaves who ran away, however. The possibility that the enemy potentially lived within their own households terrified secessionist slaveholders. Missouri slaves frequently reported their owners' secessionist activities, which ranged from lending material aid and comfort to Confederate bushwhackers to burning railroad bridges and riding with the guerrillas. In a reversal of decades of Missouri law that would not allow for the testimony of blacks against whites, the provost marshals used the testimony of slaves as they built cases against white Missourians accused of disloyalty. Some owners, such as Richard Pitman and Whitney Fowler, attempted to suppress loquacious slaves through intimidation, violence, imprisonment in local jails, or taking them south. Assistant Provost Marshal O. A. A. Gardner reported from Mexico, Missouri, that local "seceshionists have threatened to shoot every black who gives us any information and have already made way with several in this and adjoining counties." Archer Alexander reported to a local Union man that local secessionists had tampered with a railroad bridge, and he afterwards was forced to flee his owner when he learned that he was suspected of informing. Bushwhackers also beat and permanently crippled Isaac Fowler for providing information to Union men.[39]

Slaves suffered at the hands of Union troops as well: groups of jesting soldiers chased and terrorized slave children; some stole slaves' personal property and roused slave women from their beds to cook for them; and others threatened those who chose to remain with their owners. As a little boy, Robert Bryant was separated from his mother for days when soldiers attacked the wagon in which his family rode, and federal soldiers threatened a Saline County slave man because he chose to remain on his owner's place. The state generally was a dangerous place for African Americans during the war years, and they often did not know where to turn for help. Bondpeople might find assistance within their own communities and occasionally from sympathetic whites, but trusting the wrong person could be fatal. It was well known in Sullivan County, for example, that a slave man named Nels Dell had amassed a small fortune

both through a legacy from his deceased owner and by his own labor. During the war, men claiming to help him to freedom in Iowa robbed and murdered him instead.[40]

In the summer of 1862, the Union army began to enlist African American men as soldiers. Jim Lane organized one of the first African American regiments, primarily made up of former Missouri slaves who had escaped into Kansas, and these men engaged in the first armed military action by African American troops during the Civil War at the Battle of Island Mound, just over the border from Kansas, in late October 1862. Many other former Missouri slaves crossed over the state line into Iowa and Illinois, filling the ranks of the African American forces recruited in those states. Men still living in Missouri could not officially enlist until November 1863 when General John Schofield, another commander of the Department of the Missouri, authorized the recruitment of all slave men regardless of their owners' loyalties. Missouri slave men flocked into the Union army after official recruitment began in November 1863. By this point, they understood that enlistment would result in their immediate freedom, would allow them to assert their manhood and rights to citizenship, and might result in the liberation of their families as well. Alexander Marshall remembered the circumstances of his brother John Jackson's enlistment: "We were hauling fodder, and some recruiting officer came out" with another slave man and "asked John how old he was and he said 17 or 18 and that same evening John went to either Palmyra or Hannibal and that was the last time we see him." Jackson's mother did not want him to leave, but the recruiting officer and other neighborhood slave men pressured him to enlist.[41]

A few Unionist slaveholders encouraged enlistment because they recognized that their slave men would enroll with or without their permission, and, at the very least, African American soldiers would help meet

FIGURE 13 (previous page). *The Skirmish at Island Mound*. In *Harper's Weekly*, March 14, 1863. This illustration of the battle at Island Mound appeared in *Harper's Weekly* four months after the actual engagement on October 29, 1862. The Bates County, Missouri, skirmish was the site of the first military action during the Civil War in which African American troops engaged southern forces. The First Kansas Colored Volunteers, primarily made up of former Missouri slaves, was formed in the summer of 1862. The Union force fought secessionist guerrillas at a site along the Marais des Cygnes River in late October 1862, driving off the enemy but suffering casualties in the process. Courtesy of Ellis Library, University of Missouri–Columbia.

FIGURE 14. *Private Elijah Madison.* Charcoal and pastel drawing on paper, artist and date unknown, after a photograph taken between 1864 and 1866, most likely at Benton Barracks, St. Louis, Missouri. Elijah Madison (1841–1922) was enslaved on the St. Louis County property of his owner, Robert G. Coleman, along with twenty-two other people, before he enlisted in the Union army on March 17, 1864, at Benton Barracks. He served in the 68th United States Colored Troops, which saw service in the Lower South, eventually rising to the rank of corporal in October 1865 before he was discharged from service in early February 1866. After the war, he returned to St. Louis and married Elizabeth West, with whom he had fifteen children. Madison farmed for many years, as well as worked as a minister. Courtesy of the Missouri History Museum Collections, St. Louis.

the local draft quota. William Thomas actually asked the local provost marshal to force the enlistment of his slave blacksmith, Anderson, who was "loafing about for the last six months rendering service to no one." In addition, Unionist slaveholders also hoped to capitalize on monetary compensation for their slaves, which they believed was promised them by the federal government. Early in 1864, three of Paulina Stratton's young slave men enlisted in the Union army at nearby Tipton, Missouri. Stratton did not agonize over their enlistment, perhaps believing as a loyal slaveholder she would be compensated for her losses. Stratton and hundreds of other Missourians filed slave compensation claims with the United States government, but in the end they were never reimbursed for the loss of their slave property.[42]

Many other slaveholders discouraged and even physically intimidated their slaves to keep them from enlisting, however. Spotswood Rice's master attempted to bribe him by promising to give him land and a house if he would stay and manage his farming affairs. Rice remained for a few months, but eventually he and his fellow slave men ran off to enlist. Others threatened their slave men or their families with violence or locked up the men or their clothes and shoes at night to thwart enlistment. Many slave men risked their lives as they journeyed to recruitment stations. Slaveholders and guerrillas patrolled the roads at night in order to apprehend slave men on their way to enlist. Thomas Vaughn traveled to a recruiting station farther away from his home in order to avoid the local slaveholders who guarded the road to the closer Brunswick, Missouri, station. In an extremely egregious act of brutality, a Pike County slaveholding woman paid a neighbor $5 to shoot and kill her slave man after

FIGURE 15 (opposite page). *Instrument of Torture Used by Slaveholders.* In *Harper's Weekly*, February 15, 1862. This image was accompanied by a letter dated January 24, 1862, and sent by Sergeant Charles O. Dewey, who was serving with Dodge's Battery, 4th Regiment Iowa Volunteers, in Montgomery City, Missouri. A secessionist slave master Dudley Wells affixed to his slave man a "heavy iron ring, fitting closely round the neck, from which extended three prongs, each two feet in length, with a ring on the end," to which a chain might be attached, presumably to keep him from running away. The slave man had worn the collar for two months by the time he made it within Union lines. The soldiers undertook the difficult task of filing off the "Instrument of Torture" and promptly arrested Wells, who was described as being "destitute of all humanity." Courtesy of the Miller Nichols Library, University of Missouri–Kansas City.

he was captured while attempting to run away to enlist. Field officers routinely argued that the military should more actively protect those attempting to enlist, recognizing that the continued violence against recruits would dampen the prospect of future enlistees.[43]

While calculating the risks of enlistment, slave men considered the consequences of their actions for their kin as well. Some slave women and children followed their husbands and fathers to army posts, but many more initially remained with their owners. Slave women often suffered abuse because of the decisions made by their husbands and sons. Owners expected that the work of the farm would continue even after their slave men left, and many slave women complained that they now were required to do the "work formerly performed by men." Some owners treated women and children cruelly while others callously rid themselves of women and children, who now were considered a financial liability. A Paris, Missouri, slave woman complained to her husband that her owners were "treating me worse and worse every day." The provost marshal stationed in Lincoln County reported that a number of women and children were turned out by their masters after the men enlisted, he believed in an attempt to discourage future recruits. Martha Glover reported to her husband, Richard, that her owners "abuse me because you went & say they will not take care of our children & do nothing but quarrel with me all the time and beat me scandalously the day before yesterday." Glover placed greater blame on her husband, however, blasting him for leaving her "in the fix I am in." Her list of grievances was long: she was forced to suffer the abuse of her owners; she had to care for "these little helpless children" without his help; she was unable to attend a party to which she was invited; and she did nothing but "grieve all the time about you." She emphatically informed him that she would not encourage any other local married men to enlist. Martha Glover's situation became dire soon after, when her owner attempted to send her and the three youngest of their six children to Kentucky for sale, but Brigadier General William A. Pile, who was already aware of the abuse, intervened before the family was taken out of the state.[44]

Many soldiers agonized over the fate of their loved ones, pleading with Union military officials to intercede on their behalf. Some, such as Spotswood Rice, argued that their military service guaranteed the freedom and protection of their family members. As did Rice, Sam Bowmen threatened the owner of his wife and children, informing him that he must allow his wife to leave if she chose because a "Soldiers wife is free." Others took matters into their own hands and liberated their family members who remained in bondage. In March 1864, the assistant provost marshal stationed in Howard County reported that some local slave men, who had recently enlisted in the army, had returned from St. Louis "with some white soldiers and [were] hauling off tobacco from their former masters and owners and taking their wives and children." These return trips were made at great risk, as a former Platte County slave named Sam Marshall learned when he ran afoul of local Missouri State Militia soldiers, who severely beat him as he attempted to take his children with him to Leavenworth, Kansas.[45]

In the end, over 8,300 Missouri slaves served in the five United States Colored Infantry regiments that were recruited in the state, but many more enlisted in nearby Kansas, Illinois, and Iowa. The men who served in Missouri regiments constituted nearly 39 percent of the state's African American men of service age. Missouri men enlisted primarily in late 1863 and early 1864, but by the summer of 1864 recruiters found it difficult to locate many more men willing to enroll. Most Missouri slave men had achieved their freedom by then and were now more interested in working for local farmers, many of whom were offering good wages or share-cropping arrangements.[46]

As the war progressed, Missouri slaves became less tolerant of slaveholders' abuse because they knew that, although the risks were great, they had the option to leave. Like many white Missourians, they hoped that the federal government would safeguard their rights, and they repeatedly asked the provost marshals and other military officials for relief from abusive owners, rights of free passage, material aid, and assistance in disputes over their freedom. One couple who believed they were being held in slavery in "violation of law" made "nightly journeys to neighboring towns and military stations in search of imaginary Prov. Marshalls" to help them secure their freedom.[47]

With the assistance of the army and refugee aid organizations, as well as of their own volition, Missouri slaves left for the surrounding free states by the thousands after the summer of 1863. In the years following the war, potential pension claimants solicited testimony from relatives and former Missouri neighbors still living in places such as Quincy, Illinois, and Leavenworth, Kansas. In March 1864, Henry Bruce escaped to Leavenworth with his intended wife, eluding the men who pursued them, riding on his master's horse. George Johnson's father pretended to take a load of grit across the border into Iowa, just as he had done for his master before the war, but instead of grit, he covered his family and another slave family with a tarp. In April 1863, a Kansas City, Missouri, newspaper reported that large numbers of freed slaves "are constantly streaming through our streets," presumably on their way to Kansas. On April 20, "a procession of six wagons, one carriage, five horsemen and ten footmen" passed through the city. "Each wagon contained from ten to twelve persons—the whole numbering from eighty-five to ninety self-emancipated 'chattels.' . . . Each family had a heterogeneous collection of household furniture, shotguns, clothing, etc., in their wagons, and all appeared well supplied with the necessaries of life." These items represented former slaves' personal wealth accumulated from a lifetime of extra work, but some freedmen and women likely "liberated" their owners' personal possessions and livestock along with their human property.[48]

Many who hazarded running away faced an uncertain future in freedom, however. Union officials and aid workers in both Missouri and the surrounding states wrote to their superiors asking for assistance in caring for the refugee women and children who were suffering in their midst. As early as July 1863, Captain G. W. Murphy reported the presence of 270 women and children in Sedalia, Missouri, who were "suffering from some thing to eat." Oftentimes, women and children followed male relatives to recruitment stations, and many remained near these military encampments because they feared guerrilla violence or capture by their former owners if they moved back into the countryside. There were some private philanthropic efforts to aid refugees, such as the St. Louis Ladies' Contraband Relief Society, but the task rested primarily with the army. Officers did not always know what to do with the overwhelming number of people who sought their protection. They could not employ all of them in camp, nor did they usually have the resources to feed, clothe, and shelter them. They often cast around, looking for solutions to the problem of caring for them. According to the historian Leslie Schwalm, individual Union soldiers sometimes arranged for the transportation of freedmen and women to their home communities where they were put to work for their families and neighbors. Formerly enslaved Missourians faced a mixed reception in these Upper Midwest communities, where racism and white supremacy was virulent and an influx of African American workers was unwelcome by many. Some commanders of military encampments requested material aid for the freedpeople living among them, whereas others asked to ship "contraband" slaves somewhere else, such as Kansas. The Union commander in Independence, Missouri, wondered if he might be allowed to put the nearly three hundred "old men, women, and children," who made his garrison their home, to work on nearby "deserted farms" that had

FIGURE 16. Emancipation Ordinance of Missouri. The Republican-dominated State Constitutional Convention abolished slavery in Missouri on January 11, 1865. By this time, many Missouri slaves had already gained their freedom. Courtesy of the Library of Congress.

been abandoned in the wake of General Order Number 11. But by and large, their appeals and accounts read similarly, newly freed people were crowded into Missouri towns and were often living in desperate conditions, suffering from disease and hunger.[49]

"The war is over and you no more slaves"

On January 11, 1865, Missouri slaves were officially emancipated by a resolution of the now Republican-controlled Missouri State Constitutional Convention, but by this time, most—especially enlistment-age men—were already free. The road to freedom had been long, stretching back to the times when enslaved Missourians regularly contested the terms of their labor and their living arrangements. The struggles between slaves and their owners were often intensely personal and frequently ended in violent confrontation. But enslaved Missourians also resisted the dehumanizing effects of slavery by forging strong emotional ties with their fellow bondpeople, in spite of the strictures placed on them by their owners. The long fight to bolster their self-esteem and maintain human connections in the face of the degradations of slavery finally was nearing its end.[50]

Former Missouri slaves remembered that they learned about emancipation in a variety of ways. The newspaper brought the news to Rhody Holsell: "Me and another little old woman done some shoutin' and hollerin' when we heard 'bout de freedom. We tore up some corn down in de field. De old missus was right there on de fence but wouldn't dare touch us den.... They thought it was awful dat dey could not whip de slaves any longer." Rachal Goings's master came to her mother's cabin to tell his slaves that they were free. When Goings called her mother by her given name, Cynthy, the master said, "Stop chile! You mustin' call her Cynthy no more. The war is over and you no more slaves. Now you must call her mammy." Goings observed that it was a matter of semantics: "[W]e kep' on living dere just de same, till Masta' died two years after de war."[51]

Like Goings and her family, many former slaves stayed with their owners for a time after emancipation because they had few resources and because they "didn't know nothing else to do." After Marie Askin Simpson's father died in the war, her mother remained with her former owners and did "the best we could to make a living." Simpson noted that the decision to stay was in part because the hostilities had left "everybody ... mad or suspicious of each other," making it "hard to find places to live." Most freedpeople had little difficulty finding work with either their former owners or local farmers and tradesmen, although the dynamics of the relationship between employers and workers were altered from slavery days, as Tishey Taylor so aptly pointed out: "After we wuz free there wus plenty of work, they couldn't whip nobody and had to pay us for the work." In theory, all Missourians were now free to negotiate the terms of their own labor, but the realities of the situation were often much more complex.[52]

Freedpeople's lives changed dramatically in the years following emancipation. Their relationships with white Missourians certainly were forever altered, but they likely were more concerned about what freedom meant for their own families and communities. The turbulence of wartime Missouri and men's enlistment separated many families during the course of the war, and thousands of women and children faced freedom without the support of their husbands and fathers, who had served, and frequently died, in the Union army. The large number of Missouri women who filed widows' and orphans' pension claims attests to appallingly high death rates among African American soldiers and the struggles faced by their families after their deaths. War widows were forced to find the means to care for their children, often casting around for help from other bondpeople, similar to the aid received by abroad wives during slavery.[53]

The end of slavery also created opportunities, however, as many of the families that had been separated during slavery by estate divisions, sales, and abroad unions, as well as dislocation during the war, were reunited under the same roof, sometimes for the first time. Margaret Nickens was reunited with her mother in eastern Missouri after years spent at the home of her master's daughter in the western part of the state. As during slavery, freedpeople worked to reconstitute their households after the war, but not all of them sheltered nuclear families. It was common for extended kin, and even neighbors, to live together under one roof. Assembling a household of individuals who could work together as an economic unit was the primary goal, but expanding the definition of family to include extended kin and those permanently separated from relatives was a priority as well. Peter Corn's aunt and uncle claimed him from his owners after his uncle returned from the war, for example. Thousands of former Missouri slave couples also legalized their unions under the state's mandated marriage statute of 1865. Most gladly paid the licensing fee believing that for the first time the law might provide the legitimacy to their marriages that they had once sought through slave wedding ceremonies. Many black Missourians, such as Mary Bell and her siblings, also had the opportunity to attend school for the first time in their lives.[54]

Missouri slaveholders had an extremely difficult time adjusting to the changes to their lives brought about by the emancipation of their slaves, and many still clung to slavery as a system of labor and racial control. Sue Steele initially would not accept that her slave woman Lucinda Patterson was free. Her husband told Patterson that they would be glad for her to stay with them, but that she was free to go if she wished. Patterson remembered Sue Steele's nasty reply and her own response, "[C]ourse she is our nigger. She is as much our nigger now as she was the day you bought her 2 years ago and paid $1500 for her. That made me mad so I left right then." No longer bound by the obligations of ownership and demoralized by their wartime experiences, many owners drove their former slaves off of their land. "They was so mad at us for being freed that they got rid of us as soon as they could, and we was only too glad to go," Charlie Richardson remembered. Other Missouri slaveholders, such as Eda Hickam's owners, made it extremely difficult for their slaves to leave. They either did not inform them of emancipation or they tried to coerce them to remain as wage laborers. Malinda Discus's owners hoped to influence their slaves to stay by trying "to make us believe that we couldn't take care of ourselves if we were free." Many people were forced to take great risks to break the bonds of their enslavement even though they already were legally free. Louis Hill's mother fled with her children in the middle of the night, and Hill explained, "Dat was after we was free but dey wouldn't let her get away in de daytime very handy." Hill's mother was given nothing but her freedom. Reflecting back from the 1930s, Hill believed that things would have turned out differently had the government compelled slaveholders to provide their slaves with "a little track of land, a cow and a horse and give 'em a start. De slave had made what de white man had." Charlie Richardson also believed that his owners owed him something for his years of labor: "We thought they was goin' to divide up the farms and give us some of it. No Sah!"[55]

Just as was the case during slavery, the relations between former owners and slaves were influenced by the intimate conditions in which they had once lived and worked. Some former owners, most often those who had treated their bondpeople humanely, continued to extend acts of kindness to their former slaves. These actions in some cases reflected former slaveholders' desire to maintain the labor of their former slaves, but a few may have felt a sense of obligation to the people who had served them for so long. The kindness of some is no more surprising than the nastiness of Sue Steele; both were logical outcomes of the intimacy fostered on Missouri's small slaveholdings. Marilda Pethy's former mistress took in her mother and three small children when they were left homeless after emancipation. Paulina Stratton also worried over her former slave women and their children after the war, making sure that they had proper clothing and decent employment situations. Clay Smith's former master employed her mother over the years in order to assist her with her house payments. A few former owners actually presented their former bondpeople with tangible gifts in order to facilitate their transition to freedom. Lewis Mundy reported of a neighboring slaveholder who gave his emancipated slaves eighty acres of land, and Mrs. Charles Douthit claimed that her mother's former mistress gave her land and built her a house that still remained in the family. Bill Messersmith had land in abundance, but most of it was not yet cleared. He gave his former slave Jim and his wife, Martha, whom he had inherited upon his father's death, the opportunity to keep half of whatever land they could clear in five years' time. Messersmith furnished his former slaves with provisions, tools, and even two white laborers to help them through the first year. Jim, his two sons, his nephew, and the two white men cleared eighty acres, fenced it, and planted it in corn and wheat. Through this arrangement Messersmith served the needs of his former bondpeople, while also furthering his own goals for his farm. In the years following the Civil War, former Missouri slaves who served in the federal army and their dependents filed thousands of pension claims. More often than not the former owners who were asked to provide evidence toward a claim did so willingly, revealing their feelings of obligation toward and possibly affection for their former slaves.[56]

Many other former owners did not graciously accept the end of the labor and social system from which they had so richly benefited. "Slavery dies hard. I hear its expiring agonies & witness its contortions in death in every quarter of my Dist.," Brigadier General Clinton Fisk reported of the situation in central Missouri in March 1865. Many freedpeople streamed into local towns or military garrisons for protection as their former owners pushed them off of the land "with nothing to eat or scarcely wear," and as they faced increased violence as white Missourians considered the possibility of a biracial democracy. Boone County slaves flooded into Columbia after a series of lynchings in the countryside in the month directly after emancipation. The Union commander in Lafayette County was forced to issue an order that stipulated that anyone who threatened freedpeople would be considered in league with the bushwhackers who were terrorizing and murdering local African Americans and would be charged as an accessory to these murders. The demographics of the Missouri countryside actually changed as a result of this postwar violence. The river counties never again could boast of as large African American populations as before the war; many people chose the relative safety of Missouri's towns and cities instead. The African American population of Little Dixie counties declined by a dramatic 19 percent between 1860 and 1870, for example, while the African American population of St. Louis increased by 325 percent (see table 7).[57]

Aware of the continued violence and skeptical that economic opportunities existed in Missouri, many freed Missourians remained in Kansas, Iowa, or Illinois, where they had fled during the war. Henry Bruce and his wife, Pauline, were two of the more than seventeen thousand African American residents of Kansas in 1870. Bruce never returned to Missouri, but instead opened a business in Leavenworth and eventually became involved in the Kansas Republican party. In 1881, he moved to Washington, D.C., where for the rest of his life he worked at federal jobs secured for him by his well-known brother, the former Mississippi Senator Blanche K. Bruce. This fortuitous connection to his kinsman allowed Henry Bruce to prosper in postwar society, whereas other formerly enslaved Missourians continued to face discrimination and poverty in their new northern homes.[58]

Antebellum Missourians' commitment to diversified agriculture made the transition to Midwestern-style farming relatively smooth in the postwar years, as they increased grain and livestock production and capitalized on the arrival of the railroads to their communities. Certainly, the prewar structure of labor on small slaveholdings, with its combination of family and slave labor, made the postwar employment of general farmhands and domestic workers a logical outcome. Yet, wartime deprivations and emancipation left emotional scars on white Missourians that were not easily healed. Many of the men, who once were the leaders of Missouri society, now found themselves dispossessed of much of their wealth and political power. Missouri slaveholders lost their slaves, but many secessionists lost their land as well. In addition, those who supported the South were publicly humiliated as they were stripped of their political offices and professional posts, as well as the franchise, if they refused to take an oath of loyalty to the United States. Missouri's conservative Unionists were disillusioned as well, however. At the start of the war, they never could have imaged a world in which their former slaves were emancipated and they were forced to hire them as paid laborers. Most Missouri slaveholders had employed enslaved men as general farmhands and women as domestic workers. White Missourians had preferred to hire slaves from neighboring slaveholders rather than employ white farmhands because they believed they could better control enslaved workers and extract more labor from them. Yet, once their slaves were freed, farmers continued to employ workers in a manner similar to the way they had before the war, although some had difficulties adapting to the new management practices of free labor. Freedmen and women could now decide what tasks they were willing to perform, as well as whether they wished to remain employed by a particular farmer, businessman, or homemaker. As a result of their new ability to choose their employment, hemp production declined precipitously following the war, as farmers found it challenging to locate men who were willing to harvest and break the crop. Some white Missourians also had trouble adjusting to the new expectations for the terms of the relations between employers and laborers, who now were paid wages and could not be physically disciplined. Having benefited from the labor of slaves for her entire life, Paulina Stratton initially was confused about how she should treat the farmhands that she now employed. She constantly equivocated over whether or not she should ask her male employees to lend her a hand with her household chores. Paulina desired this help because she and her married daughter Agnes were left to tend to their domestic affairs without the assistance of a servant, as was the case with many other Missouri farmwomen. Paulina also found herself working in the fields for the first time in her life.[59]

Former slaveholders also had trouble reconciling to the state's new political landscape. Unlike in most of the South, Missouri Republicans were not forced to give black men the vote in order to remain in power because the state's relatively small African American population and the disenfranchisement of former secessionists had made this step unnecessary. Many white Missourians were deeply dismayed, therefore, when the federal government granted African American men the vote with the Fifteenth Amendment to the Constitution. Those who had supported the Union felt especially betrayed by the act of freeing their slaves and extending them citizenship rights. In fact, the historian Aaron Astor and others have argued that white Missourians forged a postwar southern identity in the wake of their negative experiences with federal forces during the war and because of their commonly shared racial beliefs. The advent of black political power drove many former conservative Unionists into an alliance with their former secessionist foes, a political partnership that led to reinstatement of the franchise to former Confederates. Upper South migrants had once established in Missouri a society with small-scale slavery at its core. White Missourians overwhelmingly supported the system from which so many profited economically, as well as socially. Even nonslaveholding men benefited from the hire of their neighbors' slaves, as well as a shared belief in white male equality. That white Missourians—Union and Confederate alike—reconstituted their rural communities in the following years along the lines of white supremacy and racial subordination should not be surprising.[60]

White Missourians' project of reconstructing their society in the years following the war involved learning to live in a changing world in which labor relations and social hierarchies were in flux, but it also concerned the ways that they chose to remember their past. Missourians always believed that they had perfected a better and milder form of bondage in their border state. Had they not intimately lived and worked with their slaves, both in the fields and in their homes? Somehow, the constant strife and pervasive violence of small slaveholdings was overlooked in favor of the memory of a bucolic slavery system in which owners treated their slaves kindly and enslaved Missourians rewarded them with loyalty, even in the face of their freedom. Just as the conditions of small-scale slavery made it difficult for slaveholders to acknowledge their slaves' resistance and the historic pressures of Missouri's geographic location led them to promote their mild form of slavery to outsiders, the harsh realities of life in a postwar society in transition caused many white Missourians to fashion the memory of a perfect society that was destroyed by a brutal war.[61]

Missouri's freedmen and women well understood that white Missourians' tale of mild border slavery was not the reality of their life in bondage. They carried the memories—and often the scars—of the emotional and physical abuse meted out by Missouri slaveholders within these same small-slaveholding households that white Missourians described as "domestic." Enslaved Missourians diligently worked to protect the integrity of their families in the face of the many systemic abuses of slavery, as well as the unique pressures placed on slave families and communities by the small size of Missouri slaveholdings. Before the war, they labored—by and large successfully—to develop meaningful relationships with their kin and neighbors. In all cases, maintaining these human connections across farm boundaries was challenging and was undertaken with some creativity and risk, but ultimately these relations provided the little pleasure available to enslaved men, women, and children. Most formerly enslaved Missourians could not pause long to reflect on the inaccuracies of white Missourians' description of slavery, however, nor did they have the power to publicly correct it, as they struggled to make a new life in freedom, engaging in the difficult task of reconstituting families ravaged by slavery, negotiating new terms of labor, establishing households and farms, and building social institutions, such as churches, political organizations, and schools. The work was hard, but the rewards were immense.[62]

Although they recognized the significance of the moment, neither slaves nor slaveholders fully understood the implications for their future lives as they stood on the threshold of emancipation. The day Elvira Scott fled her Saline County home she wrote:

Sunday, August 31st, 1863—a day long to be remembered here. About three o'clock a procession appeared. It was headed by eleven six-mule teams drawing wagons filled with Negro women & children. Behind them was a large procession of two hundred & forty

Negro men, besides women & children. Some were playing the fiddle. The procession of Negroes had an escort of soldiers carrying a flag. The Negroes swarmed over town in search of houses. Every unoccupied house was soon filled, besides some kitchens of occupied houses. Immediately they began pillaging—gardens, chickens coops, & peach trees were stripped.

The newly freed remained in the town, scavenging by day and dancing at night. They threatened to whip all of the local bondpeople who remained with their owners. The slaveholding men and women who had for so many years exercised control over slaves' lives were now at their mercy. Elvira Scott's world and her place in it had been turned on end, and Scott's ownership of only a few slaves did not lead her to agonize less over emancipation and its implications for postwar society. She sadly acknowledged this transformation: "Nothing but soldiers & Negroes to be seen in the streets. Truly my last days in Miami are memorable; all the peaceful, pleasant days are gone." Those newly freed Missouri slaves, whose procession with fiddle and flag and escorting soldiers so frightened Elvira Scott, surely saw their emancipation as equally "memorable." The years ahead would prove to be difficult for both black and white Missourians as they forged a new relationship in freedom, but for former slaveholders and slaves, who had fashioned a troubled coexistence in small-scale slavery, the ambiguities and extremes of their lives on slavery's border had ended.[63]

TABLES

TABLE 1. Missouri population, 1810—1860

Census year	Whites	Free blacks	Slaves	Total population	Slaves as percentage of total population
1810	16,303	605	2,875	19,783	15%
1820	56,017	347	10,222	66,586	15%
1830	114,795	569	25,091	140,455	18%
1840	323,888	1,574	58,240	383,702	15%
1850	592,004	2,618	87,422	682,044	13%
1860	1,063,489	3,572	114,931	1,182,012	10%

TABLE 2. The slave population of the ten largest slaveholding counties, 1860

Slaveholding county	Total population	Slave population	Slaves as percentage of total population
Lafayette	20,098	6,374	32%
Howard	15,946	5,886	37%
Boone	19,486	5,034	26%
Saline	14,699	4,876	33%
Callaway	17,449	4,523	26%
St. Louis	190,524	4,346	2%
Pike	18,417	4,055	22%
Jackson	22,913	3,944	17%
Cooper	17,356	3,800	22%
Clay	13,023	3,455	27%
TOTAL	349,911	46,293	13%

TABLE 3. The male-female ratio of the slave population in five Missouri counties, 1850 and 1860

	Total males		Total females		Adult males		Adult females	
	N	%	N	%	N	%	N	%
1850	5,435	49	5,647	51	2,523	49	2,642	51
1860	7,145	50	7,218	50	3,367	48	3,636	52

TABLE 4. Composition of Missouri slave families

Data derived from	Abroad marriages		Resident marriages		Single parents		Orphaned children		Total marriages
	N	%	N	%	N	%	N	%	
Pension claims	79	63	29	23	20	16	2	2	126
WPA narratives	29	45	18	28	29	45	0	0	65
Total marriages	108	57	47	25	49	26	2	1	191

TABLE 5. Composition of Missouri slaveholdings, 1850 and 1860

	Male-headed holdings		Female-headed holdings		Male and female holdings		Children-only holdings		Inter-generational holdings		Total holdings
	N	%	N	%	N	%	N	%	N	%	
1850	238	10	646	28	1,055	47	328	14	301	13	2,267
1860	322	11	766	27	1,442	50	346	12	457	16	2,876

TABLE 6. Length of Missouri slave marriages

Data derived from	10–14 years (4 to 6 children)		15–19 years (7 to 9 children)		More than 20 years (10 or more children)		Total marriages (10 years or more)		Total marriages
	N	%	N	%	N	%	N	%	
Pension claims	20	25	14	18	11	14	45	57	79
Marriage records	91	34	40	15	13	5	144	54	269

TABLE 7. Demographic changes in the ten largest slaveholding counties,
1860 to 1870

County	1860 Black population	1870 Black population	% Change
Lafayette	6,410	4,039	-37
Howard	5,960	5,193	-13
Boone	5,087	4,038	-21
Saline	4,899	3,754	-23
Callaway	4,554	3,434	-25
St. Louis	6,211	26,387	+325
Pike	4,115	4,195	+2
Jackson	4,014	5,223	+30
Cooper	3,828	3,352	-12
Clay	3,498	1,846	-47
Total	48,576	61,461	+27

Notes

Abbreviations Key

AS   George P. Rawick, *The American Slave,* (Westport, Conn.: Green-wood, 1972). Most of the narratives were included in volume 11 and supplement, series 1, volume 2. The volumes and page numbers reference the George Rawick compiled collections rather than the original WPA narratives. I have indicated the volume and page numbers at the end of the citations (e.g., Marilda Pethy, *AS*, 11:277–82).

DU   Manuscript Department, William R. Perkins Library, Duke University, Durham, North Carolina.

FSSP   Freedmen and Southern Society Project, University of Maryland, College Park, Maryland.

JCHS   Jackson County Historical Society, Independence, Missouri.

MHM   Missouri History Museum, Library and Research Center, St. Louis, Missouri.

MSA   Missouri State Archives, Jefferson City, Missouri

NA   National Archives, Washington, D.C.

pen., USCT 65   Pension Claims, United States Colored Infantry, 65th Regiment, National Archives, Washington, D.C. (I also have indicated the company in which the soldier served.)

Provost
Marshall   Missouri's Union Provost Marshal Papers: 1861—1866, Union
       Provost Marshals' File of Papers Relating to Individual Civilians
       and Union Provost Marshals' File of Papers Relating to Two or
       More Civilians, War Department Collection of Confederate Re-
       cords, Record Group 109, National Archives, microfilm viewed at
       Missouri State Archives.

WHMC   Western Historical Manuscript Collection, Columbia, Missouri.

WHMC–KC   Western Historical Manuscript Collection, Kansas City, Missouri.

Introduction

1. General John Gideon Haskell, then president of the Kansas State Historical Society, commented on slavery in western Missouri during the twenty-fifth anniversary meeting of the organization in January 1901. See Haskell, "The Passing of Slavery in Western Missouri," 31, and Trexler, *Slavery in Missouri*, 19.

2. Trexler, *Slavery in Missouri*. Bruce, *The New Man*. Deyle, *Carry Me Back*, 86.

3. Missouri Division of the United Daughters of the Confederacy, *Reminiscences of the Women of the Sixties*. Trexler, *Slavery in Missouri*, 19. Haskell, "The Passing of Slavery in Western Missouri." See also Astor, "Belated Confederates."

4. Stowe, *Uncle Tom's Cabin*, chaps. 1–10. Twain, *The Adventures of Huckleberry Finn*. Dempsey, *Searching for Jim*.

5. Most of the Missouri WPA narratives are published in *AS*, vol. 11 and *AS*, supp. series 1, vol. 2. Brown, *Narrative of William Wells Brown* (1849), 133.

6. Since the 1970s, historians have redefined the study of slavery and slaveholding in the American South. A sampling of the foundational literature on American slavery includes Blassingame, *The Slave Community;* Clinton, *The Plantation Mistress;* Escott, *Slavery Remembered;* Fox-Genovese, *Within the Plantation Household;* Genovese, *Roll, Jordan, Roll;* Gutman, *The Black Family in Slavery and Freedom;* Jones, *Labor of Love, Labor of Sorrow;* and D. G. White, *Ar'n't I A Woman?*

7. The definition of a plantation is a slaveholding of twenty or more slaves. In 1860, 12 percent of slaveholders in the Deep South owned at least twenty slaves, whereas only 4 percent did in Missouri. Not even 1 percent of slaveholders in Missouri owned fifty or more slaves. Three of the largest slaveholding counties in Missouri raised the percentage of planters in the state as a whole to 4 percent. In most slaveholding counties, closer to 2 percent of slaveholders were planters. For statistics on the size of slaveholdings and the number of slaves in Missouri, see Hilliard, *Atlas of Antebellum Agriculture*, 37–38; and Hurt, *Agriculture and Slavery in Missouri's Little Dixie*, 219–22. See also R. Fogel, *Without Consent or Contract*, 178–82.

8. James Oakes argues that small slaveholders, rather than planters, shaped southern society; however, he does not address the actual experiences of slaves living on farms. For a description of upwardly mobile Southerners see Oakes, *The Ruling Race;* and W. L. Johnson, *Soul by Soul*.

9. See E. Miller and Genovese, ed., *Plantation, Town, and Country*. A few historians

have made some observations about small slaveholdings within their works on plantation slavery: Paul D. Escott, Eugene Genovese, Elizabeth Fox-Genovese, and Peter Kolchin, for example. A number of studies of slavery in individual states were published early in the last century. A good example is Trexler, *Slavery in Missouri, 1804–1865,* which was published in 1914. These early historians were influenced by the "plantation school" interpretation of slavery. Since the 1970s, there have been some excellent regional studies of slavery and slaveholding, including Campbell, *An Empire for Slavery;* Dunaway, *Slavery in the American Mountain South;* Essah, *A House Divided;* Fields, *Slavery and Freedom on the Middle Ground;* Hahn, *The Roots of Southern Populism;* Inscoe, *Mountain Masters;* Malone, *Sweet Chariot;* McCurry, *Masters of Small Worlds;* and Stevenson, *Life in Black and White.* For slave populations by county, see Hurt, *Agriculture and Slavery in Missouri's Little Dixie,* 219–20. For a discussion of the definition of a slave society and the development of slavery in early America, see Berlin, *Many Thousands Gone;* Finley, *Ancient Slavery and Modern Ideology;* Kulikoff, *Tobacco and Slaves;* E. S. Morgan, *American Slavery, American Freedom;* Parent, *Foul Means;* and P. Wood, *Black Majority.* For master's theses and dissertations that address slavery in Missouri, see Bellamy, "Slavery, Emancipation, and Racism in Missouri, 1850–65"; Duffner, "Slavery in Missouri River Counties, 1820–1865"; and McGettigan, "Slave Sales, Estate Divisions, and the Slave Family in Boone County, Missouri, 1820–1865." For monographs see H. Frazier, *Runaway and Freed Missouri Slaves and Those Who Helped Them;* H. Frazier, *Slavery and Crime in Missouri;* Hurt, *Agriculture and Slavery in Missouri's Little Dixie;* McLaurin, *Celia, a Slave;* Poole and Slawson, *Church and Slave in Perry County, Missouri, 1818–1865;* Stone, *Slavery, Southern Culture, and Education in Little Dixie, Missouri, 1820–1860;* and Trexler, *Slavery in Missouri.*

10. Pauline Stratton Collection, WHMC. In the process of extensively researching the life of Paulina Stratton while editing and annotating her diary for publication, I have determined that Paulina rather than Pauline was Stratton's given name. The archive misnamed the collection. Hereinafter I will refer to her as Paulina in the text, but will keep the archival name in the notes.

11. One could argue that the domestic rhetoric did not represent the reality in northern homes as well where servants also were employed. For excellent discussions of southern slaveholding households, see Bardaglio, *Reconstructing the Household;* Bercaw, *Gendered Freedoms;* Fox-Genovese, *Within the Plantation Household;* Glymph, *Out of the House of Bondage;* and McCurry, *Masters of Small Worlds.*

12. Genovese, *Roll, Jordan, Roll,* 3.

13. The geographic area of Little Dixie has been defined in many ways, but I generally rely on R. Douglas Hurt's designation of the seven counties (Callaway, Boone, Howard, Cooper, Saline, Lafayette, and Clay) that border the Missouri River in the central to western part of state. These were all counties with large slave populations, where slavery was a central part of the economy and society. Including these select counties in the definition of Little Dixie does not preclude other western Missouri counties, such as Platte, Jackson, and Chariton, from sharing many of these attributes; however, Hurt argues that the seven counties were among the ten largest slaveholding counties in the state in 1860 and served as the "heart" of the Little Dixie region. In 1860, the population statistics of the five selected counties are as follows: Clay County—3,455 slaves (27 percent of the total population); Chariton County—2,839

slaves (23 percent of the total population); Cooper County—3,800 slaves (22 percent of the total population); Marion County—3,017 slaves (16 percent of the total population); and Ste. Genevieve County—617 slaves (8 percent of the total population). Slave Schedules, Chariton County, Clay County, Cooper County, Marion County, and Ste. Genevieve County, Missouri, 1850 and 1860, United States Census. Census Browser, fisher.lib.virginia.edu/collections/stats/histcensus/. See Hurt, *Agriculture and Slavery in Missouri's Little Dixie*, ix–xiv, and 219–22.

14. Gerteis, *Civil War St. Louis*.

15. There were only 3,572 free blacks living in Missouri in 1860, and 1,865 of them (52 percent) lived in St. Louis. 1860, Missouri, United States Census. See Finkelman, *Dred Scott v. Sandford: A Brief History with Documents;* and "Before Dred Scott: Freedom Suits in Missouri," Missouri State Archive website, http://www.sos.mo.gov/archives/resources/africanamerican/intro.asp. See also Kennington, "River of Injustice"; and Clamorgan, *The Colored Aristocracy of St. Louis*.

16. Brown, *Narrative of William W. Brown;* Bruce, *The New Man;* Eliot, *The Story of Archer Alexander;* Andrews, ed., *Six Women's Slave Narratives;* Missouri narratives, *AS,* vol. 11; Missouri narratives, *AS,* supp., ser. 1, vol. 2; pension claims, 65th USCT, NA; and additional pension records found in the papers of a Chariton County attorney, Benecke Family Papers, 1816–1989, WHMC.

17. For selected discussions of the use of WPA slave narratives, see Rawick, *From Sundown to Sunup;* Escott, *Slavery Remembered;* Blassingame, *The Slave Community;* Spindel, "Assessing Memory"; and Crawford, "Quantified Memory." There was also a second set of interviews conducted by researchers at Fisk University, which are called the Fisk narratives.

18. For an analysis of the use of Civil War pension records as historical evidence for slavery, see Kaye, *Joining Places,* 14–19. See also Skocpol, *Protecting Soldiers and Mothers,* and Orloff, *The Politics of Pensions*.

19. See Bruce, *The New Man;* Eliot, *The Story of Archer Alexander;* Brown, *Narrative of William Wells Brown;* Andrews, ed., *Six Women's Slave Narratives;* Benecke Family Papers, 1816–1989, WHMC; and pension claims, USCT 65, NA.

Chapter 1

1. October 1854–April 1855, Pauline Stratton Collection, WHMC.

2. Ibid.

3. Ibid.

4. If the Strattons had lived in Cooper County in 1850 they would have been counted among the top 14 percent of slaveholding households. In that year, 86 percent of slaveholders owned nine or fewer slaves and 63 percent owned four or fewer. In 1860, the Strattons were in the upper 15 percent of slaveholding families. In that year, 85 percent of slaveholders owned nine or fewer slaves and 72 percent owned four or fewer. The average number of slaves owned per household was 4.8. Within their actual township of New Lebanon, the average slaveholding was only two. Slave Schedule, New Lebanon Township, 1850 and 1860 Cooper County, Missouri, United States Census. 1855, Pauline Stratton Collection, WHMC. See also Hurt, *Agriculture and Slavery in Missouri's Little Dixie,* 54–55, 221, 309–10.

5. The first African slaves were brought to Missouri to work the Mine La Motte in 1720. For a discussion of slavery in colonial Missouri, see Foley, *The*

Genesis of Missouri, 1–28; Trexler, *Slavery in Missouri*, 21; and Aron, *American Confluence*.

6. Aron, *American Confluence*, quotations xii and 67.

7. See Foley, *The Genesis of Missouri*, 15–130; Brackenridge, *Recollections of Persons and Places in the West*, 24–26; Gerlach, *Settlement Patterns in Missouri*, 1–14; and Stepenoff, *From French Community to Missouri Town*.

8. The population of Ste. Genevieve was 691 settlers, 287 of them slaves. St. Louis had a population of 597, with 198 slaves. Some Upper Louisiana slaves were of Native American descent, although the Spanish colonial government officially outlawed Indian slavery in 1769 in order to decrease the unrest among local tribes that was often caused by the abuses of the trade in Indian slaves. This ban was rarely enforced, however, since most owners kept their property after an official review. See Foley, *Genesis of Missouri*, 101–30; Gerlach, *Settlement Patterns in Missouri*, for above statistics, 11; Trexler, *Slavery in Missouri*, 57–81; and Stepenoff, *From French Community to Missouri Town*, 121–35. For the historical debate on the question of whether slave conditions were better in the American South or in Latin American countries, see Patterson, *Slavery and Social Death*; and Genovese, *Roll, Jordan, Roll*. Stafford Poole and Douglas J. Slawson, historians of the Catholic Church in Missouri, argue that Catholic slaveholders did indeed treat their slaves better than Protestants during the antebellum years. They focus on the southeastern Missouri county of Perry, which is located in the traditional center of French settlement in the state. See Poole and Slawson, *Church and Slave in Perry County, Missouri*. For more extensive information on the treatment of slaves and the law in colonial Missouri see Foley, *Genesis of Missouri*, 115–16; Aron, *American Confluence*, 47–48; and H. Frazier, *Slavery and Crime in Missouri*, 7–25. See also Brackenridge, *Recollections of Persons and Places in the West*, 23.

9. See Trexler, *Slavery in Missouri*; Gerlach, *Settlement Patterns in Missouri*, 1–14; Foley, *Genesis of Missouri*, 15–100; Aron, *American Confluence*, 69–105; Stepenoff, *From French Community to Missouri Town*; and Hardeman, *Wilderness Calling*.

10. See Aron, *How the West Was Lost*; Aron, *American Confluence*; Hardeman, *Wilderness Calling*, 3–38; William Murphy Biographical Material, n.d., "History of William Murphy and His Descendants, 1798–1958," WHMC; and Fischer and Kelly, *Bound Away*, 150–52.

11. Gerlach, *Settlement Patterns in Missouri*, 6–14; Flint, *Recollections of the Last Ten Years in the Valley of the Mississippi*, 64–74; Hardeman, *Wilderness Calling*; Foley, *Genesis of Missouri*; C. Phillips, *Missouri's Confederate*, 10–15; Belko, *The Invincible Duff Green*; Aron, *How the West Was Lost*; and Aron, *American Confluence*.

12. The Third Treaty of San Ildefonso returned Louisiana, but not Florida, to France. In return, Spain received the Italian province of Tuscany in order to provide a position for the Duke of Parma, the husband of a Spanish royal princess. See Foley, *Genesis of Missouri*, 78, 132–33; Palmer, *The World of the French Revolution*; and Foner, *Nothing But Freedom*, 1–73.

13. For information on Missouri slave codes, see Foley, *Genesis of Missouri*, 131–58; Gerlach, *Settlement Patterns in Missouri*, 6–14; Hurt, *Agriculture and Slavery in Missouri's Little Dixie*, 24–50; Trexler, *Slavery in Missouri*, 57–81; and H. Frazier, *Slavery and Crime in Missouri*, 26–81. For accounts of the lower Missouri River valley during these years, see Hurt, *Agriculture and Slavery in Missouri's Little Dixie*, 2–4; Johnson, *History of Cooper County, Missouri*, vol. 1; and Levens and Drake, *A History of Cooper*

County, Missouri. For quotation, see "Boon's Lick Country," 468. For descriptions of early Missouri, see Duden, *Report on a Journey to the Western States of North America;* Peck, *Forty Years of Pioneer Life;* and Flint, *Recollections of the Last Ten Years.* For information about Missourians' experiences during the War of 1812, see Foley, *Genesis of Missouri,* 215–37.

14. For discussions of Missouri's admission to statehood, see McCandless, *A History of Missouri,* 2:1–30; Foley, *Genesis of Missouri,* 283–98; Shoemaker, *Missouri's Struggle for Statehood;* Forbes, *The Missouri Compromise and Its Aftermath;* Gudmestad, *A Troublesome Commerce,* 35–61; and Strickland, "Aspects of Slavery in Missouri, 1821," 505–26. For a discussion of the preponderance of settlers from the Upper South, see McCandless, *History of Missouri,* 2:31–66; Gerlach, *Settlement Patterns in Missouri,* 6–29; and Foley, *Genesis of Missouri,* 238–68.

15. The estimate of 250,000 free people who hailed from the Upper South states accounts only for those who were still living in 1860; thus the number of actual migrants would have been higher. Harrison Trexler estimated that of the 1,063,489 white Missourians in 1860, 273,808 were born in southern states. In 1850, 34 percent of the population of Missouri was born either in Kentucky, Tennessee, Virginia, or North Carolina, while another 53 percent was born in the state of Missouri. In 1860, the percentage of those born in the southern states and their Missouri descendants was similar to the percentage of the population of the same group in 1850. The 1860 census was only the second to specify place of birth: Missouri—475,246; Kentucky—99,814; Tennessee—75,594; Virginia—53,957; and North Carolina—20,259. See McCandless, *History of Missouri,* 2:37; Gerlach, *Settlement Patterns in Missouri,* 15, 31; Trexler, *Slavery in Missouri,* 9; Trexler, "Slavery in Missouri Territory," 181; and Bellamy, "Slavery, Emancipation, and Racism in Missouri," 35.

16. Small slaveholders and yeomen migrated into the southwestern frontier as well, but were marginalized over time as the plantation economy became more fully developed. Conversely, Virginia gentry migrated to the bluegrass region of Kentucky, where they established sizable plantations and horse farms. For migration studies see Baptist, *Creating an Old South;* Cashin, *A Family Venture;* Censer, *North Carolina Planters and Their Children, 1800–1860;* J. Miller, *South by Southwest;* Oakes, *The Ruling Race;* A. Rothman, *Slave Country;* Aron, *How the West Was Lost;* Aron, *American Confluence;* and Fischer and Kelly, *Bound Away.* For a description of the cultural roots of Upper South settlers, see Fischer, *Albion's Seed.*

17. For quotation, see "The Boon's Lick Country," 447. For additional statistics, see Hilliard, *Atlas of Antebellum Agriculture,* 37–38, 57–77; Hurt, *Agriculture and Slavery in Missouri's Little Dixie,* 219–22; and McCandless, *History of Missouri,* 2:37.

18. See "The Boon's Lick Country"; Gerlach, *Settlement Patterns in Missouri;* Hurt, *Agriculture and Slavery in Missouri's Little Dixie;* and C. Phillips, *Missouri's Confederate.*

19. Some historians have argued that small slaveholders were in the vanguard of migration to all regions of the South, having less to risk financially than large planters. See Tadman, *Speculators and Slaves,* 42–43; Craven, "The Turner Theories and the South," 311; and U. B. Phillips, *American Negro Slavery,* 169–86. For quotation, see Flint, *Recollections of the Last Ten Years in the Valley of the Mississippi,* 146–47. Although the slave population of Missouri increased numerically during these years, it decreased as a percentage of the total population. In 1830, slaves made

up 18 percent of the total population, but by 1860 they accounted for 10 percent. This was due to a large influx of non-southern migrants after 1840. For population statistics, see Gibson and Jung, "Historical Census Statistics on Population Totals by Race," www.census.gov.

20. For statistics, see Hurt, *Agriculture and Slavery in Missouri's Little Dixie*, 219–22. The cotton belt had a growing season ranging from 210 to 270 days, whereas Missouri had a growing season ranging from only 180 to 210 days. One small pocket of land in the extreme southeastern corner of the state was suitable for commercial cotton production, but extensive cultivation of cotton awaited the Mississippi Delta reclamation projects of the late nineteenth century. For information on the production of cotton in Missouri, see Hurt, *Agriculture and Slavery in Missouri's Little Dixie*; Gerlach, *Settlement Patterns in Missouri*; Atherton, ed., "Life, Labor, and Society in Boone County, Missouri," parts 1 and 2; Hilliard, *Atlas of Antebellum Agriculture*; and Fuenfhausen, *The Cotton Culture of Missouri's Little Dixie, 1810–1865 and Growing Upland Cotton in Central Missouri*, "Cotton Growing File," Cooper County Historical Society, Pilot Grove, Missouri.

21. See Bellamy, "Slavery, Emancipation, and Racism in Missouri," 91; and H. Frazier, *Runaway and Freed Missouri Slaves and Those Who Helped Them*. For quotations, see J. A. Reinhardt to John Dalton, January 20, 1851, Placebo Houston Collection, DU; Thomas P. Copes to Joseph Copes, October 31, 1846, Copes Papers, Howard-Tilton Memorial Library, Tulane University, New Orleans, Louisiana, as quoted in Deyle, *Carry Me Back*, 86. See also June and July 1851, February 1852, and January 1853, Archibald Little Hager Diary, WHMC.

22. See Bellamy, "Slavery, Emancipation, and Racism in Missouri"; McCandless, *History of Missouri*, vol. 2; and Abiel Leonard Papers, WHMC. For a discussion of Missourians' responses to free soilers in Kansas Territory, see Etcheson, *Bleeding Kansas*. Historians have argued that some nonslaveholding Southerners chose to move to free states in order to escape competition from slave labor, but most did not hold enlightened racial views. In 1840, three-fourths of the heads of households in Sugar Creek came from Kentucky, Tennessee, and the upcountry regions of Virginia or the Carolinas, for example. In his comprehensive study of this central Illinois community, the historian John Mack Faragher argues that many southern yeomen who felt constrained economically by slavery settled in Sugar Creek precisely because slavery was outlawed in Illinois. See Faragher, *Sugar Creek*, 44–52. The historian Philip Schwartz calculates that half of Virginia migrants moved to slave states and half moved to free states, most often to the states of the Old Northwest. Schwartz also argues that many Virginians moved to free states because they either were against slavery or simply wished to get away from it. See P. Schwartz, *Migrants Against Slavery*, and Fischer and Kelly, *Bound Away*.

23. For discussions of early travel to Missouri, see Gerlach, *Settlement Patterns in Missouri*, 12; and Flint, *Recollections of the Last Ten Years In the Valley of the Mississippi*, 64–75. William Murphy Biographical Material, n.d., "History of William Murphy and His Descendants, 1798–1958," WHMC.

24. S. C. Slater to John Slater, July 3, 1848, Missouri History Papers, MHM. Spring 1855, Pauline Stratton Collection, WHMC. Bruce, *The New Man*, 22–23. See also McCandless, *History of Missouri*, 2:137.

25. Sarah Waggoner, a former slave, also reported that it took about six weeks to

come overland with her owners from Kentucky to northwestern Missouri. For descriptions of traveling westward and of travelers, see Flint, *Recollections of the Last Ten Years in the Valley of the Mississippi*, 146–47; Mrs. Walter Raleigh Lenoir to Miss Eliza Mira Lenoir, February 16, 1836, in "Life, Labor and Society in Boone County, Missouri," ed. Atherton, part 1, 285–91; Martha J. Woods Diary, Arrow Rock Tavern Board Papers, 1826–1923, WHMC, for quotation see April 24, 1857; Sarah Ann Chandler Diary, 1836, WHMC; Sarah Ann Quarles Chandler Papers, WHMC; Guthrie-Maury Family Papers, 1815–1836, WHMC; Eliza Dyer Price, "Recollections of My Father, Samuel Dyer," 1905, WHMC; "Travel Notes of William Massilon Campbell from Lexington, Virginia to St. Charles Co, MO, in the Year 1829," Missouri History Papers, MHM; Bruce, *A New Man*, 16; and Sarah Waggoner, *AS*, 11:355–64. For a discussion of migrating with kin, see Billingsley, *Communities of Kinship*.

26. See Gerlach, *Settlement Patterns in Missouri*, 6–29. In addition to primary sources, my analysis of the various types of early settlers relies heavily on the work of Perry McCandless in *History of Missouri*, 2:31–66, especially 41–42. For Nicholas Patterson's description, see "The Boon's Lick Country."

27. For descriptions of squatters and their methods of settlement, see "The Boon's Lick Country," 451, 459, 466; and McCandless, *History of Missouri*, 2:41–42.

28. Although Missourians were always short on cash, the state was better off than most because of the many migrants who brought species from land sales in the East, silver bullion from the Santa Fe trade, and the infusion of capital from westward pioneers buying supplies in the state. Still, letter after letter from migrants complained of the shortage of money. For a discussion of land grants and sales, see McCandless, *History of Missouri*, 2:42–43; Hurt, *Agriculture and Slavery in Missouri's Little Dixie*, 24–50; Foley, *Genesis of Missouri*, 131–46; Gerlach, *Settlement Patterns in Missouri*, 6–14; and Aron, *American Confluence*, 186–219. For quotation, see J. Calvin Berry to J. H. Harmon, April 16, 1842, J. Calvin Berry Letter, 1842, WHMC.

29. For descriptions of temporary landowners, see McCandless, *History of Missouri*, 2:42–43; and Hardeman, *Wilderness Calling*. For quotation, see W. P. Johnson to "Dear Brother," October 28, 1844, Waldo P. Johnson Letters, 1839–1872, WHMC. For examples of those who moved from Missouri to Texas, Oregon, and California, see W. A. Wilson to Abiel Leonard, January 3, 1851, November 28, 1851, January 22, 1852, and February 7, 1852, and Abiel Leonard to Jeanette Leonard, January 29, 1852, Abiel Leonard Papers, WHMC; McCormack Family Papers, 1777–1873, WHMC; Hardeman, *Wilderness Calling*; Coleman-Hayter Family Papers, 1839–1900, WHMC; and William B. Napton Papers, Missouri History Papers, MHM.

30. See McCandless, *History of Missouri*, 2:42–43. For a discussion of the importance of those who remained, see Faragher, *Sugar Creek*, 51–52, and Valenčius, *The Health of the Country*, 202.

31. The six counties encompassing the Platte Purchase, which included Andrew, Atchison, Buchanan, Holt, Nodaway, and Platte Counties, were annexed to the state of Missouri in 1837 after the Sac and the Fox Indian tribes agreed to a treaty relinquishing their rights to the land the year before. Before that time, the western boundary of the state was a line running north and south directly through the mouth of the Kansas (Kaw) River at the site of present-day Kansas City. After the Platte Purchase, the northwestern boundary of the state was the Missouri River. The geographer Russel Gerlach observed, "[T]he settlement frontier did not proceed through Missouri along

a north-south axis. Rather than one frontier, several frontiers existed simultaneously, with each influenced by somewhat different factors and each proceeding at its own pace." See Gerlach, *Settlement Patterns in Missouri*, 6–29; for above quotation see 20. For quotation, see Wm. L. Irwin to "Dear Brother [John W. Simonton]," Richwoods [Miller County, Missouri], June 9, 1859, W[illiam] L[aird] Irwin Letter, 1859, WHMC. See also "The Boon's Lick Country," 459.

32. For a discussion of prairies versus woodlands, see Faragher, *Sugar Creek*, 61–78. For a discussion of farming implements in antebellum Missouri, see Hurt, *Agriculture and Slavery in Missouri's Little Dixie*, 155–86.

33. For discussions of the patterns of farm development and the costs of moving and settlement, see McCandless, *History of Missouri*, 2:31–66; Hurt, *Agriculture and Slavery in Missouri's Little Dixie*, 51–79; and Valenčius, *The Health of the Country*, 214–18.

34. Walter R. Lenoir to William B. Lenoir, November 26, 1834, in "Life, Labor, and Society in Boone County, Missouri," ed. Atherton, part 1, 283–84. W. R. Lenoir to General Edmond Jones, December 30, 1834, Walter Raleigh Lenoir Letter, 1834, WHMC. James Robinson to Jacob Van Lear, February 9, 1829, Missouri History Papers, MHM. 1854 and 1855, Pauline Stratton Diary, WHMC. See also Hardeman, *Wilderness Calling*; McCandless, *History of Missouri*, 2:45; and J. D. Martin, *Divided Mastery*, 34–43.

35. See Abiel Leonard Papers, WHMC. William B. Napton Papers, MHM. For quotation, see W. P. Johnson to Brother, October 28, 1844, Waldo P. Johnson Letters, 1839–1872, WHMC. In contrast, the historian Michael Cassity argues that in Pettis County, Missouri, initially the settlers had little need for lawyers because they were less connected to the market economy and, therefore, had few legal disputes. Pettis County had no access to the river system and so residents remained self-sufficient for longer. See Cassity, *Defending a Way of Life*, 33–35; Inscoe, *Mountain Masters, Slavery, and the Sectional Crisis in Western North Carolina*; Fischer and Kelly, *Bound Away*, 212–15; Valenčius, *The Health of the Country*, 196–98; Oakes, *The Ruling Race*; and Cashin, *A Family Venture*.

36. For quotations, see Jesse Mellon to Mary Ewers, May 24, 1839, Jesse Mellon Letter, 1839, WHMC; and Mrs. Walter Raleigh Lenoir to Miss Eliza Mira Lenoir, February 16, 1835, in "Life, Labor, and Society in Boone County, Missouri," ed. Atherton, part 1, 285–91.

37. In *Communities of Kinship*, Carolyn Earle Billingsley argues that kin were often the determining factor in migration decisions. Entries from late 1854 and early 1855, Pauline Stratton Collection, WHMC. June 24 and 26, 1846, "From Virginia to Missouri in 1846. The Journal of Elizabeth Ann Cooley," ed. Jervey and Moss, 162–206. W. P. Johnson to Mother, March 22, 1845, Waldo P. Johnson Letters, 1839–1872, WHMC. A. A. Edwards to Uncle, February 12, 1834, Harvey Family Papers, 1834–1873, WHMC. For additional information on the westward movement, see Cashin, *A Family Venture*, and J. Miller, *South by Southwest*. For additional historical examples, see "History of Reverend William Murphy and His Descendants, 1798–1958," n.d., WHMC; Martha J. Woods Diary, Arrow Rock Tavern Board Papers, 1826–1923, WHMC; Sarah Ann Chandler Diary, 1836, WHMC; and Sarah Ann Quarles Chandler Papers, WHMC.

38. Brackenridge, *Recollections of Persons and Places in the West*, 236–37. Flint, *Recollections of the Last Ten Years*, 130. 1855, Pauline Stratton Collection, WHMC.

For discussions of migrants' experiences in their new homes, see Valenčius, *Health of the Country*, and Hurt, *Agriculture and Slavery in Missouri's Little Dixie*, 54–55, 221, 309–10. See also Baptist, *Creating the Old South*.

39. Flint, *Recollections of the Last Ten Years*, 146–47.

40. Jonathan Pritchett uses regression analysis to calculate the numbers of slaves brought through the domestic trade at around 50 percent. Michael Tadman argues that the rate was between 60 and 70 percent depending on the decade. I agree with Anthony Kaye's decision to combine the two figures. See Pritchett, "Quantitative Estimates of the United States Interregional Slave Trade, 1820–1860," 267–75; Tadman, *Speculators and Slaves*, 11–12; Deyle, *Carry Me Back*, 283–96; Gudmestad, *A Troublesome Commerce*, 18–20; and Kaye, *Joining Places*, 21–50, 234 n. 21. See also Bancroft, *Slave-Trading in the Old South*, and W. L. Johnson, *Soul by Soul*.

41. Michael Tadman uses the rate of natural increase for the entire southern slave population for specific decades and imposes it on the slave population of Missouri. He finds that the number of slaves in Missouri in each decade expanded above the percentage from natural increase. For example, he calculates that 5,460 slaves were brought to Missouri between 1810 and 1819; 10,104 slaves between 1820 and 1829; 24,287 slaves between 1830 and 1839; 11,406 slaves between 1840 and 1849; and 6,314 slaves between 1850 and 1859. He argues that by the 1850s Missouri had become both an importing and exporting state. Slaveholders in western Missouri continued to import slaves, at the same time that those in the eastern part of the state were beginning to sell some of their slaves to southern markets. For a further discussion of slave trading within Missouri, see Chapter 3 of this book. See also Tadman, *Speculators and Slaves*, 11–46, statistics 12; Deyle, *Carry Me Back*, 45, 74–76; and Baptist, *Creating the Old South*, 60–87.

42. *Liberty Tribune*, February 9, 1849, vol. 3, no. 45, and May 18, 1849, vol. 4, no. 7, SHSM. Emma Knight, *AS*, 11:218–21. Malinda Discus, *AS*, supp., ser. 1, 2:166–70. Marilda Pethy, *AS*, 11:277–82. See Tadman, *Speculators and Slaves*, 3–46.

43. Malinda Discus, *AS*, supp., ser. 1, 2:166–70. Margaret Nickens, *AS*, 11:264.

44. Flint, *Recollections of the Last Ten Years*, 146–47. March and February 1855, Pauline Stratton Collection, WHMC. Sarah Graves, *AS*, 11:126–38. Charles Washington pen., USCT 65B, NA. Benjamin Reeves to Abiel Leonard, January 20, 1853, Abiel Leonard Papers, WHMC. Melinda Napton to William Napton, July 29, 1843, [1846], January 18, 1846, February 15, 184[6], Napton Papers, MHM. Henry Fleetwood pen., USCT 65K, NA. Included are some of the many references to the migration of slaves with their owners: William R. Wisley/ Riley (alias) pen., USCT 65E, NA; Matthew Carroll pen., USCT 65E, NA; John Carter pen., USCT 65A, NA; Lewis Washington pen., USCT 65C, NA; John Jackson pen., USCT 65J, NA; Jonah Edwards pen., USCT 65G, NA; Emanuel Gatewood pen., USCT 65F, NA; Peter Dawson pen., USCT 65E, NA; Jacob Robinson pen., USCT 65J, NA; John George pen., USCT 65B, NA; Arthur Jackson / Major (alias) pen., USCT 65G, NA; Henry Smith pen., USCT 65H, NA; William Powell pen., USCT 65A, NA; and Moses and Washington Combs pen., USCT 65D, NA. See also Steve Brown, *AS*, 11:56–57; Peter Corn, *AS*, 11:85–95; Lewis Mundy, *AS*, 11:258–60; Clay Smith, *AS*, 11:318–20; Fil Hancock, *AS*, 11:147–61; and Esther Easter, *AS*, 7:88–91.

45. For discussions of owners going to the Upper South to purchase slaves or enlisting relatives to purchase for them, as well as the practices of slave traders, see

Gudmestad, *A Troublesome Commerce*, 11–13, and Deyle, *Carry Me Back*, 94–141, 160–66. Thomas F. Houston to John Dalton, May 11, 1857, Placebo Houston Papers, DU. Benjamin Reeves to Abiel Leonard, January 20, 1853, Abiel Leonard Papers, WHMC. Leonard Property Book, MHM. Melinda Napton to William Napton, July 29, 1843, [1846], January 18, 1846, February 15, 184[6], Abiel Leonard Papers, WHMC.

46. For discussions of the slave family and community in the eighteenth- and nineteenth-century Chesapeake, see Berlin, *Many Thousand Gone*; P. Morgan, *Slave Counterpoint*; Kulikoff, *Tobacco and Slaves*; Stevenson, *Life in Black and White*; and Kaye, *Joining Places*, 21–50. For migration from the eastern seaboard to North Florida, see Baptist, *Creating the Old South*, 65–67. January–April 1855, Pauline Stratton Collection, WHMC.

47. Sarah Waggoner, *AS*, 11:355–64. Arthur Jackson/Major (alias) pen., USCT 65G, NA. Charles Washington pen., USCT 65B, NA. Sarah Graves, *AS*, 11:126–38. Lewis Washington pen., USCT 65C, NA. Drew, *A North-Side View of Slavery*, 280–82.

48. Tadman argues that migrating owners brought all of their slaves with them to the West despite their age, but Gudmestad claims that some did selectively decide whom to bring in order to assemble the most productive labor force. In fact, he claims that owners sometimes bought and sold slaves in order to strike the right balance. I believe that this selectivity may account for a demographic structure that suggests the dominance of the interstate slave trade. See Tadman, *Speculators and Slaves*, 228–36, and Gudmestad, *A Troublesome Commerce*, 8–11. Cassity, *Defending a Way of Life*, 28. Walter R. Lenoir to William Lenoir, May 1, 1836, in "Life, Labor, and Society in Boone County, Missouri," ed. Atherton, part 1, 303. October 1854–April 1855, Pauline Stratton Collection, WHMC.

49. 1855 and 1856, Pauline Stratton Collection, WHMC. C. P. Tate to mother, Mrs. Jane Tate, December 14, 1823, Missouri History Papers, MHM. For discussions of the acclimation process of slaves, see Valenčius, *The Health of the Country*, 22–34, 235–40; Baptist, *Creating the Old South*, 61–87; and Kaye, *Joining Places*, 21–50.

50. Ethelbert W. Lewis to brother William W. Lewis, January 20, 1837, Ethelbert W[allis] Lewis Letters, 1837–1851, WHMC.

51. Frances D. Fackler to sister Ann Burrus, February 13, 1834, Missouri History Papers, MHM. Martha and Abiel Leonard to Jeanette Leonard, June 11, 1845, and June 30, 1845, Abiel Leonard Papers, WHMC. See also Jeanette Leonard to Abiel Leonard, June 11, 1845; Missouri Reeves to sister, April 11, 1850; and Martha Leonard to Jeanette Leonard, July 18, 1851; Abiel Leonard Papers, WHMC. Octavia Blackwell Chilton to Mrs. Betsey Blackwell, November 8, 1842, Octavia Blackwell Chilton Letter, 1842, WHMC. Robert W. Brown to Dear Parents, Saline County, Missouri, March 23, 1839, Missouri History Papers, MHM. See also Robert Brown to Parents, February 15, 1840, Missouri History Papers, MHM.

52. For a discussion of chain migration, see Billingsley, *Communities of Kinship*. For quotation, see "Boon's Lick Country," 468.

53. For information about the early settlement of New Lebanon, Missouri, see Cordry, *The History of New Lebanon Cooper County Missouri*, 21–50.

54. For a comprehensive history of John and Catherine Cordry and their descendants, see Cordry, *Descendants of Virginia, Kentucky, and Missouri Pioneers*, 1–141.

55. S. Ralston to Col. D. W. Jordan, April 2, 1843, in "A Southern Family on the Missouri Frontier," ed. Overdyke, 218. W. P. Johnson to Mother, March 28, 1845, Waldo P. Johnson Letters, 1839–1872, WHMC. Thomas C. Duggins to parents, Mr. Thomas Jackson, June 12, 1840, Thomas C. Duggins Letter, 1840, WHMC. Octavia Blackwell Chilton to Mrs. Betsey Blackwell, November 3, 1842, Octavia Blackwell Chilton Letter, 1842, WHMC. D. Waldo to dear Sir, September 24, 1843, Waldo P. Johnson Letters, 1839–1872, WHMC. Ethelbert Lewis to Brother, November 20, 1837, and September 24, 1838, Ethelbert W[allis] Lewis Letters, 1837–1851, WHMC.

56. For quotations and references, see J. R. Bohannon to his cousin Mrs. Judith Clore, January 27, 1837, Charles Van Ravensway Collection, 1820–1971, WHMC; A. A. Edwards to Mother, February 12, 1834, Harvey Family Papers, 1834–1873, WHMC; William Powell to Henry A. Powell, n.d., January 1, 1839, July 1, 1839, William Powell Letters, 1839–40, WHMC; Martha Allen to Aunt and Uncle, March 15, 1857, Martha Allen Letter, 1857, WHMC; John T. Burch to his uncle, William Townshend, n.d., John T. Burch Letter, WHMC; and Justus Post to brother, John, December 5, 1817, Justus Post Letter, 1817, WHMC.

57. W. R. Lenoir to General Edmond Jones, December 30, 1834, Walter Raleigh Lenoir Letter, 1834, WHMC. Clarinda Tate to Jacob Van Lear, Callaway County, Missouri, October 1, 1823, James Robinson to brother Jacob Van Lear, Washington County, Missouri, February 9, 1829, and S. C. Slater to John Slater, St. Joseph, Missouri, July 3, 1848, Missouri History Papers, MHM.

58. Southerners also observed that people of African descent did not contract as virulent cases of the ague, leading them to believe that they were more suited to labor in harsh southern climates. They had no way to know that many African Americans carried a limited genetic immunity to malaria. For additional discussions about people of African descent and malaria, see P. Wood, *Black Majority*, 63–91. For discussions of sickness and concerns about the land, see Valenčius, *Health of the Country*, 24–25, 79–108, 114–32, 237–40, quotation, 2. Nathan Haley, Herculanuem, Jefferson County, Missouri, to Jeremiah Haley, Great Horton, Yorkshire, May 20, 1823, in Erickson, *Invisible Immigrants*, 416, as quoted in Valenčius, *Health of the Country*, 217. W. R. Lenoir to General Edmond Jones, December 30, 1834, Walter Raleigh Lenoir Letter, 1834, WHMC.

59. See Justus Post to brother, John, December 5, 1817, Justus Post Letter, 1817, WHMC; John Burch to uncle, William Townsend, n.d., John T. Burch Letter, WHMC; and William Powell to brother, Henry A. Powell, n.d., and November 10, 1840, William Powell Letters, 1839–40, WHMC. Potential migrants to Missouri also received advice from migration guidebooks that described in great detail the topography of the region and the circumstances of Missouri's many counties and towns. Each community's businesses, schools, and churches were listed, as well as the general economic prospects of the area. Migrants also received information from advice letters published in newspapers in the southeastern states. For examples, see Wetmore, *Gazetteer of the State of Missouri*; Beck, *A Gazetteer of the States of Illinois and Missouri*; A North Carolinian to the *Patriot*, September 1839 and April 23, 1843, St. Louis, Missouri, printed in the Greensborough, North Carolina, *Patriot* on October 8, 1839, October 15, 1839, and May 31, 1842, Missouri History Papers, MHM; and Thomas Lenoir Letters, 1839–1843, WHMC. See also J. Miller, *South by Southwest*.

60. For a description of a migrant who had to defend his decision to stay in

Missouri, see W. P. Johnson to Brother, July 20, 1845, Waldo P. Johnson Letters, 1839–1872, WHMC. For those who disliked Missouri, see William A. Richards to brother, April 8, 1842, William A. Richards Letters, 1841–1854, WHMC; and J. Calvin Berry to J. H. Harmon, April 16, 1842, J. Calvin Berry Letter, 1842, WHMC. See also Justus Post to brother, John, December 5, 1817, Justus Post Letter, 1817, WHMC; John Burch to uncle, William Townsend, n.d., John T. Burch Letter, WHMC; and William Powell to brother, Henry A. Powell, n.d., and November 10, 1840, William Powell Letters, 1839–40, WHMC.

61. For the development of Little Dixie, see Hurt, *Agriculture and Slavery in Missouri's Little Dixie,* 51–79.

62. For quotation, see Peck, *Forty Years of Pioneer Life,* 135. See also Hurt, *Agriculture and Slavery in Missouri's Little Dixie;* Gerlach, *Settlement Patterns in Missouri;* Atherton, ed., "Life, Labor, and Society in Boone County, Missouri," parts 1 and 2; and Hilliard, *Atlas of Antebellum Agriculture.*

63. The large number of slaves living on units with fewer than ten slaves was much higher in Missouri than in any other slaveholding state (with the exception of Delaware). In 1860, 58.5 percent of Missouri slaves lived on holdings smaller than ten, and in 1860, 60.1 percent of slaves lived on these holdings. The border state of Kentucky had the next highest percentage of slaves living on small slaveholdings. In 1850, 49 percent of slaves lived on units smaller than 10, and in 1860, 48.9 percent of slaves lived on these holdings. In contrast, in 1850, 19.6 percent of Alabama slaves lived on small slaveholdings, and in 1860, only 18.4 percent lived on units with fewer than ten slaves. For statistics on the percentages of slaves living on small slaveholdings, see Gray, *History of Agriculture in the Southern United States to 1860,* 1:530. For the percentages of small slaveholders, see Hilliard, *Atlas of Antebellum Agriculture,* 36–38, 57–77, and Hurt, *Agriculture and Slavery in Missouri's Little Dixie,* 219–22.

64. For counties with the largest slaveholding populations, see Hurt, *Agriculture and Slavery in Missouri's Little Dixie,* 219–20. For information on the peak of migration, see Hurt, *Agriculture and Slavery in Missouri's Little Dixie,* 52.

Chapter 2

1. Edwards and Sprague, eds., *The World's Laconics,* 124.

2. Martha McDonald Diary, Charles B. France Papers, WHMC.

3. For quotation, see January 1, 1860, Martha McDonald Diary, Charles B. France Papers, WHMC. 1860 Buchanan County, Missouri, United States Census.

4. See July 1856, and for quotations, January 1, 1860, July 1, 1856, and July 9, 1856, Martha McDonald Diary, Charles B. France Papers, WHMC. Slave Schedule, 1860 Buchanan County, Missouri, United States Census. For a discussion of middle-class domesticity in Kentucky, another border state, see Barton, "Good Cooks and Washers."

5. For foundational works on the ideologies of separate spheres and domesticity in the North, see Kerber, *Women of the Republic;* Ryan, *Cradle of the Middle Class;* Welter, "The Cult of True Womanhood," 151–74; and Smith-Rosenberg, *Disorderly Conduct.*

6. For discussions of Southerners' reading habits, see Wells, *The Origins of the Southern Middle Class;* McCardell, *The Idea of a Southern Nation;* Fox-Genovese, *Within the Plantation Household;* Fox-Genovese and Genovese, *The Mind of the*

Master Class; and Weiner, *Mistresses and Slaves.* See also Nord, "Religious Reading and Readers in Antebellum America"; Schantz, "Religious Tracts, Evangelical Reform, and the Market Revolution in Antebellum America"; and Vásquez, "The Portable Pulpit."

7. For selected works on southern women, families, households, and gender roles, see Bardaglio, *Reconstructing the Household;* Bercaw, *Gendered Freedoms;* Bleser, ed., *In Joy and Sorrow;* Censer, *North Carolina Planters and Their Children;* O. V. Burton, *In My Father's House Are Many Mansions;* Clinton, *The Plantation Mistress;* Fox-Genovese, *Within the Plantation Household;* Friend and Glover, eds., *Southern Manhood;* Glymph, *Out of the House of Bondage;* Jabour, *Scarlett's Sisters;* McCurry, *Masters of Small Worlds;* A. F. Scott, *The Southern Lady;* Stevenson, *Life in Black and White;* Stowe, *Intimacy and Power in the Old South;* and Weiner, *Mistresses and Slaves*.

8. For readings on slaveholding women's power and influence and the southern version of domestic ideology, see Bleser, ed., *In Joy and Sorrow;* Faust, *Mothers of Invention;* Fox-Genovese, *Within the Plantation Household;* Glymph, *Out of the House of Bondage;* McCurry, *Masters of Small Worlds;* A. F. Scott, *The Southern Lady;* Stevenson, *Life in Black and White;* and Weiner, *Mistresses and Slaves.*

9. See Byrne, *Becoming Bourgeois,* 77–120, and Wells, *The Origins of the Southern Middle Class,* 17–65, 111–32.

10. See Dunaway, *Slavery in the American Mountain South;* Faragher, *Sugar Creek;* Hahn, *The Roots of Southern Populism;* Inscoe, *Mountain Masters;* McCurry, *Masters of Small Worlds;* and Osterud, *Bonds of Community.*

11. For a discussion of small slaveholders' economic strategies, see Hahn, *The Roots of Southern Populism,* and McCurry, *Masters of Small Worlds.* This was also the case for merchant and professional families living in Missouri towns. See also Byrne, *Becoming Bourgeois,* and Wells, *The Origins of the Southern Middle Class,* 111–50.

12. Pauline Stratton Collection, WHMC. Woods-Holman Family Collection, WHMC. Haines Family Collection, WHMC. Elvira Ascenith Weir Scott Diary, 1860–1887, WHMC. Charles France Collection, WHMC. Coleman-Hayter Family Collection, WHMC. Patton-Scott Family Collection, WHMC. Helm-Davidson Family Collection, WHMC. Abiel Leonard Papers, WHMC. William Napton Papers, MHM.

13. For examples of couples who limited the size of their families, see Patton-Scott Family Papers, WHMC, and Elvira Ascenith Weir Scott Diary, 1860–1887, WHMC.

14. For discussions of the expense to slaves in the context of slaveholders' aspirations of domesticity, see Glymph, *Out of the House of Labor,* and Barton, "Good Cooks and Washers."

15. For discussions of southern marriage, see Fox-Genovese, *Within the Plantation Household;* Weiner, *Mistresses and Slaves;* Bardaglio, *Reconstructing the Household;* Bleser, ed., *In Joy and Sorrow;* Stevenson, *Life in Black and White;* and Stowe, *Intimacy and Power in the Old South.*

16. See Byrne, *Becoming Bourgeois,* 77–120, and Wells, *The Origins of the Southern Middle Class,* 111–16.

17. For a further discussion of small-slaveholding neighborhoods, see Chapter 6 of this book. 1859–1865, Pauline Stratton Collection, WHMC. William Napton to Melinda Napton, December 12, 1858, and Melinda Napton to William Napton, December 5, 1857, William Napton Papers, MHM. Winter 1862, Martha McDonald Diary, Charles B. France Papers, WHMC.

18. Mary Belt to Henry Coleman, Weston, Missouri, January 19, 1860, Coleman-Hayter Family Papers, WHMC. December 1, 1862, January 28, 1862, September 3–8, 1865, Pauline Stratton Collection, WHMC. William Napton to Melinda Napton, Jefferson City, [1845], William Napton Papers, MHM. For a discussion of southern women's concerns about marriage, see Jabour, *Scarlett's Sisters*, 89–96, 113–80. For the power of white southern men, see Fox-Genovese, *Within the Plantation Household;* Bercaw, *Gendered Freedoms;* Clinton, *The Plantation Mistress;* and Bardaglio, *Reconstructing the Household.*

19. No date, Priscilla Thomas Ingram Patton Diary, Patton-Scott Family Papers, WHMC. Martha McDonald to Charles France, August 3, 1864, and August 7, [1864], and Sarah McDonald to My Dear Children, December 13, 1864, Charles B. France Papers, WHMC. For courtships of elite southern couples, see Jabour, *Scarlett's Sisters*, 113–49; Stevenson, *Life in Black and White*, 37–62; Stowe, *Intimacy and Power in the Old South*, 50–121; and Wyatt-Brown, *Southern Honor*, 199–225.

20. Boman, *Abiel Leonard, Yankee Slaveholder, Eminent Jurist, and Passionate Unionist.* Abiel Leonard Papers, WHMC. C. Phillips, *The Making of a Southerner*, 6–53. William Napton Papers, MHM. Bartels, compiler, *Missouri: Just Married: Cooper County, Missouri, 1848–1867.* 1850 Cooper County, Missouri, United States Census. 1860 Cooper County, Missouri, United States Census. See Jabour, *Scarlett's Sisters*, 113–80, and Billingsley, *Communities of Kinship.*

21. January 1861, November 1861, November 1867, Pauline Stratton Collection, WHMC.

22. For the importance of choosing a proper marriage partner, see Clinton, *The Plantation Mistress*, 59–86; Fox-Genovese, *Within the Plantation Household*, 207–10; Stevenson, *Life in Black and White*, 37–94; and Jabour, *Scarlett's Sisters*, 113–80.

23. For a discussion of divorce, see Stevenson, *Life in Black and White*, 140–56; Jabour, *Scarlett's Sisters*, 165–66; and J. D. Rothman, *Notorious in the Neighborhood*, 169–98. *Laws of the State of Missouri; Revised and Digested by Authority of the General Assembly in Two Volumes*, 1:330–33. *Laws of a Public and General Nature of the State of Missouri Passed Between 1824 and 1836*, 2:360–61. For divorce in Missouri, see E. Martin, "Frontier Marriage and the Status Quo."

24. C. Phillips, *Missouri's Confederate*, 53–74, 91–93. Justina Woods to Zelia, August 29, 1850, September 29, 1850, Woods-Holeman Family Papers, WHMC.

25. O'Byran v. O'Bryan, in *Reports of Cases Argued and Determined in the Supreme Court of the State of Missouri by William Robards, Attorney General and ex-officio Reporter*, ed. Houck, 13:16–22. See J. D. Rothman, *Notorious in the Neighborhood*, 169–98; Stevenson, *Life in Black and White*, 140–56; and Bynum, *Unruly Women*, 59–87.

26. Hawkins v. The State, in *Reports of Cases Argued and Determined in the Supreme Court of the State of Missouri from 1840–1842 by S.M. Bay, Attorney General and ex-officio Reporter*, ed. Houck, 8:98–100. It was difficult to determine slave-ownership status for either of these households because they could not be found in the census; however, the cases reflect the prevalence of violence within Missouri households regardless of slaveholding status. It should be noted that the authorities did not take Wise's claims of slave perpetrators seriously, and he eventually was convicted on circumstantial evidence. State of Missouri v. James Layton, 1842, St. Francois, Missouri Supreme Court Records, Box 20, Folder 2, 16A/4/2, and State of Missouri v. John Weis/Wise, 1860, Perry County, Missouri Supreme Court Records, Box 448, Folder 4, 15B/4/8 (Weis is used in

the case title, but is spelled Wise in the actual court documents), MSA. For discussions of the violent results of the gap between expectations and reality see J. D. Rothman, *Notorious in the Neighborhood;* and W. L. Johnson, *Soul by Soul.*

27. Paulina Donald to Thomas Stratton, December 15, 1841, and diary, 1844–1865, Pauline Stratton Collection, WHMC. For a good description of married couples as helpmates, see Ulrich, *Good Wives.*

28. March 1856, June 14, 1862, February 1863, July 1858, April 1862, later 1861, July 20, 1866, July 15, 1861, June 1860, October 1860, June 1, 1860, September 1856, October 13, 1861, November 1861, January and February 1862, late 1861, and April 14, 1869, May and June, 1855, and April 20, 1862, Pauline Stratton Collection, WHMC.

29. September 1856, April and May 1856, March 1858, October 1851, November 4, 1855, ibid.

30. June 14, 1862, ibid.

31. C. Phillips, *The Making of a Southerner,* 6–53. William Napton Papers, MHM. Slave Schedule, 1850 Saline County, Missouri, United States Census. Slave Schedule, 1860 Saline County, Missouri, United States Census.

32. William Napton to Melinda Napton, November 31, 1845, January 25, 1847; and Melinda Napton to William Napton, March 11, 1846, April 1, 1848, April 25, 1858, William Napton Papers, MHM.

33. For a discussion of architecture in the Little Dixie region of Missouri, see Marshall, *Folk Architecture in Little Dixie;* and van Ravenswaay, *The Arts and Architecture of German Settlements in Missouri.* See also Vlach, *Back of the Big House.*

34. Marshall, *Folk Architecture of Little Dixie,* 30–71, and van Ravenswaay, *The Arts and Architecture of German Settlements in Missouri.* Steve Brown, *AS,* 11:56. Smoky Eulenberg, *AS,* 11:109. Justina Woods to Zelia, August 29, 1850, Woods-Holeman Papers, WHMC. For an extant log structure covered with clapboard, see the James Family Farm, Kearney, Missouri.

35. Marshall, *Folk Architecture of Little Dixie,* 30–71. For extant examples of "big house" vernacular architecture, see "Pleasant Green," Pilot Grove, Missouri; "Wornall House," Kansas City, Missouri; and "Bethany," Watkins Woolen Mill State Park, Lawson, Missouri.

36. Slaves shared news of sales and local and national politics with one another. They also reported about the relations between white members of the household. It was not unusual for slaves' stories about the activities within the white household to end up in criminal cases of spousal abuse and murder. For examples of this activity see Chapters 4, 6, and 7 of this book, as well as Camp, *Closer to Freedom,* and Hahn, *A Nation Under Our Feet.* For a discussion of the big house as a site of work, see Glymph, *Out of the House of Bondage.*

37. March 24, 1860, Elvira Ascenith Weir Scott Diary, 1860–1887, WHMC. Elizabeth Coleman to James and Sarah Hayter, February 19, 1855, Coleman-Hayter Family Papers, WHMC. For examples, see J. George Cranmer will, December 2, 1832, and Nelly C. Read, will, December 25, 1855, Cooper County Probate Court, Will Record Book B, June 10, 1841–August 11, 1867, Cooper County, Missouri, MSA; and *The Missouri State Gazetteer & Business Directory,* 202–3, SHSM. For consumption within merchant families, see Byrne, *Becoming Bourgeois,* 94–97. For a discussion of Victorian American homes, see Ames, *Death in the Dining Room and Other Tales of Victorian Culture.* By the 1850s, the vast array of manufactured items transported westward by

river was astounding. For an excellent inventory of frontier consumer goods see the items recovered from the site of the sinking of the steamboat *Arabia*. The Steamboat Arabia Museum, Kansas City, Missouri.

38. 1855–1865, Pauline Stratton Collection, WHMC. Lizzie Helm to Sally Helm, October 24, 1852, Helm-Davidson Family Papers, WHMC. Slave Schedule, 1860 Marion County, Missouri, United States Census.

39. William Napton to Melinda Napton, May 12, 1859, November 11, 1859, William Napton Papers, MHM.

40. Cott, *The Bonds of Womanhood*; Kerber, *Women of the Republic*; Mintz, *Huck's Raft*; and Ryan, *Cradle of the Middle Class*.

41. For descriptions of planter families, see Censer, *North Carolina Planters and Their Children*, 20–54, especially 53; Jabour, *Scarlett's Sisters*, 17–45; Stowe, *Intimacy and Power in the Old South*, 164–249; and Wyatt-Brown, *Southern Honor*, 117–98.

42. For a discussion of contraception in nineteenth-century America, see D'Emilio and Freedman, *Intimate Matters*, 59–61, 246–47. For discussions of pregnancy, childbirth, and motherhood in the antebellum South, see McMillen, *Motherhood in the Old South*, and Censer, *North Carolina Planters and Their Children*, 24–28. See January 27, 1847, August 1846, September 17, 1847, and November 19, 1851, Pauline Stratton Collection, WHMC.

43. Byrne, *Becoming Bourgeois*, 77–120.

44. Mary Belt to Elizabeth Coleman, December 1, 1859, and Mary Belt to Henry Coleman, January 19, 1860, Coleman-Hayter Family Papers, WHMC. Melinda Napton to William Napton, March 27, [1847], April 10, 1850, November 10, 1857, and April 25, 1858, William Napton Papers, MHM. See McMillen, *Motherhood in the Old South*; Censer, *North Carolina Planters and Their Families*, 34–36; and Stevenson, *Life in Black and White*, 105.

45. April 1853, August 29, 1853, May 1857, and January 10, 1858, Pauline Stratton Collection, WHMC.

46. 1860 Marion County, Missouri, United States Census. Slave Schedule, 1860 Marion County, Missouri, United States Census. To Sister from Brother Ben Helm, c. 1861; and Lizzie Helm to Sallie Helm, October 24, 1852; Helm-Davidson Family Papers, WHMC.

47. Gus Smith interview, *AS*, 11:321–32.

48. February 21, 1847, Fall 1852, and August 14, 1853, Pauline Stratton Collection, WHMC. Priscilla Thomas Ingram Patton Diary, Patton-Scott Family Papers, WHMC. March 30–31, and September 30, 1855, and January 21 and 28, 1860, Elvira Ascenith Weir Scott Diary, 1860–1887, WHMC. For evangelical child rearing and the influence of alternate sources of discipline, see Greven, *The Protestant Temperament*, 27; Friedman, *The Enclosed Garden*, 36–37; and Mintz, *Huck's Raft*, 80–81, 168–69. For a discussion of the pervasive violence in slaveholding homes, see Glymph, *Out of the House of Bondage*.

49. Mary Helm to Sallie Helm, July 23, 1852, Helm-Davidson Family Papers, WHMC. December 2, 1861, Martha McDonald Diary, Charles B. France Papers, WHMC. Melinda Napton to William Napton, November 25, 1849; William Napton to Melinda Napton, November 3, 1850; Melinda Napton to William Napton, December 5, 1857; William B. Napton Papers, MHM. Mary Leonard to Abiel Leonard, January 16, 1845; Abiel Leonard to Martha Leonard, January 24, 1845; Abiel

Leonard Papers, WHMC. See Formanek-Brunell, *Made to Play House,* and Mintz, *Huck's Raft,* 136.

50. March 30, 1855, Priscilla Thomas Ingram Patton Diary, Patton-Scott Family Collection, WHMC. April 1853, August 29, 1853, May 1857, and January 10, 1858, Pauline Stratton Collection, WHMC.

51. March 1861, Priscilla Thomas Ingram Patton Diary, Patton-Scott Family Papers, WHMC.

52. Thomas Jefferson, *Notes on the State of Virginia,* Query XVIII. Lucinda Patterson, *AS,* 11:269–76. Sarah Graves, *AS,* 11:126–38. Stevenson, *Life in Black and White,* 137–38.

53. Justina Woods to Zelia [Holeman], August 29, 1850, Woods-Holeman Papers, WHMC.

54. For the household education of slaveholding children, see Melinda Napton to William B. Napton, December 9, 1857, and January 26, 1858, William B. Napton Papers, MHM; Jeanette to Abiel Leonard, [1840s]; Mary Leonard to Abiel Leonard, August 11, 1840, Abiel Leonard Papers, WHMC; and Filler, *The New Stars.*

55. McCandless, *A History of Missouri,* 2:190–97. Hurt, *Agriculture and Slavery in Missouri's Little Dixie,* 203. Cordry, *Descendants of Virginia, Kentucky, and Missouri Pioneers,* 340–57.

56. Pauline Stratton Collection, WHMC. Cordry, *Descendants of Virginia, Kentucky, and Missouri Pioneers,* 340–57.

57. Hurt, *Agriculture and Slavery in Little Dixie,* 199–203. McCandless, *A History of Missouri,* 2:198–201.

58. Hurt, *Agriculture and Slavery in Little Dixie,* 199–203. Columbia Female Academy Papers, Columbia, Missouri, WHMC. Clay Seminary for Young Ladies, Liberty, Missouri, WHMC. Christian College, Columbia, Missouri, WHMC. Blandin, *History of Higher Education of Women in the South Prior to 1860,* 204–16. Farnham, *The Education of the Southern Belle.* See also Clinton, "Equally Their Due," 39–60; Jabour, *Scarlett's Sisters,* 83–112; and McCardell, *The Idea of a Southern Nation,* 177–226.

59. Clay Seminary, Liberty, Missouri, WHMC. Petrillo, "Missouri Schoolgirls, 1840–1870." See also Wells, *The Origins of the Southern Middle Class,* and Byrne, *Becoming Bourgeois.*

60. William Napton to Melinda Napton, January [18], 1852, March 31, 1859, November 13, 1859, June 10, 1859, WMHC. C. Phillips, *The Making of a Southerner,* 47, 119–20.

61. William Napton to Melinda Napton, November 15, 1857, WHMC. William Napton to Claiborne Fox Jackson, September 16, 1857, Dr. John Sappington Papers, WHMC.

62. Henry Coleman to Dear Son, Weston, Missouri, July 5, 1852, Coleman-Hayter Family Papers, WHMC. See Stevenson, *Life in Black and White,* 123; Glover, "Let Us Manufacture Men," 22–48; and Jabour, *Scarlett's Sisters,* 52–61.

63. Jane Turner Censer claims that among elite families in antebellum North Carolina, one in four children did not reach their first birthday. Censer, *North Carolina Planters and Their Families,* 28–31. For health conditions in Missouri, see Valenčius, *The Health of the Country.*

64. Henry Coleman to Dear Son, July 5, 1852, Weston, Missouri, Coleman-Hayter Family Papers, WHMC. Jonathan Haines to "Respected Brother [Nathan Haines]

mother and Sisters," May 26, 1843; Jonathan Haines to "Respected Brother [Nathan Haines] and Sisters," April 27, 1845; Randolph County, Missouri, Haines Family Papers, WHMC.

65. C. Phillips, *The Making of a Southerner*, 93–95. See also C. J. Carter, *Single Blessedness*.

66. November 1863, November 1850, December 1850, January 29, 1851, February 1851, December 7, 1863, May 1870, May 1867, and Summer 1869, Pauline Stratton Collection, WHMC. Elizabeth Haines to "Respective brother [Nathan Haines]," Randolph County, Missouri, February 21, n.d., Haines Family Papers, WHMC. See K. Wood, *Masterful Women*. See all wills from Cooper County Probate Court, Will Record Book A, and Will Record Book B, MSA.

67. Joseph Staples will, May 12, 1859, Cooper County Probate Court, Will Record Book B, MSA. Travese Davis will, April 28, 1824, Cooper County Probate Court, Will Record Book A, MSA.

68. I have included only the wills of those individuals who mentioned slaves. Undoubtedly there were additional slaveholders included among the testators who simply stipulated to equally divide their property. See all wills from Cooper County Probate Court, Will Record Book A, and Will Record Book B, MSA.

69. Cooper County Probate Court, Achilles Eubank will, August 26, 1838, Will Record Book A, MSA; Alfred Wilson will, July 1855, and Joseph Arnold will, June 7, 1854, Will Record Book B, MSA.

70. Alfred Wilson will, July 1855, Will Record Book B, MSA.

Chapter 3

1. "I At Home," ed. Jensen, part 1, 30–56; part 2, 283–317; part 3, 59–96; part 4, 272–88; part 5, 38–48; part 6, 224–47; part 7, 61–94; part 8, 180–206; and part 9, 410–45. For quotation from chapter title, see January 22, 1829, in "I At Home," ed. Jensen, part 9, 411.

2. "I at Home," ed. Jensen, parts 1–9.

3. J. Clemens to J. Pawling, October 4, 1816, Missouri History Collection, MHM.

4. For selected works on the ways in which antebellum Southerners racialized and gendered labor, see Genovese, *Roll, Jordan, Roll*; Fox-Genovese, *Within the Plantation Household*; Clinton, *The Plantation Mistress*; Weiner, *Mistresses and Slaves*; Glymph, *Out of the House of Bondage*; Stevenson, *Life in Black and White*; Berry, *Swing the Sickle for the Harvest Is Ripe*; D. G. White, *Ar'n't I a Woman?*; and B. Wood, *Women's Work, Men's Work*.

5. In 1860, the ten largest slaveholding counties with the aggregate slave population and the percentage of slaves as part of the total population included: Lafayette, 6,374 (32% slave); Howard, 5,886 (37% slave); Boone, 5,034 (26% slave); Saline, 4,876 (33% slave); Callaway, 4,523 (26% slave); St. Louis, 4,346 (2% slave); Pike, 4,055 (22% slave); Jackson, 3,944 (17% slave); Cooper, 3,800 (22% slave); and Clay, 3,455 (27% slave). St. Louis had the sixth-largest slave population at 4,346, but it also had 186,178 white residents. See table 2. For discussion of the stability and profitability of slavery in Missouri, see Bellamy, "Slavery, Emancipation, and Racism in Missouri," 71–100. Gerlach, *Settlement Patterns in Missouri*, 23–24. Hurt, *Agriculture and Slavery in Missouri's Little Dixie*, 220–21. Historical Census Browser, fisher.lib.virginia.edu/collections/stats/histcensus/.

6. The following section on agriculture in Missouri relies heavily on R. Douglas Hurt's comprehensive study of agricultural practices in Missouri's Little Dixie. See Hurt, *Agriculture and Slavery in Missouri's Little Dixie*.

7. For an excellent study of the development of corn and livestock production in what became the Midwest, see J. C. Hudson, *Making the Corn Belt*. For a description of livestock production in the Upper South, see Gray, *History of Agriculture in the Southern United States to 1860*, 2:831–57, 1042. See also Hurt, *Agriculture and Slavery in Missouri's Little Dixie*, 125–86, and Inscoe, *Mountain Masters, Slavery, and the Sectional Crisis in Western North Carolina*, 11–58. *Compendium of the Enumeration of the Inhabitants and Statistics of the United States* (1841). DeBow, *The Seventh Census of the United States: 1850*. Kennedy, *Agricultural Census of the United States in 1860*.

8. For excellent discussions of the agricultural practices of yeomen and small-slaveholding Southerners, see Hahn, *The Roots of Southern Populism*, and McCurry, *Masters of Small Worlds*.

9. Protective federal tariffs passed in the 1840s encouraged the increased production of American-grown hemp. By 1850, Missourians produced 17,113,784 pounds of tobacco, 16,028 tons of mostly dew-rotted hemp, 36,214,537 bushels of corn, 2,981,652 bushels of wheat, and livestock valued at $19,887,580, as well as $3,367,106 of slaughtered animals. By 1860, Missourians produced 25,086,196 pounds of tobacco, 19,267 tons of mostly dew-rotted hemp, 72,892,157 bushels of corn, 4,227,586 bushels of wheat, and livestock valued at $53,693,673, as well as $9,844,449 of slaughtered animals. In comparison, Kentucky produced 108,126,840 pounds of tobacco, 39,409 tons of hemp, 64,043,633 bushels of corn, 7,394,800 bushels of wheat, and livestock valued at $61,868,237, as well as $11,640,738 of slaughtered animals in 1860. *Compendium of the Enumeration of the Inhabitants and Statistics of the United States* (1841), 310–21. DeBow, *The Seventh Census of the United States: 1850*, 675–82. Kennedy, *Agricultural Census of the United States in 1860*, 62–65, 88–95. Population statistics taken from Hurt, *Agriculture and Slavery in Missouri's Little Dixie*, 220. See also M. W. Eaton, "The Development and Later Decline of the Hemp Industry in Missouri," and Hurt, *Agriculture and Slavery in Missouri's Little Dixie*, 80–154.

10. This description of tobacco cultivation in Missouri relies heavily on R. Douglas Hurt's excellent analysis of tobacco production in Missouri's Little Dixie, *Agriculture and Slavery in Missouri's Little Dixie*, 80–102.

11. For quotation, see Trexler, *Slavery in Missouri*, 23–24. For excellent descriptions of hemp cultivation in Missouri, see Hurt, *Agriculture and Slavery in Missouri's Little Dixie*, 103–24, and M. W. Eaton, "The Development and Later Decline of the Hemp Industry in Missouri."

12. George Lemmer argues that Missouri farmers fell below the United States average in their investment in labor-saving agricultural equipment per acre of farm land. Whereas the average for the entire country was fifty-two cents per acre in 1850 and sixty cents in 1860, in Missouri it was only forty cents in 1850 and forty-four cents ten years later. What's more, Missourians' increased investment was slight, a fact he attributes to a near doubling in the number of farm acres brought into production during the decade. Still, Missourians were making significant investments in labor-saving technology, despite slavery. Historians have long argued that Southerners had less need for agricultural machinery because they had access to slave labor. See Lemmer, "Farm Machinery in Antebellum Missouri," "Agitation for Agricultural

Improvement in Central Missouri Newspapers Prior to the Civil War," and "Early Leaders in Livestock Improvement in Missouri"; Gray, *History of Agriculture in the Southern United States to 1860*, vol. 2; and Hurt, *Agriculture and Slavery in Missouri's Little Dixie*, 125–86. See also Conard, *Encyclopedia of the History of Missouri*, 4:400; and the *Valley Farmer; A Monthly Journal of Agriculture, Horticulture, Education, and Domestic Economy, Adapted to the Wants of the Cultivators of the Soil in the Valley of the Mississippi*, 2, nos. 1–12 (January–December 1850), SHSM. DeBow, *The Seventh Census of the United States: 1850*, 675–82. Kennedy, *Agricultural Census of the United States in 1860*, 62–65, 88–95.

13. The total population of all residents of the ten largest slaveholding counties accounted for 29.6 percent (349,911 people) of the total population of the state, but excluding St. Louis County the percentage was only 13.48 (159,387 people). Construction of the Hannibal and St. Joseph Railroad was completed in 1859, and the Pacific Railroad had reached Otterville in southwestern Cooper County by the start of the Civil War. For information on early Missouri railroads, see McCandless, *A History of Missouri*, 2:143–50, 256; and W. J. Burton, *The History of the Missouri Pacific Railroad*, 216–17, MSA. Kennedy, *Agricultural Census in 1860*, 88–95. Aggregate census data, Missouri, 1860 United States Census.

14. Robert W. Frizzell argues that historians should reconsider the importance of slavery to the Little Dixie region of Missouri. He calculates that the demographics of many individual townships resembled those in the plantation regions of the South where the slave population approached 50 percent. He reasoned that this was the case even when the total slave population of many of these counties was only between 20 and 35 percent in 1860. Although these demographics are undisputed, Missouri slaveholdings were still small in comparison to those of large southern planters. For example, in Richmond Township in Howard County, where Frizzell notes that slaves made up 51.1 percent of the population, the average slaveholding was 8, and out of 152 owners there were 9 slaveholders who owned 20 to 29 slaves and 3 who owned between 30 and 49. The vast majority of slaveholdings were fewer than 20 slaves. The statistics in other large townships with a large percentage of slaves are similar. See Frizzell, "Southern Identity in Nineteenth-Century Missouri: Little Dixie's Slave-Majority Areas and the Transition to Midwestern Farming." For slave and slaveholder statistics, see Slave Schedules, Missouri Counties, 1860 United States Census; and Historical Census Browser, fisher.lib.virginia.edu/collections/stats/histcensus/.

15. For selected discussions of paternalism and white men's mastery, see Genovese, *Roll, Jordan, Roll*; Fox-Genovese, *Within the Plantation Household*; Kolchin, *Unfree Labor*; Jeffrey R. Young, *Domesticating Slavery*; McCurry, *Masters of Small Worlds*; and Bercaw, *Gendered Freedoms*. For discussions of the worldview of yeomen and small-slaveholding Southerners, see Hahn, *The Roots of Southern Populism*, and McCurry, *Masters of Small Worlds*.

16. Melinda Napton to William Napton, November 15, 1849, November 21, 1849, November 4, 1857, June 21, 1846; and William Napton to Melinda Napton, January 27, 1850, and February 4, 1850, William Napton Papers, MHM. See also C. Phillips and J. L. Pendleton, eds., *The Union on Trial*, 1–77.

17. Nathaniel Leonard to Abiel Leonard, December 24, 1836, January 24, 1837, April 22, 1837, January 22, 1841, and April 19, 1846, Abiel Leonard Papers, WHMC.

18. R. Douglas Hurt believes that there were a number of tenant farmers in Little

Dixie, although the pre-1880s censuses do not denote them as such. See Hurt, *Agriculture and Slavery in Missouri's Little Dixie*, 63–69. L. Hall to "My dear Children," January 1, 1841, Williard P. Hall Papers, MHM. "Remarks by the Editor of the Valley Farmer," *Valley Farmer*, 11 (November 1850), 33, SMSM. Thomas H. Coleman to John C. Coleman, Weston, Missouri, November 18, 1855, Coleman-Hayter Family Papers, WHMC. Susan A. Brown to Dear Mother, July 30, 1838, Saline County, Missouri, Missouri History Collection, MHM. J. Calvin Iserman to Brother William, October 3, 1858, and September 5, 1858, Iserman Letters, 1858–63, JCHS. White laborers often engaged in skilled occupations. A number of slaveholders, including Abiel Leonard, hired white carpenters and bricklayers to work with their slaves in various building projects, for example. In addition, large numbers of Irishmen worked at railroad construction in the state in the years preceding the Civil War. See Jeanette Leonard to Abiel Leonard, October 20, 1846, and Abiel Leonard to Jeanette Leonard, November 1, 1849, and November 2, 1849, Abiel Leonard Papers, WHMC; and New Lebanon Township, 1860 Cooper County, Missouri, United States Census.

19. For discussions of southern domesticity, see Weiner, *Mistresses and Slaves*; Glymph, *Out of the House of Bondage*; and Barton, "Good Cooks and Washers." For a discussion of the housework of nineteenth-century American women and the cultural value placed on it, see Boydston, *Home and Work*.

20. For the work of southern women, see Clinton, *The Plantation Mistress*; Fox-Genovese, *Within the Plantation Household*; Glymph, *Out of the House of Bondage*; and A. F. Scott, *The Southern Lady*. See also Boydston, *Home and Work*; Jensen, *With These Hands*; and Osterud, *Bonds of Community*.

21. Trexler, *Slavery in Missouri*, 22, 54–55. William Napton to Melinda Napton, December 18, 1859; and Melinda Napton to William Napton, May 25, 1858, William Napton Papers, MHM. J. D. Martin, *Divided Mastery*, 108–9.

22. See Hurt, *Agriculture and Slavery in Missouri's Little Dixie*, and Gerlach, *Settlement Patterns in Missouri*.

23. For the best discussion of slave hiring in the antebellum South, see J. D. Martin, *Divided Mastery*.

24. Historians have calculated annual hiring rates from 5 percent of the total southern slave population to nearly 20 percent of slaves in some locations. According to Brenda Stevenson, 34 percent of adult slaves were hired out in Loudoun County, Virginia, in 1860, and Sarah Hughes has argued that nearly all Elizabeth City County, Virginia, slaves were hired out at some point in their lives. The many references to slave hiring found in the historical record suggest that the labor practice was extremely prevalent in Missouri. For examples of historical literature on slave hiring, see Fogel and Engerman, *Time on the Cross*, 53–56; Stevenson, *Life in Black and White*, 184; S. S. Hughes, "Slaves for Hire"; Genovese, *Roll, Jordan, Roll*, 390; Fields, *Slavery and Freedom on the Middle Ground*; Bancroft, *Slave Trading in the Old South*; Campbell, "Research Notes: Slave Hiring in Texas"; C. Eaton, "Slave-Hiring in the Upper South"; Barton, "Good Cooks and Washers"; and Trexler, *Slavery in Missouri*, 28–37. Slave Schedule, Rocheport, 1860 Boone County, Missouri, United States Census. Slave Schedule, Palmyra (First–Third Wards), 1860 Marion County, Missouri, United States Census. Slave Schedule, Liberty Township, 1860 Marion County, Missouri, United States Census. For a good discussion of the census enumerators' instructions, see David E. Paterson, "The 1850 and 1860 Census, Schedule 2, Slave Inhabitants," http://

www.afrigeneas.com/library/slave_schedule2.html/. See also *Measuring America: The Decennial Census from 1790-2000*, 11-13, http://www.census.gov/prod/2002pubs/polo2marv-pt2.pdf/.

25. The free population of Liberty Township was 929 in 1860. Slave Schedule, Rocheport, 1860 Boone County, Missouri, United States Census. Slave Schedule, Palmyra (First-Third Wards), 1860 Marion County, Missouri, United States Census. Slave Schedule, Liberty Township, 1860 Marion County, Missouri, United States Census.

26. For discussions of hiring in the South's urban areas and in industry, see Starobin, *Industrial Slavery in the Old South*; Dew, *Bond of Iron*; Wade, *Slavery in the Cities*; and Goldin, *Urban Slavery in the American South*. See also Abiel Leonard Papers, WHMC, and Bruce, *The New Man*. Slave Schedule, Rocheport, 1860 Boone County, Missouri, United States Census. Slave Schedule, Palmyra (First-Third Wards), 1860 Marion County, Missouri, United States Census. Slave Schedule, Liberty Township, 1860 Marion County, Missouri, United States Census. For discussions of the hiring out of slave children, see J. D. Martin, *Divided Mastery*, 57-65; Barton, "Good Cooks and Washers"; and Drew, "Isaac Riley," in *A North-Side View of Slavery*, 209.

27. Brown, *Narrative of William Wells Brown*. Buchanan, *Black Life on the Mississippi*. "I At Home," ed. Jensen, part 8, 205. Bruce, *The New Man*, 70-72. Slave Schedule, Rocheport, 1860 Boone County, Missouri, United States Census. Slave Schedule, Palmyra (First-Third Wards), 1860 Marion County, Missouri, United States Census. D. D. Buie to Abiel Leonard, January 6, 1855, and December 22, 1855, Abiel Leonard Papers, WHMC. Mrs. Walter Lenoir to Thomas Lenoir, November 18, 1851, in "Life, Labor, and Society in Boone County, Missouri, 1834-1852," ed. Atherton, part 2, 420-21. Green, Kremer, and Holland, *Missouri's Black Heritage*, 22. Cozzens, "The Iron Industry in Missouri."

28. For discussions of the economic advantages to owners of hiring out their slaves, see J. D. Martin, *Divided Mastery*; and Barton, "Good Cooks and Washers"; and C. Eaton, "Slave-Hiring in the Upper South." For quotations, see J. D. Martin, *Divided Mastery*, 19, and Barton, "Good Cooks and Washers," 440.

29. The Walter Raleigh Lenoir family of Boone County, Missouri, is an excellent case study of the ways in which small slaveholders used the hire of slaves as a source of income. "Life, Labor, and Society in Boone County, Missouri, 1834-52," ed. Atherton, parts 1 and 2. For citations see Walter Raleigh Lenoir to William B. Lenoir, November 26, 1834, and Mrs. Walter Raleigh Lenoir to William A. Lenoir, September 11, 1835, in "Life, Labor, and Society in Boone County, Missouri," ed. Atherton, part 1, 284. Jeremiah Coleman to Henry Coleman, October 24 and November 25, 1848, Coleman-Hayter Collection, WHMC. McGettigan, "Boone County Slaves," part 2, citation 273. Thomas J. Brown to Zeno Brown, December 16, 1859, Joseph C. and Charles A. Killian Papers, 1821-1935, WHMC. For a discussion of the strategy to hire out slaves with limited economic value, see Barton, "Good Cooks and Washers," 436-60. Over time, many larger slaveholdings were divided when slaves were given to slaveholding children or when estates were dispersed at the death of owners. See McGettigan, "Boone County Slaves." See also McCurry, *Masters of Small Worlds*, and Hahn, *The Roots of Southern Populism*.

30. Marie Askin Simpson interview, *AS*, supp., ser. 1, 2:230-34. John Jackson pen., USCT 65J, NA. George R[odney] Jacobs, Account Book, 1853-77, WHMC. Bruce, *The New Man*, 64-81. Elizabeth Coleman to James and Sarah Hayter, February 19, 1855,

Coleman-Hayter Collection, WHMC. Mrs. Walter Raleigh Lenoir to Thomas Lenoir, November 18, 1851, Atherton, ed., "Life, Labor, and Society in Boone County, Missouri," part 2, 422. See also Thomas Vaughn pen., USCT 65K, NA.

31. McGettigan, "Boone County Slaves," part 2, 276. Mrs. Walter Raleigh Lenoir to Thomas Lenoir, January 15, 1851, and November 18, 1851, in "Life, Labor, and Society in Boone County, Missouri," ed. Atherton, part 2, 418–23. While there is no way to confirm the identity of [N.] Spenny, it appears that he was Weedon Spenny, a sixty-five-year-old miller living in Cooper County in 1850 with a three-year-old child, Mary, and who owned eleven slaves. Weedon Spenny, 1850 Cooper County, Missouri, United States Census. Weedon Spenny, Slave Schedule, 1850 Cooper County, Missouri, United States Census. N. Spenny Will, January 8, 1858, and William Chambers Will, October 19, 1842, Cooper County Probate Court, Will Record Book B, June 10, 1841–August 11, 1867, MSA. George King Will, February 4, 1852, George King Family Papers, 1778–1925, WHMC. "I at Home," ed. Jensen, parts 7–9.

32. Harrison Trexler's slave-hiring rate for male slaves (around 14 percent) was similar to that found by Clement Eaton for the South as a whole (12 to 15 percent). Sarah Hughes found slightly higher rates for Elizabeth City County, Virginia, during an earlier period. See Trexler, Slavery in Missouri, 1804–1865, 32; C. Eaton, "Slave-Hiring in the Upper South"; and S. S. Hughes, "Slaves for Hire." Mrs. Walter Raleigh Lenoir to Thomas Lenoir, November 18, 1851, in "Life, Labor, and Society in Boone County, Missouri," ed. Atherton, part 2, 420–21. Nathaniel Leonard to Abiel Leonard, January 5, 1840, Abiel Leonard Papers, WHMC. Slave Schedule, Rocheport, 1860 Boone County, Missouri, United States Census. Slave Schedule, Palmyra (First–Third Wards), 1860 Marion County, Missouri, United States Census. Slave Schedule, Liberty Township, 1860 Marion County, Missouri, United States Census. J. R. Bohannon to Judith Clore, January 27, 1837, Lilburn Kingsbury Collection, WHMC. 1841 account with Dr. F. Gilmer, Samuel Smiley Papers, WHMC. Phillip Curtis slave-hiring contract, February 14, 1859, Slaves and Slavery Collection, 1772–1950, MHM. W. H. Bedford to A. M. Bedford, December 16, 1850, Bedford Family Papers, WHMC. Bruce, The New Man, 67–68. Hurt, Agriculture and Slavery in Missouri's Little Dixie, 242–43.

33. Slave Schedule, Rocheport, 1860 Boone County, Missouri, United States Census. Slave Schedule, Palmyra (First–Third Wards), 1860 Marion County, Missouri, United States Census. Bancroft, Slave-Trading in the Old South, 145–46. McGettigan, "Boone County Slaves," part 2, 277. Bruce, The New Man, 66–67. M. M. Frazier, ed., Missouri Ordeal. J. D. Martin, Divided Mastery, 106. For a discussion of nonslaveholders who hired slaves, see J. D. Martin, Divided Mastery, and Campbell, "Research Notes: Slave Hiring in Texas." For a discussion of the southern aspirations to middle-class domesticity, see Barton, "Good Cooks and Washers"; Byrne, Becoming Bourgeois; McCurry, Masters of Small Worlds; and Weiner, Mistresses and Slaves.

34. William Garner and James Culbertson, 1860 Marion County, Missouri, United States Census, and Slave Schedule, 1860 Marion County, Missouri, United States Census. Slave Schedule, Liberty Township, 1860 Marion County, Missouri, United States Census. Nathaniel Leonard to Abiel Leonard, December 24, 1836, December 30, 1839, January 5, 1840, January 22, 1841, and April 19, 1846, Abiel Leonard Papers, WHMC.

35. Nathaniel Leonard to Abiel Leonard, January 5, 1840, and Henry Cook to Rev. C. S. Hawkes, December 15, 1847, Abiel Leonard Papers, WHMC. Bruce, The New Man. J. R. McDearmon to Martha McDearmon, January 21, 1831, J. R. McDearmon

Letters, WHMC. For the work of slave trading and hiring agents, see J. D. Martin, *Divided Mastery;* Buchanan, *Black Life on the Mississippi;* and Deyle, *Carry Me Back.*

36. N. G. Elliott to Lewis Criglar receipt, May 2, 1851, Newton G. Elliott Collection, MHM. See "I at Home," ed. Jensen, parts 1–4. For specific examples, see "I at Home," ed. Jensen, part 1, 41, 55; and "I at Home," part 7, 65, 71, 78. Isabelle Henderson, *AS,* supp., ser. 1, 2:193–95. October 1856 and November 1858, Pauline Stratton Collection, WHMC. Walter Lenoir to William B. Lenoir, June 15, 1838, in "Life, Labor, and Society in Boone County, Missouri," ed. Atherton, part 2, 415. Abiel Leonard to Jeanette Leonard, August 28, 1850, Abiel Leonard Papers, WHMC.

37. Pauline Stratton Collection, WHMC. Thomas Vaughn pen., USCT 65K, NA. John Lewis Farm Journals, James Keyte Collection, 1818–1876, WHMC. "I at Home," ed. Jensen, parts 1–4.

38. "I at Home," ed. Jensen, part 8, 185. Hire contract, January 17, 1859, Joel Franklin Chiles Family Papers, 1832–69, JCHS. A. M. Bedford to W. H. Bedford, December 16, 1850, Bedford Family Papers, WHMC. See also Bancroft, *Slave-Trading in the Old South,* 161, and Trexler, *Slavery in Missouri, 1804–1865,* 29–30.

39. Mary Rollins to James Rollins, January 7, 1849, James Rollins Papers, WHMC. Reese slave hire bill, 1855, James Lawrence and W. W. Walker Slave Rental 1855, JCHS. John Ryan hire bill, January 4, 1861, John W. Hudson Papers, 1838–1908, JCHS. Phillip Curtis slave-hiring contract, February 14, 1859, Slaves and Slavery Collection, 1772–1950, MHM. Nathaniel Leonard to Abiel Leonard, December 24, 1845, Abiel Leonard Papers, WHMC.

40. Trexler, *Slavery in Missouri,* 35–36. Bruce, *The New Man,* 78. November 1858 and July 1859, Pauline Stratton Collection, WHMC. *Missouri Republican,* July 12, 1824, July 19, 1824, SHSM. A. H. Co[nsow] receipt, July 27, 1857, James Harris Papers, 1806–1918, WHMC. See also H. Frazier, *Slavery and Crime in Missouri,* 149–51; Hurt, *Agriculture and Slavery in Missouri's Little Dixie,* 239; and J. D. Martin, *Divided Mastery,* 161–87, and 223 n. 3 for historiography of self-hiring.

41. McGettigan, "Boone County Slaves," part 1, 187–93. Mrs. Steele, *A Summer Journey,* 188–89. For examples of the literature on the southern slave trade, see Bancroft, *Slave-Trading in the Old South;* Deyle, *Carry Me Back;* Gudmestad, *A Troublesome Commerce;* W. L. Johnson, *Soul by Soul;* and Tadman, *Speculators and Slaves.*

42. J. Bull to Abiel Leonard, October 25, 1845, Abiel Leonard Papers, WHMC. For a discussion of the connection between slaveholder paternalism and the domestic slave market, see Deyle, *Carry Me Back,* 206–44; W. L. Johnson, *Soul by Soul;* and Tadman, *Speculators and Slaves,* 47–132.

43. Bill Sims, *AS,* 6:8–13. Brown, *The Narrative of William W. Brown* (1847), 62–64. Melinda Napton to William Napton, April 9, 1858, William Napton Papers, MHM. Emma Knight, *AS,* 11:218–21.

44. George O'Hockaday to Abiel Leonard, February 27, 1849, Abiel Leonard Papers, WHMC. Rhody Holsell, *AS,* 11:191–202. William Napton to Melinda Napton, March 31, 1850, April 2, 1850, November 3, 1850, November 11, 1850; and Melinda Napton to William Napton, April 10, 1850; William Napton Papers, MHM.

45. "I at Home," ed. Jensen, part 4, 274–75. October 1855, Archibald Little Hager Diary, WHMC. William Anderson to Bob, August 7, 1855, Chinn Family Papers, 1820–1868, MHM.

46. The newly elected governor of Missouri, Claiborne Fox Jackson, estimated the

value of Missouri slaves at $100,000,000 in 1861. Bellamy, "Slavery, Emancipation, and Racism in Missouri," 164. The *St. Louis Herald* as quoted in Deyle, *Carry Me Back*, 60. William Napton to Melinda Napton, March 7, 1847, William Napton Papers, MHM. Jonathan Haines to "Respected Brother [Nathan Haines] and Sisters," April 27, 1845, Haines Family Papers, WHMC. John Hambright slave bill, March 12, 1849, Thomas J. Hudspeth Papers, JCHS. Trexler, *Slavery in Missouri*, 37–45. See also Chinn Family Papers, MHM; Slaves and Slavery Collection, MHM; and Hurt, *Agriculture and Slavery in Missouri's Little Dixie*, 215–44.

47. For discussions of selling patterns in Missouri, as well as local sales in general, see Hurt, *Agriculture and Slavery in Missouri's Little Dixie*, 230–38; McGettigan, "Boone County Slaves," parts 1 and 2; McGettigan, "Slave Sales, Estate Divisions, and the Slave Family in Boone County, Missouri"; Trexler, *Slavery in Missouri*, 37–56; Trexler, "The Value and Sale of the Missouri Slave." Steven Deyle suggests that it was a routine business practice among traders to keep advertisements running continuously in local newspapers. Deyle, *Carry Me Back*, 157–73, 107, 131–38, and Tadman, *Speculators and Slaves*. For additional information on the effects of estate divisions on slave families, see Chapter 5 of this book.

48. Tishey Taylor, *AS*, 11:342–47. See also Deyle, *Carry Me Back*, 142–73, 206–44.

49. Bruce, *The New Man*, 102. Eliot, *The Story of Archer Alexander*, 97–100. Marilda Pethy, *AS*, 11:277–82. Trexler, *Slavery in Missouri*, 45. Bancroft, *Slave-Trading in the Old South*, 135–44. Tadman, *Speculators and Slaves*, 47–82. Deyle, *Carry Me Back*, 74–76, 86–87, 347–48. McGettigan, "Boone County Slaves," parts 1 and 2. McGettigan, "Slave Sales, Estate Divisions, and the Slave Family in Boone County, Missouri."

50. Trexler, *Slavery in Missouri*, 45–48. Trexler, "The Value and Sale of the Missouri Slave," 69–85. Bruce, *The New Man*, 102. Eliot, *The Story of Archer Alexander*, 100. See also Bancroft, *Slave-Trading in the Old South*; Tadman, *Speculators and Slaves*; W. L. Johnson, "Masters and Slaves in the Market"; and W. L. Johnson, *Soul by Soul*.

51. Chinn Family Papers, MHM. John R. White Book, 1816–1868, WHMC. William B. Shelby, March 23, 1860, Dorsey-Fuqua Family Collection, 1851–1939, WHMC. *Columbia Missouri Statesman*, 15 (July 17, 1857), SHSM. Brown, *The Narrative of William W. Brown* (1847), 39–62. J. W. King was sold with his mother and his siblings to a man bound for the Lone Star State, leaving his father in Missouri. See J. W. King, *AS*, supp., ser. 2, 6.5:2211–18. See also McGettigan, "Boone County Slaves," part 1, 187; "I at Home," ed. Jensen, part 3, 91; Tadman, *Speculators and Slaves*; W. L. Johnson, "Masters and Slaves in the Market"; W. L. Johnson, *Soul by Soul*; and Deyle, *Carry Me Back*.

52. W. L. Johnson, *Soul by Soul*; for quotations see 45–77. Chinn Family Papers, MHM. John R. White Book, 1816–1868, WHMC. Brown, *The Narrative of William W. Brown* (1847), 38–63, quotation, 63. Gudmestad, *A Troublesome Commerce*, 111. Bruce, *The New Man*, 102. Eliot, *The Story of Archer Alexander*, 97–100. Trexler, *Slavery in Missouri, 1804–1865*, 45. See also Bancroft, *Slave-Trading in the Old South*, 135–44; Tadman, *Speculators and Slaves*, 47–82; and W. L. Johnson, "Masters and Slaves in the Market."

53. Hannah Jones, *AS*, 11:214–17. W. C. Parson Allen, *AS*, 11:18–19. Brown, *The Narrative of William W. Brown* (1847), 80–84. Trexler, *Slavery in Missouri*, 45 and 52. W. A. Hall to Abiel Leonard, January 3, 1847, Abiel Leonard Papers, WHMC.

54. J. L. Morgan, *Laboring Women*, quotation 129. Aga's baby girl died a month after her birth, and Paulina was concerned that Aga had smothered her infant. January

1857, May 1857, June 1858, December 1858, February 1859, Pauline Stratton Collection, WHMC. Henry Pratt pen., USCT 65A, NA. Thomas Houston to J. H. Dalton, May 11, 1857, Placebo Houston Papers, DU. For selective discussions of the reproductive labor of slave women, see Fox-Genovese, *Within the Plantation Household;* Jones, *Labor of Love, Labor of Sorrow;* Berry, *Swing the Sickle for the Harvest Is Ripe;* Schwalm, *A Hard Fight for We;* and D. G. White, *Ar'n't I a Woman?* For discussions of slave breeding, see Sutch, "The Breeding of Slaves for Sale and the Western Expansion of Slavery, 1850–1860"; Tadman, *Speculators and Slaves,* 121–29; Steckel, *The Economics of U.S. Slave and Southern White Fertility;* W. L. Johnson, "Masters and Slaves in the Market," 258; and Deyle, *Carry Me Back,* 46–49.

55. Bruce, *The New Man,* 14–15, 19–20. See also W. L. Johnson, *Soul by Soul,* 20–24, quotation, 1; and J. D. Martin, *Divided Mastery,* 138–60.

56. For discussions of American slaves' labor for their owners, see Genovese, *Roll, Jordan, Roll;* Hurt, *Agriculture and Slavery in Missouri's Little Dixie;* Jones, *Labor of Love, Labor of Sorrow;* Berry, *Swing the Sickle for the Harvest Is Ripe;* Schwalm, *A Hard Fight for We;* Weiner, *Mistresses and Slaves;* D. G. White, *Ar'n't I a Woman?;* and B. Wood, *Women's Work, Men's Work.*

57. William Napton Papers, MHM. Abiel Leonard Papers, WHMC. Sappington Family Papers, 1819–1895, WHMC. Sappington Family Papers, 1831–1939, WHMC. Dr. John Sappington Papers, 1803–1887, WHMC. Slave Schedule, 1860 Howard County, Missouri, United States Census. Slave Schedule, 1860 Saline County, Missouri, United States Census. See also Boman, *Abiel Leonard;* C. Phillips, *Missouri's Confederate;* C. Phillips, *The Making of a Southerner;* and C. Phillips and J. L. Pendleton, eds., *The Union on Trial.* For additional discussions of small slaveholders who engaged in other business and professional activities, see Byrne, *Becoming Bourgeois;* Hurt, *Agriculture and Slavery in Missouri's Little Dixie;* and Inscoe, *Mountain Masters.*

58. Jeanette Leonard to Abiel Leonard, April 29, 1845, Abiel Leonard Papers, WHMC. William Napton to Melinda Napton, January 18, 185[3/4]; and Melinda Napton to William Napton, January 29, 1850; William Napton Papers, MHM. Charles Yancey to Mary Yancey, Thursday night, October 27, [1853], Charles Yancey Letters, 1839–65, WHMC.

59. Abiel Leonard Papers, WHMC. George Bollinger, *AS,* 11:36–43. Bruce, *The New Man,* 90. Trexler, *Slavery in Missouri,* 25–26. Charlie Richardson, *AS,* 11:290–97. Richard Kimmons, *AS,* supp., ser. 2, 6.5:2193–98.

60. Hattie Matthews, *AS,* 11:249–51. Rhody Holsell, *AS,* 11:191–202. April 1856 and October 1855, Pauline Stratton Collection, WHMC. "I at Home," ed. Jensen, parts 1–9. John Lewis Farm Journal, James Keyte Collection, WHMC.

61. Tobacco is also mentioned in a reference to the crops grown in 1846, although there is no indication that the Lewis family grew this cash crop in later years. John Lewis Farm Journal, James Keyte Collection, WHMC. Henry Lewis, Slave Schedule, 1850 Howard County, Missouri, United States Census. Henry Lewis, 1850 Howard County, Missouri, United States Census. Henry Lewis, John F. Lewis, Eugene Lewis, Wilbur Lewis, Slave Schedule, 1860 Howard County, Missouri, United States Census. Henry Lewis, 1860 Howard County, Missouri, United States Census.

62. John Lewis Farm Journal, James Keyte Collection, WHMC. 1841 "Hemp Brake," Franklin Burt Papers, WHMC. For slave men working with white craftsmen

in building projects, see Helm-Davidson Family Papers, 1824–1970, WHMC; Abiel Leonard Papers, WHMC; and William Napton Papers, MHM.

63. 1841 "Hemp Brake," Franklin Burt Papers, WHMC. Malinda Discus, *AS*, supp., ser. 1, 2:166–70. Pauline Stratton Collection, WHMC. William B. Napton Papers, MHM. James Monroe Abbot, *AS*, 11:1–5.

64. Abiel Leonard Papers, WHMC. 1855–1865, Pauline Stratton Collection, WHMC. For excellent discussions of slave mobility, see Camp, *Closer to Freedom;* Kaye, *Joining Places;* and O'Donovan, *Becoming Free in the Cotton South.*

65. For a discussion of the labor of small-slaveholding and yeomen women, see Mc-Curry, *Masters of Small Worlds,* and McCurry, "Producing Dependence."

66. 1855–1860, Pauline Stratton Collection, WHMC, see especially May 17, 1855, October 14, 1855, December 9, 1855, January 12, 1856, February 14, 1856, and March 11, 1860. For fireplace quotation, see Sarah Waggoner, *AS*, 11:361–62. Elvira Ascenith Weir Scott Diary, 1860–1887, WHMC. Coleman-Hayter Family Papers, WHMC. See also Boydston, *Home and Work.*

67. A few former slaves remembered their mothers performing specific tasks, usually cooking or weaving. For examples, see Madison Frederick Ross, *AS*, 11:298–300; Clara McNeely Harrell, *AS*, 11:169; and Richard Kimmons, *AS*, supp., ser. 2, 6.5:2193–98. For citations, see Marilda Pethy, *AS*, 11:277–82; Mollie Renfro Sides, *AS*, 11:310; Nathaniel Leonard to Abiel Leonard, January 5, 1840, Abiel Leonard Papers, WHMC; and Sarah Waggoner, *AS*, 11:355–64. See also Marie Askin Simpson, *AS*, supp., ser. 1, 2:230–34; John McGuire, *AS*, 11:238–40; and Mrs. Eli Daniel, *AS*, 11:203–4. Both Paulina Stratton and Melinda Napton detailed the work performed by female servants throughout their writings. See Pauline Stratton Collection, WHMC, and William B. Napton Papers, MHM.

68. "Boon's Lick Country," 453. M. M. Frazier, *Missouri Ordeal,* August 27, 1862, entry, 66–67. March 1860, Elvira Ascenith Weir Scott Diary, 1860–1887, WHMC. October 1855, Pauline Stratton Collection, WHMC. For discussions of the impact of slave ownership on the labor of slaveholding women, see Barton, "Good Cooks and Washers"; Fox-Genovese, *Within the Plantation Household,* 68, 166; McCurry, *Masters of Small Worlds,* 37–91; and Weiner, *Mistresses and Slaves.* For a discussion of the nature of women's domestic work and how it was dependent on the life cycle, see Ulrich, *A Midwife's Tale.*

69. For references to the division of labor regarding care of poultry and dairy cows, see April 1859, Pauline Stratton Collection, WHMC; and Melinda Napton to William Napton, December 5, 1857, Thursday evening, [April] 1858, and November 10, 1858, William B. Napton Papers, MHM. Melinda Napton relied more heavily on slaves to assist her with the garden when her children were younger. Apparently, the Naptons hoped to free their slave women for more important tasks. Melinda Napton to William B. Napton, Thursday evening, William B. Napton Papers, MHM.

70. The records of Missouri's small-slaveholding women abound with references to textile production through the Civil War. February 1856, November 27, 1856, February 1860, November 1860, and December 1860, Pauline Stratton Collection. Melinda Napton to William B. Napton, November 4, 1857, and March 26, 1858, William B. Napton Papers, MHM. Martha Leonard to Abiel Leonard, September 11, [1840]; Abiel Leonard to Jeanette Leonard, January 24, 1852; and Abiel Leonard to Martha Leonard, January 22, 1852; Abiel Leonard Papers, WHMC. See also Sarah Ann Chandler to son

Robert, June 6, 1865, Sarah Ann Chandler Diary, WHMC; and March 7, 1856, Mary B. Hardin Diary, WHMC. For a discussion of southern manufactured and domestic cloth production in nineteenth-century America, see Fox-Genovese, *Within the Plantation Household*, 68, 120–28, 166, 178–85, 434 n. 63; McCurry, *Masters of Small Worlds*, 77–78; McMillen, *Southern Women*, 103; Faust, *Mothers of Invention*, 45–52; Foster, *New Raiments of Self;* Goldfarb, "A Note on Limits to the Growth of the Cotton-Textile Industry in the Old South"; J. Harris, ed., *5,000 Years of Textiles*, 255–57; Terrill et al., "Eager Hands: Labor for Southern Textiles, 1850–1860"; Ulrich, *The Age of Homespun;* and Hood, *The Weaver's Craft*.

71. For examples of slave children as nurses, see Margaret Nickens, *AS*, 11:263–65; and Marie Askin Simpson, *AS*, supp., ser. 1, 2:230–34. For the household education of slaveholding children, see William B. Napton Papers, MHM, and Filler, ed., *The New Stars*. For more on the care of slave children by small-slaveholding mistresses, see Chapters 4 and 5 of this book. See also Fox-Genovese, *Within the Plantation Household*, 148, and Sarah Graves, *AS*, 11:126–38.

72. Melinda Napton to William B. Napton, Wednesday evening, [December 1857], and January 26, 1858, William B. Napton Papers, MHM. Pauline Stratton Collection, WHMC. Elvira Ascenith Weir Scott Diary, 1860–1887, WHMC.

73. James Goings, *AS*, 11:120. Charlie Richardson, *AS*, 11:290–97. Malinda Discus, *AS*, supp., ser. 1, 2:166–70. Mary Bell, *AS*, 11:25–31. Sarah Waggoner, *AS*, 11:355–64. Peter Corn, *AS*, 11:85–93. Margaret Nickens, *AS*, 11:263–65. Isabelle Henderson, *AS*, supp., ser., 1, 2:193–95. Louis Hamilton, *AS*, 11:145–46. Lewis Mundy, *AS*, 11:258–60. Madison Frederick Ross, *AS*, 11:298–300.

74. Emma Knight, *AS*, 11:218–21. Louis Hill, *AS*, 11:184–90. Marie Askin Simpson, *AS*, supp., ser. 1, 2:230–34. Malinda Murphy, *AS*, 11:261–62. James Monroe Abbot, *AS*, 11:1–5. Bruce, *The New Man*, 21–22.

75. Abiel Leonard to Martha Leonard, January 22, 1852, Abiel Leonard Papers, WHMC. Filler, ed., *The New Stars*, 30. July 1860 and July 1861, Pauline Stratton Collection, WHMC. Melinda Napton to William Napton, October 28, 1857, April 25, 1858, April 6, 1851, and April 13, 1851, William Napton Papers, MHM. Mary Leonard to Abiel Leonard, January 1851, Abiel Leonard Papers, WHMC. It is interesting to note that in 1850 Nathaniel Leonard had thirteen slaves living on his farm, including six slave men of prime working age. Given Leonard's penchant for hiring slave men and the fact that the Cooper County census taker did not enumerate hired slaves, it is possible that some of the men were hired. Therefore, the composition of Leonard's labor force may have differed a year later. Nathaniel Leonard, Slave Schedule, 1860 Cooper County, Missouri, United States Census. Mark Discus, *AS*, supp., ser. 1, 2:171–76. See also Stone, *Slavery, Southern Culture, and Education in Little Dixie, Missouri, 1820–1860*.

76. George Bollinger, *AS*, 11:342–47. Tishey Taylor, *AS*, 11:342–47. Henry Dant, *AS*, 11:98–99. Sarah Graves, *AS*, 11:126–38. Charlie Richardson, *AS*, 11:290–97. John Lewis Farm Journal, James Keyte Collection, WHMC.

Chapter 4

1. Missouri mistress Paulina Stratton wrote these lines shortly before migrating from the Kanawha Valley of western Virginia to central Missouri. I have used the incident because Paulina's sentiments closely echoed her feelings after she moved to

Missouri. In addition, the nature of the relationship with her slaves did not change dramatically after her move to Missouri. Western Virginia was also a region of small-slaveholding and yeoman farmers. Slaveholding migrants brought to Missouri methods of slave management learned in their original homes in the small-scale slavery districts of the Upper South. October and November 1852, Pauline Stratton Collection, WHMC.

2. See Trexler, *Slavery in Missouri*, 19. Many other Missourians remembered slavery in a similar light, see Filler, *The New Stars;* William Henry Schrader Reminiscences, WHMC; Eliot, *The Story of Archer Alexander;* and Bruce, *The New Man.*

3. See Haskell, "The Passing of Slavery in Western Missouri," 28–39.

4. For discussions of slave resistance on plantations, see Blassingame, *The Slave Community;* Escott, *Slavery Remembered;* Faust, *James Henry Hammond and the Old South;* Fox-Genovese, *Within the Plantation Household;* Genovese, *Roll, Jordan, Roll;* Jones, *Labor of Love, Labor of Sorrow;* Kolchin, *Unfree Labor;* and D. G. White, *Ar'n't I A Woman?* See also J. C. Scott, *Weapons of the Weak.*

5. For discussions of the ideology of paternalism, see Genovese, *Roll, Jordan, Roll;* Fox-Genovese, *Within the Plantation Household;* Kolchin, *Unfree Labor;* Kolchin, *American Slavery;* and Jeffrey R. Young, *Domesticating Slavery.*

6. Some historians have argued that plantation slaves preferred fieldwork over housework because physical distance from the master and mistress lessened the opportunity for slaveholder abuse and provided room for a slave community. In many cases the close proximity in which small slaveholders and their slaves lived and worked resembled the situation within plantation big houses. See Blassingame, *The Slave Community;* Fox-Genovese, *Within the Plantation Household;* Genovese, *Roll, Jordan, Roll;* Jones, *Labor of Love, Labor of Sorrow;* and D. G. White, *Ar'n't I a Woman?* Joseph Higgerson, *AS,* 11:173–78. Steve Brown, *AS,* 11:56–57. Nelson Danforth, *AS,* supp., ser. 1, 2:160–63.

7. Lewis Washington pen., USCT 65C, NA. Katie Leonard to Abiel Leonard, April 13, 1856, and April 15, 1856; Abiel Leonard to Jeanette Leonard, April 19, 1856; and Abiel Leonard to Katie Leonard, April 20, 1856; Abiel Leonard Papers, WHMC. March 1850, December 1852, and January 1853, Archibald Little Hager Diary, WHMC. See also Tishey Taylor, *AS,* 11:342–47.

9. Jeanette Leonard to Abiel Leonard, July 6, 1845; Benjamin Reeves to Abiel Leonard, November 20, 1845, and December 20, 1845; Abiel Leonard to Jeanette Leonard, April 17, 1847, March 12, 1850, and July 3, 1850; Abiel Leonard Papers, WHMC.

10. Mary Glasgow to Sarah Lane Glasgow, December 28, 1858, and Sarah Lane Glasgow to Anne E. Lane, November 9, 1858, Lane Collection, MHM. Abiel Leonard Papers, WHMC. William B. Napton Papers, MHM.

11. Mary Armstrong, *AS,* supp., ser. 2, 2:68–74. Mary Estes Peters, *AS,* 10.5, 323–31. Peter Corn, *AS,* 11:85–95. For the story of the extreme isolation of a slave woman who was raised in a Missouri slaveholding household, see Schreck, "Her Will Against Theirs."

12. December 13, 1836, Slave Emancipation and Fugitive Legal Papers, WHMC. July 27, 1857, and February 12, 1859, James Harris Papers, 1806–1882, WHMC. Nelly C. Read will, December 25, 1855, John Lacy will, June 26, 1855, Hugh Rogers will, September 24, 1860, and William Spud will, May 29, 1855, Cooper County Probate Court, Will Record Book B, June 10, 1841–August 11, 1867, Cooper County, Missouri, MSA.

Gus Smith, *AS*, 11:321–332. Austin King Petition, 1846, Missouri, Boone County, Citizen's Petition, 1846, WHMC. For more examples of wills and emancipation deeds, see also Hugh Dunbar—Deed of Emancipation, 1846, WHMC; Jesse Evans Emancipation Deed, May 1846, George King Family Papers, 1778–1925, WHMC; Slave Emancipation and Fugitive Legal Papers, WHMC; Slaves and Slavery Collection, 1772–1950, n.d., MHM; and Missouri, Cape Girardeau County Records, WHMC.

13. The relations between small slaveholders and slaves were in many ways similar to those scholars have found between mistresses and slave women on southern plantations, who also lived and worked closely together. See Fox-Genovese, *Within the Plantation Household*; Clinton, *The Plantation Mistress*; Glymph, *Out of the House of Bondage*; D. G. White, *Ar'n't I a Woman?*; and Weiner, *Mistresses and Slaves*.

14. See Crawford, "Quantified Memory"; and Escott, *Slavery Remembered*, 55–58.

15. Richard Kimmons, *AS*, supp., ser. 2, 6.5:2193–98. Andrew Prewitt pen., USCT 65D, NA.

16. There is no mention of slave women cooking for the entire slave community as on plantations. Rachal Goings, *AS*, 11:121–25. Hannah Allen, *AS*, 11:8–17. Fil Hancock, *AS*, 11:147–51. Sarah Waggoner, *AS*, 11:355–64. Hattie Matthews, *AS*, 11:249–51.

17. Charlie Richardson, *AS*, 11:290–99. Smokey Eulenberg, *AS*, 11:109. Tishey Taylor, *AS*, 11:342–47. Fil Hancock, *AS*, 11:147–51. For discussions of enslaved people's diets, see Genovese, *Roll, Jordan, Roll*, 540–49, and Savitt, *Medicine and Slavery*, 86–98.

18. Mark Discus, *AS*, supp., ser. 1, 2:173–74. See Genovese, *Roll, Jordan, Roll*, 535–40, and Penningroth, *The Claims of Kinfolk*, 45–78.

19. Eugene Genovese argues that slaves on smaller holdings were likely to go hungry if their owners' farms were economically vulnerable. Genovese, *Roll, Jordan, Roll*, 7–11. Harriet Casey, *AS*, 11:73–75. Louis Hill, *AS*, 11:184–90.

20. Hard times during the 1930s could not account for the fact that slaves on smaller holdings from throughout the South reported better food than on plantations. Emily Camster Green, *AS*, 11:139–42. Harry Johnson, *AS*, supp., ser. 2, 6.5:1994–2004. Perry Sheppard, *AS*, 11:308. See Crawford, "Quantified Memory."

21. Sarah Ann Chandler to son Robert, June 6, 1856, Sarah Ann Chandler Diary, 1836, WHMC. March 7, 1856, Mary B. Hardin Diary, WHMC. March and December 1856, and March and December 1857, Pauline Stratton Collection, WHMC. Sarah Graves, *AS*, 11:126–38. Sarah Waggoner, *AS*, 11:355–64. Malinda Murphy, *AS*, 11:258–60. J. B. Harrison to Capt. W. D. Swinney, December 10, 1845, Abiel Leonard Papers, WHMC. Lewis Mundy, *AS*, 11:258–60. Mark Discus, supp., ser. 1, 2:171–77. Louis Hill, *AS*, 11:184–90. Hattie Matthews, *AS*, 11:249–51. John Woods to William Woods, January 14, 1850, Woods-Holman Family Papers, WHMC. See Camp, *Closer to Freedom*, 60–92; Genovese, *Roll, Jordan, Roll*, 550–61; Savitt, *Medicine and Slavery*, 83–86; S. White and G. White, *Stylin'*, 5–62.

22. Mark Discus, *AS*, supp., ser. 1, 2:1731–77. Steve Brown, *AS*, 11:56–57. Madison Frederick Ross, *AS*, 11:298–300. Emma Knight, *AS*, 11:218–21. Rhody Holsell, *AS*, 11:191–202. Malinda Murphy, *AS*, 11:261–62. Jeanette Leonard to Abiel Leonard, February 3, 1835, Abiel Leonard Papers, WHMC.

23. A majority of those interviewed by the WPA were children during slavery. Slave owners rarely bought slave children shoes, which may partly account for the many complaints by those interviewed. Rachal Goings, *AS*, 11:121–25. Fil Hancock, *AS*, 11:147–61.

24. Frank Duncan pen., USCT 65F, NA. Tishey Taylor, AS, 11:342–47. See also Mark Discus, AS, supp., ser. 1, 2:171–77; Clara McNeely Harrell, AS, 11:169–72; Charlie Richardson, AS, 11:290–300; Emily Camster Green, AS, 11:139–42; Rachal Goings, AS, 11:121–25; Annie Bridges, AS, 11:44–51; Madison Frederick Ross, AS, 11:298–300; and Sarah Graves, AS, 11:126–38. See Vlach, *Back of the Big House*.

25. Sarah Graves, AS, 11:126–38. Hannah Allen, AS, 11:8–17. Lucinda Patterson, AS, 11:269–76. Sarah Waggoner, AS, 11:355–64. See also Madison Frederick Ross, AS, 11:298–300; Smokey Eulenberg, AS, 11:109–12; Rachal Goings, AS, 11:121–25; Mollie Renfro Sides, AS, 11:310; and Marie Askin Simpson, AS, supp., ser. 1, 2:230–4.

26. Archibald Little Hager Diary, WHMC. See also Valenčius, *The Health of the Country*.

27. Rhody Holsell, AS, 11:191–202. George Bollinger, AS, 11:36–43. Gus Smith, AS, 11:321–32. Nathaniel Leonard to Abiel Leonard, October 10, 1845, Abiel Leonard Papers, WHMC. See also Fett, *Working Cures*; Savitt, *Medicine and Slavery*; and M. J. Schwartz, *Birthing a Slave*.

28. Nathaniel Leonard to Abiel Leonard, December 16, 1846, Abiel Leonard Papers, WHMC. See also Henry Smith pen., USCT 65H, NA; John Lewis Farm Journal, January 2, 1852, James Keyte Collection, WHMC; Melinda Napton to William Napton, January 18, 1846, William B. Napton Papers, MHM; and Zifney Woods to J. J. Woods, June 24, 1852, Woods-Holman Family Papers, 1805–1906, WHMC.

29. Mary Leonard and Jeanette Leonard to Abiel Leonard, January 29, 1847; Mary Leonard to Abiel Leonard, January 24, 1847; Jeanette, Martha, and Mary Leonard to Abiel Leonard, July 12, 1846; and Nathaniel Leonard to Abiel Leonard, May 23, 1848; Abiel Leonard Papers, WHMC. 1860, Elvira Ascenith Weir Scott Diary, 1860–1887, WHMC.

30. Justina Woods to sister, January 3, 1855, Woods-Holman Family Papers, WHMC. For examples of the medical treatment of slaves, see Henry E. Rice Jr. Notes, n.d., WHMC; file 706, Ste. Genevieve, Missouri, Archives, 1756–1930, WHMC; and Estate of Russel Farnham, 1827, and B. Jones Estate, 1837–1839, Slaves and Slavery Collection, 1772–1950, MHM. See Savitt, *Medicine and Slavery*.

31. Nathaniel Leonard to Abiel Leonard, December 21, 1842; Benjamin Reeves to Abiel Leonard, January 20, 1843; and Charlotte L. Daley to Abiel and Jeanette Leonard, May 8, 1843; Abiel Leonard Papers, WHMC. William Napton to Melinda Napton, October 30, 1858, and October 31, 1858; and Melinda Napton to William Napton, April 9, 1858, October 22, 1858, October 31, 1858, and November 3, 1858; William B. Napton Papers, MHM.

32. Pauline Stratton Collection, WHMC. Daniel Lewis pen., #2, USCT 65J, NA. John Gunn pen., USCT 65B, NA. For examples of doctors delivering slave babies, see Robert Anderson pen., USCT 65K, NA; and George Delaney pen., USCT 65E, NA. See also M. J. Schwartz, *Birthing a Slave*.

33. Melinda Napton to William Napton, October 31, 1858, William B. Napton Papers, MHM. The nursing incident occurred within months of the Strattons' migrating to Missouri from Kanawha County, Virginia. January 1855, Pauline Stratton Collection, WHMC. Sarah Graves, AS, 11:126–38. Bottle-feeding was the least desirable method of infant nourishment because unsanitary conditions often led to infant death. For a discussion of antebellum southern women's commitment to nursing, see McMillen, "Mothers' Sacred Duty," 333–35. For examples of slave wet nurses, see

Lewis Washington pen., USCT 65C, NA; John Jackson pen., USCT 65J, NA; and Mat Beasley pen., USCT 65F, NA.

34. Will Daily, *AS*, 4:269–72.

35. The Strattons were substantial slaveholders by Missouri standards: they owned two slave women, one adult male slave, two elderly slave women over ninety, and four children under the age of ten in 1860. Thomas Stratton, Slave Schedule, 1860 United States Census, Cooper County, Missouri. For quotation, see February 1847, Pauline Stratton Collection, WHMC.

36. July 1853 and January 1853, Pauline Stratton Collection, WHMC.

37. John R. White to R. Brown, November 9, 1839, Abiel Leonard Papers, WHMC. Sallie Bedford to dear sister, June 27, 1851, Charles Yancey Letters, 1839–65, WHMC. Delaney, *From the Darkness Cometh the Light or Struggles for Freedom*, 21. James Monroe Abbot, *AS*, 11:1–5. Melinda Napton to William B. Napton, Friday evening, [1840s], William B. Napton Papers, MHM. Abiel Leonard to Jeanette Leonard, January 18, 1846, and Jeanette Leonard to Abiel Leonard, January 19, 1846, Abiel Leonard Papers, WHMC.

38. Bruce, *The New Man*, 64, 70–72. J. D. Martin, *Divided Mastery*, 129–30.

39. Smokey Eulenburg, *AS*, 11:109–12. Lucinda Patterson, *AS*, 11:269–76. Jonathan Ramsay to Abiel Leonard, January 12, 1836, Abiel Leonard Papers, WHMC.

40. Lucinda Patterson, *AS*, 11:269–76. Esther Easter, *AS*, 7:88–91.

41. Charles Yancey to Mary Yancey, October 27–28, 1853; Mary Yancey to Charles Yancey, October 13, 1854; Charles Yancey to Mary Yancey, October 16, 1855; Mary Yancey to Charles Yancey, Sunday evening, [1855]; and Charles Yancey to Mary Yancey, November 1, 1855, quotation; Charles Yancey Letters, 1839–65, WHMC. January 1857 and March 1863, Pauline Stratton Collection, WHMC. Abiel Leonard Papers, WHMC. Bruce, *The New Man*, 66–67. See also J. D. Martin, *Divided Mastery*, 134–35. Melinda Napton also managed the family farm in her husband's absence and was troubled by recalcitrant slaves. Melinda Napton to William B. Napton, Friday evening, [1840s], William B. Napton Papers, MHM. For discussions of the authority of slaveholding women, see Fox-Genovese, *Within the Plantation Household;* Glymph, *Out of the House of Bondage;* McCurry, *Masters of Small Worlds;* Weiner, *Mistresses and Slaves;* and K. Wood, *Masterful Women.*

42. For economic resistance of slaves on plantations, see Blassingame, *The Slave Community;* Escott, *Slavery Remembered;* Faust, *James Henry Hammond and the Old South;* Fox-Genovese, *Within the Plantation Household;* Genovese, *Roll, Jordan, Roll;* Jones, *Labor of Love, Labor of Sorrow;* Kolchin, *Unfree Labor;* and D. G. White, *Ar'n't I a Woman?*

43. Melinda Napton to William Napton, Friday evening, [1840s], May 28, 1840, December 5, 1857, William B. Napton Papers, MHM. December 1855 and January 1862, Pauline Stratton Collection, WHMC. F. F. Peake to Abiel Leonard, September 19, 1837; and Jeanette Leonard to Abiel Leonard, August 18, 1841, and April 29, 1845; Abiel Leonard Papers, WHMC.

44. Another former Missouri slave recalled an almost identical story about stolen biscuits, which provokes the question of whether these two accounts have their roots in slave tales rather than reality. William Napton to Melinda Napton, May 12, 1859, William Napton Papers, MHM. Eliza Overton, *AS*, 11:266–68. John Coffman, Slave Schedule, 1860 Ste. Genevieve County, Missouri, United States Census. January 10,

1857, Pauline Stratton Collection, WHMC. Charlie Richardson, *AS*, 11:290–97. Hattie Matthews, *AS*, 11:249–51.

45. Mary Rollins to James Rollins, February 7, 1862, James S. Rollins Papers, WHMC. Martha and Abiel Leonard to Jeanette and Mary Leonard, June 30, 1845, Abiel Leonard Papers, WHMC. Melinda Napton to William B. Napton, Friday evening, [1840s], William B. Napton Papers, MHM. See Levine, *Black Culture and Black Consciousness*, 81–135.

46. February 14, 1858, June 14, 1862, March 1863, and January 10, 1857, Pauline Stratton Collection, WHMC.

47. Brown, *The Narrative of William W. Brown* (1847), 21–26. Betty Abernathy, *AS*, 11:6–7. West v. Forrest, 1856, described in Catteral, *Judicial Cases concerning American Slavery and the Negro*, 5:195–96. For additional hiring cases also presented in Catteral, see Blanton v. Knox, April 1834; Fulkerson v. Steen, June 1834; Trimsley v. Riley, June 1838; Ellett v. Bobb, May 1840; Perkins v. Reeds, July 1843; Dudgeon v. Teass, January 1846; Adams v. Childers, July 1847; Lee v. Sparr, March 1851; Garneau v. Herthel, October 1851; Caldwell v. Dickson, March 1853; and Peters v. Clause, February 1866. See J. D. Martin, *Divided Mastery*, 138–60.

48. There was a young slave woman listed as living in Daniel Buie's household in 1850, but no slaves in 1860. A number of young white tradesmen lived with the Buies at this later date. Leonard may have sent Wesley to live with the Howard County planter W. D. Swinney, who employed an overseer for the sixty-nine slaves who resided in his household in 1860. There were other Swinneys in the general area, however. D. D. Buie to Abiel Leonard, January 6, 1855, and December 22, 1855; Jeanette Leonard to Abiel Leonard, July 15, 1855, January 23, 1856, January 28, 1856, February 14, 1856, October 16, 1859, and October 21, 1859; Abiel Leonard to Jeanette Leonard, January 26, 1856, and October 21, 1859; William A. Wilson to Abiel Leonard, January 3, 1856; and William Swinney to Abiel Leonard, October 10, 1856; Abiel Leonard Papers, WHMC. Daniel D. Buie, 1850 Saline County, Missouri, United States Census. D. D. Buie, 1860 Saline County, Missouri, United States Census. Slave Schedule, 1850 Saline County, Missouri, United States Census. Slave Schedule, 1860 Saline County, Missouri, United States Census. W. D. Swinney, 1860 Howard County, Missouri, United States Census. Slave Schedule, 1860 Howard County, Missouri, United States Census.

49. Pauline Stratton Collection, WHMC. October 18, 1855, Priscilla Thomas Ingram Patton Diary, Patton-Scott Papers, WHMC.

50. Elizabeth Coleman to James and Sarah Hayter, February 19, 1855, Coleman-Hayter Family Papers, 1839–1900, WHMC. Benjamin Reeves to Abiel Leonard, February 14, 1847; and Jeanette Leonard to Abiel Leonard, March 6, 1847; Abiel Leonard Papers, WHMC. October 18, 1855, Priscilla Thomas Ingram Patton Diary, Patton-Scott Papers, WHMC. Pauline Stratton Collection, WHMC. For discussions of planter women's protestations against slavery, see Clinton, *The Plantation Mistress;* Fox-Genovese, *Within the Plantation Household;* and Weiner, *Mistresses and Slaves*.

51. Melton McLaurin argues that Celia, who was accused of murdering her master, was provided with a first-rate attorney to defend her case precisely because the Callaway County judge was concerned that the trial appear legitimate to an audience outside of Missouri. Harriet Frazier also suggests that throughout Missouri's early history, slave defendants usually were provided with highly capable and dedicated attorneys. See McLaurin, *Celia, a Slave*, and H. Frazier, *Slavery and Crime in Missouri*,

1773–1865. Gus Smith, *AS*, 11:321–32. Lucinda Patterson, *AS*, 11:269–76. Another example was James Monroe Abbot who claimed that he could hear the cries of a slave man on the neighboring farm when his master, George Swan, whipped him with a cat-o-nine tails. See James Monroe Abbot, *AS*, 11:1–5, and Annie Bridges, *AS*, 11:44–51.

52. William Eliot did not deny that cruelty existed in Missouri. He simply argued that slavery was more humane in Missouri than in the rest of the South. Eliot, *The Story of Archer Alexander;* for a description of slavery in a border state, see 90–106, and for quotation, see 39. William Schrader Reminiscences, WHMC. Eustace v. White, August 1839 and August 7, 1839; and John R. White to Abiel Leonard, November 8, 1839; Abiel Leonard Papers, WHMC. September and October 1845, Lexington Presbyterian Church Record Book, 1839–1851, WHMC. Carpenter v. State, in Catteral, *Judicial Cases concerning American Slavery*, 5:162. H. Frazier, *Slavery and Crime in Missouri, 1773–1865*, 125–44.

53. For selected discussions of violence, see Glymph, *Out of the House of Bondage*, and Berlin, *Generations of Captivity*.

54. Summer 1845, September 1849, Archibald Little Hager Diary, WHMC. September 1860, Pauline Stratton Collection, WHMC. Margaret Montgomery Zogbaum, "The Life of Mary Ann Phelps Montgomery, 1846–1942," 1967, WHMC. Lucinda Patterson, *AS*, 11:269–76. For discussions of slave truancy, see Camp, *Closer to Freedom*, and Franklin and Schweninger, *Runaway Slaves*.

55. Rachal Goings, *AS*, 11:121–24. Madison Frederick Ross, *AS*, 11:298–300. See Krauthamer, "In Their 'Native County,'" 100–120; Naylor-Ojurongbe, "Born and Raised among These People, I Don't Want to Know Any Other," 161–91; May, *African Americans and Native Americans in the Creek and Cherokee Nation;* and Purdue, *Mixed Blood Indians.*

56. For information on runaway and truant slave women, see D. G. White, *Ar'n't I a Woman?*, 70–75; Camp, *Closer to Freedom*, 35–59; and Franklin and Schweninger, *Runaway Slaves*, 63–65.

57. See Camp, *Closer to Freedom*, 35–59; Franklin and Schweninger, *Runaway Slaves*, 63–65; and O'Donovan, *Becoming Free in the Cotton South.*

58. For discussions of the ways in which Missouri's history and geography affected slavery, see Bellamy, "Slavery, Emancipation, and Racism in Missouri, 1850–65"; Bellamy, "The Persistency of Colonization in Missouri"; Bierbaum, "Frederick Starr, A Missouri Border Abolitionist"; Etcheson, *Bleeding Kansas;* Foley, *A History of Missouri*, vol. 1; H. Frazier, *Runaway and Freed Missouri Slaves and Those Who Helped Them;* Green, "The Slavery Debate in Missouri"; Sengupta, *For God and Mammon;* Hurt, *Agriculture and Slavery in Missouri's Little Dixie;* McCandless, *A History of Missouri*, vol. 2; McLaurin, *Celia, a Slave;* Merkel, "Antislavery and Abolition in Missouri, 1819–1854: A Preliminary Study"; Merkel, "The Antislavery Movement in Missouri, 1819–1854"; Merkel, "The Underground Railroad and the Missouri Borders, 1840–1860"; Merkel, "The Abolition Aspects of Missouri's Antislavery Controversy, 1819–1865"; J. Neely, *The Border Between Them;* Nelson, "Missouri Slavery, 1861–1865"; and Trexler, *Slavery in Missouri.*

59. Thompson, *Prison Life and Reflections.* H. Frazier, *Runaway and Freed Missouri Slaves and Those Who Helped Them*, 124–67, 183–84. May 1846, Archibald Little Hager Diary, WHMC. Doy, *The Narrative of John Doy.* August 6, 1859, Joseph C. and Charles A. Killian Papers, 1821–1935, WHMC. For a warning to a local church to discontinue

preaching against slavery, see Dr. E. Bailey et al. to Messrs. Oyler and Wilson, Monroe City, Mo., May 1, 1858, Slavery and Slavery Collection, 1772–1950, n.d., MHM. See also Earle, *John Brown's Raid on Harper's Ferry*.

60. Twain, *Huckleberry Finn*. William Russell runaway advertisement, October 1, 1847, and A. King advertisement, August 7, 1854, Slaves and Slavery Collection, 1772–1950, MHM. Richard Graham petition, 1854, Slave Emancipation and Fugitive Slave Legal Papers, WHMC. Doy, *The Narrative of John Doy*.

61. Trexler, Slavery in Missouri, 1804–65, 34–35. Brown, *The Narrative of William W. Brown* (1847), 87–110. For examples of lawsuits against riverboat owners and railroads, see Russel v. Taylor, June 1837; Eaton v. Vaughn, January 1846; Price v. Thornton, March 1846; Perry v. Beardslee, March 1847; Doughtery v. Tracy, October 1847; Beardslee v. Perry, March 1851; Calvert v. Rider, October 1854; Withers v. Steamboat El Paso, January 1857; Ridley v. Steamboat Reindeer, October 1858; Welton v. Railroad Co., January 1864; Rogers v. Railroad, July 1864; McClure v. Railroad, July 1864; and Harris v. Railroad, February 1866; described in Catteral, *Judicial Cases concerning American Slavery*, 123–225.

62. George Bollinger, *AS*, 11:36–43. Madison Frederick Ross, *AS*, 11:298–30. J. B. Harrison to Capt. W. D. Swinney, December 10, 1845, and December 28, 1845, Abiel Leonard Papers, WHMC. Anne E. Lane to William C. Lane, September 4, 1851, and Anne E. Lane to Sarah Lane, [1851], Lane Collection, MHM.

63. Only sixty outstanding fugitives were listed in the 1850 United States Census (0.0686% of the total slave population) and a mere ninety-nine fugitives were listed in 1860 (0.0860% of the total slave population). See Bellamy, "Slavery, Emancipation, and Racism in Missouri, 1850–65," 91. "I at Home," ed. Jensen, part 2, 304, and part 5, 45. Summer 1845, September 1849, March 1847, March 1850, June 1850, August 1850, June 1851, November 1855, and August 1859, Archibald Little Hager Diary, WHMC. H. Frazier, *Runaway and Freed Missouri Slaves and Those Who Helped Them*, 106–23.

64. Brown, *The Narrative of William W. Brown* (1847), 66–73. One slave was James Rollins's and another belonged to Rollins's brother John. Jim Rollins to James Rollins, October 26, 1857; Jim Rollins to Mary Rollins, November 1857 and December 5, 1857; Mary Rollins to Jim Rollins, April 4, 1858; James S. Rollins Papers, WHMC. William Schrader, "William Schrader Reminiscences," manuscript, 1–3, WHMC. Washington Castleman pen., USCT 65F, NA.

65. Sam Ralston to D. W. Jordan, January 8, 1844, in "A Southern Family on the Missouri Frontier," ed. Overdyke, 216–37. For a discussion of slave patrols, see Hadden, *Slave Patrols*, and Trexler, *Slavery in Missouri*, 173–207.

66. Emma Knight, *AS*, 11:218–21. Mary Martha Bolden, *AS* supp., ser. 1, 2:150–51. Esther Easter, *AS*, 7:88–91. William Anderson to Bob, August 7, 1855, Abiel Leonard Papers, WHMC.

67. John Woods to William Woods, January 14, 1850, and April 16, 1850, Woods-Holman Family Papers, 1805–1906, WHMC. Mary A. Bell, *AS*, 11:25–31.

68. January 12, 1856, Pauline Stratton Collection, WHMC. James Monroe Abbot, *AS*, 11:1–5. Mary Armstrong, *AS*, supp., ser. 2, 2:66–74.

69. Fil Hancock, *AS*, 11:147–61. Hattie Matthews, *AS*, 11:249–51. Samuel Ralston to Colonel Jordan, January 8, 1844, in "A Southern Family on the Missouri Frontier," ed. Overdyke, 224. Brown, *The Narrative of William W. Brown* (1847), 17–20.

70. James Fenton to Abiel Leonard, May 3, 1835, Abiel Leonard Papers, WHMC.

Brown, *The Narrative of William W. Brown* (1847), 40. The *Liberty Tribune*, August 27, 1852, SHSM. Bruce, *The New Man*, 75–76. N. L. Sutherland to Samuel H. Sutherland, April 10, 1860, Samuel H. Sutherland Letters, 1858–1861, WHMC. See also H. Frazier, *Slavery and Crime in Missouri, 1773–1865*, 109–24, 167–209.

71. Jane v. State, Catteral, *Judicial Cases concerning American Slavery*, 5:139. H. Frazier, *Slavery and Crime in Missouri, 1773–1865*, 109–24, 167–209.

72. H. Frazier, *Slavery and Crime in Missouri, 1773–1865*, 109–24, 167–209. McLaurin, *Celia, a Slave.*

73. H. Frazier, *Slavery and Crime in Missouri, 1773–1865*, 109–24, 167–209. Catteral, *Judicial Cases concerning American Slavery*, 5:134–35. Trexler, *Slavery in Missouri*, 57–81. *Liberty Tribune*, May 3, 1850, SHSM.

74. *St. Louis Democrat*, quoted in *The Liberator*, July 8, 1859, and *Lewis County Reporter*, quoted in *The Liberator*, January 18, 1850, as cited in Aptheker, *American Negro Slave Revolts*, 336, 341–42, 353. Trexler, *Slavery in Missouri*, 57–81. *Liberty Tribune*, November 23, 1849, SHSM. Dempsey, *Searching for Jim*, 129–30. See also Genovese, *From Rebellion to Revolution*, and Reynolds, *Texas Terror.*

75. For examples, see March 1857, September 14, 1862, and February 1863, Pauline Stratton Collection, WHMC. Brown, *The Narrative of William W. Brown* (1847), 84–87.

76. Escott, *Slavery Remembered*, 47. According to the WPA interviews, the percentage of Missouri slaves whose fathers were white was 11.76. Statistics taken from the 102 WPA narratives of former Missouri slaves: Missouri narratives primarily in *AS*, vol. 11 and supp., ser. 1, vol. 2. 1850 and 1860, Slave Schedules, Chariton County, Clay County, Cooper County, Marion County, and Ste. Genevieve County, Missouri, United States Census. For discussions of the sexual exploitation of slave women on plantations, see Fox-Genovese, *Within the Plantation Household*; Jones, *Labor of Love, Labor of Sorrow*; McLaurin, *Celia, a Slave*; and D. G. White, *Ar'n't I a Woman?*

77. Phannie Corneal, *AS*, supp., ser. 2, 1:311–13. Charles Younger, *AS*, 11:379–82. Alice Freeman, *AS*, supp., ser. 2, 1:397–98. Mrs. James O'Donnel, *AS*, supp., ser. 2, 1:338–39. Eliza Overton's aunt was bought by a Mr. Jones, who fathered her two children. See Eliza Overton, *AS*, 11:266–68.

78. Schreck, "Splitting Heirs," quotation 99.

79. Annie Bridges, *AS*, 11:44–51. Harriet Casey, *AS*, 11:73–75. See also Bardaglio, *Reconstructing the Household*, and J. D. Rothman, *Notorious in the Neighborhood.*

80. Brown, *The Narrative of William W. Brown* (1847), 46–48. Eliot, *The Story of Archer Alexander*, 95–97. McLaurin, *Celia, a Slave*. Mary Estes Peters, *AS*, 10.5:323–31.

81. Ruth Allen, *AS*, supp., ser. 1, 2:101–4. George Jackson Simpson, *AS*, supp., ser. 1, 2:219–29. McLaurin, *Celia, a Slave*. Lewis Washington pen., USCT 65C, NA.

82. Mary Estes Peters, *AS*, 10.5:323–31. Ruth Allen, *AS*, supp., ser. 1, 2:101–4. Rachal Goings, *AS*, 11:121. See also Lewis Washington pen., USCT 65C, NA.

83. McLaurin, *Celia, a Slave*, 22–23, 117. Mary Estes Peters, *AS*, 10.5:323–31. Justina Woods to sister, July 3, 1856, Woods-Holman Family Papers, WHMC. For discussions of white women's responses to their husband's indiscretions, see Fox-Genovese, *Within the Plantation Household*, 238, 325; and J. D. Rothman, *Notorious in the Neighborhood.*

84. Captain Richard J. Hinton testimony, December 14, 1863, New York City, American Freedmen's Inquiry Commission, Letters Received by the Office of Adjutant General, M619, RG 94, reel 201, File 8, NA. For an excellent analysis of the

relationships, between white women and black men and a lengthy discussion of Hinton's testimony, see Hodes, *White Women, Black Men,* especially 125–46.

85. Captain Richard J. Hinton testimony, December 14, 1863, New York City, American Freedmen's Inquiry Commission, Letters Received by the Office of Adjutant General, M619, RG 94, reel 201, File 8, NA.

86. Preston B. Reed to S. Kirtley, December 28, 1846, Abiel Leonard Papers, WHMC. Jane Baker, *AS,* 11:24. Brown, *The Narrative of William W. Brown* (1847), 21–26.

87. William Black, *AS,* supp., ser. 1, 2: 147–49. J. D. Martin, *Divided Mastery,* 57–65.

88. Mary Bell, *AS,* 11:25–31. Brown, *The Narrative of William W. Brown* (1847), 13–16. James Monroe Abbot, *AS,* 11:1–5. Harriet Casey, *AS,* 11:73–75. Peter Corn, *AS,* 11:85–95.

89. Louis Hill, *AS,* 11:184–90. Mark Discus, *AS,* supp., ser. 1, 2:171–77. Annie Bridges, *AS,* 11:44–51. Gus Smith, *AS,* 11:323. Ed Craddock, *AS,* 11:96–97. Charlie Richardson, *AS,* 11:295. Tishey Taylor, *AS,* 11:342–47.

90. I agree with Glymph that it is a mistake to view white women's violence as an anomaly; however, my research on Missouri leads me to believe that there was the possibility of kind treatment by some mistresses. Emma Knight, *AS,* 11:218–21. Margaret Nickens, *AS,* 11:263–65. Mary Armstrong, *AS,* 4:25–30. Esther Easter, *AS,* 7:88–91. Mary Estes Peters, *AS,* 10.5:323–31. See Glymph, *Out of the House of Bondage,* 1–62, as well as Clinton, *The Plantation Mistress;* Fox-Genovese, *Within the Plantation Household;* and Weiner, *Mistresses and Slaves.*

91. Eliza Overton, *AS,* 11:266–68. Sarah Graves, *AS,* 11:126–38. Hannah Allen, *AS,* 11:8–17. Marilda Pethy, *AS,* 11:277–82. Brown, *The Narrative of William W. Brown* (1847), 27. Eliot, *The Story of Archer Alexander,* 91–93.

92. Sarah Graves, *AS,* 11:126–38.

Chapter 5

1. Mary Bell, *AS,* 11:25–31. [Private Spotswood Rice] to My Children, [September 3, 1864]; Spotswood Rice to Kittey diggs, [September 3, 1864]; and F. W. Diggs to Genl. Rosecrans, September 10, 1864, D-296 1864, Letters Received, ser. 2593, Dept. of the Missouri, RG 393, Pt. 1, NA, in *The Black Military Experience,* ed. Berlin, Reidy, and Rowland, 689–91. F. W. Diggs and Benjamin Lewis, Slave Schedule, Howard County, Missouri, United States Census. F. W. Diggs, Howard County, Missouri, United States Census. See also Steven Niven, "From Ota Benga to Elmo: One Writer's Journey through the AANB," oxfordaasc.com; and the biographical sketch of Rev. Spotswood Rice, in William G. Cutler, *History of the State of Kansas,* Labette County, part 10, kancoll.org/books, cutler/labette.

2. Mary Bell, *AS,* 11:25–31. [Private Spotswood Rice] to My Children, [September 3, 1864]; Spotswood Rice to Kittey diggs, [September 3, 1864]; and F. W. Diggs to Genl. Rosecrans, September 10, 1864, D-296 1864, Letters Received, ser. 2593, Dept. of the Missouri, RG 393, Pt. 1, NA, in *The Black Military Experience,* ed. Berlin, Reidy, and Rowland, 689–91. See also Steven Niven, "From Ota Benga to Elmo: One Writer's Journey through the AANB," oxfordaasc.com; and the biographical sketch of Rev. Spotswood Rice, in William G. Cutler, *History of the State of Kansas,* Labette County, part 10, kancoll.org/books, cutler/labette.

3. For historical works on the slave family, see Bercaw, *Gendered Freedoms;* Berry,

Swing the Sickle; Blassingame, *The Slave Community;* Dunaway, *The African-American Family in Slavery and Emancipation;* Escott, *Slavery Remembered;* Fox-Genovese, *Within the Plantation Household;* Genovese, *Roll, Jordan, Roll;* Gutman, *The Black Family in Slavery and Freedom;* L. Hudson, *To Have and to Hold;* Jones, *Labor of Love, Labor of Sorrow;* Kaye, *Joining Places;* McMillen, *Southern Women;* Malone, *Sweet Chariot;* Penningroth, *Claims of Kinfolk;* Schwalm, *A Hard Fight for We;* Stevenson, *Life in Black and White;* Weiner, *Mistresses and Slaves;* E. West, *Chains of Love;* and D. G. White, *Ar'n't I a Woman?* For discussions of Louisiana and Appalachian slave families, see Malone, *Sweet Chariot,* and Dunaway, *The African-American Family in Slavery and Emancipation.*

4. The demographics of five representative river counties, Chariton, Clay, Cooper, Marion, and Ste. Genevieve, were quite stable from 1850 to 1860. There were slightly more women in the five combined counties because female slaves outnumbered male slaves in Marion County due to the large number of women living in the towns of Hannibal and Palmyra. The number of women working as domestics in these large towns increased the number of women in these counties, but it may also reflect increased activity of slave traders in the Mississippi River counties. Those slaves sixteen and older were counted as adults. All percentages are rounded up or down. See table 3. The demographics also demonstrate the small number of slaves held on the typical Missouri slaveholding. In Chariton, Clay, Cooper, Marion, and Ste. Genevieve Counties in 1850 the average number of slaves per holding was 4.9. Of the 2,267 slaveholders, only 38 (1.7 percent) owned more than 20 slaves. A total of 243 slaveholders (11 percent) owned 10 or more slaves. In 1860, there was an increase in slaveholders, but the average slaveholding and the percentage of larger slaveholders actually remained the same. There were a few slaveholders who owned more than 50 slaves, but most of the planters owned 20 to 30 slaves. The average number of slaves owned by slaveholders in Clay, Cooper, and Chariton Counties (5.3 slaves in 1850 and 5.1 slaves in 1860) was representative of most of the largest slaveholding counties in the state. Only Howard, Lafayette, and Saline Counties had average slaveholdings of 6 or 7 slaves. In contrast, Marion and Ste. Genevieve Counties had average slaveholdings of 4.2 in 1850 and 4.3 in 1860. Slave Schedules, Chariton County, Clay County, Cooper County, Marion County, and Ste. Genevieve County, Missouri, 1850 and 1860, United States Census. See Hurt, *Agriculture and Slavery in Missouri's Little Dixie,* 219–22, and Hilliard, *Atlas of Antebellum Agriculture,* 37–38. Slave Schedule, Chariton County, Clay County, Cooper County, Marion County, and Ste. Genevieve County, Missouri, 1850 and 1860, United States Census.

5. Although they only briefly addressed the issue, Herbert Gutman and Eugene Genovese made some valuable observations about abroad marriages. See Gutman, *The Black Family in Slavery and Freedom,* 131–38, and Genovese, *Roll, Jordan, Roll,* 472–75. A few scholars of the slave family have downplayed the existence of these marriages; see Malone, *Sweet Chariot.* Paul Escott gathered his data from reports of slave marriages in WPA interviews taken from throughout the South. Escott, *Slavery Remembered,* 50–52. See also Crawford, "Quantified Memory." A few historians have explored the issue of abroad marriages, arguing that they were common and viable unions. See E. West, *Chains of Love,* and Stevenson, *Life in Black and White,* 230–31.

6. Most of the individuals who were interviewed by the WPA in the 1930s were children during slavery and could only provide information about their parents'

marriages. In contrast, although orphans, siblings, and parents of soldiers filed a number of dependent claims, most pensioners were the widows of Union soldiers. The pension claims provide information about the marital status of a large number of couples. Of the two types of evidence, the testimony of the pension claimants is most representative when it comes to determining numbers of abroad unions; therefore, the percentage of abroad marriages in Missouri was likely closer to the 63 percent of marriages found in the pension claims. It was integral to the success of a pension case that applicants describe their marital circumstances, and those deposed often testified that the couples lived separately but maintained strong marriages through frequent visiting. In contrast, not all individuals interviewed by the WPA indicated the living arrangements of their parents, and, therefore, many of those who remained silent were possibly members of abroad families. Some of the women who appear to be single or widowed may have been abroad wives. The pension claims do not show as a high a rate of one-parent families because the evidence was biased toward marriages that survived until the soldier's enlistment. The statistical data includes only the interviews and claims that provide information about slave marriages. The total percentages in table 4 do not add up to 100 percent because a number of marriages fell into multiple categories. In addition, all percentages are rounded. See table 4. See interviews of Missouri slaves, *AS*, primarily contained in volume 11 and supp., ser. 1, volume 2. See also Benecke Family Papers, WHMC, and Civil War Pension Claims, 65th USCT, NA.

7. William Wells Brown's mistress wanted to purchase the woman Brown loved in order to unite the couple. He believed his mistress's offer to buy his girlfriend was an attempt to make him content in his enslavement and less of a flight risk. Brown, *The Narrative of William W. Brown* (1847), 85–87.

8. Alfred Smith pen., USCT 65C, NA. Benjamin Hubbard pen., USCT 65K, NA. Thomas Vaughn, Benecke Family Papers, file 2646, WHMC. Thomas Vaughn pen., USCT 65K, NA. Charles Elliot pen., USCT 65C, NA. Caleb Jones, Benecke Family Papers, file 2559, WHMC. See also George Bollinger, *AS*, 11:36–43; and Betty Abernathy, *AS*, 11:6–7.

9. Bill Sims, *AS*, 16.1:8–13. Harre Quarls, *AS*, 5:222–24. Peter Corn, *AS*, 11:85–93. See Fraser, *Courtship and Love Among the Enslaved in North Carolina*.

10. For information on Natchez slave couples and the use of pension records to describe marriages, see Kaye, *Joining Places*, 51–82. See also Bercaw, *Gendered Freedoms*. William Hamilton pen., USCT 65C, NA.

11. Hattie Matthews, *AS*, 11:249–52. Peter Corn, *AS*, 11:85–93. Isaac Davis pen., USCT 65A, NA. Isaac Smith, Benecke Family Papers, file 2634, WHMC. William Miller, Benecke Family Papers, file 2579, WHMC. Alfred Smith pen., USCT 65C, NA. The historian Brenda Stevenson argues that although some scholars have located the origins of the broomstick ceremony in African culture, the evidence points toward a western European pre-Christian marriage ritual. See Fraser, *Courtship and Love among the Enslaved in North Carolina*; O'Neil, "Bosses and Broomsticks"; Poole and Slawson, *Church and Slave in Perry County, Missouri*; Stevenson, *Life in Black and White*, 228–29; and E. West, *Chains of Love*, 33.

12. Asbury Warden, Benecke Family Papers, files 2653–54, WHMC. Peter Woods, Benecke Family Papers, file 2672–73, WHMC. Lewis Washington pen., USCT 65C, NA. Emanuel Gatewood pen., USCT 65F, NA. See also E. West, *Chains of Love*, 19–42.

13. Richard Kimmons, *AS*, supp., ser. 2, 6.5:2193–98. Henry Berry pen., USCT 65F,

NA. Washington Castleman pen., USCT 65F, NA. For more examples of the participation of slaveholding women in wedding preparations and the location of weddings in slaveholders' homes, see Filler, ed., *The New Stars;* Sandy Farrer pen., USCT 65E, NA; and David Farmer, Benecke Family Papers, file 2509, WHMC.

14. Bill Sims, *AS,* 16.1:8–13. Matthew Carroll pen., USCT 65C, NA. Mollie Renfro Sides, *AS,* 11:310.

15. Jacob Priest pen., USCT 65J, NA. Washington Castleman pen., USCT 65F, NA. Isaac Davis pen., USCT 65A, NA. Benjamin Madis pen., USCT 65J, NA. John Gunn pen., USCT 65B, NA. Thomas Jackson pen., USCT 65J, NA. For additional discussions of the distances traveled by abroad men, see Sandy Farrer pen., USCT 65E, NA; Emanuel Gatewood pen., USCT 65F, NA; and Henry Rodgers pen., USCT 65H, NA.

16. Asbury Warden, Benecke Family Papers, files 2653–54, WHMC. Charles Elliot pen., USCT 65C, NA. Alfred Smith pen., USCT 65C, NA. See also Hadden, *Slave Patrols,* 105–36.

17. For discussions of matrifocality within slave households, see Malone, *Sweet Chariot,* and Stevenson, *Life in Black and White.*

18. For discussions of the reproductive labor of slaves, see Berry, *Swing the Sickle;* Jones, *Labor of Love, Labor of Sorrow;* Malone, *Sweet Chariot;* Schwalm, *A Hard Fight for We;* Stevenson, *Life in Black and White;* and D. G. White, *Ar'n't I a Woman?*

19. Justina Woods to sister, June 18, 1856, Woods-Holman Family Papers, 1805–1906, WHMC. Sarah Graves, *AS,* 11:126–38. Annie Bridges, *AS,* 11:44–51. Hattie Matthews, *AS,* 11:249–52. Jackson, *The Story of Mattie J. Jackson,* 9. Louis Hamilton, *AS,* 11:145–46. Tishey Taylor, *AS,* 11:342–47. See also King, *Stolen Childhood,* and M. J. Schwartz, *Born in Bondage.*

20. See L. Hudson, *To Have and to Hold,* and Penningroth, *Claims of Kinfolk.* For additional examples, see Henry Rodgers pen., USCT 65H, NA; Gerret Smith pen., USCT 65F, NA; Charles Lewis pen., USCT 65G, NA; Jonah Edwards pen., USCT 65G, NA; Archibald Edward pen., USCT 65A, NA; Jefferson Reeves pen., USCT 65H, NA; Mat Beasley pen., USCT 65F, NA; Matt Carroll pen., USCT 65C, NA; William Powell pen., USCT 65A, NA; and Jacob Priest pen., USCT 65J, NA.

21. "I at Home," ed. Jensen, part 9, 439. William Nelson, *AS,* 16.4:74–75. John Carter pen., USCT 65A, NA. Gus Smith, *AS,* 11:322. George Bollinger, *AS,* 11:36–43.

22. Sarah Graves, *AS,* 11:126–38. Bruce, *The New Man,* 72. John Carter pen., USCT 65A, NA. Gus Smith, *AS,* 11:321–32. Alfred Smith pen., USCT 65C, NA. Moses and Washington Combs pen., USCT 65D, NA.

23. In 1829, Stephen Hempstead visited a free black man named Willis, who was employed as a carpenter and "had bought his own freedom many years Since." See "I at Home," ed. Jensen, part 9, 416, 423, 428. Mary Rollins to James Rollins, December 7, 1846, James Rollins Papers, WHMC. November 1858 and June 1859, Pauline Stratton Collection, WHMC. Hannah Allen, *AS,* 11:7–13. Bruce, *The New Man,* 72. See also March 1850, December 1852, and January 1853, Archibald Little Hager Diary, WHMC. For discussions of bondpeople's interest in clothing, see Camp, *Closer to Freedom,* 60–92, and S. White and G. White, *Stylin',* 5–62. See Chariton County Circuit Court Records, Volume B; and Fraser v. State, September 1839; Skinner v. Hughes, March 1850; State v. Guyott, October 1857; Missouri Supreme Court Cases located in Catteral, *Judicial Cases concerning American Slavery and the Negro,* 5:154–55, 180, and 206.

24. Sarah Graves, *AS*, 11:126–38. Eliza Overton, *AS*, 11: 266–68.

25. There is no indication that Missouri slave women felt empowered by their enhanced role in abroad households. For discussions of the division of labor within slave households and the financial contributions of slave men, see Blassingame, *The Slave Community*; Genovese, *Roll, Jordan, Roll*, 483–501; and D. G. White, *Ar'n't I a Woman?* 142–60. For a discussion of the more limited economic contributions of abroad husbands, see M. J. Schwartz, *Born in Bondage*, 50–53. Eliza Overton, *AS*, 11:266–68.

26. H. Frazier, *Slavery and Crime in Missouri, 1773–1865*, 197–98. See also J. D. Rothman, *Notorious in the Neighborhood*, 133–63.

27. Few WPA interviews reported slaves separated from their mothers. In this specific sample of slave families, slave women were not commonly sold from their young children. See *AS*, primarily volume 11 and supp., ser. 1, vol. 2. Tishey Taylor, *AS*, 11:342. Mary Armstrong, *AS*, supp., ser. 2, 2:66–74. See Stevenson, "Gender Convention, Ideals, and Identity Among Antebellum Virginia Slave Women," 169–90.

28. Lewis Mundy, *AS*, 11:258–60. Harry Johnson, *AS*, supp., ser. 2, 6.5:1994–2004. Fil Hancock, *AS*, 11:147–61. Richard Kimmons, *AS*, supp., ser. 2, 6.5:2193–98. Tishey Taylor, *AS*, 11:342–47. See Webber, *Deep Like the Rivers*, and Stone, *Slavery, Southern Culture, and Education in Little Dixie, Missouri*.

29. Henry Pratt pen., USCT 65A, NA. Henry Berry pen., USCT 65F, NA. Hannah Jones, *AS*, 11:214–17. Harre Quarls, *AS*, 5:222–24. September 14, 1862, and March 1863, Pauline Stratton Collection, WHMC. William Cheatham pen., USCT 65F, NA. For discussions of polygamy and adultery in abroad marriages and in the slave community, see Genovese, *Roll, Jordan, Roll*, 473–74; Gutman, *The Black Family in Slavery and Freedom*, 67–74; Jones, *Labor of Love, Labor of Sorrow*, 34; Kaye, *Joining Places*, 51–82; and Stevenson, *Life in Black and White*, 233–34.

30. Asbury Warden pen., Benecke Family Papers, files 2653–54, WHMC.

31. See Stevenson, *Life in Black and White*, 233–34, and Berry, *Swing the Sickle*, 82–83.

32. Henry Pratt pen., USCT 65A, NA. Caleb Jones, Benecke Family Papers, file 2559, WHMC. Reuben Banks pen., USCT 65K, NA.

33. Mary Rollins to James Rollins, January 7, 1849, James Rollins Papers, WHMC. Mary Bell, *AS*, 11:25–31. Sarah Graves, *AS*, 11:126–38.

34. J. W. King, *AS*, supp., ser. 2, 6.5:2211–18. Emily Camster Green, *AS*, 11:139–42.

35. McGettigan, "Boone County Slaves," part 1, 195. "Life, Labor, and Society in Boone County, Missouri," ed. Atherton, part 2, 418–23. February 16, 1843, Smiley Family Papers, WHMC. Copybook and 1852 Will of George King, George King Family Papers, 1778–1925, WHMC.

36. "I at Home," ed. Jensen, part 3, 78–79, and part 6, 242–43. February 16, 1843, Smiley Family Papers, WHMC. Hiram Sloan Slaves, *AS*, supp., ser. 1, 2:235–39. McGettigan, "Boone County Slaves," part 2, 286–87. Robert Coleman to H. Coleman, December 26, 1856, Coleman-Hayter Family Papers, 1839–1900, WHMC. For examples of wills and emancipation deeds, see Slave Emancipation and Fugitive Slave Legal Papers, WHMC; Missouri, Cape Girardeau County Records, WHMC; and Slaves and Slavery Collection, 1772–1950, n.d., MHM. For additional information on the division of slaveholders' estates, see McGettigan, "Boone County Slaves," parts 1 and 2, and Chapter 2 of this book.

37. Pauline Stratton Collection, March 1862, WHMC. Eliza Williams slave bill,

1858, Dorsey-Fuqua Family Collection, 1851–1939, WHMC. Slave bill, 1854, Edmond Rutter Papers, 1853–55, WHMC. Margaret Nickens, *AS*, 11:263–65.

38. William Melton Will, 1829, Corby Family Papers, 1804–1905, WHMC. Malinda Discus, *AS*, supp., ser. 1, 2:166–70. Will Daily, *AS*, 4.1:269–72. Annie Bridges, *AS*, 11:44–51. Slave bill, December 15, 1859, Alfred B. Jones Collection, 1825–1860, WHMC. Slave bill, July 27, 1853, Slaves and Slavery Collection, MHM. Robert Davis to Abiel Leonard, January 30, 1847, Abiel Leonard Papers, WHMC. Brown, *The Narrative of William W. Brown* (1847), 48–58. "Life, Labor, and Society in Boone County, Missouri," ed. Atherton, part 2, 412–13.

39. Brown, *The Narrative of William W. Brown* (1847), 63–79. George Johnson, *AS*, supp., ser. 1, 2:115–17. Marilda Pethy, *AS*, 11:277–82. Emily Camster Green, *AS*, 11:139–42. John Jackson pen., USCT 65J, NA. Mark Discus, *AS*, supp., ser. 1, 2:171–77.

40. Bruce, *The New Man*, 102–3. Hiram Sloan Slaves, *AS*, supp., ser. 1, 2:235–39. Giles T. Clarke Broadside, 1855, WHMC. Malinda Discus, *AS*, supp., ser. 1, 2:166–70. Eliot, *The Story of Archer Alexander*, 41–42. Charlie Richardson, *AS*, 11:290–97.

41. T. T. Bradley to A. Higgans, July 11, 1859, T. T. Bradley Letter, 1859, WHMC. See also Brown, *The Narrative of William W. Brown*, 38–62; George Bollinger, *AS*, 11:36–43; Harriet Casey, *AS*, 11:73–75; and Mark Discus, *AS*, supp., ser. 1, 2:171–77.

42. Matthew Carroll pen., USCT 65C, NA. For discussions of selling patterns in Missouri, see Chapter 3 of this book.

43. Mary Leonard Everett to Jeanette Leonard, December 20, 1852, Abiel Leonard Papers, WHMC. Susan (Sukey) & Ersey to Dear Master [Beverley Tucker], St. Louis, October 24, 1842, in Blassingame, ed., *Slave Testimony*, 13–14. William Wiseley pen., USCT 65E, NA. Frank Cochran pen., USCT 65F, NA. Frank Duncan pen., USCT 65F, NA. Jonathan Ramsay to Abiel Leonard, June 12, 1836, Abiel Leonard Papers, WHMC. Sarah Lane Glasgow to Anne E. Lane, February 4, 1852, Lane Collection, MHM. Eliot, *The Story of Archer Alexander*, 41–42. Thomas Vaughn pen., USCT 65K, NA.

44. W. A. Wilson to Abiel Leonard, January 3, 1851, and January 22, 1852; Leonard account book, March 28, 1846; Nathaniel Leonard to Abiel Leonard, January 9, 1845; Abiel Leonard Papers, WHMC. Leonard Property Book, MHM. See also William Hamilton pen., USCT 65C, NA; and Thomas Vaughn pen., USCT 65K, NA.

45. John Ewing pen., Benecke Family Papers, file 2507, WHMC. Henry Smith pen., USCT 65H, NA.

46. Charles Douthit, *AS*, 11:107. Gus Smith, *AS*, 11:321–32.

47. The WPA narratives and the pension claims point toward the prevalence of local sales. The gender parity found in the county slave schedules also suggests that there was not an epidemic of selling slaves, especially young men, to the Deep South. For statistics, see table 3. For citations, see Matthew Carroll pen., USCT 65C, NA; Malinda Discus, *AS*, supp., ser. 1, 2:160–70; and Jesse Brown pen., USCT 65H, NA. For additional examples, see Lewis Washington pen., USCT 65C, NA; Charles Elliot pen., USCT 65C, NA; and Henry Pratt pen., USCT 65A, NA.

48. See Bercaw, *Gendered Freedoms;* Penningroth, *Claims of Kinfolk;* and L. Hudson, *To Have and to Hold.*

49. The manuscript slave censuses for Chariton, Clay, Cooper, Marion, and Ste. Genevieve Counties were used to determine the demographic make-up of Missouri's slaveholdings. A slaveholding was classified as headed by a female if it consisted of only female slaves sixteen and older with or without children. The same follows

for male-headed holdings. A holding was classified as a male and female holding if it consisted of both adult male and female slaves. The slaveholding was classified as a children-only holding if it consisted of only children fifteen years and younger. A holding was classified as intergenerational if it appears that there were adult household members from two generations. Obviously, a slaveholding could fall into both intergenerational and one of the three adult categories at the same time. In addition, all percentages were rounded off, which accounts for the totals not always adding up to 100 percent. See table 5. Slave Schedules, Chariton County, Clay County, and Cooper County, Marion County, and Ste. Genevieve County, Missouri, 1850 and 1860, United States Census. Gutman also suggested that abroad slave women may have gained assistance from family members on their home plantations. See Gutman, *The Black Family in Slavery and Freedom*, 137–40. See also Mat Beasley pen., USCT 65F, NA; Jefferson Reeves pen., USCT 65H, NA; Berry Twyman pen., USCT 65C, NA; and James W. Hensley pen., USCT 65B, NA.

50. Dallis Price, Benecke Family Papers, file 2608, WHMC. Alfred Smith pen., USCT 65C, NA. See also Berry Twyman pen., USCT 65 C, NA.

51. Henry S. Fowler/ Scott [alias] pen., USCT 65E, NA.

52. Statistics from the WPA interviews were taken from the following volumes: *AS*, primarily contained in volume 11 and supp., ser. 1, vol. 2. Statistics of the lengths of slave marriages also were taken from the pension claims and from Boone and Chariton County marriage records. The pensioners recorded the dates of their weddings, so it is possible to ascertain the actual number of years they were married. Therefore, the pension statistics are the most reliable for determining the length of abroad marriages. Using the county marriage records for statistical analysis requires making some assumptions. There are no wedding dates in these records, but the length of marriages can be estimated based on the number of years it would have taken to produce a certain number of children. For example, a couple with four to six children was married approximately ten to fourteen years, taking into account both nursing patterns and high rates of slave childhood mortality. Using the number of children to calculate lengths of marriages most certainly underestimates the number of years that some couples were married since many slave couples likely had lost one or more children. The other weakness inherent to this particular evidence is that all of these marriages survived slavery and lasted until the Civil War. With the exception of the evidence from the WPA narratives, there is little way to gauge the number of marriages cut short by the deprivations of slavery. See table 6. Bartels, *Boone County Colored Marriages*. Chariton County Marriage Record Book, Volume A and Volume 1–A. Civil War Pension Claims, USCT 65, NA. Annette Curtis provides a transcript of the 1865 marriage statute. Curtis, *Jackson County, Missouri Marriage Records of Citizens of African Descent, 1865–1881*. There are many examples of long-term slave marriages found in the pension claims, including Isaac Allen pen., USCT 65K, NA; Benjamin Arnold pen., USCT 65K, NA; and Isham Handy pen., USCT 65E, NA.

53. Lewis Washington pen., USCT 65C, NA. Thomas Vaughn pen., USCT 65K, NA. Emanuel Gatewood pen., USCT 65F, NA. See also Henry Fleetwood, Benecke Family Papers, file 2514, WHMC.

54. Clara McNeely Harrell, *AS*, 11:169.

Chapter 6

1. Archibald Little Hager Diary, 1844–1870, WHMC.

2. Ibid.

3. Alfred Smith pen., USCT 65C, NA.

4. Ibid. 1860 Agricultural Census Data, Missouri, Census Browser, fisher.lib.virginia.edu/collections/stats/histcensus/.

5. For suggested works on the nature of antebellum southern society, see O. V. Burton, *In My Father's House Are Many Mansions*; Fox-Genovese, *Within the Plantation Household*; Genovese, *Roll, Jordan, Roll*; Genovese, *The World the Slaveholders Made*; Genovese, *The Political Economy of Slavery*; Fogel and Engerman, *Time on the Cross*; Fox-Genovese and Genovese, *The Fruits of Merchant Capitalism*; Fredrickson, "Masters and Mudsills"; Kolchin, *Unfree Labor*; McCurry, *Masters of Small Worlds*; Oakes, *The Ruling Race*; Oakes, *Slavery and Freedom*; and Owsley, *Plain Folk of the Old South*. For examples of studies of backcountry and border communities, see Dunaway, *Slavery in the American Mountain South*; Stevenson, *Life in Black and White*; Hahn, *The Roots of Southern Populism*; and Inscoe, *Mountain Masters*. For discussions of rural communities in the North, see Faragher, *Sugar Creek*, and Osterud, *Bonds of Community*.

6. New Lebanon Township in Cooper County, Missouri, was the home of Thomas and Paulina Stratton. All listed households were included in the statistics referenced in the text; however, a unique historical event may have slightly skewed the numbers. In 1860, the town of Otterville, Missouri, was filled with Irish immigrants who were working on the railroad line from Tipton. Railroad men headed thirty-two New Lebanon Township households. The temporary presence of these men artificially increased the number of nonslaveholding households in the township. In addition, only two of the railroad men owned any personal property. If these thirty-two households are removed, the percentage of slaveholding households increased to 19 percent. Slaveholders then owned 58 percent of the personal property. Population Census and Slave Schedules, 1860 Cooper County, Missouri, United States Census. For slaveholding population statistics, see Gray, *History of Agriculture in the Southern United States to 1860*, 1:482. Missouri's yeomen also seemed comfortable with slaveholders representing them politically. In 1850 and 1860, slaveholders represented a much larger percentage of the state legislature than their numbers in the general population might suggest. In 1850, 35.9 percent of representatives and 41.2 percent of senators owned slaves. In 1860, 58.8 percent of representatives owned slaves, but there is no information available on senators. The vast majority owned fewer than ten slaves, although the number of those owning ten to forty-nine slaves had increased slightly by 1860. The legislators also owned more property than average Missourians. For statistics on Missouri politicians, see Wooster, *Politics, Planters, and Plain Folk*, 36–40, 168. For a discussion of Missouri politics, see McCandless, *A History of Missouri*, vol. 2.

7. Walter Raleigh Lenoir to William B. Lenoir, November 26, 1834, in "Life, Labor, and Society in Boone County," ed. Atherton, part 1, 408–29. Abiel Leonard Papers, WHMC. Hurt, *Agriculture and Slavery in Missouri's Little Dixie*, 62–65.

8. Howard Female College Rules, 1859, WHMC. Columbia Female Academy Papers, WHMC. Clay Seminary for Young Ladies, Liberty, Missouri, Papers, 1855–1864, WHMC. Kemper Family School, Boonville, Missouri, Papers, 1873–1890, WHMC.

Masonic College of Missouri, Lexington, Missouri, Consecration Program, 1845, WHMC. Erodelphian Literary Society, Lexington, Missouri, Records, 1851–1859, WHMC. Petrillo, "Missouri Schoolgirls, 1840–1870." McCurdy, *Stump, Bar, and Pulpit*, 25–45. Potts, "Franklin Debate Society," 1–21. McCandless, *A History of Missouri*, 2:163–226. Parrish, *Turbulent Partnership*. Trexler, *Slavery in Missouri*. Green, "The Slavery Debate in Missouri, 1831–1855," Hurt, *Agriculture and Slavery in Missouri's Little Dixie*, 187–214, 273–300.

9. For quotations see *Jefferson City Examiner*, December 5, 1858, as quoted in *St. Louis Missouri Democrat*, January 11, 1859, and found in Deyle, *Carry Me Back*, 168–69. Laver, "Refuge of Manhood," 1–21, quotation, 3. See Hadden, *Slave Patrol;* McCurdy, *Stump, Bar, and Pulpit*, 47–146; Hurt, *Agriculture and Slavery in Missouri's Little Dixie*, 187–214; Byrne, *Becoming Bourgeois*, 13–40; and Wells, *The Origins of the Southern Middle Class, 1800–1861*, 19–39.

10. Slave Schedule, Rocheport, 1860 Boone County, Missouri, United States Census. Slave Schedule, Palmyra (First–Third Wards), 1860 Marion County, Missouri, United States Census. Slave Schedule, Liberty Township, 1860 Marion County, Missouri, United States Census. M. M. Frazier, ed., *Missouri Ordeal*. Hurt, *Agriculture and Slavery in Missouri's Little Dixie*, 62–65.

11. William Napton Papers, MHM. Charles B. France Papers, WHMC.

12. Pauline Stratton Collection, WHMC. Abiel Leonard Papers, WHMC. William Napton Papers, MHM. Boman, *Abiel Leonard, Yankee Slaveholder, Eminent Jurist, and Passionate Unionist*, 87–88. C. Phillips, *The Making of a Southerner*, 34–35. Elvira Ascenith Weir Scott Diary, 1860–1887, WHMC. For discussions of kinship networks, see Billingsley, *Communities of Kinship*.

13. Slaveholders headed ten of the twelve wealthiest households in New Lebanon. Two nonslaveholding merchants were among the wealthiest individuals, owning thousands of dollars worth of merchandise. All of the slaves living in a household were included when calculating the number of slaves per household. The average slaveholding in Cooper County as a whole was 4.8. There were times when there was more than one slaveholder—often dependents—living in the same household. Population Census and Slave Schedules, 1860 Cooper County, Missouri, United States Census. 1855–1865, Pauline Stratton Collection, WHMC. Cordry, *Descendants of Virginia, Kentucky, and Missouri Pioneers*, 210–24, 342–57. Cordry, *History of New Lebanon, Cooper County, Missouri*, 59–72.

14. The only time that Paulina mentioned her German neighbors was to note that they were the targets of Confederate guerrilla violence during the war. 1855–1865, Pauline Stratton Collection, WHMC. Population Census and Slave Schedules, 1860 Cooper County, Missouri, United States Census. Boonville Turn and Gesang Verein Papers, 1852–1925, WHMC. Levens and Drake, *A History of Cooper County, Missouri*.

15. A sampling of the literature on the slave community includes Blassingame, *The Slave Community;* Camp, *Closer to Freedom;* Escott, *Slavery Remembered;* Fett, *Working Cures;* Fox-Genovese, *Within the Plantation Household;* Genovese, *Roll, Jordan, Roll;* Gutman, *The Black Family in Slavery and Freedom;* Hahn, *A Nation Under Our Feet;* Hudson, *To Have and to Hold;* Jones, *Labor of Love, Labor of Sorrow;* Kolchin, *Unfree Labor;* Joyner, *Down by the Riverside;* Kaye, *Joining Places;* Penningroth, *The Claims of Kinfolk;* Schwalm, *A Hard Fight for We;* and D. G. White, *Ar'n't I a Woman?* For discussions of slavery in small-slaveholding regions, see Dunaway, *Slavery in the*

American Mountain South; Stevenson, *Life in Black and White;* Hahn, *The Roots of Southern Populism;* Fields, *Slavery and Freedom on the Middle Ground;* Campbell, *An Empire for Slavery;* and Inscoe, *Mountain Masters.*

16. See Schreck, "Her Will Against Theirs," and McLaurin, *Celia, a Slave.* See also George Bollinger, *AS,* 11:40–43, and Sarah Waggoner, *AS,* 11:355–64.

17. See Camp, *Closer to Freedom,* and Kaye, *Joining Places.*

18. See *AS,* primarily volume 11 and supp., ser. 1, volume 2, and Civil War Pension Claims, 65th USCT, NA. The words "neighbor" or "neighborhood" are frequently used in the pension records to describe the local community. For examples, see Mat Beasley pen., USCT 65F, NA; Nat Tarrel [alias] / Mat pen., USCT 65D, NA; Alexander Giboney pen., USCT 65E, NA; and Ephraim Craig, Benecke Family Papers, file 2492, WHMC.

19. Matthew Carroll pen., USCT 65C, NA. Jacob Priest pen., USCT 65J, NA.

20. Thomas Vaughn, Benecke Family Papers, file 2646, WHMC. John Jackson pen., USCT 65J, NA. Matthew Carroll pen., USCT 65C, NA. Charles Elliot pen., USCT 65C, NA. Alfred Smith pen., USCT 65C, NA. Caleb Jones, Benecke Family Papers, file 2559, WHMC. For a discussion of slave mobility for work purposes in rural Georgia, see O'Donovan, *Becoming Free in the Cotton South,* 10–58.

21. For a discussion of slavery as a system of bodily and time control, see Camp, *Closer to Freedom;* Kaye, *Joining Places;* and Smith, *Mastered by the Clock.*

22. Flint, *Recollections of the Last Ten Years,* 130. November 21, 1834, Jacob Lanius Journal, WHMC. Pauline Stratton Collection, WHMC. Cordry, *History of New Lebanon.*

23. Thomas Stratton also appears to have withheld financial support from the New Lebanon Cumberland Presbyterian Church. Although she never mentioned it in the diary, Paulina must have been embarrassed to have been one of the few members of the congregation not to support the subscription to raise funds to build a new church building. Her daughters attended the dedication ceremony in June 1860, while she remained at home. See Cordry, *History of New Lebanon,* 19–67, 71–72. May and June 1855, April 20, 1862, Pauline Stratton Collection, WHMC. Jacob Lanius Journal, WHMC. Some historians have argued that many southern men found their wives' evangelical faith threatening to their position as head of the household. For discussions of nineteenth-century American women and religion, see Friedman, *The Enclosed Garden;* Herryman, *Southern Crosses;* Juster, "In a Different Voice," 34–62; A. Mathews, "The Religious Experience of Southern Women"; D. G. Mathews, *Religion in the Old South;* and Welter, "The Feminization of American Religion."

24. Malinda Discus, *AS,* supp., ser. 1, 2:166–70. Isabelle Henderson, *AS,* supp., ser. 1, 2:193–95. See Samuel Smiley Papers, file 37, WHMC. For discussions of enslaved members of southern churches, see D. G. Mathews, *Religion in the Old South;* Snay, *Gospel of Disunion,* 78–109; and Raboteau, *Slave Religion.*

25. For selected examples, see Ethelda Henry Collection, file 1972, WHMC; September and October 1845, Lexington Presbyterian Church Record Book, 1839–51, WHMC; Prairie Point Baptist Church, Cooper County, Missouri, Records, 1842–97, 1913–49, WHMC; and Mt. Nebo Baptist Church, Cooper County, Missouri, May 1829–August 1855, WHMC. For quotations, see 1845, Lexington Presbyterian Church Record Book, 1839–51, WHMC. For a discussion of evangelical courts, see McCurry, *Masters of Small Worlds.*

26. May 1829–August 1855, quotation, July 1836, Mt. Nebo Baptist Church, Cooper County, Missouri, WHMC.

27. For the social-control element of slave conversion, see Gallay, "The Origins of Slaveholders' Paternalism"; Genovese, *Roll, Jordan, Roll,* book 2, part 1; and D. G. Mathews, *Religion in the Old South,* 136–46. Malinda Discus, *AS,* supp., ser. 1, 2:166–70. Louis Hill, *AS,* 11:184–90. Steve Brown, *AS,* 11:56–57. Lewis Mundy, *AS,* 11:258–60. 1855–1865, Pauline Stratton Collection, WHMC. Mount Nebo Baptist Church Records, WHMC. Robert Bryant, *AS,* 11:61–69. Tishey Taylor, *AS,* 11:342–47. December 12, 1838, Jacob Lanius Diaries, 1833–1842, WHMC.

28. See Pauline Stratton Collection, WHMC. For discussions of the duty of evangelical women to convert household members, see P. Johnson, *A Shopkeeper's Millennium,* 99–100, and D. G. Mathews, *Religion in the Old South,* 98–100.

29. April 1, May 2, May 23, and May 25, 1834; June 6, 1835; March 6, 1836; February 18–19, 1837; October 2, 1839; and March 21–22, 1840; Jacob Lanius Diaries, 1833–1842, WHMC. See also Bellamy, "The Persistency of Colonization in Missouri."

30. Jacob Lanius Diaries, 1833–1842, WHMC. Mary Bell, *AS,* 11:25–31. Tishey Taylor, *AS,* 11:342–47. W. C. Parson Allen, *AS,* 11:18–19. See Raboteau, *Slave Religion;* Genovese, *Roll, Jordan, Roll;* D. G. Mathews, *Religion in the Old South;* and Jason R. Young, *Rituals of Resistance.*

31. Malinda Discus, *AS,* supp., ser. 1, 2:166–70. Harriet Casey, *AS,* 11:73–75. For a selected discussion of slave religion, see Genovese, *Roll, Jordan, Roll;* D. G. Mathews, *Religion in the Old South;* Raboteau, *Slave Religion;* and Jason R. Young, *Rituals of Resistance.*

32. Thomas Vaughn pen., USCT 65K, NA. Wyatt Williams, Benecke Family Papers, file 2671, WHMC. Matthew Carroll pen., USCT 65C, NA.

33. Mark Discus, *AS,* supp., ser. 1, 2:171–77. April 20, 1835, October 18, 1836, and July 3–5, 1840, Jacob Lanius Diary, WHMC. Pauline Stratton Collection, WHMC. Matthew Carroll pen., USCT 65E, NA.

34. November 1844, November 1846, April 1850, and December 1860, Archibald Little Hager Diary, WHMC. William Black, *AS,* 11:32–35. "History of Reverend William Murphy and His Descendents, 1798–1958," WHMC. Henry Berry pen., USCT 65F, NA. Matthew Carroll pen., USCT 65C, NA. Bruce, *The New Man,* 74.

35. Emanuel Gatewood pen., USCT 65F, NA. For discussions of slave weddings see O'Neil, "Bosses and Broomsticks"; Fraser, *Courtship and Love among the Enslaved in North Carolina,* 88–100; and E. West, *Chains of Love,* 19–42.

36. Sarah Waggoner, *AS,* 11:355–64. Tishey Taylor, *AS,* 11:342–47. Bruce, *The New Man,* 72. For discussions of the slave community, see Genovese, *Roll, Jordan, Roll;* Blassingame, *The Slave Community;* Camp, *Closer to Freedom;* Joyner, *Down by the Riverside;* Kaye, *Joining Places;* Levine, *Black Culture and Black Consciousness;* and Stuckey, *Slave Culture.*

37. Louis Hamilton, *AS,* 11:145. Eliza Madison, *AS,* 11:241–42. Malinda Discus, *AS,* supp., ser. 1, 2:166–70. Tishey Taylor, *AS,* 11:342–47. Gus Smith, *AS,* 11:321–32. Abiel Leonard to Jeanette Leonard, December 20, 1849; and Nathaniel Leonard to Abiel Leonard, December 29, 1850, and January 5, 1851; Abiel Leonard Papers, WHMC.

38. Mary Leonard and Martha Leonard, October 18, 1846; and Jeanette Leonard to Abiel Leonard, October 17, 1847; Abiel Leonard Papers, WHMC. Fil Hancock, *AS,* 11:147–61. William Wisley/ Riley [alias] pen., USCT 65E, NA. Thomas Vaughn pen., USCT 65K, NA. John W. Fultz / Bruce, Benecke Family Papers, files 2519–20, WHMC. For discussions of slave kin networks, see Gutman, *The Slave Family in Slavery and*

Freedom; Hudson, *To Have and to Hold;* Kaye, *Joining Places;* and Penningroth, *Claims of Kinfolk.*

39. See Civil War Pension Claims, 65th USCT, NA, and Benecke Family Papers, WHMC. For an excellent discussion of the limitations of pension records as a historical source to study slavery, including the fact that some witnesses were paid and some gave fraudulent testimony, see Kaye, *Joining Places,* 14–19.

40. Bruce, *The New Man,* 78–83, 96–98.

41. See H. Frazier, *Slavery and Crime in Missouri; Marshall Democratic,* August 20, 1858, as quoted in Dyer, "A Most Unexampled Exhibition of Madness and Brutality," part 1, 273; Buchanan, *Black Life on the Mississippi,* 19–51, 123–47; and Trexler, *Slavery in Missouri,* 66–68.

42. Bruce, *The New Man,* 99. See also Camp, *Closer to Freedom,* 122–47, and Hahn, *A Nation Under Our Feet,* 13–159. For examples of the slave grapevine, see Rhody Holsell, *AS,* 11:191–202, and Mary Bell, *AS,* 11:25–31.

43. Bruce, *The New Man,* 78–83, 96–98. George Bollinger, *AS,* 11:36–43. See also Mary Bell, *AS,* 11:25–31.

44. See McLaurin, *Celia, a Slave;* Hurt, *Agriculture and Slavery in Missouri's Little Dixie;* Frederick Starr Jr. Papers, 1850–1963, WHMC; Jordan O'Bryan Letter, 1854, WHMC; and Robert M. Stewart Papers, 1858–1860, WHMC. Harriet Casey, *AS,* 11:73–75. Marilda Pethy, *AS,* 11:277–82. Bruce, *The New Man,* 78–83, 96–98. See also Dyer, "A Most Unexampled Exhibition of Madness and Brutality," part 1.

45. The term "rival geography" was coined by Edward Said, in *Culture and Imperialism.* See also Camp, *Closer to Freedom,* 1–34, and Kaye, *Joining Places,* 21–50.

46. Eliza Madison, *AS,* 11:241–42. Tishey Taylor, *AS,* 11:342–47. Marilda Pethy, *AS,* 11:277–82. William Black, *AS,* 11:32–35.

47. Bruce, *The New Man,* 97. See also Camp, *Closer to Freedom,* 60–92.

48. Henry Rodgers pen., USCT 65H, NA. Annie Bridges, *AS,* 11:44–51. Margarett Hughes to Abiel Leonard, March 25, 1850; and P. R. Hayden to Abiel Leonard, May 21, 1849; Abiel Leonard Papers, WHMC. Skinner et al. v. Hughes, Supreme Court of Missouri, July Term, 1850. See also Chariton County Circuit Court Records, B; and Fraser v. State, September 1839; Skinner v. Hughes, March 1850; and State v. Guyott, October 1857; Missouri Supreme Court Cases described in Catteral, *Judicial Cases concerning American Slavery and the Negro,* 5:154–55, 180, and 206. Alfred Smith pen., USCT 65C, NA. See also H. Frazier, *Slavery and Crime in Missouri, 1773–1865,* and Camp, *Closer to Freedom,* 87–89.

49. Eliza Overton, *AS,* 11: 266–68. Fil Hancock, *AS,* 11:147–61. See D. G. Mathews, *Religion in the Old South;* Raboteau, *Slave Religion;* and Jason R. Young, *Rituals of Resistance.*

50. Henry Bruce went on to contend that enslaved Missourians were less susceptible to the wiles of conjurers than enslaved people living in Virginia and what he described as "the more extreme Southern states." He claimed that enslaved Missourians were more intelligent and less superstitious, supporting his argument of a less harsh form of slavery in Missouri. George Bollinger, *AS,* 11:36–43. Tishey Taylor, *AS,* 11:342–47. Bruce, *The New Man,* 52–59. See also Eliza Madison, *AS,* 11:241–42. See Fett, *Working Cures,* 84–108, and Hahn, *A Nation Under Our Feet,* 13–61.

51. Mary Bell, *AS,* 11:25–31. Bruce, *The New Man,* 85–86. See Stone, *Slavery, Southern Culture, and Education in Little Dixie, Missouri,* 38 and 54.

52. Mary Bell, *AS*, 11:25–31. Madison Frederick Ross, *AS*, 11:299–300. Lucinda Patterson, *AS*, 11:269–76. John McGuire, *AS*, 11:238–40. Bruce, *The New Man*, 67. Charlie Richardson, *AS*, 11:290–97. Sarah Waggoner, *AS*, 11:355–64. Smokey Eulenberg, *AS*, 11:109–12. See also George Bollinger, *AS*, 11:36–43.

53. See H. Frazier, *Slavery and Crime in Missouri, 1773–1865*.

54. Ephraim Craig, Benecke Family Papers, file 2492, WHMC. Mat Beasley pen., USCT 65F, NA. Jacob Jacoby pen., USCT 65G, NA.

55. Thomas Vaughn pen., USCT 65K, NA. Henry Whitson pen., USCT 65F, NA. Ira Cottrell pen., USCT 65K, NA. Alfred Smith pen., USCT 65C, NA. Bruce, *The New Man*, 87–88.

56. Frank Cochran pen., USCT 65F, NA. David Cheatham pen., USCT 65F, NA. John Whittenbury pen., USCT 65E, NA. Henry Berry pen., USCT 65F, NA. Sandy Farrer pen., USCT 65E, NA.

57. Benjamin Hubbard pen., USCT 65K, NA. David Cheatham pen., USCT 65F, NA. Jacob Priest pen., USCT 65J, NA. Washington and Moses Combs pens., USCT 65D, NA. Matthew Carroll pen., USCT 65E, NA. John Jackson pen., USCT 65J, NA. See also Isham Parks, Benecke Family Papers, file 2595, WHMC.

58. For information on the political situation in Missouri during the 1850s, see McLaurin, *Celia, a Slave*, 53–67; Hurt, *Agriculture and Slavery in Missouri's Little Dixie*, 273–306; McCandless, *A History of Missouri*, vol. 2; Merkel, "The Antislavery Movement in Missouri, 1819–1865"; Parrish, *Turbulent Partnership;* and Trexler, *Slavery in Missouri*.

59. Gerlach, *Settlement Patterns in Missouri*, 1–30. Bellamy, *Slavery, Emancipation, and Racism in Missouri, 1850–1865*, 82. Northern-born legislators accounted for 14.1 percent of members and foreign-born legislators accounted for 2.5 percent of members. Wooster, *Politics, Planters, and Plain Folk*, 31–32. Hurt, *Agriculture and Slavery in Missouri's Little Dixie*, 220–21.

60. Jordan O'Bryan to John Miller, February 6, 1854, Jordan O'Bryan Letter, 1854, WHMC. Frederick Starr to father and all the others, November 29, 1854; Frederick Starr to father, March 31, 1855; Frederick Starr Jr. Papers, 1850–1863, WHMC. For additional information on the border conflict, see McLaurin, *Celia, a Slave*, 53–67; Hurt, *Agriculture and Slavery in Missouri's Little Dixie*, 273–300; Etcheson, *Bleeding Kansas;* Cassity, *Defending a Way of Life*, 41–42; Robert M. Stewart Papers, 1858–1860, WHMC; and David Atchison Papers, WHMC.

61. Frederick Starr to sister Caroline, December 1, 1852; Frederick Starr to father, August 1, 1854, August 21, 1854, September 19, 1854, January 15, 1855, February 22, 1855, February 26, 1855, March 19, 1855, and March 31, 1855; Frederick Starr to Father, Mother, and boys, October 18, 1854; Frederick Starr to Father and all, October 30, 1854; Frederick Starr to father and all the others, November 29, 1854, and December 29, 1854; Frederick Starr to father, [April 1855]; Frederick Starr Jr. Papers, 1850–1863, WHMC. J. Calvin Iserman to Brother William, October 3, 1858, and September 5, 1858, Iserman Letters, 1858–63, JCHS. W. B. Napton to C. F. Jackson, W. B. Napton Letter, 1857, WHMC. *New Orleans Crescent*, July 5, 1858, as quoted in Deyle, *Carry Me Back*, 86–87. See also Merkel, "The Antislavery Movement in Missouri, 1819–1865."

62. This incident is described in great detail in Thomas Dyer's excellent article. See Dyer, "A Most Unexamined Exhibition of Madness and Brutality," parts 1 and 2; the quotation is found in part 2 on 383.

63. Barbara Fields refers to Maryland as the "middle ground," see Fields, *Slavery and Freedom on the Middle Ground.* See also Parrish, *Turbulent Partnership;* Hurt, *Agriculture and Slavery in Missouri's Little Dixie,* 273–300; Fellman, *Inside War,* 3–22; and Astor, "Belated Confederates," 19–93.

64. William Barclay Napton served on the Missouri State Supreme Court from 1839–1857. W. B. Napton to C. F. Jackson, W. B. Napton Letter, 1857, WHMC.

Chapter 7

1. [Private Spotswood Rice] to My Children, [September 3, 1864], and Spotswood Rice to Kittey Diggs, [September 3, 1864], both enclosed in F. W. Diggs to Genl. Rosecrans, September 10, 1864, D-296 1864, Letters Received, ser. 2593, Dept. of the Missouri, RG 393, Pt. 1, NA, in *The Black Military Experience,* ed. Berlin, Reidy, and Rowland, 689–91. F. W. Diggs, 1860 Howard County, Missouri, United States Census. F. W. Diggs, Slave Schedule, 1860 Howard County, Missouri, United States Census.

2. Postmaster F. W. Diggs to Genl. Rosecrans, September 10, 1864, D-296 1864, Letters Received, ser. 2593, Dept. of the Missouri, RG 393, Pt. 1, NA, in *The Black Military Experience,* ed. Berlin, Reidy, and Rowland, 689–91.

3. Mary Bell, *AS,* 11:25–31.

4. For a discussion of the politics of wartime Missouri and conservative Unionism, see Parrish, *Turbulent Partnership,* 1–76; Astor, "Belated Confederates," 19–93; and Whites, *Gender Matters,* 25–83.

5. See Parrish, *Turbulent Partnership,* 1–76; C. Phillips, *Missouri's Confederate,* 213–73; Siddali, ed., *Missouri's War,* 58–83; and Gerteis, *Civil War St. Louis,* 97–125.

6. A series of military commanders was placed in charge of the St. Louis post during the early years of the war. Nathaniel Lyon twice replaced the more conciliatory General William Harney. General John C. Frémont, the son-in-law of Thomas H. Benton and a friend of the powerful Blair family, eventually replaced Lyon. See Parrish, *Turbulent Partnership,* 1–76.

7. Parrish, *Turbulent Partnership,* 1–76. Fellman, *Inside War.* Astor, "Belated Confederates," 19–162. Geiger, "Missouri's Hidden Civil War." For statistics on Missouri's white population, see Blassingame, "The Recruitment of Negro Troops in Missouri During the Civil War," 326–38.

8. Union troops stationed in Missouri increasingly were sent to military operations in the east. For a discussion of guerrillas, see Parrish, *Turbulent Partnership,* 149–77; Fellman, *Inside War;* Goodrich, *Black Flag;* and Stiles, *Jesse James.*

9. See Fellman, *Inside War;* Astor, "Belated Confederates"; and Taylor, *The Divided Family in Civil War America.*

10. Elvira Ascenith Weir Scott Diary, 1860–1887, WHMC. Bruce, *The New Man,* 103–4, 111. Filler, *The New Stars,* 149. Lizzie E. Brannock to Brother Edwin, January 13, 1864, Lizzie E. Brannock Letters, 1864, WHMC. M. M. Frazier, *Missouri Ordeal,* January 30, 1862, entry. See also Luckett Family Scrapbook, 1854–1936, WHMC; Hardeman, ed., "Bushwhacker Activity on the Missouri Border"; and Fellman, *Inside War.*

11. James Monroe Abbot, *AS,* 11:1–5. Marilda Pethy, *AS,* 11:277–82. George Bollinger, *AS,* 11:36–43. Joe Casey, *AS,* 11:76–78. Rhody Holsell, *AS,* 11:191–202. November 1864, August 1862, and August 1863, Pauline Stratton Collection, WHMC.

12. July 1862, Elvira Ascenith Weir Scott Diary, 1860–1887, WHMC. M. M. Frazier, *Missouri Ordeal,* July 1862.

13. August 1863, Elvira Ascenith Weir Scott Diary, 1860–1887, WHMC. Fellman, *Inside War,* 165. For the motivations of the guerrillas, see Ross, ed., *Autobiography of Samuel S. Hildebrand;* and Fellman, *Inside War.*

14. Wes Lee, *AS,* 11:227–29. 1861–65, Pauline Stratton Collection, WHMC. Fellman, *Inside War,* 44–52.

15. J. B. Colgrove, NA M345 reel 54, Provost Marshal, NA, viewed at MSA, MSA reel F 1141. For information on the Provost Marshal Papers, see the MSA website: http://www.sos.mo.gov/archives/.

16. March 9, 1862, and August and September 1863, Elvira Ascenith Weir Scott Diary, 1860–1887, WHMC. March 12, 1862, Priscilla Thomas Ingram Patton Diary, Patton-Scott Family Papers, WHMC. Fellman, *Inside War,* 39–40, 252.

17. April 26 and July 21, 1862, Elvira Ascenith Weir Scott Diary, 1860–1887, WHMC. M. M. Frazier, *Missouri Ordeal,* November 13, 1862, entry. September 1861, Pauline Stratton Collection, WHMC. See M. E. Neely Jr., *The Fate of Liberty,* 32–50, 168–69, quotation 46; Gerteis, *Civil War St. Louis,* 169–201; and Hesseltine, "Military Prisons in St. Louis, 1861–1865."

18. See also 1st Lieut. Eugene E. Kent to Gen. Fisk, August 9, 1864, Letters Received [No id number on document, located toward back of box], Series 3537, District of North Missouri, Records of U.S. Army Continental Commands, RG 393, Pt. 2, No. 226, NA, viewed at FSSP [C216]. For a description of a similar situation in wartime New Orleans, see Rable, "Missing in Action," and Faust, *Mothers of Invention,* 196–219. For a discussion of the effects of border warfare on gender roles, see Beilein Jr., "The Presence of These Families"; Bowen, "The Changing Role of Protection on the Border"; Kempker, "The Union, the War, and Elvira Scott"; and Whites, "Forty Shirts and a Wagon Load of Wheat."

19. For a discussion of secessionist households' support of guerrillas, see Beilein Jr., "The Presence of These Families." Elvira Ascenith Weir Scott Diary, 1860–1887, WHMC. Priscilla Thomas Ingram Patton Diary, Patton-Scott Family Papers, WHMC.

20. Fellman, *Inside War,* 23–80. Ross, ed., *Autobiography of Samuel S. Hildebrand.* For a discussion of the assault on the sanctity of the household in wartime St. Louis, see Whites, *Gender Matters,* 45–64. See also Niepman, "General Orders No. 11"; Brownlee, *Gray Ghosts of the Confederacy,* 118–19; J. Neely, *The Border Between Them,* 96–131; C. F. Harris, "Catalyst for Terror," 290–305; Castel, "Order Number 11 and the Civil War on the Border"; and Goodrich, *Black Flag,* 60–95.

21. Whites, "Forty Shirts and a Wagon Load of Wheat." Beilein Jr., "The Presence of These Families," 18–19. For information on Missouri refugees and Order No. 11, see Fellman, *Inside War,* 73–80; J. Neely, *The Border Between Them,* 124–25, 145; and Niepman, "General Orders No. 11 and Border Warfare During the Civil War," 96–121. Drew Gilpin Faust has explained that during the Civil War the term refugee was used to describe wealthy southern families who voluntarily fled their homes, whereas those who had fewer resources and little choice were referred to as displaced. I have chosen to use refugee as it is currently used because I believe that the word best describes Missourians' situation. It is my belief that most Missourians left their homes after they were forced out or because they feared for their lives. See Faust, *Mothers of Invention.*

22. Nan P. Cooper, "Mother's Trip Across the Plains," 1901, WHMC. Johnson, *History of Cooper County, Missouri,* 960–61. Cordry, *History of New Lebanon, Cooper County, Missouri,* 89–92. March 1863, Pauline Stratton Collection, WHMC. John D.

Starke, Co. H, 45th Rgt. Missouri Infantry, and Co. B, 48th Rgt. Missouri Infantry, Military Service Records, M 405, Rolls #678 and #687, NA. Mrs. Silliman to My Dear Brother, [1862], Silliman Family Letters, 1862–1865, WHMC. Priscilla Thomas Ingram Patton Diary, Patton-Scott Family Papers, WHMC. Elvira Ascenith Weir Scott Diary, 1860–1887, WHMC. See also Haley Family Papers, WHMC. For Missouri refugees, see Fellman, *Inside War*, 73–80; Benedict, *Jayhawker*; and J. Neely, *The Border Between Them*, 132–70.

23. See Bruce, *The New Man*, 103. See also Astor, "Belated Confederates."

24. Eliot, *The Story of Archer Alexander*, 42–43. Bruce, *The New Man*, 99–100. Jackson, *The Story of Mattie J. Jackson*, 9–13. See also Camp, *Closer to Freedom*, 114–16.

25. Eliot, *The Story of Archer Alexander*, 59. Parrish, *Turbulent Partnership*, 123–48. Mary Bell, *AS*, 11:25–31. See Nelson, "Missouri Slavery, 1861–1865," 260–74. See also Bellamy, "Slavery, Emancipation, and Racism in Missouri."

26. August 1862, Elvira Ascenith Weir Scott Diary, 1860–1887, WHMC. Bruce, *The New Man*, 188, 103.

27. Mrs. Silliman to brother, [1862], Silliman Family Letters, 1862–1865, WHMC. March 1862, Elvira Ascenith Weir Scott Diary, 1860–1887, WHMC. For a discussion of the forays of Kansas troops into Missouri during the war, see Benedict, *Jayhawkers*.

28. For an example of Kansas troops liberating Missouri slaves, see Edward M. Samuel et al. to His Excellency Abraham Lincoln, September 8, 1862, enclosing statement of Edward M. Samuel, September 8, 1862, President 197 1862, Letters Received from the President & Executive Departments, RG 107, NA, in *The Destruction of Slavery*, ed. Berlin et al., 436; and Brig. Gen. B. M. Loan to Lt. Col. C. W. Marsh, September 26, 1862, Letters Sent, Series 3372, vol. 225/525 DMo, p. 34, District of Central Missouri, Records of the U.S. Army Continental Commands, Record Group 393, part 2, NA, viewed at FSSP [C-7123]. Mrs. Waller to friend, February 7, 1863, Coleman-Hayter Family Papers, WHMC. Wylie Miller, *AS*, 11:256–57. 1861–65, Pauline Stratton Collection, WHMC. For an excellent discussion of slaves' recognition of the meaning of the presence of the Union military, see Blight, *A Slave No More*, 1–162.

29. M. M. Frazier, *Missouri Ordeal*, January 15, August 28, October 30, and November 7, 1862. Thos. to My Dear Wife, November 14, 1862, Civil War Letter, WHMC. M. P. Cayce to Maj. Gen. Schofield, July 31, 1863, C-655 1863, Letters Received, ser. 2593, Dept. of the Missouri, RG 393 Pt. 1, NA, in *The Destruction of Slavery*, ed. Berlin et al., 460. See Parrish, *Turbulent Partnership*, 101–21, and McPherson, *Battle Cry of Freedom*, 497–98.

30. Major Genl. H. W. Halleck to General Asboth, December 26, 1861, Vol. 10 DMO, pp. 109–10, Letters sent by Maj. Gen. Henry W. Halleck, ser. 2576, Dept. of the Missouri, RG 393 Pt. 1, NA, in *The Destruction of Slavery*, ed. Berlin et al., 423–24. Col. Jno. C. Kelton to Asst. Ajt. Genl., October 6, 1861, Letters Received, ser. 5486, Western Dept., RG 393 Pt. 1, NA, in *The Destruction of Slavery*, ed. Berlin et al., 416. Brig. Genl. J. M. Schofield to Col. J. O. Kelton, March 3, 1862, S-271 1862, Letters Received, ser. 2593, Dept. of the Missouri, RG 393 Pt. 1, NA, in *The Destruction of Slavery*, ed. Berlin et al., 429. John M. Richardson to Hon. Simon Cameron, December 1, 1861, R-134 1861, Letters Received Irregular, RG 107, NA, in *The Destruction of Slavery*, ed. Berlin et al., 417–19. Major Geo. E. Waring Jr. to Acting Maj. Gen. Asboth, December 19, 1861, enclosed in Actg. Maj. Gen. Asboth to Colonel W. Scott Ketchum, December 23, 1861, A-68, 1861, Letters Received, ser. 2593, Dept. of the Missouri, RG 393 Pt.

1, in *The Destruction of Slavery*, ed. Berlin et al., 421–23. T. A. Russell to Maj. Genl. Halleck, February 12, 1862, enclosed in Col. W. H. Worthington to Captain, February 17, 1862, W-151 1862, Letters Received, ser. 2593, Dept. of the Missouri, RG 393, Pt. 1, NA, in *The Destruction of Slavery*, ed. Berlin et al., 427–29. For a general discussion of Union military policy regarding fugitive slaves in Missouri, see Berlin et al., eds., *The Destruction of Slavery*, 395–412. See also Parrish, *Turbulent Partnership*, 101–21; McPherson, *Battle Cry of Freedom*, 497–98; Gerteis, *From Contraband to Freedman*; Siddali, *From Property to Person*; Berlin et al., eds., *The Wartime Genesis of Free Labor: The Upper South*, 564; and Astor, *Belated Confederates*, 19–93.

31. Capt. Wm. R. Butler to A. A. Genl. Central Division, October 1, 1862, B-18 1862, Letters Received, ser. 2593, Dept. of the Missouri, RG 393 Pt. 1, NA, in *The Destruction of Slavery*, ed. Berlin et al., 437. General Orders, No. 35, Head Quarters, Department of the Missouri, December 24, 1862, Orders & Circulars, ser. 44, RG 94, NA, in *Destruction of Slavery*, ed. Berlin et al., 441–44. John F. Ryland et al. to His Excellency Governor Gamble, June 4, 1863, R-44 1863, Letters Received, ser. 2786, Provost Marshal General, Dept. of the Missouri, RG 393 Pt. 1, NA, in *The Destruction of Slavery*, ed. Berlin et al., 457–58. See also Siddali, *From Property to Person*, and Gerteis, *From Contraband to Freedman*.

32. John R. Moore to Honble. E. M. Stanton, April 5, 1862, M-455 1862, Letters Received, RG 107, in *The Destruction of Slavery*, ed. Berlin et al., 429–31.

33. Charles Jones to His Excellency Abraham Lincoln, March 24, 1863, J-198 1863, Letters Received, RG 107, in *The Destruction of Slavery*, ed. Berlin et al., 450–53. Charles Jones to Gen. Davidson, March 24, 1863, Unentered Letters Received, Series 2594, Dept. of the Missouri, RG 393 Pt. 1, NA, referenced in *The Destruction of Slavery*, ed. Berlin et al., 453, and viewed at FSSP [C-175].

34. Tishey Taylor, *AS*, 11:342–47. For an excellent discussion of the disillusionment of Missouri Unionists, see Astor, "Belated Confederates." Col. Samuel M. Wirt to Brig. Genl. Clinton B. Fisk, April 20, 1864, Letters Received, ser. 3537, Dist. of North Missouri, RG 393 Pt. 2 No. 226, NA, in *The Wartime Genesis of Free Labor*, ed. Berlin et al., 604–5.

35. Richard Kimmons, *AS*, supp., ser. 2, 6.5:293–98.

36. Capt. Stephen E. Jones to Col. Dick, April 15, 1863, B-128 1863, Letters Received, ser. 3514, Dept. of the Ohio, RG 393 Pt. 1, NA, in *The Destruction of Slavery*, ed. Berlin et al., 453–54. Esther Easter, *AS*, 7:88–91. Hattie Matthews, *AS*, 11:249–52. Mark Discus, *AS*, supp., ser. 1, 2:171–77. Henry Bruce claimed that slaves were almost valueless by 1862 because there were no interested buyers. Bruce, *The New Man*, 102. Prime male and female slaves routinely sold for $1000 and above in the years preceding the war. Prime male slaves sold for $300 to $400 in 1863, and less than $200 in 1864. See Nelson, "Missouri Slavery"; Bellamy, "Slavery, Emancipation, and Racism in Missouri"; J. S. Hughes, "Lafayette County and the Aftermath of Slavery"; and John and Phoebe Hopkins, Bill of Sale, 1862, WHMC.

37. M. M. Frazier, *Missouri Ordeal*, December 22, 1862, entry. December 1862, Elvira Ascenith Weir Scott Diary, 1860–1887, WHMC. William Black, *AS*, 11:32–34. Bruce, *The New Man*, 100.

38. For bushwhacker deprivations, see Berlin et al., eds., *The Genesis of Free Labor: The Upper South*, 596–97, 604–5, 616. Brig. Genl. Thomas Ewing, Jr., to Lt. Col. C. W. Marsh, August 3, 1863, B-604, 1863, Letters Received, series 2593, Dept. of the

Missouri, RG 393 Pt. 1, NA, in *The Black Military Experience*, ed. Berlin, Reidy, and Rowland, 228–30. For the rape of Missouri women, see Fellman, *Inside War*, 207–12. Harry Johnson, *AS*, supp., ser. 2, 6.5:1994–2004. Hannah Jones, *AS*, 11:214–17. Eliza Madison, *AS*, 11:241–42.

39. For examples, see William Irwin, NA M345 Reel 140, MSA Reel F 1137, Henry and Lee Ashbrook, NA M345 Reel 10, MSA Reel F 1219, Eli Andrews, NA M345 Reel 8, MSA Reel F 1137, Archer Alexander, NA M345 Reel 4, MSA Reel F 1218, Alex Becker, NA M345 Reel 22, Reel F MSA 1228, Whitney Fowler, NA M345 Reel 96, MSA Reel F 1322, C. M. France, NA M345 Reel 96, MSA Reel F 1322, Provost Marshal, NA, viewed at MSA. See also Nelson, "Missouri Slavery, 1861–1865," and Bellamy, "Slavery, Emancipation, and Racism in Missouri." Asst. Pro. Mar. O. A. A. Gardner to Maj. Genl. Curtis, February 16, 1863, G-34 1863, Letters Received, ser. 2593, Dept. of the Missouri, RG 393 Pt. 1, NA, in *The Destruction of Slavery*, ed. Berlin et al., 445–46. Eliot, *The Story of Archer Alexander*, 46–48. Henry S. Fowler/ Scott [alias] pen., USCT 65E, NA.

40. For examples of the abuse of slave children by soldiers, see Louis Hill, *AS*, 11:184–90; Marilda Pethy, *AS*, 11:277–82; and Wylie Miller, *AS*, 11:256–57. For thefts by guerrillas and soldiers and the work of slave women, see Charlie Richardson, *AS*, 11:290–97; Harriet Casey, *AS*, 11:73–75; Fil Hancock, *AS*, 11:147–61; and Rachal Goings, *AS*, 11:121–24. Robert Bryant, *AS*, 11:61–69. September 1863, Elvira Ascenith Weir Scott Diary, 1860–1887, WHMC. Missouri Sullivan County Papers, 1844–1943, WHMC.

41. John Jackson pen., USCT 65J, NA. In February 1864, the *Columbia Missouri Statesman* reported that enlistment of slave men had been brisk during the previous three months. See "No Color Line." See also Civil War pension claims, 65th USCT, NA. Cullen, "I's a Man Now." For descriptions of the process of enlisting Missouri slaves and their numbers, see Blassingame, "The Recruitment of Negro Troops in Missouri During the Civil War"; Nelson, "Missouri Slavery, 1861–1865"; and Berlin, Reidy, and Rowland, eds., *The Black Military Experience*, 188–89, 236–38. For discussions of African American troops recruited in Kansas, see Tabor, "The Skirmish at Island Mound," and Benedict, *Jayhawkers*. For a discussion of African American households in the postwar South, see Bercaw, *Gendered Freedoms*.

42. Anderson, NA M345 Reel 7, MSA Reel F 1217, Provost Marshal, NA, viewed at MSA. March 1864, Pauline Stratton Collection, WHMC. Stratton filed slave compensation forms for her slave men after the war, and these forms were placed in the soldiers' military service records. The United States Congress passed two acts in 1864 and 1866 providing for financial compensation for loyal slaveholders whose slaves either enlisted ($300) or were drafted ($100) into the Union army. Many former Missouri slaveholders took advantage of this opportunity in the years following the war even if their conduct during the war was less than loyal. Congress established a commission to examine the claims of the thousands of loyal slaveholders, mostly from the border states, who filed claims. In the end, none of the claims were allowed because in 1867, the Republican controlled Congress passed legislation putting an end to the program. Samuel Stratton, military service record, USCT 68E, NA. Lauda Stratton, military service record, USCT 67K, NA. Green Webb, military service record, USCT 67K, NA. For additional information on slave compensations, see Mallory, ed., *Claims by Missourians for Compensation of Enlisted Slaves*.

43. Mary Bell, *AS,* 11:25–31. William Fuller et al. to Maj. General W. S. Rosecrans [February 1864], and Lt. Col. A. Jacobson to Major Genl. Rosecrans, February 17, 1864, J-49 1864, Letters Received, ser. 2593, Dept. of the Missouri, RG 393 Pt. 1, NA, in *The Black Military Experience,* ed. Berlin, Reidy, and Rowland, 238–42. Liet. Jeff A. Mayhall to Col. Jas. O. Broadhead, December 17, 1863, M435, 1863, Letters Received, series 2786, Provost Marshal General, Dept. of the Missouri, Records of the U.S. Continental Commands, RG 393 Pt. 1, NA, viewed at FSSP [C-190]. March 1864, Pauline Stratton Collection, WHMC. Thomas Vaughn pen., USCT 65K, NA. Affidavit of Aaron Mitchell, January 4, 1864, Unentered Letters Received, Series 2574, Dept. of the Missouri, RG 393 Pt. 1, NA, in *The Black Military Experience,* ed. Berlin, Reidy, and Rowland, 237–38. See J. S. Hughes, "Lafayette County and the Aftermath of Slavery, 1861–1870," 54.

44. Ann to My Dear Husband, January 19, 1864, enclosed in Brig. Genl. Wm. A. Pile to Maj. O. D. Greene, February 11, 1864, P-91 1864, Letters Received, ser. 2593, Dept. of the Missouri, RG 393 Pt. 1, NA, the letter is addressed to "Andrew Valentine Co E 2nd Mo Colored Inft A D Benton Barracks St. Louis Mo.," in *The Black Military Experience,* ed. Berlin, Reidy, and Rowland, 686–87. Martha to My Dear Husband [Richard Glover], December 30, 1863, enclosed in Brig. Genl. Wm. A. Pile to Maj. O. D. Greene, February 11, 1864, P-91 1864, Letters Received, ser. 2593, Dept. of the Missouri, RG 393, Pt. 1; and Brig. Genl. Wm. A. Pile to Maj. Genl. Rosecrans, February 23, 1864, enclosed in Brig. Genl. Wm. A. Pile to Maj. O. D. Greene, March 17, 1864, P-197 1864, Letters Received, ser. 2593, Dept. of the Missouri, RG 393 Pt. 1, NA, in *Black Military Experience,* ed. Berlin, Reidy, and Rowland, 244–45.

45. Maj. A. C. Marsh to Col. J. P. Sanderson, April 5, 1864, M-454 1864, Letters Received, ser. 2786, Provost Marshal General, Dept. of the Missouri, RG 393 Pt. 1, in *The Destruction of Slavery,* ed. Berlin et al., 482–83. Lt. A. A. Rice to Col., March 31, 1864, Letters Received, ser. 2786, Provost Marshal General, Dept. of the Missouri, RG 393 Pt. 1, NA, in *The Wartime Genesis of Free Labor,* ed. Berlin et al., 600–601. [Private Spotswood Rice] to My Children, [September 3, 1864]; Spotswood Rice to Kittey diggs, [September 3, 1864]; and F. W. Diggs to Genl. Rosecrans, September 10, 1864, D-296 1864, Letters Received, ser. 2593, Dept. of the Missouri, RG 393, Pt. 1, NA, in *The Black Military Experience,* ed. Berlin, Reidy, and Rowland, 689–91. Sam Bowmen to Dear Wife, May 10, 1864, filed with W-497 1864, Letters Received, ser. 2593, Dept. of the Missouri, RG 393 Pt. 1, in *The Destruction of Slavery,* ed. Berlin et al., 484–86. Asst. Adjt. Genl. J. Rainsford to Brig. Genl. E. B. Brown, March 6, 1864, Unentered Letters Received, ser. 2594, Dept. of the Missouri, RG 393 Pt. 1, dispatch from J. P. Lewis, March 6, 1864, NA, in *The Destruction of Slavery,* ed. Berlin et al., 479–80. Maj. Gen. S. R. Curtis to General, March 13, 1864, Unentered Letters Received, ser. 2594, Dept. of MO, RG 393 Pt. 1, NA, in *The Destruction of Slavery,* ed. Berlin et al., 480–81. See also Greer W. Davis to Major General Curtis, February 24, 1863, D-83 1863, Letters Received, ser. 2593, Dept. of the Missouri, RG 393, Pt. 1, NA, in *The Black Military Experience,* ed. Berlin, Reidy, and Rowland, 449–50. See also Berlin, Reidy, and Rowland, eds., *The Black Military Experience,* 481–86.

46. There were 701 free black men and 20,466 slave men or 21,167 total who were of service age. There were 8,344 men attributed to Missouri regiments. In addition, there were 2,080 Kansas men, 1,811 Illinois men, and 440 Iowa men, many of whom were likely Missouri slaves. See Berlin, Reidy, and Rowland, eds., *The Black Military*

Experience, 12. Affidavit of Aaron Mitchell, January 4, 1864, Unentered Letters Received, Series 2574, Department of the Missouri, RG 393 Pt., NA, in *The Black Military Experience*, ed. Berlin, Reidy, and Rowland, 237–38. See J. S. Hughes, "Lafayette County and the Aftermath of Slavery," 54. For descriptions of the process of enlisting Missouri slave men and their numbers, see Blassingame, "The Recruitment of Negro Troops in Missouri During the Civil War"; Nelson, "Missouri Slavery, 1861–1865"; Berlin, Reidy, and Rowland, eds., *The Black Military Experience*, 188–89, and 236–38; Berlin et al., eds., *The Destruction of Slavery*; quotation found on 409–10. For the end of recruitment in Missouri, see Brig. Genl. Wm. A. Pile to Brig. Genl. L. Thomas, May 21, 1864, P-163 1864, Letters Received, ser. 360, Troops Division, RG 94, in *The Wartime Genesis of Free Labor*, ed. Berlin et al., 607–8; and Lt. J. M. Gavin to Capt. R. L. Ferguson, August 3, 1864, A-162 1864, Letters Received, ser. 2786, Provost Marshal General, Dept. of the Missouri, RG 393 Pt. 1, NA, in *The Black Military Experience*, ed. Berlin, Reidy, and Rowland, 250–51.

47. Richard Booth, NA M345 Reel 30, MSA Reel F 1232, Provost Marshal, NA, viewed at MSA.

48. The historian Earl Nelson estimates that less than 20 percent of Missouri slaves fled the state in the first two years of the war, but in the spring of 1863 "[s]laves left the State in droves." See Nelson, "Missouri Slavery, 1861–1865," 266–70. Bruce, *The New Man*, 108–11. George Johnson, *AS*, supp., ser. 1, 2:115–17. Women and children often followed men to recruitment stations in the free states such as that in Quincy, Illinois, just over the Missouri state line. For quotation from the *Kansas City Journal of Commerce*, April 9 and 21, 1863, see Nelson, "Missouri Slavery, 1861–1865," 269. Berlin et al., eds., *The Genesis of Free Labor*, 586–87. For examples of letters of officers, see Berlin et al., eds., *The Genesis of Free Labor*, 579, 586–92, 595.

49. [Egbert B. Brown] to Major Genl. J. M. Schofield, July 14, 1863, vol. 225/525 DMo, pp. 184–85, Letters Sent, ser. 3372, Dist. of Central Missouri, RG 393 Pt. 2, No. 217, NA, in *The Wartime Genesis of Free Labor*, ed. Berlin et al., 576. Capt. H. B. Johnson to General, August 14, 1863, vol. 186 DMo, Letters Received, ser. 3107, Dist. of the Border, RG 393 Pt. 2 No. 200, NA, in *The Wartime Genesis of Free Labor*, ed. Berlin et al., 577–78. Maj. J. Nelson Smith to 1st Lt. E. L. Burthoud, March 15, 1864, Letters Received, ser. 3379, Dist. of Central Missouri, RG 393 Pt. 2 No. 217, NA, in *The Wartime Genesis of Free Labor*, ed. Berlin et al., 589–90. Lt. J. H. Smith to General E. B. Brown, April 14, 1864, Unentered Letters Received, ser. 2594, Dept. of the Missouri, RG 393 Pt. 1, NA, in *The Wartime Genesis of Free Labor*, ed. Berlin et al., 602. Surg. Robt. Richardson and Capt. Theo. S. Case to General, May 18, 1864, Letters Received, ser. 3379, Dist. of Central Missouri, RG 393 Pt. 2 No. 217, NA, in *The Wartime Genesis of Free Labor*, ed. Berlin et al., 605–7. Schwalm, "Overrun with Free Negroes." Schwalm, *Emancipation's Diaspora*. See also Downs, "The Other Side of Freedom," 78–103.

50. An election was held in November 1864 to choose delegates for the State Constitutional Convention, but southern sympathizers were not allowed to participate. Those elected represented the new face of Missouri's population and politics. Nearly half of the delegates were born in free states or in foreign countries. In contrast, the secession convention of 1861 overwhelmingly consisted of Southerners. See Parrish, *Turbulent Partnership*, 178–207; Nelson, "Missouri Slavery, 1861–1865"; and Emancipation Resolution, Missouri State Constitutional Convention, WHMC.

51. Rhody Holsell, *AS*, 11:191–202. Rachal Goings, *AS*, 11:121–24.

52. Smokey Eulenberg, *AS*, 11:109. Marie Askin Simpson, *AS*, supp., ser. 1, 2:230–34. Tishey Taylor, *AS*, 11:342–47. For discussions of the transition from slavery to freedom and the alteration of relations between slaves and owners, see Foner, *Nothing But Freedom*; Jones, *Labor of Love, Labor of Sorrow*, 11–109; Hahn, *A Nation Under Our Feet*; Hunter, *To Joy My Freedom*; Schwalm, *A Hard Fight for We*, 75–186; and Weiner, *Mistresses and Slaves*, 155–233.

53. Almost a third of the soldiers from three black regiments recruited in Missouri died while in service, see Berlin, Reidy, and Rowland, eds., *The Black Military Experience*, 486–87.

54. Margaret Nickens, *AS*, 11:263–65. Peter Corn, *AS*, 11:85–95. Bartels, *Boone County Colored Marriages, 1865–1882*. Chariton County Marriage Record Book, Volume A and Volume 1-A. Civil War Pension Claims, USCT 65, NA. Annette Curtis provides a transcript of the 1865 marriage statute. See Curtis, *Jackson County, Missouri Marriage Records of Citizens of African Descent, 1865–1881*. For an example of Missouri schools, see Mary Phelps to Brig. Gen. J. W. Sprague, March 10, 1866, and Brig. Gen. J. W. Sprague to Maj. Genl. O. O. Howard, March 27, 1866 [Phelps letter forwarded to Howard], P-530 1866, Letters Received, ser. 231, Arkansas Assistant Commissioner, Records of the Bureau of Refugees, Freedmen, and Abandoned Lands, RG 105, NA, viewed at FSSP [A-2292]. Mary Bell, *AS*, 11:25–31. For a discussion of freedpeople's postwar households, see Bercaw, *Gendered Freedoms*.

55. Lucinda Patterson was bought before the war, likely in 1860, five years earlier. Delicia Ann Wiley [Lucinda] Patterson, *AS*, 11:269–76. Mat Beasley pen., USCT 65F, NA. Charlie Richardson, *AS*, 11:296–97. Schreck, "Her Will Against Theirs." Malinda Discus, *AS*, supp., ser. 1, 2:166–70. Louis Hill, *AS*, 11:184–90. See also Roark, *Masters Without Slaves*; Foner, *Nothing But Freedom*; Astor, "Belated Confederates"; and Hahn, *A Nation Under Our Feet*.

56. Delicia Ann Wiley [Lucinda] Patterson, *AS*, 11:269–76. Marilda Pethy, *AS*, 11:277–82. August 28, 1866, July 27, 1867, February 23, 1868, and March 29, 1869, Pauline Stratton Collection, WHMC. Clay Smith, *AS*, 11:318–20. Lewis Mundy, *AS*, 11:258–60. Charles Douthit, *AS*, 11:107. Gus Smith, *AS*, 11:321–32. See also Missouri Civil War Pension Claims, NA.

57. Brig. Genl. Clinton B. Fisk to Jas. E. Yeatman, Esq., March 25, 1865, vol. 284 DMo, p. 276, Letters Sent, ser. 3530, Dist. of North Missouri, RG 393 Pt. 2, No. 226, NA, in *The Destruction of Slavery*, ed. Berlin et al., 489. F. T. Russell to Gen'l., February 21, 1865, Letters Received, ser. 3537, Dist. of North Missouri, RG 393 Pt. 2 No. 226; and J. H. Lathrop to Gen. Clinton Fisk, March 8, 1865, Unentered Letters Received, ser. 2594, Dept. of the Missouri, RG 393 Pt. 1, NA, in *The Wartime Genesis of Free Labor: The Upper South*, ed. Berlin et al., 616–19. General Orders No. 7, Head Quarters 4, Sub. Dist., Cent. D, Mo.., April 25, 1865, vol. 383/942 DMo, General Orders, ser. 3367, 4th Subdist. of Central Missouri, RG 393 Pt. 2 No. 216, NA, in Berlin et al., ed., *The Wartime Genesis of Free Labor: The Upper South*, 622. Astor includes Callaway, Boone, Howard, Cooper, Chariton, Saline, and Lafayette Counties in his population statistics for Little Dixie. He also observes that the population of Kansas grew from "625 African Americans in 1860 to 17,108 in 1870." For population statistics, see Astor, "Belated Confederates," 196–97. See also table 7 for population changes in the ten Missouri counties with the largest slave populations.

58. Bruce, *The New Man*. See Schwalm, "Overrun with Free Negroes," and Schwalm, *Emancipation's Diaspora*.

59. See Frizzell, "Southern Identity in Nineteenth-Century Missouri"; Neely, *Divided in the Middle*, 132–252; Geiger, "Missouri's Hidden Civil War," 142–98; and Astor, "Belated Confederates," 162–336. M. W. Eaton, "The Development and Later Decline of the Hemp Industry in Missouri." 1865–1870, Pauline Stratton Collection, WHMC.

60. Neely, *Divided in the Middle*, 132–252; Geiger, "Missouri's Hidden Civil War," 142–98; Astor, "Belated Confederates," 162–336; G. Andrews, "The Radical Politics of Reconstruction in Ralls County, Missouri, 1865–1870"; and C. Phillips, *Missouri's Confederate*.

61. For a discussion of postwar Missouri, see Astor, "Belated Confederates," and J. Neely, *The Border Between Them*. See also Missouri Division of the United Daughters of the Confederacy, *Reminiscences of the Women of the Sixties*. For a discussion of the memory of the Civil War, see Blight, *Race and Reunion*.

62. For discussions of African Americans' lives in postwar Missouri, see Greene, Kremer, and Holland, *Missouri's Black Heritage*, 75–139; Schreck, "Her Will Against Theirs"; Christensen, "Black Education in Civil War St. Louis"; and McKerley, "Citizens and Strangers."

63. August 31 and September 1863, Elvira Ascenith Weir Scott Diary, 1860–1887, WHMC.

BIBLIOGRAPHY

Primary Archives

JCHS
Jackson County Historical Society
Independence, Missouri

DU
Manuscript Department
William R. Perkins Library
Duke University
Durham, North Carolina

FSSP
Freedmen and Southern Society
    Project
University of Maryland
College Park, Maryland

MHM
Missouri History Museum
Library and Research Center
St. Louis, Missouri

MSA
Missouri State Archives, Jefferson
    City, Missouri

NA
National Archives
Washington, D. C.

SHC
Southern Historical Collection
University of North Carolina
Chapel Hill, North Carolina

WHMC
Western Historical Manuscript
    Collection
University of Missouri
Columbia, Missouri

Published Primary Sources

Andrews, William L., ed. *Six Women's Slave Narratives.* Oxford: Oxford University Press, 1988.

Atherton, Lewis E., ed. "Life, Labor, and Society in Boone County, Missouri, 1834–52, As Revealed in the Correspondence of an Immigrant Slave Owning Family from North Carolina." Part 1. *Missouri Historical Review* 38 (April 1944): 277–304.

———, ed. "Life, Labor, and Society in Boone County, Missouri, 1834–52, As Revealed in the Correspondence of an Immigrant Slave Owning Family from North Carolina." Part 2. *Missouri Historical Review* 38 (July 1944): 408–29.

Babcock, Rufus. *Forty Years of Pioneer Life.* Carbondale: Southern Illinois University Press, 1965.

Bartels, Carolyn M. *Boone County Colored Marriages, 1865–1882.* Shawnee Mission, Kans.: Carolyn M. Bartels, 1980s.

———, comp. *Missouri: Just Married: Cooper County, Missouri, 1848–1867.* Shawnee Mission, Kans.: Carolyn M. Bartels, 1988.

Beck, Lewis C. *A Gazetteer of the States of Illinois and Missouri.* Albany, N.Y.: C. R. and G. Webster, 1823.

Berlin, Ira, Joseph Patrick Reidy, and Leslie S. Rowland, eds. *Freedom: A Documentary History of Emancipation, 1861–1867. Series II. The Black Military Experience.* Cambridge: Cambridge University Press, 1982.

Berlin, Ira, et al., eds. *Freedom: A Documentary History of Emancipation, 1861–1867.* Series 1, vol. 1, *The Destruction of Slavery.* Cambridge: Cambridge University Press, 1985.

———. *Freedom: A Documentary History of Emancipation, 1861–1867.* Series 1, vol. 2, *The Wartime Genesis of Free Labor: The Upper South.* Cambridge: Cambridge University Press, 1993.

Blassingame, John W., ed. *Slave Testimony: Two Centuries of Letters, Speeches, Interviews, and Autobiographies.* Baton Rouge: Louisiana State University Press, 1977.

"Boon's Lick Country: Two Gospel Preachers Explore a New Settlement." *Missouri Historical Society Bulletin* 6 (July 1950): 442–90.

Brackenridge, Henry Marie. *Recollections of Persons and Places in the West.* Philadelphia: James Kay, Jun., and Brother, 1834.

Breeden, James O., ed., *Advice among Masters: The Ideal in Slave Management in the Old South.* Westport, Conn.: Greenwood Press, 1980.

Brown, William W. *Narrative of William W. Brown.* Boston: Antislavery Office, 1847.

———. *The Narrative of William W. Brown.* London: Charles Gilpin, 1849.

Bruce, Henry C. *The New Man: Twenty-Nine Years a Slave, Twenty-Nine Years a Free Man: Recollections of H. C. Bruce.* York, Penn.: A. G. Brown, 1880.

Burr, Virginia Ingraham, ed. *The Secret Eye: The Journal of Ella Gertrude Clanton Thomas, 1848–1889.* Chapel Hill: University of North Carolina Press, 1990.

Carson, Wm. G. B., ed. "The Diary of Matt Field." Part 1. *Missouri Historical Society Bulletin* 5 (January 1949): 91–108.

———, ed. "The Diary of Matt Field." Part 2. *Missouri Historical Society Bulletin* 5 (April 1949): 157–84.

Catteral, Helen Tunnicliff. *Judicial Cases concerning American Slavery and the Negro.* Vol. 5. Washington, D.C.: Carnegie Institution of Washington, 1937.

Clamorgan, Cyprian. *The Colored Aristocracy of St. Louis.* Edited by Julie Winch. 1858. Reprint, Columbia: University of Missouri Press, 1999.

Compendium of the Enumeration of the Inhabitants and Statistics of the United States. Washington: Thomas Allen, 1841.

Cornet, Florence D., ed. "The Experiences of a Midwest Salesman in 1836." *Missouri Historical Society Bulletin* 29 (July 1973): 227–35.

Curtis, Annette W. *Jackson County, Missouri, Marriage Records of Citizens of African Descent, 1865–1881.* Independence, Mo.: J. C. Eakin, c. 1992.

DeBow, J. D. B. *The Seventh Census of the United States: 1850.* Washington: Robert Armstrong, 1853.

Delaney, Lucy. *From the Darkness Cometh the Light or Struggles for Freedom.* St. Louis: J. T. Smith, c. 1891.

Douglass, Frederick. *Narrative of the Life of Frederick Douglass, An American Slave. Written by Himself.* Reprint, Garden City, N.Y.: Anchor Books, 1973.

Doy, John. *The Narrative of John Doy, of Lawrence, Kansas.* New York: Thomas Holman, 1860.

Drew, Benjamin. *A North-Side View of Slavery: The Refugee: or the Narratives of Fugitive Slaves in Canada.* Boston: J. P. Jewett, 1856.

Duden, Gottfried. *Report on a Journey to the Western States of North America and a Stay of Several Years Along the Missouri (During the Years 1824, '25, '26, '27).* An English translation, edited by James W. Goodrich et al. Reprint, Columbia: University of Missouri Press, 1965.

Edwards, Tyron, and William Bueel Sprague, ed. *The World's Laconics; Or, the Best Thoughts of the Best Authors.* New York: M. W. Dodd, 1853.

Eliot, William G. *The Story of Archer Alexander: From Slavery to Freedom.* Boston: Cupples, Upham, 1885.

Erickson, Charlotte. *Invisible Immigrants: The Adaptation of English and Scottish Immigrants in Nineteenth-Century America.* Ithaca, N.Y.: Cornell University Press, 1972.

Filler, Louis, ed. *The New Stars: Life and Labor in Old Missouri.* Yellow Springs, Ohio: Antioch Press, 1949.

Flint, Timothy. *Recollections of the Last Ten Years in the Valley of the Mississippi.* Edited by George Brooks. Reprint, Carbondale: Southern Illinois University Press, 1968.

Frazier, Margaret Mendenhall, ed. *Missouri Ordeal, 1862–1864, Diaries of Willard Hall Mendenhall.* Newhall, Calif.: Carl Boyer, 1985.

Fuller, Berenice M. *Missouri Plantation Life.* St. Louis: Missouri Historical Society, 1935.

Gustorf, Frederick. *The Uncorrupted Heart: Journals and Letters of Frederick Julius Gustorf.* Columbia: University of Missouri Press, 1969.

Hardeman, Nicholas P., ed. "Bushwhacker Activity on the Missouri Border: Letters to Dr. Glen O. Hardeman, 1862–1865." *Missouri Historical Review* 58 (April 1964): 265–77.

Hawkins v. The State. *Reports of Cases Argued and Determined in the Supreme Court of the State of Missouri from 1840–1842 by S. M. Bay, Attorney General and ex officio Reporter.* Vol. 3. Edited by Louis Houck. St. Louis: Gilbert Book Co.

Isley, Elise Dubach. *Sunbonnet Days.* Caldwell, Idaho: Caxton Printers, 1935.

Jackson, Mattie. *The Story of Mattie J. Jackson.* Recorded by Dr. L. S. Thompson (formerly Mrs. Schuyler). Lawrence, Mass.: Lawrence Sentinel Office, 1866.

Jefferson, Thomas. *Notes on the State of Virginia, 1781–1782.*

Jensen, Dana O., ed. "I At Home, By Stephen Hempstead, Sr." *Missouri Historical Society Bulletin,* part 1, 13 (October 1956): 30–56; part 2, 13 (April 1957): 283–317; part 3, 14 (October 1957): 59–96; part 4, 14 (April 1958): 272–88; part 5, 15 (October 1958): 38–48; part 6, 15 (April 1959): 224–47; part 7, 22 (October 1965): 61–94; part 8, 22 (January 1966): 180–206; and part 9, 22 (July 1966): 410–45.

Jervey, Edward D., and James E. Moss, eds. "From Virginia to Missouri in 1846: The Journal of Elizabeth Ann Cooley." *Missouri Historical Review* 60 (January 1966): 162–206.

Kennedy, Joseph C. G. *Agricultural Census of the United States in 1860; Compiled from the Original Returns of the Eighth Census.* Washington: Government Printing Office, 1864.

Krug, Mark M., ed. *Mrs. Hill's Journal—Civil War Reminiscences.* Chicago: R. R. Donnelly and Sons, 1980.

Laws of a Public and General Nature of the State of Missouri Passed Between 1824 and 1836. 2 vols. Vol. 2. Jefferson City, Mo.: Lusk and Son, 1842.

Laws of the State of Missouri; Revised and Digested by Authority of the General Assembly in Two Volumes. Vol. 1. St. Louis: E. Charless for the State, 1825.

Missouri Division, United Daughters of the Confederacy, comp. *Reminiscences of the Women of Missouri during the Sixties.* Dayton, Ohio: Morning House Press, 1988.

"No Color Line." *Missouri Historical Review* 38 (July 1944): 497.

O'Bryan v. O'Bryan. *Reports of Cases Argued and Determined in the Supreme Court of the State of Missouri by William Robards, Attorney General and ex-officio Reporter.* Vol. 13. Edited by Louis Houck. Cape Girardeau, Mo., 1871

O'Hanlon, John. *Life and Scenery in Missouri.* Dublin: James Duffy, 1890.

Overdyke, W. Darrell, ed. "A Southern Family on the Missouri Frontier: Letters from Independence, 1843–1855." *Journal of Southern History* 17 (May 1951): 216–37.

Peck, J[ohn] M[ason]. *Forty Years of Pioneer Life: Memoir of John Mason Peck.* Introduction by Paul M. Harrison. Reprint, Carbondale: Southern Illinois University Press, 1965.

———. *A Guide for Emigrants: Containing Sketches of Illinois, Missouri, and Adjacent Parts.* Boston: Lincoln and Edmands, 1831.

Phillips, Christopher, and Jason L. Pendleton, eds. *The Union on Trial: The Political Journals of Judge William Barclay Napton, 1829–1883.* Columbia: University of Missouri Press, 2005.

Rawick, George P., ed. *The American Slave: A Composite Autobiography.* 41 vols. Westport, Conn.: Greenwood Press, 1977.

Ross, Kirby, ed. *Autobiography of Samuel S. Hildebrand.* 1870. Reprint, Fayetteville: University of Arkansas Press, 2005.

Schroeder, Adolf E., and Carla Schultz-Geisberg, eds. *Hold Dear, As Always: Jette, a German Immigrant Life in Letters.* Columbia: University of Missouri Press, 1988.

Shippee, Lester B., ed. *Bishop Whipple's Southern Diary.* Reprint, New York: Da Capo, 1965.

Steele, Mrs. *A Summer Journey.* New York: John S. Taylor, 1841.

Stowe, Harriet Beecher. *Uncle Tom's Cabin, or, Life among the Lowly.* 1852.

Thompson, George. *Prison Life and Reflections.* Oberlin, Ohio: James M. Fitch, 1847.

Twain, Mark. *The Adventures of Huckleberry Finn.* 1884.

Wetmore, Alphonso. *Gazetteer of the State of Missouri.* St. Louis: C. Keemle, 1837.

Windell, Marie G., ed. "The Road West in 1818, the Diary of Henry Vest Bingham." Part 1. *Missouri Historical Review* 40 (October 1945): 21–54.

———, ed. "The Road West in 1818, the Diary of Henry Vest Bingham." Part 2. *Missouri Historical Review* 40 (January 1946): 172–204.

Secondary Sources

Ames, Kenneth L. *Death in the Dining Room and Other Tales of Victorian Culture.* Philadelphia: Temple University Press, 1992.

Andrews, Gregg. "The Radical Politics of Reconstruction in Ralls County, Missouri, 1865–1870," in *The Other Missouri History: Populists, Prostitutes, and Regular Folk,* 8–30. Columbia: University of Missouri Press, 2004,

Aptheker, Herbert. *American Negro Slave Revolts.* Reprint, New York: International Publishers, 1952.

Aron, Stephen. *American Confluence: The Missouri Frontier from Borderland to Border State.* Bloomington: Indiana University Press, 2006.

———. *How the West Was Lost: The Transformation of Kentucky from Daniel Boone to Henry Clay.* Baltimore: Johns Hopkins University Press, 1996.

Astor, Aaron. "Belated Confederates: Black Politics, Guerrilla Violence, and the

Collapse of Conservative Unionism in Kentucky and Missouri, 1860–1872."
PhD diss., Northwestern University, 2006.

Bancroft, Frederic. *Slave-Trading in the Old South*. Baltimore: J. H. Furst, 1931.

Baptist, Edward. *Creating an Old South: Middle Florida's Frontier before the Civil War*. Chapel Hill: University of North Carolina Press, 2002.

Bardaglio, Peter W. *Reconstructing the Household: Family, Sex, and the Law in the Nineteenth-Century South*. Chapel Hill: University of North Carolina Press, 1995.

Barton, Keith C. "'Good Cooks and Washers': Slave Hiring, Domestic Labor, and the Market in Bourbon County, Kentucky." *Journal of American History* 84 (September 1997): 436–60.

Beilein, Joseph M., Jr. "'The Presence of These Families Is the Cause of the Presence There of the Guerrillas': The Influence of Little Dixie Households on the Civil War in Missouri." MA thesis, University of Missouri, 2006.

Belko, Stephen. *The Invincible Duff Green: Whig of the West*. Columbia: University of Missouri Press, 2006.

Bellamy, Donnie D. "The Persistency of Colonization in Missouri." *Missouri Historical Review* 72 (October 1977): 1–24.

———. "Slavery, Emancipation, and Racism in Missouri. 1850–65." PhD diss., University of Missouri, 1971.

Benedict, Bryce. *Jayhawkers: The Civil War Brigade of James Henry Lane*. Norman: University of Oklahoma Press, 2009.

Bercaw, Nancy. *Gendered Freedoms: Race, Rights, and the Politics of Household in the Delta, 1861–1875*. Gainesville: University Press of Florida, 2003.

Berlin, Ira. *Generations of Captivity: A History of African-American Slaves*. Cambridge, Mass.: Belknap Press, 2003.

———. *Many Thousands Gone: The First Two Centuries of Slavery in North America*. Cambridge, Mass.: Belknap Press, 1998.

———. *Slaves Without Masters: The Free Negro in the Antebellum South*. New York: Pantheon Books, 1974.

Berry, Daina Ramey. *Swing the Sickle for the Harvest Is Ripe: Gender and Slavery in Antebellum Georgia*. Urbana: University of Illinois Press, 2007.

Bierbaum, Milton E. "Frederick Starr, a Missouri Border Abolitionist: The Making of a Martyr." *Missouri Historical Review* 58 (April 1964): 309–25.

Billingsley, Carolyn Earle. *Communities of Kinship: Antebellum Families and the Settlement of the Cotton Frontier*. Athens: University of Georgia Press, 2004.

Blandin, Mrs. I. M. E. *History of Higher Education of Women in the South Prior to 1860*. Reprint, Washington, D.C.: Zenger, 1975.

Blassingame, John W. "The Recruitment of Negro Troops in Missouri during the Civil War." *Missouri Historical Review* 58 (April 1964): 326–38.

———. *The Slave Community: Plantation Life in the Antebellum South*. New York: Oxford University Press, 1979.

Bleser, Carol, ed. *In Joy and Sorrow: Women, Family, and Marriage in the Victorian South*. New York: Oxford University Press, 1991.

Blight, David W. *Race and Reunion*. Cambridge, Mass.: Belknap Press, 2001.

———. *A Slave No More: Two Men Who Escaped to Freedom*. Orlando: Harcourt, 2007.

Boman, Dennis K. *Abiel Leonard, Yankee Slaveholder, Eminent Jurist, and Passionate Unionist*. Lewiston, N.Y.: Edwin Mellen Press, 2002.

Bowen, Rebekah Weber. "The Changing Role of Protection on the Border: Gender and the Civil War in Saline County." In *Women in Missouri History: In Search of Power and Influence*, ed. LeeAnn Whites, Mary C. Neth, and Gary R. Kremer, 119–33. Columbia: University of Missouri Press, 2004.

Boydston, Jeanne. *Home and Work: Housework, Wages, and the Ideology of Labor in the Early Republic*. New York: Oxford University Press, 1990.

Brownlee, Richard S. *Gray Ghosts of the Confederacy: Guerrilla Warfare in the West, 1861–1865*. Baton Rouge: Louisiana State University Press, 1958.

Buchanan, Thomas C. *Black Life on the Mississippi: Slaves, Free Blacks, and the Western Steamboat World*. Chapel Hill: University of North Carolina Press, 2004.

Burke, Diane Mutti. "'Mah pappy belong to a neighbor': The Effects of Abroad Marriages on Missouri Slave Families." In *Searching for Their Places: Women in the South Across Four Centuries*, ed. Thomas H. Appleton Jr. and Angela Boswell. Columbia: University of Missouri Press, 2003.

———. "'May we as one family live in peace and harmony': Relations between Mistresses and Slave Women on Missouri's Farms, 1821–1865." In *Women in Missouri History: In Search of Power and Influence*, ed. LeeAnn Whites, Mary C. Neth, and Gary R. Kremer. Columbia: University of Missouri Press, 2004.

Burton, Orville Vernon. *In My Father's House Are Many Mansions: Family and Community in Edgefield, South Carolina*. Chapel Hill: University of North Carolina Press, 1985.

Burton, W. J. *The History of the Missouri Pacific Railroad*. St. Louis, 1956.

Bynum, Victoria. *Free State of Jones: Mississippi's Longest Civil War*. Chapel Hill: University of North Carolina Press, 2002.

———. *Unruly Women: The Politics of Social and Sexual Control in the Old South*. Chapel Hill: University of North Carolina Press, 1992.

Byrne, Frank J. *Becoming Bourgeois: Merchant Culture in the South, 1820–1865*. Lexington: University of Kentucky Press, 2006.

Camp, Stephanie H. M. *Closer to Freedom: Enslaved Women and Everyday Resistance in the Plantation South*. Chapel Hill: University of North Carolina Press, 2004.

Campbell, Randolph B. *An Empire for Slavery: The Peculiar Institution in Texas, 1821–1865*. Baton Rouge: Louisiana State University Press, 1989.

———. "Research Notes: Slave Hiring in Texas," *American Historical Review* 93 (February 1988): 107–14.

Carter, Christine Jacobson. *Southern Single Blessedness: Unmarried Women in the Urban South, 1800–1865.* Urbana: University of Illinois Press, 2006.

Carter, Dan T. *When the War Was Over: The Failure of Self-Reconstruction in the South, 1865–1867.* Baton Rouge: Louisiana State University Press, 1985.

Cashin, Joan E. *A Family Venture: Men and Women on the Southern Frontier.* Oxford: Oxford University Press, 1991.

———. "The Structure of Antebellum Planter Families: 'The Ties That Bound Us Was Strong.'" *Journal of Southern History* 56 (February 1990): 55–70.

Cassity, Michael. *Defending a Way of Life: An American Community in the Nineteenth Century.* Albany: State University of New York Press, 1989.

Castel, Albert. "Order Number 11 and the Civil War on the Border." In *The Civil War in Missouri,* ed. William E. Parrish, Columbia: The State Historical Society of Missouri, 2006, 140–52.

Catteral, Helen Tunnicliff. *Judicial Cases concerning American Slavery and the Negro.* Vol. 5. Reprint, New York: Negro Universities Press, 1968.

Censer, Jane Turner. *North Carolina Planters and Their Children, 1800–1860.* Baton Rouge: Louisiana State University Press, 1984.

Christensen, Lawrence O. "Black Education in Civil War St. Louis," in *The Civil War in Missouri,* ed. William E. Parrish, Columbia: The State Historical Society of Missouri, 2006, 168–84.

Clinton, Catherine. "Equally Their Due: The Education of the Planter Daughter in the Early Republic." *Journal of the Early Republic* 2 (April 1982): 39–60.

———. *The Plantation Mistress: Women's World in the Old South.* New York: Pantheon Books, 1982.

Conard, Howard Lewis. *Encyclopedia of the History of Missouri.* Vol. 4. St. Louis: Southern History, 1901.

Cordry, Eugene Allen. *Descendants of Virginia, Kentucky, and Missouri Pioneers.* Eugene Allen Cordry, 1973.

———. *History of New Lebanon, Cooper County, Missouri.* Fort Worth, Texas: VKM Publishing, 1976.

Cott, Nancy. *The Bonds of Womanhood: Woman's Sphere in New England, 1780–1835.* New Haven: Yale University Press, 1977.

Cozzens, Authur. "The Iron Industry in Missouri." *Missouri Historical Review* 35 (1941): 509–38, and 36 (1942): 48–60.

Craven, Avery. "The Turner Theories and the South." *Journal of Southern History* 5 (1939): 291–314.

Crawford, Stephen. "Quantified Memory: A Study of the W.P.A. and Fisk University Slave Narrative Collections." PhD diss., University of Chicago, 1980.

Crighton, John C. *A History of Columbia and Boone County.* Columbia, Mo.: Computer Color-Graphics, 1987.

Cullen, Jim. "'I's a Man Now': Gender and African American Men." In *Divided Houses: Gender and the Civil War,* ed. Catherine Clinton and Nina Silber, 76–91. New York: Oxford University Press, 1992.

Cutler, William G. *History of the State of Kansas*. Labette County, part 10, kancoll.org/books, cutler/labette.

D'Emilio, John, and Estelle B. Freedman. *Intimate Matters: A History of Sexuality in America*. New York: Harper and Row, 1988.

Dempsey, Terrell. *Searching for Jim: Slavery in Sam Clemens' World*. Columbia: University of Missouri Press, 2003.

Dew, Charles B. *Bond of Iron: Master and Slave at Buffalo Forge*. New York: W. W. Norton, 1994.

Deyle, Steven. *Carry Me Back: The Domestic Slavery Trade in American Life*. New York: Oxford University Press, 2005.

Dorsett, Lyle W. "Slaveholding in Jackson County, Missouri." *Bulletin of the Missouri Historical Society* 20 (October 1963): 25–37.

Downs, Jim. "The Other Side of Freedom: Destitution, Disease, and Dependency among Freedwomen and Their Children during and after the Civil War," in *Battle Scars: Gender and Sexuality in the American Civil War*, ed. Catherine Clinton and Nina Silber. New York: Oxford University Press, 2006.

Duffner, Robert W. "Slavery in Missouri River Counties, 1820–1865." PhD diss., University of Missouri, 1974.

Dunaway, Wilma. *The African-American Family in Slavery and Emancipation*. Cambridge: Cambridge University Press, 2003.

———. *Slavery in the American Mountain South*. Cambridge: Cambridge University Press, 2003.

Dunson, A. A. "Notes on the Missouri Germans on Slavery." *Missouri Historical Review* 59 (April 1965): 335–66.

Dyer, Thomas. "'A Most Unexampled Exhibition of Madness and Brutality': Judge Lynch in Saline County, Missouri, 1859." Part 1. *Missouri Historical Review* 89 (April 1995): 269–89.

———. "'A Most Unexampled Exhibition of Madness and Brutality': Judge Lynch in Saline County, Missouri, 1859." Part 2. *Missouri Historical Review* 89 (July 1995): 367–83.

Earle, Jonathan. *John Brown's Raid on Harper's Ferry*. New York: Bedford St. Martins, 2008.

Eaton, Clement. "Slave-Hiring in the Upper South: A Step toward Freedom." *Mississippi Valley Historical Review* 46 (March 1960): 663–78.

Eaton, Miles W. "The Development and Later Decline of the Hemp Industry in Missouri." *Missouri Historical Review* 43 (July 1949): 344–59.

Edwards, Laura. *Gendered Strife and Confusion: The Political Culture of Reconstruction*. Urbana: University of Illinois Press, 1997.

———. *Scarlett Doesn't Live Here Anymore: Southern Women in the Civil War Era*. Urbana: University of Illinois Press, 2000.

Elkins, Stanley. *Slavery: A Problem in American Institutional and Intellectual Life*. Chicago: University of Chicago Press, 1959.

Engerman, Stanley, and Eugene Genovese, eds. *Race and Slavery in the Western Hemisphere: Quantitative Studies*. Princeton, N.J.: Princeton University Press, 1975.

Escott, Paul D. *Slavery Remembered: A Record of Twentieth-Century Slave Narratives*. Chapel Hill: University of North Carolina Press, 1979.

Essah, Patience. *A House Divided: Slavery and Emancipation in Delaware, 1638–1865*. Charlottesville: University Press of Virginia, 1996.

Etcheson, Nicole. *Bleeding Kansas: Contested Liberty in the Civil War Era*. Lawrence: University Press of Kansas, 2004.

Faragher, John Mack. "History from the Inside Out: Writing the History of Women in Rural America." *American Quarterly* 33 (Winter 1981): 537–57.

———. *Sugar Creek: Life on the Illinois Prairie*. New Haven: Yale University Press, 1986.

Farnham, Christie Anne. *The Education of the Southern Belle: Higher Education in the Antebellum South*. New York: New York University Press, 1994.

Faust, Drew Gilpin. *James Henry Hammond and the Old South: A Design for Mastery*. Baton Rouge: Louisiana State University Press, 1982.

———. *Mothers of Invention: Women of the Slaveholding South in the American Civil War*. Chapel Hill: University of North Carolina Press, 1996.

Fellman, Michael. *Inside War: The Guerrilla Conflict in Missouri during the American Civil War*. New York: Oxford University Press, 1989.

Fett, Sharla. *Working Cures: Healing, Health, and Power on Southern Slave Plantations*. Chapel Hill: University of North Carolina Press, 2002.

Fields, Barbara Jeanne. *Slavery and Freedom on the Middle Ground: Maryland during the Nineteenth Century*. New Haven: Yale University Press, 1985.

Finley, M. I. *Ancient Slavery and Modern Ideology*. New York: Penguin Books, 1980.

Finkelman, Paul. *Dred Scott v. Sandford: A Brief History with Documents*. New York: Bedford St. Martins, 1997.

Fischer, David Hackett. *Albion's Seed: Four British Folkways in America*. New York: Oxford University Press, 1989.

Fischer, David Hackett, and James C. Kelly. *Bound Away: Virginia and the Westward Movement*. Charlottesville: University of Virginia Press, 2000.

Flanders, Ralph Betts. *Plantation Slavery in Georgia*. Chapel Hill: University of North Carolina Press, 1933.

Fogel, Robert. *Without Consent or Contract*. New York: W. W. Norton, 1989.

Fogel, Robert, and Stanley Engerman. *Time on the Cross: The Economics of American Negro Slavery*. Boston: Little, Brown, 1974.

Foley, William E. *The Genesis of Missouri: From Wilderness Outpost to Statehood*. Columbia: University of Missouri Press, 1989.

———. *A History of Missouri*. Vol. 1, *1673–1820*. Columbia: University of Missouri Press, 1971.

Foner, Eric. *Nothing But Freedom: Emancipation and Its Legacy.* Baton Rouge: Louisiana State University Press, 1983.

———. *Reconstruction: America's Unfinished Revolution.* New York: Harper and Row, 1988.

Forbes, Robert Pierce. *The Missouri Compromise and Its Aftermath.* Chapel Hill: University of North Carolina Press, 2007.

Ford, Lacy K., Jr. *Origins of Southern Radicalism: The South Carolina Upcountry, 1800–1860.* New York: Oxford University Press, 1988.

Formanek-Brunell, Miriam. *Made to Play House: Dolls and the Commercialization of American Girlhood.* New Haven: Yale University Press, 1993.

Foster, Helen Bradley. *New Raiments of Self: African American Clothing in the Antebellum South.* New York: Berg Publishers, 1997.

Foushee, Kenneth. "Some Aspects of Slavery and the Slave Law in Antebellum Missouri." MA thesis, Southeast Missouri State University, 1973.

Fox-Genovese, Elizabeth. *Within the Plantation Household: Black and White Women of the Old South.* Chapel Hill: University of North Carolina Press, 1988.

———. "Women in Agriculture during the Nineteenth Century." In *Agriculture and National Development,* ed. Lou Ferleger. Ames: Iowa State University Press, 1990.

Fox-Genovese, Elizabeth, and Eugene Genovese. *The Fruits of Merchant Capitalism: Slavery and Bourgeois Property in the Rise and Expansion of Capitalism.* New York: Oxford University Press, 1983.

———. *The Mind of the Master Class: History and Faith in the Southern Slaveholders' Worldview.* Cambridge: Cambridge University Press, 2005.

Franklin, John Hope, and Loren Schweninger. *Runaway Slaves: Rebels on the Plantation.* New York: Oxford University Press, 1999.

Fraser, Rebecca J. *Courtship and Love among the Enslaved in North Carolina.* Jackson: University Press of Mississippi, 2007.

Frazier, Harriet. *Runaway and Freed Missouri Slaves and Those Who Helped Them, 1763–1865.* Jefferson, N.C.: McFarland, 2004.

———. *Slavery and Crime in Missouri, 1773–1865.* Jefferson, N.C.: McFarland, 2001.

Fredrickson, George. "Masters and Mudsills: The Role of Race in the Planter Ideology of South Carolina." In *The Arrogance of Race: Historical Perspectives on Slavery, Racism, and Social Inequality.* Middletown, Conn.: Wesleyan University Press, 1988.

Friedman, Jean E. *The Enclosed Garden: Women and Community in the Evangelical South, 1830–1900.* Chapel Hill: University of North Carolina Press, 1985.

Friend, Craig Thompson, and Lorri Glover, eds. *Southern Manhood: Perspectives on Masculinity in the Old South.* Athens: University of Georgia Press, 2004.

Frizzell, Robert W. "Southern Identity in Nineteenth-Century Missouri: Little Dixie's Slave-Majority Areas and the Transition to Midwestern Farming." *Missouri Historical Review* 99 (April 2006): 238–60.

Fuenfhausen, Gary Gene. *The Cotton Culture of Missouri's Little Dixie, 1810–1865, and Growing Upland Cotton in Central Missouri.* Boonville, Mo.: Little Dixie Publications, 2001.

Gallay, Alan. "The Origins of Slaveholders' Paternalism: George Whitefield, the Bryan Family, and the Great Awakening in the South." *Journal of Southern History* 54 (August 1987): 371–94.

Gaspar, David Barry, and Darlene Clark Hine, eds. *More Than Chattel: Black Women and Slavery in the Americas.* Bloomington: Indiana University Press, 1996.

Geiger, Mark W. "Missouri's Hidden Civil War: Financial Conspiracy and the Decline of the Planter Elite, 1861–1865." PhD diss., University of Missouri, 2006.

Genovese, Eugene D. *From Rebellion to Revolution: Afro-American Slave Revolts in the Making of the New World.* New York: Vintage Books, 1981.

———. *The Political Economy of Slavery: Studies in the Economy and Society of the Slave South.* New York: Pantheon Books, 1965.

———. *Roll, Jordan, Roll: The World the Slaves Made.* New York: Pantheon Books, 1974.

———. *The World the Slaveholders Made: Two Essays in Interpretation.* New York: Pantheon Books, 1969.

Gerlach, Russel L. *Settlement Patterns in Missouri.* Columbia: University of Missouri Press, 1986.

Gerteis, Louis. *Civil War St. Louis.* Lawrence: University Press of Kansas, 2001.

———. *From Contraband to Freedman: Federal Policy toward Southern Blacks, 1861–1865.* Westport, Conn.: Greenwood Press, 1973.

Gibson, Campbell, and Kay Jung. "Historical Census Statistics on Population Totals by Race, 1790 to 1990, and by Hispanic Origin, 1970 to 1990, for the United States, Regions, Divisions, and States." www.census.gov.

Giffen, Jerena East. "Add a Pinch and a Lump: Missouri Women in the 1820s." *Missouri Historical Review* 65 (July 1971): 478–504.

Glover, Lorri. "'Let Us Manufacture Men': Educating Elite Boys in the Early National South." In *Southern Manhood: Perspectives on Masculinity in the Old South,* ed. Craig Thompson Friend and Lorri Glover, 22–48. Athens: University of Georgia Press, 2004.

Glymph, Thavolia. *Out of the House of Bondage: The Transformation of the Plantation Household.* New York: Cambridge University Press, 2008.

Goldfarb, Stephen J. "A Note on Limits to the Growth of the Cotton-Textile Industry in the Old South." *Journal of Southern History* 48 (November 1982): 544–46.

Goldin, Claudia Dale. *Urban Slavery in the American South, 1820–1860: A Quantitative History.* Chicago: University of Chicago Press, 1976.

Goodrich, Thomas. *Black Flag: Guerrilla Warfare on the Western Border, 1861–1865.* Bloomington: Indiana University Press, 1995.

Gray, Lewis Cecil. *History of Agriculture in the Southern United States to 1860.* 2 vols. New York: Peter Smith, 1941.

Green, Barbara L. "The Slavery Debate in Missouri, 1831–1855." PhD diss., University of Missouri, 1980.

Greenberg, Kenneth. *Honor and Slavery: Lies, Duels, Noses, Masks, Dressing as a Woman, Gifts, Strangers, Humanitarianism, Death, Slave Rebellions, the Proslavery Argument, Baseball, Hunting, and Gambling in the Old South.* Princeton, N.J.: Princeton University Press, 1996.

Greene, Lorenzo J., Gary R. Kremer, and Antonio F. Holland. *Missouri's Black Heritage.* St. Louis: Forum Press, 1980.

Greven, Phillip J. *The Protestant Temperament: Patterns of Child-Rearing, Religious Experience, and the Self in Early America.* New York: Knopf, 1977.

Gudmestad, Robert. *A Troublesome Commerce: The Transformation of the Interstate Slave Trade.* Baton Rouge: Louisiana State University Press, 2003.

Gutman, Herbert G. *The Black Family in Slavery and Freedom, 1750–1925.* New York: Pantheon Books, 1976.

Hadden, Sally E. *Slave Patrols: Law and Violence in Virginia and the Carolinas.* Cambridge, Mass.: Harvard University Press, 2001.

Hahn, Steven. *A Nation Under Our Feet: Black Political Struggles in the Rural South from Slavery to the Great Migration.* Cambridge, Mass.: Harvard University Press, 2003.

———. *The Roots of Southern Populism: Yeoman Farmers and the Transformation of the Georgia Upcountry, 1850–1890.* New York: Oxford University Press, 1983.

Hardeman, Nicholas Perkins. *Wilderness Calling: The Hardeman Family in the American Westward Movement, 1750–1900.* Knoxville: University of Tennessee Press, 1977.

Harris, Charles F. "Catalyst for Terror: The Collapse of the Women's Prison in Kansas City." *Missouri Historical Review* 89 (April 1995): 290–305.

Harris, Jennifer, ed. *5,000 Years of Textiles: An International History and Illustrated Survey.* New York: Harry N. Abrams, 1993.

Harris, J. William. *Plain Folk and Gentry in a Slave Society: White Liberty and Black Slavery in Augusta's Hinterlands.* Middletown, Conn.: Wesleyan University Press, 1985.

Haskell, J. G. "The Passing of Slavery in Western Missouri." *Transactions of the Kansas State Historical Society* 7 (1901–2): 28–39.

Herryman, Christine. *Southern Crosses: The Beginnings of the Bible Belt.* New York: Alfred A. Knopf, 1997.

Hesseltine, William B. "Military Prisons in St. Louis, 1861–1865." In *The Civil War in Missouri: Essays from the Missouri Historical Review, 1906–2006,* ed. William E. Parrish, 121–39. Columbia: State Historical Society of Missouri, 2006.

Hilliard, Sam Bowers. *Atlas of Antebellum Agriculture*. Baton Rouge: University of Louisiana Press, 1984.

Hodes, Martha. *White Women, Black Men: Illicit Sex in the Nineteenth-Century South*. New Haven: Yale University Press, 1997.

Hood, Adrienne D. *The Weaver's Craft: Cloth, Commerce, and Industry in Early Pennsylvania*. Philadelphia: University of Pennsylvania Press, 2003.

Houck, Louis. *A History of Missouri*. Chicago: R. R. Donnelley and Sons, 1908.

Hudson, John C. *Making the Corn Belt: A Geographical History of Middle-Western Agriculture*. Bloomington: Indiana University Press, 1994.

Hudson, Larry. *To Have and to Hold: Slave Work and Family Life in Antebellum South Carolina*. Athens: University of Georgia Press, 1997.

Hughes, John Sarrett. "Lafayette County and the Aftermath of Slavery, 1861–1870." *Missouri Historical Review* 75 (October 1980): 51–63.

———. "Slavery and Emancipation in Lafayette County, Missouri." MA thesis, St. Louis University, 1955.

Hughes, Sarah S. "Slaves for Hire: The Allocation of Black Labor in Elizabeth City County, Virginia, 1782–1810." *William and Mary Quarterly* 35 (April 1978): 260–86.

Hunter, Lloyd A. "Slavery in St. Louis, 1804–1860." *Bulletin of the Missouri Historical Society* 30 (July 1944): 233–65.

Hunter, Tera. *To Joy My Freedom: Southern Black Women's Lives and Labors after the Civil War*. Cambridge, Mass.: Harvard University Press, 1997.

Hurt, Douglas. *Agriculture and Slavery in Missouri's Little Dixie*. Columbia: University of Missouri Press, 1992.

Inscoe, John. *Mountain Masters, Slavery, and the Sectional Crisis in Western North Carolina*. Knoxville: University of Tennessee Press, 1989.

Jabour, Anya. *Scarlett's Sisters: Young Women in the Old South*. Chapel Hill: University of North Carolina Press, 2007.

Jensen, Joan. *Promised to the Land: Essay on Rural Women*. Albuquerque: University of New Mexico Press, 1991.

———. *With These Hands: Women Working on the Land*. New York: Feminist Press, 1981.

Johnson, Paul. *A Shopkeeper's Millennium: Society and Revival in Rochester, New York, 1815–1837*. New York: Hill and Wang, 1978.

Johnson, W. F. *History of Cooper County, Missouri*. 1 vol. Topeka: Historical Publishing, 1919.

———. *History of Cooper County, Missouri*. Vols. 1 and 2. Reprint, Fort Worth, Texas: VKM Publishing, 1978.

Johnson, Walter Livezey. "Masters and Slaves in the Market: Slavery and the New Orleans Trade, 1804–1864." PhD diss., Princeton University, 1995.

———. *Soul by Soul: Life Inside the Antebellum Slave Market*. Cambridge, Mass.: Harvard University Press, 1999.

Jones, Jacqueline. *Labor of Love, Labor of Sorrow.* New York: Basic Books, 1985.

Jordan, Winthrop. *White Over Black: American Attitudes toward the Negro, 1580–1812.* Chapel Hill: University of North Carolina Press, 1868.

Joyner, Charles. *Down by the Riverside: A South Carolina Slave Community.* Urbana: University of Illinois Press, 1984.

Juster, Susan. "'In a Different Voice': Male and Female Narratives of Religious Conversion in Post-Revolutionary America." *American Quarterly* 41 (March 1989): 34–62.

Kaye, Anthony. *Joining Places: Slave Neighborhoods in the Old South.* Chapel Hill: University of North Carolina Press, 2007.

Kempker, Erin. "The Union, the War, and Elvira Scott." *Missouri Historical Review* 95 (April 2001): 287–301.

Kennington, Kelly. "River of Injustice: St. Louis's Freedom Suits and the Changing Nature of Legal Slavery in Antebellum America." PhD diss., Duke University, 2009.

Kerber, Linda. "Separate Spheres, Female Worlds, Woman's Place: The Rhetoric of Women's History." *Journal of American History* 75 (June 1988): 9–39.

———. *Women of the Republic: Intellect and Ideology in Revolutionary America.* Chapel Hill: University of North Carolina, 1980.

King, Wilma. *Stolen Childhood: Slave Youth in Nineteenth Century America.* Bloomington: Indiana University Press, 1995.

Kolchin, Peter. *American Slavery, 1619–1877.* New York: Hill and Wang, 1993.

———. *Unfree Labor: American Slavery and Russian Serfdom.* Cambridge, Mass.: Belknap Press, 1987.

Krauthamer, Barbara. "In Their 'Native Country': Freedpeople's Understandings of Culture and Citizenship in the Choctaw and Chickasaw Nations." In *Crossing Waters, Crossing Worlds: The African Diaspora in Indian Country,* ed. Tiya Miles and Sharon P. Holland, 100–120. Durham, N.C.: Duke University Press, 2006.

Kulikoff, Allan. *Tobacco and Slaves: The Development of Southern Cultures in the Chesapeake, 1860–1800.* Chapel Hill: University of North Carolina Press, 1986.

Laver, Harry S. "Refuge of Manhood: Masculinity and the Militia Experience in Kentucky," in *Southern Manhood: Perspectives on Masculinity in the Old South,* ed. Craig Thompson Friend and Lorri Glover, 1–21. Athens: University of Georgia Press, 2004.

Lee, George F. "Slavery and Emancipation in Lewis County, Missouri." *Missouri Historical Review* 65 (April 1971): 294–317.

Lemmer, George. "Agitation for Agricultural Improvement in Central Missouri Newspapers Prior to the Civil War." *Missouri Historical Review* 37 (July 1943): 371–85.

———. "Early Leaders in Livestock Improvement in Missouri." *Missouri Historical Review* 37 (October 1942): 29–39.

———. "Farm Machinery in Antebellum Missouri." *Missouri Historical Review* 40 (July 1946): 467–80.

Levens, Henry C., and Nathaniel M. Drake. *A History of Cooper County, Missouri.* St. Louis: Perrin and Smith, 1876.

Levine, Lawrence W. *Black Culture and Black Consciousness: Afro-American Folk Thought from Slavery to Freedom.* Oxford: Oxford University Press, 1977.

Libby, David J. *Slavery and Frontier Mississippi, 1720–1835.* Jackson: University Press of Mississippi, 2004.

Mallory, Rudena Kramer. *Claims by Missourians for Compensation of Enlisted Slaves.* Kansas City, Mo.: Rudena Kramer Mallory, 1992.

Malone, Ann Patton. *Sweet Chariot: Slave Family and Household Structure in Nineteenth-Century Louisiana.* Chapel Hill: University of North Carolina Press, 1991.

Marshall, Howard Wright. *Folk Architecture in Little Dixie: A Regional Culture in Missouri.* Columbia: University of Missouri Press, 1981.

Marten, James. *The Children's Civil War.* Chapel Hill: University of North Carolina Press, 1998.

Martin, Edeen. "Frontier Marriage and the Status Quo." *Westport Historical Quarterly* (March 1975): 99–108.

Martin, Jonathan D. *Divided Mastery: Slave Hiring in the American South.* Cambridge, Mass.: Harvard University Press, 2004.

Mathews, Alice. "The Religious Experience of Southern Women." In *Women and Religion in America,* vol. 2. *The Colonial and Revolutionary Periods,* ed. Rosemary Radford Ruether and Rosemary Skinner Keller. San Francisco: Harper and Row, 1983.

Mathews, Donald G. *Religion in the Old South.* Chicago: University of Chicago Press, 1977.

May, Katja. *African Americans and Native Americans in the Creek and Cherokee Nation, 1830 to 1920s: Collision and Collusion.* New York: Garland, 1996.

McCandless, Perry. *A History of Missouri.* Vol. 2, *1820–1860.* Columbia: University of Missouri Press, 1972.

McCardell, John. *The Idea of a Southern Nation: Southern Nationalists and Southern Nationalism, 1830–1860.* New York: W. W. Norton, 1979.

McCurdy, Frances Lea, *Stump, Bar, and Pulpit: Speechmaking on the Missouri Frontier.* Columbia: University of Missouri Press, 1969.

McCurry, Stephanie. *Masters of Small Worlds: Yeoman Households, Gender Relations, and Political Culture of the Antebellum South Carolina Low Country.* Oxford: Oxford University Press, 1995.

———. "Producing Dependence: Women, Work, and Yeomen Households in Low-Country South Carolina." In *Neither Lady Nor Slave: Working Women of the Old South,* ed. Susanna Defino and Michele Gillespie, 55–71. Chapel Hill: University of North Carolina Press, 2002.

McGettigan, James W., Jr. "Boone County Slaves: Sales, Estate Divisions, and Families, 1820–1865." Part 1. *Missouri Historical Review* 72 (January 1978): 176–97.

———. "Boone County Slaves: Sales, Estate Divisions, and Families, 1820–1865." Part 2. *Missouri Historical Review* 72 (April 1978): 271–95.

———. "Slave Sales, Estate Divisions, and the Slave Family in Boone County, Missouri, 1820–1865." MA thesis, University of Missouri, 1976.

McKerley, John. "Citizens and Strangers: The Politics of Race in Missouri from Slavery to the Era of Jim Crow." PhD diss., University of Iowa, 2008.

McLaurin, Melton A. *Celia, a Slave: A True Story of Violence and Retribution in Antebellum Missouri*. Athens: University of Georgia Press, 1991.

McMillen, Sally G. *Motherhood in the Old South: Pregnancy, Childbirth, and Infant Rearing*. Baton Rouge: Louisiana State University Press, 1990.

———. "Mothers' Sacred Duty: Breast-feeding Patterns among Middle- and Upper-Class Women in the Antebellum South." *Journal of Southern History* 51 (August 1985): 333–56.

———. *Southern Women: Black and White in the Old South*. Arlington Heights, Ill.: Harlan Davidson, 1992.

McPherson, James M. *Battle Cry of Freedom: The Civil War Era*. New York: Oxford University Press, 1988.

Merkel, Benjamin G. "The Abolition Aspects of Missouri's Antislavery Controversy, 1819–1865." *Missouri Historical Review* 44 (April 1950): 232–53.

———. "Antislavery and Abolition in Missouri, 1819–1854: A Preliminary Study." MA thesis, Washington University, 1932.

———. "The Antislavery Movement in Missouri, 1819–1865." PhD diss., Washington University, 1939.

———. "The Underground Railroad and the Missouri Borders, 1840–1860." *Missouri Historical Review* 37 (April 1943): 271–85.

Miller, Elinor, and Eugene Genovese, eds. *Plantation, Town, and Country: Essays on the Local History of American Slave Society*. Urbana: University of Illinois Press, 1974.

Miller, James. *South by Southwest: Planter Emigration and Identity in the Slave South*. Charlottesville: University of Virginia Press, 1991.

Mintz, Steven. *Huck's Raft: A History of American Childhood*. Cambridge, Mass.: Belknap Press, 2004.

Mohr, Clarence. *On the Threshold of Freedom: Masters and Slaves in Civil War Georgia*. Athens: University of Georgia Press, 1986.

Morgan, Edmund S. *American Slavery, American Freedom: The Ordeal of Colonial Virginia*. New York: W. W. Norton, 1975.

Morgan, Jennifer L. *Laboring Women: Reproduction and Gender in New World Slavery*. Philadelphia: University of Pennsylvania Press, 2004.

Morgan, Philip. *Slave Counterpoint: Black Culture in the Eighteenth-Century Chesapeake and Lowcounty*. Chapel Hill: Published for the Omohundro Institute of Early American History and Culture, by the University of North Carolina Press, 1998.

Nagel, Paul C. *Missouri: A Bicentennial History.* New York: Norton, 1977.

Naylor-Ojurongbe, Celia. "'Born and Raised among These People, I Don't Want to Know Any Other': Slaves' Acculturation in Nineteenth-Century Indian Territory." In *Confounding the Color Line: The Indian-Black Experience in North America,* ed. James F. Brooks, 161–91. Lincoln: University of Nebraska Press, 2002.

Neely, Jeremy. *The Border Between Them: Violence and Reconciliation on the Kansas-Missouri Line.* Columbia: University of Missouri Press, 2007.

———. "Divided in the Middle: A History of the Kansas-Missouri border, 1854–1896." PhD diss., University of Missouri–Columbia, 2004.

Neely, Mark E., Jr. *The Fate of Liberty: Abraham Lincoln and Civil Liberties.* New York: Oxford University Press, 1991.

Nelson, Earl J. "Missouri Slavery, 1861–1865." *Missouri Historical Review* 28 (July 1934): 260–74.

Niepman, Ann Davis. "General Orders No. 11 and Border Warfare During the Civil War." In *Kansas City, America's Crossroads: Essays from the Missouri Historical Review, 1906–2006,* ed. Diane Mutti Burke and John P. Herron, 96–121. Columbia: University of Missouri Press, 2007.

Niven, Steven. "From Ota Benga to Elmo: One Writer's Journey through the AANB," oxfordaasc.com.

Nord, David Paul. "Religious Reading and Readers in Antebellum America," *Journal of the Early Republic* 15 (Summer 1995): 241–72.

Oakes, James. *The Ruling Race: A History of American Slaveholders.* New York: Vintage Books, 1983.

———. *Slavery and Freedom: An Interpretation of the Old South.* New York: Vintage Books, 1991.

O'Donovan, Susan. *Becoming Free in the Cotton South.* Cambridge, Mass.: Harvard University Press, 2007.

O'Neil, Patrick. "Bosses and Broomsticks: Ritual and Authority in Antebellum Slave Weddings," *Journal of Southern History* 75 (February 2009): 29–48.

Orloff, Ann S. *The Politics of Pensions: A Comparative Analysis of Britain, Canada, and the United States, 1880–1940.* Madison: University of Wisconsin Press, 1993.

Osterud, Nancy Grey. *Bonds of Community: The Lives of Farm Women in Nineteenth-Century New York.* Ithaca, N.Y.: Cornell University Press, 1991.

Otto, John Solomon. "The Migration of the Southern Plain Folk: An Interdisciplinary Synthesis." *Journal of Southern History* 51 (May 1985): 183–200.

Owsley, Frank Lawrence. *Plain Folk of the Old South.* Baton Rouge: Louisiana State University Press, 1949.

Palmer, R. R. *The World of the French Revolution.* New York, Harper, 1971.

Parent, Anthony, Jr. *Foul Means: The Formation of a Slave Society in Virginia, 1660–1740.* Chapel Hill: University of North Carolina Press, 2003.

Parrish, William E. *Turbulent Partnership: Missouri and the Union, 1861–65.* Columbia: University of Missouri Press, 1963.

Patterson, Orlando. *Slavery and Social Death: A Comparative Study.* Cambridge, Mass.: Harvard University Press, 1982.

Penningroth, Dylan. *The Claims of Kinfolk: African American Property and Community in the Nineteenth-Century South.* Chapel Hill: University of North Carolina Press, 2003.

Petrillo, Lauren. "Missouri Schoolgirls, 1840–1870: 'The Breath of enchantment was lingering near us.'" Undergraduate capstone paper, University of Missouri–Kansas City, 2008.

Phifer, Edward W. "Slavery in Microcosm: Burke County, North Carolina." In *American Negro Slavery: A Modern Reader,* ed. Allen Weinstein. New York: Oxford University Press, 1968.

Phillips, Christopher. *The Making of a Southerner: William Barclay Napton's Private Civil War.* Columbia: University of Missouri Press, 2007.

———. *Missouri's Confederate: Claiborne Fox Jackson and the Creation of Southern Identity in the Border West.* Columbia: University of Missouri Press, 2000.

Phillips, Ulrich B. *American Negro Slavery.* Baton Rouge: Louisiana State University Press, 1966.

Poole, Stafford, and Douglas J. Slawson. *Church and Slave in Perry County, Missouri, 1818–1865.* Lewiston, N.Y.: Edwin Mellen Press, 1986.

Potts, Louis. "Franklin Debate Society: Culture on the Missouri Frontier." *Missouri Historical Review* 86 (October 1991): 1–21.

Pritchett, Jonathan B. "Quantitative Estimates of the United States Interregional Slave Trade, 1820–1860." *Journal of Economic History* 61 (June 2001).

Purdue, Theda. *Mixed Blood Indians: Racial Constructions in the Early South.* Athens: University of Georgia Press, 2003.

Rable, George. "'Missing in Action': Women of the Confederacy." In *Divided Houses: Gender and the Civil War,* ed. Catherine Clinton and Nina Silber, 134–46. New York: Oxford University Press, 1992.

Raboteau, Albert J. *Slave Religion: The "Invisible Institution" in the Antebellum South.* Oxford: Oxford University Press, 1978.

Rawick, George. *From Sundown to Sunup: The Making of the Black Community.* Westport, Conn.: Greenwood, 1972.

Reichard, Maximilian. "Black and White on the Urban Frontier: The St. Louis Community in Transition, 1800–1830." *Missouri Historical Society Bulletin* 33 (October 1976): 3–17.

Reynolds, Donald. *Texas Terror: The Slave Insurrection Panic of 1860 and the Secession of the Lower South.* Baton Rouge: Louisiana State University Press, 2007.

Roark, James L. *Masters Without Slaves: Southern Planters in the Civil War and Reconstruction.* New York: W. W. Norton, 1977.

Rothman, Adam. *Slave Country: American Expansion and the Origins of the Deep South.* Cambridge, Mass.: Harvard University Press, 2005.

Rothman, Joshua D. *Notorious in the Neighborhood: Sex and Families across the Color Line in Virginia, 1787–1861.* Chapel Hill: University of North Carolina Press, 2003.

Ryan, Mary. *Cradle of the Middle Class: The Family in Oneida County, New York, 1790–1865.* Cambridge: Cambridge University Press, 1981.

Said, Edward. *Culture and Imperialism.* New York: Knopf, 1993.

Saville, Julie. *The Work of Reconstruction: From Slave to Wage Laborer in South Carolina, 1860–1870.* New York: Cambridge University Press, 1994.

Savitt, Todd L. *Medicine and Slavery: The Diseases and Health Care of Blacks in Antebellum Virginia.* Urbana: University of Illinois Press, 1978.

Scarpino, Philip V. "Slavery in Callaway County, Missouri: 1845–1855." Part 1. *Missouri Historical Review* 71 (October 1976): 22–43.

———. "Slavery in Callaway County, Missouri: 1845–1855." Part 2. *Missouri Historical Review* 72 (April 1977): 267–83.

Schantz, Mark S. "Religious Tracts, Evangelical Reform, and the Market Revolution in Antebellum America." *Journal of the Early Republic* 17 (Fall 1997): 425–66.

Schreck, Kimberly. "Her Will Against Theirs: Eda Hickam and the Ambiguity of Freedom in Postbellum Missouri." In *Beyond Image and Convention: Explorations in Southern Women's History,* ed. Janet L. Coryell et al. Columbia: University of Missouri Press, 1998.

———. "Splitting Heirs: Gender, Race, and the Properties of Unreconstructed Households." PhD diss., University of Missouri, 2004.

Schwalm, Leslie. *Emancipation's Diaspora: Race and Reconstruction in the Upper Midwest.* Chapel Hill: University of North Carolina Press, 2009.

———. *A Hard Fight for We: Women's Transition from Slavery to Freedom in South Carolina.* Urbana: University of Illinois Press, 1997.

———. "'Overrun with Free Negroes': Emancipation and Wartime Migration in the Upper Midwest." *Civil War History* 50, no. 2 (2004): 145–74.

Schwartz, Marie Jenkins. *Birthing a Slave: Motherhood and Medicine in the Antebellum South.* Cambridge, Mass.: Harvard University Press, 2006.

———. *Born in Bondage: Growing Up Enslaved in the Antebellum South.* Cambridge, Mass.: Harvard University Press, 2000.

Schwartz, Philip J. *Migrants Against Slavery: Virginians and the Nation.* Charlottesville: University Press of Virginia, 2001.

Scott, Anne Firor. *The Southern Lady: From Pedestal to Politics.* Chicago: University of Chicago Press, 1970.

Scott, James C. *Weapons of the Weak: Everyday Forms of Peasant Resistance.* New Haven: Yale University Press, 1985.

Sengupta, Gunja. *For God and Mammon: Evangelicals and Entrepreneurs, Masters and Slaves in Territorial Kansas, 1854–1860.* Athens: University of Georgia Press, 1996. Shoemaker, Floyd Calvin. *Missouri's Struggle for Statehood, 1804–1821.* Reprint, New York: Russell and Russell, 1969.

Siddali, Silvana R. *From Property to Person: Slavery and the Confiscation Acts, 1861–1862.* Baton Rouge: Louisiana State University Press, 2005.

———, ed. *Missouri's War: The Civil War in Documents.* Athens: Ohio University Press, 2009.

Skocpol, Theda. *Protecting Soldiers and Mothers: The Political Origins of Social Policy in the United States.* Cambridge, Mass.: Harvard University Press, 1993.

Smith, Mark. *Mastered by the Clock: Time, Slavery, and Freedom in the American South.* Chapel Hill: University of North Carolina Press, 1997.

Smith-Rosenberg, Carroll. *Disorderly Conduct: Visions of Gender in Victorian America.* New York: Oxford University Press, 1986.

Snay, Mitchell. *Gospel of Disunion: Religion and Separatism in the Antebellum South.* Chapel Hill: University of North Carolina Press, 1993.

Sommerville, Diane Miller. *Rape and Race in the Nineteenth-Century South.* Chapel Hill: University of North Carolina Press, 2004.

Spindel, Donna J. "Assessing Memory: Twentieth-Century Slave Narratives Reconsidered." *Journal of Interdisciplinary History* 27 (Autumn 1996): 247–61.

Stampp, Kenneth. *The Peculiar Institution: Slavery in the Antebellum South.* New York: Knopf, 1956.

Starobin, Robert S. *Industrial Slavery in the Old South.* New York: Oxford University Press, 1970.

Steckel, Richard H. *The Economics of U.S. Slave and Southern White Fertility.* New York: Garland, 1985.

Stepenoff, Bonnie. *From French Community to Missouri Town: Ste. Genevieve in the Nineteenth Century.* Columbia: University of Missouri Press, 2006.

Stevenson, Brenda E. "Gender Convention, Ideals, and Identity among Antebellum Virginia Slave Women." In *More Than Chattel: Black Women and Slavery in the Americas,* ed. David Barry Gaspar and Darlene Clack Hine, 169–90. Bloomington: Indiana University Press, 1996.

———. *Life in Black and White: Family and Community in the Slave South.* New York: Oxford University Press, 1996.

Stiles, T. J. *Jesse James: Last Rebel of the Civil War.* New York: Alfred A. Knopf, 2002.

Stone, Jeffrey C. *Slavery, Southern Culture, and Education in Little Dixie, Missouri, 1820–1860.* New York: Routledge, 2006.

Stowe, Steven Mac. *Intimacy and Power in the Old South: Ritual in the Lives of the Planters.* Baltimore: Johns Hopkins University Press, 1987.

Strickland, Arvarh E. "Aspects of Slavery in Missouri, 1821." *Missouri Historical Review* 65 (July 1971): 505–26.

Stuckey, Sterling. *Slave Culture: Nationalist Theory and the Foundations of Black America.* New York: Oxford University Press, 1988.

Sutch, Richard. "The Breeding of Slaves for Sale and the Western Expansion of

Slavery, 1850–1860." In *Race and Slavery in the Western Hemisphere: Quantitative Studies,* ed. Stanley Engerman and Eugene Genovese, 173–320. Princeton, N.J.: Princeton University Press, 1975.

Tabor, Chris. *The Skirmish at Island Mound, Mo.* Bates County Historical Society, 2001.

Tadman, Michael. *Speculators and Slaves: Masters, Traders, and Slaves in the Old South.* Madison: University of Wisconsin Press, 1989.

Tallant, Harold D. *Evil Necessity: Slavery and Political Culture in Antebellum Kentucky.* Lexington: University Press of Kentucky, 2003.

Taylor, Amy Murrell. *The Divided Family in Civil War America.* Chapel Hill: University of North Carolina Press, 2005.

Terrill, Tom E., et al. "Eager Hands: Labor for Southern Textiles, 1850–1860." *Journal of Economic History* 36 (March 1976): 84–99.

Thornton, J. Mills. *Politics and Power in a Slave Society. Alabama, 1800–1860.* Baton Rouge: Louisiana State University Press, 1978.

Trexler, Harrison A. *Slavery in Missouri, 1804–1865.* Baltimore: Johns Hopkins University Press, 1914.

———. "Slavery in Missouri Territory." *Missouri Historical Review* 3 (April 1909): 179–97.

———. "The Value and Sale of the Missouri Slave." *Missouri Historical Review* 8 (January 1914): 69–85.

Ulrich, Laurel Thatcher. *The Age of Homespun: Objects and Stories in the Creation of an American Myth.* New York: Vintage, 2002.

———. *Good Wives: Image and Reality in the Lives of Women in Northern New England, 1650–1750.* New York: Alfred A. Knopf, 1982.

———. *A Midwife's Tale: The Life of Martha Ballard, Based on Her Diary, 1785–1812.* New York: Vintage Books, 1990.

Valenčius, Conevery Bolton. *The Health of the Country: How American Settlers Understood Themselves and Their Land.* New York: Basic Books, 2002.

van Ravenswaay, Charles. *The Arts and Architecture of German Settlements in Missouri: A Survey of a Vanishing Culture.* Columbia: University of Missouri Press, 1977.

Vásquez, Mark G. "The Portable Pulpit: Religious Tracts, Cultural Power, and the Risk of Reading." *American Transcendental Quarterly* 16 (June 2002): 89–100.

Vlach, John Michael. *Back of the Big House: The Architecture of Plantation Slavery.* Chapel Hill: University of North Carolina Press, 1993.

Wade, Richard C. *Slavery in the Cities: The South, 1820–1860.* New York: Oxford University Press, 1964.

Webber, Thomas. *Deep Like the Rivers: Education in the Slave Quarter Community, 1831–1865.* New York: Norton, 1978.

Weiman, David F. "Staple Crops and Slave Plantations: Alternative Perspectives on Regional Development in the Antebellum Cotton South." In *Agriculture and National Development,* ed. Lou Ferleger. Ames: Iowa State University Press, 1990.

Weiner, Marli F. *Mistresses and Slaves: Plantation Women in South Carolina, 1830–1880.* Urbana: University of Illinois Press, 1998.

Wells, Jonathan Daniel. *The Origins of the Southern Middle Class, 1800–1861.* Chapel Hill: University of North Carolina Press, 2004.

Welter, Barbara. "The Cult of True Womanhood, 1820–1860." *American Quarterly* 18 (Summer 1966): 151–74.

———. "The Feminization of American Religion." In *Dimity Convictions: The American Woman in the Nineteenth Century.* Athens: Ohio University Press, 1976.

West, Carroll Van. *Trial and Triumph: Essays in Tennessee's African-American History.* Knoxville: University of Tennessee Press, 2002.

West, Emily. *Chains of Love: Slave Couples in Antebellum South Carolina.* Urbana: University of Illinois Press, 2004.

———. "Debate on the Strength of Slave Families." *Journal of American Studies* 33 (August 1999): 221–41.

———. "Surviving Separate: Cross-Plantation Marriages and the Slave Trade in Antebellum South Carolina." *Journal of Family History* 24 (April 1999): 212–31.

White, Deborah Gray. *Ar'n't I a Woman?* New York: W. W. Norton, 1985.

White, Shane, and Graham White. *Stylin': African American Expressive Culture from Its Beginnings to the Zoot Suit.* Ithaca, N.Y.: Cornell University Press, 1998.

Whites, LeeAnn. *The Civil War as a Crisis in Gender: Augusta, Georgia, 1860–1890.* Athens: University of Georgia Press, 1995.

———. "Forty Shirts and a Wagon Load of Wheat: Women, the Domestic Supply Line, and the Civil War on the Western Border." *Civil War History* (forthcoming).

———. *Gender Matters: Civil War, Reconstruction, and the Making of the New South.* New York: Palgrave Macmillan, 2005.

Wiethoff, William E. *The Insolent Slave.* Columbia: University of South Carolina Press, 2002.

Wolfe, Margaret Ripley. *Daughters of Canaan: A Saga of Southern Women.* Knoxville: University Press of Kentucky, 1995.

Wood, Betty. *Women's Work, Men's Work: The Informal Slave Economies of Lowcountry Georgia.* Athens: University of Georgia Press, 1995.

Wood, Kristen. *Masterful Women: Slaveholding Widows from the Revolution to the Civil War.* Chapel Hill: University of North Carolina Press, 2004.

Wood, Peter. *Black Majority: Negroes in Colonial South Carolina from 1670 through the Stono Rebellion.* New York: W. W. Norton, 1974.

Wooster, Ralph. *Politics, Planters, and Plain Folk: Courthouse and Statehouse in the Upper South, 1850–1860.* Knoxville: University of Tennessee Press, 1975.

Wright, Gavin. *The Political Economy of the South: Households, Markets, and Wealth in the Nineteenth Century.* New York: W. W. Norton, 1978.

Wyatt-Brown, Bertram. *Southern Honor: Ethics and Behavior in the Old South.* Oxford: Oxford University Press, 1982.

Young, Jason R. *Rituals of Resistance: African Atlantic Religion in Kongo and the Lowcountry South in the Era of Slavery.* Baton Rouge: Louisiana University Press, 2007.

Young, Jeffrey Robert. *Domesticating Slavery: The Master Class in Georgia and South Carolina, 1670–1837.* Chapel Hill: University of North Carolina Press, 1999.

Index

CPSIA information can be obtained at www.ICGtesting.com
Printed in the USA
LVOW08s1632080813

346991LV00006B/544/P

On Slav